1 MONTH OF
FREE
READING

at

www.ForgottenBooks.com

By purchasing this book you are eligible for one month membership to ForgottenBooks.com, giving you unlimited access to our entire collection of over 1,000,000 titles via our web site and mobile apps.

To claim your free month visit:

www.forgottenbooks.com/free197846

ISBN 978-0-267-83273-6
PIBN 10197846

THOMAS WINNINGTON ESQ.ᴿ

ob. 1746.

From the original at Holland House.

Published, with Permission by Edward Jeffery, 1826.

MEMOIRS

OF THE

LIFE AND ADMINISTRATION

OF

SIR ROBERT WALPOLE,

Earl of Orford,

IN THREE VOLUMES.

BY

WILLIAM COXE, M.A. F.R.S. F.A.S.

RECTOR OF BEMERTON.

A NEW EDITION.

=====

VOL. II.

LONDON:

PRINTED FOR T. CADELL, JUN. AND W. DAVIES,
IN THE STRAND.

1800.

Luke Hanſard, Printer,
Great Tuınſtile, Lincoln's-Inn Fields.

MEMOIRS

OF

SIR ROBERT WALPOLE.

PERIOD THE FOURTH:

From the Acceſſion of GEORGE the Second, to
the Reſignation of Lord TOWNSHEND :
1727—1730.

CHAPTER THE THIRTY-FIRST: 1727.

Acceſſion and Charaɛ̃er of George the Second.—Education—Charaɛ̃er—
Perſon—Conduɛ̃—and Influence of Queen Caroline.—Account of Mrs.
Howard, afterwards Counteſs of Suffolk.

GEORGE the Second, ſon of George the
Firſt, by Sophia, princeſs of Luneburgh
Zell, was born at Hanover the 30th of Oɛ̃ober
1683, and principally educated under the direction of his grandmother, the eleɛ̃reſs Sophia. Being at a very early period initiated into the pro-
feſſion of arms, he made the campaign of 1708
with the allied army in the Netherlands, under the
command of the duke of Marlborough. He
greatly diſtinguiſhed himſelf as a volunteer at the
battle of Oudenard, where he charged the enemy

at the head of the Hanoverian dragoons, and had his horfe fhot under him *. In 1708, he was created duke of Cambridge, and knight of the garter; and at the acceffion of George the Firft, was fo elated, that he faid to an Englifh gentleman, " I have not one drop of blood in my veins which is not Englifh, and at the fervice of my father's fubjects †." He accompanied the king to England; foon after he had taken his feat in the privy council, was created prince of Wales; and during the king's abfence in 1716, was appointed guardian and lieutenant of the realm.

The unfortunate mifunderftanding which took place between him and his father, has been already related; and although a reconciliation was effected through the interpofition of Devonfhire and Walpole, yet it was more apparent than real: the king gave a ftrong proof that his jealoufy was not abated, by never again configning to him the government of affairs during his abfence. Notwithftanding this caufe of diffatisfaction, the prince, from the period of the reconciliation, feldom formally oppofed his father's government; but paffed a retired life, confining himfelf principally to a fmall circle of felect friends, with whom he lived in habits of ftrict intimacy: of thefe, the earl of Scarborough and Sir Spencer Compton were the moft favoured.

George the Second was, at the time of his acceffion, in the 45th year of his age; and bore the character

* Rimius's Memoirs of the Houfe of Brunfwick.
† Polnitz, vol. iv. p. 230. 232.

character of a prince of high integrity, honour, and veracity. His countenance was pleafing, dignified, and expreffive, with prominent eyes, and a Roman nofe. In perfon he was well proportioned, but much below the middle fize; to which the ballad on the feven wife men alludes, fpeaking of Richard, afterwards lord Edgecumbe, who was very diminutive :

"When Edgecumbe fpoke, the prince in fport
    Laugh'd at the merry elf;
Rejoic'd to fee within his court
    One fhorter than himfelf.

I am glad (cry'd out the quibbling fquire)
My *lownefs* makes your highnefs *higher*."

He poffeffed one great advantage over his father, that he was not ignorant of the language and conftitution of England, although his knowledge of both was limited. He was naturally referved, except to thofe who belonged to his houfehold, or were admitted to his familiar fociety, fond of bufinefs, and of great application whenever application was neceffary; well acquainted with the ftate of foreign affairs; and his obfervations, and replies to the notes of his minifters, dictated by the occafion, prove good fenfe, judgment, and rectitude of intentions *. His temper was warm, vehement, and irritable; prone to fudden emotions of anger, and not eafily appeafed. He was flow in deliberation, cautious in decifion; but his opinion once formed, he became inflexible, and impatient

of

* Correfpondence, Period IV.

of remonſtrance, He was ſtrictly œconomical, punctual in the diſcharge of his expences; ſo peculiarly methodical in all his actions and occupations, that, to uſe the expreſſion of a nobleman much about his perſon, " he ſeemed to think his having done a thing to-day, an unanſwerable reaſon for his doing it to-morrow *." He was rigidly attached to etiquette and punctilious forms, and fond of military parade; without the ſmalleſt taſte for the arts, or love of ſcience, like his father, he gave no patronage to literature, unleſs from the ſuggeſtions of his queen, or the interceſſion of his miniſters. Cold and phlegmatic in his general appearance, he at the ſame time poſſeſſed a high degree of ſenſibility; of which he gave many proofs, particularly on the death of his queen, and the reſignation of Sir Robert Walpole, which would appear incredible to thoſe who are not acquainted with his domeſtic character. The love of women was his predominant weakneſs; but it did not lead him into any exceſſes which affected his public character, or interfered with the intereſts of his kingdom. He had ſeen, and lamented, that his father had been governed by his miſtreſſes; and was ſo extremely cautious to avoid a ſimilar error, that the counteſs of Yarmouth, the only one among them who poſſeſſed any real influence over him, could ſeldom venture to exert her intereſt in public concerns. She once requeſted Horace Walpole to procure a trifling place for one of her

ſervants,

* Lord Hervey to H. Walpole, Oct. 31, 1735.

servants, but charged him not to mention to the king that it was at her requeft; " becaufe (fhe added) if it is known that I have applied, I have no chance of fucceeding *.

But his conduct was far different in regard to queen Caroline, of whofe judgment and good fenfe he had the higheft opinion, and in whom he ever placed the moft implicit confidence. Some of the French writers call hiftory *la fable convenue*, and not without fome degree of reafon; for moft hif-tories are written either by authors who have been themfelves interefted in the events which they re-late, and glofs over the tranfactions of their own party, or are compofed by writers who have not accefs to original papers, know little more than common occurrences, and derive the principal information from uncertain publications, tradi-tional reports, gazettes, and news-papers. The perfonage whofe character I am attempting to delineate, will afford a ftriking example of the truth of thefe obfervations; for it is a remarkable fact, that the hiftorians of the reign of George the Second, fcarcely mention the name of queen Ca-roline, who almoft entirely governed the king dur-ing the firft ten years of his reign; who bore her faculties fo meekly, and with fuch extraordinary prudence, as never to excite the leaft uneafinefs even in a fovereign highly tenacious of his autho-rity, but contrived that her opinion fhould appear as if it had been his own; who folely occafioned the

* From Lord Walpole.

the continuance of Sir Robert Walpole in the miniftry; who patronifed and promoted Herring,
Hoadley, Clarke, Hare, Sherlocke, Butler, and
Pearce; and without whofe recommendation or
concurrence, fcarely any fituation in church or
ftate was conferred.

Her education,
character, and
perfon.

Carolina Wilhelmina, daughter of John Frederic, Margrave of Anfpach, by the princefs of
Saxe-Eyfenach, was born in 1683. Having loft her
father when fhe was very young, and her mother
marrying John George the Fourth, electtor of
Saxony, fhe was left under the guardianfhip of
Frederic, electtor of Brandenburgh, afterwards king
of Pruffia; paffed part of her early days at the
court of Berlin *, and received her education under the fuperintendance of her aunt, the accomplifhed Sophia Charlotte †, fifter of George the

Firft,

---

* Polnitz.

† Sophia Charlotte, the fecond wife of Frederic, was the daughter
of Erneft Auguftus, electtor of Hanover. This elegant and accomplifhed
princefs was born in 1668; and in 1681, having efpoufed Frederic,
then electtoral prince, became, on his acceffion to the throne, the great
ornament of his fplendid court. Her features were regular, yet expreffive; her form, though below the middle ftature, was elegant and
graceful; her demeanour dignified and polite; and her conduct ever
irreproachable. She never interfered in affairs of ftate, though always
ready, when called upon, to aid with her counfels, journies, and correfpondence, the views of the king. Her underftanding was highly cultivated; fhe fpoke the principal languages of Europe with fuch eafe
and fluency, that fhe ufually addreffed herfelf to foreigners in their
refpective tongues; fhe was well verfed in hiftory, converfant in different branches of natural philofophy, and not unacquainted even with
fcholaftic divinity. Though her learning was fo profound, that fhe was
ftiled the Female Philofopher, fhe was not only extremely diffident, but
careful to avoid the affectation of wifhing to difplay her multifarious ac-
quirements. She was no ftranger to the polite accomplifhments, fond of
dancing, and did not difdain to be an actrefs in plays which were performed by her command: fhe excelled in mufic, fung and compofed
with tafte; and was the great patronefs of fcience and the arts. She
drew Leibnitz to Berlin, and aftonifhed that great philofopher with the
extent of her capacity, the depth of her refearches, and the folidity of her

             obfervations.

Firſt. From her example and inſtructions, ſhe im-
bibed that politeneſs of demeanour and dignity of
character, thoſe ſentiments of philoſophy, that ardent love of learning, and fondneſs for metaphy-
ſical knowledge, which merited the eulogium of
Clarke and Leibnitz.

She gave an early inſtance of her attachment to
the proteſtant religion. The fame of her beauty
and accompliſhments attracted the notice of the
archduke Charles, ſon of the emperor Leopold the
Firſt, and afterwards Emperor himſelf, who made
a tender of his hand. Not allured by the ſplendor
of the family into which ſhe might have been
adopted, ſhe declined the offer without heſitation:
" But Providence (obſerves Addiſon) kept a ſtore
in reward for ſuch an exalted virtue ; and, by the
ſecret methods of its wiſdom, opened a way for
her

obſervations. She died at Hanover in 1705, on a viſit to her mother the
electreſs Sophia, in the 37th year of her age; and diſplayed on her
death-bed the utmoſt calmneſs and reſignation. To the king her huſ-
band ſhe wrote a tender letter, thanking him for his care, and recommending her domeſtics to his protection. To her brother, who was diſ-
confolate at her approaching diſſolution, ſhe ſaid, " Nothing is ſo natural as death ; I have long conſidered it as a debt ; and though I am
young enough to have lived a few years longer, yet I feel no regret in
dying." When La Bergerie, a Calviniſt miniſter, offered his ſpiritual
aſſiſtance, ſhe ſaid ; " Friends are proved in time of neceſſity ; you
offer your aſſiſtance at a moment when I can no longer ſerve you ; accept my thanks, which are all that I can beſtow." Then turning to
him, as he was going to exhort her, ſhe continued ; " For twenty years
I have ſeriouſly examined my religion ; I have peruſed the books which
treat on that ſubject with too much attention to be in the ſmalleſt doubt ;
you can ſay nothing to me which I do not know ; and I can aſſure you,
that I depart in tranquillity." Her phyſician repreſenting to her that
ſhe increaſed her complaint by ſpeaking ; " Adieu then, La Bergerie
(ſhe added) ; I remain your good friend." Obſerving one of her attendants weeping, ſhe exclaimed, " Why do you weep ? could you
think that I was immortal ?" And then ſtretching out her hand to her
brother ; " Dear brother, (ſhe cried) I am ſuffocated ;" and in an
inſtant expired.

Period IV. her to·become the greateſt of her ſex among thoſe
1727 to 1730. who profeſs that faith to which ſhe adhered with
ſo much Chriſtian magnanimity *."

Caroline eſpouſed, in 1705, George the Second,
then electoral prince of Hanover. She was eſteemed
handſome before ſhe had the ſmall-pox, and became too corpulent. Tickell did not flatter her in
his poem of Kenſington Gardens, when he ſaid ;

> " Here England's daughter, darling of the land,
> Sometimes, ſurrounded with her virgin band,
> Gleams through the ſhades. She, tow'ring o'er the reſt,
> Stands faireſt of the fairer kind confeſt ;
> Form'd to gain hearts that Brunſwick's cauſe deny'd,
> And charm a people to her father's ſide †."

She had a hand and arm greatly admired for its
whiteneſs and elegance, a penetrating eye, " and
a ſmile celeſtial ‡," an expreſſive countenance,
great ſweetneſs and grace, particularly when ſhe
ſpoke. But theſe charms of her perſon were far
ſurpaſſed by the endowments of her mind. She
poſſeſſed quickneſs of apprehenſion, a natural good
underſtanding, which had been duly cultivated ;
and obtained a conſiderable knowledge in many
branches of uſeful and polite literature §.

Her levees were a ſtrange picture of the motley
character and manners of a queen and a learned
woman. She received company while ſhe was at
her toilette ; prayers, and ſometimes a ſermon,
were read ; learned men and divines were inter-
mixed

---

* Freeholder, No. 21.
† Tickell's Kenſington Gardens, p. 258.
‡ Tickell.   § Rimius.

mixed with courtiers and ladies of the houfehold: the converfation turned on metaphyfical fubjects, blended with repartees, fallies of mirth, and the tittle-tattle of a drawing-room. She had a happy turn for converfation, and a readinefs in adapting her difcourfe to the perfons with whom fhe talked; poffeffed peculiar talents for mirth and humour; excelled in mimicry, and was fond of difplaying it; was pleafed with making a repartee herfelf, and with hearing it from others. Her conduct, during the unfortunate mifunderftanding which took place between George the Firft and her hufband, when prince of Wales, was fo prudent and dignified, that the late king always behaved to her with marks of due refpect and affection, though he never cordially loved her. Yet notwithftanding her courtefy, affability of deportment, condefcenfion to men of letters, and fondnefs for focial intercourfe, fhe had a high notion of the regal ftation, and was partial to the etiquette of a court; fhe feldom forgot that fhe was a queen, and always kept up a due ftate both in public and private. She would occafionally dine with Sir Robert Walpole at Chelfea; but even her vifits to a favourite minifter were fubjected to form and etiquette: fhe fat down to table with lady Walpole, the royal family whom fhe brought with her, and the lady in waiting: Sir Robert always ftood behind her chair, and gave her the firft plate; then retired into another apartment, where dinner was ferved for him and the queen's houfehold *.

Queen

* From Lord Orford.

Period IV.
1727 to 1730.

Queen Caroline was fond of conversing and cor-
responding with men of learning, and particularly
with divines, whom she often perplexed with
questions concerning the doctrines of the different
churches, and consulted with a view of settling
her faith. Hoadley, Clarke, Hare, and Sherlocke,
were among the number to whom she principally
applied. She carried on a correspondence on these
subjects, by means of her bed-chamber woman,
Mrs. Clayton, afterwards lady Sundon, who had
acquired a powerful ascendancy over her. The
divine whom she most particularly noticed, and
by whose conversation she often owned that she
was most instructed, was Dr. Clarke, whose profound learning, in all branches of sacred and profane literature, was scarcely ever equalled, whose
piety was unquestioned, and whose playful manners and placid temper rendered him as amiable
as he was learned. Dr. Clarke had only the rec-
tory of St. James's, which was given him by queen
Anne, and the mastership of Wigston Hospital;
and queen Caroline proposed placing him on the
bench, an honour which Clarke invariably declined. Finding that he persisted in his refusal,
she desired Sir Robert Walpole to try the powers
of his rhetoric, which had never been employed
in vain on a similar occasion. The minister
obeyed; and in a conference at Kensington palace, used every argument in his power to prevail on Clarke to accept the proffered dignity;
when Clarke declined, he continued to press it;
and the conference was so long, that the candles

were

were burnt down in the sockets; and the pages came into the apartment to know if fresh lights were not wanted *. But the rhetoric of the minister had no effect, and the queen was highly disappointed, that she was prevented from placing Dr. Clarke on the bench of bishops.

Queen Caroline maintained a correspondence with Leibnitz on the most abstract sciences, in which she supremely delighted; and in the course of this literary intercourse, the German philosopher having insinuated some suspicions that the foundations of natural religion were in danger of being hurt by the doctrines of Sir Isaac Newton, she applied to Clarke for an answer to this suggestion. The answer brought on a reply, and the reply a second answer, and the controversy was carried on with all the spirit and learning which those great philosophers could throw into such dry subjects as the principles of natural religion and philosophy, and free-will and fatality. They submitted their respective arguments to the princess as to an umpire; and vied in unfolding their systems in as conspicuous a manner as the nature of so intricate a subject would allow. The princess was highly flattered with this arbitration, and permitted Dr. Clarke, whose opinion she seems to have embraced, to dedicate to her the account of the controversy. In this dedication, the learned author has not omitted to pay a tribute to her desire of knowledge and love of truth, in a strain of

panegyric

* From Lord Orford and Etough's Papers.

Period IV. panegyric which could hardly be avoided on such
1727 to 1730. an occafion.   Nor was it folely dictated by flattery; for Whifton * informs us, that he often
heard Clarke fpeak with admiration of her mar-
vellous fagacity and judgment, in the feveral parts
of the difpute.

But although this accomplifhed princefs poffeffed confiderable influence over George the Second, fhe had acted with fo much caution, and
behaved with fuch moderation and prudence, that
fhe was confidered at the time of his acceffion,
by the party in oppofition, as a mere cypher, and
the whole power and influence over the king was
fuppofed to be lodged in the hands of Mrs. Howard, afterwards countefs of Suffolk.

Character of   Henrietta, fifter of John, the firft earl of Buck-
Mrs. Howard, inghamfhire, was eldeft daughter of Sir Henry
Countefs of
Suffolk.   Hobart †, of Blickling, in Norfolk, and efpoufed
Charles Howard, younger fon of Henry, fifth earl
of Suffolk, whom fhe accompanied to Hanover
before the death of queen Anne.   Having ingratiated herfelf into the favour of Caroline, then
electoral princefs, fhe accompanied her to England, and became her bed-chamber woman.   If
we were to draw an eftimate of the underftanding
and character of Mrs. Howard, from the reprefentations of Pope ‡, Swift, and Gay, during the
time

---

* Whifton's Hiftorical Memoirs of Clarke.

† Collins's Peerage.

‡ See Pope's Letters to Swift, October 25th, 1725.—Mifcellanies.
Swift's Character of Mrs. Howard.—Gay's Epiftle to Pope; and
other parts of their refpective works.

time of her favour, we might suppose that she
possessed every accomplishment and good quality
which were ever the lot of a woman.

The real truth is, that Mrs. Howard was more
remarkable for beauty than for understanding,
and the passion which the king entertained for her,
was rather derived from · chance * than from any
combination of those transcendant qualities, which
Swift and Pope ascribed to their court divinity.
She had been long wholly unnoticed by the prince,
who was enamoured of another lady that was
more cruel to the royal lover than Mrs. Howard.
This lady was the beautiful and lively Mary Bellenden, daughter of lord Bellenden †, maid of
honour to queen Caroline, when princess of Wales,

and

* From Lord Orford.

† Sir William Bellenden, created a peer after the restoration of
Charles the Second, died unmarried, making a conveyance of his
estate and honour to John Ker, a younger son of William, the second
earl of Roxburgh, who then changed his name to Bellenden, and took
the arms. He married Mary, widow of William Ramsay, third earl of
Dalhousee, and daughter of Henry Moore, first earl of Drogheda, by
Alice his wife, daughter of William lord Spencer, by Penelope,
daughter of Henry Wriothesly, earl of Southampton.

WILLIAM Lord SPENCER—PENELOPE WRIOTHESLY.

HENRY, First Earl of SUNDERLAND,   ALICE—Lord DROGHEDA.
    1643.

        MARY MOORE—Lord BELLENDEN.

MARY BELLENDEN—JOHN CAMPBELL,
            afterwards Duke
            of Argyle.

JOHN Duke   Lord FREDERICK CAMPBELL.   CAROLINE,
of Argyle.   m. 1st. Charles Bruce,
                                         Earl of Aylesbury,
                                         2d. Field Marshal Conway.

and a great friend of Mrs. Howard. Gay alludes
to her, in his ballad entitled Damon and Cupid,
as one of the reigning beauties :

> " So well I'm known at court,
>   " None aſks where Cupid dwells;
> " But readily reſort,
>   " To *Bellenden*'s or Lepell's."

She is alſo thus deſcribed in an old ballad, made
upon the quarrel between George the Firſt and
the prince of Wales, at the chriſtening, when the
prince and all his houſehold were ordered to quit
St. James's :

> " But *Bellenden* we needs muſt praiſe,
>   " Who, as down the ſtairs ſhe jumps;
> " Sings over the hills and far away,
>   " Deſpiſing doleful dumps."

This lovely and elegant woman rejected the ad-
dreſſes of the prince, and eſpouſed, in 1720, John
Campbell, then groom of the bed-chamber to the
prince of Wales, and afterwards duke of Argyle.
She was highly favoured by queen Caroline, and
univerſally admired as an accompliſhed pattern of
good ſenſe, and exemplary conduct.

The prince, after having communicated his paſ-
ſion for Miſs Bellendon to Mrs. Howard, and
being rejected, became enamoured of his confi-
dante.

The queen's behaviour to Mrs. Howard.

Lord Cheſterfield has obſerved, in the unfavourable portrait * which he has drawn of queen Caroline, *that ſhe even favoured and promoted the ga-*

lantries

* Cheſterfield's Letters to his Son, alſo in Miſcellaneous Works,
vol. 3.

antries of the king. But this severe reprefentation
is totally devoid of truth, and proves little knowledge of her real difpofition. It was a·principle
with her not to difguft the king with remonftrances, or to appear diffatisfied with his attentions to other women. But certainly never wife
felt or lamented a hufband's infidelities more than
herfelf; although fhe had too much good fenfe
and prudence, and too much refpect for her character to treat her rivals with marks of ill humour,
or to fhew, by her outward behaviour, fymptoms
of jealoufy and difpleafure. She was always able
to difguife her feelings and conceal her uneafinefs.
It was thus that her behaviour to Mrs. Howard
led many to fuppofe that fhe was in high eftima-
tion; and Swift, Pope, and Gay, repeatedly call
her the chief favourite of the queen.

To her particular friends, queen Caroline was
not wanting in complaints of the king's infidelities, and fhe ufed to call his favourite, by way
of banter, her fifter Howard : this expreffion was
confidered by the friends of the miftrefs as a
proof of the queen's partiality and kindnefs,
whereas it was in reality the ftrongeft mark of
averfion and contempt. But, in fact, the forced
complacency of her outward behaviour, was a violent effort of prudence and difcretion, and fhe
never failed to oppofe the rife of thofe who paid
their court to the miftrefs. Among many inftances which may be enumerated, I fhall felect
thofe of Gay, Swift, and Chefterfield.

Gay

Gay disap-
pointed in his
expectations
from her pro-
tection.

Gay began paying his court to her when she was
electoral princess, and while he accompanied the
earl of Clarendon as his secretary to Hanover.
But the embassy lasted only nineteen days; and
being disappointed of his hopes of preferment by
the death of queen Anne, the poet turned himself towards the rising sun, and soon after the accession of George the First, drew the character
of Caroline in a high strain of panegyric *.

The princess, not insensible to praise, received
Gay, soon after her arrival in England, with great
kindness, and gave him hopes of promotion. From
this period he commenced courtier, paid a regular
attendance, and was honoured with many marks
of her patronage and protection. He continued,
however, his attendance at court for twelve years
without obtaining a solid reward of his assiduity.
At her command, he wrote his fables for the duke
of Cumberland, and being of a sanguine disposition,
formed high expectations of promotion when the
accession of George the Second would permit his
patroness to provide for him. When that event
took place, his hopes were greatly magnified on
the queen's telling Mrs. Howard, in allusion to
the fable of the Hare and many Friends †, that
she would take up the hare. But his expectations were by these means raised so high, that he
considered the offer of the place of gentleman
                                        usher

* An Epistle to a Lady, occasioned by the Arrival of the Princess
of Wales.

† Swift's Works, vol. 16. p. 170.

usher to the princess Louisa, though above £.200 a year, as an insult, and rejected it with scorn.

Swift was convinced that the minister had prevented the bounty of queen Caroline from being shewn to the author of the Hare and many Friends, and he observes, alluding to it in a copy of verses addressed to Gay;

> " Fain would I think our female friend sincere,
> " Till *Bob, the poet's foe*, possest her ear, &c."

In another place, Swift asserts, that it was principally owing to the dedication, prefixed to the Pastorals, in honour of Bolingbroke, and to some expressions in his fables, which displeased the court. He repeats this accusation in his letters and works, and had even the rudeness to hint it to Sir Robert Walpole himself, when he dined with him at Chelsea *. Gay was of the same opinion, and in the second part of his fables, which were not printed till after his death, is full of sarcastic and splenetic allusions to the minister. But as Walpole was neither of a jealous or vindictive disposition, there is no reason to give credit to the aspersions of his enemies, and to suppose that he used his influence over queen Caroline, for the purpose of injuring Gay, particularly when another and a more natural motive of her conduct may be suggested.

In fact, Gay was the innocent cause of his own disgrace, for he thought that Mrs. Howard was all powerful at court, and that he, whom Swift humorously

* Swift's Works, vol. 16. p. 169.

Period IV. humoroufly calls * one of her led captains, fhould
1727 to 1730. rife by her recommendation. Pope alfo, in a letter to Swift, alluding to Mrs. Howard, fays, *Gay*
puts his whole truft in that lady whom I defcribed to
you, and whom you take to be an allegorical crea-
ture of fancy. And Gay thus expreffes himfelf
to Swift; " Mrs. Howard has declared herfelf very
ftrongly, both to the king and queen, as my protector †." But in thefe words, they unconfci-
oufly declare the caufe of his disfavour. The
queen's jealoufy of the interference and credit of
the miftrefs, obftructed his promotion; and his
own indifcretion afterwards, deftroyed every hope.
Soon after this difappointment, he produced the
Beggar's Opera; and both his converfation and
writings were fo full of invectives againft the
court, that all expectations of farther notice from
the queen were obvioufly relinquifhed.

Swift. Swift alfo proved the ill policy of attempting
to ingratiate himfelf with the queen through the
medium of Mrs. Howard. With a view of
changing his preferments in Ireland for other in
England, which the princefs feemed to exprefs an
inclination to promote, he maintained a correfpondence with Mrs. Howard, whom he praifed
in the moft fulfome manner, and courted with the
moft affected affiduity, by letters when he was
abfent, and by conftant perfonal attendance when
he was in England. But as foon as the efforts of
Mrs. Howard proved unfuccefsful, Swift turned
his

* Swift's Works, vol. 16. p. 168.
† Swift's Works, vol. 19. p. 252.

his fatire against her, on whom he had heaped
fuch unbounded encomiums, imputed his failure
folely to her want of fincerity; and reproached
her in very bitter and difrefpectful terms. Lady
Betty Germaine, and his friend Gay, in vain endeavoured to juftify Mrs. Howard, and to prove
that fhe was not to blame; but the mifanthropic
Swift, when he had once formed his opinion, was
not eafily convinced by any arguments. He fays,
in a letter to lady Betty Germaine, " For thefe
reafons, I did always, and do ftill think, Mrs.
Howard, now lady Suffolk, an abfolute courtier."
When this character was fhewn to lady Suffolk,
fhe mildly obferved, " It is very different from
that which he fent me himfelf, and which I have
in his own hand writing *."

The earl of Chefterfield is another remarkable
inftance. He had long coveted the poft of fecretary of ftate, and an arrangement had been made
in his favour. After an audience of the queen,
to which he was introduced by Walpole, and
thanking her for her concurrence, he had the imprudence to make a long vifit to the miftrefs; the
queen was informed of the circumftance, and his
appointment did not take place †. At another
time, he had requefted the queen to fpeak to the
king for fome trifling favour. The queen promifed, but forgot it; a few days afterwards, recollecting her promife, fhe expreffed regret at
her forgetfulnefs, and added, fhe would certainly
                                            mention

* From lord Orford.
† Etough.—From the communication of Sir Robert Walpole.

C 2

mention it that very day. Chesterfield replied, that her majesty need not give herself that trouble, for lady Suffolk had spoken to the king. The queen made no reply, but on seeing the king, told him she had long promised to mention a trifling request to his majesty, but it was now needless, because lord Chesterfield had just informed her, that she had been anticipated by lady Suffolk. The king, who always preserved great decorum with the queen, and was very unwilling to have it supposed that the favourite interfered, was extremely displeased, both with lord Chesterfield and his mistress. The consequence was that in a short time lady Suffolk went to Bath for her health and returned no more to court; Chesterfield was dismissed from his office of lord steward of the household, and never heard the reason until two years before his death, when he was informed by the late earl of Orford, that his disgrace was owing to his having offended the queen by paying court to lady Suffolk *.

* Her husband having succeeded to the title of earl of Suffolk, on the death of his brother in June 1731, she became countess of Suffolk. At the period of her retirement from court, she was a widow, her husband having died on the 28th of September 1733, and she espoused, in July 1735, George Berkley, fourth son of Charles, second earl of Berkley. Lady Suffolk lived to an advanced age, not dying till 1767; she left no issue, an only son, which she had by her first husband, dying in 1745 unmarried.

CHAPTER THE THIRTY-SECOND.

1727.

Rumours of a Change in Administration.—Intrigues of the Tories, Pulteney, and Bolingbroke.—Character of Sir Spencer Compton, who declines the Office of prime Minister.—Continuation of Townshend and Walpole, by the Intervention of Queen Caroline.—The good Effects of her Influence over the King.

THE news of the king's death had no sooner reached London, than a general belief was current that the administration would be totally changed. It was credited, that Sir Robert Walpole had irretrievably offended the new king, when prince of Wales, as he had been frequently heard to protest, that when he came to the throne, that minister should never be employed. Rumours of a change of ministry.

Pulteney, before their open rupture, had informed the prince of Wales of some disrespectful expressions used on a former occasion, and told him that he was sold to his father's ministers, by persons who considered nothing but themselves and their own interest, and were in haste to make their fortunes *. Since their quarrel, he had undoubtedly exaggerated this representation, and, as he continued on good terms at Leicester House, naturally used his whole credit against Walpole. Intrigues of Pulteney:

Bolingbroke and the Tories had also caballed at Leicester House, and were supported by the whole weight Of Bolingbroke and the Tories,

* Answer to one Part of an infamous Libel.

C 3

Period IV.
1727 to 1730.

weight and influence of the favourite, Mrs. How-ard. Swift alſo, in a letter to his friend Dr. She-ridan, mentions the hopes of the Tories, and the certain diſmiſſion of Walpole.

In fact, Walpole himſelf was at this moment convinced of his removal, and yet was well ſa-tisfied that his excluſion could not be of long continuance. In conformity with theſe ſentiments, he ſaid to his friend Sir William Yonge, " I ſhall certainly go out ; but let me recommend you not to go into violent oppoſition, as we muſt ſoon come in again" *.

In this moment of probable diſgrace, Walpole was deſerted by many of his friends ; and Sir Spencer Compton, whom the king had already avowed his intention of appointing miniſter, be-came the idol of the day. But the event turned out otherwiſe, and the public expectations were diſappointed.

Walpole ſupported by queen Caro-line.

It is now well known, that the continuance of the new adminiſtration was principally owing to the influence of queen Caroline ; and writers of great credit, but not acquainted with the interior ſituation of Leiceſter Houſe at that period, have not ſcrupled to aſcribe her patronage of Sir Ro-bert Walpole, ſolely to the offers which he made to obtain from parliament a jointure of £.100,000 a year, when Sir Spencer Compton could only venture to propoſe £.60,000, as if motives of ſordid intereſt had *alone* induced the queen to protect

* From Sir George Yonge.

protect the minifter; and as if her conduct was
derived from an inftantaneous impulfe, uncon- nected with any previous communication or inter- courfe. The offer had doubtlefs its due effect; but a number of circumftances combined to in- fluence her in favour of Sir Robert Walpole.

The queen was by no means ignorant of his character and abilities. While he was in oppofi- tion to government, from 1717 to 1720, he had continued in the higheft favour with the prince of Wales. During this period, a woman of her good fenfe, could not fail of diftinguifhing that capa- city for bufinefs, thofe powers of intellect, which raifed him to the head of his party; and his wife and able conduct upon the failure of the South Sea fcheme, naturally increafed this prepoffeffion in his favour.

He had, in conjunction with lord Townfhend, gratified the prince of Wales, by obtaining from the king the garter for the earl of Scarborough. And count Broglio, the French embaffador, ob- ferves * on this occafion, " That minifters not un- frequently procured places for thofe perfons who were attached to the prince, from the confideration that the time might come, when fuch a conduct would turn out to their advantage."

The duke of Devonfhire, who had always been the great friend and fupporter of Walpole, had continued on good terms with the princefs of Wales.

* Count Broglio to the king of France, 24 July, 1724. Corref- pondence, Period III.

C 4

Wales. He had ftrongly impreffed her with fentiments of high regard for his abilities and minifterial capacity, and had reprefented him as the
perfon who had principally counteracted the intrigues of the Jacobites, difcovered the plot of
bifhop Atterbury, and whofe good offices were
effentially employed in preferving the family on
the throne. Nor can a ftronger proof be alledged
of the height to which this confidential intercourfe
was carried, than that the refolution which he
had once formed to refign, was communicated by
the duke of Devonfhire to the princefs, and that
fhe perfuaded him to relinquifh the defign *.

But the principal caufe which fecured to him
the protection of the queen, was his prudent behaviour in regard to Mrs. Howard. He had pe-
netration fufficient to forefee, that George the
Second would be governed by his wife, whom he
adored, and of whofe abilities and good fenfe he
had formed the higheft idea, and not by his miftrefs, of whofe judgment he never entertained any
favourable opinion. The minifter had always
treated the princefs of Wales with the higheft
refpect, and declined paying court to Mrs. Howard; a mode of conduct, which, according to the
opinion of fuperficial obfervers, would inevitably
bring on his difgrace, but which, in effect, contributed to his continuance in office. A contrary
mode of proceeding had infpired the queen with
an invincible averfion to Pulteney, Bolingbroke,
and

* Onflow's Remarks: Correfpondence, Period IV.

and the Tories. Hence she used all her influence
with the king not to change the administration.

The account of the king's death was brought first to the minister at Chelsea, in a dispatch from lord Townshend, who had accompanied George the First to the continent. He instantly repaired to the palace at Richmond. The king was then retired, as was his usual custom, to his afternoon's nap. On being informed that his father was dead, he continued for some time incredulous, until he was told that the minister was waiting in the anti-chamber with the express. He at length started up, and made his appearance half dressed; but he still retained his unbelief, until the dispatch from Townshend was produced. Walpole having knelt down, and kissed his hand, inquired whom his majesty would be pleased to appoint to draw up the declaration to the privy council? "Compton," replied the king with great abruptness, and Walpole quitted the apartment under the most mortifying impressions. He immediately waited on Sir Spencer Compton with the king's commands, who, unacquainted with the etiquette and forms of expression used on the occasion, avowed his ignorance, and requested the minister to draw up the declaration. Walpole complied, and Compton conveyed it to the king *.

Sir Spencer Compton was second surviving son of James earl of Northampton; after having received a liberal education, and improved himself by foreign travel, he was introduced into parliament

* From lord Orford.

ment at an early period, and deserted the principles of his family, who were Tories, by adhering
to the Whigs. He was made treasurer to the
prince of Denmark, appointed manager for the
trial of Sacheverel, was chairman in several important committees of elections and privileges, in
which he acquitted himself with much satisfaction,
and made himself master of the forms and proceedings of the House. At the accession of George
the First, he was appointed treasurer to the prince
of Wales; and his constant adherence to the
Whigs, his intimate acquaintance with Walpole,
his numerous connections, and a character he had
acquired for dispatch of business, secured him the
place of speaker without opposition. With that
honourable office he united, in 1721, the post of
paymaster of the forces, and treasurer of Chelsea
Hospital. He was created knight of the bath on
the revival of that order. Compton was not distinguished for brilliancy of genius, or eminence of
abilities. His formal and solemn manner contributed to the support of his authority as speaker,
and seemed to denote extent of knowledge and
profundity of thought, while his assiduity in business, and punctuality in accounts, rendered him
respectable in the opinion of George the Second,
who being extremely regular in all his proceedings,
loved regularity in others, and esteemed it one of
the most essential requisites in a minister. Such
was the person whom George the Second had se-
lected; and as the monarch was usually deemed

9   inflexible

inflexible in his refolutions, the appointment feemed irrevocably fixed.

Walpole paffed the two days which immedi-ately followed the acceffion of the new king, in great agitation and concern, and held feveral con-ferences with his friends at Devonfhire Houfe. Scrope *, fecretary to the treafury, who was ad-mitted to one of thefe meetings, defcribed the whole company, abforbed in gloom and confter-nation. Either the next, or the following day, Scrope repeated his vifit to the defponding mi-nifter, and found no alteration in his mien and appearance. He firft encouraged him in general terms to hope, and then added reafons for that en-couragement, which he had from one, whofe name he could not divulge. His friend had informed him, that queen Caroline was difpleafed with Compton, who had been deficient in deference and refpect, and had conceived a high opinion of Walpole's ability for finance. She ufed to con-verfe with George the Firft at chapel, on political fubjects; and once in particular, having obferved that a want of proper funds would oblige him to difband his Hanover troops, he replied, " No, for Walpole can convert ftones into gold †." This anecdote recurred to her recollection; fhe com-municated it to the king, and exerted herfelf to abate his predilection for Compton, and influence him in favour of Walpole. The truth of the in-formation

---

* Minutes of Scrope's Converfations with Etough. Corref-pondence, Period IV.   † See chapter 30.

formation foon appeared; the queen was affiduoufly employed in removing the prejudices of the
king. She reprefented the folly and hazard of
difmiffing a well eftablifhed miniftry, and of forming a motley cabinet of Whigs and Tories; and
artfully took an opportunity of hinting the imprudence of placing a man at the head of the miniftry, who could not draw up the declaration to
be laid before the privy council, but was compelled to have recourfe to him who was about to
be difmiffed; fhe alfo hinted to him, that Sir Robert Walpole had agreed to carry through the
houfe of commons, an augmentation of £.130,000
to the civil lift.

Thefe reprefentations had their effect; and with
them, many other caufes co-operated to change
the king's fentiments. Sir Spencer Compton found
himfelf unequal to the weight of government, and
was not eager to take upon him fo refponfible an
office. He was convinced, that he could not bear
up againft the oppofition of Sir Robert Walpole,
who had fo much weight in the houfe of commons, and who would be fupported by the united
interefts of Newcaftle, Devonfhire, Townfhend,
and the great leaders of the Whigs, unlefs a Tory
adminiftration was formed. George the Second
was averfe to throw himfelf into the hands of the
Tories, and yet could not form a new miniftry,
which promifed ftability, without taking that ftep.
Pulteney, the only man of great weight and influence among the Whigs in oppofition, was by
no means attached to the Tories, and would not

have

have heartily coalefced with them. Bolingbroke was fo extremely unpopular, that his re-eftablifh-ment in the houfe of lords, and his admiffion into the miniftry, would have occafioned great mur-murs and difcontents among thofe who ufually fupported government. Lord Carteret, the only man of abilities who was cordially inclined to join the Tories, had little perfonal confequence, was not the leader of any party, and did not poffefs the fmalleft influence in the houfe of commons.

The fituation of foreign affairs alfo no lefs con-tributed to confirm the king in his refolution not to remove the miniftry. The treaty of Hanover had been recently concluded, and the negotiations for the confummation of that alliance were in great forwardnefs. They had been planned and were conducting by lord Townfhend, in co-operation with France. The oppofition had warmly refifted the treaty, and might have introduced a new plan, which muft have deranged and overturned the whole fyftem of foreign politics. Cardinal Fleury, who then governed France, was intimately con-nected with Horace Walpole; he had adopted the pacific fentiments which influenced the Englifh cabinet, and deprecated the change of that fyftem which had kept Europe in peace for fo long a pe-riod. When the news of the king's death reached Paris, Horace Walpole requefted and obtained an immediate conference, which took place at Ver-failles on the enfuing day. In this conference, the French minifter conveyed, in the ftrongeft terms, profeffions of friendfhip from Louis the Fifteenth

to

to George the Second; and in his own name declared his firm refolution to maintain the good
underftanding between the two crowns. He alfo
expreffed thefe fentiments in a letter which he
wrote on the fame day to Horace Walpole. Immediately after the conference *, Horace Walpole
quitted Paris, without waiting for leave of abfence,
repaired to London, and delivered his letter to the
king in perfon. The king was at firft extremely
diffatisfied with him for quitting his ftation fo
abruptly; but during the conference, which lafted
two hours †, he gradually foftened, as Horace
Walpole explained, with great addrefs, the relative
fituations of England and France, effaced the ill
impreffions that he had entertained of his and his
brother's conduct, and confirmed the fentiments
of the French cabinet, which were contained in
the letter from cardinal Fleury. Accordingly, the
king wrote, with his own hand, a letter ‡ to the
cardinal, in which he declared his refolution to
purfue the fame meafures as were purfued by his
father, and to continue the fame minifters who
had conducted thofe meafures.

Under thefe circumftances, the offer which had
been made to Compton, was the only remaining
impediment to the continuance of Walpole. The
manner of furmounting this difficulty was previoufly

---

* Memoires de Montgon, tome 4. p. 401, 403.

† Etough. From Horace Walpole, Period V.

‡ Duke of Newcaftle to Mr. Robinfon and the earl of Waldegrave.
Correfpondence. Montgon mentions the conference between Fleury
and Horace Walpole, and afferts that cardinal Fleury wrote a letter to
the king of England; but this letter was to Horace Walpole. Memoires de Montgon.

oufly concerted. The queen having, in the prefence of Walpole,. repeated to Compton 'the intimation that the king intended to place him at the
head of the treasury; Walpole inftantly declared
his ready acquiefcence, and gave affurances of. his
beft affiftance and fupport. Compton was extremely affected at this inftance of, his mafter's
kindnefs, and fhed tears, as he declared his incapacity to undertake fo arduous a truft *.

While this fcene was paffing in the clofet, the
door of Sir Spencer Compton's houfe in St. James's
Square was befieged by perfons of all ranks, who
crowded to pay their court to the new minifter.
As Walpole was paffing through the fquare in his
carriage, he faid to a friend who was with him,
" Did you obferve how my houfe is deferted, and
how that door is crowded with carriages ? To-morrow the fcene will be changed : that houfe will be
deferted, and mine will be more frequented than
ever."

As his continuance in office was the work of the
queen, it was through her that it was firft made
known to the public. On the firft drawing-room
which fhe held at Leicefter Houfe, lady Walpole,
among others, prefented herfelf; but as there was
a great crowd, and her hufband was fuppofed to
have received his difmiffion, no one retired, till
the queen perceiving her at fome diftance, beck-
oned to her, and faid, " There I am fure ! fee a
friend;" inftantly the whole company made way.

She

* Communicated by Sir Robert Walpole to bifhop Wefton. Etough
Papers.

She approached the queen, and kissed her hand;
her majesty spoke to her in a most gracious manner, and lady Walpole, in relating the anecdote to
her son *, from whom I received it, added, " and
in returning I might have walked upon their heads,
so eager were they to pay their court to me."

From this moment Walpole was courted, Compton in his turn deserted, and the ministry, with
very few alterations, continued in their former
offices. On the 24th of June, the very day in
which Swift said the ministry would be changed,
Walpole was re-appointed first lord commissioner
of the treasury and chancellor of the exchequer,
and lord Townshend again received the seal of secretary of state. An attempt ┼ was finally made
by the party, through Mrs. Howard, to prevail on
the king to confer an earldom on lord Bathurst;
but that measure being thwarted by the influence
of the queen, they relinquished all hopes of success, and Bolingbroke retired from London in
disgust.

Queen Caroline possessed great art in bending
the king's mind to the purposes which his English
minister thought advantageous and necessary, and
in counteracting the Hanoverian cabals. She always affected to retire when the minister came
into the closet, declared she did not understand
business, and only remained as if to obey the king's
commands, and not out of inclination or curiosity.
She never appeared to listen; never gave her opinion unless solicited, and then delivered it with a
modestly

* From Lord Orford.   ┼ Ibid.

modefty and humility which captivated and charmed the king. She was extremely fond of power, though fhe affected the contrary, and preferved her influence over the king by confummate difcretion. She was a friend to peace, and appreciated and enforced the pacific fyftem of Sir Robert Walpole, as the only means of preferving the interior tranquillity, and preventing a rebellion; as the great caufe of the national profperity, of the increafe of commerce, and of the improvement of manufactures and agriculture.

The interpofition of queen Caroline, and the affiftance which fhe gave to the miniftry, in regulating the conduct of affairs, was of the higheft advantage both to them and the country. She was not unacquainted with the conftitution of England; and fhe often prepared and fmoothed the way towards obtaining the king's confent to meafures which he had firft oppofed, becaufe they often ran counter to his German prejudices, or to his paffion for military glory.

From the time of his acceffion, to the hour of her death, the king always appointed her, during his abfence, regent of the kingdom, and an act of parliament was paffed for the exprefs purpofe of exempting her from taking the oaths. He uniformly expreffed as much fatisfaction, when the affairs of government were conducted by her, as when they were conducted by himfelf; an honourable teftimony of his confidence, which fhe amply merited by her confummate good fenfe and difcretion. The reliance which George the Second

placed

Period IV. placed on the queen, is evidently proved by some
1727 to 1730. expreſſions in a letter from Da Cunha, the Portu-
gueſe miniſter at the Hague, to Azevedo in Lon-
don . " As to your journey to Hanover, I have already given my opinion; it is certain neither the
king will do any thing without the queen, nor the
queen without the king: and therefore, in point
of diſpatch of buſineſs, London is Hanover, and
Hanover is London *."

CHAPTER THE THIRTY-THIRD:

1727—1729.

*Walpole obtains an Increaſe of the Civil Liſt, and a Jointure of
£.100,000 for Queen Caroline.—Meeting and Proceedings of the New
Parliament.—State of the Oppoſition.—Important Diſcuſſion on the
State of the Sinking Fund and National Debt.—Report of the Houſe of
Commons on that Subject.—The King refuſes to make Charles Stanhope
a Lord of the Admiralty.—Foreign Affairs.—Tranſactions with Spain
and the Emperor.—Alliance with Brunſwick.—Act of the Pardo.—
Congreſs of Soiſſons.—Treaty of Seville.*

New miniſtry
confirmed.

IN conſequence of the re-appointment of Towſ-
hend and Walpole, not a ſingle member of the
cabinet council was removed, excepting the earl
of Berkley, firſt lord of the admiralty, who was replaced by Sir George Byng, viſcount Torrington,
the confidential friend of Walpole; and the power
of the miniſter was increaſed by the nomination of
ſeveral of his friends to ſubordinate offices in the
treaſury, admiralty, and other boards of government.

* July 3d 1736. Orford Papers.

ment. The wifdom of continuing the adminiftration, was proved by the unanimity with which affairs were at firft conducted in parliament; and
the acceffion of George the Second, which the
Jacobites abroad and at home had impatiently
expected as the fignal of a new revolution, took
place with the moft perfect tranquillity. They
founded their principal hopes on the removal of
the minifter. The fecretary of lord Orrery, had
obferved to the exiled bifhop of Rochefter, that
if the project to deftroy Sir Robert Walpole was
fuccefsful, he had more hopes of feeing the Che-
valier reftored, to the fatisfaction of himfelf and
fubjects, than from any Alberoni or foreign affiftance in the world. Atterbury himfelf alfo acknowledged that the king knew his intereft too well to
encourage any attempts againft the minifter *.
The general defpondency which they now teftified, was equal to the ardour of their former expectations, and fufficiently proves that he was confidered as the great fupport of the proteftant fucceffion, and the bulwark of the religion and conftitution.

The oppofition feems to have been ftunned with
the re-appointment of the minifter, whofe difgrace
they had fondly anticipated, and the bufinefs was
carried through the houfe of commons almoft with
perfect unanimity. The day after the arrival of
the exprefs, with official intelligence of the death

of

* Secret Intelligence from Paris, September 24th, 1727.—Walpole
Papers.

of George the Firſt, the parliament aſſembled in conformity to the act of ſettlement, and was prorogued by commiſſion to the 27th. On that day, the king came to the houſe of peers, and in his ſpeech from the throne, after expreſſing his concern for the death of his father, his determination to preſerve the conſtitution inviolable, and to ſecure to all his ſubjects the full enjoyment of their religious and civil rights; he gave his full ſanction to the late meaſures. The addreſs of condolance and congratulation, moved by Sir Paul Methuen, and ſeconded by Walpole, was carried without oppoſition. It was drawn up in ſuch terms as ſufficiently proved that he thought himſelf ſecure of all the influence and power which he had hitherto poſſeſſed *. On the 3d of July, he propoſed that the entire revenue of the civil liſt, which produced about £.130,000 more than the £.700,000 granted to the late king, might be ſettled on his majeſty during life. Although this motion was conſidered as the price of his continuance in office, yet no one ventured to oppoſe it, except Shippen, who after a long ſpeech, moved, that no more than £.700,000 ſhould be ſettled; but as he was not ſeconded, the original motion paſſed without a diviſion †.

On

---

* Journals.—Tindal, vol. 20. p. 4.—Hiſtorical Regiſter, 172.—Chandler.

† It is a curious obſervation of Smollett (vol. 2. p. 131.) which muſt tend to ſhew with how much partiality and inaccuracy he compiled his hiſtory. That " to theſe particulars (namely, in the ſpeech of Shippen) which were indeed *unanſwerable,* no reply was made. Even this mark of decency was laid aſide, as idle and *ſuperfluous.*" The fact was, that no reply was made, not becauſe the arguments were unanſwerable, but becauſe no one ſeconded the motion; a circumſtance

of

On the 9th, in confequence of a meffage requefting the houfe to fettle a jointure on the queen, if fhe fhould fervive the king; it was unanimoufly agreed that £.100,000 fhould be granted for that purpofe. On the 17th, the king made a fpeech from the throne, in which, after thanking the parliament for this mark of attachment and affection, he gave another and a ftronger fanction to the conduct of the minifters, and adverted to the flourifhing ftate of the country. The parliament was then prorogued to the 29th of Auguft, and foon afterwards diffolved. Thus was this fhort feffion of parliament conducted with an unanimity and zeal unexampled in the annals of this country.

As the fame men were continued in office, of courfe the fame meafures were purfued both at home and abroad. At home, to continue the public tranquillity, to counteract the fchemes of the Jacobites, to promote commerce, to encourage agriculture and manufactures were the great efforts of adminiftration, and in thefe Walpole took an active and leading part. The new houfe of commons, which affembled on the 23d of January 1728, was of the fame temper and difpofition as the laft; and the members in favour of adminiftration were foon found to exceed the complement in the former parliament. Sir Spencer Compton,

Meeting of the new parliament.

of which Smollett takes no notice. Belfham alfo obferves (vol. 1. p. 172.) with no lefs inaccuracy, "The amendment was rejected *with a great majority*," which would lead the reader to fuppofe, that there was a divifion. But in fact, there was no amendment duly moved and feconded, and the original motion, of courfe, paffed unanimoufly.

Period IV. ton, who had occupied the chair, having been
1727 to 1730. created a peer, Arthur Onflow was elected fpeaker,
with an unanimity which could only be infpired
by an opinion of his integrity and abilities, an
opinion which his fubfequent conduct fully juftified, by an able and impartial difcharge of his
duty, during a period of thirty-feven years *. The

King's fpeech. fpeech from the throne was remarkable for an appearance of franknefs and fincerity. The king firft
alluded to the uncertain fituation of affairs abroad,
to the difficulties which had attended the execution of the preliminaries with Spain, and to the
unavoidable neceffity of not difcontinuing warlike
preparations; and then, after the ordinary profeffions of frugality, and willingnefs to reduce the
national expences, exhorted the commons to take
into confideration the encouragement of feamen in
general, that they might be invited rather than
compelled to enter into the fervice of their country, a confideration, he obferved, worthy of the reprefentatives of a people great and flourifhing in
trade and navigation. To this purpofe, he propofed an addition to the fund of Greenwich ho-
fpital, and concluded with recommending unanimity, zeal, and difpatch.

Addrefs. This fpeech was heard with general fatisfaction.
The addrefs paffed the lords without oppofition;
being prefented to the commons for their approbation, Shippen propofed, with a view to caft a
reflection on the minifters, after the words *difagreeable*

* Tindal.

greeable, and uncertain state of affairs, to add, *at his majesty's accession to the throne.* He then took occasion to launch out into the most bitter invectives, and particularly taxed the squadron as useless and insignificant, for not having rifled the galleons at Carthagena, and plundered Porto Bello. Sir William Wyndham seconded the motion with his usual energy, and observed, that the languid measures adopted by government, tended only to remove the negotiations from Paris and Madrid to Cambray, and would not assist in removing the difficulties into which this dilatory mode of proceeding had plunged the nation. But these declamatory objections did not accord with the temper of the house; they rather excited so much indignation among the independent members, that the opposition did not venture to call for a division, and the address was carried unanimously. In fact, this conduct of opposition, not only displeased the nation, but even hurt their cause in the only court, where it was likely to have any effect. For the great objection which cardinal Fleury had raised against the counsels of England, was derived from their precipitancy and violence; and Bolingbroke had laboured to impress this notion on his partisans. The ministers availed themselves of this circumstance, and in conformity to their instructions, earl Waldegrave, who in the absence of Horace Walpole conducted the affairs of England at Paris, represented with due effect to the cardinal, that the same measures to which he objected, as

too

Period IV.   too prompt and decisive, were reprobated in Eng-
1727 to 1730. land, as deficient in spirit and energy [*].

Debate on the   The first question which met with much oppo-
Hessian troops. sition, was that made by Horace Walpole, that
February 14.
£.230,923 should be granted for maintaining
12,000 Hessians in the British pay, In the debate
on this motion, the minority seem to have first
recovered from their surprise; the Pulteneys and
Sir William Wyndham spoke with great weight
and art on a question which has been so often discussed, and which still continues to agitate the
public mind, concerning the expediency of taking
foreign troops into British pay. The argument in
favour of the question was, in substance, that the
late king had thought fit to provide these troops,
in order to obtain the ends of the treaty of Hanover; that they were ready at hand, and much
cheaper than raising national troops; that a disappointment, from the defection of the king of Prus-
sia, one of the contracting parties in the alliance,
was a special reason for retaining them; that time
had manifested this to have been a prudential measure, it having prevented a war in Germany; that
the reasons for taking them into pay still subsisted,
and therefore their continuance was necessary till
the intended congress at Cambray was finished,
84 divided against 280 [†].

The opposi-   It was at this period, in which Walpole, con-
tion.
fiding on the support of queen Caroline, took the

lead

* George Tilson to the earl of Waldegrave, February 2d and 5th,
1727-8. Waldegrave Papers.   † Journals. Chandler.

lead in the administration, and became in reality
the first minister, although lord Townshend still
ostensibly retained the name; that the opposition
began to form itself into consistency, and to com-
pose a firm and compact phalanx, which resisted
all the efforts and influence of the minister to divide them, and which finally drove him from the
helm.

Until the death of George the First, the com-
ponent parts of this heterogeneous body, which
consisted of a few disappointed Whigs, Tories, and
Jacobites, did not cordially coalesce. Many of
those Whigs and moderate Tories, who looked up
to that event as a prelude to their own admission
into the ministry, kept aloof from those who, as
being professed Jacobites, or violent Tories, could
not expect the same success. But no sooner had
the continuance of Walpole in office annihilated
their hopes, than the whole body became compact
and united. In this respect, the Whigs became
Tories, the Tories Whigs; and the Jacobites af-
sumed every shape which tended to promote their
views, by distressing government, and harassing the
minister, whom they considered as the great supporter of the house of Brunswick.

The chief aim of the minister was to comprehend almost all the Tories as enemies to the government, by the name of Jacobites, or at least to
give that stigma to every one who was not a pro-
fest and known Whig. With this view, his own
administration being naturally supported on a Whig
foundation, he endeavoured to attach to himself
all

Period IV. all thofe who had been dependent on Sunderland.
1727 to 1730. With fome he fucceeded, but not with all; and of
thofe whom he could not gain, feveral remained
in their employments, becaufe they were protected
by the Hanover junto. This body of Whigs, fmall
but of confiderable eminence, remained his enemies to the time of the king's death, watching for
every opportunity to ruin him; and from the ac-
- ceffion of George the Second, commenced the oppofition which became afterwards fo troublefome
and formidable *. Pulteney was the great leader
of this body; under him were ranged his kinfman
Daniel Pulteney, Sir John Barnard, Sandys, and
afterwards lord Polwarth, Pitt, Littleton, and the
Grenvilles. Sir William Wyndham was the great
chief of the Tories, and William Shippen was at
the head of the Jacobites, who did not form lefs
than fifty members. Thofe who fupported the minifter were lord Hervey, whofe character and talents have been fcandaloufly depreciated by Pope,
Henry Pelham, Sir William Yonge, whom Johnfon calls the beft fpeaker in the houfe of commons, Winnington, and his brother Horace Walpole, whofe talents for negotiation, indefatigable
affiduity in bufinefs, and acquaintance with foreign
tranfactions, rendered him an able co-adjutor.

Debates on the
finking fund
and the na-
tional debt.

During this feffion, a very important queftion,
on the ftate of the national debt, was brought before the houfe, in which the minifter of finance was
deeply engaged. In the debates which took place

on

* For the characters of the leading members of Oppofition, fee Onflow's Remarks, Correfpondence, Period IV.

on this fubject, the oppofition had declaimed
againft the profufe expenditure of the public money. They declared, that although large fupplies
were annually voted during the laft reign, and the
produce of the finking fund had been applied to
the difcharge of the debt, during a period of almoft
uninterrupted tranquillity, yet the public burthens
were *increafed* inftead of being diminifhed; and
they obferved, that if the war with Spain fhould
continue, and new troubles arife in Europe, frefh
taxes muft be perpetuated to the lateft pofterity,
and the nation muft inevitably fink under fuch an
accumulated load.

In proof of thefe arguments, Pulteney had publifhed a well written pamphlet, " On the State of
the National Debt." Many fimilar ftatements had
appeared in the Craftfman, attempting to fhew,
that the finking fund had been of no fervice to the
purpofe for which it was originally intended. Walpole knew that this pofition was defended by the
moft able pens, and oftentatioufly fupported by
laborious calculations, which the people could not
comprehend. As thefe affertions raifed great clamours at home, and had a confiderable effect
abroad, in decrying the credit of the nation, it
became neceffary to confute, or at leaft to contradict them, in the fame pofitive manner in which
they were advanced. With this view, the minifter
determined, through the medium of the houfe of
commons, to make a folemn appeal to the nation
againft their ftatements; and his refolution was
unwittingly forwarded by oppofition, who did not
know

Period IV.
1727 to 1730.

know that in repeating their attacks, they supplied him with the very weapons of defence, which he could not so easily have acquired without their concurrence.

February 22.

In laying before the commons an account of the sinking fund, Walpole declared, that since 1716, it had discharged above six millions of the debt, but that as new debts had been contracted, the national burthens had upon the balance been diminished about two millions and a half. Pulteney in reply asserted, that notwithstanding the great merit which some persons had arrogated to themselves from the establishment of the sinking fund, it appeared that the debt had *increased*, instead of being diminished, since the commencement of that pompous project. To this Sir Nathaniel Gould, an eminent merchant, observed, that he apprehended the gentleman had taken this notion from a treatise, intituled, " The State of the National Debt ;" that if he understood any thing, it was numbers, and that he would stake his credit, to shew the fallacy of the author's calculations and inferences. Pulteney defended his calculations, and added, that he was not at present prepared to prove his assertions, but that he would do so in a few days, and would also stake his reputation on their truth. The minister supported the opinion of Sir Nathaniel Gould, and added, that he would also stake his reputation on the truth of what he advanced *. Walpole now exerted himself in preparing

* George Tilson to the earl of Waldegrave, February 22d, 1727-8, Correspondence.—Chandler.

paring fpecific ftatements of the produce of the
finking fund, of the debts which had been liquidated, and of thofe which had been contracted
fince its eftablifhment, with a view of fubmitting
them to parliament on the firft opportunity, which
was foon fupplied by the leading member of oppofition.

On the 29th of February, the king's anfwer
was given to an addrefs, requefting a fpecific account of £.250,000 which had been charged for
fecret fervices; he trufted the houfe would repofe
the fame confidence in him as they had repofed
in his royal father; and declared, that a fpecific
account of the difburfements could not be given,
without manifeft prejudice to the public. This
meffage had no fooner been delivered by Sir Paul
Methuen, comptroller of the houfehold, than
Pulteney rofe: with great animation he inveighed
againft fuch a vague and general way of account-
ing for the public money, as tending to render
parliament infignificant and ufelefs, to cover em-
bezzlements, and to fcreen corrupt and rapacious
minifters. He again urged the increafe of the national debt, and infifted on having that important
affair debated in a grand committee. The minifter oppofed the immediate difcuffion of the
queftion, but moved to adjourn the debate only
to the 4th of March, when after the examination
of the revenue officers, he fhould be ready to lay
before the houfe, the ftate of the national debt.
This motion was carried by 202 againft 66 *.

Accord-

* Journals.

Accordingly, on the 4th of March, the commons, in a committee of the whole houfe, confidered the ftate of the national debt, and examined at the bar the proper officers of the revenue. At the conclufion of this examination,
with a view to avoid all general cavils, and to reduce the affertions of the adverfaries to a fpecific
account, a motion was made by the friends of the
minifter, " That the monies already applied towards difcharging the national debts incurred before Chriftmas 1716, together with £.220,435,
which will be iffued at Lady Day 1728, amount
to £.6,648,762."

In reply to this propofition, the minority argued, that for the purpofe of fwelling the amount
of the fums faid to be iffued for the liquidation
of the debt, the minifter had put down no lefs
than three millions, which had been advanced in
1720, to make the irredeemables redeemables;
and which could not properly be called a payment
of debts. They alfo infifted, that he had omitted
feveral large fums, particularly one million raifed
upon the credit of the civil lift, and deficiences
of the land tax, malt, and other funds. They
concluded, that thefe defalcations from the fums
paid, and additions to the ftanding debts, would
reduce the £.6,648,762, which, according to the
boafts of the minifter, was fuppofed to be liquidated, to lefs than one third.

Walpole, on the other hand, maintained with
no lefs pofitivenefs the accuracy of his own ftatements, expatiated on the ftate of the nation, and

§   of

of the public debts, explained the operation and
efficacy of the finking fund, and supported the
motion. The oppofition then propofed that the
fpeaker fhould refume the chair, but this being
negatived by 250 againft 97, the original queftion
was put, and carried without a divifion.

The minifter having obtained this victory, refolved to bring forwards his public appeal to the
nation, by prefenting a report from the houfe of
commons to the king, ftating, in certain refolutions, the amount of the national debt, and the
fums which had been liquidated by means of the
finking fund. With this view, four refolutions
were fubmitted to a committee of the whole
houfe, on the 8th of March; the firft of which
repeated, in the fame words, the motion made on
the 4th, that £.6,648,762 had been difcharged.

The oppofition, recollecting their former defeat
by a large majority, and feeing that the houfe
wholly differed from their reprefentations, did not
lay their wonted ftrefs on the main queftion, but
loudly called again upon the minifter for an account of the fum lately employed in fecret fervice.
To thefe clamours Walpole made the ufual reply,
that it had been expended in negotiations too
delicate to be fpecified. In the midft of his
fpeech, an account was tranfmitted by lord Townfhend, that the convention with Spain was figned
at the Pardo *. Walpole availed himfelf of this
information; and acquainting the houfe with the
news, added, " That the nation would be now
relieved

* See the conclufion of this chapter.

relieved from the burthen of the late, expences, and that he could affure the members who called fo loudly for a fpecification of the fecret .fervice money, that it had been expended in obtaining the conclufion of that peace, the preliminaries of which were now figned. The defigns of thofe (he faid) who had laboured to difturb the tranquillity of Europe, were thus defeated ; and the purchafe of peace, and the prevention of war, on terms fo cheap, were highly beneficial to the public." This information fpread general fatisfaction through the houfe ; the queftion was inftantaneoufly called for, and the refolutions paffed without a divifion*. On a fubfequent meeting, thefe refolutions were formed into a report, which was drawn up by the minifter, and laid before the houfe, to be prefented to the king.

April 8th.
Report on the
ftate of the
finking fund
and national
debt.
This is a very elaborate performance †, and deferves the ftricteft attention. After laying down the fubject of the report, which was to examine how much of the additional debt incurred before the 25th of December 1716 had been difcharged, and what new debts had been contracted fince that time ; it proceeds with making fevere reflections againft the arts which had been practifed to miflead the people in this important inquiry, " by publifhing and promoting, with the greateft induftry, moft notorious mifreprefentations of the

true

---

* Lettre de Monfieur Le Coq, au Roi de Pologne, de Londres, 23 Mars, 1728. Alfo, a letter from a foreign minifter, dated $\frac{12}{23}$ March, 1728. De la Faye to earl Waldegrave, March $\frac{11}{22}$, 172$\frac{6}{8}$. Correfpondence, Period III.

† Tindal, vol. 20. p. 24.

true ſtate of our debts, and of the proviſions
made for the diſcharge of them; and by infuſing
groundleſs jealouſies and inſinuations, as if the
produce of the ſinking fund had been but little
and inconſiderable, or that by wrong and impru‑
dent meaſures, bad œconomy, neglect, or miſ‑
management, unneceſſary expences had been made,
and new debts contracted, that not only equalled,
but exceeded by ſeveral millions, the amount of
the old debts that had been diſcharged *." It
then adopts a method that is plain, eaſy, and in‑
telligible to the meaneſt capacity, by giving, in
two tables, the amounts of the debts diſcharged
and incurred ſince the 25th of December 1716,
juſt before the eſtabliſhment of the ſinking fund:

Debts incurred ſince De‑			
cember 25th 1716, and			
ſince diſcharged - - -	6,626,404	16	9½
Debts contracted and in‑			
curred ſince December			
25th 1716, and now ſub‑			
ſiſting - - - - -	3,927,988	7	11¼
Difference, or decreaſe of			
the national debt - -	2,698,416	9	7¼

It then gives the new debts under the proper
heads of the ſervices for which they were con‑
tracted; and after having related the beginning,
eſtabliſhment, and beneficial effects of the ſinking
fund, obſerves, that by reducing the intereſt of
the

* Journals.

the greateſt part of the. debts from 6 to 4 per cent. there is a ſaving of one third of the intereſt, which is equal to a diſcharge of one third of the principal; and that as the annual produce of the fund was gradually raiſed from £.400,000 to £.1,200,000 the addition of £.800,000, if valued at twenty-five years purchaſe, the current price of annuities, would give a real profit to the public of £.20,000,000.

It concludes by ſaying, " This is the happy ſtate of the ſinking fund, taken ſeparately, and by it-ſelf; ,but, if we caſt our eyes upon the ſtate of our public credit in general, it muſt be an additional ſatisfaction to us, that by preſerving the public faith inviolable, by the diſcharge of the old ex-chequer bills, and the reduction of the high in-tereſt on all our ſtanding debts, the whole credit that is taken on the annual.funds, for carrying on the current ſervice of the year, is and may be ſup-plied for the future at £.3 per cent. or leſs, for intereſt, premium, and charges, by exchequer bills, juſt as the occaſions of the public require, without any loans, or being obliged to any perſons, for money to. be advanced or lent on the credit of them; and ſo far is the public from being under the former neceſſities of allowing extravagant in-tereſt, premiums, or diſcounts, for any money they want, that the only conteſt now among the cre-ditors of the public is, that every one of them de-ſires to be the laſt in courſe of payment."

" Permit us then, moſt gracious ſovereign, to congratulate your majeſty on the comfortable pro-
ſpect

ſpect we have now before us, if, notwithſtanding
the many difficulties this nation has laboured under ſince the happy acceſſion of your majeſty's
late royal father to the throne, notwithſtanding the
unnatural rebellion which ſoon after broke out,
and the many heinous plots and conſpiracies which
have ſince been formed and carried on for overturning the religion and liberties of our country,
and the proteſtant ſucceſſion in your moſt illuſ-
trious family; the many diſturbances which have
ariſen, and the uncertain and embroiled condition
of the affairs of Europe, not a little fomented and
encouraged by the falſe intelligence, and malicious
inſinuations which have been induſtriouſly ſpread
abroad by your majeſty's and our enemies, of the
uneaſy and perplexed ſtate of our affairs at home,
as if that had rendered it almoſt impoſſible for
this nation, effectually to exert themſelves in
defence of their own juſt rights and poſſeſſions, and
for eſtabliſhing and ſecuring the public peace and
tranquillity; if, notwithſtanding theſe and many
other difficulties which we laboured under, and
while the ſinking fund was yet in its infancy, and
ſo much leſs than it now is, we have been able to
diminiſh the national debts ſo much already, what
may we not hope for in regard to a more ſpeedy
and ſenſible diſcharge of them for the future, now
the ſinking fund is ſo greatly increaſed, and our
public credit in ſo flouriſhing a condition *."

Such was the ſubſtance of this remarkable report,

* Journals.

port, which was carried by 243 againſt 77 [*]. It

was preſented to the king, and drew a favourable

anſwer, expreſſing his extreme ſatisfaction for the
removal of groundleſs jealouſies and apprehenſions,
for the happy effects to be derived from the flouriſhing ſtate of public credit, for the proviſion made
for the gradual diſcharge of the national debt, and
concluded by obſerving, " You may be aſſured, it
ſhall be my particular care and ſtudy to maintain
and preſerve the public credit, and to improve the
ſinking fund, and to avoid all occaſions of laying
any new burthens upon the people [†]."

The effects of the report, both at home and
abroad, were incalculably beneficial to the credit
of the miniſter. Whatever were the opinions of
individuals, whatever might be the cavils of thoſe
who oppoſed government, the ſtatement of the
miniſter was approved by more than *two thirds of
the national repreſentatives, aſſembled in parliament,
and was ſolemnly ſanctioned by the king.* At home
the diſcontents viſibly ſubſided; abroad the national credit was eſtabliſhed on ſtronger grounds
than ever. It was proved, in oppoſition to the
clamours of the diſaffected, that the kingdom
could ſupport the expences of a war. France
courted our alliance with redoubled ardour; Spain
was confirmed in her wiſhes for peace; the Emperor and Ruſſia ſhrunk from a conteſt with Great
Britain; and the diſpatches from Paris, Seville,
and Vienna, ſufficiently announced the weight and
influence which the counſels of England had gained
by

---

[*] Journals.   [†] Ibid.

by the opinion, which now generally prevailed in favour of her finances.

In this session occurred one of those difficult and critical cases, in which Walpole was reduced to the necessity of complying with the will of the sovereign, contrary to his own judgment, or of resigning. Great complaints had been made of the deficiency of the civil list, and upon an examination of the revenue officers, a motion was made by Scrope, secretary to the treasury, that the sum of £.115,000 be granted to his majesty, not as a deficiency, but as an arrear. It appeared that there was no deficiency, yet the house rejected a motion for a secret committee, and passed the act, by a majority of 241 against 115. In the lords, the bill met with strenuous opposition, and though carried, very strong protests were entered on the Journals, and signed by fourteen peers. This transaction gave great pain to Walpole: he is said to have used every effort of address and reasoning to dissuade the prosecution of the demand, so much as even to offend the king. The enemies of his administration were not ignorant of his resistance, and some of the leading Tories made secret proposals to the king, that if he would discard Walpole, they would not only obtain the sum required, but add to it £.100,000. Thus circumstanced, the minister reluctantly complied, and subjected his character to much obloquy *.

This inflexibility of George the Second exposed Walpole

* Journals. Chandler. Tindal. Etough's Papers.

E 3

Walpole not only to many difficulties in his public
career, but to many unmerited reproaches in his
character, as a man of veracity. Great embarraffment to a minifter muft be derived from the occafional reluctance of the fovereign to confirm the
promifes made to individuals of particular offices,
either of honour or truft; and on fuch occafions,
he naturally incurs the blame of either indifference,
negligence, or duplicity. · Thus he had not been
able to obtain for his friend the duke of Devonfhire the prefidentfhip of the council, which high
office was, by the interpofition of Sunderland, conferred on lord Carleton, who, fince his elevation to
the peerage, had feldom voted with the Whigs.

But perhaps no failure affected him more, or
caufed more reproaches, than the refufal of the fovereign to make Charles Stanhope, elder brother
of the earl of Harrington, a lord of the admiralty.
The real caufe of the king's non-compliance, arofe
from his averfion to Charles Stanhope, which was
difclofed to the minifter, under the ftricteft injunctions of fecrecy. George the Second had
found, among his father's papers and letters, a
memorial from lord Sunderland, written in the
hand of Charles Stanhope, highly expreffive of
ftrong diflike to the prince of Wales, and recommending the adoption of the moft violent meafures againft him. The perufal of this paper excited the higheft indignation as well againft the
memory of lord Sunderland, as againft the fecretary who had written it. In regard to Charles
Stanhope, the king declared, that no confideration
fhould

should· induce him to affign to him 'any place of · truft or honour ; and he kept his word.' For when. Sir Robert Walpole efpoufed ·his intereft ‑ with much ardour, he offended the king, who re- jected the application, with fome expreffions of refentment againft the minifter for having recom- mended him *.

When George the Firft left England, things wore the appearance of a general pacification. In virtue of the preliminaries figned by the Imperial and Spanifh embaffadors, a courier from Spain was hourly expected to announce, that the fiege of Gibraltar was raifed, and the prizes reftored. But the death of the king put a momentary fufpenfion to thefe hopes.

Philip received the preliminaries on the 10th of June, and before he iffued orders in conformity with his promifes, the news of that event arrived. The acceffion of the new fovereign had been an- nounced by the Jacobites abroad, as likely to meet with numerous obftacles, and at all events, it was fuppofed that the helm of government would not be directed by fo fteady a hand, when Townfhend and Walpole were removed. Under·thefe impref- fions, Philip, infpired with the hopes of breaking the ftrict alliance between France and England, and of again engaging the Emperor in his fupport, while he affected to agree to the terms accepted by his embaffador, delayed, under various pre- tences,

* Lord Townfhend to Stephen Poyntz, June 3d, 1728. Cor- refpondence, Period IV.

E 4

tences, to raife the fiege of Gibraltar, and to reftore the Prince Frederic, a fhip belonging to the South Sea company, which had been feized under the pretence of carrying on a contraband trade.

The Emperor juftified this conduct, by declaring, that the king of Spain was not obliged by the preliminaries to take thofe fteps; and by his preparations, gave unequivocal figns of intentions hoftile to England. The only method therefore of bringing Philip to reafon, was to attack his ally in Germany, and to purfue fuch vigorous meafures as might deter the court of Vienna from fupporting Spain by invading the electorate and the United Provinces, the only parts in which the allies of Hanover were vulnerable, and which the Englifh would be bound in honour to defend. This meafure was ftill more neceffary, becaufe the conventions made by the Emperor with the electors and princes of the empire, and the fubfidies which he was to pay with Spanifh money, in virtue of thofe conventions, were not expired. The allies were, by the management of the courts of Vienna and Madrid, in the fame ftate of uncertainty as to peace or war, as they were before the preliminaries were figned.

Among all thefe conventions made by the Emperor, none had a more fatal tendency than that with Brunfwick Wolfenbuttel. The Emperor had already drawn the electors of Mentz, Cologne, Treves, and Bavaria, and the Elector Palatine, into his intereft. His near confanguinity to the prince of Saxony, feemed to fecure to him, at leaft, the neutrality

neutrality of that proteftant electorate; and he
had found means to' draw off the king of Pruffia,
by the promife of guarantying to him the fucceffion of Berg and Ravenftein. ' In cafe of a rupture,
he had fecured Mentz as a place of arms, which
gave him the command of Suabia, Franconia, and
the Rhine.

The Elector of Mentz had already permitted
him to put a garrifon into Erfurt, which, by its
fituation, made him in effect mafter of Upper
Saxony : but ftill Lower Saxony, in which circle
the dominions of Hanover are fituated, remained
inacceffible, till he found means to make a treaty
with the duke of Brunfwick Wolfenbuttel, by
which he was to grant that prince a fubfidy of
200,000 florins a year. In a fecret article of that
treaty, it was farther ftipulated, that the conjuncture of affairs requiring it, clofer engagements
fhould be entered into between them; as well for
augmenting the duke's fubfidies and troops; as in
relation to the town of Brunfwick. In confequence of this convention, another fubfidiary treaty
was opened between the court of Ruffia and the
duke; under the influence and direction of the
Emperor. Had he been permitted to garrifon
Brunfwick, not only a fatal difunion would have
been produced between the branches of the king's
family; but the fituation of that place would have
enabled the Emperor to pour into the electorate
his own troops, as well as the 30,000 men which
by the treaty with Ruffia, were to have been introduced into the empire, under pretence of recovering

vering Slefwick for the duke of Holftein; the
greater part of Weftphalia would have been laid
under contribution, even to the frontiers of Holland; and the kings of Denmark and Sweden
would have been kept in awe, by being forced to
provide for the fafety of their own poffeffions on
the fide of Germany.

In this dangerous fituation of affairs, when the
king's German dominions, and through them the
United Provinces, were threatened by the combined arms of Auftria, Ruffia, and Pruffia, and
when the poffeffion of Brunfwick, as a place of
arms for the allies of Vienna, would have enabled
the Emperor to penetrate into Lower Saxony, and
bring on a general war, a treaty was negotiated
and concluded with the duke of Brunfwick Wolfenbuttel, which put an inftant check to the views
of the Emperor, and to the hopes of Spain.   This
treaty, negotiated between lord Townfhend and
count Dehn, the confidential minifter of the duke
of Brunfwick, was figned at Wolfenbuttel, on the
23d of November 1727. It ftipulated a renewal of
the family compact, according to the treaty of the
6th of May 1661, by which Brunfwick was to be
kept for the common fafety of the houfe of Lunenburgh, and not delivered up to any other power; a
mutual guaranty of dominions; mutual affiftance
in cafe of attack; a fubfidy of £. 25,000 a year, during four years, to the duke of Brunfwick, who was
to furnifh at leaft 5,000 men. This treaty, if confidered in its general effects and tendency to the
pacification

pacification of Germany, was a mafter-piece of policy: it united the two branches of the houfe of
Lunenburgh, who had been long at variance; and
by preventing the progrefs of the Imperial arms,
faved the electorate of Hanover from hoftile inroads.

Thefe prudent and vigorous meafures had the
effect for which they were defigned. The Emperor was reduced to a ftate of inaction; and
Spain, unable to maintain an unequal conteft
with the allies of Hanover, fubmitted with reluctance, and ratified the preliminaries of peace
at the Pardo, a royal palace near Madrid, in conformity to a declaration fettled between Horace
Walpole and cardinal Fleury, and made by count
Rothembourg, the French minifter in Spain. In
confequence of this act, the congrefs of Soiffons
was held, where the plenipotentiaries of all the
powers concerned in the late troubles were affembled; and although nothing material was tranfacted, yet the negotiations were managed, on
the part of the Hanover allies, in fuch a manner
as to create a divifion between the courts of Vienna and Madrid. The project of a provifional
treaty, negotiated between the Imperial, Britifh,
and French plenipotentiaries, had fo alarmed the
king of Spain, and created fo much uneafinefs in
the queen, that they required from the Emperor
a pofitive declaration on the fubject of marrying
the two archducheffes to the two Infants of Spain,
and his refufal to explain himfelf, excited their
refentment to fuch a degree, as to give England
and

Period IV. and France an opportunity of detaching them
1727 to 1730. from the Emperor.

Treaty of Se-
ville.

    The breach being now made, a reconciliation
fpeedily took place between the allies of Hanover
and Spain. Philip facrificed the Emperor, as the
Emperor, by declining to co-operate in the fiege
of Gibraltar, had facrificed him, figned the preliminaries at Pardo, and concluded, at Seville,
1729.   the 29th of November, with Great Britain and
France, a treaty of peace, union, and mutual
defence. This treaty, befides the reftoration of
peace, and the renewal. of all former treaties between Great Britain and Spain, ftipulated the introduction of fix thoufand Spaniards, inftead of
neutral troops, as fpecified by the quadruple alliance, into Tufcany, Parma, and Placentia, for
fecuring to Don Carlos the eventual fucceffion to
thofe duchies, in cafe the reigning fovereigns
fhould die without iffue male; and if the Emperor would not acquiefce, forcible means were
to be ufed for effectuating the introduction.

    In return for this fingle article granted to Spain,
Great Britain obtained immediate redrefs of fome
grievances, the promife of redrefs in others, new
guaranties of all her poffeffions, and of all her
rights of trade, and a tacit exclufion of any claim
to Gibraltar, upon which to be filent, after the
clamorous demands made by Spain, was the fame
as a public renunciation *.

Although

* The contents of the part of this chapter which relates to foreign
affairs, have been principally drawn from the various difpatches of
Horace Walpole and William Stanhope, in the Walpole and Stan-
4   hope

Although Walpole fuffered the negotiations to be oftenfibly managed by Townfhend, and feemed to take no part in the various tranfactions, yet he watched with a jealous eye the progrefs of the bufinefs. In the fecret correfpondence which he conftantly held with his brother Horace, whofe opinion had a great influence over Townfhend, he directed all his advice and views to the final eftablifhment of peace. He was on the one hand equally ftudious not to offend the Emperor beyond hopes of recovery, who he well knew, in cafe of a reconciliation between France and Spain, could alone in future prevent the aggrandifement of the houfe of Bourbon, and on the other fide, was equally anxious to facilitate an accommodation with Spain, for the fake of reftoring the Britifh commerce, which had received a deep blow from the rupture with that country. The treaty of Seville, was indeed principally owing to his interference or directions; and Townfhend's repugnance to this plan of pacification, was overruled by the prudence and difcretion of his colleague.

Chapter 33.
1727 to 1729.

Walpole promotes the peace.

hope papers, and from the ftate of the negotiation, from June 1728 to June 1730, drawn up by Mr. Robinfon, the minifter at Vienna, in the Grantham papers.

CHAPTER THE THIRTY-FOURTH:

1727—1729.

Debates in Parliament on a supposed Promise of George the First to restore Gibraltar to Spain.—Mistakes generally entertained on that Subject.—True State of Facts.—Conduct of the Regent.—Of the King and Queen of Spain, and its Consequences.

Period IV. 1727 to 1730.

Parliamentary proceedings respecting Gibraltar.

IN the midst of these transactions, an outcry was raised against administration, for having degraded the king, and disgraced the nation, by breaking a promise made to Philip the Fifth, for the restitution of Gibraltar, which, it was urged, had induced that monarch to accede to the quadruple alliance; and therefore the war was unjust on the part of England, because he only claimed his right in virtue of that promise, and offered to commence a negotiation for peace, when it was fulfilled. To these assertions Walpole replied, that the promise having been given when he was not in administration, he was in no respect answerable for it; but that if it had ever been made, he durst aver, that it was conditional, and rendered void by the refusal of Spain to comply with the terms on which it was founded, and that whenever the performance of that agreement was mentioned to him, he always maintained that Gibraltar should not be granted without the consent of parliament *. When Sandys moved,

February 6, 1727.

" for

* Chandler.

" for addreffing the king to communicate to this
houfe, copies of the declaration, letter, or engagement, on which the king of Spain founded
his peremptory demand for the reftitution of that
fortrefs," he was feconded, and ftrenuoufly fupported by Sir William Wyndham, Hungerford,
and Pulteney, who took notice of a letter written
in 1721, to one of the Emperor's plenipotentiaries at Cambray, wherein a promife of ceding
Gibraltar was exprefsly mentioned; they were
oppofed by Henry Pelham, Brodrick, Horace
Walpole, and Sir Robert Walpole, who faid, that
the communication of the declaration or letter
was altogether impracticable and unprecedented;
the private letters of princes being almoft as facred as their very perfons *.

But although this remark at that time impofed
a refpectful filence on the houfe of commons,
yet the queftion was again revived in the upper
houfe, and the letter being produced, fome of
the lords in oppofition moved the refolution,
" That effectual care be taken, in the treaty then
in agitation, that the king of Spain do renounce
all claims and pretenfions to Gibraltar and Mi-
norca, in plain and ftrong terms." But the motion being overruled, another was carried, " That
the houfe relies upon the king for preferving the
undoubted right to Gibraltar and Minorca."
This refolution being fent down to the commons,
lord Malpas propofed and carried an addrefs for
a copy of the letter to the king of Spain; which

. being

* Chandler, vol. 6. p. 384.

Period IV. being laid before the houfe, a warm debate en-
1727 to 1730. fued. Many fevere reflections were levelled at
thofe who advifed the king to write fuch a letter, as implied, or at leaft was confidered by the Spaniards as fignifying a pofitive promife of giving up Gibraltar, and was therefore the principal occafion of the king of Spain's refentment, and of the difficulties in promoting a pacification. To thefe infinuations, Walpole replied as on the former occafion, and added, that the letter did not contain any pofitive promife; and that effectual care had been taken in the prefent negotiation to fecure the poffeffion of Gibraltar. But the party in oppofition declaring themfelves diffatisfied with this explanation and anfwer, moved an addition to the refolution of the lords, that all pretenfions on the part of Spain to Gibraltar and Minorca, fhould be fpecifically given up; but the queftion being negatived by a large majority of 156 voices, the refolution of the lords was carried without a divifion. Thus ended this bufinefs in parliament, which had created fo much ill-will, occafioned fo many falfe reports at the time, and which has fince been mifreprefented by thofe who inculpate the minifter for breaking a promife which he never made, and for violating the national honour, when, in fact, he defended and fupported it.

Errors of hif-   Although the bufinefs was thus concluded in
torians. parliament, yet the affertions of the minifter did not fatisfy oppofition, and as the affair was again renewed in the Craftfman, and other periodical
                  publications,

publications, with increafed rancour and exaggerated invective, to which Walpole never con-
defcended to make any reply, thefe invectives
have been adopted by fubfequent hiftorians with
no lefs afperity, and have been confidered as authentic facts. . Nor is this mifreprefentation, confined to the authors of this country : Many of the
French writers are, totally miftaken in the account
of this negotiation, in afferting, that George the
Firft promifed unconditionally to reftore Gibraltar.

Thus, particularly, Anquetil prefumes, that in
the peace which Spain concluded with France and
England, in 1720, there was a fecret article by
which the *king of England promifed to reftore Gi-*
braltar to Spain ; and he grounds this prefumption,
not unfairly, on the two following paffages from
the Memoirs of Villars. March 10, 1727: The
pope's nuncio at Madrid, wrote to the nuncio in
France, that the king of Spain offered to agree to
the fufpenfion of the trade from Oftend, and at
the fame time demanded Gibraltar, *infifting that*
the reftitution of it had been promifed by the king of
England. November 2, 1727: Count Rothembourg, the French embaffador at Madrid, relates,
that the queen of Spain complained of the Englifh, and fpeaking of Gibraltar, took out an original letter from the king's cabinet, *in which*
George the Firft promifed the reftitution of Gibral-
tar [*]. As therefore the accounts given of this
tranfaction

* Vol. 2. p. 411. See alfo Belfham's Hiftory, vol. 1. p. 251.

Period IV.
1727 to 1730. tranfaction are in general erroneous, and as the inquiry itfelf is not uninterefting, I fhall ftate a narrative of the negotiations relative to the reftitution of Gibraltar, drawn from authentic documents.

Correct ftatement of the fact.
In 1715, George the Firft, for the purpofe of avoiding a rupture with Spain, gave full powers to the regent, duke of Orleans, to offer the reftoration of Gibraltar ; the hoftilities which followed, annulled the promife, and afterwards the king of Spain acceded purely and fimply to the quadruple alliance, without ftipulating the ceffion. The regent, however, with a view to ingratiate himfelf with the king of Spain, and to promote the double marriage between the two infants and his two daughters, repeatedly renewed the offer in the name of George the Firft, and infpired Philip with the moft fanguine hopes of recovering fo important a fortrefs. Thefe expectations being urged by Philip with great warmth, and with little difcretion, obliged the king to declare that he did not confider himfelf as bound by his former conditional promife. The regent being reproached by the queen of Spain with a breach of his word, difpatched the count de Saneterre to England, to reprefent the danger and delicacy of his fituation. He declared, that he confidered the king's promife as full and pofitive, and that he would as foon confent to his utter ruin, as to the difhonour of failing in fo public an engagement. Thefe ftrong expreffions from the regent, who had proved himfelf fo faithful an ally, and whofe affiftance in dif-

covering

covering and counteracting the schemes of the Jacobites was so neceffary, perplexed the king, and
induced him to use his utmost endeavours to gratify him and the king of Spain, with this view, earl
Stanhope founded the difpofition of the upper
houfe, by infinuating an intention to obtain a bill,
empowering the king to difpofe of Gibraltar, for
the advantage of the nation. But this hint produced a violent ferment. The public were roufed
with indignation on the fimple fufpicion, that at
the clofe of a fuccefsful war, unjuftly begun by
Spain, fo important a fortrefs fhould be ceded.
General murmurs were at the fame time excited
by a report induftrioufly circulated by oppofition,
that the king had entered into a pofitive engagement for that purpofe; virulent pamphlets were
publifhed to alarm the people, and to perfuade
them rather to continue the war, than to give up
Gibraltar. The minifters were compelled to yield
to the torrent, and to adopt the prudent refolution
of waving the motion, left it fhould produce a
contrary effect, by a bill, which might for ever
tie * up the king's hands. The interference of
France in this affair, and the extreme eagernefs to
obtain the reftitution, was of great detriment. The
alarm was indeed fo ftrong, that fufpicions were
entertained that the regent was meditating the defertion of the alliance with England, and made
Gibraltar a pretext to juftify a change of fyftem.

                                                           Thefe

* Earl Stanhope to Sir Luke Schaub, Paris, March 28, 1720.
Hardwicke Papers.

Thefe apprehenfions induced the king to fend earl Stanhope to Paris, with a view of reprefenting the true fituation of affairs, and to ftate the unpopularity of the meafure, and the impracticability of carrying it againft the general fenfe of the people.

The letter which Stanhope conveyed from the king to the regent on this occafion, was firm, difcreet, and fatisfactory. He acknowledged that he had made the offer of ceding Gibraltar, folely with a view of preventing the rupture, and that Spain might have obtained it, had fhe then acceded to the propofed conditions. But it was now too late to revive the demand, as the king of Spain had proved himfelf the aggreffor. It never could be underftood that a voluntary offer of this nature, to prevent a war, was binding as a preliminary of peace. He concluded by obferving, that he had never given his confent, fince the rupture, to the renewal of the offer, and had received no communication from the regent of any intention to bring it forward *. The duke of Orleans was fully fatisfied with this reprefentation. He owned, that although he could not avoid continuing to prefs for the reftitution which he had fo folemnly promifed in the king's name, yet that he would employ every indirect means in his power, to prevent its being indifcreetly and improperly urged, and teftified his refolution to make a feparate peace with Spain.

The king, however, being ftill inclined to gratify the regent, if he could do it without difobliging

* The king to the duke of Orleans. Walpole Papers.

ing his subjects, referred the object of dispute to the congress at Cambray, hoping that in the course of negotiations, the Spanish plenipotentiaries might urge such motives and arguments in its favour, as would influence the parliament and people *. Under the same impressions, he made another effort. By his order, earl Stanhope wrote to secretary Craggs, to lay before the lords justices the advantages which would result from ceding Gibraltar for Florida, or the eastern part of St. Domingo, and for certain commercial advantages. This proposal being laid before the council, lord Townshend at first warmly opposed, but finally agreed, if a suitable equivalent, particularly Florida, could be obtained. Accordingly, the cession seemed ultimately determined, if it met with the approbation of parliament. But the obstinacy of the king of Spain, rendered this proposal ineffectual. He declined yielding Florida in exchange, and insisted on Gibraltar without giving any equivalent †. This claim on his part was so warmly and repeatedly insisted on, as the indispensable requisite for acceding to the terms of pacification, that it was deemed a prudent art of policy not to retard the conclusion of peace, by a positive denial. Philip having requested, as an ostensible vindication of the peace, which was reprobated in Spain as highly

* Sir Luke Schaub to Grimaldo, Madrid, June 17, 1720. Hardwicke Papers.

† Secretary Craggs to earl Stanhope, August 2 and 26, 1720. Stanhope Papers. Earl Stanhope to secretary Craggs, Hanover, October 1, 1720. Hardwicke Papers.

Period IV. highly difhonourable, a letter conveying a promife
1727 to 1730. of reftoring Gibraltar, George the Firft complied,
and expreffed himfelf with great difcretion on this

The king's letter. delicate fubject. " I no longer balance (he obferved) to affure your majefty of my readinefs to
fatisfy you with regard to your demand, touching
the reftitution of Gibraltar, *upon the footing of an
equivalent,* promifing you to make ufe of the firft
favourable opportunity to regulate this article,

April 29, with confent of my parliament." When the Bri-
1721. tifh minifter delivered this letter, both the king
and queen of Spain made fo many objections, particularly to the word equivalent, that at his fug-

June 1, 1721. geftion the king confented to write another letter,
in which thofe words were omitted, under the full
conviction that the letter, even in that mutilated
ftate, left the affair entirely to the parliament, who
might refufe to part with Gibraltar upon any
terms; or if they agreed to the ceffion, might
equally infift upon an equivalent *.

Haughty and unreafonable conduct of the king of Spain. This was the memorable letter †, which was
the caufe of fo much obloquy. Philip confidered
it as a pofitive promife, and his minifter infifted
upon a pure and fimple reftitution, without any
equivalent. The king of England, on the contrary, afferted that the ceffion muft folely depend
on the confent of parliament, which would not

be

* Difpatch from William Stanhope to lord Carteret, Aranjuez,
May 29, 1721. Hardwicke Papers.

† This letter is printed in the Journals of the lords and commons,
in the Political State of Europe, Hiftorical Regifter, Chandler, and
Tindal, with an omiffion of the words marked in Italics.

be eafily obtained. In the midft of thefe claims
on one fide, and counter declarations on the other,
which agitated the plenipotentiaries during two
years, the diffolution of the marriage between
Louis the Fifteenth and the Infanta, occafioned
the rupture between France and Spain. Philip
broke up the congrefs at Cambray without having agreed to the preliminaries, and the queftion
of Gibraltar remained undecided. After ineffectually endeavouring to detach England from
France, and whilft he was fecretly preparing for a
reconciliation with the houfe of Auftria, he renewed his claims, and accompanied them with
bitter reproaches.

In the midft of thefe altercations, Ripperda,
having publicly declared at Vienna that England
would be compelled to reftore Gibraltar, colonel
Stanhope was commanded to obtain an immediate
acknowledgment from Madrid, whether this declaration of Ripperda was made by order, or
fimply on his own authority *. The king of
Spain, and his firft minifter Grimaldo, both replied, that Ripperda had furpaffed his orders, in
faying that a rupture with England would enfue,
unlefs Gibraltar was reftored; and Stanhope was
defired to acquaint his court with this declaration.
Stanhope prepared his difpatch, and the courier
was on the point of taking his departure, when
he received a letter from Grimaldo, informing
him that the continuation of the friendfhip and
com-

* Letter from colonel Stanhope to lord Townfhend, July 14, 1725.

F 4

commerce between England and Spain, would depend on the fpeedy compliance with this demand. On inquiry, he found that the caufe of this fudden change in opinion, proceeded from the news juft brought of the ratification of the treaty of Vienna. In fact, both the king and queen of Spain were fo little acquainted with the conftitution and temper of the Englifh nation, that they infifted on an *immediate* reftitution of Gibraltar as the only means of avoiding a rupture. Againft this extraordinary demand, Stanhope remonftrated in an audience with the king and queen of Spain; he declared, that they infifted upon an impoffibility, fince what they required could not be effected without confent of parliament; whereas there was then no parliament affembled, nor could poffibly be affembled, before the king's return to England in the fpring. "No!" faid the queen, "Let then the king your mafter return prefently into England, and call a parliament exprefsly for this purpofe, it being no more than what we might expect from his friendfhip for us; and I am affuredly and pofitively informed, that the matter once fairly propofed, would not meet with one negative in either houfe; let this fhort argument be once made ufe of: either give up Gibraltar, or your trade to the Indies and Spain; and the matter, I will anfwer for it, won't admit of a moment's debate *."

The

---

* Letter from W. Stanhope to lord Townfhend, Auguft 6, 1725; Stanhope and Harrington Papers.

The confequence of this infolent and peremptory demand being a refufal on the part of England, Philip commenced the fiege of Gibraltar,
and alledged as an excufe for the aggreffion, the
breach of promife on the fide of George the
Firft. When the defertion of the Emperor compelled him to accept the preliminaries of peace,
he clogged the negotiation by renewing his claims
on Gibraltar, and furnifhed the oppofition in
England with matter of reproach to the minifter,
who juftified himfelf in parliament. The objeét
of Philip was to bring the difpute before the
congrefs of Soiffons; that of the Englifh plenipotentiaries was to prevent it. The prudent
manner in which they fucceeded in that defign,
does honour to their diplomatic abilities; and
the treaty of Seville was, as I have already obferved, concluded without any ftipulation or mention of Gibraltar.

CHAPTER THE THIRTY-FIFTH:

1728.

Rise, Disgrace, Imprisonment, Escape, and Arrival of Ripperda in England.—Reception and Conferences with the Ministers.—Dissatisfaction and Departure.—Enters into the Service of the Emperor of Morocco.

Ripperda in England.

THE arrival of the duke of Ripperda in England, his clandestine reception, and temporary concealment under the protection of Townshend and Walpole, form a remarkable event in this year. The papers committed to my inspection, contain several curious particulars of this extraordinary man, who negotiated the treaty of Vienna, and who afterwards betrayed the secret articles to the court of London.

Memoirs of Ripperda.

William, baron and duke of Ripperda, was descended from a noble family in the lordship of Groningen, one of the United Provinces; he received a learned education, and acquired an intimate knowledge of the French, Spanish, and Latin languages. He served as colonel during the war of the Spanish succession. In the midst of his military occupations, he applied himself with indefatigable industry to the study of trade and manufactures; and being no less distinguished for his insinuating address, was deputed, soon af-

Envoy to Madrid.
1715.

ter the peace of Utrecht, envoy to Madrid, for the purpose of settling the commercial disputes

2

between

between **Spain** and the Dutch republic. · While
he was labouring to adjuft that difficult bufinefs,
he contributed to promote the conclufion of a
commercial treaty between Spain and England,
for which fervice Townfhend commends his good
offices in terms of high approbation. *.

During his refidence at Madrid, his ardent imagination, confummate addrefs, and extreme facility in writing difpatches and drawing memorials in various languages, recommended him to
cardinal Alberoni, who employed him in affairs of
a moft fecret and delicate nature. The fervices
which he performed, and the grateful acknowledgments of the minifter, infpired him with the
moft fanguine expectation of obtaining a fplendid
fituation in a country where, fince the acceffion
of a foreign king, aliens had been frequently promoted to the higheft offices of government ; and
as Alberoni alledged as an excufe that he could
not be promoted on account of his religion, he
made a public abjuration, and was admitted into
the Roman Catholic church. He was then appointed fuperintendant of a cloth manufactory,
recently eftablifhed, by his own fuggeftion, at
Guadalaxara, and received the grant of a penfion
and an eftate. During this period of his life, he
was penfioned by the Emperor, and feems to have
received occafional prefents from the Englifh
court. He was fo unprincipled, that he had even
the affurance to call upon the envoy Bubb, afterwards Dodington, for 14,000 piftoles, in the
name

* Townfhend Papers.

name of cardinal Alberoni, which he appropriated to his own use *, and this tranſaction probably contributed to his removal. Having brought the manufactory to a high degree of improvement, and enjoying frequent opportunities of converſing with the king and queen, he excited the jea-louſy of Alberoni, and 'was removed from the ſuperintendance. Ripperda, however, diſſembled his reſentment, while he ſtill continued in public on terms of amity with the prime miniſter, ſe-cretly repreſented to Daubenton and Grimaldo, who were diſguſted with Alberoni, many errors and inſtances of mal-adminiſtration, which the confeſſor laid before the king, and perſuaded him to conſult Grimaldo, through the channel of the poſtmaſter-general.

In the courſe of the difficult and complicated tranſactions in which Spain was involved with the Emperor, France, and England, the opinion of Ripperda was alſo demanded. He accordingly drew up a report, in which he declared, that the king could never ſucceed in his deſigns againſt the Emperor, unleſs he could obſtruct the opera-tions of England. With this view, he recom-mended that the troops deſtined to invade Sicily, ſhould be landed, with great ſtores of arms and ammunition, on the coaſts of Scotland or Ire-land, to aſſiſt in replacing the Pretender on the throne. If that event ſhould take place, the prince would in gratitude reſtore Gibraltar, Mi-norca, Jamaica, and all the American ſettle-ments

* Stanhope's Diſpatches, Harrington Papers.

ments wrefted from Spain by the Englifh, and the Italian provinces would be eafily recovered. This advice, though rejected by the influence of Alberoni, who perfevered in the reduction of Sicily, made a deep impreffion on the king's mind, and gave him a favourable opinion of Ripperda's genius and fpirit, which was increafed, when the repeated predictions of Ripperda, that the rafh and ill-concerted meafures of Alberoni would fail, were verified by the event. The difgrace of the cardinal being the confequence of his ill-fuccefs, the fuperintendancy of the manufactures at Guadalaxara was reftored to Ripperda, and his influence over the king and queen was promoted by the ftrong recommendations which the duchefs of Parma, at the fuggeftions of the Imperial court, made in his favour, to her daughter the queen of Spain, and by the orders given to marquis Scotti, the minifter of Parma at Madrid, to ferve as a channel of communication between him and the queen. Hence Ripperda obtained private audiences of the king and queen of Spain, in which he laid down plans for the improvement of trade, and the increafe of the marine; flattered the queen, with promoting the aggrandifement of her family, and ftill more ingratiated himfelf in her favour, by propofing the marriage of Don Carlos with an archduchefs.

Depending on her protection, he aimed at the miniftry of ftate, of the marine and the Indies; he had even difpofed the king to remove the minifters, when Scotti betrayed the fecret to Daubenton

His ambitious views.

benton and Grimaldo. Daubenton prevented the immediate appointment of Ripperda, by re-prefenting the danger and impropriety of entruft-ing the adminiftration to a new convert; and when the death of Daubenton, and the offer of a cardinal's hat to the new confeffor, father Bermu-das, feemed likely to facilitate his elevation, his expectations were annihilated by the abdication of Philip. During the fhort reign of Louis, the queen maintained a private correfpondence with Ripperda, and followed his advice, in fending large fums of money and her jewels to Parma.

Soon after Philip's refumption of the crown. when the cabinet of Madrid formed a project of reconciliation with the Emperor, Ripperda was fe-lected as the fitteft perfon to carry that delicate negotiation into execution. He was accordingly deputed to Vienna, with fecret inftructions to make a peace with the Emperor, to conclude a marriage between Don Ferdinand and the fecond archduchefs, and to fecure, on the death of the Emperor without iffue male, the Italian provinces and the Netherlands to Spain, and the reverfion of Tufcany and Parma to Don Carlos. · Before his departure, he delivered in a project for pre-paring a fleet 100 fhips, an army of 100,000 in-fantry, and 30,000 horfe. The expences he pro-pofed to difcharge from the revenues of the In-dies alone, by new modelling the trade to the fet-tlements, and fecuring the profits, which were almoft totally abforbed by the Englifh and French nations, and the Spanifh minifters. He alfo un-dertook

dertook to save an annual sum of 10,000,000 crowns; and obtained from the king a promise, that on his return from Vienna, he should be appointed prime minister to carry his project into execution.

Ripperda performed the object of his mission with great address. He departed from Spain in the latter end of October, and arrived at Vienna in November, where he resided in the suburbs, under the fictitious name of the baron of Pfaffenberg. It does not appear that the English court had any notice of his arrival from St. Saphorin, their agent at Vienna, before the 18th of February; when he received intelligence from Petkum, minister of the duke of Holstein, that a Dutchman, the description of whose person answered to that of Ripperda, held long and secret conferences with count Zinzendorf by night. This man was soon discovered to be Ripperda; but all the information which St. Saphorin could procure concerning the object of his mission, amounted to no more than a conjecture, that a marriage between an archduchess and an infant of Spain, was the subject of their conferences; but whether with the prince of Asturias or Don Carlos, was a matter of which he was wholly ignorant.

Ripperda was anxious to finish his mission, that he might return to Spain, and obtain those honours which awaited him; but with a view to render the queen of Spain more tractable, he changed his instructions, and proposed that the eldest

eldeſt archduchefs fhould be given to her ſon,
Don Carlos, and that Mademoiſelle de Beaujo-
lois, who had been affianced to him, fhould be
transferred to the prince of Aſturias. The queen
inftantly approved and promoted a plan fo congenial to her wiſhes, by which the imperial dignity,
and the hereditary dominions of the houſe of
Auftria, would devolve on her iffue. Having
thus fecured the queen, he gained the court of
Vienna, by affirming, that if he was placed at the
helm of government in Spain, a faving would be
made of 50,000,000 crowns, out of which five or
fix millions fhould be annually remitted to Vienna. He accordingly received a verbal, if not a
written promife, from count Zinzendorf, in the
name of the Emperor, that the eldeſt archduchefs
fhould be affianced to Don Carlos.

While this bufinefs was in agitation, the diffolution of the marriage between the infanta and
Louis the Fifteenth, and the refufal of England
to accept the fole meditation, excited the refentment of the king and queen of Spain to fuch a
degree, that inftant orders were tranfmitted to Vienna, for concluding a treaty on any terms. Ripperda found no difficulty from the Emperor.

Under thefe aufpices, Ripperda concluded the
treaty of Vienna; the news of which, on reaching Madrid, infpired the king and queen with
the moft extravagant joy, and the populace,
delighted at their deliverance from French interference, fhouted, " Long live the auguft houfe
                                              of

of Auftria *." Count Konigfeck, deputed embaffador to Madrid, was received with the moft
flattering marks of efteem and confideration, and
foon acquired fuch an afcendancy, that he wholly
governed the counfels of Spain.

The fecrecy with which the whole negotiation
was conducted, was fo well maintained, that the
contents of the treaty, which was figned on the
2'ift of May, were fcarcely fufpected, until they
were hinted at by the Emperor himfelf, who
could not contain his joy on the occafion, and
then divulged by the Imperial minifters, with a
view to infult and intimidate the cabinet of England. The veil of fecrecy being now removed,
Ripperda came forth in the public character of
embaffador from Spain. The fplendour of his
houfehold, the liberality of his donations, and
the punctuality of his payments, attracted efteem
and fecured popularity. He at the fame time
difplayed the natural warmth and prefumption of
his temper. He poured forth, in public companies, the moft bitter invectives againft England,
and made repeated declarations, that a refufal to
give up Gibraltar, or to guaranty the engagements recently concerted between the two contracting powers, would be followed by an immediate attempt to affift the Pretender.

Ripperda quitted Vienna in the beginning of
November. He paffed through Italy, and taking

* Count Staremberg to the Emperor, June 8, 1725. Harrington
Papers.

Period IV. ing ſhip at Genoa, diſembarked at Barcelona.
1727 to 1730. On landing there, he gave to the officers of the
garriſon, who crowded to pay their reſpects, an
ample account of the tranſactions at Vienna, declaring that the Emperor had 150,000 troops ready
to march at an hour's *, warning, and that as
many more could be brought into the field in ſix
months. He ſpoke contemptuouſly of France,
threatened the Hanoverian allies, if they ſhould
preſume to oppoſe the deſigns of the Emperor
and Philip; declared that France ſhould be pil-
laged, that the king of Pruſſia would be cruſhed
in one campaign, and that George the Firſt
would be deprived of his German territories by
the Emperor, and of his Britiſh dominions by the
Pretender. At the concluſion of theſe rodomon-
tades, he continued his journey without delay, and
rode poſt to Madrid, where he arrived on the 11th
of December, in the afternoon; after a ſhort interview with his wife, he repaired to the palace
without changing his dreſs, and went to the anti-
chamber. Applying to the lord in waiting for admiſſion, he was informed that Grimaldo, the ſecretary of ſtate, was with the king and queen of
Spain, and that he could not be immediately admitted. He expreſſed, in terms of deriſion, his
impatience and ſurpriſe that Grimaldo continued
ſo long, and on his coming out took no notice of
him, but deſired the lord in waiting to announce
his arrival.

He

* W. Stanhope to lord Townſhend, December 27.

He was inftantly admitted, and received with
the higheft marks of kindnefs and fatisfaction *.
The conference was long; and on the following
day he was nominated minifter and fecretary of
ftate, in the room of Grimaldo; all the other minifters, councils, and foreign embafladors were ordered to tranfact bufinefs with him; and without
the name of prime minifter, he was invefted with
the fame uncontrouled authority as had been enjoyed by Alberoni. But he poffeffed more turbulence, felf-fufficiency, and haughtinefs than the
cardinal, without his addrefs, refources, and incor-
ruptible integrity, and the Britifh embaflador,
who knew his character well, obferved, that without the fpirit of prophecy, " One might forefee
ten Alberonis in this Ripperda, as Scylla did ten
Mariufes in Julius Cæfar."

It foon appeared that Ripperda poffeffed neither
addrefs or abilities fufficient to carry his gigantic
fchemes into execution; and the king, irritated
by the difappointment of his fanguine hopes, and
angry at having been the dupe of this fuperficial
pretender, repeatedly told the queen, that Ripperda was a madman, and muft be removed:.

Swoln with vanity and prefumption, he feemed,
however, to defy all oppofition. " I know," he
faid, ".that the Spanifh minifters and nation are
irritated againft me; but I laugh at their attempts.
The queen, to whom I have rendered the moft
effential fervices, will protect me." And another
                                                  time

* Memoires de Montgon, tome i. p. 207, 208.

G 2

time he exclaimed at a public levee, that he was shielded by six friends who would defend him against all intrigues, God, the Blessed Virgin, the emperor and empress, the king and queen of Spain *. But although Ripperda owed his elevation to the union he had formed between the courts of Vienna and Madrid, and appears, from this expression, to have perfectly understood, that his continuance in power could only be secured by supporting that system; yet such was his caprice or vanity, that soon after his establishment, he began to deviate from the line of conduct by which he had attained it. He relaxed in his attentions to count Konigseck, the imperial embassador, and was suspected of endeavouring to form an union with those of Great Britain and Holland. This conduct rendered Konigseck his enemy; the incapacity of the minister became daily more apparent, and his vain-glorious boasting, produced nothing but the contempt and derision of the statesmen of every nation.

Under these circumstances, Don Joseph and Louis de Patinho, secured the protection of the queen, by the private recommendation of her confessor, Don Domingo da Guerra, who represented them as persons highly qualified to direct the helm of government, and well inclined to support the plans of Ripperda as far as they related to the aggrandisement of Don Carlos. They also gained the interest of count Konigseck by offers of supplying

* Memoires de Montgon, tome i. p. 210.

plying the imperial court with the promifed fubfidies. Both the queen and Konigfeck now fuffered the king's refentment againft Ripperda to
break out; they no longer counteracted the cabals
of the Spanifh minifters, nor concealed the clamours of the nation againft an upftart, a convert,
and a foreigner.

Ripperda at length perceiving that he was de-
tefted by the people, thwarted by the Spanifh minifters, oppofed by Konigfeck, defpifed by the
king, and declining in the favour of the queen,
paid great court to the Britifh and Dutch embaffadors, and made the moft humble profeffions of
refpect and duty to the king of England. In the
midft of thefe continued apprehenfions and alarms,
he was difmiffed from the fuperintendance of the
finances, under the pretence of delivering him from
part of the burthen of government. Forefeeing
that this would be fpeedily followed by the lofs
of all his employments, he, requefted the king's
permiffion to retire from his fervice; but his demand was not complied with, and he continued
to tranfact bufinefs till the 14th of May, when he
received a letter from the marquis de la Paz, that
the king accepted his refignation, and conferred
on him a penfion of 3,000 piftoles. The general
fatisfaction which this event diffufed, and the tu-
multuous acclamations of the populace, who affembled in large bodies before his houfe, filled him
with apprehenfions of being maffacred; and after
writing a fubmiffive letter to the king, he took re-

G 3

fuge

fuge in the hotel of the British embaffador, who was with the court at Aranjuez.

On his return to Madrid, the evening of the 15th, Stanhope had a difficult part to act. It was of the greateft importance to obtain from Ripperda a communication of the fecrets of the Spanifh cabinet, and particularly an account of the negotiations which had recently taken place, and were then tranfacting between the courts of Vienna and Madrid, and yet be careful not to offend the king of Spain, by appearing to countenance a difcarded minifter, in oppofition to the will of the fovereign in whofe court he refided. The caution and prudence with which he conducted himfelf on this delicate occafion, reflects honour on his judgment, and contributed greatly to his future elevation. He contrived to give protection to the ex-minifter, and to detain him in his houfe, until he had extorted from him all the fecrets which he was willing or able to communicate.

Ripperda now betrayed to him the fecret articles of the treaty of Vienna, and probably exaggerated the defigns of the Emperor and the king of Spain, with a view to ingratiate himfelf with the king of England, and to exafperate the nation againft thofe two monarchs who had occafioned his difgrace. He, who in the height of his power was fo giddy and prefumptuous, was now become fo abject, that his whole frame fhook with agitation, he appeared to be in the greateft agonies, and wept like a child.

For

'For the purpose of conveying the intelligence communicated by Ripperda, which was of too much importance to be fent by the poft, or even to be entrufted in a difpatch by a common courier, Keene, then conful general, afterwards embaffador in Spain, was difpatched to England. After communicating in perfon, the fecret with which he was entrufted to the duke of Newcaftle and the other minifters of ftate, he drew up, by order of the king, a letter to the duke of Newcaftle, containing the fubftance of Ripperda's converfation, which is inferted in the correfpondence *.

After a negotiation of a few days, which paffed between the Spanifh court and the Britifh embaffador, Ripperda was taken by force from his houfe, and transferred to the caftle of Segovia, from whence he made his efcape, after a confinement of fifteen months.

The governor of the caftle and his wife, being both infirm, could not pay conftant attention to their prifoners, and the fervant maid +, being feduced by the duke, contrived his efcape, and effected it with the affiftance of a corporal, who was one of the guards; while his faithful valet, with unexampled attachment, remained in his apartment, and for fome time prevented intrufion, by declaring

---

* See Period IV. Article Ripperda.

† Campbell, in his Memoirs of the duke of Ripperda, has converted the fervant maid into the daughter of a Caftilian nobleman, and the antiquated wife of the governor, into a fprightly and beautiful young woman.

declaring that his mafter was indifpofed *. The duke had juft recovered from a fevere fit of the gout, and not without the greateft difficulty defcended the ladder of ropes which was let down from the window of his apartment, and repaired to the place where a mule and a guide waited for him. Unable to continue riding he gave his mule to the guide, and hired a carriage, but proceeded fo flowly that he employed five days in travelling to a_ fmall village on the frontiers of Portugal, where he remained until he was joined by his two confidants. With them he arrived at Miranda de Ducro, the firft town in Portugal, and from thence continued to Oporto, where he embarked for England, on board the Charity, under the name of Don Manuel de Mendofa †.

Arrives in England.

The veffel was forced by contrary winds into Corke, and in the beginning of October, he landed at Comb-martin, in Devonfhire, with the young woman, the corporal, and a fervant, and paffed a few days at Exeter. Townfhend and Walpole, apprifed of his arrival and departure from Exeter, difpatched Corbiere, under fecretary of ftate, to meet him on the weftern road, who conveyed him in a coach and four to Eton, where he was lodged incognito, in an apartment belonging to Dr. Bland, dean of Durham, and head mafter of the fchool. There he was met by Townfhend, who received him with the greateft marks of at_

tention,

* See letter from Keene to the duke of Newcaftle, giving an account of Ripperda's efcape.—Correfpondence, Article Ripperda.
† Memoires de Montgon. Political State of Great Britain.

tention, with a view to obtain from him fuller
and more accurate information concerning the fecret articles of the treaty of Vienna. After a refidence of a few days at Eton, he departed with
the fame fecrecy to London, where he arrived on
the 13th. After continuing for fome time incognito, he took a large houfe in Soho fquare, and
a villa, and lived in a magnificent ftyle. During
his refidence in England, he maintained an occafional correfpondence with Walpole, and having
made a rapid proficiency in the Englifh language,
conceived the chimerical hope of filling fome high
department in adminiftration. While the differences with Spain were under difcuffion, and a pof-
fibility of a rupture with that country continued,
the minifters kept up an amicable intercourfe
with Ripperda, which probably fed his delufion,
and inflamed his ambition. But when the conclufion of the treaty of Seville, contrary to his
views and remonftrances, rendered his information
no longer ufeful, he felt the pain of difappointed
felf-importance, and in the year 1731, withdrew
in difguft to Holland.

Animated by a fpirit of vengeance againft Spain, Adventures
which he could not fatisfy among the powers of in Morocco.
Europe, he embarked for Barbary, at the inftigation of the embaffador from Morocco, entered
into the fervice of the emperor Muley Abdallah,
embraced the Mahometan religion, was created a
bafhaw, obtained the command of the army and
the office of prime minifter; and gained the entire confidence of the emperor. After feveral fucceffes

Period IV.
1727 to 1730.

ceffes over the Spaniards, and defeating a competitor for the throne of Morocco, in which he gave
figns of great courage and fkill, he was worfted
near Ceuta, and preferved his life, by refigning
his command.   He deferted Muley Abdallah,
when dethroned by Muley Ali, and finally retired
to Tetuan, where he lived under the protection
of the bafhaw, and died in 1737, at a very advanced age *.

Death.

Cawthorn, in his poem on the Vanity of Human
Enjoyments, has well delineated the capricious
and motley character of Ripperda.

O paufe, left virtue every guard refign,.
And the fad fate of Ripperda be thine.
This glorious wretch indulged at once to move
A nation's wonder and a monarch's love;
Bleft with each charm politer courts admire,
The grace to foften, and the foul to fire,
Forfook his native bogs with proud difdain,
And, though a Dutchman, rofe the pride of Spain.
This hour the pageant waves the Imperial rod,
All Philip's empire trembling at his nod;
The next difgrac'd, he flies to Britain's ifle,
And courts the funfhine of a Walpole's fmile.
Unheard, defpifed, to fouthern climes he fteers,
And fhines again at Sallé and Algiers;
Bids pale Morocco all his fchemes adore,
And pours her thunder on th' Hefperian fhore:
All nature's ties, all virtue's creeds belied,
Each church abandon'd, and each God denied;
Without a friend his fepulchre to fhield,
His carcafe from the vultures of the field,
He dies, of all ambition's fons the worft,
By Afric hated, and by Europe curft.

---

* This account of Ripperda is principally drawn from the difpatches of St. Saphorin at Vienna, of William Stanhope at Madrid,
and from " An Account of Ripperda," by two Sicilian abbots, in the
Walpole Papers.

CHAPTER THE THIRTY-SIXTH:

1730.

Sanguine Hopes of Opposition that Walpole would be removed.—Their Efforts in Parliament.—Debates on the Imperial Loan—on the Penfion Bill—on Dunkirk—and the Renewal of the Eaft India Company's Charter.—Arrangement of the Miniftry on the Refignation of Lord Townfhend.—Characters of the Duke of Newcaftle and Lord Harrington.

ALTHOUGH the Tories had hitherto joined the difcontented Whigs in their attacks againft the minifter, yet their coalition had never been hearty and fincere. They formed a feparate body; and as they did not amount to lefs than one hundred and ten members, they confidered themfelves, both from their fuperior numbers and weight as country gentlemen, entitled rather to give than receive an impulfe from the other parts of the minority. They did not therefore chufe to pay that regular attendance in parliament, which a conftant and uniform warfare required from all thofe who, however differing in many points, were united in that of diftreffing the minifter. But in the feffion which opened in 1730, a regular and fyftematic plan was formed by Bolingbroke, and carried into execution by means of his addrefs and activity. His connection with Pulteney, as the joint manager of the Craftfman, gave him an influence over the Whigs; and his intimacy with Sir William Wyndham, fecured to him the acquiefcence

Coalition of the Tories and difcontented Whigs.

Period IV. quiescence of the Tories.. He had persuaded the
1727 to 1730. whole body, that notwithstanding the signature
of the convention at Pardo, a peace with Spain
still met with insuperable difficulties. That Philip
had not relinquished his demand of Gibraltar;
that the Spanish depradations would still continue
to be committed with impunity; that the British
commerce with Spain would either be suspended
or annihilated. Measures were therefore concerted
to call the ministers to account for their supineness and pusillanimity. The clamours thus excited, extremely popular in a nation jealous of
its honour, and anxious to secure its commercial
advantages, occasioned great discontents, as well
amongst the friends as the enemies of the minister.

Conduct of   Although the conclusion of the treaty of Se-
Bolingbroke. ville, which was highly favourable to the commercial interests of England, and honourable to
her national glory, disconcerted opposition, and
overset the schemes of Bolingbroke in this particular, yet he was too able not to form another
plan of attack. Having made a coalition between
the discordant parties in the minority, and appointed a general muster in parliament, he still
continued to animate the mass with fresh spirit.
His labours were now turned to sow discord
among the Hanoverian allies, to avail himself of
a growing misunderstanding which had recently
appeared between England and France, to encourage the emperor to persist in his refusal to
admit Spanish garrisons into Parma and Tuscany,
and thus to counteract the execution of the treaty

I

of

of Seville. Under his auspices, and by his direction, the opposition brought forwards many questions calculated to harrass government, and to
render themselves popular. The expectations
formed by the disaffected were highly sanguine;
and a notion prevailed both at home and abroad *,
that the fall of the minister was unavoidable.
Their hopes of success were founded on the difunion in the cabinet; on the supposed aversion
of the king to Walpole, and on the disgust of
those Whigs who adhered to Townshend.

The first trial of their strength was made on the
question concerning the Imperial loan. The Emperor, by the treaty of Seville, having been deprived of liberal remittances from Spain, attempted
to borrow £.400,000 in London. A bill was accordingly presented to the commons for preventing loans to foreign powers, without licence from
the king under his privy seal. Had the ministry
permitted the loan, they would have been abun-
dantly and deservedly reproached: Advocates,
however, against the prohibition were not wanting. The hardships of all restraints, the disadvantage to us, and the advantage to the Dutch,
were specious pretences. Walpole took an active share in combating the arguments of opposition, and the question was carried †. A sufficient justification of the measure was, that the want
of money compelled the court of Vienna to submit to terms of accommodation.

The

---

* Secret intelligence from Paris. Walpole Papers.
† Journals.

Period IV.   The most popular and plausible measure pro-
1727 to 1730. posed by opposition was, the pension bill, which
On the pension was now first introduced, and which from this
bill.
period, became a never-failing topic of antiminif-
February 16. terial attack, and of ministerial defence. Sandys
moved for leave to bring in a bill to disable all
persons from sitting in parliament, who had any
pension, or any offices held in trust for them from
the crown, directly or indirectly; and for the
purpose of enforcing this exclusion, he proposed
that every member, on taking his seat, should
swear that he had not any pension, directly or
indirectly, did not enjoy any gratuity or reward,
or hold any office or place of trust; and that after
having accepted the same, he would signify it to the
house within fourteen days. Walpole, who knew
the unpopularity of the arguments which could
be urged against the bill, and appreciated the effect of those which would be brought in its favour, declined taking any active part against it,
notwithstanding the express injunctions of the
king *, who called it a villanous bill, and the
disgust of Townshend, who was unwilling that the
odium of its rejection should be cast upon the
house of lords. He does not seem to have spoken
in the debate, or to have exerted his usual influence; for while most of the questions supported
or opposed by government, were passed or thrown
out by a majority of more than two to one, the
bill was only carried by 144 against 134 †. It
was

---

* Note from the king to lord Townshend. Correspondence.
† Journals. Tindal.

was negatived by the houfe of lords after a long
debate *, and a proteſt entered, by twenty-fix
peers. A fimilar fate attended it the next feſ-
fion; and during his whole adminiſtration, Sir
Robert Walpole never made any ſtrong oppofition
to it, but left it to be rejected by the upper
houfe. It was now the generally received opinion,
and not without foundation, that the miniſter
fuffered the penfion bill to pafs the houfe of commons, becaufe he knew that it would be thrown
out by the peers. Sandys therefore, in the ſub-
fequent feffion, brought forward a motion for appointing a committee, to inquire whether any
members had, directly or indirectly, any penfions,
or any offices from the crown held in truſt for
them, in part, or in the whole. Walpole ventured to oppofe it; he called it a motion for
erecting the houfe into a court of inquifition, and
urged, that it juſtified the treatment which the
bill had met with in the upper houfe. He declared that the act, if paſſed, could not anſwer
the end for which it was propofed; unlefs the
houfe fhould affume to itfelf a power unknown
to the conſtitution, namely, a power of compelling every member that was fufpected, to accufe
himfelf, not of any thing criminal, for it could
not be criminal to take either place or penfion
from the crown, and in confequence of that conſtruction, to difpoffefs half the counties and boroughs in England of their reprefentatives. The
arguments and influence of the miniſter prevailed,
and

* Lords Debates. ' Tindal.

and the bill was thrown out, by 206 againſt 143 [*]. Yet ſuch was the unpopularity of the rejection, that many members, ſuſpected of having penſions or places held in truſt, voted for it, leſt their oppoſition might diſoblige their conſtituents.

On the affair
of Dunkirk.

The ſtipulation to deſtroy the harbour of Dunkirk, made at the peace of Utrecht, and renewed in the treaty with France of 1717, had never been fully complied with. The French cabinet, always anxious to retain the uſe of a harbour, which, in caſe of a war with Great Britain, was ſituated ſo advantageouſly for the annoyance of our trade, continued clandeſtinely to prevent the demolition of the works. Frequent remonſtrances were made by the Engliſh government, and promiſes extorted from the French cabinet, that the treaty ſhould be carried into effect : but the inhabitants, either by the ſuggeſtion or connivance of the French government, kept the harbour and works in a ſtate of repair.

This was a ſubject which gave great uneaſineſs to the miniſter, on which he frequently expatiated in his letters to his brother, and even reproached him for neglecting to enforce the demolition. It was a point, however, of ſo much delicacy, that cardinal Fleury, though he conſtantly avowed his readineſs to accede to the demands of the Britiſh miniſter, yet always eluded them, probably not daring to irritate the people of France by the enforcement of ſo diſagreeable a command. The delays on this ſubject afforded to oppoſition a

ground

* Journals.

ground for infinuating that the miniftry were in
connivance with the court of France, to fanction
the repairs of that harbour. Bolingbroke was
well aware · that nothing would more exafperate
the public mind, than the perfuafion that the
French were employed in the reparation of that
harbour ; and if that fact could be proved, that
the fufpicion of conniving at it would fall upon
the miniftry : he was no lefs convinced, that it
would weaken the credit of the minifter abroad,
if he, could prove that France did not fulfil its
engagements, and that a mifunderftanding had
arifen between the two kingdoms. To obtain
evidence in fupport of thefe points, he fent his
fecretary, Brinfden, to infpect the ftate of the
works at Dunkirk.

On the imperfect and exaggerated report of this
agent, was founded a motion for an addrefs, that
" the king fhould direct that all orders, inftructions, reports, and proceedings, had in regard to
the port and harbour of Dunkirk, fince its demolition, be laid before the houfe." The king having agreed to this addrefs, the neceffary docu-
ments· were produced, which being read, and wit-
neffes examined, Sir William Wyndham moved,
that in what, had been done relating to the harbour of Dunkirk, there was a manifeft violation
of the treaties between the two crowns. But
before he was feconded, the other fide made a
motion for an addrefs of thanks to the king, " for
his attention to the interefts of the nation, in
caufing a proper application to be made to the

Period IV. court of France, not only for putting a stop to
1727 to 1730. the works carrying on, but for demolishing such
as had been made by the inhabitants of Dun-
kirk, for repairing the port and channel there;
and to express their satisfaction in the good effects
which his majesty's instances had had, by obtaining express orders from the most Christian king,
for causing to be destroyed all the works that
might have been erected at Dunkirk, contrary to
the treaties of Utrecht and the Hague; and their
reliance upon their being punctually executed;
and further to declare their satisfaction in the firm
union and mutual fidelity, which so happily subsisted, and were so strictly preserved between the
two nations *."

This unexpected motion, which prevented the
discussion of that proposed by Sir William Wyndham, occasioned a long and warm debate, in which
Walpole seems to have particularly distinguished
himself. The great object of opposition was to
draw over the Whigs, who usually supported government, and had lately wavered under the plausible notion that the conduct of the minister had
been in this instance contradictory to the principles and interests of their party. The object of
the minister was to prove to the Whigs, that their
principles and interests were no ways affected by
this controversy, and that it was simply a Tory
question. With great art he introduced a personal application, and made a most vigorous attack.

8

* Tindal, vol. 20, p. 71.

tack on Bolingbroke, who was particularly obnoxious to the Whigs, at whofe inftigation he infinuated this inquiry was made, and whofe character and fpirit of oppofition he drew in the moft
unfavourable colours. Sir William Wyndham,
provoked by the philippic againft his friend, defended him with uncommon energy, and drew a
comparifon between him and Walpole, in which
he attempted to fhew that Bolingbroke was by no
means inferior in honefty and integrity to the minifter. This comparifon called up Henry Pelham,
who ably feconded the attack againft Bolingbroke,
and excited fuch a general indignation among the
Whigs, that the addrefs was carried by 274 againft
149 *. The lofs of this queftion by fo large a
majority, which the oppofition expected to have
carried triumphantly, increafed the popularity of
the minifter, and his credit abroad ; and Horace
Walpole, who took a confiderably fhare in the
debate, obferves in a letter to Poyntz, this was
the greateft day, both with refpect to the thing
itfelf, and the confequences, that had ever occurred within his memory, for the king and miniftry, and muft prove a thunder-bolt to their adverfaries in England, as well as abroad, as it contradicted the affertions of oppofition, that the king
and the Whigs were diffatisfied with his brother's
adminiftration †.

Another object of great national intereft, brought
forward by oppofition, was to prevent the renewal

* See Journals.

† Horace Walpole to lord Harrington and Stephen Poyntz. March 2d, 1730. Correfpondence.

of

of the charter of the Eaſt India company, which was near its expiration, and to form another incorporated ſociety without the excluſive privileges, which ſhould grant licences, upon certain conditions, to all perſons inclined to trade to the Eaſt Indies. The leading men in the minority, foreſeeing that the company would apply to the legiſlature for the renewal of their charter, had ſecretly prevailed on many reſpectable merchants in the city to engage in the ſcheme. It had a popular tendency, from the general averſion which is always entertained againſt monopolies and excluſive privileges, by thoſe who derive no immediate ſhare from the emoluments; and was ſtill farther recommended by the plauſible pretence of eaſing the public burthens, by obtaining a large ſum of money from the new incoroporated ſociety.

Having obtained information of their views, the miniſter laboured to counteract them. He was convinced that the trade could only be carried on by an excluſive company. The perſons who were to form the new ſociety, were wholly unacquainted with the ſecrets of the buſineſs, and unleſs the company could be induced to communicate information, and to part with its forts and ſettlements in the country, the trade might be reduced or annihilated. Having concerted his plan with a few of the directors, in whom he placed implicit confidence, and aware that the chief hopes of ſucceſs conceived by oppoſition, were founded on the popular ground of obtaining

9

ſums

fums of money for the ufe of the public, he anticipated their views, by infinuating to the houfe,
that a part of his ways and means would be derived
from the Eaft India company. This unexpected
turn furprifed the minority, and wholly difconcerted their plan before it was brought to maturity. They had however proceeded fo far in opening private fubfcriptions, and making engagements, that they could not recede *. A petition
was therefore prefented to the houfe by feveral
merchants, traders, and others, offering to ad-
vahce £.3,200,000 at five payments, before the
25th of May 1733, at an intereft of 5 per cent. to
redeem the fund and trade of the Eaft India company, provided the lenders might be incorporated and vefted with their whole trade, yet fo
as not to trade with their joint ftock, or in a corporate capacity, but the trade be open to all his
majefty's fubjects, upon licence from fuch propofed new company, defiring the fame, on proper
terms and conditions ; and provided the trade be
exercifed to and from the port of London only ;
and be fubject to redemption at any time upon
three years notice, after a term of thirty-one years,
and repayment of the principal.

After a long debate, the petition was rejected
by a majority of 223 againft 138 †.

The oppofition, however, were not intimidated
by the rejection of this propofal. They had been
taken

---

* Horace Walpole to lord Harrington, March 2. Correfpondence.
† Journals.

taken unawares, and compelled, by the addrefs of
the minifter, to bring it forward before it had been
fully digefted. They refolved therefore to introduce the bufinefs again, and employed the in-
tervening time in publifhing anonymous letters,
effays in periodical papers, and pamphlets, againft
exclufive companies in general, and particularly
againft the Eaft India company. All the arguments * which had ever been advanced againft
monopolies in this and other mercantile companies,
were retailed on this occafion, and all the benefits
which were fuppofed to refult from a free trade,
were magnified with great art and fubtilty. The
minifters and the Eaft India company were not,
on their part filent ; they likewife defended, with
no lefs fkill, the advantages of an united company,
vefted with exclufive privileges, and bound by
peculiar regulations, under the controul of the
legiflature. The petition was again prefented to
the houfe of commons, on the 9th of April, and
rejected without a divifion. While it was depending, the minifter brought in his bill, which
prolonged the charter to 1766, on the condition
of paying £.200,000 towards the fupply of the year,
and of reducing the intereft of the money advanced
to the public, from £.160,000 to £.120,000, or
one per cent. by which bargain, the nation was
benefited to the amount of at leaft a million.

An act which paffed this feffions, though trifling
in itfelf, yet muft not be omitted, as it formed

part

* The reader will find the arguments, pro and con, in Anderfon's
Hiftory of Commerce, who has treated the queftion with great judgment. Vol. 3. p. 156—162.

part of thofe commercial regulations which the
minifter was endeavouring gradually to introduce,
by taking off feveral reftraints that fhackled foreign commerce. It feems to have been the firft
deviation from a general principle which had been
eftablifhed by the European nations who had dominions in America, to maintain an exclufive intercourfe between the mother country and the co-
lonies. The narrow fpirit of this impolitic reftriction, from which incredible advantages were
fuppofed to refult, but which in reality was productive of great inconveniencies, did not efcape
the notice of the minifter; and he fuffered an exception to be made of rice, as a perifhable commodity. An act accordingly was paffed, for granting liberty to carry rice from Carolina directly to
any part of Europe, fouth of Cape Finifterre, in
Britifh bottoms, navigated by Britifh failors *.
In confequence of this beneficial act, the plantations of rice were confiderably increafed in the
province of Carolina. The good effects of this
regulation induced the minifter afterwards to extend the privilege to the colony of Georgia. And
it is the obfervation of an eminent commercial
writer, " that the confequence of both thefe well-
judged laws has been, that the rice of the American plantations has been preferred to the rice of
Verona and Egypt, which had before a general
fale †."

The

* Tindal, vol. 20. p. 76.
† Anderfon's Origin of Commerce, vol. 3. p. 164.

The oppofition moved in the courfe of the feffion for various papers, relating to foreign affairs.
Of thofe they obtained, little ufe feems to have
been made, except to furnifh matter to the writers of pamphlets and effays in periodical papers.
Thefe publications now affumed fuch an air of
violence and audacity, as feems to have alarmed
the minifter, perhaps too much, for it induced
him to make it one of the topics of animadverfion
in the fpeech from the throne which terminated
the feffion.

The fame day on which the houfe was prorogued,
Townfhend refigned. Lord Harrington was appointed fecretary of ftate, Henry Pelham fecretary
at war, and the privy feal was given to the earl of
Wilmington, on whofe affiftance oppofition had
relied with the moft perfect fecurity. In a few
months after, he was created lord prefident of the
council, which high office he held till the removal
of Sir Robert Walpole.

The charge of foreign affairs now oftenfibly de-
volved on the duke of Newcaftle and lord Harrington, whofe characters form a remarkable con-
traft, though they acted together with the utmoft
cordiality.

Thomas Pelham Holles, duke of Newcaftle,
was fon of Thomas lord Pelham, by Grace, fifter
of John Holles, duke of Newcaftle. He was born
in Auguft 1693-4, and on the death of his father,
in 1712, fucceeded to the barony of Pelham : he
inherited a large part of the great eftate of his uncle, who had no iffue male, and took the name
of

of Holles. Being of a great Whig family, he ftrenuoufly promoted the ƒuccefſion: of the line of
Brunfwick.   Soon after the accefſion of George
the Firſt, he was created earl of Clare, and in 1715,
duke of Newcaſtle. He ſupported the adminiftration of his brother-in-law * lord Townſhend; but
on the fchiſm of the Whig adminiftration in 1717,
he attached himſelf to Sunderland, by whoſe influence he was appointed lord chamberlain of the
houſehold, and inveſted with the order of the garter.
On the coalition which took place in 1720, between Sunderland and Townſhend, he joined his
former friend.   During the ſtruggle in the cabinet
between Townſhend and Walpole on one ſide, and
Carteret and Cadogan on the other, he uniformly
attached himſelf to the brother miniſters.   His
devotion to their cauſe was ſo warm, and his conſequence as one of the great Whig leaders ſo highly
appreciated, that he was ſolely admitted into the
moſt intimate confidence, and entruſted with the
moſt ſecret tranſactions.   In their private correſpondence, they invariably ſtyle him their good
friend : Townſhend repeatedly deſires Walpole to
give information to the duke.   In one place he
expreſsly ſays, " When I deſire you to communicate this to no one, I always except the duke of
Newcaſtle;" and Walpole no leſs frequently aſ-
ſures his correſpondent, that he has no reſerve for
their common friend.   When it became neceſſary

to

---

* The firſt wife of Charles viſcount Townſhend was Elizabeth,
daughter of lord Pelham by his firſt wife, Elizabeth, daughter and
heir of Sir William Jones, attorney general to Charles the Second.

Period IV. to remove Carteret from the office of secretary of
1727 to 1730. ftate, Newcaftle was felected as the fitteft perfon
to fill that ftation, which in confequence of the
alliance with France, was a poft of the higheft delicacy and importance.

Newcaftle was thirty years of age when he was
raifed to this office, and as he fucceeded Carteret,
whofe knowledge of foreign affairs, and talents for
bufinefs were duly appreciated, his appointment
to fo important a truft was contemptuoufly fpoken
of, and the new fecretary was confidered as not
capable of fully difcharging the duties of his office. His outward appearance and manners, feemed to juftify this obfervation. He was trifling and
embarraffed in converfation, always eager and in a
hurry to tranfact bufinefs, yet without due method. He was unbounded in flattery to thofe
above him, or whofe intereft he was defirous to
conciliate, and highly gratified with the groffeft
adulation to himfelf. The facility with which
he made and broke his promifes, became almoft
proverbial. He was not fufficiently confiderate
to his fecretaries and fubordinate clerks, exacting
from them a large facrifice of time and labour ;
and to his immediate dependants he was fretful
and capricious.

With thefe unfavourable appearances, he gave
few fymptoms of the talents which he undoubtedly poffeffed. In fact, he had much better abilities than are ufually attributed to him. He had
a quick comprehenfion ; he was an ufeful and frequent debater in the houfe of peers ; had an anfwer
ready

ready on all occasions; and spoke with great animation, though with little arrangement, and without grace or dignity. He wrote with uncommon facility, and with such fluency of words, that no one ever used a greater variety of expressions; and it is a remarkable circumstance, that in his most confidential letters, written with such expedition as to be almost illegible, there is scarcely a single erasure or alteration.

His temper was peevish and fretful, and he was always jealous of those with whom he acted. Of this jealousy, Townshend occasionally complained in his private correspondence with Horace Walpole, and in one instance, he particularly observes, "This was my view in sending a projet mitoyen, but my dear friend the duke looks upon the thoughts of any body else as reflections upon his own; and instead of considering the use that may be made of what is suggested by another, looks upon it as a personal thing, and runs out into a long justification of his own performances, which nobody finds fault with *." Sir Robert Walpole also repeatedly insinuated to his correspondents, not to omit writing confidentially to Newcastle; and exhorted them rather to neglect him than the duke, who would be grievously offended by the smallest omission. This jealousy, suppressed in some measure during his subordinate situation under lord Townshend, increased as he advanced in years, was highly troublesome to the minister of the house of commons,

---

* Walpole Papers.

mions, and created so much difguft, as to occafion. frequent altercations.

George the Second had conceived a very early and violent antipathy to the duke of Newcaftle, which was augmented by the difcordancy of their tempers and habits, particularly by his deficiency in method and exactnefs, which the king confidered as effential characteriftics of a minifter. The reprefentations of Walpole, on the neceffity of conciliating a man fo powerful from family and party connections, induced the king to moderate or conceal his repugnance; but his diflike broke out occafionally into bitter expreffions of contempt and averfion. In one of thefe difcontented moods, he faid to a confidential perfon, " You fee that I am compelled to take the duke of Newcaftle to be my minifter, who is not fit to be chamberlain in the fmalleft court of Germany."

With thefe habits, and this difpofition, and under the neceffity of ftruggling againft the deep-rooted averfion of George the Second, it is a matter of furprife that he fo long retained his power; for if we reckon from his firft promotion to the poft of lord chamberlain, to his refignation at the commencement of the reign of George the Third, he continued to fill a high fituation at court for a period of fix and forty years. This long continuance in office was owing to his fituation as the chief leader of the Whigs, to his princely fortune and profufion of expence, to the high integrity and difintereftednefs of his character, and to the uni-

form,

form fupport which he gave to the houfe of Brunf-.
wick.

As a fubordinate minifter, acting under fuperior
influence, his zeal and activity were highly ufeful;
and his want of order, and warmth of temper, were
counteracted and modified by the method and,
prudence of Walpole. But when he was placed,
at the head of affairs, he became diftracted * with
the multiplicity of bufinefs, yet unwilling to divide it with others. Weaknefs of counfels, fluc-
tuation of opinion, and deficiency of fpirit, marked
his adminiftration during an inglorious period of
fixteen years; from which England did not recover, until the mediocrity of his minifterial talents, and the indecifion of his character, were
controuled by the afcendency of Pitt.

His colleague in office, William Stanhope, (de- Character of
fcended from Sir John Stanhope, brother of Philip lord Harring-
the firft earl of Chefterfield) was third fon of John ton.
Stanhope of Elvafton, in Derbyfhire. After receiving a learned education, he entered into the profeffion of arms; ferved in Spain under his kinfman James, afterwards earl Stanhope, and after feveral promotions, obtained, in 1715, a regiment
of horfe. He was chofen in the firft parliament
of the reign of George the Firft, for the town of
Derby; and in 1717, appointed envoy extraordinary and plenipotentiary to the king of Spain.
On the rupture between Spain and England in

1718,

* Lord Harvey, in a letter to Horace Walpole, faid of him, " that
he did nothing in the fame hurry and agitation, as if he did every
thing." Correfpondence, Period V.

1718, he was named envoy and plenipotentiary to the court of Turin. In May 1721 he served as a volunteer in the French army commanded by marſhal Berwick, which laid ſiege to Fontarabia, During this war, he concerted a plan for the deſtruction of three Spaniſh ſhips of the line, and a great quantity of naval ſtores, in the port of St. Andero, in the Bay of Biſcay; an Engliſh ſquadron effected that enterprize; he himſelf contributed to the execution, by accompanying a detachment of troops, which Berwick ſent at his ſolicitation, and was the firſt that leaped into the water when the boats approached the ſhore *.

On the peace with Spain, he was conſtituted brigadier general, and returned to Madrid in the ſame character as before. During his reſidence at that court, he was witneſs to many extraordinary events, which he has ably detailed in his diſpatches: the abdication of Philip the Fifth, the ſucceſſion and death of Louis, the reſumption of the crown by Philip, the return of the Spaniſh infanta, the ſeparation of Spain from France, and union with the houſe of Auſtria, and the riſe and fall of Ripperda. He manifeſted great firmneſs and diſcretion when that miniſter was forcibly taken from his houſe; and his conduct on this occaſion, principally impreſſed the king and the miniſters with a deep ſenſe of his diplomatic talents, and contributed to his future elevation.

On the rupture with Spain, which commenced with the ſiege of Gibraltar, he returned to England,

* Collins's Peerage.

land, was appointed vice chamberlain to the king,
and foon afterwards nominated, in conjunction
with Horace Walpole and Stephen Poyntz, plenipotentiary at the congrefs of Soiffons.

He had now two great objects in view, a peerage, and the office of fecretary of ftate. But he
had to ftruggle as well againft the ill-will of the
king, who was highly difpleafed with his brother
Charles Stanhope, as againft the prejudices of Sir
Robert Walpole, who, deeply impreffed with a
recollection of the conduct of earl Stanhope at
Hanover, had taken an averfion to the very name.
It required all the influence of the duke of Newcaftle, and the friendfhip of Horace Walpole, to
furmount thefe obftructions; which were not removed until he had gained an acceffion to his diplomatic character, by repairing to Spain, and
concluding the treaty of Seville. His merits in
that delicate negotiation, extorted the peerage
from the king; and on the refignation of lord
Townfhend, he was nominated fecretary of ftate.
In that office, his knowledge of foreign affairs, his
application to bufinefs, his attention to diplomatic
forms, the folemnity of his deportment, the precifion of his difpatches, and his propenfity to the
adoption of vigorous meafures againft France, on
the death of Auguftus the Second, rendered him
highly acceptable to the king. Having offended
queen Caroline, by affecting to fet up an intereft
independent of her, he would have been removed,
had not his prudence and caution again conciliated
her favour.

He

Period IV. He never cordially coalefced with Sir Robert
1727 to 1730. Walpole ; and although he almoſt uniformly acted
in fubfervience to his views, he looked up to the
duke of Newcaſtle as his patron and friend, and
gave many inſtances in which he facrificed his
own intereſts, even in oppofition to the commands.
of the king, to gratitude and friendſhip. He
was a man of ſtrong fenfe and moderation ; of high
honour and difintereſted integrity ; and fo tenacious of his word, that Philip of Spain faid of
him, " Stanhope is the only foreign miniſter who
never deceived me *." He was of a mild and even
temper, and contracted, by long habit, fo much
patience and phlegm, that he was characterifed
by the Portuguefe miniſter, Don Azevedo ✝, as
" not being accuſtomed to interrupt thofe who fpoke to
him." A contemporary hiſtorian ‡ has alfo farther defcribed him as one whofe moderation, good
fenfe, and integrity, were fuch, that he was not
confidered as a party man, and had few or no perfonal enemies. Although he never fpoke in the
houfe of peers, yet he was highly ufeful in recommending to the cabinet the moſt prudent method
of attack or defence, and in fuggeſting hints to
thofe who were endowed with the gift of the
tongue.

* Stephen Poyntz to Thomas Townſhend, Auguſt 4, 1729. Correfpondence. ✝ Orford Papers. ‡ Tindal.

CHAPTER THE THIRTY-SEVENTH:

1730.

Origin and Progress of the Disagreement between Townshend and Walpole.—Resignation—Retreat and Death of Townshend.

THE treaty of Seville was the concluding act of Townshend's administration; it was signed on the 9th of November 1729, and on the 16th of May he retired in disgust from the office of secretary of state. His resignation was owing to a disagreement with his brother-in-law and co-adjutor, Sir Robert Walpole, which had long subsisted. It had been occasionally compromised by the interference of common friends, but finally broke into a rupture, which rendered the continuance of both in office incompatible.

Causes of the disagreement between Townshend and Walpole.

The causes of this misunderstanding were various, and originated from the difference of temper, from disagreement on subjects of domestic and foreign politics, from political and private jealousy.

Townshend was frank and impetuous, long accustomed to dictate in the cabinet, and fond of recommending bold measures. Walpole was mild, insinuating, pliant, and good-tempered; desirous of conciliating by lenient methods, but prepared to employ vigour when vigour was necessary.

The

The impetuous manners of Townſhend, began to alienate the king, and diſguſt the queen ; ſeveral members of the cabinet were no leſs diſſatisfied with him. Newcaſtle, in particular, was anxious to remove a miniſter, who abſolutely directed all foreign affairs, and who rendered him a mere cypher ; he wiſhed to procure the appointment of lord Harrington, who already owed his peerage to him, and who, he flattered himſelf, would act in ſubſervience to his dictates.

To theſe public cauſes of miſunderſtanding, derived from a deſire of pre-eminence, a private motive was unfortunately added. The family of Townſhend had long been the moſt conſpicuous, and accuſtomed to take the lead, as the only one then diſtinguiſhed by a peerage, in the county of Norfolk ; the Walpoles were ſubordinate both in eſtate and conſequence, and Houghton was far inferior in ſplendour to Rainham *. But circumſtances were much altered. Sir Robert Walpole was at the head of the treaſury, a peerage had been conferred on his ſon, the increaſe of his paternal domains, the conſtruction of a magnificent ſeat, the acquiſition of a ſuperb collection of paintings, a ſumptuous ſtile of living, and affable manners, drew to Houghton a conflux of company, and eclipſed the more ſober and leſs ſplendid eſtabliſhment at Rainham.

Walpole had long been conſidered as the firſt miniſter in all buſineſs relating to the internal affairs :

---

* Rainham was built by Inigo Jones for Sir Roger Townſhend.

fairs : he was the principal butt of oppofition, for the name of Townfhend fcarcely once occurs in the Craftfman, and the other political papers againft government; while that of Walpole is feen in almoft every page.

His influence over the queen had, on the acceffion of George the Second, prevented the removal of Townfhend. He managed the houfe of commons; and was fupported by a far greater number of friends than his brother minifter could boaft; who had little parliamentary influence; and ftill lefs perfonal credit.

Walpole felt, in all thefe circumftances, his fuperior confequence ; he was confcious that he fhould be fupported by the queen, and was unwilling to continue to act in a fubordinate fituation ; while Townfhend, who had long been ufed to dictate, could not bear any oppofition to his fentiments, or any refiftance to his views. He confidered his brother minifter as one who had firft enlifted himfelf under his banners; and who ought to continue to act with the fame implicit obedience to his commands. Hence a ftruggle for power enfued.

Townfhend had been hitherto the principal difpenfer of ecclefiaftical preferments. This great object of minifterial influence was naturally coveted by Walpole, and had occafioned frequent difputes. In many points of domeftic adminiftration, the violence of Townfhend's meafures was reprobated and oppofed by Walpole, particularly in the bufinefs of Wood's coinage ; in the haughty

I 2   manner

manner of writing to the duke of Grafton, then lord lieutenant of Ireland; and in the meafures adopted in the riots in Scotland in 1725. In foreign affairs, Walpole affected not to interfere, declaring that he did not underftand them, and that they did not belong to his department; yet he always oppofed, as much as lay in his power, all complicated engagements, and uniformly objected to the too lavifh expenditure of the public money in the formation of alliances, which he often confidered as ufelefs and chimerical. His remonftrances had produced a fenfible effect in oppofition to the fentiments of Townfhend; but it was particularly in the negotiation for the treaty of Hanover, that a wide difference of opinion had fubfifted. He expreffed his difapprobation at the precipitate manner in which it was concluded, and was offended that fuch an important ftep had been taken without a due communication to him.

He was ftill more diffatisfied when the Danifh fubfidy became due. For as France avoided paying her fhare, and the whole burthen fell upon England, he, as minifter of finance, was under the neceffity of finding refources to fupply the deficiency.

In feveral difpatches from the foreign minifters in 1725 and 1726, frequent mention is made of the growing mifunderftanding between Townfhend and Walpole, and a rupture is defcribed as unavoidable. Yet thefe bickerings and occafional inftances of difcordant fentiments, did not alien-

ate

ate the brother ministers. They continued to act
together, and on the accession of George the Second, the removal of one would have been followed with the resignation of the other. Their
union at this period was so close, and the opinion
which Walpole entertained of Townshend so favourable, that in 1727, when Townshend was in
imminent danger, Walpole expressed, in terms of
affection and concern, his apprehensions of the
loss which the cause would sustain from his death;
" he considered him as the bulwark of the constitution; and trusted *that Providence would interpose
to save the man, without whom all must fall to the
ground* *.*"

These disputes had been frequently allayed by
the interposition of lady Townshend; she had,
like an Octavia between Anthony and Augustus,
by a discreet exertion of her influence as wife and
sister, moderated the asperities of the contending
politicians. But her mediation had unfortunately
ceased by her death, which happened in March
1726.

Queen Caroline observed the growing misunderstanding between the brother ministers, and
when the rupture became unavoidable, gave her
support to Walpole in preference to Townshend.
By her influence, he soon obtained the preponderance.

Townshend, thus reduced to act a secondary
part, was resolved to make an effort to recover
his

* See Correspondence, Period IV.

I 3

his former power, by removing the duke of Newcaftle, whofe official jealoufy, and attempts to
raife lord Harrington to the office of fecretary of
ftate, had difpleafed him, and placing his friend
lord Chefterfield, who had long afpired to that
ftation, in his ftead. Full of thefe projects, he
accompanied the king to Hanover; and being
the only Englifh minifter of the cabinet abroad, embraced the favourable opportunity of ingratiating
himfelf. He became more obfequious to the king's
German prejudices, paid his court with unceafing
affiduity, and appeared to have gained fo much
influence, that he thought himfelf capable of obtaining the appointment of Chefterfield, who was
embaffador at the Hague, and had confiderably
diftinguifhed himfelf in his diplomatic capacity.
At the fuggeftion of lord Townfhend, he waited
on the king in his paffage through Holland, and
obtained permiffion to attend his majefty to London. When Chefterfield received the offer of the
fecretaryfhip of ftate, he inquired of Lord Townfhend whether the queen was fecured; the anfwer
implied no doubt. But as he had offended her
majefty by the court he paid to lady Suffolk, fhe
exerted all her influence, which was feldom exerted in vain, to fruftrate the fcheme.

Altercation be-
tween Town-
fhend and
Walpole.

Such an attempt, however fecretly conducted,
could not efcape the obfervation of Walpole. He
conferred with the queen on the proper means of
averting the defign, and the communications he
received from her in this and other particulars,
inflamed his refentment. On quitting the palace
after

after one of thefe conferences, he met Townfhend
at colonel Selwyn's, in Cleveland Court, in the prefence of the duke of Newcaftle, Mr: Pelham, colonel and Mrs. Selwyn. The converfation turned on a foreign negotiation, which at the defire of Walpole had been relinquifhed. Townfhend, however, ftill required that the meafure fhould be mentioned to the commons, at the fame time that the houfe fhould be informed that it was given up. Walpole objecting to this propofal as inexpedient, and calculated only to give unneceffary trouble, Townfhend faid, " Since you object, and the houfe of commons is your concern more than mine, I fhall not perfift in my opinion; but as I now give way, I cannot avoid obferving, that upon my honour I think that mode of proceeding would have been moft advifable." Walpole, piqued at thefe expreffions, loft his temper, and faid, " My lord, for once, there is no man's fincerity which I doubt fo much as your lordfhip's, and I never doubted it fo much as when you are pleafed to make fuch ftrong profeffions." Townfhend, incenfed at this reproach, feized him by the collar, Sir Robert caught hold of him in return, and then both, at the fame inftant, quitted their grafp, and laid their hands upon their fwords. Mrs. Selwyn, alarmed, attempted to call the guards, but was prevented by Pelham. But although their friends interpofed to prevent an immediate duel, yet the contumelious expreffions ufed on this occafion, rendered all attempts to heal the breach ineffectual.

Great

Period IV.
1727 to 1730.
Their differ-
ence as to fo-
reign affairs.

. Great difference of opinion had alſo ariſen in regard to foreign affairs. When Townſhend accompanied the king abroad, in May 1729, he conſidered the Emperor as the ſole cauſe of the obſtacles which impeded a general pacification, and immediately on his arrival at Hanover, plunged into the chaos of German politics. He was ſo much incenſed againſt the Emperor, and ſo vehemently inclined to compel him to accede to the admiſſion of Spaniſh garriſons into Parma and Leghorn, that he promoted, to the utmoſt of his power, the concluſion of a ſubſidiary alliance with the four electors of the Rhine, by which England could not have guarantied the pragmatic faction during the exiſtence of that alliance. On the contrary, Walpole, anxious not to do any thing which might render England incapable for a time to gratify the Emperor in his favourite project, ſecretly oppoſed the concluſion of the treaty, and laboured to reconcile the diſcordant politics of Spain and Auſtria, or if that was impoſſible, to conciliate Spain without too much irritating the Emperor.

This colliſion of opinions naturally increaſed the miſunderſtanding, led them to counteract each other, and to ſtrive for pre-eminence in the cabinet.

Townſhend
ineffectually
recommends
Methuen.

Having failed in raiſing Cheſterfield to the office of ſecretary of ſtate, Townſhend made a laſt attempt to obtain that place for Sir Paul Methuen; in which he was equally unſuccefsful. Theſe diſappointments increaſed his natural irritability,

tability, which he vented in peevish expreſſions
againſt lord Harrington; and theſe reproaches,
probably exaggerated by the duke of Newcaſtle,
increaſed the animoſities in the cabinet.

At length the conteſt was brought to a criſis.
Townſhend ſeems to have obtained the good-will
of the king by repreſenting, that he was the only
ſupport of his German intereſt, that lord Harrington neglected preſſing the plan of operations
againſt the Emperor, and that Hanover would be
ſacrificed by the new arrangements. Under theſe
circumſtances, the duke of Newcaſtle, with the
approbation of the Walpoles, drew up a diſpatch
to the plenipotentiaries at Soiſſons, diſſuading an
attack of the Auſtrian Netherlands, adviſing that
an army ſhould be aſſembled on the banks of the
Rhine, for the purpoſe of threatening the frontiers of Bohemia; and ſtrongly recommending,
that before this plan was concerted with France,
propoſals of accommodation ſhould be preſented
to the Emperor. But before the letter was ſub-
mitted to the king, Townſhend had written to
his majeſty, enforcing the neceſſity of forming a
plan of hoſtile operations before any declaration
was made, for the purpoſe of compelling the king
of Pruſſia to ſubmit, and reducing the Emperor
to accept of the terms dictated by England and
her allies.

The king approved this advice, and ordered
Townſhend to communicate his reſolution to the
duke of Newcaſtle and Horace Walpole, that inſtructions might be forwarded to the plenipotentiaries,

tiaries, in conformity to that opinion. Townfhend accordingly fent the letter, with the king's
anfwer, to Horace Walpole, and went into Norfolk for a few days. In this dilemma, the duke
defpaired of fuccefs, and propofed to act agreeably to the dictates of Townfhend. But Sir Robert Walpole communicated Newcaftle's difpatch
to the queen, and obtained, through her influence, the affent of the king, who expreffed his
full approbation of the contents.

Refigns.

Townfhend, finding that his perfonal influence
with the king was not fufficient to counteract the
exertions of his rivals, oppofed by the queen, and
deferted by the remaining members of the cabinet,
gave in his refignation, and retired from public
affairs.

**Explains the
caufes of his
refignation.**

In feveral letters to his confidential correfpondents abroad, which are ftill extant in the
Rainham Collection, Townfhend attributes his refignation principally to the effects of his dangerous illnefs in 1727, which rendered him incapable of fupporting the fatigues of his place, but
hints at the fame time with great delicacy at the
coolnefs and mifintelligence which had arifen between him and Sir Robert Walpole, and at the
difguft he had recently received from that quarter.
At the fame time he adds, with great fpirit and dignity, he is happy to announce that his retreat has
not made any alteration in public affairs, and that
he never could have refolved to quit his fituation,
if he had not been fully convinced that Walpole
would follow the fame principles, and carry on
the

the fame meafures which had been hirtherto purfued. In his letter to Slingelandt, he obferves,
" the king has had the goodnefs to permit me to
retire in the moft obliging manner, and has moft
gracioufly received the affurances, which I took
the liberty to make, that notwithftanding my refignation, I fhould always be ready to furnifh all
the eclairciffements in my power whenever it fhall
be deemed neceffary for his fervice."

. Townfhend retired with a moft unfullied character for integrity, honour, and difintereftednefs,
and gave feveral ftriking proofs that he could
command the natural warmth of his temper, and
rife fuperior to the malignant influence of party
and difappointed ambition. The opppofition, who
had formed fanguine expectations from the difunion in the cabinet, were prepared to receive
him with open arms, but he refilted their advances, and firmly perfevered in his original determination. Soon after Chefterfield commenced his
ardent oppofition to Walpole, he went to Rainham, and requefted Townfhend to attend an important queftion in the houfe of lords. Townfhend
replied, that he had formed a refolution which he
could not break, of never again engaging in political contefts. " I recollect," he added, " that
lord Cowper, though a ftaunch Whig, had been
betrayed by perfonal pique and party refentment,
in his oppofition to the miniftry, to throw himfelf into the arms of the Tories, and even to fupport principles which tended to ferve the caufe of
the Jacobites. I know that I am extremely
warm;

warm; and I am apprehenfive if I fhould attend the houfe of lords, I alfo may be hurried away by the impetuofity of my temper, and by perfonal refentment, to adopt a line of conduct, which in my cooler moments I may regret." He maintained this honourable and truly patriotic refolution; and thus proved himfelf worthy of the higheft eulogium.

He paffed the evening of his days in the purfuit of rural occupations and agricultural experiments; his improvements ameliorated the ftate of hufbandry, his hofpitality endeared him to his neighbours, and the dignity of his character infured refpect. Apprehenfive of being tempted again to enter into thofe fcenes of active life, which he had refolved totally to abandon, he never revifited the capital, but died at Rainham, in 1738, aged 64.

Death.

Notwithftanding the afperity with which this conteft was conducted, the brother minifters feem to have renounced their friendfhip without forfeiting their efteem for each other. Townfhend did not indulge in peevifh expreffions againft his fuccefsful rival, and Sir Robert Walpole never blamed the minifterial conduct or depreciated the abilities of lord Townfhend. He was always unwilling to enter into the caufes of their difunion; when an intimate friend preffed him on the fubject fome years afterwards, he made feveral attempts to evade the queftion, and at length replied, " It is difficult to trace the caufes of a difpute between ftatefmen, but I will give you the hiftory history in a few words ; as long as the firm of the house was Townshend and Walpole, the utmost harmony prevailed ; but it no sooner became Walpole and Townshend, than things went wrong, and a separation ensued *."

* The contents of this chapter are derived from the letters in the Correspondence —Etough's Papers.—The late Earl of Hardwicke's Memorandums.—Maty's Life of Lord Chesterfield.—Communications from the late earl of Orford, lord Sydney, and his brother Charles Townshend, esquire.

PERIOD THE FIFTH:

From the Refignation of Lord Townshend to
the Diffolution of the Parliament:

1730—1734:

CHAPTER THE THIRTY-EIGHTH:

1730—1731.

*Walpole inclines to a Reconciliation with the Emperor.—Negotiations
which preceded and terminated in the Treaty of Vienna.—Treaty of
Seville carried into Execution.—Tranfactions in Parliament.—General Satisfaction.—Character of Earl Waldegrave, the new Embaffador at Paris.*

Walpole con-
ducts foreign
affairs.

THE refignation of Townshend placed Walpole in a new point of view. Hitherto he
had taken no public part in foreign affairs, and
only indirectly influenced the current negotiations,
either through the private interpofition of the
queen, or the medium of his brother, affecting to leave the fole direction of thofe matters
to the fecretary of ftate. But the removal of
Townshend inftantly changed his fituation. The
duke of Newcaftle for fome time continued to act
the fame fubordinate part as before; and the new
fecretary, lord Harrington, received his impulfe
from the minifter of the finance, or from his brother
Horace.

Horace. Walpole, therefore, now took a more
open and decided place in the regulation of foreign transactions, and his opinion seems to have
principally contributed to the renewal of the ancient connection with the houfe of Auftria, with
whom England had been fo long in a ftate of open
defiance.

He had fagacioufly appreciated the advantages
which refulted to England from the alliance
with France, convinced that an union with that
power had effectually hurt the caufe of the Pretender, and counteracted the fchemes of the Jacobites. He was aware that France, during the
minority of Louis the Fifteenth, or under the government of a prime minifter like Cardinal Fleury,
of a pacific and timid difpofition, was a very
proper ally in a defenfive treaty, to check and
prevent the defigns of the Emperor, who had
formed fchemes and alliances detrimental to the
fecurity and commerce of England. He well knew
that minifters of a free nation muft fometimes be
obliged to contract new engagements, in oppofition
to thofe powers with whom they would have been
willing to have lived in the ftricteft friendfhip,
upon juft and honourable terms *.

He had therefore concurred with Townfhend, in
warmly promoting the alliance with France, and was
not deterred by the popular outcry, that the meafures
of the cabinet were directed to lower our natural
ally, the houfe of Auftria, and exalt France, our
natural enemy, from purfuing a plan which fecured

* The intereft of Great Britain fteadily purfued, p. 26.

cured to England internal tranquillity and external peace. The improvement of our commerce and manufactures were a full juftification of this wife meafure.

But things were now confiderable changed. The folid eftablifhment of the houfe of Hanover on the throne of Great Britain, and the number of Jacobites who, on the quiet acceffion of George the Second, renounced their principles, had leffened the danger of internal commotions, and rendered the co-operation of France in favour of the Pretender, lefs an object of alarm.

State of the French cabinet. The relative fituation of France was no lefs changed. Morville, the friend of England, had been difmiffed from the office of fecretary of ftate, and his fucceffor, Chauvelin, the enemy of England, governed Cardinal Fleury. A reconciliation had taken place between France and Spain, and the ancient jealoufy between France and England began to revive on both fides.

In confequence of this alteration of circumftances, France acted from policy an indecifive and wavering part. When the Emperor, in oppofition to the arrangements made by the allies of Seville, declared, that if Spanifh troops fhould enter Tufcany, he would drive them out, it became neceffary either to force him te execute that treaty, or to prevail upon him, by the guaranty of his favourite object, the pragmatic fanction. Cardinal Fleury affected to co-operate with England, in obtaining the confent of the Emperor, either by force or perfuafive means ; but artfully threw

*

obftacles

obftacles in the way of both. Various fchemes
for effecting that end were propofed. It was the
great object of England to prevent the invafion
of the Low Countries, and to confine principally
the feat of war to Sicily, or at leaft to Italy: It
was the view of the French to extend it to the other
parts of the Auftrian dominions, under the hopes
of making conquefts on the fide of Germany and
the Low Countries.

· When the two nations were actuated with fuch
different views, no co-incidence of opinion could
be expected. France objected to all fchemes,
either of compulfion or compromife, and endeavoured to throw the blame of inactivity on the
Englifh and Dutch. Meanwhile Spain complained
bitterly that the treaty of Seville was not executed,
and that Parma and Tufcany, for the attainment
of which fhe had acceded to the quadruple alliance, were on the point of being loft.

Walpole now perceived that the ftrict alliance
with France could no longer be maintained. He
had two objects in view, the one, according to his
own expreffions, to avoid a war with the Emperor, for fear of its confequences, and the other
with Spain, on account of our trade, and the only
method of effecting both thefe purpofes was to
renew the ancient connection with the houfe of
Auftria, and to lure the Emperor to accede to the
treaty of Seville, with a promife of guarantying
the pragmatic fanction.

On thefe interefting topics he maintained a
correfpondence with his brother, Horace Walpole,

embaffador at Paris; combated his opinion in favour of continuing the friendfhip with France,
and gradually brought him over to approve a
negotiation with the houfe of Auftria.

The Emperor had, before the treaty of Seville,
endeavoured to open a feparate negotiation with
England, and fince its conclufion had thrown out
hints to our embaffador at Vienna, that a thorough reconciliation might eafily be effected. In
confequence of thefe infinuations, the Britifh cabinet decided on making the attempt, and lord
Harrington announced this refolution in an official difpatch to Mr. Robinfon, who had fucceeded earl Waldegrave in the embaffy to Vienna *.

An anfwer being tranfmitted, that the Imperial
court was inclined, with every appearance of fincerity on their part, to renew their ancient connection with England, on fair and reafonable conditions, farther inftructions were forwarded from
the fecretary of ftate, together with the plans of
treaties and declarations to be figned by the Emperor, both in regard to the difputes with England, and to the king's German affairs †.

While this negotiation was pending, the delay
gave fuch umbrage to the king of Spain, that he
Jan. 29. declared, by the Marquis of Caftellar, his embaffador at Paris, that he confidered himfelf free
from all engagements contracted on his part by
the treaty of Seville, and at full liberty to adopt
                                              fuch

* September 14-25, 1730. Correfpondence, Period V.
† Lord Harrington to Mr. Robinfon, Dec. 4-15, 1730.

such measures as should be most suitable to his interests.

Soon after these transactions, the duke of Parma Death of the died; the duchess, his widow, declared herself duke of Par- pregnant: the Emperor, with the secret conni- ma. vance of England, took possession of Parma, mak- ing at the same time a declaration, that if the duchess should be delivered of a son, the intro- duction of the Spanish troops should take place; if of a daughter, Don Carlos should instantly re- ceive the investiture of Parma and Placentia, from the Emperor and empire.

In opening this negotiation, the British cabinet Parliamentary had declared the determined resolution of the proceedings. king to make the treaty of Seville the basis of the new alliance, and the securing to Don Carlos the succession to Tuscany and Parma was held out as an indispensable article. The minister was aware that the best method to obtain peace was to be prepared for war, and that the only suc- cessful means for carrying the treaty of Seville into effect, were to be ready to enforce its exe- cution by vigorous measures. The speech which Jan. 21. the king delivered from the throne on the meet- ing of parliament, was drawn up by him in con- formity with these sentiments. After declaring, that every measure was adopted to prevent, by an accommodation, the fatal consequences of a ge- neral rupture; and that it was impossible to state the supplies which would be required for the current service of the year, until peace or war

should

ſhould be decided upon, it concluded with theſe
ſtrong expreſſions :

" The time draws near, which will admit of
no farther delays. If the tranquillity of Europe
can be ſettled without the effuſion of blood, or
the expence of public treaſure, that ſituation will
certainly be moſt happy and deſirable. But if
that bleſſing cannot be obtained, honour, juſtice,
and the ſacred faith due to ſolemn treaties, will
call upon us to exert ourſelves, in procuring by
force, what cannot be had upon juſt and reaſon-
able terms *."

The negotiation was carried on with ſo much
addreſs and ſecrecy, that although ſome rumour
of it tranſpired, and hints were thrown out in
the Craftſman, yet the debate on the ſide of the
minority was conducted on a ſuppoſition, that
England was preparing to execute the treaty of
Seville by force, and an amendment to the addreſs was propoſed, that the king ſhould be re-
queſted not to concur in a war againſt the Emperor, either in Flanders or on the Rhine. But
when this propoſition was negatived, a more plauſible amendment was ſuggeſted by oppoſition, who
artfully availed themſelves of the prejudice conceived againſt the king for his attachment to
Hanover; they propoſed to inſert, that they would
ſupport his majeſty's engagements, ſo far as they
related to the intereſt of Great Britain. In anſwer to this propoſal, Walpole did not heſitate to
                                            declare,

* Journals.

declare, " That fuch an expreffion in their addrefs would feem to infinuate, that the king had
entered into engagements that did not relate to
the interefts of Great Britain, which would be a
great inftance of ingratitude towards the king,
who in all his meafures had never fhewed the leaft
regard to any thing but the intereft of Great Britain, and the eafe and fecurity of the people ; as all
thofe who had the honour to ferve him could tef-
tify, and upon their honour declare ; he hoped
every member of that houfe was convinced, that
the king would never enter into any engagement
that was not abfolutely neceffary for procuring the
happinefs, and infuring the fafety, of his fubjects,
and therefore it was quite unneceffary to confine
the words of their addrefs to fuch engagements as
related to the intereft of Great Britain *."

Nothing was faid directly in anfwer to this affertion, though fo much might have been faid.
It was only urged, that to fupport any hoftile
operations againft the Emperor on the Rhine, was
abfolutely deftructive to the interefts of Great
Britain, tending to the total fubverfion of the balance of power ; that the houfe had good reafon
to believe that no minifter would dare to advife
the king to fuch a meafure ; and the member who
ufed thefe ftrong expreffions, concluded by oppofing the amendment as unneceffary : the addrefs
was therefore carried without a divifion. It was
alfo drawn up by the minifter, and after acknow-
ledging,

* Chandler.

K 3

ledging, in terms of gratitude, the king's goodnefs, " in endeavouring to have the conditions
of the treaty of Seville fulfilled and executed, in
fuch manner as might beft fecure a general pacification, and be conformable to his engagements
with his allies," declared, " that they would, with
all chearfulnefs, grant fuch fupplies as fhould be
neceflary for the fervice of the enfuing year, and
effectually enable the king to make good his engagements *."

Unanimity and zeal.   The unanimity and vigour of this addrefs, which
was equally adopted by the houfe of peers, had a
great effect on the tranfactions abroad, and gave
energy to the negotiations of Vienna.

In confequence of the adoption of thefe meafures, lord Harrington expreffed to the Britifh
minifter at Vienna, the king's difapprobation of
the delays and obftacles with which the Imperial
court clogged the progrefs of the negotiations, replied to the counter project of the Emperor,
gave farther inftructions, and fent the ultimatum
of the cabinet.

Obftructions to the Auftrian alliance.   Notwithftanding thefe remonftrances,' the miniftry well knew that the obftacles were derived
no lefs from the pertinacity of the Hanoverian,
than the haughtinefs of the Imperial court, and
one of the great difficulties which occurred in
concluding an accommodation, arofe from blending the affairs of Germany with thofe of England.

Mr. Ro-

* Chandler.

Mr. Robinfon had been particularly ordered* " to continue the greateft friendfhip and confi- dence towards Dieden, the Hanoverian agent at Vienna, and act in perfect concert with him in every thing, wherein the king's interefts were concerned: And to employ his beft offices and inftances with the Imperial minifters, for procuring the moft effectual redrefs and fatisfaction to the king upon the feveral demands which Dieden was inftructed to make for that purpofe to the court of Vienna."

Thefe objects of contention between the Emperor and the king, as elector of Hanover, were fo various, complicated, and delicate, that the treaty would never have been concluded, had the Britifh minifter at Vienna infifted, according to his official orders, upon a full and fatisfactory anfwer to all the points in difpute. Fortunately, *Removed* the cabinet of London, influenced by Walpole, had the courage to cut the gordian knot, which it could not unloofe; lord Harrington, in a private letter, inftructed Mr. Robinfon † to fign the treaty with England, and to refer the German affairs to a future decifion.

Another great difficulty in conducting this ne- *Farther diffi-* gotiation, arofe from an erroneous opinion, formed *culties obvi-* by the Emperor, that the minifters of the Englifh *ated.* cabinet were difunited, and from a jealoufy that the two Walpoles, who were known to direct the

helm

* Grantham Papers. Difpatch from lord Harrington to Mr. Robinfon, 4/15 December, 1730. Correfpondence.

† Lord Harrington to Mr. Robinfon. January 28th—February 8th, 1731. Correfpondence.

helm of government, were favourable to the alliance with France, and confequently hoftile to the
houfe of Auftria. This notion had been fupported
by the duchefs of Kendal, in her correfpondence
with the Emprefs, and corroborated by fome leading members of oppofition, who had long held a
private intercourfe of letters with the Emperor or
his minifters.

This falfe opinion, together with the difficulty of
fettling the German affairs, fufpended the fignature of the treaty. In this moment of doubt and
uncertainty, a letter * from Horace Walpole to
Mr. Robinfon, conveying the ftrongeft affurances
of his own and his brother's fentiments in favour
of the Emperor, decided the Imperial cabinet, and
haftened the conclufion.

Second treaty
of Vienna.
The treaty was figned on the 16th of March,
and is ufually called the fecond treaty of Vienna,
to diftinguifh it from that which was concluded
in 1725. It was a defenfive alliance, and ftipulated a reciprocal guaranty of mutual rights and
poffeffions; on the part of England, to guaranty
the Emperor's fucceffion, according to the pragmatic fanction; on that of the Emperor, to abolifh the Oftend company, and all trade to the
Eaft Indies, from any part of the Auftrian Netherlands, to fecure the fucceffion of Don Carlos
to Parma and Tufcany, and not to oppofe the introduction of Spanifh garrifons.

Effects of the
treaty.
Thus was this great and difficult tafk of preventing a general war, accomplifhed with an addrefs

* February 9—20, 1732. Correfpondence.

drefs and fecrecy that reflected high honour on
thofe who conducted it. The treaty of Seville
was carried into execution without force, and
without breach of faith to any other power: to
Don Carlos, Parma was fecured, with the confent
of the Emperor, and the eventual fucceffion of
Tufcany guarantied; Spain was fatisfied with England; and the Emperor, gratified with the guaranty of the pragmatic fanction, confidered this
union as the commencement of a new æra to the
houfe of Auftria.

The fatisfaction in England was full and com--
plete. In fact, no event more difconcerted oppofition, or raifed the minifter higher in the eftima-
tion of the public. It had long been a favourite
theme of popular declamation, that his meafures
had a tendency to lower the houfe of Auftria, and
to exalt the power of France. Their arguments
were therefore now turned againft themfelves;
the breach of the French alliance, and reconciliation with Auftria, took away one plaufible topic
of raillery and invective.

The only popular objection to the management
of foreign affairs now was, that England was en-
tangled in a multiplicity of treaties and guaranties; that no rupture could take place in Europe,
in which we fhould not be obliged to interfere as
principals; that it was the fteady intereft of Great
Britain to contract no burthenfome engagements,
and to truft to her naval ftrength and infular fituation for repelling all foreign attempts.

To

Period V.
1730 to 1734.
Answered.
To this general objection a general answer was returned ; that a nation, whose strength depends upon the flourishing state of trade and credit, (inseparable from that of public tranquillity) whose commerce extends to all parts of the world, and is founded on compacts and stipulations with powers of different and incompatible interests ; who has as many enviers as neighbours, as numerous rivals as there are commercial powers, must have a more extensive and particular interest to foresee and obviate those troubles, which, if not prevented in time, might occasion great disturbances, might place so large a share of dominion in the hands of once prince, as to endanger the liberties of the rest, and consequently interrupt her trade. A people thus situated, must provide themselves with foreign support, proportionable to the attempts that may be apprehended from the continental powers to their prejudice, which cannot possibly be secured but by reciprocal engagements on their part, and by interesting themselves as deeply in the welfare of other nations, as they expect those nations to interest themselves on their behalf.

Treaty of Seville carried into execution.
This compact having secured the consent of the Emperor to the introduction of Spanish troops, Philip revoked the marquis de Castelar's declaration, and acceded to the new treaty of Vienna ; and the execution of it, which speedily followed, proved the sincerity of the Imperial and British courts. After a few altercations between the Emperor

peror and Don Carlos, the one claiming Parma as
an inheritance, and the other infifting on confer-
ring it as a fief of the empire, the Spanifh troops
landed át Leghorn, on the 20th of Oftober, un,
der convoy of the Britifh and Spanifh fleet. Don
Carlos himfelf arrived there on the 26th of December, and was put in full poffeffion of Parma
and Placentia,

In opening this negotiation, Walpole had been Charaſter and
anxious not to irritate France, before he had con- earl of Walde-
ciliated the court of Vienna. He judged it pru- grave.
dent to fend in the place of his brother Horace,
who had returned from his embaffy at Paris, a
perfon agreeable to Cardinal Fleury, and in whom
he could implicitly confide. Lord Chefterfield
had been recommended for that poft, as a prelude
to his being appointed fecretary of ftate; but
Horace Walpole reprefented to his brother, that
his temper and habits would not accord with
thofe of the Cardinal, and fuggefted the earl of
Waldegrave, as more proper for fo delicate a fituation, who was accordingly nominated.

James earl of Waldegrave was defcended from
an ancient family in Northamptonfhire, whofe anceftors may be traced in a direct line to times an-
terior to the conqueft. They were lords of the
towns of Waldegrave, Twywell and Slipton, in
the county of Northampton * ; Sir Richard Wal-

degrave

* As the account of the Waldegrave family given by Collins, is
incorreſt in many particulars, a more accurate ftatement is here added from family documents, communicated by the countefs of Waldegrave. "Waldegrave, a Saxon by lyneall defcent, lord of the
" county of Northampton, had at the conqueft one only daughter, and
. " her

degrave was fpeaker of the houfe of commons in 1382; and fome of his anceftors received the eftates of Naveftock and Borely, in Effex, and Chewton in Somerfetfhire, as grants from Henry the Eighth.

In 1643 Sir Edward Waldegrave was made a baronet, and his great grandfon, Sir Henry Waldegrave, was, in 1685, created a peer, by the title of baron Waldegrave, of Chewton *, in Somerfetfhire, where the family then principally refided. On the revolution he followed the fortunes of James the Second, whofe natural daughter, Henrietta, by Arabella Churchill, he had efpoufed, and to whom he had many and great obligations. He died at Paris in 1689.

His eldeft fon and fucceffor James, of whom we are now treating, was born in 1684, and educated in the Roman Catholic religion. In 1722 he entered into the communion of the church of England,

---

" her he married, by the conqueror's commandment, to Guerim or
" Waiin de Waldegrave of Normandie, by means of which mar_
" riage Waldegrave the Saxon had a pardon granted him by the con_
" queror, of his life and land, notwithftanding he bore arms againft
" him at Battle Abbey, on king Harold's part, which pardon is yet ex_
" tant, and was lately in the hands of the lords of the manor of Wal_
" degrave, &c. in the county of Northampton. This town and ma_
" nor was fold by Sir William Waldegrave, knight, in the reign of
" king Henry the Eighth."

Waldegrave is of Saxon derivation, from *Walde*, and *Grave*, fig_
nifying the ruler of a *Walde* or foreft. The anceftors of the prefent
earl refided in different counties at different periods. A Sir Richard
Waldegrave, who was fpeaker of the houfe of commons in 1382, mar_
ried the heirefs of Sylvefter of Buers, in the county of Suffolk, and
either himfelf or fome of his defcendants, more than once reprefented
that county.—The grants of Naveftock, Borely, and Chewton, pro_
bably occafioned the fale of the family inheritance in Northampton_
fhire.

* Collins's Peerage. Collinfon's Hiftory of Somerfetfhire.—Article Chewton.

England, and took his feat in the houfe of peers., His uncle, the duke of Berwick, being defirous to mortify him for having renounced his faith, inquired of him whether he had made his abjuration from political or religious motives, and ufed the expreffion, " *confefs* the truth," to which he plied, " I changed my religion to avoid *confeffion.*"

When it was thought neceffary to fend an embaffador to Vienna, for the purpofe of executing the articles agreed upon in the preliminaries figned between England, France, and the Emperor at Paris, 'and of conciliating the Emperor, who had been diffatisfied with the king of England, lord Waldegrave was felected as the perfon whofe mild and affable demeanour beft qualified him for that negotiation. George the Firft, who confidered the miffion as too great a condefcenfion after the ill ufage he had received from the Emperor, fent word that he approved the perfon, though he difliked the errand *.

Lord Waldegrave fet out in May 1727, and arrived at Paris on the 14th of June. The difficulty of fettling the complicated negotiations, and the events which followed the death of George the Firft, detained him in France nearly a year. He went to Vienna in April 1728. During his refidence in that capital, he corrected the miftatement which the oppofition in England had tranfmitted of their ftrength, and of the weaknefs of the party that efpoufed the meafures of government; and plainly fhewed that the divifions in the

* Earl of Waldegrave's Diary.

the cabinet would not diminish the weight and influence of Great Britain abroad. He proved to the Imperial minifters, that the preliminaries with Spain contained no conditions hoftile to the houfe of Auftria, and were ftrictly conformable to the articles of the quadruple alliance. He threw out hopes to the Emperor of a future accommodation with England, and that the guaranty of the pragmatic fanction might be the confequence of acceding to the introduction of Spanifh garrifons into Parma and Leghorn. He obtained a ratification of the preliminary articles between the Emperor, England, and France, and laid the foundation of the reconciliation, which Mr. Robinfon carried into execution. He then returned to Paris, where he was appointed embaffador extraordinary on the refignation of Horace Walpole.

He filled this difficult employment ten years, during a period in which the difunion between France and England was gradually increafing to an open rupture.

For his fervices at Vienna, he was created vifcount Chewton and earl of Waldegrave, and his exertions at Paris were rewarded with the garter. In 1740 he obtained leave to return for the recovery of his health. He embarked for England, October 1740, and died at his feat at Naveftock in Effex, on the 11th of April 1741, in the 57th year of his age.

He was in high confidence with Sir Robert Walpole, and was the foreign embaffador in whom, next to his brother, the minifter principally con-

8   fided.

fided: Several letters which paffed between them,'
and are printed in the correfpondence, prove the
truth of this affertion. He conducted himfelf in
his embaffies with confummate addrefs, and particularly diftinguifhed himfelf by obtaining fecret information in times of emergency. Though
a man of pleafure, he purfued bufinefs, when bufinefs was neceffary, with indefatigable diligence.
His letters are written with great fpirit, perfpicuity, and good fenfe, and are peculiarly entertaining. He had fo little the appearance of a
man of bufinefs, that he was confidered as incapable of writing fuch excellent difpatches as he
tranfmitted to England, and they were principally
attributed to his fecretary, Mr. Thompfon. But
this unjuft imputation was foon proved to be
falfe, when the embaffador left France, and the
fecretary remained chargé d'affaires. The inferio-
rity of his letters, to thofe which were written
during Waldegrave's embaffy, was ftriking, and
carried a full conviction, that they were of his
own compofition. I am enabled alfo to do juftice
to the abilities of the earl of Waldegrave in this
refpect. A complete collection of his letters and
difpatches, from 1727 to 1740, is preferved at
Naveftock, and the greater number are original
draughts written in his own hand, with fuch era-
fures and alterations as fully prove that they were
folely his compofition. They do honour to his diplomatic talents, and prove found fenfe, an infinuating addrefs, and elegant manners.

The

The renewal of the ancient alliance with the house of Auftria, had greatly difpleafed the French cabinet, and particularly difgufted cardinal Fleury, whofe fentiments were always inclined to the adoption of pacific meafures, who (however influenced by the counfels of Chauvelin) was convinced that the peace of Europe had been principally owing to the union between France and England, who appreciated the fentiments of Sir Robert Walpole as congenial to his own, and who from long habits of intimacy and confidence, had contracted a partiality for Horace Walpole, which he was unwilling to relinquifh. He confidered this alliance as a prelude to inceffant bickerings and future contefts ; and, being well acquainted with the domineering fpirit of the houfe of Auftria, and the eagernefs of Charles the Sixth, to obtain from all the powers of Europe, the guaranty of the pragmatic fanction, fufpected that his affent to the treaty of Vienna was purchafed with a promife on the part of England, to compel France to accede to that guaranty, and expreffed in ftrong terms of indignation, his apprehenfion of fecret articles derogatory to the interefts of France.

The candid anfwer of the Britifh cabinet, conveyed through the earl of Waldegrave, removed the jealoufies of the cardinal. The king and cabinet in England, had now adopted, however unwillingly, the principles of the pacific minifter, and De la Faye, under fecretary of ftate, fpoke the fentiments of Walpole, when he obferved,

that

that no one but a perfon totally ignorant of the Britifh conftitution, could for a moment have en- tertained fuch an opinion. The king, he remarked, could not engage in war without money, and muft apply to parliament for fupplies, if fuch a misfortune fhould occur. The parliament, who Removed. fpoke the voice of the nation, might be induced to grant fupplies for the purpofe of keeping out the Pretender, protecting merchants, preferving, trade, or maintaining Gibraltar; but it would have been a monftrous conduct to propofe an annual fupply of five millions for the purpofe of compelling France to guaranty the pragmatic fanction. The nation could never bear fuch a propofition, and the minifter who had the folly to make it, would juftly incur the indignation of the people *.

The earl of Waldegrave being recalled from Vienna, it became neceffary to depute a perfon of confidence to that court, on whom the Walpoles could no lefs implicitly depend; nor can a greater proof of their fuperior afcendancy in the cabinet be given, than that Mr. Robinfon was the perfon who was chofen to fill this important fituation at this critical juncture.

Thomas Robinfon, afterwards knight of the Miffion and Bath, and lord Grantham, was fourth fon of Sir character of Mr. Robinfon. William Robinfon, baronet, of the county of York, by Mary, daughter of George Aiflabie, of

Studley

* De la Faye to the earl of Waldegrave, Auguft 16th, 1731. Correfpondence.

Studley Royal. He was brought up at Weftminfter fchool, and completed his education at Trinity College, Cambridge, of which he became a
fellow in 1719. In 1723, he accompanied Horace Walpole as fecretary to the embaffy at Paris,
and was diftinguifhed by him with the higheft
marks of confidence and efteem ; under his inftructions, and from his example, he acquired a
confummate experience in diplomatic concerns.
During the abfence of the embaffador, he was entrufted with the management of the Englifh affairs in France, and conducted himfelf with fo
much addrefs and ability, that he was not duped
even by the affected candour of cardinal Fleury,
nor deluded by the artifices of Chauvelin. Great
command of temper, patience of contradiction,
dignity of manner, franknefs in receiving, and
quicknefs in anfwering objections, rendered him
peculiarly adapted to counteract the chicanery of
the Imperial court, to foften the domineering
and punctilious character of the Emperor Charles
the Sixth, and to conciliate the difcordant tempers of the four minifters of the conference *. He
continued at the court of Vienna from 1730 to
1748, when he was deputed embaffador and joint
plenipotentiary with the earl of Sandwich, to conclude the peace of Aix la Chapelle.

His difpatches are clear and perfpicuous, fo explicit and defcriptive, as to convey a faithful picture of the tempers and characters of thofe with
whom

---

* Prince Eugene, count Zinzendorff, count Staremberg, and the
bifhop of Bamberg.

whom he negotiated; and it was truly said of
him, that he not only set down every word that
was uttered in his conferences with the Imperial
ministers, but noted even their looks and ges-
tures These interesting documents contain a co-
pious, and almost uninterrupted narrative of the
trarsactions between England and the court of Vienna, during a period of eighteen years, big with
events, that threatened the downfal of the house
of Austria, which was averted by the heroism of
Maria Theresa, and the interposition of England.
In 1742 he was made knight of the Bath, and
soon after the conclusion of the peace of Aix la
Chapelle, returned to England. He was succes-
sively appointed lord of trade, master of the great
wardrobe, and secretary of state. In 1761 he was
created a peer, by the title of lord Grantham,
and died in 1770, aged seventy-three.

CHAPTER THE THIRTY-NINTH:

1731.

*Biographical Memoirs of William Pulteney.—Origin and Progress of his
Misunderstanding with Walpole.*

TWO errors are principally to be avoided by
an author, that undertakes to write the life
of a minister, who directed, during so long a period, the helm of government, and whose conduct
materially affected the interests of Great Britain

and

and the fate of Europe: the firft is fuch a bias
of affection and partiality, as to draw a panegyric
rather than a hiftory; the fecond, an indifcriminate prejudice againft thofe who headed the oppofition; and who, becaufe they were enemies to
Sir Robert Walpole, have been held forth by
his partifans as devoid of all principle, and ufing,
in every inftance, their reprobation to his meafures, as a cloak for malice and rancour. This
laft is the ufual error of biographers; yet it appears extraordinary to a candid mind, that in order to raife the character of one great man, it
fhould feem neceffary to debafe all his opponents,
and that no allowance fhould be made for difference of opinion, or inveterate habits and pre-
poffeffions. Becaufe the party writers of oppofition have loaded Walpole with invective, is it juft
to afperfe his adverfaries with equal virulence?

But in no inftance has prejudice been carried to
a greater height, then in drawing the character and
conduct of Pulteney, the great leader of oppofition.
He, above all others, has been expofed to the
fiery ordeal of party; not only by the friends of
the minifter whom he drove from the helm, but
alfo by thofe who were once joined with him, and
who, difcontented at the difpofal of offices on the
change of adminiftration, railed at their former
leader, becaufe they were not promoted to thofe
places which they claimed as the reward of their
long perfeverance.

William

William Pulteney * ·was· defcended from an ancient family, who took their furname from a place
of that appellation in Leicefterfhire. His grand- Family,
father, Sir William Pulteney, was member of par- birth, and
liament for the city of Weftminfter, and highly Pulteney.
diftinguifhed himfelf in the houfe of commons
for his manly and fpirited eloquence.

Of his father, William Pulteney, I find little
upon record, except his birth, marriage, and
death.

William Pulteney ✝, his eldeft fon, was born in
1682, received his education at Weftminfter
fchool, where he greatly improved in claffical literature; and being removed to Chrift Church,
Oxford, fo highly diftinguifhed himfelf by his talents and induftry, that he was appointed, by
dean Aldrich, to make the congratulatory fpeech
to queen Anne, on her vifit to the college.

Having travelled through various parts of Eu- Comes into
rope, he returned to his native country, with a parliament.

mind

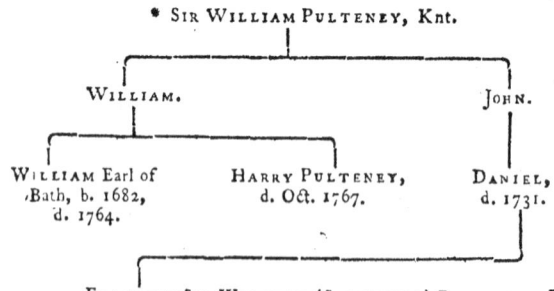

* Sir William Pulteney, Knt.

William.

John.

William Earl of Bath, b. 1682, d. 1764.

Harry Pulteney, d. Oct. 1767.

Daniel, d. 1731.

Frances═Sir William (Johnstone) Pulteney, Bart.

Henrietta Laura, Baronefs Bath.

✝ I am indebted to the kindnefs of the bifhop of Salifbury (Dr.
Douglas) for fome of thefe anecdotes, which relate to the early part of
Mr. Pulteney's life.

mind highly improved ; and came into parliament
for the borough of Heydon, in Yorkſhire, by the
intereſt of Mr. Guy, his protector and great be-
nefactor.

Being deſcended from a Whig family, and educated in revolution principles, the young ſenator
warmly eſpouſed that party, and during the whole
reign of queen Anne oppoſed the meaſures of the
Tories.

He firſt ſpoke in the houſe on the place bill,
which he warmly ſupported, and ſome amendments being made by the lords, the diſcuſſion,
was, by the intervention of the miniſtry, poſtponed for three days; during which interval,
means were found to gain over ſeveral who had
oppoſed the bill, and the amendments ſeemed
likely to be carried.

The young ſenator, indignant at this apoſtacy,
and irritated that ſeveral had, in a few days, totally changed their opinions, animadverted in a few
words on ſuch political baſeneſs and alluding to
Sir James Montague *, who after having diſtinguiſhed himſelf in oppoſition to the amendments,
now voted for them, obſerved, " Cerberes has
received his ſop, and barks no more ;" a remark
which ſtruck the houſe as ready and pertinent.

He had formed a juſt notion, that no young
member ought to preſs into public notice with
too much forwardneſs, and fatigue the houſe with
long orations, until he had acquired the habit of
order and preciſion. He was often heard to de-

clare,

---

* Afterwards ſolicitor and attorney general.

clare, that hardly any perſon ever became a good
orator, who began with making a ſet ſpeech. He
conceived that circumſtances of the moment ſhould
impel them to the delivery of ſentiments, which
ſhould derive their tenor and application from the
courſe of the debate, and not be the reſult of
previous ſtudy or invariable arrangement.

Pulteney and his partiſans accuſed Walpole of
being "a wretch who could not raiſe £.100 upon
his own ſecurity;" in the ſame manner, the advocates of Walpole accuſed Pulteney, with equal
injuſtice, of having received favours ana bribes
from the crown, and of ingratitude in forſaking
the miniſter, to whom he owed great obligations.
But both accuſations were equally devoid of truth.
Pulteney inherited from his father a very confiderable eſtate, and had received from Henry
Guy, the intimate friend of his grandfather, and
guardian of his youth, and who had been ſecretary
to the treaſury, a legacy of £.40,000, and an eſtate
of £.500 a year. He received alſo with his wife
Anna Maria, daughter of John Gumley, of Iſle-
worth, a very large portion, and increaſed this
property, by the moſt rigid œconomy, which his
enemies called avarice; but which did not prevent him from performing many acts of charity
and beneficence.

During the whole reign of queen Anne, Pulteney uniformly eſpouſed the ſide of the Whigs;
and ſupported, both by his eloquence and fortune,
the proteſtant ſucceſſion in the houſe of Hanover.
On the proſecution of Sacheverel, he ably diſtin-

guiſhed

guifhed himfelf in the houfe of commons, in defence of the revolution, againft the doctrines of
paffive obedience and non-refiftance. When the
Tories came into power, in 1710, he was fo obnoxious to them, that his uncle, John Pulteney,
was removed from the board of trade. He not
only took a principal fhare in the debates of the
four laft years of queen Anne, while the Whigs
were in oppofition, but was alfo admitted into
the moft important fecrets of his party, at that
critical time, when the fucceffion of the Hanover
family being fuppofed to be in danger, its friends
thought themfelves obliged to engage in very
bold enterprifes to fecure it. He was a liberal
fubfcriber to a very unprofitable and hazardous
loan, then fecretly negotiated by the Whig party,
for the ufe of the Emperor, to encourage him to
refufe co-operating with the Tory adminiftration
in making the peace of Utrecht.

On the profecution of Walpole for high breach
of truft and corruption, Pulteney warmly vindicated his friend ; and on his commitment to the
Tower, was amongft thofe who paid frequent vifits to the prifoner, whom he, with the reft of
the Whigs, confidered as a martyr to their caufe *.
He alfo engaged with Walpole in defending the
Whig adminiftration, and wrote the ironical dedication to the earl of Oxford, prefixed to Walpole's account of the parliament, which I have
before taken notice of.

Soon

* Pulteney's Anfwer.

Soon after the death of queen Anne, and before a meffage had been received from George the
Firft, Pulteney, in anfwer to thofe who oppofed
the claufe moved by Horace Walpole, for giving
£.100,000 for apprehending the Pretender fhould
he land, or attempt to land, in any of the king's
dominions, obferved, "That the proteftant fucceffion was in danger, as long as there was a popifh
Pretender, who had many friends both at home
and abroad; that the late queen was fenfible of
that danger, when fhe iffued her proclamation
againft him; and that the cafe was not altered
by her demife: that the nation would be at no
charge if the Pretender did not attempt to land,
and if he did, £.100,000 would be well beftowed
to apprehend him*."

His parliamentary abilities and uniformity of
conduct gave him a very honourable claim to dif-
tinction on the acceffion of George the Firft.
Accordingly, on the king's arrival, and before a
meeting of the new parliament, he was appointed
privy counfellor and fecretary at war, even in oppofition to the inclination of the duke of Marlborough, who, as commander in chief, thought
himfelf entitled to recommend to that poft †.
He was chofen a member of the committee of fecrecy, nominated by the houfe of commons to
examine and report the fubftance of the papers
relating to the negotiation for peace; and on the
fuppreffion of the rebellion which broke out in
Scotland, he moved for the impeachment of lord
Widrington,

* Tindal, vol. 18. p. 298.   † Letter to Pulteney, p. 29.

Period V.
1730 to 1734.

Widrington, and oppofed the motion to addrefs the king, for a proclamation, offering a general pardon to all who were in arms in Scotland, who fhould lay their arms down within a certain time. ;

He was at this period fo much connected with Stanhope and Walpole, that in allufion to the triple alliance between Great Britain, France, and Holland, which was then negotiating by general Stanhope, fecretary of ftate, they were called the three *grand allies* ; and a proverbial faying was current " are you come into the triple alliance ?" *

Refigns.

But when Stanhope and Walpole took different fides, on the fchifm between the Whigs, when Townfhend was difmiffed, and Walpole refigned, . Pulteney followed his friends example, and gave up his place of fecretary at war.

Origin of his difagreement with Walpole.

When Walpole made a reconciliation between the king and the prince of Wales, and negotiated with Sunderland to form a new adminiftration, in which he and lord Townfhend bore the moft confpicuous part, then were firft fown thofe feeds of difguft and difcontent which afterwards burft forth.

The caufes of this unfortunate mifunderftanding, may be traced from the authority of the parties themfelves, or their particular friends. Pulteney was offended becaufe Walpole had negotiated with the prince of Wales and Sunderland, without communicating the progrefs to him, although he had told it to Mr. Edgecumbe,

who

* Memoirs of the Life and Conduct of William Pulteney, efq; p. 17.

who indifcreetly gave an account daily to Pulteney *

Another caufe of difguft was, that Pulteney, who had hitherto invariably proved his attachment to Townfhend and Walpole, expected to receive fome important employment, whereas he was only offered a peerage, and when he declined it, more than two years elapfed before any farther overtures were made; and though Pulteney at length folicited † and obtained the office of
cofferer

---

* The account of this tranfaction is thus given by Pulteney himfelf, feveral years afterwards, when he was in the height of oppofition. " You fent to him one day, as he was going out of town, defiring to fpeak with him, that, when he came, you told him of the reconciliation between the late k— and the then p— of W——; and that a bargain was made for thofe *Whigs*, who had refigned their employments, to be put in again by degrees. To this the gentleman replied, ' *Who pray is it, that hath had authority to make this bargain?*' Your anfwer was, ' *I have done it with the miniftry, and it was infifted on that nobody but lord Towfhend fhould know of the tranfaction. Neither lord* Cowper, *the* Speaker, *nor any one elfe knew it; and therefore we hope you will not take it amifs, that it was kept fecret from you.*'—' Not I,' faid the gentleman, ' *but I think it very odd, that any one fhould prefume to take a plenary authority upon himfelf, to deal for fuch numbers as were concerned, in an affair of this confequence.*'—' *We have not,*' faid you again, ' *had our own interefts alone in view. We have bargained for all our friends, and in due time they will be provided for. I am to be,* faid you, *at the head of the treafury. Lord* Sunderland *had a great defire to retain the difpofition of the* fecret fervice money *to himfelf; but* I *would by no means confent to that, knowing the chief power of a minifter (and I prefume his profit alfo) depends on the difpofition of it.*' You named feveral others, who were to come into employments; *and* faid to *this gentleman, ' We know, Sir, that you do not value any thing of that kind; fo we have obtained a peerage for you.*' It feems you did not, at that time, pretend that the *gentleman* either *expected,* or *infifted on any employment;* and therefore told him, that the king had confented to make him a *peer.* To this the *gentleman* replied with fome warmth, ' *Sir, if ever I fhould be mean enough to fubmit to being fold, I promife you that you fhall never have the felling of me. A* peerage *is what, fome time or other, I may be glad of accepting, for the fake of my family; but I will never obtain it by any bafe method, or fubmit to have it got for me on fuch terms by you.*" ‡

† Pulteney's Anfwer.

---

‡ An Anfwer to one Part of a late infamous Libel, intituled " Remarks on the Craftfman's Vindication of his Two honourable Patrons," p. 54, 55.

Period V.
1730 to 1734. cofferer of the houſhold, in the room of the earl of Godolphin, who received a penſion of £. 5,000 per annum to make way for him, he deemed that place far below his juſt expectations.

Notwithſtanding, however, theſe ſecret cauſes of diſguſt, Pulteney continued to ſupport the adminiſtration. On the communication of the plot in which biſhop Atterbury was involved, he moved for an addreſs to congratulate the king on the diſcovery of ſo dangerous and unnatural a confederacy. Chairman of the ſecret committee. He was chairman of the committee appointed by the houſe of commons in the proſecution; and the report which he drew up on that occaſion, is a maſter-piece of perſpicuity and order. But the diſdainful manner in which he conceived he had been treated by Walpole, had made too deep an impreſſion on his mind to be eradicated. Finding that he did not poſſeſs the full confidence of adminiſtration, or diſapproving thoſe meaſures which tended, in his opinion, to raiſe the power of France on the ruins of the houſe of Auſtria, and which in his opinion ſacrificed the intereſts of Great Britain to thoſe of Hanover, topics on which he afterwards expatiated with great energy and unuſual eloquence in parliament, he became more and more eſtranged from his former friends, and expreſſed his diſapprobation of their meaſures both in public and private. Joins oppoſition. At length, his diſcontent arrived to ſo great a height, that he declared his reſolution of attacking the miniſter in parliament.

M

Walpole

Walpole perceived his error in difgufting fo able
an affociate, and with a view to prevent his oppofition to the payment of the king's debts, hinted
to him in the houfe of commons, that at the removal of either of the fecretaries of ftate, the
minifters defigned him for the vacant employment. To this propofal Pulteney made no anfwer, but bowed and fmiled, to let him know he
underftood his meaning *.

Chapter. 39.
1731.
Walpole at-
tempts t° co^R-
ciliate him.

Pulteney now came forward as the great op-
pofer of government, and his firft exertion on
the fide of the minority, was on the fubject of the
civil lift. A meffage being delivered from the king,
by Sir Robert Walpole, praying the commons to
affift him in difcharging the debts of the civil lift,
Pulteney moved for an addrefs, that an account
fhould be laid before the houfe, of all the monies paid for fecret feryice, penfions, bounties,
&c. from the 25th of March, 1725. This addrefs being voted, a motion was made for the
houfe to go into a grand committee, to confider
of the king's meffage; but Mr. Pulteney reprefented, "The houfe having ordered an addrefs for
feveral papers relating to the civil lift, and other
expences, they ought, in his opinion, to put off
the confideration of the meffage, till thofe papers
were laid before the houfe; it being natural to
inquire into the caufes of a difeafe, before remedies are applied." This being oppofed by Walpole, Pulteney replied, " He wondered how fo
great a debt could be contracted in three years
time;

April 8th,
1725.

April 9th.

* Pulteney's Anfwer, p. 51.

time ; but was not surprised some persons were so eager to have the deficiencies of the civil lift made good, since they and their friends had so great a share in it ; and desired to know, whether this was all that was due, or whether they were to expect another reckoning ?" To this it was answered in general, " There was indeed a heavy debt on the civil lift, and a great many pensions ; but moft of thefe had been granted in king William and queen Anne's reign ; some by king Charles the Second, and very few by his present majefty. Since the civil lift was firft settled for his majefty, an expence of above £.90,000 per annum had happened, which could not then be foreseen, and therefore was left unprovided for. Upon examination of the account of the civil lift debts, it would appear, that moft of those expences were either for the neceffary support of the dignity of the crown and government, or for the public good. There was indeed a pension of £.5,000 of another nature, upon the account of the cofferer's place, but which could not well be avoided, for both lord Godolphin, who was in that office, and his father, had so well deferved of the government, that they could not handfomely remove him without a gratuity, and therefore they gave him a pension of £.5,000 to make room for the worthy gentleman who now enjoys the poft." *

Pulteney opposed the motion in every ftep, until the third reading, when he voted for the

payment

* Tindal, vol. 19. p. 524, 525.

payment of the king's debts; and he himfelf thus
accounts for his conduct in this particular: " The
late king had of himfelf, or as he was advifed by
his *minifters*, frequently tried *the gentleman* on this
point, and ufed to perfuade him to be for it.   He
ufed all the arguments he could; urged to him
all the motives he thought could poffibly engage
him, but all to no purpofe.   He continued inflexible.   At length, the *king* faid to him, *it is
hard you will not let me be an honeft man*.   What
would you, contiued his majefty, *think yourfelf of
one, who refufed to pay his butcher, his baker, ana
other honeft tradefmen ?*—To this the *gentleman* replied, not a little affected with his majefty's laft
argument, *God forbid that he fhould prevent his majefty from acting fuch an honeft part*.   It was not his
intention.   *What he meant to do was confiftent with
his duty as a* fervant to his majefty, *and agreeable
to his duty as a* reprefentative of the people.   *He
meant only to expofe that unneceffary profufion which
had been made* in fecret fervice money, penfions,
&c.   *That the money which fhould have paid his*
honeft tradefmen, *was by thefe means divertea.*
His view therefore was to get a cenfure of *fuch
practices*, and to prevent their becoming *precedents*;
nor had he any defign of depriving the *honeft creditors* of their juft debts; and this was the reafon, when he came to the laft inftance, why *this
gentleman* voted for the queftion; which his majefty underftood very well to be agreeable to the
promife he had made, however myfterious it might
appear to others, and which the gentleman was
                                              fully

Period V. fully perfuaded to be juft in itfelf, and confiftent
1730 to 1734. with his duty as *a fervant to the crown* *.

Difmiffed. He was foon afterwards difmiffed from his
place of cofferer of the houfhold, and from this
period entered a fyftematic oppofition to the minifter. Pulteney proved himfelf fo formidable,
that Walpole again endeavoured to gain him
over, and about the time of Townfhend's refignation, queen Caroline ✝ offered him a peerage,
together with the poft of fecretary of ftate for foreign affairs, if he would again join his old co-

Refufes to be adjutor; but Pulteney rejected the offer, and
fecretary of
ftate. declared his fixed refolution never again to act
with Sir Robert Walpole.

The moft violent altercations paffed in the houfe
of commons between them; their heat againft
each other feemed to increafe in proportion with
their former intimacy, and neither was deficient
in farcaftic allufions, violent accufations, and virulent invectives.

On the ninth of February, 1726, Pulteney,
made a plaufible motion for the appointment of a
committee to ftate the public debts, as they ftood
on the 25th of December, 1714, with the debts
which had been incurred fince that time, till the
25th December 1725, diftinguifhing how much of
the faid debts had been provided for, and how
much remained unprovided for by parliament.
He was feconded by Daniel Pulteney, and fupported by Sir Jofeph Jekyl. In oppofition, Walpole

* Anfwer to the Remarks on the Craftfman's Vindication of his
Two honourable Patrons, p. 52, 53.
✝ From the earl of Orford. Life of bifhop Newton.

pole, endeavoured to shew, that such an inquiry was unreasonable and preposterous, and that it might give a dangerous wound to public credit at this critical juncture, when monied men were already too much alarmed by the appearances of an approaching war, urging, that in the present posture of affairs, the commons could not better express their love to their country, than by making good their promises and assurances, at the beginning of this session, and by raising, with the greatest dispatch, the necessary supplies, to enable the king to make good his engagements, for the welfare of his subjects, to disappoint the hopes of the enemies to his government, and to repel any insults that might be offered to his crown and dignity. Barnard, member for the city of London, confirmed the assertion of the minister, as to the danger of increasing the alarm of monied men, which had already so much affected public credit, that the stocks had within a few weeks fallen 12 or 14 per cent. Sir Thomas Pengelly having spoken for the motion, Walpole again replied; on which Pulteney declared, " He made this motion with no other view, than to give that *great man* an opportunity to shew his integrity to the whole world, which would finish his sublime character." To this Walpole answered, " This compliment would have come out with a better grace, and appeared more sincere, when that fine gentleman had himself a share in the management of the public money, than now he was out of

　　　　M　　　　place.

place, * Such petulant altercations between thefe-
two able fpeakers, caufed much diffatisfaction to
thofe independent members who wifhed well to
the Hanover line, and who generally fupported or
oppofed all queftions from conviction, without
being influenced by party motives. This oppofition of Pulteney was fo apparently dictated by
perfonal refentment, that feveral who would otherwife have confidered the motion juft and reafonable, voted againft it. Many deemed it ill-timed,
and calculated to hurt public credit, and to draw
an odium on the houfe of commons, and accordingly fupported the minifter; for thefe reafons the motion was negatived by 262 againft
89. †

. Pulteney now placed himfelf at the head of the
difcontented Whigs. In conjunction with Bolingbroke, his ancient antagonift, he became the principal fupporter of the Craftfman, to which paper
he gave many effays, and furnifhed hints and obfervations.

Courted by fo-
reign powers. At this period, Pulteney was greatly courted
by the foreign minifters of thofe powers who were
difpleafed with the meafures of the Britifh cabinet, and by none more than by Palm, the Imperial embaffador, who caballed with oppofition
and endeavoured to overturn the miniftry. ‡

The

---

* Chandler.

† Thomas Brodrick to lord chancellor Midleton, February 10,
1726. Midleton Papers. Journals.

‡ Letter from Palm to the Emperor, December 17, 1726. Correfpondence.

The controversy in 1731, which passed between
Pulteney and Walpole's friends and pamphleteers,
widened the breach, and rendered it irreparable.
The Craftsman was full of invectives against Walpole, and the measures of his administration. In
answer to this paper, a pamphlet was published
under the title of Sedition and Defamation Displayed; in a letter to the author of the Craftsman, with a motto from Juvenal,

Ande aliquid brevibus Gyaris, & carcere dignum,
Si vis esse aliquis.——

It contained a violent, and, according to the spirit of the political pamphlets of the times, a scurrilous abuse of Pulteney and Bolingbroke. The
character of Pulteney is pourtrayed in the colours
of party, in a dedication to the patrons of the
Craftsman; and his opposition is wholly attributed to disappointed ambition and personal
pique. In answer to this pamphlet, which he
supposed to be written by lord Hervey, the great
friend and supporter of Sir Robert Walpole, he
wrote, " *A proper Reply to a late scurrilous Libel, in-*
tituled Sedition and Defamation Displayed, in a Let-
ter to the Author; by Caleb D'Anvers, of Gray's
Inn, Esq."

In this pamphlet, Mr. Pulteney introduces the
character of Sir Robert Walpole, which it must
be confessed does not yield, either in scurrility or
misrepresentation, to that of Pulteney, given in
Sedition and Defamation Displayed.

In

In this publication, the author treated lord Hervey * with such contempt, and lashed him with

* John lord Hervey, eldest son of John the first earl of Bristol, was born in 1696. He came first into parliament soon after the accession of George the First; was appointed vice-chamberlain to the king in 1730; in 1733 was created a peer; and in 1740 was constituted lord privy seal, from which post he was removed in 1742. He died in 1743. He took a considerable share in the political transactions of the times, and was always a warm advocate on the side of Sir Robert Walpole. Tindal † has observed, " that history ought to repair the injury that party has done to some part of his character,'' and in fact, it is necessary; for never was man more exposed to ridicule, and lashed with greater severity, than lord Hervey has been exposed and lashed by the satirical pen of Pope. If we may credit the satirist, who has delineated his character under the name of Sporus, he was below all contempt ; a man without talents, and without one solitary virtue to compensate for the most ridiculous foibles, and the most abandoned profligacy,

     " Let Sporus tremble.—A. What that thing of silk,
     " Sporus, that mere white curd of asses milk ?
     " Satire or sense, alas ! can Sporus feel ?
     " Who breaks a butterfly upon a wheel ?
     " P. Yet let me flap this bug with gilded wings,
     " This painted child of dirt, that stinks and sings, &c.
     " Eternal smiles his emptiness betray,
     " As shallow streams run dimpling all the way.
     " Whether in florid impotence he speaks,
     " And, as the prompter breathes, the puppet squeaks;
     " Or at the ear of Eve, familiar toad,
     " Half froth, half venom, spits himself abroad, &c.
     " Amphibious thing ! that acting either part,
     " The trifling head, or the corrupted heart,
     " Fop at the toilet, flatt'rer at the board,
     " Now trips a lady, and now struts a lord.
     " Eve's tempter thus the Rabbins have exprest,
     " A cherub's face, a reptile all the rest,
     " Beauty that shocks you, parts that none will trust,
     " Wit that can creep, and pride that licks the dust."

However I may admire the powers of the satirist, I never could read this passage without disgust and horror ; disgust at the indelicacy of the allusions, horror at the malignity of the poet, in laying the founda_ tion of his abuse on the lowest species of satire, personal invective, and what is still worse, on sickness and debility. The poet has so much distorted this portrait, that he has in one instance made the ob. ject of his satire, what ought to have been the subject of his praise, the rigid abstinence to which lord Hervey unalterably adhered, from

the

† Vol. 20. p. 83.

with such ridicule, in allusion to his effeminate
appearance, as a species of half-man and half-
woman,

the necessity of preserving his health. Lord Hervey having felt some attacks of the epilepsy, entered upon, and persisted in a very strict regimen, and thus stopt the progress, and prevented the effects of that dreadful disease. His daily food was a small quantity of asses milk, and a flour biscuit; once a week he indulged himself with eating an apple: he used emetics daily. To this rigid abstemiousness, Pope malignantly alludes, when he says,

" The mere white curd of asses milk."

In short, I agree with the ingenious editor of Pope, " Language cannot afford more glowing or more forcible terms to express the utmost bitterness of contempt. We think we are here reading Milton against Salmasius. The raillery is carried to the very verge of *railing*, some will say *ribaldry*. He has armed his muse with a scalping knife."

May we not ask, with the same author, " Can this be the nobleman whom Midleton, in his dedication to the History of the Life of Tully, has so seriously, and so earnestly praised, for his strong good sense, his consummate politeness, his real patriotism, his rigid temperance, his thorough knowledge and defence of the laws of his country, his accurate skill in history, his unexampled and unremitted diligence in literary pursuits, who added credit to this very history, as Scipio and Lælius did to that of Polibius, by revising and correcting it, and brightening it, (as he expresses it) by the strokes of his pencil?" May we not also ask, Is this the nobleman who wrote some of the best political pamphlets which appeared in defence of Walpole's administration? who, though sometimes too florid and pompous, was a frequent and able speaker in parliament, and who, for his political abilities, was raised to the post of lord privy seal? In truth, lord Hervey possessed more than ordinary abilities, and much classical erudition; he was remarkable for his wit, and the number and appositeness of his repartees.

Although his manner and figure were at first acquaintance highly forbidding, yet he seldom failed to render himself, by his lively conversation, which Pope calls,

" The well whipp'd cream of courtly common sense,"

an entertaining companion to those whom he wished to conciliate. Hence he conquered the extreme prejudice which the king had conceived against him, and from being detested, he became a great favourite. He was particularly agreeable to queen Caroline; as he helped to enliven the uniformity of a court, with sprightly repartees and lively sallies of wit.

His cool and manly conduct in the duel with Pulteney, proved neither want of spirit to resent an injury, or deficiency of courage in the hour of danger, and he compelled his adversary to respect his conduct, though he had satirised his person.

His defects were extreme affectation, bitterness of invective, prodigality of flattery, and great servility to those above him.

Horace

Period V. woman, which Pope, in his character of Sporus,
1730 to 1734. has no lefs illiberally adopted, that lord Hervey
Duel with lord was highly offended, a duel * enfued, and Pulte-
Hervey. ney flightly wounded his antagonift. It afterwards appeared that lord Hervey did not compofe
this pamphlet; and Pulteney acknowledged his
miftake, and imputed it, without fufficient authority, to Walpole himfelf. †

As one great fource of obloquy vented by the
minifterial writers againft Pulteney, was his junction with Bolingbroke, who, when driven from
his country, had efpoufed the party of the Pretender, a letter by Bolingbroke appeared in the
Craftfman of May 22, 1731, with the fictitious
name of Old-caftle, which, after heaping many
charges on the minifter, drew the characters of
Pulteney and Bolingbroke in a moft favourable
light, and vindicated them from the imputations
of the writers on the fide of government.

This letter produced an anfwer, intituled, " *Re-
marks on the Craftfman's Vindication of his Two
Honourable Patrons, in his Paper of May 22, 1731.*
Par nobile fratrum;

In which the two characters commended by the
Craftfman, were attacked with increafing afperity,
and

Horace, earl of Orford, has given a lift of his political writings, in
the catalogue of Royal and Noble Authors; and among the Orford
Papers, are draughts of feveral of thofe pamphlets which were fubmitted to Sir Robert Walpole. Some are corrected by him, in others,
the minifter made confiderable additions. See Warton's Pope, vol. 4.
p. 44, 45, 46. Opinions of Sarah duchefs of Marlborough, Article,
lord Hervey.

* An Account of the duel is given in a letter from Thomas Pelham
to earl Waldegrave, January 28, 1731. Correfpondence, Period V.

† It was written by Sir William Yonge, fecretary at war, as he
himfelf informed the late lord Hardwicke.

and Pulteney, was loaded with the moft virulent perfonal, abufe, by ranfacking his private life, prying into his domeftic concerns and family tranf- actions, by accufing him of acting folely from dif- appointment and revenge, of being governed by veteran Jacobites, of difrefpect to the king, in- gratitude to the minifter, of fharing the bounties, and adding to the penfions of the crown, and of having obtained the fee-fimple of £.9,000 per annum, by the favour, indulgence, and affiftance of the minifter, whom he had fworn to deftroy.* Perhaps he would have acted a more prudent and dignified part, in not making any reply to the in- vective of a party pamphlet ; but, as he conceived it to have been written, or at leaft the materials to have been furnifhed by the minifter, his in- dignation was roufed, and he publifhed an ani- mated defence of himfelf and his own conduct, a work to which I have frequently alluded, as con- taining much curious information on the origin and progrefs of the quarrel between him and Wal- pole. It is ftyled, *An anfwer to One Part of a late infamous Libel, intituled,* " *Remarks on the Craftf- man's Vindication of his Two Honourable Patrons ;*" *in which the character and conduct of Mr. P. is fully vindicated.* Addreffing it to Sir Robert Wal- pole, he fays of the pamphlet in which he had been fo indecently abufed, " There are feveral " paffages of *fecret* hiftory in it, falfely ftated and " mifreprefented, which could come from nobody " but yourfelf. You might, perhaps, employ " fome

* P. 37.

M 4

" fome of your mercenaries to work them up 'for " you; but the' ingredients are certainly your " own."

In the courfe of the defence, Mr. Pulteney gives us his account of the converfation about making him fecretary of ftate, which 'he accufes Walpole of having difclofed, and mifreprefented. And as Walpole had thrown out to him the bait of the fecretaryfhip, to prevent, if poffible, his oppofing the payment of the king's debts, the fecret hiftory of that tranfaction, as far as Pulteney was concerned, is laid before the public. Having gone through that part of his defence, he proceeds, " Since now we are upon the heads of *fecret hiftory, which you have opened,* I muft explain another point in this gentleman's defence, concerning the reconciliation between his late majefty and the prefent king, from whence it will appear, whether you or this gentleman was moft greedy of employments, and who difcovered the trueft zeal for the honour of his prefent majefty." * That part of his fecret converfation which related to George the Second, then prince of Wales, is here fubjoined.

" *But pray, Sir* (continued the *gentleman) fince you acquaint me with the terms you have made for me, what are thofe you have made for the* P—, *who hath acted fo honourable and fteady a part to thofe with whom he engaged, and who are now in oppofition to the court?* To this you anfwered with a fneer, *Why He is to go to court again, and he will,*
have

---

* Anfwer to an infamous Libel, p. 53.

have his DRUMS *and his* GUARDS, *and such* FINE
THINGS.   At this the *gentleman* was aftonifhed,
and thought proper to prefs you a little further,
by afking you, *whether the* P— *was to be left regent again, as he had been when the king went out
of England ?*——*No,* faid you, WHY SHOULD HE?
What ! replied the *gentleman, have you ftipulated
for a fhare of royalty for* yourfelf, *on the king's departure, and is the* P— *to live like a* private fubject; *of no confequence in the kingdom ?*—The *gentleman* avers upon his *honour,* that your anfwer was
this : HE DOES NOT DESERVE IT.—WE HAVE
DONE TOO MUCH FOR HIM; AND IF IT WAS
TO BE DONE AGAIN, WE WOULD NOT DO
SO MUCH:—Upon this, the *gentleman* went directly to the P— (with whom he then had fome
credit) and humbly reprefented upon what terms
the reconciliation was founded. He told him
that he was fold to his *father's minifters,* by *perfons* who confidered nothing but *themfelves* and
their own intereft, and were in hafte to make
their fortunes. This was thought by him to have
had fome weight, at that time, with the P—,
though the gentleman did not think it proper to
tell him the whole that had paffed, and relate
what you faid of him in fo ungrateful a manner." *

"The difclofure of this fecret converfation, and
of the contemptuous expreffions which Walpole
is faid to have uttered againft the king, when
prince of Wales, inftead of irritating him againft
the minifter, only raifed his refentment higher
    againft

Struck out of
the lift of privy
counfellors.

---

* Anfwer to an infamous Libel, p. 55, 56.

againſt Pulteney. Franklin, the printer of the pamphlet, was arreſted ; Pulteney's name was ſtruck out of the liſt of privy counſellor's, and he was put out of all commiſſions of the peace, * meaſures which tendered to render the breach irreparable. Such was indeed the bitterneſs of party, and the animoſity againſt the miniſter, that Pulteney does not heſitate to declare, that " the oppoſition had come to a determined reſolution, not to liſten to any treaty whatſoever, or from whomſoever it may come, in *which the firſt and principal condition ſhould not be to deliver him up to the juſtice of the country*." †

When ſuch virulent invectives paſſed on both ſides, it was hardly poſſible, to ſuppoſe that any compromiſe could be effected. Pulteney continued invariably to oppoſe the meaſures of Walpole, and was principally inſtrumental in driving him from the helm of affairs. But although in the zeal of party, and in the warmth of debate, theſe two great men reviled each other with ſo much acrimony, yet even in the houſe of commons, they frequently entered into converſation on the moſt amicable terms; and as Pulteney always, though in oppoſition, ſat on the treaſury bench, theſe opportunities were very frequent, Dr. Pearce, biſhop of Rocheſter, has recorded an anecdote of their eaſy manner of converſing, which reflects high honour on both parties.

" Mr. Pulteney ſitting upon the ſame bench with Sir Robert Walpole in the houſe of commons,

* Tindal, v. 20. p. 104.
† Mr. Pulteney's Anſwer, p. 47.

mons, faid, "Sir Robert, I have a favour to afk
of you." O my good friend Pulteney, faid Sir
Robert, what favour can you have to afk of me ?
It is, faid Mr. Pulteney, that Dr. Pearce may not
fuffer in his preferment for being my friend. I
promife you, returned Sir Robert, that he fhall
not. Why then I hope, faid Mr. Pulteney, that
you will give him the deanery of Wells. No, replied Sir Robert, I cannot promife you that for
him, for it is already promifed."

Sir Robert having afterwards obtained for him
the deanery of Winchefter, his friend Mr. Pulteney, congratulating him on his promotion, faid
to him, " Dr. Pearce, though you may think
that others befides Sir Robert have contributed
to get you that dignity, yet you may depend
upon it, that he is all in all, and that you owe it
entirely to his good-will towards you ; and therefore, as I am now fo engaged in oppofition to him,
it may happen, that fome who are of *our* party
may, if there fhould be any oppofition for members of parliament at Winchefter, prevail upon
me to act there in affiftance of fome friend of
our's ; and Sir Robert, at the fame time, may
afk your affiftance in the election for a friend of
his own, againft one whom we recommend. I
tell you, therefore, beforehand, that if you comply with my requeft, rather than Sir Robert's, to
whom you are fo much obliged, I fhall have the
worfe opinion of you. Could any thing be more
generous

Period V. generous to the dean as a friend, or to Sir Ro-
1730 to 1734. bert, to whom in other refpects he was a declared
opponent ?" *

CHAPTER THE FORTIETH:

1733.

*Walpole propofes to take Half a Million from the Sinking Fund, for the
Service of the current Year.—Encroachments from its firft Eftablifhment to this Motion.—Oppofition to the Bill.—Subftance of the Reafons
on both Sides.—It paffes the Houfe.—Subfequent Encroachments.—
Beneficial Confequences which would have been derived from appropriating the Produce to the Liquidation of the Debt.—Ill Confequences
of alienating it.—Motives which induced the Minifter to take that
Method of raifing Supplies.*

THE laft accounts which I had occafion to
give of the parliamentary proceedings and
domeftic events, were carried down only to May
1730. The hopes of a divifion amongft the
Whigs, and of the minifters, gave energy to
the leaders of oppofition; but the ill fuccefs of
their exertions, and the uninterrupted profperity
of the country, during the two fucceeding years,
render the domeftic hiftory barren of events, and
afford little worthy of mention in the life of the
minifter. But the fixth feffion of the third feptennial parliament, which opened on the 17th of
January 1733, is diftinguifhed by two meafures
of Sir Robert Walpole; of which the firft, to
take half a million from the finking fund, though
contrary to the national intereft, was carried by
a large majority; and the fecond, which was the

excife

* Life of Pearce.

excife fcheme, though evidently calculated for
the advantage of the country, met with fuch violent oppofition, as induced the minifter to relinquifh it.

This chapter will be confined to the difcuffion
of the important queftion concerning the alienation of the finking fund; a meafure which has
incurred the bitter cenfure of moft writers who
have fpeculated on the fubject of finance, and
which feems to be the greateft blot in the adminiftration of the minifter. In this difquifition, I
fhall endeavour to ftate, the deviations from, and
encroachments on the finking fund, until it was
finally perverted from its original ufe, and inftead
of being employed in the liquidation of the national debt, became a fund for the current fervice
of the year; to fhew the beneficial confequences
which would have refulted from following the original defign; and to confider the motives which
induced the minifter to counteract his own great
eftablifhment, and to entail a debt on the nation,
which, if it could not have been entirely paid
off, might at leaft have been confiderably diminifhed.

When the houfe of commons paffed an act for
the eftablifhment of a fund for applying the furpluffes of duties and revenues to the liquidation
of the national debt, called in fubfequent acts
the finking fund, the words to appropriate them
to that purpofe were as ftrong as could be found,
to and for none other ufe, intent, or purpofe whatfo-
ever.

During

During the whole reign of George the Firſt it was invariably appropriated to its original purpoſes, and rather than encroach upon it, money was borrowed upon new taxes, when the ſupplies in general might have been raiſed, by dedicating the ſurpluſſes of the old taxes to the current ſervices of the year. * Even in the infancy of the eſtabliſhment, when its operations were neceſſarily very confined, great advantages were derived even from this ſmall ſurplus; the national intereſt was immediately reduced from 6 to 5 per cent.; £.750,000 in old exchequer bills were paid off in 1719; and it appeared, by the report of the houſe of commons, that from 1717 to 1728, it had diſcharged £.2,698,416, and that its average amount was £.1,200,000.

Appropriated
to other uſes.
ꝰIt no ſooner attained this progreſſive power, that its operations were ſuſpended. Between 1727 and 1733, ſeveral encroachments were made, either by alienating the taxes which yielded the ſurpluſſes, or by charging the intereſt of ſeveral loans upon the ſurpluſſes appropriated to the payment of the debt. But although this meaſure was in effect the ſame as depriving it of groſs ſums (there being no difference between taking the annual intereſt of a ſum, and that ſum itſelf) yet as theſe encroachments were not literally direct invaſions of the fund, they ſeem to have met with little oppoſition.

However, in 1733 an open attack was made. Half a million being voted for the ſervice of the enſuing

year,

* Price's Appeal on the National Debt. Sinclair, p. 106.

year, the minifter propofed to take that fum from
the finking fund; and by that means to continue
the land tax at one fhilling in the pound; adding, that if this motion fhould be objected to,
he fhould move for a land tax of two fhillings in
the pound, there being no other means of providing for the current expences.

I This motion juftly occafioned a long and violent debate, and the ftrength of the argument
undoubtedly lay on the fide of oppofition. The
whole fubftance of the reafons, which the minifter could urge in defence of this violation of his
own principles, was the neceffity of giving eafe
to the landed intereft, and the dread of the public creditors to have their debts difcharged. On
this occafion he advanced this remarkable pofition, that the fituation of the country, and the
cafe of the public creditors was altered fo much
fince the eftablifhment of the finking fund, that
the competion among them was not who fhould
be the firft, but who fhould be the laft to be
paid, an affertion, which none of the oppofition
ventured to contradict, and therefore may be
confidered as true. He alfo added, that although
the finking fund was eftablifhed for the payment
of the debts, yet it was ftill fubject to the difpofal of parliament; and whenever it appeared,
that it could be more properly and beneficially
applied to fome other ufe, the legiflature had a
power, and ought to difpofe of it in that manner.

On the other fide, the oppofition argued, that
the facred depofit for difcharging the debts and
abolifhing

Period v. abolifhing the taxes, ought not to be applied to
1730 to 1734·any ufe, except in cafes of extreme neceffity,
which were not now apparent ; that the affenting
to the motion was in fact robbing pofterity of
£.500,000, and the progreffive intereft of that
fum, for a trifling cafe to themfelves. They reminded him of his inconfiftency, in deftroying his
own darling project, and undermining the boafted
monument of his own glory.; and Sir John Barnard emphatically urged, " that the author of
fuch an expedient muft expect the curfes of pofterity."

Thefe arguments, however, did not affect the
decifion of the houfe of commons. The influence
of the minifter, aided by the co-operation of the
landed, monied, and popular interefts, triumphed
over oppofition; and the motion was carried by
a majority of 110 voices; 245 againft 135.

Farther en-
croachments.

The practice of alienating the finking fund having been once fanctioned by parliament, was continued without intermiffion. In 1734 £.1,200,000,
or the whole produce of the year, was taken from
it ; in 1735 and 1736, it was anticipated and
mortgaged. " Thus expired," obferves Dr. Price,
perhaps with more enthufiafm than truth, " after
an exiftence of a few years, the finking fund ;
that facred bleffing (as it was once thought) and
the nation's only hope. Could it have efcaped, it
would long before this time have eafed Britain of
all its debts, and left it fafe and happy."

Speculations
on the fubject.

In regard to the beneficial confequences which
muft have refulted from the due adminiftration

of

of the finking fund, many words are not wanting to prove that point. Without eftimating the advantages as highly as the opponents of the minifter, or Dr. Price, it may fairly be inferred, from the ftatement of Walpole himfelf, that had the produce been applied to that purpofe, from its firft eftablifhment in 1716 to 1739, the year in which the war with Spain commenced, more than 20 millions of the national debt might have been eafily paid off, whereas only £.7,190,740 were difcharged. *

The ill confequences of alienating the finking fund are fo evident, that it is not my intention to juftify Sir Robert Walpole; on the contrary, he deferves and has fufficiently incurred the cenfure of pofterity. But while we blame this conduct in its full latitude, let us not follow the example of thofe fpeculative writers, who do not fufficiently weigh exifting circumftances, neglect to confider the temper of the times and the fituation of the country, and who judge of the meafures purfued by government in 1733, from thofe which have been purfued in fubfequent times. In juftice to the

* The oppofition computed, but on very erroneous calculations, that at Chriftmas 1733, £.25,000,000 might have been paid off more than had been difcharged, and Dr. Price obferves, " Had it, from the year 1732, been allowed to increafe beyond this (except from the intereft of debts paid by it,) and been applied for the firft twenty-five years to the payment of debts, bearing 4 per cent. intereft, and afterwards to the payment of debts, bearing 3 per cent. it would (in the prefent year 1781) have completed the redemption of more than one hundred and fixty millions of debt, leaving the public, during this whole period, in poffeffion of all the furpluffes which have arifen in the revenue beyond £.1,212,000, except thofe produced by redemptions." Price on Annuities, vol. 1. p. 220.

the memory of a minifter, who feems to have facrificed every object for the prefervation of interior tranquillity and external peace, let us confider the motives which induced him to propofe
the alienation of the finking fund, which cannot
be better illuftrated than in the words of a very
judicious writer on finance.

"Thefe fteps of adminiftration I ·neither cenfure or approve of. I muft fuppofe every ftatef-
man· to have good reafons for doing what· he
does, unlefs I can difcover that his motives are
bad. May not the landed intereft, who compofed the parliament, have infifted upon fuch a
diminution of their load; May not the proprietors of the public debts have infifted, on their
fide, that no money out of the finking fhould be
thrown into their hands, while the bank was
making loans upon the land and malt duties at 3
per cent. ? Might not the people have been averfe
to an augmentation of taxes ? When three fuch
confiderable interefts concur in a fcheme, which
in its ultimate though diftant confequences, muft
end in the notable prejudice of perpetuating the
debts, although opportunities offer to diminifh
them, what can government do ? They muft fubmit ; and, which is worfe, they cannot well avow
their reafons.

"Such combinations muft occur, and frequently too, in every ftate loaded with debts,
where the body of the people, the landlords, and
the creditors, find an advantage in the non-pay-
ment

ment of the national debt. It is for this reafon, I imagine, the beft way to obviate the bad
confequences of fo ftrong an influence in parliament, would be, to appropriate the amount
of all finking funds in fuch a manner, as to put
it out of a nation's power to mifapply them, and
by this means force them either to retrench their
extraordinary expences, or to impofe taxes for
defraying them." *

Thefe obfervations are perfectly juft, and con-
fonant to the fpirit and temper of the times; nor
did any meafure of Walpole's adminiftration more
conciliate the favour of the landholders, monied
men, and people, than the alienation of the finking fund, fo juftly deprecated by pofterity, yet
fo much applauded by his contemporaries.

For a long period after the acceffion of George
the Firft, the greater part of the landed intereft
uniformly oppofed government. With a view to
ingratiate the new family with thefe perfons, who
formed a large party in the houfe of commons,
the minifter lowered the land tax to three and
then to two fhillings in the pound; this meafure
effectually galled oppofition, brought over many
friends to government; and it was truly faid by
Henry Pelham, in the houfe of commons, " Gentlemen may talk as they pleafe of what was done in
laft feffion of parliament; but I can fay, that in
all places were I have fince been, I have had the
pleafure

* Steuart's Political Œconomy, vol. 2, page 391.

Period v. pleafure of receiving the thanks of the people, for
1730 to 1734. the cafe then given to the landed intereft; and
whatever glofs may now be put upon that affair,
yet I know that fome gentlemen, who appeared
againft it, were heard to fay at the time that affair was mentioned, it will pleafe the country too
much, and therefore we muft endeavour to render it abortive. I will, indeed, do the gentlemen the juftice to believe that they then fpoke
as they thought; and they then did what they
could to prevent the fuccefs of a defign, by which
his majefty's adminiftration has gained the favour
and the efteem of the generality of the landholders in England." *

The monied men were no lefs fatisfied. The
minifter himfelf informs us of their principles:
" The finking fund" he fays, " was now grown
to a great maturity, produced anually about
£.1,200,000, and became almoft a terror to all
the individual proprietors of the public debts.
The high ftate of credit, the low rate of intereft,
and the advanced price of the ftocks and funds
above par, made the great monied companies, and
all their peoprietors, apprehend nothing more
than being obliged to receive their principals too
faft; and it became almoft the univerfal confent
of mankind, that a million a year was as much
as the creditors of the public could bear to receive, in difcharge of part of their principal." †

As

---

* Chandler, vol. 7, p. 295.

† Some Confiderations on the Public Funds, p. 56.

As to the people at large, it is always more agreeable to them to defray the current ex- pences by alienating a finking fund, than by im- pofing a new tax. Every tax is felt, foon occa- fions murmurs, and meets with fome oppofition. In proportion as the taxes are multiplied, two difficulties arife; the people more loudly com- plain of every new impoft, and it becomes more difficult to find out frefh fubjects of taxation, or to augment the old levies. But a temporary fufpenfion of the payment of the debt is not felt, and occafions neither murmurs or complaint. To borrow therefore from the finking fund is always an obvious expedient for raifing fupplies *, and has never been known to create a national fer- ment.

The minifter muft have been more than man, had he preferred the bleffings of pofterity to the curfes of his own age, or facrificed prefent eafe to the dread of remote evils.

Yet, after making due allowance to the tem- per of the times, and the fituation of parties, the meafure itfelf cannot be juftified; the warmeft admirers of the minifter muft allow, that it is a dark fpeck in his financial adminiftration.

The fagacious mind of Walpole, might have difcovered fome method of fatisfying the public creditors, while he paid them off; he might have conciliated prefent advantage with the benefit of pofterity, combined his own intereft with that of

the

* Smith, Wealth of Nations, vol. 3. p. 418.

Period V.   the people, and by confining himfelf to a partial
1730 to 1734. alienation, have rendered it a temporary, and not
a permanent evil. *

CHAPTER THE FORTY-FIRST.

1733.

*Origin and Progrefs of the Excife.—Objeᵭ of Walpole's Scheme.—Arts
of Oppofition.—Parliamentary Proceedings.—Speech of Walpole.—
Bill abandoned.—Views and Conduᵭ of Oppofition.—Influence of Walpole.—Removals and Promotions.—Prorogation of Parliament.*

I AM now arrived at that important period in
the life of Sir Robert Walpole, which relates
to what is ufually called the EXCISE SCHEME,
or in other words, the plan for fubjecting the duties on wine and tobacco to the laws of excife; a
meafure which raifed a great ferment in the nation, becaufe it was perverted by the malignant
fpirit of party, and was not thoroughly underftood by fober and impartial perfons; but which
reafon, and the difinterefted voice of pofterity has
fanctioned and juftified.

Tucker's Eu-
logium of the
excife fcheme.
On this fubject, a judicious writer †, who well
underftood the principles of commerce, has obferved, " Without entering into a defence of all
parts

* For the hiftory and alienation of the finking fund have been confulted, An Enquiry into the Conduct of our Domeftick Affairs from
the year 1721 to 1734: Suppofed to be written by Mr. Pulteney, page
33 to 55. An anfwer to that pamphlet, intitled, Some Confiderations
concerning the Publick Funds, written by Sir Robert Walpole, page 8
to 81. Price on Annuities, vol. 1. p. 185 to 223. Sinclair on the
Revenue, vol. 1. p. 99 to 101. Smith's Wealth of Nations, vol. 3
p. 410. Stuart's Political Œconomy, vol. 2.

† Tucker's Elements of Commerce and Theory of Taxes, p. 148,
a book printed but not publifhed.

parts of his conduct, I am perfuaded that impartial pofterity will do him the juftice to acknowledge, that if ever a ftatefman deferved well of the Britifh nation, Sir Robert Walpole was the man. Indeed, the only true way of difcovering, whether we are advancing or retreating in our political and commercial capacity, is to compare the paft with the prefent, and to examine whether we have the fame quantity of pernicious taxes, and monopolizing patents, as we had formerly. If we have not, it is our bufinefs to be thankful for the deliverance we have received, and to unite our endeavours to be freed from the remainder. This is real patriotifm and public fpirit.

" One of the great merits of Sir Robert Walpole, and in which perhaps no minifter ever approached him, was that of fimplifying the taxes, abolifhing the numerous petty complicated impofts which checked commerce and vexed the fair trader, and fubftituting in their ftead more equal and fimple.

" But to omit matters of leffer note, the wifeft propofal to relieve the nation was the Excife Scheme, by means of which the whole ifland would have been one general FREE PORT, and a *magazine* and *common ftorehoufe* for all nations.

" It was not indeed a perfect fcheme at its firft appearance; but the foundation was good, and a few alterations would have rendered it a moft ufeful inftitution for the purpofes of national commerce. But the bufinefs of thofe times was not to alter, mend, or improve, but to op-

N 4   pofe,

pofe, and to raife a ferment. But even in its
moft imperfect ftate it would have defeated the
views of monopolifts, and have proved of great
national advantage. If the bill had been fo worded
as to be only *permiſſive* not *compulſory*, every man
in this kingdom would have made the excife
fcheme his own choice, that is, he would have
preferred the method of putting his goods in a
warehoufe, and paying the duties as he wanted
them, rather than paying the duties all at once
at the cuftom houfe. As a proof of this, let it
be obferved, that the very men who made the
loudeft clamour againft the excife fcheme, in a
a few years petitioned for a much worfe, the prefent law relating to tobacco; which is allowed
on all hands to be an excife fcheme in effect, and
to have inconveniences, which the excife fcheme
had not. But to give fome falvo to the matter, the
word *Permit* is changed to that of *Certificate*." *

Either the excife fcheme was not fuch as it is
here explained, or the oppofition to it was founded
on principles of error, mifreprefentation, and party.
Let me then be permitted to confider by what
means the nation in general was induced to give
fuch a decided refiftance to the bill, and to make
as public and as loud rejoicings when it was re-
liquifhed, as upon the moft glorious national victory ever gained over our enemies in times of the
greateft danger.

In

* Tucker, Theory of Laws, p. 149.

In attempting to develop these causes, it may be expedient to trace the history of the excise from its first introduction into England, until the opening of Walpole's scheme.

The first attempt to impose it was made in 1626, by a commission under the great seal, issued to thirty-three lords and others of the privy council, but the parliament having remonstrated, it was judged by both houses contrary to law, and the commission accordingly cancelled by the king. * So odious was the very name, that if we may credit Howel, Sir Dudley Carleton, then secretary of state, having only named it in the house of commons, with a view to shew the happiness which the people of England enjoyed above other nations, in being exempted from that imposition, was suddenly interrupted, called to the bar, and nearly sent to the Tower. †

During the civil wars in 1641, parliament ventured to impose an excise on beer, ale, cyder, and perry; but although they pleaded absolute necessity in excuse for this expedient, and continued it only from month to month; yet the execution of it raised riots in London. The populace burnt down the excise house in Smithfield, and nothing but a standing army, adds the Craftsman, would have forced it upon the people at that time, when they were greatly disaffected to the king and favourable to the parliament ‡.

Although Charles the First, in one of his declarations, charged parliament with imposing insupport-

---

* Craftsman, N° 333.   † Ibid.   ‡ Ibid.

fupportable taxes and odious excifes upon their fellow fubjects; yet he was afterwards under the neceffity of recurring to the fame expedient. Accordingly, excifes were laid on by both parties, though both of them declared that they fhould be continued only till the end of the war, and then abolifhed.

Soon afterwards the parliament impofed it on fugar, butcher's meat, and on fo many other commodities, that it might juftly be called general, in purfuance of a plan, laid down by Pymm, in a letter to Sir John Hotham; " That they had proceeded to the excife in many particulars, and intended to go farther; but that it would be neceffary to ufe the people to it by little and little." *

At the reftoration, the excife was abolifhed on all articles of confumption, except beer and ale, cyder and perry, which produced a clear revenue, according to Davenant, of £.666,383. Thefe duties were divided into two equal portions; the one called the hereditary excife, becaufe granted to the crown for ever, in recompenfe for the court of wards, purveyance, and the levies abolifhed by act of parliament; the other the temporary excife, becaufe granted only for the life of the king.

On the acceffion of James the Second, parliament not only renewed the temporary excife for his life, but alfo increafed it by additional duties

no

* Craftfman, N° 333, 1773. Appendix. Blackftone, B. 1. C. 8. Clarendon.

on wines, vinegar, tobacco, and fugar, which
however were fuffered to expire.

The immediate effects of the revolution were
to diminifh the excifes, fuppofed to be of a nature peculiarly obnoxious to the fpirit and principles of the conftitution. But the neceffity of
raifing money to defend our religion and liberties
became fo urgent, that even this fpecies of impofition was adopted. Excife on falt, on the diftil-
lery, and on malt, fince known by the name of
the malt tax, were then firft introduced; an additional excife on beer produced alone £.450,000,
and the fums raifed by thofe duties, during the
reign of William, amounted to £.13,649,328, or
nearly a million per annum.

But fo great were the neceffities which the war
on the Spanifh fucceffion intailed on the nation,
during the reign of queen Anne, that the averfion to the excife did not prevent additional duties on feveral articles of confumption, and it
produced in her reign £.20,859,311, or nearly
£.1,738,275 per annum.

During the whole reign of George the Firft, no
excife was laid on, except a fmall duty on wrought
plate, under the adminiftration of Sunderland.
But the internal tranquillity of the country, and
the exemption from foreign war, increafing the
produce of the taxes, the excife yielded, in
13 years, £.30,421,451, or about £.2,340,000
per annum. Its unpopularity however was not
abated by long ufage, and the laws for the
collection were neceffarily fo fevere, and fo

I   often

often exercifed in preventing frauds and punifh-ing fmugglers, that they were confidered by many perfons as encroaching on private property and perfonal liberty.

Public aver-
fion to the
excife.
Such were the prejudices conceived againft the excife, that the principal writers on finance, government, and trade, from the revolution to the period under confideration, almoft uniformly condemn it; and a plaufible notion prevailed, that as the real income of every country originates from the land, all taxes fhould be at once impofed on landed property.*

Even Davenant, who well underftcod the nature of taxes in general, and has fo ably written on public credit, was deceived in this particular. Becaufe at that time the excife had the effect of finking the price of the fubject excifed inftead of raifing the price of the produce †, he concluded that all excifes fall ultimately upon the land, and propofed, as more equitable, the poll tax and land tax.

The authority of Locke alfo contributed to fpread the fame notion, and his opinion againft the eftablifhment of the excife, was quoted with due effect by the Craftfman. That great philofopher, whofe writings tended fo much to expand and enlighten the human mind, had without due confideration afferted, that all impofitions on articles

* For a refutation of this fyftem, fee Smith's Wealth of Nations. Neckar on Finances, vol. 1. c. 6. Steuart's Political Economy. Sinclair, vol. 2. p. 113.

† The excife upon malt had the effect of lowering the price of barley, inftead of raifing the value of beer. Steuart's Political Eeconomy, vol. 2. p. 362.

ticles, of confumption fell ultimately upon land.
The natural confequence therefore of that pofition,
was, that any additional duties on wine and tobacco could not ultimately eafe the landholder,
and therefore could not fulfil the intention held
forth to the country gentlemen, as, an argument,
in favour of the bill.

This fyftem, though exploded * by a more in-
telligent age, had a furprifing influence on all ranks
and defcriptions of men at that time, when the
principles of commerce and taxation were little
underftood, and lefs followed. The oppofition,
laid great ftrefs on this argument; and in conformity to the exifting opinion, Sir William Wyndham did not fcruple to declare it, "as demon-
ftrable as any propofition in Euclid, that if we actually paid a land tax of ten fhillings in the pound,
without paying any other excifes or duties, our liberties would be much more fecure, and every
landed gentleman might live at leaft in as much
plenty, and might make a better provifion for
his

* Sir John Sinclair has, in a few words, ably fhewn the abfurdity
of impofing all the taxes on land. " Were it admitted, though it can
hardly be ferioufly maintained in a commercial country, that the whole
income of the nation arofe from the cultivation of the foil, yet ftill, by
impofing duties on confumptions, a greater revenue may be raifed, than
by a direct tax on land. By the latter method you only tax the pro-
prietor of the foil, who has only a certain portion of the produce, and
a confiderable part of which is neceffarily taken from him for the fubfiftence of others. Whereas by the former method, the public fhares
in the profits of thofe individuals who derive any benefit from the foil
by any means, whether directly or indirectly. And hence, whilft the
tax of four fhillings in the pound on land is feverely felt by many individuals in England, though it yields only two millions per annum, a
tax on barley, in all its various ftages of confumption, to the amount
of above three millions and a half, is levied without murmur." Sinclair
on the Revenue, vol. 2. p. 113.

his family, than under the prefent mode of taxation."

Walpole's mo-
tives for ex-
tending it.   On the contrary, the fagacity of Walpole led
him to perceive, that a tax on landed property
was a greater burthern to the fubject than taxes
on articles of confumption. He was fully aware,
that the excife laws obftruct the operations of the
fmugglers more effectually than the laws of the
cuftoms; that the method of levying taxes in ufe,
was more burthenfome upon trade, and more expenfive to the merchants, than the raifing of them
by excife, and that it would be more beneficial
to commerce, and would confiderably increafe the
revenue, if all, or the greater part of the cuftoms
were converted into excifes. But as he well knew
the averfion which the nation entertained againft
the excife, and as he was unwilling to deviate from
his own great principle of government, *not to roufe
things which are at reft*, he propofed gradually to
introduce his plan by abolifhing the land tax, and
fubftituting other methods, until he could venture to come forwards with the propofal of his
great fcheme for extending the excife.

With this view he made an alteration in the
duties on coffee, tea, and chocolate, by abolifhing the import duties, and fubjecting them to
inland duties, and to the fame mode of collection as is practifed in the excife. But as he ftill
fuffered them to be levied as cuftoms, and pru-
dently omitted to mention the word excife, this
amendment met with no oppofition, and in-
                                    creafed

creafed the duties on tea, coffee, and chocolate
about £.120,000 a year.*

For the fame purpofe he proposed the revival of
the falt duty, which had been abolished in 1729,
becaufe he conceived, that a revival of excife duties on commodities formerly fubjeded to that
mode of collection, would not be regarded with
fo jealous an eye, as a new impoft in the fame
line.

But though he thus endeavoured to conceal his
intended purpofe, yet the oppofition penetrated
his fcheme; in the debate which took place on
that fubject, they firft threw down the gauntlet,
and dwelt with unabated energy on the apprehenfions of a general excife, as the war whoop to
fpread an alarm throughout the country, and as
the death warrant of national liberty. It was then
that, provoked by the petulance of his adverfaries,
and entertaining too great a contempt of their arguments, with more fpirit than judgment, and
with more attention to the dictates of truth, than
to the temper of the times, he anticipated the
intended mention of his extenfive views, and laid
down the great plan before it was fufficiently ma-
tured, and before the nation was able to confider
and

---

* The difference between the cuftoms and excife is thus defined by
Sir Robert Walpole himfelf. "The duties known by the name of
cuftoms are certain rates impofed by authority of parliament upon all
commodities imported from abroad, which rates are either to be paid
by the importer, upon the entry at importation, with different allow-
ances and difcounts for prompt payment, or they muft be fecured by
bond, payable in a certain number of months, and, as well as the duties paid down, are repaid and drawn back again upon re-exportation,
as the bonds given, vacated and difcharged; or in fhort, cuftoms are
duties paid by the merchant, upon *importation*: Excifes, duties payable
by the retail trader upon confumption." Orford Papers.

and appreciate its excellence. He unequivocally declared, that the land tax was the moft unequal, moft grievous, and the moft oppreffive tax ever known in this country; a tax not to be raifed but in times of the greateft neceffity; and in anfwer to thofe who oppofed the revival of the falt duties, becaufe it was partly levied under the excife, he ventured to declare, that an excife is only a word for a tax levied in a different manner. He added, " If it be found by experience, that the prefent method of raifing our taxes is more burthenfome upon our trade, and more inconvenient and expenfive than the excife, I fee no manner of reafon why we fhould be frightened by thefe two words, ' general excife,' from changing the method of collecting the taxes we now pay, and choofing that which is moft convenient for the trading part of the nation."*

This manly avowal of his fentiments in favour of the excife laws, was naturally deemed by oppofition the prelude to his adoption of them, and magnified into a fcheme for a general excife all the neceffaries of life.

Aware of having prematurely advanced notions which the age could not comprehend, a pamphlet was publifhed on this fubject, under his aufpices, intitled, " *Some general Confidera-tions concerning the Alteration and Improvement of the Revenues ;*" in which an attempt was made to inform the people, that the fcheme was founded on the firft principles of commerce and taxation, and

in

* Chandler.

in no degree derogatory from the liberties of the
fubject.

But in this progreffive plan he was baffled by oppofition, who employed againft him all the powers of wit and eloquence, which they pof-feffed in fo abundant a degree; and it muft be confeffed the fcheme was not defended with equal energy and fpirit. The nation took the alarm; and before the fcheme was underftood, even be-fore it was formally propofed, the writers in op-pofition, more particularly the Craftfman, deli-neated fuch a hideous picture of the EXCISE, as raifed among the people the moft terrible appre-henfions. Thefe weekly effays, collected and pub-lifhed under the title of " *Arguments againft Ex-cifes*," contributed to pervert the judgment, and excite the rage of the deluded multitude. Againft the united fhafts of fophiftry, wit, and ridicule, adapted to the prejudices and conceptions of the people, the weapons of fober truth and reafon had no effect.

The grand object of the bill was to give eafe to the landed intereft, by the total abolition of the land tax; to prevent frauds; to decreafe fmug-gling; to augment the revenue; to fimplify the taxes, and facilitate the collection of them at the leaft poffible expence.

The great outlines of the plan were, to convert the cuftoms into duties of excife, and to meliorate the laws of the excife in fuch a manner, as to ob-viate their abufes or oppreffions.

Such

Such were the object and general outlines of the plan. The specific propositions were, to divide the commodities into taxed and not taxed, and to confine the taxed commodities to a few articles of general consumption. To comprehend among the untaxed commodities, the principal necessaries of life, and all the raw materials of manufacture. The free importation of the necessaries of life would, by rendering those necessaries cheaper, reduce the price of labour. The reduction of the price of labour would diminish the price of home manufactures, and increase thereby the demand in all foreign markets, by underselling those of other nations. The free importation of raw materials would reduce the price of manufactures, and the cheapness of the goods would secure both the home consumption, and a great command in the foreign markets; and it was this regulation which induced Tucker to say, that by means of this scheme the whole island would become *one general* FREE PORT.

So much for the commodities untaxed. But even the trade of the taxed commodities would be augmented, and both the foreign and home trade would enjoy considerable advantages. The foreign trade would be benifited, because the commodities delivered out of the warehouse for exportation, being exempted from all imposts, would be perfectly free; and the carrying trade, under these regulations, would be highly increased. The home trade would be benefited, because the im-

9   porter,

porter, not being obliged to advance the duty on the commodities delivered for interior consumption, until he difpofed of his goods, would afford to fell them cheaper, than if he had been obliged to advance the duty at the moment of importation.

Such, according to the opinion of a very judicious writer *, was the object of the famous excife fcheme.

Preparatory to its introduction, a committee had been appointed to infpect into the frauds and abufes committed in the cuftoms; and on the 7th of June, 1732, Sir John Cope, the chairman, prefented their report to the houfe. Though it was of infinite importance, and of fo great length as to comprife, when printed, 103 pages in folio; yet the committee were fo fenfible that they had not fully explored all the receffes of fraud, and had left great part of their tafk unaccomplifhed, that they accompanied this elaborate document with an apology for its imperfections, in which they obferved, that the fhortnefs of the feffion would not allow them to make it fo complete as they might otherwife have done, and that the number and intricacy of the various frauds, rendered a thorough difquifition almoft impracticable.

In this report they adverted to the frauds committed by traders in tobacco, tea, brandy, and wine, and in the courfe of it difplayed fcenes of difho-

* Smith's Wealth of Nations, vol. 3. p. 358.

diſhoneſty, perjury, informing, violence, and murder, which would appear to ſanction almoſt any
meaſure, however violent, by which ſo horrible
a ſtigma could be removed from the mercantile
body, and from the fiſcal laws of the country. It
was proved by undeniable evidence, that by perjury, forgery, and the moſt impudent colluſion,
in the article of tobacco, the revenue was frequently defrauded to the amount of one third of
the duties, and that in many caſes, an allowance
had been diſhoneſtly obtained, as a drawback on
re-exportation, exceeding the ſum originally received by government, which in the port of London only, ſuſtained by theſe means a loſs of
£. 100,000 per annum. The ſmuggling of tea and
brandy was conducted ſo openly and ſo audaci-
ouſly, that ſince Chriſtmas 1723, a period only
of nine years, the number of cuſtom houſe officers beaten and abuſed amounted to 250; and
ſix had been murdered. 251,320 pounds weight
of tea, and 652,924 gallons of brandy had been
ſeized and condemned; and upwards of 2,000
perſons proſecuted. 229 boats and other veſſels
had been condemned, 185 of which had been
burnt, and the remainder retained for the ſervice
of the crown. The ſmuggling of wine was managed with ſo much art, or the connivance of the
revenue officers ſo effectually ſecured, that within
the period of nine years, only 2,208 hogſheads
had been condemned, though it appeared, from
depoſitions on oath, that in the ſpace of two
years, 4,738 hogſheads had been run in Hamp-
shire,

fhire, Dorfetfhire, and Devonfhire only, and on,
inquiry, 30 officers were difmiffed, and informations entered againft 400 perfons; 38 were committed to jail, 118 admitted evidence, and 45
had compounded.

Notwithftanding the facts contained in this report, and the endeavours ufed to enlighten the
public mind, the oppofition had been fo affidu-
ous and fuccefsful in the diffemination of flander
and fufpicion, that they looked forward with impatience to the introduction of the minifter's plan,
as the certain means of triumph to them, and of
difgrace to him: Indeed, confidering the nature
of the conteft, they could hardly be thought too
fanguine in their expectations of the event. The
members of any adminiftration propofing meafures
for giving additional ftrength to government, for
reftraining the turbulent, or fuppreffing fraud, are
open to every fpecies of calumny, affailable by
all the weapons of eloquence, wit, ridicule, per-
fonality, and mifreprefentation; while in their
defence, they are reftricted to the ufe of thofe topics which make their impreffion only by force
of time and experience. The majefty of argu-
mentative eloquence, and the glare of wit, are
undervalued, when eloquence is fuppofed to be
biaffed by intereft, and wit is divefted of per-
fonality and cauftic fatire, which alone can make it
pleafing to the multitude.

The writers in the intereft of oppofition had
founded the trumpet of alarm from one end of
the kingdom to the other: they afferted that the
minifter's plan would not tend to prevent fraud,

decreafe

decreafe fmuggling, or augment the revenue; but would deftroy the very being of parliament; undermine the conftitution, render the king abfolute, and fubject the houfes, goods, and dealings of the fubject, to a ftate inquifition. They reprefented the excife as a monfter feeding on its own 'vitals;' and 'compared it' to the Trojan horfe, which contained an army in its belly.

Having by thefe means agitated the public mind to a frenzy of oppofition, the enemies of the minifter were anxious to follow their advantage, and to urge him to bring forward his plan before the people had leifure for fober reflection. London, and many places in the country, had given exprefs inftructions to their reprefentatives, to oppofe the excife fcheme in all its forms, and to ufe every method to impede its progrefs; and the members were fo anxious to fhew that they had not been unmindful of thefe dictates, that they feized every opportunity, long before the meafure was officially announced to the houfe, of adding to the impreffions of horror already entertained againft it.

On the opening of the feffion, the king, in his fpeech from the throne, recommended to the houfe, *that in all their deliberations, as well upon raifing the annual fupplies, as the diftribution of the public revenues, they fhould purfue fuch meafures as would moft conduce to the prefent and future eafe of their conftituents.* In another part of his fpeech, he admonifhed them *to avoid unreafonable heats and animofities, and not fuffer themfelves to be diverted by any*

fpecious

fpecious pretences, from fteadfaftly purfuing the true
intereft of the country.

On the motion for the addrefs, Sir John Barnard made thefe obfervations. " The honourable
" gentleman who moved the addrefs, propofes for
" us to fay, *That we will raife the fupplies in fuch*
" *manner as will moft conduce to the prefent, and fu-*
" *ture eafe of the fubject.* Now, there feems to be
" a great jealoufy without doors, as if fomething
" were intended to be done in this feffion of par-
" liament, that may be deftructive to our liber-
" ties, and detrimental to our trade : from whence
" this jealoufy hath arifen, I do not know ; but
" it is certain that there is fuch a jealoufy among
" all forts of people, and in all corners of the
" nation ; and therefore, we ought to take the
" firft opportunity to quiet the minds of the
" people, and to affure them that they may depend
" upon the honour and integrity of the members
" of this houfe ; and that we will never confent
" to any thing that may have the leaft appearance
" of being deftructive to their liberties, or detri-
" mental to their trade ; for which reafon, I move
" that thefe words, *and fuch as fhall be confiftent*
" *with the trade, intereft, and liberty of the nation,*
" may be added as an amendment."

In fupport of this amendment, Shippen obferved, " It is certain that there are great fears,
" jealoufies, and fufpicions without doors, that
" fomething is to be attempted in this feffion of
" parliament, which is generally thought to be
" deftructive to the liberties and to the trade of

O 4 " this,

" this nation.   There is at prefent a moft remark-
" able and general fpirit among the people for
" protecting and defending their liberties and their
" trade, in oppofition to thofe attempts which they
" expect are to be made againft both : from all
" quarters we hear of meetings and refolutions
" for that purpofe; and this fpirit is fo general,
" that it cannot be afcribed to any one fet of
" men : they cannot be branded with the name
" of Jacobites or republicans; no; the whole
" people of England feem to be united in this
" fpirit of jealoufy and oppofition."

Walpole, in reply, difclaimed any knowledge of
a defign to injure the trade of the nation, and
faid, " If the people are hampered or injured in
" their trade, they muft feel it, and they will
" feel it before they begin to complain; in fuch
" cafe it is the duty of this houfe, not only to hear
" their complaints, but, if poffible, to find out a
" remedy.   But the people may be taught to
" complain; they may be made to feel imaginary
" ills, and by fuch practices they are often in-
" duced to make complaints before they feel any
" uneafinefs."   He did not, however, oppofe the
amendment, and it was carried.

This was only a prelude to feveral other fkir-
mifhes which took place before the grand attack.   In the debate of the 14th of February, on
the fubject of preventing the importation of foreign fugar, rum, &c. into the plantations in
America, Sir John Barnard again obferved, that
" It would be impoffible to prevent the running
" of

" of French rum on shore, even if we were to send
" to America the whole army of excise officers
" which we have here at home.   The sending
" them thither, might indeed, add a good deal
" to our happiness in this country; but all of
" them together could be of no service for such a
" purpose in that country."

    In the debate on alienating part of the sinking
fund, a more decided attack was made by Pulteney, who said, " Though I was aware of the mo-
" tion now made, I was in hopes that was not all
" the honourable gentleman was this day to open
" to the committee: There is another thing, a
" very terrible affair impending! A monstrous
" project! Yea, more monstrous than has ever
" yet been represented! It is such a project as
" has struck terror into the minds of most gen-
" tlemen within this house, and into the minds of
" all men without doors, who have any regard to
" the happiness or to the constitution of their coun-
" try.   I mean, THAT MONSTER, THE EXCISE!
" THAT PLAN OF ARBITRARY POWER, which
" is expected to be laid before this house in the
" present session of parliament."

    On the 27th of February, a call of the house
being moved for on that day fortnight, the excise scheme was again introduced.   Sir John
Rushout commenced an attack on the minister,
by saying, " I do not rise to oppose the call of
" the house; but there being, as I imagine, a
" certain scheme or project to be brought into
" the house, which seems to be of very great con-
" sequence to the whole nation, I wish that the
                                   " call

" call of the houfe may, be about the time that
" that fcheme is to be laid before us. We have
" long been in expectation of feeing this glori-
" ous fcheme, which is to render us all completely
" happy; we have waited for it with impatience
" ever fince the beginning of the prefent feffion.
" I do not know whether the fcheme itfelf has
" lately met with any alterations or amendments;
" but I hope, if it be to be laid before us this
" feffion, it will not be put off till towards the
" end of the feffion, when gentlemen are tired
" out with attendance, and obliged to return
" home to mind their own private affairs."

Walpole replied, " As to the fcheme men-
" tioned by the honourable gentleman who fpoke
" laft, it is certain that I have a fcheme, which I
" intend very foon to lay before you; I have
" not indeed, as yet, fully determined what my
" motion fhall be; but if the motion for the call
" of the houfe be appointed for this day fort-
" night, I believe I fhall be fully determined be-
" tween this and that time. I do not defire, I
" never did defire to furprife this houfe in any
" thing; nor had I, thank God, ever any occa-
" fion to ufe the low art of taking advantage of
" the end of the feffion for any thing I had to
" propofe; but when the houfe does refolve it-
" felf into a committee, which I mean to move
" for, I will lay before that committee a fcheme
" which I have long thought of, which I am
" convinced is for the good of the nation; and
" which, if agreed to, will improve both the trade

" and

" and; the public. revenue. As for the fcheme's
" having received alterations and amendments, I
" do not know but it may; I never thought my-
" felf fo wife, as to ftand in no need of affift-
" ance; on the contrary, I have taken from others
" all the advice and affiftance I could obtain;
" and in all my inquiries, I have chofe to con-
" fult with thofe who I knew had a perfect know-
" ledge of fuch affairs, and had no particular in-
" tereft in view, nor any private end to ferve:
" from thofe who have by-ends of their own, I
" can never expect impartial counfel, and there-
" fore I have in this, as well as every other af-
" fair, thought it ridiculous to afk their advice."
He concluded by obferving, " That if a project
" could be framed to prevent the frauds com-
" mitted in the revenue, the author of fuch pro-
" ject would deferve the thanks of his country,
" and of every fair trader; becaufe, whenever a
" tax is laid on, and not collected regularly and
" duly, from every man fubject to its operation,
" it is really making the fair trader pay to the
" public what the fraudulent trader puts into
" his own private pocket; by which means the
" fmuggler underfells the fair trader in every
" commodity, and by which the fair trader muft
" be at laft ruined and undone."

Sir William Wyndham followed, and affected
to affume, as an abftract ftatement, that the queftion was, " Whether we fhould facrifice the con-
" ftitution to the prevention of frauds in the re-
" venue?" Sir John Barnard feized this opportunity

'tunity of making a popular fpeech, in which' he faid, " If I have been rightly informed, this' " fcheme, in its firft conception, was for a *ge-* " *neral excife,* but that, it feems, was afterwards " thought too much at once, and therefore, we " are now to fingle out only one or two branches, " in order that they may firft be hunted down. " But the very fame reafon may prevail with us, " to fubject every branch to thofe arbitrary laws; " and as fuch laws are, in my opinion, abfolutely " inconfiftent with liberty, therefore I muft think' " that the queftion upon this fcheme, even al- " tered as it feems it is, will be, Whether we " fhall endeavour to prevent frauds in the col- " lection of the public revenues, at the expence " of the liberties of the people?" " For my own " part," added he, " I never was guilty of any " fraud, and therefore I fpeak againft my own " intereft, when I fpeak againft any method that " may tend towards preventing frauds; but I will " never put my private intereft in balance with " the intereft or happinefs of the nation. *I had* " *rather beg my bread from door to door, and fee* " *my country flourifh, than be the greateft fubject* " *in the nation, and fee the trade of my country de-* " *caying, and the people enflaved and oppreffed.*"

In the interval between the debate and the call of the houfe the minifter was preparing to bring forward his fcheme in a manner as little exception-able as poffible, and the oppofition were exerting all their powers and influence to form a ftrong party

8   againft

againſt it, and to excite the public to clamour for
its rejection, whatever might be its merits.

On the 7th of March, the miniſter moved, and
carried, that on that day ſe'nnight, the houſe
ſhould reſolve itſelf into a committee, to conſider
of the moſt proper methods for the better ſecurity
and improvement of the duties and revenues already charged upon and payable from tobacco and
wines. It was farther ordered, that the proper
accounts, returns, and other papers, ſhould be referred to the ſaid committee, and the commiſſioners of the cuſtoms and exciſe ſhould attend.

On this occaſion, all the arts and influence of
oppoſition were called forth to excite clamours
againſt the meaſure. Not only the members ſoli-
cited the attendance of their friends, but letters
were delivered by the beadles, and other officers
in the pariſhes and wards of the city, to induce a
numerous party to aſſemble at the doors, and in
the avenues to the houſe, to overawe the proceedings of the legiſlature. Walpole was apprized
of theſe proceedings, but not to be deterred from
the proſecution of his deſign. On the 15th of
March, the houſe having reſolved itſelf into a committee, he opened the buſineſs, and ſaid:

" As * I had the honour to move that the
houſe ſhould reſolve itſelf into this committee, I
think it incumbent on me to open to you, what

was

---

* The ſubſtance of this ſpeech is principally taken from heads and
memorandums, in the hand writing of Sir Robert Walpole, among the
Orford Papers. A few connecting ſentences have been ſupplied from
the printed ſpeech in the contemporary publications: Political State;
Hiſtorical Regiſter. See alſo Chandler.

was then intended' to be proposed as the subject of your consideration. This committee is appointed for the better security of the duties and revenues already charged and payable upon tobacco. This can be done in no way so proper and effectual, as by preventing the commission of those frauds by which the revenue has already sustained such great injuries. As the proposed improvement is to be made by an alteration in the method of collecting and managing, the duties already imposed, without any addition, or subjecting to the same duties any articles not already chargeable, I might have avoided stating this project to a committee of the whole house; but I have deserted the old road, and proposed a supply not immediately necessary for the current service of the year, that I might leave a greater freedom of consideration, by taking away every appearance of pressing necessity. I shall therefore only observe, that some previous provision must be made for the future application of the increased sum which, should the plan I am about to propose to be adopted, will be received into the exchequer.

" The contest, in the present instance, is between the unfair trader, on one side; the fair trader, the planter, and the public, on the other; but to the public must be referred my most forcible appeal, as they, in truth, bear the whole weight of the injury: for though the fraudulent factor seems to make the planter, retailer, and confumer equally his prey, yet the landed intereft ultimately

timately fuffers the whole effect of the fraud, by
making good what the fubject pays, and the government does not receive.

" In fuch a caufe, I might reafonably expect
the approbation of the fair trader, and the affiftance of parliament ; for affuredly, if in thefe
times any caufe can poffibly be confidered exempt
from the operations of party, it is the caufe now
before the committee. But, Sir, I am not to
learn, that whoever attempts to remedy frauds,
artempts a thing very difagreeable to all thofe
who have been guilty of them, or who expect to
derive future benefits from them. I know that
thefe men, who are confiderable in their numbers,
and clamorous in their exertions, have found abet-
tors in another quarter, in perfons much worfe
than themfelves ; in men who are fond of improving every opportunity of ftirring up the
people to mutiny and fedition. But as the fcheme
I have to propofe, will not only be a great improvement to the revenue, an improvement of
two or three hundred thoufand pounds by the
year, but alfo great benefit to the fair trader, I
fhall not be deterred, either by calumny or clamour, from doing my duty as a member of this
houfe, and bringing forward a meafure, which my
own confcience juftifies me in faying, will be attended with the moft important advantages to
the revenues and commerce of my country.

> *Juftum et tenacem propofiti virum,*
> *Non civium ardor prava jubentium,*
> *Mente quatit folidâ.*

" Amongft

" Amongſt the many ſlanders to which the report of this project has expoſed me, I cannot
avoid mentioning one, which has been circulated
with an aſſiduity proportioned to its want of truth,
that I was about to propoſe *a general excife.* In
all plans for the benefit of government, two eſſential points muſt be conſidered, juſtice and prac-
ticability: many things are juſt which would not
be practicable; but ſuch a ſcheme would be neither one or the other. Various are the faults of
miniſters, various their fates: few have had the
crimes of all; none till now found that the imputation of crime to him, became a merit in others.
Yet if I were to propoſe to you ſuch a ſcheme,
popular opinion would run exactly in that channel. It would be a crime in me to propoſe, a
crime in you to accept; and the only chance left
to the houſe of retaining the favour of the people,
would be the unqualified rejection of the project.
But *I do moſt unequivocally aſſert, that no ſuch ſcheme
ever entered my head, or, for what I know, into the
head of any man I am acquainted with.* Yet though
I do not wiſh to do wrong, I ſhall always retain
a proper ſhare of courage and ſelf-confidence to
do what I judge right, and in the meaſures I am
about to propoſe, ſhall reſt my claim to ſupport
and approbation on the candid, the judicious,
and the truly patriotic.

" My thoughts have been confined ſolely to
the revenue ariſing from the duties on wine and
tobacco; and it was the frequent advices I had
of the ſhameful frauds committed in theſe two
branches,

branches, and the complaints of the merchants
themfelves, that induced me to turn my attention
to difcover a remedy for this growing evil. I am
perfuaded, that what I am about to propofe, will,
if granted, be an effectual remedy. But, if gentlemen will be prevailed on by induftry, artifice,
and clamour, to indulge the fuggeftions of party
prejudice, they and their pofterity muft pay dear
for it, by the grievous entail of a heavy land tax,
which they will have fanctioned by their pufillanimity, in not daring to brave the outrages of the
fraudulent and felf-interefted. For myfelf, I fhall
only fay, I have fo little partiality for this fcheme,
except what a real and conftitutional love of the
public infpires, that if I fail in this propofal, it
will be the laft attempt of the kind I fhall ever
make, and I believe, a minifter will not foon be
found hardy enough to brave, on the behalf of
the people, and without the flighteft motive of
intereft, the worft effects of popular delufion and
popular injuftice.

" I fhall for the prefent, confine myfelf entirely
to the tobacco trade, and to the frauds practifed
in that branch of the revenue. If there is one fubject
of taxation more obvious than another, more immediately within the direct aim of fifcal impofition
than another, it is fuch an article of luxury as depends
for its ufe on cuftom or caprice, and is by no means,
effential to the fupport of real comfort of human life.
If there is a fubject of taxation where it is more immediately the province of the legiflature to fupprefs fraud, and ftrictly to infift on the payment;
of every impoft, it muft be that where the wrong

is felt by every clafs of perfons, and none are benefited, except the moft difhoneft and profligate
part of the community.   Both thefe defcriptions
apply to the fubject before us.   For though the
ufe of tobacco is perhaps lefs fanctioned by natural reafon than any other luxury, yet fo great
is the predilection for it, in its various forms, that
from the palace to the hovel there is no exemption from the duty ; and furely it muft be confidered an intolerable grievance, that by the frauds
which are daily committed, the very pooreft of
the peafantry are obliged to pay this duty twice:
once in the enhanced price of the article ; for
though the fraudulent trader contrives to fave to
himfelf the amount of the tax impofed by parliament, yet he does not fell it cheaper to the public ; and a fecond time, in the tax that is neceffarily fubftituted to make good the deficiency
which has been by thefe means occafioned.   Did
it ever happen till now, that when an abufe of
this kind was to be remedied, endeavours were
ufed to make the attempt unpopular ?

" In difcuffing this fubject, it will be neceffary
firft to advert to the condition of our planters of
tobacco in America.   If they are to be believed,
they are reduced to the utmoft extremity, even
almoft to a ftate of defpair, by the many frauds
that have been committed in that trade, and by
the ill ufage they have fuftained from their factors
and correfpondents in England, who from being
their fervants, are become their tyrants.   Thefe
unfortunate people have fent home many reprefentations

fentations of the bad ftate of their affairs; they have lately deputed a gentleman with a remon-ftrance, fetting forth their grievances, and praying for fome fpeedy relief: this they may obtain by means of the fcheme I intend now to propofe; but I believe it is from that alone they can expect any relief.

"The next thing to be confidered is, the ftate of the tobacco trade with refpect to the fair trader. The man who deals honourably with the public, as well as individuals, the man who honeftly pays all his duties, finds himfelf forcftalled in almoft every market within the ifland, by the fmuggler and fraudulent dealer. As to our foreign trade in tobacco, thofe who have no regard to honour, to religion, or to the welfare of the country, but are every day contriving ways and means for cheating the public by perjuries and falfe entries, are the greateft gainers; and it will always be fo, unlefs we can contrive fome method of putting it out of their power to carry on fuch frauds for the future.

"We ought to confider the great lofs fuftained by the public, by means of the frauds committed in the tobacco trade, and the addition that muft certainly be made to the revenue, if thofe frauds can be prevented in future. By this addition, parliament will acquire the means of exercifing one of its moft enviable privileges, that of diminifhing the burthens of the country, the power of doing which will thus be prefented to them in various forms. If it fhould be the pre-

vailing

vailing opinion, that the discharge of the national
debt should be accelerated, this increase offers an
abundant resource. If the idea should prevail,
that those taxes ought to be alleviated which fall
heaviest on our manufacturers and the labouring
poor, as soap and candles, this increase will replace the difference. Or if it should be judged
that more immediate attention ought to be paid
to the current service, the fund may be referved
for that use : and it is manifestly unjust and impolitic, that the national debt should be continued, and the payment postponed ; or that the
heavy duties on our manufactures should remain,
which are justly paid, and without fraud ; or that
ways and means for the current service should be
annually imposed, if the present revenues will answer all or any of these purposes. This, I am
convinced, will be the effect of the scheme I am
to propose, and whoever views it in its proper
light, must see the planters, the fair traders, and
the public, ranged on one side in support of it ;
and none but the unfair traders and tobacco factors, on the other.

" I am aware that the evidence to be adduced
in proof of the existence of the frauds I am about
to enumerate, is not such as would be sufficient
to induce a court of justice to pronounce the
guilt of those to whom they may be imputed.
But as I do not undertake the task of inculpa-
tion, if I make out such a case to the committee,
as will enable them to decide on the existence of
the crime, they will not hesitate to apply the remedy.

medy. They will consider the deficiency of strict legal proof, as a motive for their interference, rather than their forbearance; more particularly when they reflect, that if persons are with difficulty induced to give testimony in such a case as this, where the good of the country only is to be pursued, without injury to any one, they will be still less easily brought forward to give such information as will tend to the ruin of others. In this case it is hardly too much to say, that gentlemen should learn from the example of those interested, how to conduct themselves: they have, with an alacrity and unblushing eagerness which proves, which confesses their guilt, hastily inferred the most violent intentions in the friends of government; they have assumed facts, and inferred intentions, without the smallest data on which to found their presumptions. I ask no more than this: if I succeed in making it appear that gross frauds are daily practised, and the revenue injured in a most daring and profligate manner; that the proposed remedy, should it appear adequate and applicable, may be resorted to, without subjecting me to the necessity of procuring that which is, in fact, unattainable, such precise proof as would satisfy the administrators of the laws in the disposal of property, or deciding on guilt. Such evidence, and such facts as I have been able to collect, it is my duty to lay before you; and it is your duty to support me, unless my plan appears totally void of reason and justice."

P 3   The

The minifter then proceeded to give fuch preliminary ftatements and calculations, as were neceffary to render his plans intelligible, to make
the abufes obvious, and to demonftrate the propriety and neceffity of reform. From thefe ftatements it appeared, · that the exifting duties on
tobacco amounted to fixpence and one-third of a
penny on every pound. The difcounts, allow-
ances, and drawbacks, were a total drawback on
re-exportation; ten per cent. on prompt payment; and fifteen per cent. on bonded duties.
The grofs produce of the tax, at a medium,
£.754,131. 4s. 7d. the nett produce only
£.161,000.

Having made thefe ftatements with the utmoft
exactnefs and perfpicuity, he proceeded :

" I fhall now point out as clearly as I can, and
as amply as my knowledge will enable me, the
principal frauds and moft glaring inftances of dif-
honefty, which occafion this amazing difpropor-
tion. And firft I fhall mention one, which feems
alone capable of diverting from its proper channel the amount of any tax. I mean that of ufing
light weights inwards, and heavy weights out-
wards, of paying by the firft, and taking the
drawback by the laft, and charging the planter,
and taking commiffion by the whole. This evil
is farther enhanced by negligence; for it is cuf-
tomary to weigh a few hogfheads only, and if
they anfwer, the whole pafs according to the numbers in the cocket,

" A par-

"ᵃ A particular inſtance of this fraud came
lately to our knowledge by mere accident: one
Mitford, who had been a conſiderable tobacco
merchant in the city, happened to fail, at a time
when he owed a large ſum of money on bond
to the crown. An extent was immediately iſſued
againſt him, and government obtained poſſeſſion
of all his books, by which the fraud was diſcovered. For it appeared, as may be ſeen by one
of his books, which I have in my hand, that
upon the column where the falſe quantities which
had been entered at the importation were marked,
he had, by a colluſion with the officer, got a ſlip
of paper ſo artfully paſted down, that it could
not be diſcovered, and upon this ſlip of paper
were written the real quantities which were entered, becauſe he was obliged to produce the
ſame book when that tobacco was entered for
exportation. But upon exportation, the tobacco
was entered and weighed according to the quantities marked on this ſlip of paper, by which he
ſecured a drawback, or his bonds returned, to
near double the value of what he had actually
paid duty for upon importation. Yet this Mitford was as honeſt a man, and as fair a trader, as
any in the city of London. I deſire not to be
miſunderſtood; I mean, that before he failed,
before theſe frauds came to be diſcovered, he was
always reckoned as honeſt a man, and as fair a
trader, as any in the city of London, or in any
other part of the nation."

After enumerating ſeveral other inſtances where
govern-

government had been defrauded of a full third of
the duties impofed, and legally payable, he came
to Peele's cafe, which is fingular from its enor-
mity. " In September 1732, this Peele entered
in the James and Mary, from Maryland, 310
hodgfheads of tobacco, for which he paid the
duty in ready money. In October following, he
fold 200 hogfheads to one Mr. Hyam, for exportation, and they were immediately exported. It
appears on thefe 200 hogfheads, that the duties
paid at importation, according to the weights in
the land-waiters books, were fhort of the real
weights by 13,292 pounds. The certificates fworn
to for Mr. Peele to obtain debentures, were to
difcharge bonds given on a former entry of Vir-
ginia tobacco, imported in November 1731. The
indorfement on the cocket made by Mr. Peele,
in order to receive the debentures, exceeded the
real weights actually fhipped by 8,288 pounds, fo
that the total of the pounds weight gained by this
fraud, amounts to 21,580.

" The next fraud to which I fhall direct your
attention, is that of receiving the drawback on
tobacco for exportation, and relanding it. The
effects of this practice are too obvious to require
elucidation, and it has been carried to fuch an
extent, that a great number of fhips were employed at Guernfey, Jerfey, and the Ifle of Man,
in receiving and relanding fuch tobacco. Nor
was the evil confined to thefe ports; a very intel-
ligent gentleman, Mr. Howel, who refided many
years in Flanders, has frequently obferved feveral
quantities

quantities of tobacco imported into Oftend and Dunkirk, and there repacked in bales of one hundred pounds each, and put on board veffels which waited there to reland it in England or Ireland. About twelve months ago, nine Britifh veffels were employed in taking cargoes for this purpofe at Dunkirk.

" The third fraud to which I fhall direct the attention of the committee, is that of receiving the whole drawback for a commodity of almoft no value, namely, the ftalks of the tobacco, which it is ufual, after the leaf has been ftripped off, to prefs flat and cut, and by mixing this offal with fand and duft, impofe on the revenue officers, and obtain the fame drawback as for an equal weight of the entire plant. This miferable ftuff, when the fraudulent purpofe has once been anfwered, is either thrown into the fea, or relanded and fold at three farthings a pound, with an allowance of 1,010 pounds weight in five hogfheads.

" The fourth fraud I fhall advert to, is one of very great confequence, known by the name of focking; which is a cant term for pilfering and ftealing tobacco from fhips in the river. This iniquitous practice, which was difcovered in 1728 and 1729, was chiefly carried on by watermen, lightermen, tide-waiters, and city porters, called gangs-men : the commodity fo pilferred was depofited in houfes from London Bridge to Woolwich, and afterwards fold, frequently to eminent merchants. Five hundred examinations have been
taken

taken on the fubject, from which it appears, that, in the fpace of one year, fifty tons were focked on board fhips and on the quays. Sixteen tons were feized, but that quantity was reckoned an inconfiderable part of the whole. In confequence of thefe informations, 150 officers were difmiffed, nine were convicted, of whom fix are ordered for tranfportation, three to be whipt : thefe profecutions were all carried on at the expence of government ; and it is not a little remarkable, when we recollect the profeffions of patriotifm, virtue, and difintereftednefs, which are now fo copioufly poured forth, that not a fingle merchant, though the facts were fo notorious and fhameful, affifted the ftate, either by information or pecuniary exertion, to fupprefs the fraud, or bring the delinquents to punifhment.

" The laft grievance I fhall mention, cannot fo properly be denominated a fraud, as an abufe arifing from the nature of the duties paid, and the manner of paying them ; I mean the advantage afforded to the merchant of trading with the public money, or making government pay more than they receive. Bonds are given for eighteen months, three years are allowed for the exportation of the article, and new importations difcharge old bonds. The loffes which refult to government from the failure of the obligors in thefe bonds, is immenfe; befides the ungracious tafk to which it fubjects them of fuing the fureties, who had no intereft in the contract. The rich trader has another advantage ; he avoids giving bonds, by paying the amount

amount of his duties in ready money, for which
he is allowed a difcount of ten per cent. Now it
is very common, and not out of the line of fair
trade, for a merchant to pay this duty, receive
the difcount, and by immediately entering the
fame commodity for exportation, gain an advantage (I will not fay defraud the revenue) of ten
per cent. without lofs, rifque, or expenditure.

" The frauds which I have here enumerated
are, I apprehend, fufficiently proved to fatisfy
the committee of their exiftence, and their enor-
mity is obvious enough to demand active interference. The only remedy I can devife, is that
of altering the manner of collecting the duties.
Frauds become practicable by having but one
check at importation, and one at exportation; if
there is but one fentinel at a garrifon, and he
fleeps, or is corrupted, the caftle is taken; but
if there are more than one, it is in vain to corrupt the firft, without extending the fame influence to thofe who remain; and when difficulties
are fo multiplied, the project becomes hazardous
and uncertain, and is abandoned.

" If the grievance then is admitted, it only remains to mention the remedy, and to confider
whether it is effectual, or whether it is worfe than
the difeafe.

" The laws of the cuftoms are manifeftly infufficient to prevent the frauds which already
exift; I therefore propofe to add the laws of excife; and by means of both, it is probable, I may
fay

say certain, that all such frauds will be prevented in future.

"I have already stated to the committee, that the several imposts on tobacco amount to six pence and one third of a penny per pound, all of which, must be paid down in ready money upon importation, with the allowance of ten per cent. upon prompt payment; or there must be bonds given, with sufficient sureties, for payment, which is often a great loss to the public, and always a great inconvenience to the merchant importer. Whereas, by what I shall propose, the whole duty will amount to no more than four pence three farthings per pound, and will not be paid till the tobacco is sold for home consumption; so that if the merchant exports his tobacco, he will be quite free from all payment of duty, or giving security; he will have nothing to do but re-load his tobacco for exportation, without being at the trouble of attending to have his bonds cancelled, or taking out debentures for the drawbacks: all which, I conceive, must be a great ease to the fair trader; and to every such trader the prevention of frauds must be a great advantage, because it will put all the tobacco traders in Britain on the same footing, which is but just and equitable, and what ought, if possible, to be accomplished.

"Now, in order to make this ease effectual to the fair trader, and to contribute to his advantage, by preventing, as much as possible, all frauds for the future, I propose, as I have said, to join the laws of excise to those of the customs, and to leave

leave the one penny, or rather three farthings per
pound, called the farther fubfidy, to be ftill
charged at the cuftom houfe, upon the importation of tobacco, which three farthings fhall be
payable to his majefty's civil lift as heretofore ; and
I propofe for the future, that all tobacco, after
being weighed at the cuftom-houfe, and charged
with the faid three farthings per pound, fhall be
lodged in a warehoufe or warehoufes, to be appointed by the commiffioners of excife for that
purpofe, of which warehoufe the merchant importer fhall have one lock and key, and the warehoufe-keeper to be appointed by the faid commiffioners fhall have another, that the tobacco may
lie fafe in that warehoufe, till the merchant finds
a market for it, either for exportation or home
confumption : if his market be for exportation,
he may apply to his warehoufe-keeper, and take
out as much for that purpofe as he has occafion
for, which, when weighed at the cuftom-houfe,
fhall be difcharged of the three farthings per pound
with which it was charged upon importation, fo
that the merchant may then export it without any
farther trouble. But if his market be for home
confumption, he fhall pay the three farthings
charged upon it at the cuftom-houfe upon importation, and then, upon calling his warehoufe-
keeper, he may deliver it to the buyer, on paying
an inland duty of four pence per pound, to the
proper officer appointed to receive the fame.

" And whereas all penalties and forfeitures to
become due by the laws now in being, for regulating

lating the collection of the duties on tobacco, or at leaft all that part of them which is not given to informers, now belong to the crown, I now propofe that all fuch penalties and forfeitures, in fo far as they formerly belonged to the crown, fhall for the future belong to the public, and be applicable to the fame ufes to which the faid duties fhall be made applicable by parliament ; and for that purpofe I have the king's commands to acquaint the houfe, that he, out of his great regard for the public good, with pleafure confents that they fhall be fo applied ; which is a condefcenfion in his majefty, that I hope every gentleman in this houfe is fully fenfible of, and will freely acknowledge.

" Having thus explained my fcheme to the committee, I fhall briefly touch on the advantages to be derived from, and anticipate fome of the objections which may probably be made to it.

" Firft then, turning duties upon importation into duties on confumption, is manifeftly a great benefit to the merchant importer. The paying down of duties, or bonding, are heavy burthens. The payment of duties requires a treble ftock to what would elfe be requifite in trade ; and the afking fecurities, befides numerous other inconveniences, fubjects the merchant to the neceffity of returning the favour. It hardly requires to be mentioned, that it is a very great accommodation to be obliged to provide for the payment of one

penny

penny only, inftead of fix pence and one third of a penny.

" The next benefit is the great abatement on the whole duty. The inland duty being four pence per pound, and the remaining fubfidy three farthings, gives an abatement of 10 per cent. and of 15 per cent. upon the whole : whereas, the 25 per cent. is at prefent given only on the money paid down, which is not a fifth of the whole, and but 15 per cent. allowed on the four fifths which is bonded. Thus a duty of five pence farthing is paid on four fifths of the tobacco, and four pence three farthings on the other fifth ; while by the plan I propofe, no more than four pence three farthings will be paid on the whole. It is eafy to calculate how great the advantage muft be to the planter and fair trader from this arrangement, which demands fo fmall an advance, exempts them from all the inconveniences of finding fureties, and requires no payment of any confequence, till the moment when a purchafer prefents himfelf to refund the coft.

" If it fhould be objected againft this project, that it makes the tobacco trade a ready money bufinefs, which it cannot bear; I anfwer, that it may be fo or not, as the parties themfelves may chufe to arrange it ; for if the merchant gives the confumer credit, as he now does, for the duties as well as the commodity, the objection ceafes to have any weight.

" The great advantage to the public will be this, that no duty being paid on tobacco defigned

for

for exportation, an immediate ftop will be put to the fraud on drawbacks, and to moſt of the diſ-graceful efforts of diſhoneſty, which I have pre-viouſly enumerated. This faſt does not require to be verified by an experiment; it is ſufficiently proved by the ſucceſs and facility which attend the collection of the malt duty.

" I come now to the main point, and which alone can admit of debate; the grand objection of making the dealers in tobacco ſubject to the laws of exciſe. I am aware, that on this ſubject I have arguments or rather aſſertions to encounter, which are of great import in ſound, though of very little in ſenſe. Thoſe who deal in theſe ge-neral declamations ſtigmatize the ſcheme in the moſt unqualified manner, as tending to reduce thoſe ſubjected to it to a ſtate of ſlavery. This is an aſſertion, the fallacy of which can only be determined by compariſon. There are already ten or twelve articles of conſumption ſubjected to the exciſe laws; the revenue derived from them amounts to about £.3,200,000 per annum, which is appropriated to particular purpoſes. A great number of perſons are, of courſe, involved in the operation of theſe laws: yet, till the preſent mo-ment, when ſo inconſiderable an addition is pro-poſed, not a word has been uttered about the dreadful hardſhips to be apprehended from them. Theſe clamours of intereſted and diſaffected per-ſons are beſt anſwered by the contented tacitur-nity of thoſe in whoſe behalf their arguments, if of any force, ought to operate. Are the brewers

and

and maltſters ſlaves, or do they reckon themſelves ſo? Are they not as free in elections, to elect or be elected, as any others?· or let any gentleman preſent ſay, if he ever met with any oppoſition from, or by means of an exciſeman?

"'I quit this general topic to advert to more particular and ſpecific objections: The chief of them are, houſes liable to be ſearched; the being ſubject to the determination of commiſſioners without appeal, who are neceſſarily creatures of the crown; the number of exciſe officers; the injury the ſubject will ſuſtain in being tried with-out a jury; and the particular intereſt of the crown in this alteration.

" To all theſe objections one general obſerva-tion will apply; that if for theſe reaſons this ſcheme is to be relinquiſhed, the whole ſyſtem of exciſe laws ought to be abandoned. But I ſhall examine them one by one. I begin with the laſt, the moſt cruel and unjuſt, becauſe it tends to ſet up an improper diſtinction, and draw a ſtrong line of oppoſition between the intereſts of the crown and the intereſts of the people; that is to ſay, between the eſtate and particular property of the crown, and the eſtate and particular property of the public: this naturally leads to a general con-ſideration of the public revenues.

" The revenues may be computed at £.6,700,000 per annum. The public has of this, as its parti-cular intereſt and property, about £.5,900,000 per annum, namely, the appropriated funds and annual fupplies. The proportion remaining to the crown, £.800,000, is not an eighth part of the whole. And here, in order to obviate a general mifreprefentation, it is neceffary to ftate, that the civil lift revenues, in five years, from Midfummer 1727 to Midfummer 1732, have fallen fhort of the fum they are fuppofed to produce by upwards of £.26,000 a year on the average. Happy indeed would be the ftate of the country, if the appropriated duties would anfwer all the proper engagements, and leave a furplus fufficient for the current fervice! But if that great object is not attainable, it is furely well worth the attention of parliament to provide for a moiety, or even a fourth part of the current fervice. The appropriated duties were funds for paying the intereft of the national debt. There had been deficiencies in feveral, but now a fupply is made; a finking fund for gradually difcharging the principal. A million per annum has for feveral years been applied, and that, by the public creditors, is now thought more than fufficient.

" If under the prefent management, the duties produce much lefs than ought to be paid to the public, has the public a right to make the moft of their own revenues, or are they alone excluded from doing themfelves juftice ? To object againft the improvement of the king's part, is to fay, that the public had better be defrauded of feven parts in eight, than that juftice fhould be done to the crown in the eighth. If manifeft frauds were dif-covered in a branch belonging entirely to the civil lift,

lift, the poft office for example, would you rather
fanction the wrong than do juftice to the crown?
Why then this unreafonable jealoufy in the prefent
inftance? I call the jealoufy unreafonable, becaufe
in this propofition all poffible care has been taken
to avoid the imputation of being defigned for
the benefit of the crown. The penny which goes
to the civil lift is left to be paid at the cuftom-
houfe. All increafe from the inland duty is not
to go to the crown, but to the public. All fines,
forfeitures, and penalties arifing from the inland
duties, are renounced by the crown, and appropriated to the public. In a word, the crown will
have no intereft in the inland duty, but as truftee
for the public.

" This fact, duly confidered, anfwers the great
objection to the determination of commiffioners.
For granting, for a moment, that commiffioners are
to be fuppofed corrupt, venal, and creatures of the
crown, what influence can their regard for the
crown have on them, to induce them to opprefs
the people, when the crown has no intereft in
their determination? But though this anfwer
might reafonably be deemed fatisfactory and fufficient, yet to obviate even fpeculative objections,
a remedy is fupplied for this fuppofed grievance,
by invefting three of the twelve judges with a
power of determining, in a fummary way, all ap-
peals brought before them within the bills of mor-
tality; and in the country, the fame power is to
be vefted in one of the judges of the affize going
the next circuit. This renders it impoffible that

Q 2   the

the intereſt of the ſubject can be ſacrificed to undue influence on the one hand, or the revenue
to private ſolicitation, perſonal friendſhip, or regard on the other. While ſuch a tribunal pre-
ſents itſelf, no offender would chuſe to be carried
into Weſtminſter hall, rather than have his cauſe
judged in a ſummary way. The benefit of a trial
by jury would not induce a man to encounter
the tedious, vexatious, and expenſive proceedings
in a court of law, more burthenſome than the penalties and forfeitures in diſpute. As far as my
own obſervation enables me to judge on the preſent ſyſtem, where the commiſſioners have, in
moſt caſes, a power to determine themſelves, or
to bring informations, I have found that moſt
people, againſt whom informations have been laid,
have been deſirous that their cauſes ſhould be determined by commiſſioners; but I never yet heard
of one who was willing to take his cauſe out, of
the hands of the commiſſioners to have it tried in
Weſtminſter hall. One reaſon which contributes
to render the exerciſe of power by the commiſſioners more popular is, that they poſſeſs the privilege of mitigation, which is not entruſted to the
judges, who are merely adminiſtrators of the law
according to the letter.

" The next objection is the increaſe of revenue
officers, which fear, intereſt, and affectation have
magnified into a ſtanding army. This ſtanding
army, allowing the propoſed addition to extend to
tobacco and wine, will not, according to the eſti-
mate of the commiſſioners, exceed *one hundred and
twenty-*

twenty-fix perfons; that number, in addition to thofe already employed, will do all the duty. In this computation, warehoufe-keepers are of courfe not included, their number muft be uncertain; for the fatisfaction and accommodation of the merchants: Few houfes, however, out of London, will be fubject to the excife laws which are not fo already.

" The only remaining objection is, the power of officers to enter and fearch houfes. This objection could not poffibly have any weight, without the aid of grofs mifconception, or mifreprefentation. All warehoufes, cellars, fhops, and rooms ufed for keeping, manufacturing, or felling tobacco, are to be entered at the inland office. Thefe are to be always liable to the infpection of the officer, and it is to be made penal to keep or conceal tobacco in any room or place not entered: But no other part of the houfe is liable to be fearched without a warrant and a conftable, which warrant is not to be granted without any affidavit of the caufe of fufpicion. The practice of the cuftoms is now ftronger; they can enter with a writ of affiftance without any affidavit. But why all this folicitude in the behalf of fraud? If the powers given by either, or both the fyftems of revenue law are not fufficient (as I am informed they are not in the cafe of tea) it is an argument to add more checks, but no argument againft the application of this.

" The regulation in thefe two commodities, can affect neither trade, the poor, or the manu-

facturer.

facturer. The poor are not at all concerned in the queſtion of tobacco, as the retailer now ſells all tobacco at the rate of duty paid. The manu- facturer is concerned as little, for the ſame reaſon, and neither one or the other drinks any wine. The landed intereſt cannot be affected by it in conſequence of an advanced charge on the poor and the manufacturer. The whole clamour then is in favour of the retailer or tradeſman, and even he cannot ſuffer, unleſs guilty of frauds. " This is the ſcheme which has been repreſented in ſo dreadful and terrible a light ; this is the monſter, the many-headed monſter, which was to devour the people, and commit ſuch ravages over the whole nation. How juſtly it has been repreſented in ſuch a light, I ſhall leave to this committee and to the world without doors to judge. I have ſaid, and will repeat it, that whatever apprehen- ſions and terrors people may have been brought under from a falſe and malicious repreſentation of what they neither did, or could know or under- ſtand, I am fully perſuaded, that when they have duly conſidered the ſcheme I have now the ho- nour to open to you, they will view it in another light ; and that if it has the good fortune to meet the approbation of parliament, and comes to take effect, the people will ſoon feel the happy con- ſequences of it ; and when they experience theſe good effects, they will no longer look on thoſe perſons as their friends, who have ſo groſsly im- poſed on their underſtandings.

" I look

" I look upon it as a moſt innocent ſchême; it can be hurtful to none but ſmugglers and unfair traders.' I am certain it will be of great benefit to the revenue, and will tend to make LONDON A FREE PORT, AND BY CONSEQUENCE, THE MARKET OF THE WORLD. If I had thought otherwiſe of it I would never have ventured to propoſe it in this place."

He then concluded, by moving a repeal of the ſubſidy and additional duty on tobacco, amounting in the whole to five pence and one third of a penny in the pound weight.

The members of oppoſition were not ſilenced or diſmayed by the ample and candid manner in which the miniſter opened and explained his ſcheme; and pointed out its benefits. Though he had anticipated many of their objections, and ſhewn their futility, yet they brought them forward with as much confidence and perſeverance as if they had been perfectly juſt and entirely new. The debate was long and animated; the miniſter was principally ſupported by Mr. Yorke, then attorney general, and afterwards earl of Hardwicke, and Sir Joſeph Jekyll, maſter of the rolls. The principal orators of oppoſition were alderman Perry, Sir Paul Methuen, Sir John Barnard, Heathcote, Pulteney, and Sir William Wyndham, who peculiarly diſtinguiſhed himſelf on this occaſion.

Their efforts were generally directed to countenance the popular clamours, which they themſelves had excited: they recurred to all the inflammatory topics drawn from the introduction of

Q 4

a ſtand-a ftanding army of excifemen, giving arbitrary power to the crown, and enflaving the fubject. They depreciated the propofed fcheme, by affecting to demonftrate, that when the manner of committing a fraud was difcovered, the farther perpetration of it became impracticable. Alderman Perry, in the name of the merchants of London, offered to anfwer for all the bonds outftanding, in confideration of a difcount of £. 20,000, but he took care to except all thofe, which were defperate, and made no calculation of their probable amount. Sir John Barnard called in the commiffioners of the cuftoms, who were obvioufly interefted to prevent the completion of the excife fcheme, and afked them what they thought the frauds in the tobacco trade might amount to, one year with another? They anfwered, they had never made any computation; but one of them faid that he had, as matter of private curiofity, calculated on the fubject, and thought it might amount to thirty or forty thoufand pounds a year. Sir John then enquired; Whether it was their opinion, that if the officers of the cuftoms did their duty diligently and faithfully, it would effectually prevent all or, moft of the frauds in the tobacco trade? This was, of courfe, anfwered in the affirmative. On the bafis of this loofe unauthenticated information, and hardy affertion, the oppofition reviled the fcheme with the moft unqualified abufe, and unfparing ridicule.

Pulteney faid, " The honourable gentleman was pleafed to dwell on the generofity of the

crown

crown in giving up the fines, forfeitures, and
feizures to the public; but in my opinion, it will
be a poor equivalent for the many oppreffions and
exactions which the people will be expofed to by
this fcheme. I muft fay, that the honourable
gentleman has been, of late, mighty bountiful and
liberal in his offers to the public. He has been
fo gracious to afk us, Will you have a land tax of
two fhillings in the pound? A land tax of one
fhilling in the pound? Or will you have no land
tax at all? Will you have your debts paid? Will
you have them foon paid? Tell me but what you
want, let me but know how you can be made
eafy, and it fhall be done for you. Thefe are
moft generous offers; but there is fomething fo
very extraordinary, fo farcical in them, that, really,
I can hardly mention them without laughing: It
puts me in mind of the ftory of Sir Epicure Mam-
mon in the Alchymift. He was gulled of his money by fine promifes; he was promifed the philofopher's ftone, by which he was to get mountains of gold, and every thing elfe he could defire;
but all ended at laft, in *fome little thing for curing
the itch.*"

Sir William Wyndham made a moft able and vehement fpeech, in which he alluded to *Empfom*, and
Dudley, who, to gratify the avarice of their mafter,
drained the purfes of the fubjects, not by new taxes,
but by a fevere and rigorous execution of the laws
that had been enacted: " But what was their fate?
They had the misfortune to out-live their mafter;
and his fon, as foon as he came to the throne, took
off

off both their 'heads." " 'There never was 'a'
ſcheme," he added, " which encountered ſo much
diſlike and diſſatisfaction from the people in general; the whole nation has already ſo openly declared their averſion, that I am ſurpriſed to ſee it
inſiſted on; the very propoſing of ſuch a ſcheme
in the houſe of commons, after ſo many remonſtrances againſt it, I muſt think moſt audacious; it
is, in a manner, flying in the face of the whole
people of England."

In reply to theſe obſervations, the miniſter
ſaid, that much of the matter thrown out by the
ſpeakers on the other ſide was foreign to the debate: that the ancient hiſtorians, not only of this
but other countries, had been ranſacked to find
parallel caſes of wicked miniſters, and make affected applications. " Of late years (he ſaid) I
have dwelt but little in the ſtudy of hiſtory, but
I have a very good prompter behind me," (meaning the attorney general) " and by his means I
can recollect, that the caſe of *Empſom* and *Dudley*
was ſo different from any thing that can poſſibly
be preſumed from the caſe now before us, that I
wonder how it was poſſible to bring them into the
debate. Thoſe men had, by virtue of old and
obſolete laws, unjuſtly extorted great ſums of
money from people, under pretence that they had
become liable to penalties for the breach of ſta-
tutes, which had for many years fallen into diſuſe.
I muſt ſay (and I hope moſt of thoſe who hear
me will think) that it is very unjuſt to draw any
parallel between their characters and mine: If my
character

character is, ,or fhould ever come to be, in any refpect, like their's; I fhall deferve their fate. But while I know myfelf innocent, I fhall depend upon the protection of the laws of my country ; as long as they can protect me I am fafe ; and if that protection fhould fail, I am prepared to fubmit to the worft that can happen. I know that my political and minifterial life has by fome gentlemen been long wifhed at an end, but they may afk their own difappointed hearts, how vain their wifhes have been; and as for my natural life, I have lived long enough to learn to be eafy about parting with it.''

He then adverted to the artifices which had been ufed to exafperate the people, whom he compared to puppets, which perfons behind the curtain played, and obliged to fay whatever they pleafed. He expofed the methods which had been ufed to draw a concourfe of people to the door, fuch as fending circular letters by the beadles ; and concluded in thefe words ; " Gentlemen may fay what they pleafe of the multitudes now at our door, and in all the avenues leading to this houfe; they may call them a modeft multitude if they will; but whatever temper they were in when they came hither, it may be very much altered now, after having waited fo long at our door. It may be very eafy for fome defigning feditious perfon to raife a tumult and difor-der among them, and when tumults are once begun, no man knows where they may end; he is a greater man than any I know in the nation, that

could

could with the fame eafe appeafe them. For this reafon, I think it was neither regular or prudent to ufe any methods for bringing fuch multitudes to this place, under any pretence whatever. Gentlemen may give them what name they think fit, it may be faid they came hither as humble fupplicants, but I know whom the law calls *fturdy beggars,* * and thofe who brought them hither; could not be certain but that they might have behaved in the fame manner."

After a few words from Sir John Barnard, in which he defended the affembling of people at the doors, and affectedly gave to the phrafe *fturdy beggars,* that invidious fenfe in which it was afterwards fo much repeated by the enemies of the minifter, the queftion was called for, and paffed by a majority of 61 ; (266 againft 205.) The firft refolution being thus carried, three others were put, and agreed to without a divifion.

The debate was protracted till two o'clock in the morning, an hour at that time confidered extremely late. The people without were fo exafperated, that as Sir Robert paffed towards his carriage, fome of them caught him by the cloak, and would probably have committed fome violent outrage on his perfon, if his fon, Edward Walpole, and general Churchill had not interfered.

On the 16th Sir Charles Turner, according to order, reported to the houfe the proceedings of the

---

* I was informed, on the refpectable authority of the late much to be regretted lord John Cavendifh, that the minifter ufed the phrafe *fturdy beggars,* not as a matter of reproach, but to mark that the petitioners againft the excife, were formidable petitioners.

the committee. The debate was refumed with
increafed acrimony. Sir John Barnard, Bacon,
Sir Thomas Afton, lord Morpeth, Pulteney, and
Walter Plumer oppofed the queftion, that the
houfe fhould agree to the report. Horace Walpole, lord Hervey, Sir Thomas Robinfon, lord
Glenorchy, Clayton, and Sir Robert Walpole
fupported it; the houfe divided; the affirmative
was voted by a majority of 60 * (249 againft 189);
and Sir Charles Turner, the chancellor of the exchequer, the attorney general, the folicitor general, Dodington, Clayton, Sir William Yonge, Sir
George Oxenden, Scrope, and Edward Walpole,
were directed to prepare and bring in the bill.

The effect of this bill on the public mind was
fo great, and the ferment it occafioned fo violent,
that I have judged it proper to ftate every divifion which took place during its difcuffion. It is
unneceffary to fpecify the particulars of the debates, which, though conducted with great afperity, contained little novelty, and were often on
mere points of order, or difcuffion of precedents.

The bill was brought in, and read a firft time,
on the 4th of April. An objection was made
that fome parts of it were not within the compafs
of the refolutions, and that it fhould therefore
be withdrawn. This was overruled by a majority
of 56; † (232 againft 176). A motion being
then made for the houfe to adjourn, was negatived by 237 againft 199, and another for the
fecond reading on that day fe'nnight was carried
by

* Journals,   † Ibid.

by a majority of 36 ; * (236 againſt 200). The next day it was propoſed to print the bill, and diſtribute a proper number of copies to the members of the houſe, which being oppoſed by the miniſter, was negatived by a majority of 16 ; † (128 againſt 112.).

The lord mayor of London, however, contrived to obtain a copy, and laid it before the common council; who reſolved to petition the houſe againſt the bill, and prayed to be heard by counſel. The petition was patroniſed by Sir John Barnard, and

10th April. ordered to lie on the table ; but their being heard by counſel was over-ruled by a majority of 17 ; ‡ (214 againſt 197.) The next day ſimilar applications were made from the Towns of Nottingham and Coventry. The order of the day being then read, for the ſecond reading of the bill, Walpole moved that it ſhould be poſtponed to the twelfth

Bill relinquiſh- day of June : as it was generally underſtood, that
ed. the houſe would adjourn before that day, it was maniſeſt that the miniſter meant to abandon his ſcheme. This mode, however, of dropping it, did not pleaſe ; they wanted it to be rejected with ſome ſevere animadverſion, but though ſome hints were thrown out to that effect, yet the general ſenſe of the houſe, which was uncommonly full, was ſo apparent againſt it, that they did not think it prudent to make any ſpecific motion.

Many conjectures have been made on the motive which induced the miniſter to abandon his plan ; but I find none ſo ſatisfactory as the diſ

like

---

* Journals.   † Ibid.   ‡ Ibid.

like of counteracting the public opinion. The
decline of his majority from 61 on the firſt, to 17
on the laſt diviſion, affords no ſolution of his
motives, for the intermediate queſtions were not
of ſo much importance as the firſt, and though
ſome of his friends undoubtedly from a dread of
encountering the fury of a miſguided populace,
retired for a time from the ſcene of conteſt, I do
not find, from the printed liſt in the Hiſtorical
Regiſter, that more than four joined the ſtandard
of oppoſition. Nor is it probable that the threat
of farther deſertions alarmed the miniſter, becauſe,
if his partiſans had reſolved to abandon him, they
would have united themſelves with the oppoſition,
and have formed a conſtant majority in the houſe
againſt him. An anecdote recorded by one of his
friends, renders it ſtill more probable, that his
unwillineſs to carry any meaſure marked by popular diſapprobation, was the true motive of his
conduct.

   " On the evening before the report, Sir Robert
ſummoned a meeting of the principal members
who had ſupported the bill. It was very largely
attended. He reſerved his own opinion till the
laſt : but perſeverance was the unanimous voice.
It was urged that all taxes were obnoxious, and
there would be an end of ſupplies, if mobs were
to controul the legiſlature in the manner of raiſing
them. When Sir Robert had heard them all, he
aſſured them, " That he was conſcious of having
meant well ; that in the preſent inflamed temper
of the people, the act could not be carried into
                                    execution

execution without an armed force; that there would be an end of the liberty of England, if fupplies were to to be raifed by the fword. If, therefore, the refolution was to proceed with the bill, he would inftantly requeft the king's permiffion to refign, for he would not be the minifter to enforce taxes at the expence of blood." *

Public rejoicings.

Though the houfe did not rife, as was expected, before the 12th of June, yet they adjourned over that day, fo that the tobacco bill was dropt, and the wine bill was never brought forward. The defeat of this propofition was celebrated in London, and various parts of the kingdom, as a great national victory. Bonfires were made, effigies burnt, cockades were generally worn, infcribed with the motto of Liberty, Property, and no E x c i s e ; the Monument was illuminated, and every demonftration given of exuberant triumph and exceffive joy. The univerfity of Oxford gave into the fame folly, and carried their rejoicings to a moft indecent excefs. The gownfmen joined and encouraged the mob, jacobitical cries refounded through the town, and three days paffed in this difgraceful manner before the vice chancellor and proctors could reftore tranquillity.

Farther efforts of oppofition.

The public rejoicings, and the general averfion entertained againft the excife, infpired the oppofition with hopes that they fhould be enabled, through that medium, to embarrafs government, and effect the removal of the minifter, by compelling

* This anecdote is mentioned in " Hiftorical Remarks on the Taxation of free States, "on the authority of Mr. White, member for Retford, who lived in friendfhip with Sir Robert Walpole.

X This thin quarto volume was written by Sir William Meredith, when representative in Parliament for Liverpool. I printed twenty copies for his friends. It was never published, ...

pelling him to repeal the whole body of excise
laws. With this view, a petition from the dealers in tea and coffee, praying for relief againſt the
exciſe laws, as oppreſſive and injurious to trade,
was preſented, but it was rejected by 250 againſt
150. *

Notwithſtanding this defeat, the oppoſition
ſtill laboured under two groſs miſtakes : the firſt
was, that many members who promoted the bill,
had voted in contradiction to their real ſentiments
from ſelf intereſt; and the ſecond, that the king did
not cordially ſupport the miniſter, but waited only
for a favourable opportunity of removing him. They
had the mortification however to be fully undeceived in theſe opinions. A ſufficient proof that
they had undervalued the number of thoſe members
who were attached to the miniſter ſoon appeared,
upon a motion for appointing by ballot a committee to enquire into the frauds in the cuſtoms.
This propoſal was intended to reduce the miniſter to a dilemma. If it had been rejected, it would
have been ſaid, that he durſt not ſtand an inquiry into the facts which he had laid down as the
principle on which the exciſe bill was founded :
if it was carried, great hopes were entertained,
that in chuſing a committee by ballot, many of
thoſe members who they believed had ſupported
the miniſter from a dread of incurring his diſpleaſure, would venture to give their votes in favour of their liſt, in preference to the court liſt,
when it would not be known for which liſt each

particular

* Journals.

particular perfon gave his vote. No oppofition being made, a ballot took place, and a warm conteft enfued ; each fide acted an open and manly part. Their refpective lifts contained the names of thofe only who were ftaunch friends, and the court lift was carried by a majority of 85. This decifive victory put and end to the efforts and hopes of oppofition for this feffion of parliament. *

They were no lefs undeceived in their opinion, that the king did not cordially fupport the minifter. Some perfons of great confequence, had alfo about this period joined oppofition, and this defection was increafed from an idea which generally prevailed, that the credit of Walpole was declining, and his difgrace certain. In the houfe of peers, the oppofition, which had been rendered formidable by the junction of lord Carteret, was confiderably increafed by the defection of feveral who enjoyed very profitable pofts under the crown: The earl of Chefterfield, lord fteward of the houfhold, the earl of Burlington, captain of the band of penfioners, lord Clinton, lord of the bed chamber, and three Scotch peers, the duke of Montrofe, keeper of the great feal, the earl of Stair, vice admiral, and the earl of Marchmont, lord regifter. To thefe were added, lord Cobham, colonel of the king's regiment of horfe, and the duke of Bolton, colonel of the king's regiment of horfe guards. Many of thefe had influenced their friends in the houfe of commons, and particularly the

* De la Faye and Thomas Pelham, to the earl Waldegrave. Correfpondence, April 26.

the three brothers of lord Chesterfield, had voted against the excise bill. It was generally believed, that the number and consequence of these peers would prevent the minister from venturing to remove them, and that the king would not consent to their dismission or resignation. But the event proved otherwise. On the 11th of April the excise bill was abandoned; and on the 13th, as the earl of Chesterfield, * in company with lord Scarborough, was going up the great stair-case of the palace at St. James's, he was informed by a servant of the duke of Grafton, that his master wanted to see him on business of the greatest importance; on returning home the duke of Grafton waited on him, and acquainted him that he was come by the king's command to require the surrender of the white staff, which was immediately delivered. The dismission of Chesterfield was followed by the removal of Montrose, the earls of Stair, Burlington, and Marchmont, and lord Clinton. The resentment of the minister was carried so far, that lord Cobham and the duke of Bolton were even deprived of their regiments. †

The authority of the minister was also fully proved by the nomination of his confidential friends to the vacant offices, among whom the earl of Ilay was most conspicuous. His son, lord Walpole, was also made lord lieutenant of the

county

* Maty's Life of Lord Chesterfield. Sect. 4.
† Historical Register.

county of Devon, in the room of lord Clinton, and all doubts of his superior influence in the cabinet, were removed by the appointment of Sir Charles Wager to the office of first lord of the admiralty, vacant by the death of lord Torrington, which took place in June. His power on this occasion was far more evident, because there was no instance, since the accession of the house of Brunswick, that a commoner was raised to that high office, and because George the Second had a strong predilection for persons of rank, and had often been informed, that the family of Sir Charles Wager was not sufficiently distinguished.

It is curious to observe the veteran seaman, in a letter to Sir Robert Walpole, * founding his title to that post, not on his naval services, which no one could deny, but on a fanciful genealogy. The demur, however, was over-ruled by the minister, the king's scruples were removed, the Herald's office did not stand in his way, and he was placed at the head of the admiralty, which post he continued to fill, during the administration of Walpole, with much advantage to the minister, with great benefit to his country, and with no less credit to himself.

The king, in his speech from the throne, on the prorogation of the parliament, adverted to the artifices employed to delude the minds of the people, and to pervert the truth. "I cannot pass by unobserved, the wicked endeavours that have lately

---

* Sir Charles Wager to Sir Robert Walpole, 12 July, 1731. Correspondence, Period V.

lately been made ufe of to inflame the minds of the people, and by the moft unjuft mifreprefenta-tion to raife tumults and diforders, that almoft threatened the peace of the kingdom ; but I de-pend upon the force of truth, to remove the groundlefs jealoufies that have been raifed of de-figns carrying on againft the liberties of my peo-ple, and upon your known fidelity to defeat and fruftrate the expectations of fuch as delight in confufion. It is my inclination, and has always been my ftudy, to preferve the religious and civil rights of all my fubjects. Let it be your care to undeceive the deluded, and to make them fen-fible of their prefent happinefs, and the hazard they run of being unwarily drawn, by fpecious pretences, into their own deftruction."

CHAPTER THE FORTY-SECOND:

1734.

Character of Lord Hardwicke.—Parliamentary Proceedings.—Efforts of the Minority in Parliament.—The Excife.—The Removal of the Duke of Bolton and Lord Cobham —The Place Bill.—Motion for the Repeal of Septennial Parliaments.—Sir William Wyndham's Speech.— Walpole's Reply.—Bolingbroke's retreat to France.—The King's Speech.—Diffolution of Parliament.

IN confequence of the numerous removals and refignations among the peers, which had taken place the laft feffion, the oppofition in the upper houfe became extremely formidable, and the ma-jority of good fpeakers were ranged on that fide.

To

To counterbalance this preponderancy, Sir Philip Yorke was made lord chief juftice of the court of King's Bench.

His character.   This great lawyer, who fat fo long and with fo diftinguifhed a character for integrity and knowledge at the head of the law, had raifed himfelf folely by his eminent talents. The eloquence which he difplayed at the bar had recommended him to notice, and in 1719 he was appointed folicitor general, in the 30th year of his age; at the fame time he was re-elected for the borough of Lewes in Suffex, by the intereft of his patron, the duke of Newcaftle. In 1723 he was nominated attorney general, and highly diftinguifhed himfelf by his prudent and able fpeeches in the houfe of commons. In October, 1733, he was conftituted lord chief juftice of the King's Bench, and in November, in the fame year, called to the upper houfe, by the title of baron Hardwicke. The ftyle of his eloquence was more adapted to the houfe of lords than to the houfe of commons. The tone of his voice was pleafing and melodious, his manner was placid and dignified. Precifion of arrangement, clofenefs of argument, fluency of expreffion, elegance of diction, great knowledge of the fubject on which he fpoke, were his particular characteriftics. He feldom rofe into great animation; his chief aim was more to convince than amufe; to appeal to the judgment rather than to the feelings of his auditors. He poffeffed a perfect command over himfelf, and his even

6   temper

temper was never ruffled by petulant oppofition,
or malignant invective.

The parliament affembled on the 17th January,
and as it was the laft feffion, the minority exerted
their utmoft efforts to diftrefs the minifter, and
to increafe his unpopularity.

The plan of attack was in this, as in the feffion
of 1730, principally formed by Bolingbroke; and
under his aufpices, and by his direction, ably conducted by Sir William Wyndham, who feems to
have particularly diftinguifhed himfelf in the debates.

They firft tried their ftrength in various motions for papers and copies of inftructions which
were fent to the Britifh minifters in France and
Spain; for an addrefs to know how far the king
was engaged by his good offices in the caufes of
the war againft the Emperor; and for an account
of what application had been made by the parties
engaged in hoftilities. In thefe motions their exertions were baffled by the minifter, and the fmalleft majority in his favour was 95. Having ex-
haufted their efforts in regard to foreign tranfactions, in which he appeared to be moft vulnerable,
they directed their views to domeftic events.

They attempted to renew the public clamours
about the excife, and to accufe the minifter of not
having totally relinquifhed that fcheme; and of
waiting only for a favourable opportunity of again
introducing it. For this purpofe a petition being
again prefented from the druggifts, and other
dealers in tea, for relief againft the excife laws,

fome

fome of the leading members of oppofition attempted to revive the debate, and were inexcufa-
bly perfonal in their invectives againft the minifter. Pulteney in particular obferved, " I am perfuaded he ftill entertains the fame opinion of the
excife, and waits only for a proper opportunity
to renew it ; for which reafon he is unwilling that
we fhould go into fuch a committee as is now
propofed, left we fhould fap all the foundations
of any future project for a farther extenfion of the
excife laws." The reply of the minifter to this
infinuation was direct and manly. After repelling the attacks with equal fpirit and energy, he
faid, " As to the wicked fcheme, as the gentleman was pleafed to call it, which he would perfuade gentlemen is not yet laid afide, I, for my
part, affure this houfe, I am not fo mad as ever
again to engage in any thing that looks like an
excife, though in my own private opinion, I ftill
think it was a fcheme that would have tended
very much to the intereft of the nation, and I am
convinced that all the clamours without doors,
and a great part of the oppofition it met with
every where, was founded upon artful falfehoods,
mifreprefentations, and infinuations, that fuch
things were intended as had never entered into
the thoughts of any man with whom I am acquainted." In confequence of this explicit declaration, the affertions of the contrary fide made
little impreffion on the houfe, and the queftion

for

for referring the petition to a committee, was negatived by 233 againſt 155 *.

The ſpirit of oppoſition was·carried· to ſuch an Debates on·
exceſs, that the minority not only· reſiſted every the removal
of the duke of
meaſure of government with unabating· pertena- Bolton and
city, but brought forwards a queſtion that·.had a lord Cobham.
direct tendency to undermine and· deſtroy· the
conſtitution which they affected ſo zealouſly to
admire. In fact, this attempt had ſo direct a tendency to renew that military independance, which
in the laſt century had ſubverted the throne, and
enſlaved the people, that even thoſe writers who,
in other reſpects, invariably·decry the Walpole
adminiſtration, have not ſcrupled to reprobate this
propoſal, though it was ſupported with all the
ſtrength of their favourite party. † The motion
related to the removal of the duke of Bolton and
lord Cobham from their military commands.

Lord Morpeth, after the reading of the muti- 13th Feb,
ny bill, roſe, and concluded a ſpeech full of trite
reflections on a ſtanding army, under the influence of the crown, on the danger of arbitrary
power,· and ſome inapplicable and erroneous alluſions to the conſtitution ·of Holland and Sweden,
by moving for leave to bring in a bill " for ſecuring the conſtitution, by preventing officers, not
above the rank of colonels of regiments, from
being deprived of their commiſſions, otherwiſe
than by judgment of a court martial to be held
for

---

* Chandler. Journals.
† Smollett, book. 2. chap. 5.—Belſham, vol. 1. p. 340.

for that purpose, or by addrefs of either houfe of parliament."

This motion was argued at great length, and with uncommon warmth; but though ancient and modern hiftory was ranfacked, and every topic introduced which ingenuity could fuggeft, few obfervations worthy of record were produced. The minority were fully employed in defending their propofition againft the charges with which it was overwhelmed by the minifterial advocates.

Walpole concluded the debate, * with a fpeech replete with found principles and conftitutional doctrines. He defended not only the prerogative of the crown, but the intereft of parliament, and the well-being of the community, againft the horrible defpotifm of a ftratocracy, or army government; vindicated the purity of court martials, and deprecated the evils which would refult to the fervice from fubjecting them to the influence of intrigue, and making their decifions the mean of retaining or forfeiting a poft for life. " The behaviour of an officer, he obferved, may be influenced by malice, revenge, and faction, and on the pretence of honour and confcience; and if ever any officer of the army, becaufe the king refufed to comply with fome very unreafonable demand, fhould refolve to oppofe in every thing the meafures of government, I fhould think any man a moft pitiful minifter if he fhould be afraid of
advifing

* Lord Catherlogh faid a few words after him, but they contained a fimple diffent, unenforced by argument, expreffive only of the obligations of the army to the movers of the queftion.

advifing· his·majefty to ·cafhier fuch an officer.
On the٭contrary, I fhall leave it as ·a legacy to
all future minifters, ٭ that upon every occafion,
it is ٫their duty to advife ٫their mafter ٫that fuch
a man is unfit to have any command in his armies. Our king has, by his prerogative, a·power
of placing, preferring, and removing any officer he
pleafes, either in our army or militia : It· is by that
prerogative chiefly, he is enabled to execute our
laws, and preferve the peace of the ٫kingdom : if
a wrong ufe fhould be made of that prerogative,
his minifters are accountable for it to parliament ;
but it cannot be taken from him or diminifhed
without overturning our conftitution ; ·for our
prefent happy conftitution may be overturned by
republican, as well as by arbitrary fchemes. Therefore it muft be left to his majefty to judge by what
motives an officer acts, and if ·he thinks an officer
acts from bad motives, in duty to himfelf, he ought
to remove him." He then expatiated on the danger of a dictatorfhip from the meafure propofed,
and concluded with the conftitutional apothegm :
    " *Nolumus leges Angliæ mutari.*"
The queftion was negatived without a divifion. †

Foiled in this attempt, the oppofition renewed
the attack on a ground more plaufible and popular, that of perfonal inquiry. Sandys moved for
an addrefs, " humbly to defire his majefty, gracioufly to inform the houfe, by whofe advice he
                                              had

٭ Opinions of the Duchefs of Marlborough, p. 105. Thefe words
are erroneoufly attributed to Mr. Pelham, by Chandler.
    † Chandler. Journals.

had been pleafed to difcharge the duke of Bolton
and lord Cobham, and what crimes were alledged
againft them." Pulteney feconded the motion.
The miniftry difcerning the views of their opponents, and knowing that to difcufs the queftion
would produce the fame effect as pleading to a
fpecific charge, by letting loofe on them all the
powers of invective, and all the arts of mifreprefentation, declined the conteft ; they made no reply, but called for the queftion. Sir William
Wyndham in vain attempted, by reproaches and
invectives, to provoke a debate, the queftion was
again called for, and on a divifion, negatived by
252 againft 193. *

On the fame day the duke of Marlborough
brought into the houfe of lords, a bill fimilar to
that in the commons, but it was thrown out
after the firft reading. A motion to the fame
purport as that of Sandys was made by lord Car-
taret, but rejected. Protefts on both occafions
were entered on the journals, figned by upwards
of thirty peers, and the duke of Bolton and lord
Cobham feparately figned a fhort and manly proteft.

On the place
bill ;
Another meafure of oppofition, calculated to
render themfelves popular, was to revive a felf-
denying ordinance, which had excited much clamour in the reign of king William, and, after
great oppofition, had formed an article among the
limitations in the act of fettlement, but had been
afterwards repealed. It was intitled a bill for fecuring

* Journals.

curing the freedom of parliament, by limiting the number of officers (both civil and military) in the houfe of commons. Several friends of the mini- fter were ftrongly inclined to favour the bill, and others could not venture to oppofe fo popular a queftion at the eve of a general election.

The motion was alfo fo agreeable to the fenti-ments of many among the Whigs, who ufually fupported government, that the minifter did not ufe his influence on this occafion. He did not even fpeak in the debate, but contented himfelf with giving a filent vote, as he did on the penfion bill. For thefe reafons it was negatived by a very fmall majority of 230 againft 191. * But a fmall majority on this fingle queftion had no effect on the general ftate of parties. It fully proved the judgment of Walpole, in not committing himfelf in fubjects of fo much delicacy, or preffing his adherents to vote in oppofition to popular predi-lections.

But the queftion on which the oppofition founded their principal hopes, if not of fuccefs at leaft of embarraffing the minifter, was a pro-pofal to repeal the feptennial bill, which was firft introduced on this occafion, and afterwards an-nually renewed.

It had been long a matter of furprife, that a queftion which was fo well calculated to increafe their popularity, had not been propofed before. But the fact was, that in this particular inftance

the

* Journals.

Period V. the oppofition was divided. The Tories and Jaco-
1730 to 1734. bites, who had ftrenuoufly refifted the introduction
of the bill, could not obtain the co-operation of
the difaffected Whigs, as it feemed to imply a dereliction of their principles, to vote for the repeal
of a bill which they had once thought neceffary
for the fecurity of the Proteftant fucceffion. At
the repeated inftigations of Bolingbroke, Sir William Wyndham and the leading Tories perfifted,
and at length carried their point. The Whigs
reluctantly complied, and proved, by their manner of conducting the debate, the awkward fituation in which they were placed. The motion
was made by Bromley, and feconded by Sir John
St. Aubyn. The only Whigs of any confequence
who fpoke for the queftion, were Sir John Barnard, who faid only a few words, and Pulteney,
March 13. who rofe late in the debate. He made a fhort
fpeech, and prefaced it with an apology for his
apparent inconfiftency, in voting for the repeal of
a bill which he had fupported at the time of its
introduction.

The fpeech of Sir William Wyndham on this
occafion, is triumphantly quoted by the modern
writers who uniformly ftigmatife the Walpole adminiftration, as a mafter-piece of eloquence and
energy; they ftate his arguments as unanfwerable.
At the fame time thefe partial reporters never advert to the reply of Sir Robert Walpole, but leave
the reader to fuppofe that fcarcely any anfwer was
made,

made, and that the whole strength of the argu-

ment lay on the side of oppofition. *

To abridge or detail printed debates, without
illuftrating them by any new documents, is not
the general purport of this work. But on this
occafion, where there has been fuch a wilful fuppreffion of the argument on one fide, and fuch an
affected difplay of the reafoning on the other, it
will be almoft as great a novelty to give the fpeech
of the minifter, as if it had never been in print.
I have therefore inferted the philippic of Sir
William Wyndham, and Walpole's reply, verbatim from contemporary narratives. †

After a fhort reply to Sir William Yonge, who
preceded him, and juftifying the affertions of Sir
John Barnard, who fpoke in favour of the motion,
Sir William Wyndham vindicated the triennial

bill

VOL. I

---

* Smollett, in recording this tranfaction, has characterifed Sir William Wyndham, by faying that, "His fpeech fpoke him the unri-
valed orator, the uncorrupted Briton, and the unfhaken patriot." He
gives only that part of the fpeech which relates to the character of Walpole, and concludes, "Notwithftanding the moft warm, the moft nervous, the moft pathetic remonftrances in favour of the motion, *the queftion
was put, and it was fuppreffed by mere dint of numbers,* Vol. 2. p. 495.
If Smollett means any thing by this relation, it muft be that no reply was
made to the argument of his admired orator, but that the bufinefs was
got rid of by the cry of, *Queftion! Queftion!* Belfham has thus related
the tranfaction: "The minifter having defied the oppofition to ad-
duce a fingle inftance, in which the interefts of the nation had been injured by the operation of this bill; or, by any undue exercife of the royal
prerogative connected with it, Sir William Wyndham obferved," &c.
After quoting Sir William Wyndham's fpeech, he adds, without
taking the fmalleft notice of Sir Robert Walpole's reply, "Notwithftanding the admiration excited by this fudden burft of eloquence, and
the ability with which the motion of repeal was fupported by various
other fpeakers, it was negatived on the divifion, though not by the
accuftomed minifterial majority, the numbers being 247 againft 184."
† Political State of Great Britain.—Hiftorical Regifter.—See alfo
Chandler.

bill from the objections of those who declared that
it was introduced by the enemies of the revolution,
he added, " The learned gentleman has told us,
that the septennial law is a proper medium be-
.tween the unlimited power of the crown, and the
limitting that power too much; but before he
had fixed upon this as a medium, he should first
have discovered to us the two extremes. I will
readily allow, that an unlimited power in the
crown, with respect to the continuing of parliaments, is one extreme; but the other I cannot
really find out; for I am very far from thinking,
that the power of the crown was too much limited
by the triennial law, or that the happiness of the
nation was any way injured by it, or can ever be
injured by frequent elections. As to the power of
the crown, it is very certain, that as long as the
administration of public affairs is agreeable to the
generality of the people, were they to chuse a new
parliament every year, they would chuse such representatives as would most heartily concur in
every thing with such an administration; so that
even an annual parliament could not be any limitation of the just power of the crown; and as to
the happiness of the nation, it is certain, that
gentlemen will always contend with more heat
and animosity about being members of a long
parliament, than about being members of a short
one; and therefore the elections for a septennial
parliament must always disturb the peace, and,
injure the happiness of the nation, more than the
elections for an annual or triennial parliament: Of
this

this the elections in the city of London, mentioned by my worthy friend, are an evident de-
monstration.

" As to the elections coming on when the nation is in a ferment, it is so far from being an objection to frequent elections, that it is, in my
opinion, a strong argument in favour of them ; because it is one of the chief supporters of the freedom of the nation. It is plain, that the people
seldom or ever were in a ferment, but when encroachments were made upon their rights and
privileges ; and when any such are made, it is
very proper, nay, it is even necessary, that the
people should be allowed to proceed to a new
election, in order that they may chuse such representatives as will do them justice, by punishing those who have been making encroachments
upon them. Otherwise, one of these two effects
may very probably ensue : either the ferment will
break out into an open insurrection, or the encroachment that has been made, may happen to
be forgot before a new election comes on, and
then the invaders of the people's rights will have a
much better lay for getting such a new parliament chosen, as will not only free them from
all punishment, but will confirm the encroachments that have been made, and encourage the
making of new. Thus the rights of the people
may be nibbled and curtailed piecemeal, and ambitious criminals may at last get themselves so
firmly seated, that it will be out of the power of

the people to ftop their career, or to avoid the
chains which they are preparing.

    " Now, to return to the power of the crown,
which the learned gentleman has told us was too
much limited by the triennial law ; I think I have
made it plain, that the juft power of the crown
cannot poffibly be limited by frequent elections,
and confequently could not be too much limited
by the triennial law ; but by long parliaments the
crown may be enabled to affume, and to make
ufe of an unjuft power. By our conftitution, the
only legal method we have of vindicating our
rights and privileges againft the encroachments of
ambitious minifters is by parliament ; the only way
we have of rectifying a weak or wicked adminiftration is by parliament ; the only effectual way
we have of bringing high and powerful criminals
to condign punifhment is by parliament. But if
ever it fhould come to be in the power of the
adminiftration to have a majority of this houfe
depending upon the crown, or to get a majority
of fuch men returned as the reprefentatives of the
people, the parliament will then ftand us in no
ftead. It can anfwer none of thefe great purpofes ;
the whole nation may be convinced of the weaknefs
or the wickednefs of thofe in the adminiftration,
and yet it may be out of the nation's power, in a
legal way, to get the fools turned out, or the
knaves hanged.

    " This misfortune can be brought upon us by
nothing but by bribery and corruption ; and therefore there is nothing we ought to guard more
watchfully

watchfully· againſt. And an honourable gentleman who ſpoke ſome time ago, upon the ſame
ſide with me, has ſo clearly demonſtrated, that
the elections for a ſeptennial parliament are more
liable to be influenced by corruption than thoſe
for a triennial, that I am ſurpriſed his argument
ſhould be miſtaken or not comprehended : but it
ſeems the moſt certain maxims, the plaineſt truths,
are now to be controverted or denied. It has been
laid down as a maxim, and I think it is a moſt
infallible maxim, that a man will contend with
more heat and vigour, for a poſt, either of honour
or profit, which he is to hold for a long term,
than he will do for one he is to hold for a ſhort
term. This has been controverted : it has been
laid down as a maxim, and I think equally infallible, that 100 guineas is a more powerful bribe
than 50 ; this has been denied ; yet neverthelefs
I muſt beg leave to puſh the argument a little
farther.

" Let us ſuppoſe a gentleman at the head of
the adminiſtration, whoſe only ſafety depends
upon corrupting the members of this houſe :
this may now be only a ſuppoſition, but it is
certainly ſuch a one, as may happen ; and if ever
it ſhould, let us ſee if ſuch a miniſter might not
promiſe himſelf more ſuccefs in a ſeptennial, than
he could in a triennial parliament. It is an old
maxim, that every man has his price, if you can
but come up to it : this, I hope, does not hold true
of every man, but I am afraid it too generally
holds true ; and that of a great many it may hold
true,

true, is what I believe was never doubted of, though I don't know but it may now likewife be denied, However, let us fuppofe this diftreffed minifter applying to one of thofe men who has a price, and is a member of this houfe: in order to engage this member to vote as he fhall direct him, he offers him a penfion of £. 1,000 a year. If it be but a triennial parliament, will not the member immediately confider within himfelf, if I accept of this penfion, and vote according to direction, I fhall lofe my character in the country, I fhall lofe my feat in parliament the next election, and my penfion will then of courfe be at an end; fo that by turning rogue I fhall get but £. 3,000, this is not worth my while; and fo the minifter muft either offer him, perhaps double that fum, or otherwife he will probably determine againft being corrupted. But if the parliament were feptennial, the fame man might perhaps fay within himfelf, I am now in for feven years, by accepting of this penfion I fhall have at leaft £. 7,000, this will fet me above contempt; and if I am turned out at next election, I do not value it, I'll take the money in the mean time. Is it not very natural to fuppofe all this; and does not this evidently fhew, that a wicked minifter cannot corrupt a triennial parliament with the fame money with which he may corrupt a feptennial.

"Again, fuppofe this minifter applies to a gentleman who has purchafed, and thereby made himfelf member for a borough, at the rate of, perhaps, £. 1,500, befides travelling charges, and other little

little, expences : suppofe the minifter offers him a penfion of £.500 a year to engage his vote, willt not he naturally confider, if it be a triennial par- liament, that if he cannot get a higher penfion he will lofe money by being a member; and furely, if it be a right burgefs, he will refolve not to fell at all, rather than fell his commodity for lefs than it coft him; and if he finds he cannot fell at all, he will probably give over ftanding a candidate again upon fuch a footing; by which, not only he, but many others, will be induced to give over dealing in corrupting the electors at the next election. But in cafe it be a feptennial parliament, will he not then probably accept of the £.500 penfion, if he be one of thofe men that has a price? becaufe he concludes that for £.1,500, he may always fecure his election; and every parliament will put near £.2,000 in his pocket, befides reimburfing him all his charges. After viewing the prefent queftion in this light, is it poffible not to conclude, that feptennial par- liaments, as well as the elections for fuch, muft always be much more liable to be influenced by corruption than triennial, or elections for trien- nial.

" For my own part, I have been often chofen, I have fat in parliament above thefe twenty years, and I can fay with truth, that neither at my elec- tion, nor after my return, no man ever dared to attempt to let me know what is meant by bri- bery and corruption; but am forry to hear the impoffibility of preventing it mentioned, and men-

S 3 tioned

tioned too within thefe walls. The honourable gentleman who fpoke laft, told us, the evil of corruption was inevitable : if I were fo unhappy as to think fo, I fhould look upon my country to be in the moft melancholy fituation. Perhaps it may be the way of thinking among thofe he keeps company with ; but I thank God I have a better opinion of my countrymen ; and fince it appears to be a way of thinking among fome gentlemen, it is high time for us to contrive fome method of putting it out of their power to corrupt the virtue of the people. For we may depend upon this as a certain maxim, that thofe who think they cannot gain the affections of the people, will endeavour to purchafe their proftitution ; and the beft way to prevent the fuccefs of their endeavours, is to raife the price fo high, as to put it out of the power of any man, or of any fet of men, to come up to it. If a parliament is to be purchafed, if elections are to be purchafed, it is manifeft the corrupting of triennial muft, upon the whole, coft a great deal more than the corrupting of feptennial elections or parliaments. Therefore, in order to put it out of the power of any man, or of any adminiftration, to purchafe the proftitution of a parliament, or of the people, let us return to triennial parliaments ; and if that will not do, let us return to annual elections, which, I am very certain, would render the practice of corruption impoffible. This is now the more neceffary, becaufe of the many new pofts and places of profit which the crown has at its

difpofal,

disposal, and the great civil lift settled upon his prefent majefty, and which will probably be continued
to his fucceffors this; I fay, urges the neceffity
for frequent new parliaments, becaufe the crown
has it now more in their power than formerly, to
feduce the people, or the reprefentatives of the
people, in cafe any future adminiftration fhould
find it neceffary for their own fafety, to do fo.

"That the increafe or decreafe of corruption
at elections, or in parliament, muft always depend upon the increafe or decreafe of virtue
among the people, I fhall readily grant; but it is
as certain, that the virtue of almoft every particular man, depends upon the temptations that are
thrown in his way; and according to the quantity of virtue he has; the quantity of the temptation muft be raifed; fo as at laft to make it an
over-balance for his virtue. Suppofe, then, that
the generality of the electors in England had virtue
enough to withftand a temptation of five guineas
each, but not virtue enough to withftand a temptation of ten guineas one with another. Is it not
then much more probable, that the gentlemen
who deal in corruption, may be able to raife as
much money once every feven years, as will be
fufficient to give ten guineas each, one with another, to the generality of the electors, than that
they will be able to raife fuch a fum once in every
three years? And is it not from thence certain,
that the virtue of the people in general is in greater
danger of being deftroyed by feptennial than by
triennial parliaments? To fuppofe that every man's
vote at an election, is like a commodity, which

S 4   muft

muſt be ſold at the market price, is really to ſuppoſe that no man has any virtue at all. For. I will
aver, that when once a man reſolves to ſell his
vote at any rate, he has then no virtue left, which,
I hope, is not the caſe of many of our electors,
and therefore the only thing we are to apprehend
is, leſt ſo high a price ſhould be offered as may
tempt thouſands to ſell, who had never before any
thoughts of carrying ſuch a commodity to market. This is the fatal event we are to dread, and
it is much more to be dreaded from ſeptennial
than triennial parliaments. If we have, therefore
any deſire to preſerve the virtue of our people; if
we have any deſire to preſerve our conſtitution ;
if we have any deſire to preſerve our liberties, our
properties, and every thing that can be dear to a
free people; we ought to reſtore the triennial law ;
and if that be found to be inſignificant, we ought
to aboliſh prorogations, and return to annual
elections.

" The learned gentleman ſpoke of the prerogative of the crown, and aſked, if it had lately been
extended beyond thoſe bounds preſcribed to it by
law ? I will not ſay that there has been lately any
attempts to extend it beyond the bounds preſcribed by law.; but I will ſay, thoſe bounds have
been of late ſo vaſtly enlarged, that there ſeems
to be no great occaſion for any ſuch attempt.
What are the many penal laws made within theſe
forty years, but ſo many extenſions of the prerogative of the crown, and as many diminutions of
the liberty of the ſubject ? And whatever the neceſſity was that brought us into the enacting of
                                               ſuch

such laws, it was a fatal necessity; it has greatly
added to the power of the crown; and particular
care ought to be taken not to throw any more
weight into that scale.. Perhaps the enacting of
several of those penal laws might have been avoided; I am persuaded the enacting of the law relating to trials for treason, not only might, but
ought to have been avoided; for though it was
but a temporary law, it was a dangerous precedent; and the rebellion was far from being so general in any county, as not to leave a sufficient
number of faithful subjects for trying those who
had committed acts of treason within the county.
In former times the crown had a large estate
of its own; an estate sufficient for supporting the
dignity of the crown; and as we had no standing
armies, nor any great fleets to provide for, the
crown did not want frequent supplies; so that
they were not under any necessity of calling frequent parliaments. And as parliaments were always
troublesome, often dangerous to ministers, therefore they avoided the calling of any such as much
as possible. But though the crown did not then
want frequent supplies, the people frequently
wanted a redress of grievances, which could not
be obtained but by parliament; therefore the
only complaint then was, that the crown either
did not call any parliament at all, or did not allow them to sit long enough. This was the only
complaint; and to remedy this, it was thought
sufficient to provide for having frequent parliaments, every one of which, it was presumed, was
always

always to be a new parliament; for it is well known, that the method of prorogation was of old very rarely made ufe of, and was firft introduced by thofe who were attempting to make encroachments upon the rights of the people.

" But now the cafe is altered. The crown, either by ill management, or by prodigality and profufenefs to its favourites, has fpent or granted away all that eftate; and the public expence is fo much enlarged, that the crown muft have annual fupplies, and is therefore under a neceffity of having the parliament meet every year. But as new elections are always dangerous as well as troublefome to minifters of ftate, they are for having them as feldom as poffible; fo that the complaint is not now for want of frequent meetings or feffions of parliament, but againft having the fame parliament continued too long. This is the grievance now complained of; this is what the people defire; this is what they have a right to have redreffed. The members of parliament may for one year be looked on as the real and true reprefentatives of the people; but when a minifter has feven years to practife on them, and to feel their pulfes, they may be induced to forget whofe reprefentatives they are; they may throw off all dependance upon their electors, and may become dependants upon the crown, or rather upon the minifter for the time being, which the learned gentleman has moft ingenioufly confeffed to us, he thinks lefs dangerous than a dependance upon his electors.

" We

" We have been told in this houfe, that no faith is to be given to prophefies, therefore I fhall not pretend to prophefy; but I may fuppofe a cafe, which, though it has not yet happened, may poffibly happen. Let us then fuppofe a man abandoned to all notions of virtue or honour, of no great family, and of but a mean fortune, raifed to be chief minifter of ftate, by the concurrence of many whimfical events; afraid or unwilling to truft any but creatures of his own making, and moft of them equally abandoned to all notions of virtue and honour; ignorant of the true intereft of his country, and confulting nothing but that of enriching and aggrandizing himfelf and his favourites; in foreign affairs trufting none but fuch whofe education makes it impoffible for them to have fuch knowledge or fuch qualifications as can either be of fervice to their country, or give any weight or credit to their negotiations. Let us fuppofe the true intereft of the nation by fuch means neglected or mifunderftood, her honour and credit loft, her trade infulted, her merchants plundered, and her failors murdered; and all thefe things overlooked, only for fear his adminiftration fhould be endangered. Suppofe him next poffeffed of great wealth, the plunder of the nation, with a parliament of his own chufing, moft of their feats purchafed, and their votes bought at the expence of the public treafure. In fuch a parliament, let us fuppofe attempts made to enquire into his conduct, or to relieve the nation from the diftrefs he has brought upon it; and when

lights

lights proper for attaining thofe ends are called for, not perhaps for the information of the particular gentlemen who call for them, but becaufe nothing can be done in a parliamentary way; until thefe things be in a proper way laid before parliament. Suppofe thefe lights refufed, thefe reafonable requefts rejected by a corrupt majority of his creatures; whom he retains in daily pay, or engages in his particular intereft, by granting them thofe pofts and places which ought never to be given to any but for the good of the public; Upon this fcandalous victory, let us fuppofe this chief minifter pluming himfelf in defiances, becaufe he finds he has got a parliament, like a packed jury, ready to acquit him at all adventures. Let us farther fuppofe him arrived to that degree of infolence and arrogance, as to domineer over all the men of ancient families, all the men of fenfe, figure, or fortune in the nation ; and as he has no virtue of his own, ridiculing it in others, and endeavouring to deftroy or corrupt in all.

" I am ftill not prophefying, I am only fuppofing ; and the cafe I am going to fuppofe, I hope will never happen ; but with fuch a minifter, and fuch a parliament, let us fuppofe a prince upon the throne, either for want of true information, or for fome other reafon, ignorant and unacquainted with the inclinations and the intereft of his people, weak, and hurried away by unbounded ambition and infatiable avarice. This cafe has never happened in this nation ; I hope, I fay, it will never exift ; but as it is poffible it may,

may, could there any greater curfe happen to a
nation, than fuch a prince on the throne, advifed, and folely advifed by fuch a minifter, and
that minifter fupported by fuch a parliament.
The nature of mankind cannot be altered by human laws, the exiftence of fuch a prince, or fuch
a minifter, we cannot prevent by act of parliament; but the exiftence of fuch a parliament I
think we may: and as fuch a parliament is much
more likely to exift, and may do more mifchief
while the feptennial law remains in force, than if
it were repealed, therefore I am moft heartily for
the repeal of it."

After the intervention of a fhort fpeech from
Henry Pelham, and another from Pulteney, Sir
Robert Walpole thus addreffed the chair;

" Sir, I do affure you, I did not intend to have
troubled you in this debate, but fuch incidents
now generally happen towards the end of our debates, nothing at all relating to the fubject, and
gentlemen make fuch fuppofitions, meaning fome
perfon, or perhaps, as they fay, no perfon now in
being, and talk fo much of wicked minifters, domineering minifters, minifters pluming themfelves
in defiances, which terms, and fuch like, have been
of late fo much made ufe of in this houfe, that if
they really mean no body either in the houfe or out
of it, yet it muft be fuppofed they at leaft mean to
call upon fome gentleman in this houfe to make them
a reply; and therefore I hope I may be allowed to
draw a picture in my turn; and I may likewife

fay,

fay, that I do not mean to give a defcription of any particular perfon now in being. When gentlemen talk of minifters abandoned to all fenfe of virtue or honour, other gentlemen may, I am fure, with equal juftice, and, I think, more juftly, fpeak of anti-minifters and mock-patriots, who never had either virtue or honour, but in the whole courfe of their oppofition are actuated only by motives of envy, and of refentment againft thofe who have difappointed them in their views, or may not perhaps have complied with all their defires.

" But now, Sir, let me too fuppofe, and the houfe being cleared, I am fure no perfon that hears me can come within the defcription of the perfon I am to fuppofe. Let us fuppofe in this, or in fome other unfortunate country, an anti-minifter, who thinks himfelf a perfon of fo great and extenfive parts, and of fo many eminent qualifications, that he looks upon himfelf as the only perfon in the kingdom capable to conduct the public affairs of the nation, and therefore chriftening every other gentleman who has the honour to be employed in the adminiftration, by the name of Blunderer. Suppofe this fine gentleman lucky enough to have gained over to his party fome perfons really of fine parts, of ancient families, and of great fortunes, and others of defperate views, arifing from difappointed and malicious hearts; all thefe gentlemen, with refpect to their political behaviour, moved by him, and by him folely;

all

all they fay, either in private or public, being
only a repetition of the words he has put into
their mouths, and a fpitting out that venom
which he has infufed into them; and yet we may
fuppofe this leader not really liked by any, even
of thofe who fo blindly follow him; and hated
by all the reft of mankind. We will fuppofe this
anti-minifter to be in a country where he really
ought not to be, and where he could not have
been but by an effect of too much goodnefs and
mercy, yet endeavouring, with all his might and
with all his art, to deftroy the fountain from.
whence that mercy flowed. In that country fuppofe him continually contracting friendfhips and
familiarities with the embaffadors of thofe princes
who at the time happen to be moft at enmity
with his own; and if at any time it fhould happen
to be for the intereft of any of thofe foreign minifters to have a fecret divulged to them, which
might be highly prejudicial to his native country,
as well as to all its friends; fuppofe this foreign
minifter applying to him, and he anfwering, I
will get it you, tell me but what you want, I
will endeavour to procure it for you : upon this
he puts a fpeech or two in the mouths of fome of
his creatures, or fome of his new converts; what
he wants is moved for in parliament; and when
fo very reafonable a requeft as this is refufed,
fuppofe him and his creatures and tools, by his
advice, fpreading the alarm over the whole nation,
and crying out, gentlemen, our country is at prefent involved in many dangerous difficulties, all
which

Period V.
1730 to 1734

which we would have extricated you from; but a wicked minister and a corrupt majority refused us the proper materials; and upon this scandalous victory, this minister became so insolent as to plume himself in defiances. Let us farther suppose this anti-minister to have travelled, and at every court where he was, thinking himself the greatest minister, and making it his trade to betray the secrets of every court where he had before been; void of all faith or honour, and betraying every master he ever served. I could carry my suppositions a great deal farther, and I may say I mean no person now in being; but if we can suppose such a one, can there be imagined a greater disgrace to human nature than such a wretch as this?

" Now, to be serious, and to talk really to the subject in hand. Though the question has been already so fully and so handsomely opposed by my worthy friend under the gallery, by the learned gentleman near me, and by several others, that there is no great occasion to say any thing farther against it; yet as some new matter has been stated by some of the gentlemen who have since that time spoke upon the other side of the question, I hope the house will indulge me the liberty of giving some of those reasons which induce me to be against the motion. In general I must take notice, that the nature of our constitution seems to be very much mistaken by the gentlemen who have spoken in favour of this motion. It is certain, that our's is a mixed government, and the perfection

perfection of our conftitution confifts in this, that
the 'monarchical, ariftocratical, and democratical
forms of government are mixed and interwoven in
our's, fo as to give us all the advantages of each,
without fubjecting us to the dangers and inconveniences of either. The democratical form of
government, which is the only one I have now occafion to take notice of, is liable to thefe inconveniences, that they are generally too tedious in
their coming to any refolution, and feldom brifk
and expeditious enough in carrying their refolutions into execution : that they are always wavering in their refolutions, and never fteady in any of
the meafures they refolve to purfue ; and that they
are often involved in factions, feditions, and infur-
rections, which expofes them to be made the
tools, if not the prey of their neighbours. Therefore in all the regulations we make, with refpect
to our conftitution, we are to guard, againft running too much into that form of government
which is properly called democratical : this was,
in my opinion, the effect of the triennial law,
and will again be the effect, if ever it fhould be
reftored.

" That triennial elections would make our government too tedious in all their refolves is evident ; becaufe in fuch cafe, no prudent adminiftration would ever refolve upon any meafure of
confequence, till they had felt not only the pulfe
of the parliament, but the pulfe of the people ;
and the minifters of ftate would always labour
under this difadvantage, that as fecrets of ftate

muft

muſt not be immediately divulged, their enemies (and enemies they will always have) would have a handle for expoſing their meaſures, and rendering them diſagreeable to the people, and thereby carrying perhaps a new election againſt them, before they could have an opportunity of juſtifying their meaſures, by divulging thoſe facts and circumſtances from whence the juſtice and the wiſdom of their meaſures would clearly appear.

"Then it is by experience well known, that what is called the populace of every country, are apt to be too much elated with ſucceſs, and too much dejected with every misfortune. This makes them wavering in their opinions about affairs of ſtate, and never long of the ſame mind; and as this houſe is choſen by the free and unbiaſſed voice of the people in general, if this choice were ſo often renewed, we might expect, that this houſe would be as wavering and as unſteady as the people uſually are; and it being impoſſible to carry on the public affairs of the nation without the concurrence of this houſe, the miniſters would always be obliged to comply, and conſequently would be obliged to change their meaſures as often as the people changed their minds.

"With ſeptennial parliaments we are not expoſed to either of theſe misfortunes, becauſe, if the miniſters, after having felt the pulſe of the parliament, which they can always ſoon do, reſolve upon any meaſures, they have generally time enough before the new election comes on, to give the people a proper information, in order to ſhew

them

them, the juftice and the wifdom of the meafures
they have purfued; and if the people fhould at
any time be too much elated, or too much dejected, or fhould without a caufe change their
minds, thofe at the helm of affairs have time to
fet them right, before a new election comes on.

" As to faction and fedition, I will grant, that
in monarchical and ariftocratical governments, it
generally arifes from violence and oppreffion; but
in democratical governments, it always arifes from
the people's having too great a fhare in the government. For in all countries, and in all governments, there always will be many factious and
unquiet fpirits, who can never be at reft, either
in power or out of power. When in power they
are never eafy, unlefs every man fubmits entirely
to their direction; and when out of power, they
are always working and intriguing againft thofe
that are in, without any regard to juftice, or to
the intereft of their country. In popular governments fuch men have too much game, they have
too many opportunities for working upon and
corrupting the minds of the people, in order to
give them a bad impreffion of, and to raife difcontents againft thofe that have the management
of the public affairs for the time; and thefe difcontents often break out into feditions and in-
furrections. This would, in my opinion, be our
misfortune, if our parliaments were either annual
or triennial: by fuch frequent elections, there
would be fo much power thrown into the hands
of the people, as would deftroy that equal mix-

ture,

ture, which is the beauty of our conftitution. In ſhort, our government would really become a democratical government, and might from thence very probably diverge into a tyrannical. Therefore, in order to preferve our conftitution, in order to prevent our falling under tyranny and arbitrary power, we ought to preferve that law, which I really think has brought our conftitution to a more equal mixture, and confequently to a greater perfeƐtion than it was ever in before that law took place.

" As to bribery and corruption, if it were poſſible to influence, by fuch bafe means, the majority of the eleƐtors of Great Britain, to chufe fuch men as would probably give up their liberties; if it were poſſible to influence, by fuch means, a majority of the members of this houfe to confent to the eftablifhment of arbitrary power, I fhould readily allow, that the calculations made by the gentlemen of the other fide were juft, and their inference true ; but I am perfuaded that neither of thefe is poſſible. As the members of this houfe generally are, and muft always be, gentlemen of fortune and figure in their country, is it poſſible to fuppofe, that any of them could by a penfion or a poft be influenced to confent to the overthrow of our conftitution, by which the enjoyment, not only of what he got, but of what he before had, would be rendered altogether precarious. I will allow, that with refpeƐt to bribery, the price muft be higher or lower, generally in proportion to the virtue of the man who is to

be

be bribed; but it muft likewife be granted, that the humour he happens to be in at the time, and the fpirit he happens to be endowed with, adds a great deal to his virtue. When no encroachments are made upon the rights of the people, when the people do not think themfelves in any danger, there may be many of the electors, who, by a bribe of ten guineas, might be induced to vote for one candidate rather than another; but if the court were making any encroachments upon the rights of the people, a proper fpirit would, without doubt, arife in the nation, and in fuch a cafe I am perfuaded that none, or very few, even of fuch electors, could be induced to vote for a court candidate, no not for ten times the fum.

" There may be fome bribery and corruption in the nation, I am afraid there will always be fome. But it is no proof of it that ftrangers are fometimes chofen; for a gentleman may have fo much natural influence over a borough in his neighbourhood, as to be able to prevail with them to chufe any perfon he pleafes to recommend; and if upon fuch recommendation they chufe one or two of his friends, who are perhaps ftrangers to them, it is not from thence to be inferred, that the two ftrangers were chofen their reprefentatives by the means of bribery and corruption.

" To infinuate that money may be iffued from the public treafury for bribing elections, is really fomething very extraordinary, efpecially in thofe gentlemen who know how many checks are upon every fhilling that can be iffued from thence; and

T 3　　　　　　　how

how regularly the money granted in one year for
the fervice of the nation, muſt always be accounted
for the very next feſſions in this houfe, and likewife in the other, if they have a mind to call for
any fuch account. And as to gentlemen in offices,
if they have any advantage over country gentlemen, in having fomething elfe to depend on befides their own private fortunes, they have likewife many difadvantages: they are obliged to live
here at London with their families, by which
they are put to a much greater expence, than
gentlemen of equal fortune who live in the country. This lays them under a very great difadvantage in fupporting their intereſt in the Country.
The country gentleman, by living among the
electors, and purchafing the neceſſaries for his family from them, keeps up an acquaintance and
correſpondence with them, without putting himfelf to any extraordinary charge; whereas a gentleman who lives in London, has no other way of
keeping up an acquaintance and correſpondence
among his friends in the country, but by going
down once or twice a year, at a very extraordinary
expence, and often without any other bufinefs;
fo that we may conclude, a gentleman in office
cannot, even in feven years, fave much for diſtri-
buting in ready money at the time of an election; and I really believe, if the fact were narrowly inquired into, it would appear, that the
gentlemen in office are as little guilty of bribing
their electors with ready money, as any other fet
of gentlemen in the kingdom.

                                        " That

" That there are ferments often raifed among the people without any juft caufe, is what I am furprifed to hear controverted, fince very late experience may convince us of the contrary : do not we know what a ferment was raifed in the nation towards the latter end of the late queen's reign ? And it is well known what a fatal change in the affairs of this nation was introduced, or at leaft confirmed, by an election coming on while the nation was in that ferment. Do not we know what a ferment was raifed in the nation foon after his late majefty's acceffion? And if an election had then been allowed to come on while the nation was in that ferment, it might perhaps have had as fatal effects as the former; but, thank God, this was wifely provided againft by the very law which is now wanted to be repealed.

" It has, indeed, been faid, that the chief motive for enacting that law, now no longer exifts : I cannot admit that the motive they mean was the chief motive ; but even that motive is very far from having entirely ceafed. Can gentlemen imagine, that in the fpirit raifed in the nation not above a twelvemonth fince, Jacobitifm and difaffection to the prefent government had no fhare ? Perhaps fome who might wifh well to the prefent eftablifhment did co-operate, nay, I do not know but they were the firft movers of that fpirit ; but it cannot be fuppofed that the fpirit then raifed fhould have grown up to fuch a fer-

ment, merely from a propofition which was honeftly and fairly laid before the parliament, and
left entirely to their determination! No, the
fpirit was, perhaps, begun by thofe who are truly
friends to the illuftrious family we have now
upon the throne; but it was raifed to a much
greater height than, I believe, even they defigned,
by Jacobites, and fuch as are enemies to our prefent eftablifhment, who thought they never had a
fairer opportunity of bringing about what they
have fo long and fo unfuccefsfully wifhed for, than
that which had been furnifhed them by thofe who
firft raifed that fpirit. I hope the people have
now in a great meafure come to themfelves, and
therefore I doubt not but the next elections will
fhew, that when they are left to judge coolly, they
can diftinguifh between the real and the pretended
friends to the government. But I muft fay, if
the ferment then raifed in the nation had not
already greatly fubfided, I fhould have thought a
new election a very dangerous experiment; and
as fuch ferments may hereafter often happen, I
muft think that frequent elections will always be
dangerous; for which reafon, in fo far as I can
fee at prefent, I fhall, I believe, at all times think
it a very dangerous experiment to repeal the feptennial bill."

It is impoffible at this diftance of time to appreciate exactly the effect of the minifter's fpeech;
but a contemporary writer * afferts, that it was
one

* Tindal.

one of the beſt he ever made. The fate of theſe two ſpeeches is ſingular: Sir William Wyndham, by his diſreſpectful alluſions to the king, drew on himſelf a reproof, the juſtice of which neither himſelf or his friends have endeavoured to diſprove. It was conſidered as an intemperate effuſion, and did not loſe the miniſter a ſingle ſupporter in parliament, or a ſingle adherent in the country; yet it has been carefully inſerted by party writers, calling themſelves hiſtorians, while that of the miniſter has been no leſs invidiouſly ſuppreſſed,

Walpole's ſpeech, as far as it relates to that perſonality which ſeems to be the recommending characteriſtic of the other, has certainly leſs claim to be recorded, becauſe the character and ſituation of Bolingbroke, contraſted with his own, are leſs able to give permanence and publicity to invective. The faults of an ex-miniſter, or aſpiring leader of a party, are leſs intereſting, to the community, than thoſe of the man who holds the reins of government. But the immediate reſult of Walpole's unpremeditated reply to this ſtudied attack, was a ſenſe of ſhame in the oppoſition Whigs, and of indignation in the principal Tories, which interrupted their cordial union. Several Whigs re-united themſelves to the miniſter, and the leading Tories, aſhamed of appearing the puppets of Bolingbroke, though they continued to thwart and oppoſe the meaſures of government, did not, of themſelves, bring forward any new queſtion during the remainder of the ſeſſion.

It

It may not perhaps be improper in this place to obferve, that the fenfation which Walpole's fpeech made in the houfe of commons, and the effect which it had out of doors, in developing the intrigues of Bolingbroke with the oppofition in England, and of laying open his cabals with foreign courts and minifters, were the immediate caufe, that he quitted this country, and retired to France. Pulteney, who faw and appreciated the fatal confequences of his unpopularity among the Whigs, to which party he himfelf was always cordially attached, bitterly complained that Sir William Wyndham received too implicitly the dictates of Bolingbroke. With a view therefore to remove this ftigma from oppofition, he recommended to him a temporary retirement from England. Bolingbroke was extremely mortified, that all his repeated profeffions of honour, virtue, and difintereftednefs, did not gain credit; he found himfelf reduced to the moft wretched fituation which an afpiring mind like his could fuffer, that of being excluded from a fhare in the legiflature, and heading a party in continued oppofition, without the fmalleft hopes of ever being reftored to his feat in the houfe of lords. In his letters to Sir William Wyndham, he feelingly defcribes his own fituation, "I am ftill," he fays, "the fame profcribed man, furrounded with difficulties, expofed to mortifications, and unable to take any fhare in the fervice, but that which I have taken hitherto, and which, I think, you would not perfuade me to take in the prefent ftate of things.

My

My part is over, and he who remains on the ftage
after his part is over, deferves to be hiffed off." *

In confequence of thefe fentiments, he waited
until the meeting of the new parliament, when a
large majority ftill fupporting the minifter, during
whofe continuance in power he had no chance of
obtaining a complete reftoration, he followed
the advice of **Pulteney**, and retired in difguft to
France.

The adverfaries of the minifter had taken advantage of the inflamed ftate of the public mind,
to circulate reports, both in their fpeeches and
writings, that the liberties of the fubject were in
danger, and that he had planned a regular fyftem
of oppreffion, which, if not refifted, would erect
a defpotic and arbi rary power on the ruins of the
Britifh conftitution.

The fpeech which Walpole compofed for the
king, on the diffolution of the parliament, was
calculated to counteract thefe reports, and to conciliate the public. It was full of fentiments which
none but a free nation could underftand and appreciate ; fentiments which do honour to the minifter who compofed it, to the king who uttered
it, to the parliam ent who heard it, and to the
people who applauded it.

" The profperity and glory of my reign depend
upon the affections and happinefs of my people,
and the happinefs of my people upon my preferving to them all the legal rights and privileges,
as eftablifhed under the prefent fettlement of the
crown

---

* Lord Bolingbroke to Sir William Wyndham, Paris, November 29, 1735.—Correfpondence, Period III. Article Bolingbroke.

crown in the Proteftant line. A due execution and ftrict obfervance of the laws, are the beft and only fecurity both to fovereign and fubject : their intereft is mutual and infeparable, and therefore their endeavours for the fupport of each other ought to be equal and reciprocal. Any infringement or encroachment upon the rights of either is a diminution of the ftrength of both, which, kept within their due bounds and limits, make that juft balance, which is neceffary for the honour and dignity of the crown, and for the protection and profperity of the people. What depends upon me, fhall, on my part, be religioufly kept and obferved, and I make no doubt of receiving the juft returns of duty and gratitude from them." *

CHAPTER THE FORTY-THIRD:

1733—1734.

View of Foreign Tranfactions from the Death of Auguftus the Second to the Diffolution of Parliament.—Succefsful Hoftilities of France, Spain, and Sardinia, againft the Emperor.—Neutrality of the Dutch.—Caufes which induced England to reject the Application of the Emperor for Succours.

IF any man ever deferved the appellation of minifter of peace, that man was Sir Robert Walpole. The foreign tranfactions of this eventful period will fufficiently verify that affertion. Yet it cannot be denied, that peace itfelf may be dearly purchafed by the dereliction of national honour, by the breach of treaties, by permitting the lofs

* Chandler, vol. 8. p. 248. Journals.

of dominions to thofe whom it is our intereft to fupport, and the aggrandifement of thofe whom it is our intereft to deprefs. And it muft be confeffed, that if any cenfure can be juftly thrown on the pacific fyftem adopted by Walpole, it muft be thrown on the inactivity of England at this critical juncture; in her refufal to affift the Emperor, againft the united arms of France, Spain, and Sardinia; in fuffering the Spanifh branch of the houfe of Bourbon to wreft from the houfe of Auftria, Naples, and Sicily; and, what was ftill more hoftile to the interefts of Great Britain, in permitting the acceffion of Loraine and Bar to France. For if it be allowed, that any merit is due for preferving this country and Europe from a general War, that merit is due to Walpole; fo on the other hand, it cannot be denied, that if any blame can be imputed to the cabinet for tamenefs and pufillanimity, that blame muft alfo attach folely to him; as he alone ftood forth in oppofition to the king and part of the cabinet, and by refufing to affift the Emperor, maintained his country in peace.

I fhall confine myfelf at prefent to a brief deduction of the facts and negociations which preceded and followed the death of Auguftus the Second, interfperfed with fuch obfervations as may tend to elucidate his conduct, and difplay the motives that induced the minifter of finance to abftain from entering into offenfive operations againft France, and to fuffer the aggrandifement of the houfe of Bourbon, and the depreffion of the houfe

houſe of Auſtria; which proved afterwards ſo fatal to the intereſt of England, and of which we
now experience the evil effects. In making this
deduction, it is not my intention either to cenſure
or to commend, but ſimply to ſtate the ſum and
ſubſtance of the motives, which the papers in my
poſſeſſion have enabled me to aſſign for his
conduct.

Pacific ſtate
of Europe.

For a term of twenty years, Europe had enjoyed
an unexampled ſtate of tranquillity, only broken
by petty hoſtilities between Spain and England
in 1718 and 1727. This tranquillity had been
owing to the temporary ſeparation between France
and Spain, to the reciprocal intereſts of France
and England in the maintenance of peace, and
to the good intelligence between the two ca-
binets.

But the reconciliation between France and
Spain, and the re-union of England and Auſtria,
by the treaty of Vienna, had ſcarcely taken place,
before the jealouſies between the two nations began to revive; their counſels were no longer
guided by the ſame mutual good will and harmony. The efforts to give a king to Poland, on

February 1.

the death of Auguſtus the Second, the indignation of Elizabeth Farneſe againſt the Emperor, for
having deceived her in not accompliſhing the
marriage between her ſon, Don Carlos, and an
archducheſs, and the diſputes which aroſe concerning the ſucceſſion of Tuſcany and Parma, kin-
dled a war between the houſes of Auſtria and
Bourbon, which would have become general,

had

had not Walpole prevented the diffusion of hostilities.

The death * of Augustus the Second had no
sooner been announced, than Louis the Fifteenth
determined to support the claims of his father-in-
law to the crown of Poland, in defiance of the
Emperor and Russia, who favoured the elector of
Saxony, son of the deceased monarch. He declared
to all the foreign embassadors, that he would not
suffer any power to oppose the freedom of election in Poland. This declaration implied, that
he expected no opposition to be made to the election of Stanislaus, because the influence of France
in Poland was so great, as to preclude the choice
of any other candidate. And as Spain was prepared to act offensively against the Emperor, and
the king of Sardinia was on the point of concluding an alliance with France and Spain, Walpole had a difficult and delicate part to act. He
was no less anxious than the Emperor or Russia,
to exclude Stanislaus; and yet he was unwilling
to offend France, by taking an open and active
share in his exclusion. He was no less zealous
to promote the election of Augustus, in return for
his guaranty of the pragmatic sanction. But as
he was determined to decline entering into a war,

if

Consequences
of the death of
Augustus the
Second.

Conduct of
France:

Of England.

---

* The substance of this chapter is taken from the dispatches of Horace Walpole, lord Harrington, the duke of Newcastle, and Thomas
Robinson; Walpole, Orford, and Grantham Papers. Also from several papers drawn up by Horace Walpole, particularly, " Reflections on the present state of affairs, October 8, 1733."—" Conduct
of England, with regard to what has passed in Poland, since the death
of king Augustus, and the transactions in other parts relative thereto,
extracted from the correspondence with his majesty's ministers in foreign parts," from February to November 1733. " Continuation of
the Conduct, &c." from November 1733 to July 1734.

if it could be declined with honour, his conduct evinced the moft confummate addrefs and prudence.

Although the affurances to fecond the pretenfions of the elector, and to exclude Staniflaus, were as ftrong as words could exprefs; yet every declaration was avoided which feemed to imply, in the moft diftant degree, the co-operation of force. To the Czarina, who announced her inclination to unite with the king and the Emperor in filling the vacancy, and hoped that the choice would not fall on Staniflaus, or any French prince, it was replied, that the king would ufe his endeavours for the election of an unexceptionable perfon, and would fecond the Czarina's difpofition to fecure the public tranquillity.

To the Emperor, who declared his refolution to fupport the freedom of election, according to the conftitution of Poland, which expreffions were conftrued as meaning an exclufion of Staniflaus, and who requefted that the Englifh minifter at Warfaw might act in concert with him, Ruffia, and Pruffia, every affurance was given, that the king of England approved the refolution of promoting a new and free election in favour of an unexceptionable prince, and would forward the fame defign, as far as could be done by good offices. It was alfo urged that Mr. Woodward, the minifter at Drefden, fhould contribute as much as poffible to the fame views; and if any complaint fhould be afterwards made, that he had acted lefs warmly than might be expected againft

6   Staniflaus,

Staniflaus, he was to alledge, as an excufe, the un-
willingnefs of the king to give fuch an offence to
France, without advantage to himfelf or his allies,
and the fmall influence the king could expect to
have in the affairs of that diftant kingdom.

· At the fame time the king ordered his minifter
at Warfaw to give the ftrongeft affurances of his
affection and friendfhip towards that republic.
He was to declare upon all occafions, in the king's
name, for a free election, in favour of any prince,
who was not difpleafing. to the neighbouring
powers, and in whom the Poles might find a fecurity for their liberties. He was to act in concert with the minifters of the Emperor and the
Czarina, and affift them in obtaining the election
of Auguftus; but he was to act with the utmoft
difcretion and moderation, not to join in giving
the exclufion to any perfon, except the Pretender
or his children. He was to oppofe Staniflaus, but
not in fuch a manner as might give offence, though
he need not conceal his wifhes in favour of the
party efpoufed by the Emperor and his allies. If
any encouragement was given to the Pretender, he
was to proteft againft it, and leave the kingdom.

The Britifh cabinet carried their caution on this
occafion to the higheft degree of delicacy. The
Imperial minifters delivered to Mr. Robinfon * a
paper, importing, that France appearing determined to break the peace, a rupture might be
prevented by a ftrict union between the Emperor
and

* July 15, Walpole Papers.

and his allies. For this reason the Emperor defired to concert meafures with England and the
United Provinces, either for deterring France, or
for repelling hoftilities. The Emperor, it was
urged, had amply provided Luxemburgh, but
the remaining part of the Netherlands fhould be
jointly fecured, and the empire protected. The
concurrence of the king of England was expected,
becaufe he had *approved* all the meafures and
fentiments adopted by the Imperial court, in
regard to the Polifh election. In reply to thefe
infinuations, Mr. Robinfon was ordered to obferve, that this expreffion might be underftood as
if the king had actually *approved* the exclufion of
Staniflaus by force, that fuch an infinuation ought
not to pafs unnoticed, becaufe it was directly
contrary to the moft pofitive affurances, which had
been tranfmitted from England to the Britifh
minifter at Vienna; that the king was fo far from
having approved any defign to commit hoftilities
in Poland, that he never could believe the Emperor had entertained fuch a defign, and that he
had always declared for a free election. The truth
of this ftatement was acknowledged by the court
of Vienna; and Mr. Robinfon was again directed
to diffuade them from purfuing fuch meafures as
might caufe difturbances in Europe. Thefe ftrong
and repeated remonftrances finally prevailed on
the Emperor, not openly to employ force, but to
leave that part to the Czarina.

   In conformity to the fame principle, the Britifh
minifters at Warfaw and Vienna expreffed the
difappro-

disapprobation of the king, that the Imperial
minister at Warsaw accompanied the Russian embassador when he notified the resolution of the Czarina to exclude Stanislaus by force, and when the Emperor was solicitous to engage England in a treaty of mutual defence with Russia, the answer of the king implied, that he was ready to conclude a treaty of friendship with the Czarina, but would not agree that it should contain defensive stipulations, or engagements to assist her, if she should be attacked in Europe on account of the transactions of Poland.

During these transactions, the election took place in Poland. The French party so far prevailed in favour of Stanislaus, who in 1710 had been declared for ever incapable of being elected king of Poland, that a majority of the diet of convocation entered into a confederation to choose no one but a native, born of Roman Catholick parents, who possessed no sovereignty out of Poland, and was not supported by any foreign troops beyond the frontiers. In consequence of this resolution, which was declaring in his favour, Stanislaus secretly passed into Poland, made his appearance at Warsaw, and was chosen by the diet of election, which assembled on the 12th of September. Against this election, the Saxon party came forward, supported by a Russian army which entered Warsaw without resistance. The adherents of Stanislaus were dispersed, he himself fled to Dantzic, and the partizans of Augustus

Election of Stanislaus: April.

Counter-election of Augustus.

U 2 assembled

France, Spain, and Sardinia, declare war againſt the Emperor.

affembled at Wola, the plain of election near Warſaw, and proclaimed him king of Poland.

The indignation of Louis the Fifteenth, was not appeaſed by the profeſſions of the Emperor, that he had not acted offenſively againſt Staniſlaus, becauſe he had ſent no troops into Poland; but arguing that the co-operation of his miniſter at Warſaw with the Ruſſian and Saxon miniſters, and the aſſembling of 6,000 men on the frontiers of Poland, were the ſame as if he had openly employed force, declared war againſt him, in conjunction with Spain and Sardinia.

Their fuccefsful operations.

The declaration of war on the part of the three allied powers, was followed by inſtant hoſtilities. The French army, under Marſhal Berwick, took the fort of Kehl, and invaded Germany; another corps, under the count of Belle Iſle, overran Loraine.

The Emperor claims the aſſiſtance of England.

Nov. 1/15

The Emperor, in a memorial delivered by Count Kinſki, his embaſſador in London, claimed the ſuccours ſtipulated by the laſt treaty of Vienna, and claimed them in a manner which ſhewed his conviction, that England could not in juſtice refuſe them. In fact, he had many reaſons to ſuppoſe that he ſhould obtain the required aſſiſtance. For notwithſtanding the precautions which the Engliſh cabinet had taken to diſſuade the Emperor from uſing force in Poland, they at the ſame time ſecretly employed every effort to obtain the excluſion of Staniſlaus, the validity of whoſe election the Engliſh miniſter at Warſaw

refuſed

refufed to acknowledge. They had been highly inftrumental in promoting the conclufion of the alliance between the Emperor and Auguftus, by which the Emperor, in return for the guaranty of the pragmatic fanction, promifed affiftance to pro-cure his free nomination to the throne of Poland, in oppofition to the partizans of Staniflaus, and to fupport him, if chofen, by force of arms.

The king was decidedly in favour of affifting the Emperor; the queen, though defirous of up-holding the pacific fyftem of Walpole, did not venture to oppofe his wifhes ; and lord Harrington, who, as fecretary of ftate, principally conducted the negotiation with the court of Vienna, was inclined to the fame opinion.

In this crifis of affairs, Walpole ftood in a very delicate fituation, and was reduced to a difagree-able alternative. On one fide, he was to oppofe the earneft wifhes of the king, to act in contra-diction to the fentiments of part of the cabinet, and at the fame time to appear as if he was abet-ting the degradation of the houfe of Auftria, and promoting the aggrandifement of the houfe of Bourbon. On the other fide, he was to plunge the nation into a war for the oftenfible purpofe of giving a king to Poland, in which England had no immediate concern, in oppofition, perhaps, to the public opinion, and at the eve of a general election. But as he had for fome time forefeen that he fhould be reduced to follow one of thefe difagree-able alternatives, he had previoufly collected all

V 3   the

the information neceſſary ·to regulate his deciſion, and to enable him to purſue that conduct which ſeemed liable to the feweſt inconveniences.

The Emperor had been repeatedly exhorted to put the Auſtrian Netherlands in a ſtate of defence; from a certain apprehenſion, that unleſs that was ·effected, the barrier would be expoſed, and · the Dutch ſo alarmed, from the danger of being over-run by the French, that they would never have the ſpirit to act with vigour, in co-operation with England. But inſtead of hearkening to theſe juſt remonſtrances, Luxemburgh was alone provided with the neceſſary means of defence; the fortifi-·cations in the other parts were left in a moſt de-fenceleſs ſtate, and the care of them conſigned to the Engliſh and Dutch; a care which, the greffier Fagell obſerved in a letter to Bruyninx, "The Dutch, not yet recovered from the expences of the late war, *could not*, and the Engliſh *would not* take upon themſelves."

The Emperor had alſo been repeatedly exhorted to conclude a defenſive alliance with the king of Sardinia, who was ſtrongly inclined to prefer his friendſhip to that of France and Spain; and his co-operation, which, inſtead of opening to the French the key of Italy, would have excluded them from that country, might have been obtain-ed by trifling ſacrifices. But the emperor had, either from his uſual dilatorineſs, or from an un-willingneſs to cede any portion of the Milaneſe, declined engaging on his ſide ſo important an ally,

until

until it was too late; and Charles Emanuel* apologized to the king of England, that he had been
reluctantly compelled, for his own safety and intereft, to clofe with the offers of France and Spain,
becaufe the Emperor had refufed to comply with
his terms. In confequence of this imprudent neglect, and a total inattention to the common means
of defence, his Italian dominions were incapable
of refifting the inroads of the combined powers.

Chapter 43;
1733 to 1734.

The fituation of the United Provinces did not
afford the fmalleft profpect of inducing them to
engage in offenfive operations. The leading men
were offended with the king of England, for having given the princefs Anne in marriage to the
prince of Orange, without previous notice, and
were fufpicious that he was attempting to revive
the office of ftadtholder. The dread of being expofed to a French invafion, fhould they take an
active part in favour of the Emperor, was fo great,
that the ftates general were inclined to accept the
offers of France, to conclude a neutrality for the
Auftrian Netherlands, and to agree not to affift
the Emperor, in confequence of any events which
related to the Polifh election. Repeated remonftrances had been ineffectually made from the Britifh cabinet, againft this precipitate meafure.

State of the United Provinces.

At length Walpole, anxious to obtain the co-
operation of a power, without whom England
could not venture to act, fent his brother Horace†

Miffion of Horace Walpole to the Hague.

to

---

* Walpole papers. Letter from the King of Sardinia to George
the Second, March, 1734. Coriefpondence.

† Horace Walpole's Apology and Difpatches,

to the Hague, though not in an official capacity, for the purpofe of conciliating the leading men, over whom he had great influence, and of perfuading the ftates general to adopt a more manly and

decifive conduct. On his arrival at the Hague, he found things in a very indifferent fituation; the people in general were much diffatisfied, not only with the conduct of the court of Vienna, but with that of England, upon a miftaken notion, that the king was labouring, out of partiality to the Emperor, to force them into the prefent war, and was endeavouring to promote the interefts of the prince of Orange, at the expence of the Dutch conftitution.

The news of the miffion of the minifter's brother had an inftantaneous effect in raifing the hopes of the Imperial court*, and gave a convincing proof that the cabinet of London were ferious in their wifhes to affift the Emperor, if it could be done without endangering the fecurity of England. It however had no other confequences than to reftore the confidence between the two nations, and to conciliate the leading men in Holland. For the Dutch were fo difpirited with the defencelefs ftate of the Netherlands, fo difgufted with the conduct of the Emperor, and fo averfe to refume the burthens of war, that he could not bring them to adopt vigorous meafures, or to countenance the fmalleft hopes of joining in offencive operations.†

The

---

* Mr. Robinfon to Lord Harrington, May 11th, 1733. Grantham Papers.

† Journal of Horace Walpole. Walpole Papers.

The internal fituation of England was no lefs unfavourable to an immediate breach with France; a long period of peace and tranquillity had increaf- ed commerce, agriculture, and the refources of the country. The landed proprietors were highly fatisfied with the diminution of the land tax, the monied men were no lefs pleafed with deferring the payment of the national debt, the Jacobites were daily decreafing; the Tories, though perfonally hoftile to the minifter himfelf, began to experience the comforts of good order, derived from a fettled government. Confidence in government had taken place of diftruft; and the ftate of the country, both at home and abroad, exhibited the ftrongeft fymptoms of ftability and credit. Walpole faw and appreciated thefe happy effects, derived from external peace and internal tranquillity; he was unwilling to rifk the unpopularity of impofing new burthens; he was well aware that a war with France would renew the hopes and excite the efforts of the fallen party, and realife his conftant prediction, that the crown of England would be fought for on Britifh ground.

The refult which he drew from this combination of circumftances and events was, that it would be highly imprudent to involve the country in hoftilities, without the co-operation of Holland. He was fully convinced that the nation would not readily approve a war for a Polifh election; and that parliament would not be inclined to grant fufficient fupplies for fo chimerical and diftant a project.

He

Prudence of
Walpole. . ..

He did not think it prudent, however, to oppofe at once the decided opinion. of the king, who
was eager for a war. He infinuated the neceffity of
temporifing, till a new parliament was chofen, and
the nation could be roufed to a fenfe of the danger which would arife from the aggrandizement of
the houfe of Bourbon, and until the people were
made capable of judging, that the only foundation upon which the liberties of Europe could fub-
fift, was the indivifibility of a power like the houfe
of Auftria, fufficient to be oppofed to the houfe of
Bourbon*.

It was not however without great difficulty that
he obtained the confent of the king and cabinet
to adopt a line of conduct, which appeared no lefs
pufilanimous in itfelf, than oppofite to the tenour
of the laft treaty concluded at Vienna. But he
gained his point by firmnefs and perfeverance; by
inculcating the neceffity of mature deliberation,
and of avoiding extremities till it fhould appear
that the meafures were no lefs practicable than advantageous: and he confidered it prudent to feel
the pulfe of public opinion, which ought always
to be confulted in cafes of fuch extreme importance as a declaration of war.

Anfwer to the
Emperor.

In confequence of this determination, an anfwer was returned to the requeft of fuccours, made
by the Imperial court, to the following import,
that the king was concerned to fee the peace broken, and the Emperor attacked; that he had hitherto

* Mr. Robinfon to Mr. Pelham, Vienna, November 11, 1733.
Grantham Papers.

therto employed his beft offices, though unfuccefſ-
fully, to prevent the rupture, and would now ufe
all poffible means to accommodate matters. That
the motives hitherto alledged for the commiffion
of hoftilities, being founded upon Polifh affairs,
in which the king had taken no part,. but that of
ufing his good offices, it was far from being clear,
that he was obliged, purely upon that account,
to enter into the quarrel. That as to the demand
of fuccours, the king, though always ready: to
execute his engagements, and fhew his particular
friendfhip for the Emperor, muft yet be fatisfied
that the demand was founded on pofitive engagements, before he involved his people in a war.
He muft therefore, carefully examine the allegations on both fides, and confult his allies, particularly the States General, and put himfelf in
fuch a pofture, as might enable him to provide
effectually for his own fecurity,.and for the execution of his engagements.

The Emperor, highly indignant at the back- Artful policy
of the Em-
wardnefs of the cabinet, projected an expedient peror.
which feemed. calculated to forward the ac-
complifhment of his views. Well knowing the
averfion of England to the marriage between an
archduchefs and a prince of the houfe of Bourbon,
and the remonftrances which had been made to
him on that fubject, not only during the time
when he was at variance with England, but even
lately by Mr. Robinfon, in the ftrongeft manner,
on the mere rumour that fuch a meafure was in
agitation; he affected to open a negotiation with
                                        Spain,

Spain, to renew the propofal of a marriage between his fecond daughter and Don Carlos.

On the arrival of a courier from Vienna*, count Kinfki painted in the ftrongeft colours to the king, the great uneafinefs and danger of the Emperor's fituation; his inability to refift fingly the united arms of France, Spain, and Sardinia, and at the fame time the little dependance to be placed upon the king of Pruffia. He ftated the unpromifing conduct of feveral other princes of the empire, and the neutrality already accepted by fome of them, together with the ftrong indications of a refolution and concert among feveral, even of the electors, to prevent the empire itfelf from taking any part; and laftly, the defpair of affift-ance from the States General. He concluded thefe reprefentations with infifting in the Em-peror's name, that the king fhould no longer defer explaining his intention, but fhould immediately give a pofitive promife to come, the very next campaign, to his affiftance; without this promife, he infinuated, the Emperor muft comply with the demands of Spain, in giving his fecond daughter in marriage to Don Carlos, as the only means ftill in his power, for extricating himfelf and family from their prefent difficulties, for preventing the deftruction of the houfe of Auftria, and for pre-ferving the equilibrium in Europe.

Defeated by Walpole.
This artful expedient, however, did not fucceed. Walpole had not been fo much alarmed on a former

* Continuation of the conduct of England, &c. January 1734. Walpole Papers.

former occasion, at the rumour of such a marriage, as lord Townshend and the other ministers,
and he now conceived that matters were considerably changed. He conjectured that the Emperor
only threw out this infinuation, with a view to
alarm England, rather than with a determination
to adopt the meafure; and he was of opinion,
that even if the Emperor fhould be in earneft,
provided the eldeft of the archduchefses was
affianced to the duke of Loraine, the marriage of
the fecond with Don Carlos would not be productive of great difadvantages. In all events, to
ufe his own expreffions, " Circumftances change;
" things diftant and uncertain muft yield to
" prefent and certain dangers *."

In conformity with thefe fentiments, orders
were immediately difpatched to Mr. Robinfon, to
explain to the Imperial court, the feveral reafons
which made it impoffible for the king, even if the
Emperor's claim of fuccours was well founded, to
come fo foon as was expected to his affiftance. He
was at the fame time to declare, that the king no
longer oppofed the marriage of the fecond archduchefs with Don Carlos, it being reprefented to
him as the only means left for retrieving the Emperor's affairs, by detaching Spain from France.
Mr. Robinfon was, however, to infift, that nothing
fhould be concluded in this affair, without the
king's intervention, and that due precautions
fhould be taken for preventing the dangers that
might

* Among the Orford Papers, I find fome reflections on this fubject,
written by Sir Robert Walpole. They are without date or fignature,
but they were undoubtedly made at this period. See Correfpondence.

might be apprehended to the liberties of Europe from fuch an alliance; amongſt which, he was to inſinuate, that the marrying of the eldeſt arch-duchefs to the duke of Loraine, under the gua-ranty of Spain, was looked upon as one of the moſt effectual ſecurities.

The king offers his mediation.

. About the ſame time, finding the Dutch utterly averſe to encounter the burthens and dangers of a war, and anxious to 'prevent them from throwing themſelves into the arms of France, the miniſter enforced the abſolute neceſſity of acceeding to the neutrality, in compliance with their earneſt wiſhes. The king exhorted the Emperor to acquieſce in the neutrality for the Netherlands, and offered his mediation, in conjunction with the States General, to bring about an accommodation, and to reſtore peace.

Indignation of the Em-peror.

The declaration in favour of the marriage, which was ſuppoſed to be ſo contrary to the wiſhes of the Engliſh cabinet, and the tender of good offices only inſtead of effectual ſuccours, ſo highly irri-tated the Emperor, that his anſwer to both theſe propoſitions, contained no leſs haughtineſs and ſpirit, than if the affairs of the houſe of Auſtria had been in the moſt proſperous ſituation.

The declaration concerning the marriage, made a ſimilar impreſſion on all the imperial miniſters, They treated the ſuppoſition, that the Emperor had ever entertained the leaſt thought of marrying his ſecond daughter to the duke of Parma, as in-jurious; they even affected to doubt that Kinſki had ever ſpoken in the manner imputed to him.

And

And in the 'anfwer which was delivered by the Chapter 43.
Emperor's order to Mr. Robinfon, upon the 18th 1730 to 1734.
of February, the Emperor declared, in the moft
folemn terms, that he never had any thoughts,
nor ever would condefcend to purchafe peace on
thofe terms, and formally difavowed. Kinfki, and
all others who might ever have given the leaft hint
of that kind, declaring his determined refolution
to defend himfelf to the laft extremity.

In anfwer to the offer of good offices, the
Emperor peremptorily rejected the propofal of a
neutrality for the Netherlands; declared his firm
refolution of fupporting his caufe by force of arms,
and fo far from temporifing, he threatened the
Dutch to remove the war into Flanders, by attacking France on the fide of Luxemburgh.

With a view of rendering the interpofition of Meeting of
England more effectual, and giving weight to the Parliament.
propofal of good offices, Walpole had recourfe to
his ufual method of preventive meafures, and
adopted the refolution of putting the country in a
refpectable pofture of defence, tempering caution
with fpirit, and deliberation with energy. The
fpeech from the throne, on the opening of the
feffion, correfponded with thefe principles. After
recommending the utmoft prudence and precaution, and exhorting parliament to weigh and
confider circumftances thoroughly, before a final
determination was taken, to act in concert with
the States General, and to avoid precipitate declarations; the king added, " In the mean time,
I am perfuaded you will make fuch provifions as
fhall

shall secure my kingdoms, rights, and possessions from all dangers and insults, and maintain the respect due to the British nation: whatever part it may in the end be most reasonable for us to act, it will, in all views, be necessary, when all Europe is preparing for arms, to put ourselves in a proper posture of defence. As this will best preserve the peace of the kingdom, so it will give us a due weight and influence in whatever measures we shall take in conjunction with our allies. But should the defence of the nation not be sufficiently provided for, it will make us disregarded abroad, and may prove a temptation and encouragement to the desperate views of those, who never fail to flatter themselves with the hopes of great advantages from public troubles and disorders *."

* Journals. Chandler.

PERIOD THE SIXTH:

From the Diffolution of Parliament, to the Death
of Queen CAROLINE.

1734—1737.

CHAPTER THE FORTY-FOURTH:

1734—1735.

*Succefsful Operations of the Allies.—Embaffy of Horace Walpole to the
Hague.—Indignation of the Emperor, and his Attempts to remove
Walpole.—Origin, Progrefs, and Termination of the Secret Con-
vention.—Renewal of Hoftilities.—Fluctuating State of the Britifh
Cabinet.—Embarraffments and Firmnefs of Walpole.*

THE Emperor expofed, without the affift- Succefs of
ance of a fingle ally, to the united arms of $^{the\ allies.}$
France, Spain, and Sardinia, was reduced to a
moft difaftrous fituation. The Milanefe was wholly
fubdued by the allied forces; the victory of Bi- May 5.
tonto fecured to Don Carlos the conqueft of
Naples and Sicily; and Mantua, the only poffeffion which remained to the Emperor in Italy, was
threatened with a fiege, and unable to hold out for
any length of time. In Germany, the Imperial
forces, though commanded by Eugene, were too
inferior to refift the operations of the French; the
capture of Treves, Traerbach, and Philipfburgh,

opened

opened to the French the entrance into the Empire, and Eugene was compelled to act on the
defensive.

Preparations
in England.

This difaftrous fituation of the Auftrian affairs,
alarmed the Britifh cabinet, and though the
minifter was firmly refolved to avoid hoftilities,
yet he faw the immediate neceffity of augmenting
the forces, both in England and Holland, and to
be at all events prepared for war.

The great object was, to fecure the concurrence
of the United Provinces, and to prevail on them
to act in concert with England, that the mediation
of the two maritime powers might be accepted by
the Emperor, and refpected by France and her
allies.

Embaffy of
Horace
Walpole to
the Hague.

In order to obtain the co-operation of Holland,
Horace Walpole had been again difpatched to the
Hague, with the character of embaffador extra-

July 27, 1734. ordinary, and had warmly preffed the States
General to augment their forces; and although
his reprefentations had not been attended with due
effect, yet he had confiderably removed the jealoufy
and difagreement which had recently arifen between the two maritime powers, and gave hopes
that his attempts might prove fuccefsful.

Remon-
ftrances of
the Emperor:

While thefe tranfactions were paffing between
the king and the Republic, under the promife of
inviolable fecrecy on both fides, frequent memorials
were prefented by count Kinfki, calling upon the
king in the ftrongeft manner, to fulfil his engagements towards the Emperor, by fending inftantly
the moft effectual fuccours.

'Although

Although no specific answer could be returned whilst the negotiation at the Hague was depending, yet previous intimations had been given to the Imperial court, that no immediate assistance could be expected from England in the present situation of affairs.

But as soon as the negotiation was brought to a conclusion, and it was determined to make the offer of their joint mediation and good offices for an accommodation of the differences, Lord Harrington gave to count Kinski, an account of this resolution; and orders were transmitted to their ministers at Paris and Madrid, to propose a general pacification through the mediation of the maritime powers. The Emperor received the notification communicated by Mr. Robinson, with no less surprise than indignation, and his minister delivered in a strong and pointed memorial. In this paper, the Emperor insisted on the rectitude of his own conduct and views, the insincerity of France, and the wanton aggressions of the allies; claimed from the maritime powers effectual co-operation to insure the guaranties stipulated by existing treaties, previous to his acceptance of their proposed mediation; and added, he would never have acted as they had; and after a delay of nine months, offered his mediation instead of sending assistance*.

While the answer to this memorial was pre- paring in concert with the States General, the Emperor

---

* Reponse de la cour Imperiale aux representations de Messrs. Robinson et Brininx, 30 Juin, 1734. Walpole Papers.

Emperor became indignant at the delay; and imputing the denial of fuccours to the influence of Sir Robert Walpole, broke out into the moft intemperate expreffions againft him. Totally unacquainted with the firft principles of the Englifh conftitution, forming, from the accounts tranfmitted by count Kinfki, wrong notions of the king's power, and of the ftate of parties, and knowing that George the Second was perfonally eager for the war, he entertained the moft fanguine hopes that the nation would be brought over to his opinion.

Under thefe impreffions, he revived the chimerical plan which he had ineffectually adopted in 1726, of appealing to the nation againft the minifter. His embaffador in London caballed with oppofition; endeavoured to excite the fympathy of the nation; threw the blame of his depreffion on Sir Robert Walpole; appealed to the king's feelings, and to his inveterate hatred of the houfe of Bourbon, and endeavoured, by means of the Emprefs, to intereft queen Caroline in his favour.

Thefe imprudent attempts did not efcape the knowledge of Walpole. An intercepted letter from the Emperor to count Kinfki, fully developed the plan in agitation, and difplayed the threats which Charles the Sixth was weak enough to fuppofe would alarm the minifter, and compel him to act offenfively againft France.

Attempts to effect his removal. He even carried his refentment fo far, that he attempted to obtain the removal of Walpole, by

means

means of a meddling emiffary, who was ill calculated to fucceed in fo difficult an enterprife.

This emiffary was Strickland, bifhop of Namur,
by birth an Englifhman, and by religion a Roman
catholic. Warmly attached to the caufe of the
Pretender, he facrificed his country to his principles, and was promoted to the Abbey of Saint
Pierre de Preaux, in Normandy. In the latter
end of the reign of George the Firft, he maintained a correfpondence with the oppofition; and
through their intereft with the Emperor, he was
raifed to the bifhopric of Namur; he afterwards became a fpy to the Englifh miniftry, and rendered
himfelf fo ufeful, that he was confidered as a proper
perfon of confidence to refide at Rome, for the
purpofe of giving information with regard to the
Pretender. With this view, lord Harrington *
applied to the Emperor for his intereft to obtain
for him a cardinal's hat; and Mr. Robinfon was
ordered to fecond that recommendation with his
whole influence. The bifhop being a man of an
artful and intriguing turn, plaufible in his manner, and having gained great credit for his ftrict
regularity and difintereftednefs in the management of his diocefe, was admitted to feveral
audiences of the Emprefs, and fo far infinuated
himfelf into her good graces, that he was employed to thwart the marriage of the eldeft archduchefs with Don Carlos, to which fhe had an
infuperable averfion.

During

* Walpole and Grantham Papers. Mr. Robinfon to lord Harrington, September 8. To Horace Walpole, November 13, 1734. Correfpondence.

During thefe audiences, he artfully infinuated fuch remarks on the mifmanagement of the Imperial miniftry, as induced the Emprefs to obtain for him a private audience of the Emperor. He availed himfelf of this permiffion to prefent feveral memorials, for the amelioration of the domeftic affairs, which were well received by the Emperor, fond of new fchemes, and inclined to think unfavourably of his minifters. From thefe topics, he digreffed to lord Harrington's recommendation; and reprefented himfelf as capable either of forcing the Britifh adminiftration to enter into the war, or if that failed of fuccefs, of driving out Sir Robert Walpole, through the intrigues of oppofition. The Emperor weakly acceded to this propofal, and fupplied the bifhop of Namur with private credentials to the king and queen of England. On his departure, he was inftructed to take advantage of the decided inclination of the king to enter into the war, of the apparent lukewarmnefs of the queen to fupport the pacific fyftem, and of the difunion of fentiments in the miniftry.

The bifhop of Namur was received by the king and queen in fo gracious a manner, as to give umbrage to Sir Robert Walpole. He had a long and fecret conference with Lord Harrington * ; reports were foon in circulation, that he would draw the nation into a war, and that he was privately fupported by the king and queen, and abetted by lord Harrington ; and that the fall of the minifter would be the immediate confequence.

It

* Orford Papers. Correfpondence.

It became neceffary to difcredit thefe rumours.
Horace Walpole hinted to lord Harrington his
opinion of the bifhop, and the ill policy of ap- Counteracted
pearing to countenance fo dangerous a perfon. by Walpole.
In the private correfpondence which he held with
queen Caroline *, he alfo artfully reprefented the
impropriety of giving fuch a reception to a mif-
fionary who was fo favourable to the oppofition;
he urged the neceffity of not fuffering a perfon of
his fufpicious character to remain in England; and
infinuated that the Emperor fhould be undeceived
in his notion, that the king was of a different
opinion from the miniftry, and be pofitively informed that England could not take a part in the
war.   Walpole, in concert with his brother, fupported this meafure, and fuggefted to the queen,
that fhe fhould herfelf write to the Emprefs †, to
contradict the faife accounts fent by Kinfki and
the bifhop of Namur, and candidly to declare that
no fuccours could be given by England, until the
offer of the mediation had been rejected.   The
minifter carried his point; the bifhop of Namur
was civilly difmiffed; the king was either convinced of the neceffity of adopting pacific meafures,
or yielded reluctantly to a plan which he could not
venture to oppofe.   Lord Harrington fubmitted
to the fuperior influence of Walpole; and the
Emperor, with fome hefitation, agreed to admit
                                                        the

* Orford Papers. Letter to queen Caroline, October 18-29, 1734.
Correfpondence.

† Correfpondence.

the good offices, and to accept the mediation of the maritime powers.

Meanwhile, a secret negotiation was suddenly opened with France, which seemed at first to afford a prospect of a speedy accommodation, and on that account was eagerly embraced by Sir Robert Walpole, but which involved both him and his brother in considerable embarraffments, excited, in the course of its progress, the difpleasure of the king, and occasioned a temporary disagreement among the ministers.

Intimacy of
Horace
Walpole
with baron
Gedda,

Horace Walpole maintained an intimate correspondence with baron Gedda, the Swedish minister at Paris, for whom he procured an annual pension of £.400; and as Gedda was on good terms with cardinal Fleury, and had communicated the private sentiments of the French minister, Horace Walpole had, at the suggestion of his brother, found means to convey hints for a general accommodation.

Embarraffing
fituation of
the cabinet.

The fituation of the British cabinet was exceedingly embarraffing; being reproached on one fide by the Emperor for not fulfilling the guaranty by declaring war, and on the other by France, for not being cordially difposed to favour a peace, it became expedient to take a decided part. But the co-operation of the United Provinces was confidered by the minister as a neceffary means to infure fuccefs.

The difpofition of perfons and affairs in Holland was fo timid and fluctuating, as to afford little

little hope of terminating hoftilities, unlefs France could be induced, of her own accord, to open a negotiation. For it was fenfibly urged* by the embaffador at the Hague, that although thefe conditions might not be fuch as would be accepted by the Emperor, yet if they were once propofed to him by England and the States General, he would be undeceived in his fond expectations, that thofe powers would enter into the war for the purpofe of recovering his dominions in Italy, and be inclined to turn his attention to fome expedient for an accommodation.

With this view, Horace Walpole, with the pri-vate approbation of his brother, employed the intervention of his friend at Paris, and finally obtained the object fo much defired. Baron Gedda acquainted him, that the cardinal, impreffed with a defire to give peace to Europe, propofed to enter into a confidential correfpondence with him, for the purpofe of fettling the preliminaries for a general pacification, to be communicated to no one but the Penfionary Slingelandt †. This overture being confidered by a part of the cabinet as tending only to amufe, and as a fnare employed by France, to prevent the adoption of vigorous meafures, was at firft warmly oppofed; but being fupported by queen Caroline and Sir Robert Walpole, and thofe members of adminiftration, who adhered to their opinion, it was immediately accepted;

Overtures of cardinal Fleury.

---

* Horace Walpole to Sir Robert Walpole, Auguft 6, 1734. Correfpondence.

† Horace Walpole to the queen. Walpole Papers.

cepted; a private correspondence took place, and
the cardinal proposed to send a confidential person,
by the name of Jannel, to the Hague, to settle and
conclude the terms to which England or France
would previously accede, before they were, communicated on one side to the Emperor, and on the
other to the allies of France.

This proposition of Cardinal Fleury being approved by the cabinet, an interesting correspondence took place between him and Horace Walpole,
concerning the previous conditions to be settled
for adjusting the preliminaries. The letters of the
cardinal, and the answers of Horace Walpole,
were transmitted to England for the approbation
and direction of the king, and private accounts
were regularly forwarded to Sir Robert Walpole.

During these transactions, Sir Robert Walpole
bestowed extraordinary pains on foreign affairs.
Besides holding a secret and constant correspondence with his brother, and suggesting, through
his means, those sentiments with which he wished
to impress the queen, he examined with peculiar
attention the dispatches to and from the secretaries
of state; took notes, and made references of the
most important letters; and although he displeased the king by his firmness in suggesting pacific
measures, and in some instances was secretly thwarted by lord Harrington, who acted in deference to
the views of his sovereign, yet he would not suffer
any measure to be pursued without his approbation,
and directed or controuled the whole series of this
intricate negotiation.

In confequence of this confidential intercourfe, Jannel arrived at the Hague on the 5th of Novem- ber; continued there only three days, and had three very important conferences with Horace Walpole and the Penfionary, with fuch fecrecy, that his arrival was not fufpected, until he had taken his departure. Of thefe three confer- ences, Horace Walpole tranfmitted an accurate and well written account to the Britifh cabinet. An arrangement was taken towards fettling the preliminaries, in which the two parties, after propofing terms which could not be acceded to on either fide, gradually approached each other, and feemed to be not very diftant from the probability of coming to an amicable agreement. The terms propofed by Jannel, and oppofed or affented to by Horace Walpole, were to be referred on one fide to the cardinal, and on the other to the Britifh cabinet.

A plan for the preliminaries was now to be pro- pofed by the cabinet, and forwarded to the Hague, for regulating the conduct of the embaffador.

In order to engage England and Holland in the war, the Emperor had withdrawn all his troops from the barrier towns, and confined himfelf to the defence of Luxemburgh. He reprefented that it was more the intereft of the maritime pow- ers than his own, to preferve the Low Countries from France, and therefore he fhould leave to them the care of their defence. This refolution had been privately taken without the knowledge of
Walpole,

Walpôle, in concert with the king and lord Harrington, who were no lefs anxious than the Emperor to commence hoftilities againſt France. In
confequence of this refolution, a plan was drawn
up by lord Harrington*, to be forwarded to Horace Walpole. It was worded in a moſt artful
manner, and appeared to have no other defign
than to preferve the Low Countries from France.
The embaſſador was ordered to infinuate to the
Dutch, that if they would authorife the king to
affure the Emperor of their defign to augment
their forces, his majefty would endeavour to prevail on the Emperor to fend, without delay, a
fufficient number of men from the Rhine for the
defence of the Low Countries; and that the king,
at the requifition of the Dutch, according to the
tenour of the barrier treaty, would fupply 10,000
men, provided they would furniſh an equal
number.

This difpatch, before it was fent to the Hague,
was forwarded by a meſſenger to Sir Robert Walpole, who was then at Houghton, for his approbation. The miniſter highly difapproved the meafure, and thought it neceſſary to exprefs his difapprobation in fuch ſtrong terms, that lord Harrington totally relinquiſhed his defign. In his
anfwer to Walpole, he teſtified his concern that
the draught which he propofed to write to Horace
Walpole concerning the Netherlands, was fo
ſtrongly

* Lord Harrington to Horace Walpole, Whitehall, November
5-16th, 1734. Correſpondence.

ſtrongly condemned *: "The letter itſelf," he   Chapter 44.

added, "is not ſent."   1734 to 1735.

Soon afterwards, lord Harrington drew up, by Firm and pru-
order of the king, a plan for the preliminaries, dent conduct
of Walpole.
which was calculated to throw obſtacles in the way
of the negotiation with France; and to check the
eagerneſs of Horace Walpole, for immediately
modifying and cloſing with the propoſitions of cardinal Fleury. Theſe inſtructions were to be forwarded to the Hague, in a letter to the embaſſador
by which he was to be implicitly guided in this
delicate buſineſs †. He prepared this letter on the
12th of November; but as it was an affair of too
great importance to be precipitately decided without the concurrence of the miniſter, who was then
at Houghton, he diſpatched a meſſenger with a
letter, encloſing a copy, and requeſting his opinion. This plan met with no leſs diſapprobation
than that which related to the Netherlands; and
Walpole was never engaged in a more difficult or
delicate part. Although he well knew that to diſ-
approve or alter it, was in effect to act in direct
contradiction to the ſentiments and wiſhes of the
king, yet he did not heſitate to adopt that reſolution. He conſidered the plan as wholly formed by
lord Harrington; and in a very frank and candid
manner, gave his objections, without attempting
in the ſmalleſt degree to conceal, or even to palli-
ate his opinion. And perhaps in no inſtance were

the

---

* Sidney Papers. November 8th, 1734. Correſpondence.

† Lord Harrington to Horace Walpole, November 12, 1734.
Lord Harrington to Sir Robert Walpole, November 13, 1734. Correſpondence.

the integrity, prudence, and firmnefs of Walpole
more evident, than in the anfwer which he returned to lord Harrington on this occafion *.

Secret conven-
tion.
In the middle of December, Jannel returned
to the Hague, and the conferences were refumed.
The confequence of thefe meetings was, a project
of pacification concerted between England and the
States; as conformable as poffible to the fentiments
and defires of France, as they were explained by
the cardinal in his private correfpondence with
Horace Walpole and the Penfionary, and which
ought to have been figned at the Hague by Jannel. But as the French minifters had protracted
the negotiation, by railing new demands, and
creating frefh difficulties, it was thought expedient
to fatisfy the expectation and impatience of Europe, by publifhing the plan.

Accordingly, the king in his fpeech, which he
delivered at the opening of the new parliament,
obferved, "that in a fhort time, a plan would be
offered to the confideration of all the parties engaged in the prefent war, as a bafis for a general negotiation of peace, in which the honour and intereft
of all parties had been confulted, as far as the
circumftances of time, and the prefent pofture of
affairs would permit †."

Infincerity of
Fleury.
The French minifters affected to be diffatisfied
with this proceeding; they pretended that it was a
breach of that fecrecy which had been promifed,
and

---

* Sir Robert Walpole to lord Harrington, November $\frac{15}{26}$, 1734,
Correfpondence.

† Journals. Chandler, vol. 9. p. 3.

and remonftrated, that this hafty publication of
the conditions for a general peace, would entirely
fruftrate the good intentions of France, by alarming the allies. At the fame time, Jannel, inftead
of figning the project of the preliminaries, according to the repeated affurances of cardinal Fleury,
received a new counter project, and frefh inftructions, which the Englifh and Dutch minifters at the
Hague could not agree to, and from which he
could not venture to recede. Thus this important negotiation, which had employed fix months,
and had been conducted with the greateft fecrecy,
was fuddenly fufpended. Jannel quitted the
Hague, charged with expoftulatory letters to the
cardinal, on the unexpected mifcarriage of this
great work, which was expected to give peace to
Europe; and on the following day, Horace Walpole fet out for London, carrying with him the
unfigned project of pacification, which had been
concerted with the minifters of the Republic.

The principal articles of this project were, the
abdication of Staniflaus, on the condition of retaining his title; the evacuation of Poland by the
Ruffian Troops; the ceffion of Naples and Sicily
to Don Carlos, and of the Tortonefe, Novarefe,
and Vigevenafco to the king of Sardinia. To
the Emperor : the reftoration of all the other conquefts, the immediate poffeffion of Parma and
Placentia, and the fucceffion of Tufcany, except
Leghorn, which was to be created an independant
republic; France to guaranty the pragmatic fanction;

tion; Spain and Sardinia to renew their guaranties.
This plan to be confidered as the bafis of an immediate negotiation for a general peace, and an armiftice to be ftrenuoufly recommended by the mediators.

The Emperor having teftified his inclination to accept this plan, though he afterwards attempted to make fome alterations which were inadmiffible, it was prefented in form to the refpective minifters of the Emperor, France, Spain, and Sardinia. The Earl of Waldegrave returned to Paris, with inftructions to prefs the cardinal in the ftrongeft manner to confirm and fupport this project, according to the moft folemn affurances which he had given in his private correfpondence with Horace Walpole. But his reprefentations were not attended with effect. The opinion of lord Harrington, which had been confirmed by the earl of Waldegrave in his former difpatches from Paris, that France was infincere in thefe overtures, and only intended to deceive the Britifh cabinet, proved true, and Sir Robert Walpole was the dupe of his pacific inclinations.

Irrefolution of
Holland.
The real caufe of this failure was derived from the irrefolution and inactivity of the Dutch, of which Chauvelin, who either governed or influenced the cardinal, availed himfelf, to prevent the conclufion of the fecret convention with England.

Policy of
Chauvelin.
"One of the fundamental principles of Chauvelin's politics," obferves Horace Walpole, in a letter

letter to lord Harrington, "was to feparate, if
poffible, the States from England. The bafis of
all his meafures when he entered into the war, was
founded upon this principle; and his language and
exertions have been from time to time more or
lefs violent and haughty, in carrying it on, according to the appearance of a divifion or union
. between the king and the States; and by this fame
rule or compafs, he has dexterity enough to fteer
the cardinal's pliant temper, or to adapt his own
fentiments to the cardinal's, whenever he finds
the old gentleman's vigour, from an apprehenfion
of the maritime powers taking jointly a fhare in
this war, begin to fwerve and incline to peace."

In the prefent circumftances, Chauvelin well
knew the Dutch could never be induced to enter
into the war, as long as they had no apprehenfions
for the fafety of the Netherlands; and although
the Penfionary expreffed, in a letter to the cardinal, his fentiments in ftrong and lively terms in
favour of the project, with a view to fupport and
add weight to the reprefentations of Horace Walpole; yet the effect of his letter was fully counter-
balanced by the report made by Fenelon, the
French embaffador at the Hague, of the profound
tranquillity in Holland, and of the determined refolution of the Dutch not to engage in hoftilities.

The British cabinet now roufed itfelf from its
pacific lethargy, and Walpole himfelf was fore-
moft in recommending and enforcing the neceffity

of making the moſt active exertions. Two motions, warmly ſupported by him, were carried in the
houſe of commons, though not without great op-.
poſition *, for taking 30,000 ſeamen and 26,000
ſoldiers into pay, in addition to 12,000 men in
Ireland, and 6,000 Danes, according to the ſubſidiary treaty with Denmark.

While theſe augmentations were making with .
unuſual vigour, it was determined to lay before the
States General the ſtrongeſt repreſentations, for
the pupoſe of ſtimulating them to ſimilar exertions, though all hopes of effecting a general accommodation were not abſolutely relinquiſhed.
Horace Walpole was directed to take Paris in his
route to the Hague, to expoſtulate with the cardinal on his evaſive conduct, to induce him if poſſible to ratify the terms to which he had conſented,
if he did not ſucceed in that effort, to endeavour
at leaſt to procure an armiſtice; and at all events
to obtain the final ſentiments of France, that at
his return to the Hague, he might be able to concert proper meaſures with the States.

Horace Walpole purſued the object of his miſſion with no leſs ſpirit than addreſs. In a long conference with the cardinal, he explained the motive
and purport of his miſſion, recapitulated the riſe,
progreſs, and iſſue of the ſecret negotiation; ob-
viated the principal objections which had been
urged by the cardinal in his laſt letters, and ſupported each article of the project of pacification,
which Jannel ought to have ſigned at the Hague,

r , he

* 256 to 183, and 261 to 208. Chandler.

he ftated, in the ftrongeft manner, the fatal confequences which might refult from his refufal to
fulfil his promife, and preffed him to a fpeedy confent to the plan and armiftice. The cardinal, in
reply, pleaded the impoffibility of compliance, by
reafon of the general outcry of the French nation,
council of ftate, and allies againft the plan, as
partial and difhonorable; he particularly reprefented the impropriety of the demand, that France
fhould guaranty the pragmatic fanction, without
any advantage in return; and afferted that Tufcany, with Parma and Placentia, in addition to
the Milanefe, would render the Emperor more
formidable in Italy than he was before the rupture:
he alfo hinted at the danger of difobliging Spain,
and of compelling her to conclude a feparate accommodation with the Emperor.

To thefe objections, Horace Walpole anfwered
with fuch addrefs and force, and alarmed the cardinal fo much, by declaring that the mifcarriage
of the negotiation would be followed by a general
war, or a family alliance between the courts of
Madrid and Vienna, that he brought him in appearance to approve an armiftice, for fetting on
foot an immediate negotiation, and to promife
to ufe his influence with the king of Sardinia, and
by this means to force Spain to accede. He alfo
expreffed his willingnefs, that France and the maritime powers fhould fign a declaration, engaging
to promote, by a fecret and confidential concert,
the conclufion of a peace, on the conditions regulated in the late correfpondence. His approbation

was even carried fo far, that when Horace Walpole produced a project of a declaration, confo-
nant to the cardinal's new propofitions and wifhes,
he expreffed his readinefs to take it into confideration, and promifed to exert his whole influence to
bring the great work to a happy conclufion *.

Yet, notwithftanding thefe folemn affurances,
he either had not power, or wanted inclination to
fulfil his promife; he foon after obferved, that the
project laid before the king of France, was deemed
inadmiffible; and that the article of the armiftice,
if ratified, would cover France with fhame, and
deprive her of all her allies.

It was now evident that the cardinal could no
longer abide by his declarations of difinterestednefs,
and that he was endeavouring to fuggeft fome artful means, by which he could contradict his
own affertions, that France required nothing for
herfelf. It was plain, though he did not venture to avow it, that Loraine was the object of her
wifhes, and that as long as the allies continued to
be fuccefsful againft the Emperor, and England
and Holland did not take an active and manly part,
the ftrongeft reprefentations would have no effect.

In vain therefore Horace Walpole reproached
the cardinal with the duplicity and weaknefs of
his conduct; in vain he renewed his inftances for
a fufpenfion of arms, and reprefented the fatal
confequences which would probably refult from
his refufal; in vain he threatened to publifh an account

---

count of the whole transaction, and expose him to the world.

The cardinal was abashed and confounded, but not in the least convinced, or moved to compliance. Although he affected earnestly to desire that a plan of pacification should be formed and ratified, yet he could not be induced to explain himself, either on the terms or the method, and delivered his sentiments in so confused and inarticulate a manner, that the British embassador could collect nothing but vague promises, without any specific proposals. Horace Walpole accordingly departed from Paris, leaving the negotiation in the same state in which he found it on his arrival.

Lord Harrington in this instance spoke the una- nimous language of the British cabinet, when in his instructions to Horace Walpole *, he painted in the strongest terms, the king's concern and indignation at the cardinal's late conduct towards him and the States. He observed that this conduct, whether the effect of artifice or irresolution, made it equally unwise and inexcusable to rely, without being at the same time well provided against all events, upon any future transaction with the cardinal, for bringing about a termination of the present troubles, which threatened to subvert the balance of Europe. He said, the time was now come, in which it was indispensably incumbent

* Walpole Papers. Lord Harrington to Horace Walpole, 15th April, 1735.

Y 3

cumbent upon the maritime powers to defend the
liberties of Europe; and to lose no time in putting
themselves into a condition to act with vigour,
whenever they should find it necessary: He added,
that the king hoped the states would immediately
make the proper augmentation of their forces, as
he had himself done, by sea and land, in order to
disabuse France and her allies in their presumption
upon the supineness of the republic, and to be in
readiness to take such measures, in concert with
England, as the preservation of their own, and
the liberties of Europe might require.

Ineffectual. In vain Horace Walpole strenuously exerted himself in pursuit of these instructions. The recollection of the haughty and unfriendly conduct of
the Imperial court; of the defection of England,
at the peace of Utrecht, without securing a sufficient barrier to the States; their jealousy of the
prince of Orange, increased by his late marriage
with the princess Anne; a total disregard for the
losses of the Emperor in Italy, which they did not
consider as their immediate concern, and the security of the Low Countries, by the convention of
neutrality concluded with France on the first appearance of a rupture, contributed to prevent the
Dutch from taking any part in the war. These resolutions were fortified by the melancholy consideration of the exhausted and distressed state of the
republic; by an opinion, generally prevalent in
Holland, of the cardinal's pacific disposition,
and of the moderation of France; and particularly by the apprehension of confirming the Emperor

peror in his fuppofed averfion to peace, by any
appearance of vigour. Accordingly the States,
inftead of taking an active part, renewed their inftances to the refpective powers, for a favourable
anfwer to the plan of pacification.

- The Emperor was unwilling to agree to the
previous conditions, unlefs the maritime powers
engaged, fhould thefe conditions not be accepted
by the allies, to commence hoftilities; but they
declined taking upon them this engagement, becaufe they fufpected that the Emperor would
throw obftacles in the way of the pacification, for
the purpofe of bringing on a general war, which
was the great object of his wifhes. The Emperor
behaved peevifhly to England, and prefumptuoufly
to the States, who were diffatisfied with him, and
fufpicious that England was acting in concert with
him to their prejudice.

The fituation of affairs in Holland infpired cardinal Fleury with fufficient refolution to urge, in
a private letter to Horace Walpole, a heavy ac-
cufation againft him and the Penfionary, for
having divulged the fecret correfpondence; and to
juftify himfelf in his refufal to comply with the
conditions of the plan; and he added, that the
publication of the plan had raifed fuch indignation in the whole council, that he could not
venture to avow or efpoufe it. The main view
of this letter was to clofe the fecret correfpondence
with Horace Walpole; to ferve as a preliminary
to the anfwer of the allies, who rejected the terms
of pacification propofed by the maritime powers,

and

and to justify another campaign, which was opened with redoubled exertion.

Thus ended this important negotiation, in which cardinal Fleury, or rather Chauvelin, who governed the cardinal, deceived the British cabinet, lured the Dutch with the hopes of a pacification, and prevented them both from taking such vigorous measures as would have stopped the allies in the career of conquest.

Motives of Fleury's conduct.

Yet cardinal Fleury does not seem to deserve the reproaches for duplicity which were now lavished upon him. We are too apt to estimate the conduct of other nations, from what passes in our own, without duly considering the peculiar situation and circumstances of those with whom we are negotiating, and without knowing the real state of the public opinion, which every minister, even in the most despotic countries, is in some measure obliged to consult. The real truth seems to be, that the English cabinet expected terms from France which could not be complied with; that cardinal Fleury was probably sincere in his first overtures for peace, but was persuaded by the representations of Horace Walpole, who had gained great ascendancy over him during his embassy at Paris, to accede to conditions; which he could not afterwards venture to propose to the king and council of France. That on sober reflection, he conceived it highly dishonourable in Louis the Fifteenth to desert Stanislaus, in support of whom the war had been undertaken, merely to obtain the transfer of some dominions

in

in Italy to Don Carlos and the king of Sardinia, without either effecting this object, taking vengeance on thofe who prevented it, or obtaining fome acquifition which might ferve as an indemnity for the expences of the war, and juftify to the people in France, the dereliction of the caufe for which hoftilities had been undertaken.

The object of Spain was to drive the Emperor from Italy; the king of Sardinia expected the whole Milanefe; while France, under the mafk of moderation and profeffions of difinterestednefs, aimed at the acquifition of Loraine.

To reconcile fuch jarring interefts, and to effect a general pacification, was not in the power of a divided cabinet, whofe meafures fluctuated with continued verfatility. Orders were occafionally given by lord Harrington, in conformity to the fentiments of the king, and contrary to thofe of the firft minifter. Thefe orders were fometimes oppofed, or at leaft fecretly counteracted by Walpole; either by himfelf, in his perfonal conferences with the king and queen, or by means of the fuggeftions made by Horace Walpole, in his private correfpondence with the queen, or by the agency of the duke of Newcaftle, who at this period was devoted to him. Various inftructions were conveyed to the foreign minifters, each contrary to the other, as the inclinations of the king and lord Harrington in favour of war, or the pacific fentiments of the firft minifter, gained the afcendancy.

The

Period VI,
1734 to 1737.

Difpleafure of the king.

The king was highly difpleafed with the refufal of the minifter to enter into the war, and gave fuch unequivocal figns of his difpleafure, that queen Caroline could not venture to attempt openly to promote or juftify his meafures. But with a view to exculpate his conduct, fhe artfully threw the blame on Horace Walpole, whom fhe often rallied in the king's prefence as the principal caufe of the inactivity of England, and hinted that his brother had been directed by his advice, influence, and known interference in foreign affairs *.

CHAPTER THE FORTY-FIFTH.

1735—1736.

Event of the general Elections.—Meeting of the new Parliament.— Proceedings.—Prorogation.—Difference between Spain and Portugal, adjufted by the armed Mediation of England.—Progrefs of Hoftilities between the Allies and the Emperor.—Detail of the various Negotiations which led to the Conclufion of the Preliminaries.—King's Speech.—Unanimity of Parliament, in regard to Foreign Affairs.

THE minifter and his friends laboured under great difadvantages, and had many difficulties to encounter in the management of the general elections. The inactivity and neutrality of England, became a matter of popular infamy; and even men of profeffed impartiality, feverely cenfured Walpole, by whofe influence the inclinations of the king and the cabinet to affift the houfe of Auftria were reftrained. The common topics

* Horace Walpole's Apology. Walpole Papers.

topics of want of spirit, and the dereliction of national honour, had great effect in exciting discontents, while the advantages derived from the continuance of peace to trade, manufactures, and agriculture, being tacitly progressive, did not immediately attract public attention, or procure their deserved applause. The rapid success of the French and Spanish arms, and the humiliation of the house of Austria, increased the national dissatisfaction. But above all, the excise scheme had excited ill-humour and violent clamours, and it was imprudently introduced a short time before the dissolution of parliament. It was particularly offensive in Scotland, where the frauds in the customs were more extensive than in England. The greater part of the Whigs in Scotland were irritated against the court, and a large number manifested their dissatisfaction, in the manner of their opposition on the election of the sixteen peers. Several of the Presbyterians were averse to the minister for the continuance of the test act, the repeal of which, notwithstanding repeated declarations of his private good wishes, he had never promoted.

Walpole embarked in support of his friends in many expensive contests, and expended a large sum out of his own private fortune*. The expences of the contested election for the county of Norfolk amounted to £.10,000, and yet he failed of success. The two candidates, Morden and Coke, who stood for the Whig interest, and whom

he

---

* Etough says £. 60,000.

he fupported, were fupplanted by Bacon and Woodhoufe, who were favoured by the Tories. In confequence of thefe difficulties and defeats in his own county, the return of members who fupported his adminiftration was inferior in number to thofe who fat in the laft parliament.

The new parliament affembled on the 14th of January. The fpeech from the throne alluded to a plan, formed in concert with Holland, as a bafis for a general negotiation; mentioned the treaty with Denmark; and concluded by obferving, that while war was raging in Europe, it would be proper for Great Britain to maintain herfelf in a pofture of defence.

The oppofition to the addrefs, in both houfes, was vehement and formidable. The amendments propofed by oppofition, were fupported with great ability, and the divifions of the anti-minifterial party were in the upper houfe 37 againft 87, and in the commons 185 againft 265.

During this feffion few debates of importance occurred, and none which perfonally affected the minifter. Although he permitted feveral motions, made by oppofition, to pafs without a divifion, and in the contefted elections as many were carried againft as for adminiftration, yet the material points propofed by government were carried. The fubfidiary treaty with Denmark was approved; £.794,529 was granted for the land fervice, and 30,000 feamen were voted.

The attention of the houfe of lords was occupied by a petition from feveral Scotch peers, complaining

×

plaining

plaining of undue influence in the election of the sixteen. The minister was accused of engaging votes by various acts of corruption, and of over-awing the electors by the presence of troops. The principal persons who conducted this attack, were those who had been deprived, of their places, but though it was managed with great address and asperity, it terminated in his favour. The strength of the opposition was proved by the smallness of the majority, which on the first division was 90 against 47, and on the second, 73 against 39. Two violent protests were entered, the first signed by 33, the second by 32 peers *.

The session was closed by prorogation on the 15th of May, when the king, in his speech from the throne, expressed his intention of visiting his German dominions, and appointing the queen regent during his absence, of whose just and prudent administration, he had on the like occasion had experience. " Let me," he concluded, " earnestly recommend it to you to render the burthen of this weighty trust as easy to her as possible, by making it your constant study and endeavour, as I am sure it is your inclination, to preserve the peace of the kingdom, and to discountenance and suppress all attempts to raise groundless discontents in the minds of my people, whose happiness has always been and shall continue my daily and uninterrupted care †."

The secret correspondence with cardinal Fleury was scarcely closed, when a dispute between Spain and

---

* Lords' Debates.　　† Chandler. Journals.

and Portugal brought on another feries of intricate negotiations, and threatened to fpread ftill wider the horrors of war *.

Affairs of
Portugal.

John the Fifth, king of Portugal, had efpoufed the archduchefs Mary Ann, fifter of the Emperor Charles the Sixth, and his connection with the houfe of Auftria, had increafed the hatred which his family bore to France. For fome time after the peace of Utrecht, a great coolnefs had taken place between him and Philip the Fifth, the natural confequence of fituation and connections. At length their jealoufy and rivalfhip in fome meafure fubfided, and the two courts were recon-, ciled by a double marriage between Ferdinand, prince of Afturias, and Barbara, infanta of Portugal, and between Jofeph, prince of Brafil, and the infanta of Spain. But this marriage did not long operate in preferving harmony, and a diplo-matic difpute nearly produced an open rupture.

Difpute with
Spain.

The fervants of Don Cabral de Belmonte, the Portuguefe minifter at Madrid, being accufed of violently refcuing a malefactor from the officers of juftice, were arrefted and carried to prifon. The minifter having complained of this infult, as an infraction on the law of nations, was warmly fupported by his court: at the fame time the Spanifh embaffador at Lifbon, demanded fatisfaction

* The fubftance of the remaining part of this chapter is principally taken from the fame documents as the forty-fourth, from a fecond continuation of the paper, intitled, " Conduct of England, &c." from July to December 1734, and from " A Summary D duction of the Courfe of Public Affairs, from the Delivery of the Project of Accom-modation by the Maritime Powers, to their Application of the Vienna Preliminaries," from February 1735 to January 1736. Walpole Papers.

faction for the behaviour of the Portuguese minifter, but inftead of obtaining redrefs, he had the
mortification of feeing nineteen of his own do-
meftics arrefted and fent to prifon; and as neither
court would give the fatisfaction reciprocally demanded, the two minifters retired from their refpective embaffies, and both nations prepared for
immediate hoftilities.

Don Azevedo, envoy from the king of Portu- Claims the
gal, arrived at London, to folicit, by virtue of the affiftance of England.
fubfifting treaties, and particularly that of 1703,
the affiftance of England, in favour of the king
of Portugal, againft an attack which he apprehended from Spain. To this demand the king
returned for anfwer, that he would, agreeably to
the honour of his engagements, immediately, in
conjunction with the States General, interpofe his
good offices, and that in the mean time, to fecure
Portugal from any hoftile attempt, efpecially
againft the Brazil fleet, which was then upon its
return, a ftrong fquadron fhould be fent to Lifbon;
advifing the king of Portugal at the fame time, to
fhew a readinefs in bringing this difpute to an accommodation.

This advice was by no means acceptable to the Inclined to
king of Portugal; he had feen with a jealous eye the Emperor.
the recent fucceffes of the Spaniards in Italy; he
had beheld, not without regret, an advantageous
peace which Philip had lately concluded with the
Moors, and he expected, perhaps, that Spain
would again revive pretenfions on Portugal, which,
notwithftanding all renunciations, had never been
sincerely

Period VI. fincerely relinquifhed. During the war he had
1734 to 1737 uniformly efpoufed and approved the conduct of
the Emperor; and perfons of all ranks and diftinctions in Portugal, had expreffed their wifhes in
favour of the fame caufe. He was ftill farther
exafperated againft the court of Madrid, by the
repeated complaints of his favourite daughter
Barbara, of the ill treatment which fhe received
from the queen of Spain. Thefe concurrent circumftances roufed the refentment of John the
Fifth, a prince of great fpirit; and his violent
temper was irritated to fuch a degree, that he was
eager to commence hoftilities againft Spain, and
warmly folicited both the king of England and
the Emperor to conclude an offenfive alliance.
He faid * to lord Tyrawley, the Britifh embaffador
at Lifbon, the time was now arrived to reduce
Philip to reafon; that fo favourable an opportunity would never again occur; Spain was left in
fo defencelefs a ftate by the numerous armies employed in Italy, that a fmall number of Portuguefe
would overrun the country without oppofition;
and that the Britifh fleet would prevent the return
April 17. of the Spanifh troops from Italy. His confidential
minifters publicly declared, that if manifeftos from
the prince of Afturias were difperfed, inviting the
Spaniards to fhake off the tyranny of the queen,
and the incapacity of the king, the whole kingdom would rife in his favour; and with a view to
induce England to embrace this meafure, it was
urged,

* Walpole Papers. Lord Tyrawley to the duke of Newcaftle,
May 19, 1735.

ürged, that if the attempt of the prince of Afturias'
fucceeded, Philip would be compelled to recal his
troops from Italy, for the defence of his own
kingdom ; and that the force of the allies being
weakened, that the Imperial troops might again
acquire the afcendancy, and the houfe of Bourbon
be fruftrated in its attempts to lower the houfe of
Auftria.

Thefe negotiations concerning the difputes be-Profpect of a
tween Spain and Portugal, were neceffarily blended general war.
with thofe between the Emperor and the allies.
The Emperor received the offers of Portugal with
avidity, and gave unbounded promifes of the moft
effectual affiftance; trufting that if hoftilities fhould
take place between Spain and Portugal, England
would be drawn into the quarrel, and a general
war would be the unavoidable confequence. So
great was the difficulty of reconciling two courts,
both remarkable for pride and etiquette, and two
fovereigns equally intemperate in their anger, and
fo impoffible did it appear to forefee the confequences or controul the events, that a general and
bloody war feemed almoft inevitable. Affairs
wore fo gloomy an afpect, that Horace Walpole
* fays, in a letter to his brother, " I own I fee
nothing but black clouds gathering on all fides :
I don't fee a ray of light to difperfe them."

But Sir Robert Walpole did not behold things Englifh fqua-
in fo difcouraging a light, and the Britifh cabinet, dron fent to
directed by him, acted with no lefs fpirit than Lifbon.
caution. In the beginning of June, a fquadron
of twenty-five fhips of the line and feveral frigates

* April 29th, 1735. Correfpondence.

z failed

Period VI.
1734 to 1737.

Alarms of
France.

Accommoda-
tion between
Portugal and
Spain.

failed from Portſmouth, under the command of
Sir John Norris, and arrived in the Port of Liſbon. The deſtination of this fleet made a ſtrong
ſenſation at Paris and Madrid, and gave great
weight to the armed mediation of England. Cardinal Fleury was particularly alarmed; he repreſented to lord Waldegrave *, in a moſt pathetic
manner, that when the king of Portugal ſhould ſee
ſo *terrible a fleet* as twenty-five men of war, come to
his aſſiſtance, he would reject all offers of mediation, the friends of the Emperor at Liſbon would
encourage him to attack Spain, Spain would be
defended by France, and Portugal by England,
and a general war, of which no one could ſee the
bounds, or calculate the effects, would be the
inevitable conſequence. The Britiſh cabinet was
not affected with theſe remonſtrances; the ſquadron was not withdrawn; but a ſtrong repreſentation was made to the courts of Spain and
France, that its object was only to protect the
trade of the Engliſh ſubjects, and to defend the
coaſt and commerce of Portugal againſt any attempt: that Sir John Norris was inſtructed not
to act offenſively, nor to encourage or aſſiſt the
king of Portugal in offenſive meaſures. †

This ſpirited conduct rendered the miniſtry extremely popular in England, and greatly contributed to reſtore the tranquillity of Europe. ‡
Spain having at firſt declined the proffered inter-
poſition,

---

* Earl of Waldegrave to the duke of Newcaſtle, June 1ſt, 1735.
Correſpondence.
† Mr. Keene to the duke of Newcaſtle, June 9th, 1735. Keene
Papers.
‡ Tindal, vol. 20. p. 291.

position, proposed at length to refer the decision of the differences to England and France; and Portugal, after making ineffectual endeavours to prevail on England to act offensively; finally acquiesced in the mediation of France and the maritime powers. Hostilities, though began in America against the Portuguese colony of St. Sacrament, never reached Europe; a convention, signed at Madrid in July, 1736, under the mediation of the English, French, and Dutch plenipotentiaries, was followed by a peace, concluded at Paris, by which all differences were adjusted *.

A short time before the Portuguese minister soli- cited the assistance of England, the Imperial court delivered an answer to the plan of pacification; but this answer was only provisional, and the acceptance of the armistice was restrained to such conditions as rendered it inadmissible. It concluded by exhorting the maritime powers to make such preparations as to be in readiness to act offensively if the allies should reject the plan. The Emperor, † at the same time, stated the right which he had acquired, as well by the treaties made in 1731, as by his conduct since that period, to the friendship and assistance of the maritime powers, against the unjust attacks and ambitious views of the house of Bourbon, ‡ and made the most bitter reflections upon the unmanly and pusillanimous part, which those powers, especially the Dutch, had hitherto acted since the ruptures. It was now evident that

* Walpole Papers. Horace Walpole to Sir Robert Walpole, August 16, 1735.
  Memoire raisonnée, March 15. Grantham Papers.
  Deduction.

Z 2   the

Period VI.

1734 to 1737.

England and
Holland de-
cline affiltance.

the Emperor would not hearken to any overtures of accommodation from the maritime powers, unlefs they promifed to affift him, if the allies
rejected the plan. They deemed it neceffary,
therefore to declare, in the moft. pofitive terms,
that they would not on any. confideration engage
in the war; and to reprefent to the Imperial court,
the entering into a particular accommodation with
Spain or France; with Spain, by giving in marriage an archduchefs to Don Carlos, or with
France by exchanging Loraine for Tufcany. To
this reprefentation no immediate anfwer was given.

Indignation
and defpon-
dency at Vi-
enna.

The notification to the Imperial court, in anfwer to the memorial delivered by count Ulefeldt,
that England and Holland declined taking a part
in the war, was received at Vienna with the
ftrongeft fymptoms of furprife and defpondency;
all that Mr. Robinfon could draw from them, was
fullen and abrupt declarations of aftonifhment and
affliction to fee the Emperor thus abandoned by
the very power from whom he principally and
folely expected affiftance. Bartenftein, * the confidential, though fubordinate minifter of Charles
the Sixth, faid, that Europe was loft, the Emperor was the firft facrifice. He knew, were he
Emperor, what party he fhould take; he would
let things follow their own courfe. The war would
end of itfelf for want of matter to feed the flame.
The enemies of the houfe of Auftria would furely
not require Vienna; with his hereditary countries
the Emperor would ftill be fufficiently great for
himfelf, though not ufeful to others.

Prince

* Walpole Papeis. Mr. Robinfon to lord Harrington, July 5th,
1735.

Prince Eugene also observed, that the wifest meafure which the Emperor could purfue, was to recal all his forces into his hereditary dominions, and fuffer France to take the reft, if the maritime powers had no concern for them. But it was count Sinzendorff, who on this, as on all other occafions, ufed the moft violent expreffions of paffion and fury. Having afked the Britifh minifter, if there were no fuccours to be expected, and receiving for anfwer, that in all probability there were none, he exclaimed, " What a fevere fentence have you paffed upon the Emperor! No malefactor was ever carried with fo hard a doom to the gibbet." He was for burning Amfterdam, and for giving up Flanders; " there was, and there could be," he added, " no feparate negotiation. The only means left for the Emperor, was to fet fire to the four corners of the world, and to perifh, if he muft perifh, in the general conflagration."

Thefe violent expreffions of indignation and defpair, were foon followed by a fuitable conduct; the Emperor was alarmed at the negotiations of France, Sweden, and Turkey; at the union, concert, and progrefs of the allies in Italy; at the retreat of count Konigfegg into the Tyrol, which left Mantua to its fate.

He attributed to the treaty of 1731 all his misfortunes, which arofe from a determined refolution of the French to deftroy his fucceffion, guarantied by that treaty; and principally to the introduction of the 6,000 Spaniards into Italy;

z 3   which

Period VI.
1734 to 1737.

which enabled the French to gain over the king of Sardinia. Thus abandoned by his allies, he determined to feparate himfelf from the maritime powers, and ordered count Kinfky to exprefs his extreme aftonifhment at the conduct of England, and to affirm, that he had no other fyftem of accommodation, than to fubmit to his enemies, when deferted by his friends.

In this fituation of affairs, the mind of the Emperor was fecretly agitated to fuch a height, as to raife apprehenfions in the Emprefs, that his underftanding might be effected by the conflict. "During the dead of the night," writes Mr. Robinfon to lord Harrington, "and while he was fingly with her, he gave a loofe to his affliction, confufion, and defpair." Thefe agitations were augmented by a total diftruft of his own minifters, excepting Bartenftein, who having lefs to lofe than the others, flattered the Emperor with ideas more fuitable to romantic glory, than to ordinary prudence. "This court," he adds, "is defperate, and no prudent man can forefee what may be the effect of a violent defpair. The Emperor, as in a fhipwreck, will lay hold on the firft plank."

Peremptory requeft of the Emperor.

July 27th, 1735.

The fame fentiments were enforced by count Kinfky *, in an audience of the king at Hanover. He reprefented the fituation and ftrength of the Imperial troops, and defired his opinion upon the beft method of employing them, either by fending large detachments into Italy, or by abandoning

* Lord Harrington to the duke of Newcaftle, Walpole Papers, Deduction.

ing that territory, except Mantua, and the entries
into the Tyrol; by collecting an army on the
Rhine, to act offensively againſt France; or, laſt-
ly, by penetrating into France, on the ſide of the
Moſelle and the Netherlands. He required at
the ſame time a preciſe declaration of the king's
final intentions on the point of ſuccours, and declared, that the Emperor would conſider a delay
or ſilence on this queſtion, as an abſolute negative; and muſt then provide, as ſoon, and as well
as he could, for himſelf, by way of negotiation,
without conſulting the maritime powers, or conſi-
dering their intereſts. A demand was at the ſame
time made for a ſubſidy, either public or ſecret,
which would enable him to ſupport a large army
in the field, and to lure the king of Sardinia from
the party of France and Spain.

While the Emperor was thus appealing to the
hopes and fears of the maritime powers, and warmly
ſoliciting ſuccours and ſubſidies, he threatened to
abandon the Low Countries, and even to cede
them to France, for the recovery of his Italian
dominions, and the guaranty of the pragmatic
ſanction; a threat which excited ſtrong apprehenſions in the Britiſh cabinet, and was deprecated as an event of the utmoſt conſequence to
the commercial and political intereſts of England.

Mean time the Britiſh cabinet was employed in
endeavouring to divide the allies, and in renewing
their ſolicitations for peace, even to the very
power by which they had been recently duped

and

and deceived. Sir Robert Walpole was conscious that the only hopes of pacification depended on France, and if she could be brought to a sincere co-operation with England, the other belligerent powers, however averse, could not withold their assent. He was desirous not to offend the cardinal, by shewing disgust at his duplicity; wished not to be pecipitate in divulging the account of the secret negotiation; thought that the publication of that transaction should rather be the consequence than the forerunner or provocation of a war *. He was fully convinced, from his knowledge of the cardinal's and Chauvelin's characters, that unless the points of concession originated with them †, France would never be brought to guaranty the pragmatic sanction, which he considered as essentially necessary to the preservation of tranquillity in Europe; he was aware that the desperate situation of the Emperor's affairs in Italy, and his unwillingness to act in any degree cordially with the maritime powers, increased the difficulty of obtaining an accommodation, and that a peace would be cheaply purchased by suffering France to acquire Loraine, provided Tuscany was given in exchange to the duke of Loraine, the Milanese restored, and Parma and Placentia ceded to the Emperor, in return for the two Sicilies.

In conformity with these views, Horace Walpole

---

* Horace Walpole to Sir Robert Walpole, $\frac{9}{20}$th May 1735. Correspondence.

† Horace Walpole to Sir Robert Walpole, April $\frac{18}{29}$th 1735. Correspondence.

pole hinted, in a dispatch to lord Waldegrave,
the circulation of a rumour in Paris, that the object of France was the acquisition of Loraine,
in exchange for Tuscany. Lord Waldegrave, in
a conference with the cardinal, casually mentioned this report. The extreme pleasure which
this hint gave, the pains he took in setting forth
its expediency, and obviating all objections, sufficiently proved that this was the great point
which France had in view *.

While the British cabinet were thus exerting
themselves in favour of a pacification, and endeavouring to persuade the Emperor and France
to agree to terms of accommodation without the
knowledge of the other powers, a secret negotiation was opened between the Emperor and France,
without the concurrence of England   At the
time that cardinal Fleury was holding the private
correspondence with Horace Walpole, he made
secret overtures to the Emperor, with the hopes
of detaching him from the maritime powers. In
his anniversary letter † of compliments to the
Emperor, on occasion of the new year, dated December 12, 1734, he had added a postscript in his
own hand, expressing, in the strongest terms, his
affection and respect for the Emperor's person, as
well as his earnest desire to see the peace of Europe restored. The Emperor, besides the usual
chancery letter, returned an answer in his own
hand, dated February 16th, to the said postscript,
declaring

Overtures from Fleury to the Emperor.

---

* The earl of Waldegrave to lord Harrington, June 7th, 1735.
Walpole and Waldegrave Papers.
† Walpole Papers. Summary Deduction.

declaring his readiness, in conjunction with his allies, to listen to terms of amity, and the facility, of obtaining a peace, if the cardinal would heartily promote it. These two letters were put into the hand of the Pope's nuncio at Bruffels, to convey them to the cardinal; who, in opening the nuncio's packet (for he opened all his letters at arms length, and in the chimney) dropt the Emperor's particular letter into the fire, and could not recover it before it was defaced. The cardinal informed the nuncio, by a letter of March 10th, of this accident, and expreffed his fhame and concern. But the Emperor confidering this ftory as a mere fiction to excufe his filence, the correfpondence was interrupted.

Soon after this incident, the Emperor, finding all attempts to induce the maritime powers to act offenfively againft France ineffectual, artfully made diftant overtures to Spain, in relation to the marriage of an archduchefs with Don Carlos, with the approbation of England. The dread of a fimilar union between Spain and Auftria to that which took place in 1725, alarmed the cardinal; and he accordingly took occafion, by means of a confidential perfon at Paris, to convey to count Sinzendorff his wifhes to conclude a peace directly with the Emperor, without the intervention of any other power, and added, that he would either depute a perfon of confidence fecretly to Vienna, or the Emperor might fend one to Paris, for the purpofe of fettling the conditions of a feparate accommodation.

To

To this overture; the Emperor consented, and
at the very moment when the cardinal was luring
the British cabinet with the hopes of opening,
under their auspices, a negotiation with the Emperor, he dispatched his agent, la Beaume, to
Vienna. This transaction was carried on in so secret a manner, that although some suspicions were
entertained ; yet the first vague rumour of the
mission was communicated by the earl of Waldegrave, on the second of August, * which he had
casually derived from a spy, in the secretary of
state's office at Paris ; and when he taxed the cardinal with his duplicity, the hoary minister did
not blush to deny, the fact, and because the negotiation was at that moment suspended, offered
in the most solemn manner to take an oath on
the bible, † that no private negotiation was at
that time pending between France and Austria. La
Beaume actually passed through the army, and after holding a conference with prince Eugene, arrived and had continued five weeks at Vienna, before Mr. Robinson ‡ entertained the smallest suspicions of the fact. The first intimation which
he received from lord Harrington, appeared to
him nothing more than an uncertain report, and
it was not till after much minute inquiry, that
he found the information to be true.

Although the king, in his reply to Kinski, had
declared that he would not take upon himself to
give

* Walpole Papers. The earl of Waldegrave to the duke of Newcastle, August 2, 1735. Correspondence.
† The earl of Waldegrave to the duke of Newcastle, September
28, 1735. Correspondence.
‡ Walpole and Grantham Papers.

give any advice, and urged that it would be extremely difficult to enter into the war without the
concurrence of the Dutch; although he hinted at
the feveral fchemes of a feparate negotiation;
thought the exchange of the dutchies of Loraine
and Tufcany preferable; infinuated the readinefs
of Spain to accept the fecond archduchefs, and
offered to affift in forwarding the match, or to
adopt any other method for the purpofe of effecting a pacification; yet the Emperor, well aware
that the king was ftrongly inclined to afford active affiftance, urged his claim with redoubled inftances.

The earneft folicitations of the Emperor, his
threats to abandon the Low Countries, and the
knowledge of his fecret negotiation with France,
made a ftrong impreffion on the king and cabinet, and gave weight to the opinion of that
party which inclined for war. For it was deemed
far more eligible to encounter hoftilities, than by
a refufal of fuccours to throw the houfe of Auftria into the arms of France, or by permitting
the diminution of her territories, to enfeeble the
only power which could effectually prefent a barrier to the encroachments of the houfe of Bourbon.

This defertion of the houfe of Auftria in her
extreme diftrefs, gave great difpleafure to feveral of
the minifter's friends and co-adjutors, and to none
more than to lord Harrington; who, in his capacity of fecretary of ftate, had the mortification to
fend inftructions, and to forward meafures contrary to his own fentiments. " The reafons," he
observes,

observes, in a letter to Horace Walpole, "you
alledge to prove that the treaty of Seville was not
the caufe of the Emperor's misfortunes are unanfwerable, and I wifh you could fuggeft as good
ones (in cafe we are forced to it) for juftifying to
the Emperor our not affifting him ; but if that,
could be done, to juftify it to ourfelves and our,
country ; confidering, the prefent behaviour and
operations of France and her allies, nothing but
the moft abfolute inability can do it." *

In a fubfequent letter, lord Harrington + even
fuggefted a meafure, which if followed, would probably have involved England in the war : it was,
to propofe to the Dutch, either an augmentation
of their forces, or to join the king in requiring
from the allies a direct fpecification of the conditions on which they would conclude a peace, and
to declare peremptorily, that unlefs a pofitive anfwer was given, England and the States would
decline the mediation, and adopt the neceffary,
meafures for preferving their own fecurity, and
the equilibrium of Europe. He alfo urged, if,
the States fhould decline both thefe propofitions,
that England fhould withdraw from the mediation, and at the fame time acquaint the Emperor, that the king would endeavour to affift
him in making a feparate peace with any of his
enemies, and in failure of that attempt, would
join with him afterwards in the war, if an opportunity fhould arife of doing it with fuccefs.

The

---

* Walpole Papers. Hanover, Auguft 7th.
† Walpole Papers. Lord Harrington to Horace Walpole, Hanover, Auguft 31.

The difference of opinion was now fo great, the party for war was fo warmly fupported by the king, and that for peace by Sir Robert Walpole, as to occafion much indecifion in the meafures purfued abroad, and in the inftruƈtions fent to the foreign minifters. The French cabinet availed itfelf of thefe circumftances with confiderable effeƈt, and particularly in Holland, where Chavigny, in his paffage through the Hague to Hanover, exaggerated the divided ftate of adminif- tration. He decried the fpirited attempts made by Horace Walpole to infufe vigour and fpirit into the counfels of the States General, and publicly declared, that the fentiments of the court and minifters of England, differed from the plan of pacification delivered by Horace Walpole to the States, and from the joint refolutions of the king and States, on the fubjeƈt of the plan and armiftice, communicated to the French embaffador on the 8th of June.

Sir Robert Walpole had given weight to this opinion, in a private interview with Chavigny,* who preffed him to bring about a pacification by a fecret convention between France and England. He avowed his inclination for peace, and expreffed his defire to fettle the terms with cardinal Fleury, but denied his own power folely to carry any meafure into execution. When Chavigny confidered him in the light of prime minifter, and argued that his known credit with the king would enable him to carry any point he thought neceffary :

* Walpole Papers. Horace Walpole to Sir Robert Walpole, June. 17th, 1735. Correfpondence.

ceffary: " Let us fuppofe," replied Walpole,
" That I fhould agree to any meafure, without
confulting the duke of Newcaftle, who is fecretary of ftate for the department of France, and
the duke, on being informed of the tranfaction,
fhould oppofe it, what is to be done in that cafe?
and what opinion would you have of me, to find
things ftopt and overturned by fuch an oppofition ?"

It was impoffible that affairs could long continue in this ftate of fufpence, and that the tranquillity of Europe could be fecured, while the cabinet of England was diftracted and embarraffed.
It became, therefore, neceffary for the honour of
the minifter, as well as for the prefervation of his
fyftem, to fhew, that whatever private differences
might exift in the cabinet, their public opinion
was decidedly in favour of pacific meafures; and
to undeceive the Emperor in his expectations of
affiftance from the maritime powers, by enforcing
the neceffity of a feparate accommodation either
with France or Spain. Thefe two objects were
finally attained.

In this dilemma, Walpole acted with the moft
confummate addrefs. While the official difpatches from Vienna expreffed the ftrongeft difapprobation of the fecret negotiation with France,
and caft the moft bitter reflections on the Imperial minifters, his letters, and thofe of his brother
Horace, breathed nothing but pacific fentiments.
They * palliated the conduct of the Emperor,
and

* Horace Walpole to Sir Robert Walpole, December 9th, 1735.
Correfpondence.

Period VI. and were anxious not to offend either him or 1734 to 1737 France, by a violent and precipitate condemnation of their meafures. They. afferted, that although the alteration of the project from that offered by the maritime powers, was executed without the co-operation of England, and the king had just reafon to complain of inattention. and flight, yet as it was entirely agreeable to what England had propofed, the king could blame nothing but the form of proceeding. They obferved, that it would be highly unbecoming to take offence at mere punctilious circumftances; they eftimated the bleffings of peace too highly to fuffer etiquitte to prevail over prudence, or to object to an agreement, merely becaufe it did not exactly follow the original project; provided peace was the refult, they both repeatedly declared, it was no matter by whom or in what manner it was procured. *

Tranfmits a final anfwer to the Emperor. But though Walpole was anxious not to difoblige the Emperor, he would not fanction his demand of fuccours or fubfidies; and as the king and part of the cabinet appear to have ftrongly recommended that meafure, he was firm and decifive in enforcing his pacific fentiments. At length, after much oppofition and fome delays, a paper was tranfmitted to Mr. Robinfon at Vienna, which feems to have been drawn up by the minifter. It ftated the determined refolution of the king not to take any part in the war, to offer his intervention in favour of the Emperor,

† Horace Walpole to Thomas Robinfon. Walpole Papers.

peror, but not to fend any affiftance either in men
or money.

Having arranged thefe difficult points, his opinion triumphed, and his pacific meafures were
adopted in their fulleft latitude; the Britifh cabinet now fteered a fteady and uniform courfe, no
longer divided in counfels, or differing in fenti-
ment; and their unanimous exertions were finally
crowned with fuccefs.

It was their aim to make it the intereft of
France to co-operate ferioufly in the reftoration
of tranquillity, by candidly agreeing to fuch conditions as would juftify cardinal Fleury in defert-
ing Spain, and making a feparate accommodation
with the Emperor; and this meafure could only
be effected by facilitating the ceffion of Loraine
to France, in exchange for Tufcany, by leaving
to cardinal Fleury and Chauvelin the manner of
propofing it, and by fubmitting the fpecific plan
to the Emperor for his approbation.

The earl of Waldegrave,* in conformity to inftruCtionS fent from the queen, drew from cardinal Fleury a fpecific acknowledgment of his intentions. After increafing his alarm, at a refolution of the States, which feemed to announce the
adoption of more vigorous meafures, he reprefented the calamities ready to fall upon Europe,
from his dilatory and irrefolute proceedings; that
he forefaw nothing but ruin and deftruction from
beginning and then dropping negotiations, and
fubftituting new projects in their place. He gradually

Plan of pacifi-
cation:

* The earl of Waldegrave to the duke of Newcaftle, Auguft 24.
Correfpondence.

dually obtained, by artful queſtions; a confeſſion that the exchange of Loraine for Tuſcany, was the great object of France; and finally, under a pro-miſe of the ſtricteſt ſecrecy, he prevailed on the cardinal to lay open his ſcheme for a general paci-fication, which, with a very few exceptions, was ſimi-lar to that which had been propoſed by the mari-time powers. At the ſame time, the cardinal re-queſted that the plan ſhould be propoſed and executed by England in concert with France; and he added, that ſuch a peace, being eſtabliſhed on the foundation of juſtice and reaſon, he would abandon his allies if they did not comply.

Having thus prevailed on cardinal Fleury to acquieſce in the intervention of England, the next ſtep was to gain the conſent of the Emperor to the terms propoſed by France, to be modified by England; and this was effected with equal ability. The Britiſh miniſter at Vienna, * in a private au-dience of the Emperor, repreſented the concern of the king at the unfortunate events of the war, and his indefatigable zeal and ardent wiſhes in de-ſiring to put an end to the troubles of Europe. He obſerved, that the diſappointment which the king derived from his inability to enter into the war, was equal to that which the Emperor muſt have experienced in not having received that aſ-ſiſtance which he ſo ardently expected. He urged, that in the preſent ſituation of affairs, there ſeemed no other expedient remaining, than to de-tach one of the allies, and to carry that project into

* Thomas Robinſon to lord Harrington, Auguſt 26th. Walpole Papers.

into execution in the manner moft agreeable, the king had expreffed a defire to have the Emperor's opinion; and had been anxioufly waiting for an anfwer. He then added, that he had now to fub-mit to the Emperor's confideration, a ftrong in-ftance of the king's confidence and friendfhip, which was to communicate the offer of a fepa-rate accommodation from France, nearly con-formable to the plan propofed by the maritime powers, and acceded to by the Emperor; the ceffion of Loraine to France in exchange for Tuf-cany, the deceafe of the great duke, he concluded by faying, that the Emperor's confent to this plan would infallibly infure a fuccefsful iffue.

In reply, the Emperor, after returning his grate-ful acknowledgments to the king for this in-ftance of his friendfhip, added with much dig-nity, " Although I relied upon more fubftantial marks of friendfhip from the king, whofe word was engaged by treaty to affift me with real fuc-cours, and although in a fimilar cafe I fhould not have withheld thofe fuccours which I ftood en-gaged to by treaty, yet I am willing to believe that the difappointment which I have experienced, however fatal to myfelf and family, was lefs owing to want of inclination in the king, than to the impoffibility of acting otherwife: notwithftand-ing this difappointment, I will pay all imaginable deference to the advice now communicated, and will appreciate as it deferves this mark of confi-dence. But as it is an affair of the higheft im-portance and delicacy, and as the exchange does

not

356

not totally depend on myfelf, I cannot give the previous promife which is now defired, even if I were convinced of the fuccefs ; for the object under confideration is not fo much what fhould be done, but whether it is proper to be done. I again affure you, however, that I will pay the greateft deference to the king's advice, and after I have duly reflected upon it, and confulted my council, if you defire it, will myfelf give the anfwer."

Reply.

Thefe declarations were foon followed by various explanations from the Imperial minifters, and finally by a formal anfwer in writing. As far as could be gathered from the dubious and myfterious manner in which the court of Vienna enveloped their fentiments, it appeared as if the Emperor, on certain conditions, might be induced to accede to the overtures of cardinal Fleury, provided Tufcany was given unconditionally to the family of Loraine, and the king of Sardinia would accept the Langhes inftead of the Tortonefe.

Amidft fuch difcordant views as influenced the conduct of Auftria and France, it was not to be expected that any conditions would be finally acceded to on either fide without much altercation and delay. But it was a great point gained, that the contending parties feemed gradually drawing towards an amicable compromife. The object of England was fecretly to affift in keeping up the intercourfe recently eftablifhed between the Emperor and France, to offend neither of thofe powers by cenfuring their conduct ; but on the contrary,

Subfequent proceedings.

trary, to declare that, although the king was not
unacquainted with the fecret negotiation, yet fo far
from oppofing it, he would be defirous of facilitating its fuccefsful iffue, if it fhould be found
not inconfiftent with the equilibrium of Europe.

The British minifters at the Imperial and French
courts, were inftructed to approve the basis of
the agreement fettled between France and the
Emperor, of which they obtained certain information, and a counter project, with fome few
alterations for preventing the ceffion of Loraine
to France, without a fufficient indemnity, was
drawn up by lord Harrington, and forwarded to
Paris and Vienna. In confequence of this con- Nov. 21.
duct, the Imperial and French courts at length
acknowledged the fecret negotiation, and the Britifh embaffador at Vienna received from prince
Eugene, a project of the preliminary articles with
which the Emperor and France were contented,
and to which the concurrence of the maritime
powers was defired.

The anfwer to this project was made in the
name of Great Britain and the United Provinces;
it ftated, that as the preliminaries did not effentially differ from the plans before delivered, nor
contain any thing detrimental to the equilibrium
of Europe, the king and the Republic did not
hefitate to declare their approbation and readinefs to concur in a future treaty for bringing them
to perfection; referving to themfelves the liberty
of ftipulating the neceffary fecurity for their own
poffeffions, rights, privileges, and commerce.

The

Period VI.
1734 to 1737.

Suspension of
arms on the
Rhine,

Opposite views
of the allies.

The secret negotiation had already produced very advantageous effects in Germany; it occasioned an actual, though not a stipulated armistice on the Rhine. The French and Imperial troops did not undertake any offensive operations. Prince Eugene returned to Vienna in the month of October, and soon afterwards the two armies passed into winter quarters. But the same beneficial consequences could not take place in Italy; since the fate of the war did not wholly depend, as it did in Germany, on the *fiat* of cardinal Fleury, where no suspension of arms could take place, without the consent of the king of Spain, who, eager to accelerate the possession of Mantua, would not easily be induced to agree to an armistice at the moment when he thought himself secure of success. But what could not be accomplished by persuasion or force, was finally effected by stratagem.

One great object of the British cabinet was to prevent, or at least to protract the siege of Mantua, which was but scantily provided with ammunition and provisions. With a view to deter the French from attempting it, Horace Walpole, in a letter to the cardinal, and baron Gedda and lord Waldegrave in their conferences, represented, that although the English had declined going into the war; yet they would not see the house of Austria ruined, and that if Mantua was taken, and the Emperor was driven out of Italy, the maritime powers must come forward to his assistance. Fortunately, Mantua was the subject of contention between

between the allies in Italy. Philip was eager to
begin the siege, conscious that the possession of
that important fortress, as the key of Lombardy,
on the side of the Tyrol, would give to Spain the
controul of Italy. Cardinal Fleury himself did
not attempt to conceal his apprehensions of the
consequences that would result from the capture.
He said to the earl of Waldegrave, * that the fall
of that place into the hands of the Spaniards,
would defeat all his schemes, and render the king
and queen of Spain untractable. He even promised, and·in this instance did not belie his word,
to order the French general in Italy to protract
the opening of the trenches, and even to place
his troops in such a manner, as to permit the entrance of provisions into the town. The king of
Sardinia went still farther, and in a letter to
George the Second, declared that he was ready
to join the maritime powers, if they would enter
into the war; † expatiated on his own danger,
should the possession of Mantua encourage Spain
to deprive him of all the territories which had
been allotted to him by his engagements with
France. He pressed the king speedily to negotiate
a peace between the Emperor and'the allies, as the
only means of preventing his falling a sacrifice to
the resentment of Spain, for having delayed co-
operating in the siege of Mantua. He declared
that he would rather make a sacrifice of part of
the

* Walpole Papers. Horace Walpole to Sir Robert Walpole, Oc-
tober 4th, 1735. Correspondence.
† Walpole Papers. Lord Harrington to the duke of Newcastle,
Hanover, August 14th, 1737.

the Milanefe, that the Emperor might retain a footing in Italy, by keeping poffeffion of Mantua, with Parma, Placentia, and Tufcany, than even obtain poffeffion of the whole Milanefe, on con-dition that Mantua, with the other poffeffions in Italy, fhould be ceded to Don Carlos. *

In compliance with thefe views, he had pofi-tively refufed to furnifh a fingle piece of artillery, and fecretly obftructed every meafure which tended to facilitate the capture of that important fortrefs. By thefe manœuvres, the fiege was protracted un-til the feafon was too far advanced; and Philip was thus prevented from gaining a preponderance in Italy, which would have rendered him too powerful in that quarter, and have induced him to refufe all conditions of peace which did not confirm the total exclufion of the Emperor.

England fo-ments the jea-loufy between France and Spain.
During this whole tranfaction, cardinal Fléury was kept in continual alarm, by repeated infinu-ations from Horace Walpole and the earl of Wal-degrave, that the Dutch would act with vigour, provided France would not accede to honourable terms. † They alfo made continued reprefenta-tions to him, that the Emperor, if rendered def-perate, would throw himfelf into the arms of Spain, and agree to the marriage of Don Carlos with an archduchefs, which the French minifter feemed to deprecate as much, or even more than the king of England. For the fame purpofe, the Britifh cabinet never ceafed making overtures, both

* The duke of Newcaftle to lord Harrington, June 6, 1735. Wal-pole Papers.
† Horace Walpole's Apology.

both to the Emperor and Spain, in favour of the
marriages; and this bufinefs was fo artfully managed, that though it was conducted under the
appearance of the ftricteft fecrecy; yet it was duly
communicated to the cardinal in the manner tho
moft likely to alarm him.

The cardinal had no fooner agreed to a feparate accommodation with the Emperor, and a fecret convention with England, than the recollection of his former infincerity in his correfpondence
with Horace Walpole, and the influence of Chauvelin over him, induced the Britifh cabinet to
keep him fteady to his engagements, by oppofing
art to art, and intrigue to intrigue. They availed
themfelves of his apprehenfions of a rupture with
Spain, and of his dread left a clofe union fhould
be formed between Spain and England. Mr.
Keene, the Englifh minifter at Madrid, executed,
with much addrefs, the inftructions of his court,
on this head. From the time of the firft official
communications from cardinal Fleury, of the fecret accommodation between France and the Emperor, and the partial fufpenfion of arms in Italy,
without the knowledge or confent of Spain, he
artfully fomented the refentment which the court
of Madrid entertained againft France, for defert-
ing and betraying the common caufe. He encouraged the irritable and punctilious difpofition
of Philip the Fifth, who was piqued at being betrayed by his native country; he increafed while
he affected to allay the ungovernable fury of the
queen, who afpired to make her fon, Don Carlos,

los, mafter of Italy, and who confidered the difpofal of Parma and Tufcany to the Emperor, as
an injurious deprivation of her own inheritance.

The court of Spain was fo irritated, that Mr.
Keene obferved, in a letter to the duke of Newcaftle,* " There is fcarce any thing that they would
not do, to revenge themfelves upon the French;
you will eafily judge of their defire to do it, when,
contrary to their pride, they make fuch applications
to the king before they know the leaft of his majefty's fentiments. I wifh, indeed, that matters may
not have been pufht rather too far; 'for hitherto
I found more difpofition in them to fit down
quietly with their mortification, if there was no remedy, than I do at prefent; but they now feem
to be drove to defpair, and to be refolved to act
as people in that ftate."

Even Don Patinho, the firft minifter, who was
fo myfterious, that according to cardinal Fleury,
he always fpoke as well as wrote † in cypher,
was fo highly irritated, that he propofed, in un-
ambiguous terms, to undermine the French commerce with Spain, and particularly that with the
Indies, by increafing the Englifh trade; " and
thus we fhall," as he obferved to the Britifh minifter at Madrid, ‡ " revenge ourfelves upon the
cardinal in the moft eafy and effectual manner,
and kill him *with a ftaff of cotton*." §

The

---

* Madrid, December 10th, 1735. Keene Papers.
† The Earl of Waldegrave to the duke of Newcaftle, October 28th,
1733.
‡ Benjamin Keene to the duke of Newcaftle, November 28th.
Keene Papers.
§ Un Bâton de Coton.

The Britifh cabinet, long accuftomed to the Chapter 47. violent and changeful temper of the court of 1735 to 1736. Madrid, and well knowing that the king, though alienated by temporary difpleafure, was from principle and intereft attached to France, amicably deprecated thefe counfels, and urged the good policy as well as neceffity of acceding to the preliminaries.

The refult of all thefe wifely combined mea- Signature of fures, was the fignature of preliminaries for a ge- the prelimina- neral pacification, which was concluded on fuch ries. favourable terms, that even lord Bolingbroke, the implacable enemy of Sir Robert Walpole, obferved; "If the Englifh minifters had any hand " in it, they were wifer than he thought them; " and if not, they were much luckier than they " deferved to be." *

The opinion which truth extorted unwillingly from lord Bolingbroke, that the terms of the preliminaries were as juft and honourable as the circumftances would permit, feems to have been the opinion of the greateft part of the nation; for the annals of England give no inftance of a feffion in parliament which paffed with fo little oppofition, in regard to foreign affairs, as that in the commencement of 1736. With becoming King's fpeech. pride and fatisfaction, for having fettled the great outlines of a general peace, the fpeech from the January 15. throne expreffed the pacific fentiments of the minifter, that provided peace was made, it was no object of confideration by whom, or in what manner

ner

* Lord Hervey to Horace Walpole, December 23d, January 3d, 1735. Correfpondence.

ner it was made. After mentioning the happy turn which the affairs of Europe had taken, and after obferving, that a plan of pacification had been propofed by the king, in conjunction with the States, and that the Emperor and France had feparately concerted the preliminaries for obtaining that end, the king faid : " It appearing, upon due examination, that thefe articles do not effentially vary from the plan propofed by me and the States, nor contain any thing prejudicial to the equilibrium of Europe, or to the rights and interefts of our refpective fubjects, we thought fit, in purfuance of our conftant purpofe, to contribute our utmoft towards a pacification ; to declare, by a joint refolution, to the courts of Vienna and France, our approbation of the faid preliminaries, and our readinefs to concur in a treaty to be made for bringing them to perfection."

As an infallible fymptom of peace, he noticed, rhat a confiderable reduction would be made both by fea and land, and concluded with this pathetic exhortation to moderation and harmony at home : " I am willing to hope, this pleafing profpect of peace abroad, will greatly contribute to peace and good harmony at home. Let that example of temper and moderation, which has fo happily calmed the fpirits of contending princes, banifh from among you all inteftine difcord and diffention. Thofe who truly wifh the peace and profperity of their country, can never have a more favourable opportunity than now offers, of diftinguifhing themfelves, by declaring their fatisfaction

faction in the progress already made, towards restoring the public tranquillity, and in promoting what is still neceffary to bring it to perfection. *

On this occafion, the addrefs was carried in the houfe of commons, not only without a divifion, but without the fmalleft oppofition, and the feffion ended with fcarcely a fingle refleition on the conduct of foreign affairs ; a fingular 'phenomenon in the political annals of this country.

CHAPTER THE FORTY-SIXTH.

1736.

Parliamentary Proceedings.—Gin Act.—Motion to repeal the Teft Act, negatived.—Bill for the Relief of the Quakers paffes the Commons, but is thrown out by the Lords.—Account of Edmund Gibfon, Bifhop of London.—Prorogation.—Horace Walpole declines the Office of Secretary of State.—Accompanies the King to Hanover, as Vice Secretary. —Foreign Negotiations.—Prudence of Sir Robert Walpole.—Private Correfpondence with his Brother.—Objeits to guaranty the Provifional Succeffion to Berg and Juliers.—Oppofes the Northern League, and the Mediation between Ruffia and the Porte.—Promotes the definitive Treaty.—The Delays of the Emperor.—Ineffectual Attempt to bribe Chauvelin.—Secret Correfpondence with Cardinal Fleury, and Difmiffion of Chauvelin.

THE parliamentary proceedings of this feffion, relating to domeftic affairs, were, in general, of little importance. The only fubjects which it may be neceffary to particularize, were The *Gin Act*; the repeal of the Teft Act, and the bill for giving relief to Quakers.

The act for laying a tax on fpirituous liquors,

Parliamentary Proceedings.

Gin Act.

and

---

* Chandler, vol. 9. p. 103, 104. Journals.

and licenfing the retailers, was a meafure in which the minifter had no immediate concern, but for which he fuffered much unmerited obloquy. The bill was principally promoted by Sir Jofeph Jekyll, from a fpirit of philanthrophy, which led him to contemplate with horror the progrefs of vice, li-centioufnefs, and immorality that marked the po-pular attachment to thefe inflammatory poifons. This benevolent attempt embarraffed the minif-ter, but did not anfwer the defired end.

It was incumbent on the minifter to prevent any diminution of the revenue of the crown, and for that purpofe to fupply any deficiency which might arife from the reduced confumption of fpi-rituous liquors ; but this attention to his official duty, expofed him to much intemperate abufe, and he was reproached for wifhing to facrifice the morals of the people to financial confiderations. After many debates, in which he took an active fhare, the bill paffed, and £. 70,000. per annum was granted to the king as a compenfation for the diminution of the civil lift, to which the duty had hitherto belonged. *

The populace fhewed their difapprobation of this act in the ufual mode of riot and violence. Numerous defperados availed themfelves of the popular difcontents, and continued the clandef-tine fale of gin in defiance of every reftriction. The demand of penalties, which the offenders were unable to pay, filled the prifons, and re-moving every reftraint, plunged them into courfes more

* Chandler, vol. 9. p. 172.

more audacioufly criminal. It ·was found, that Chapter 46.
a duty and penalty fo fevere as to amount to an ·. 1736.
implied prohibition, were as little calculated to
benefit the public morality as the public revenue,
and, as Walpole predicted, a fubfequent adminiftration was obliged to modify the meafure.

Few fubjects ·were more embarraffing to the Repeal of the
minifter, than the propofed repeal of the teft act. teft act.
He had for a long time acted with the diffenters ;
he fully appreciated the advantage which the proteftant fucceffion had derived from their exertions;
he had received from them the warmeft fupport ;
he knew that they had reafon to expect relief
from a proteftant king, whom they had affifted
in placing on the throne ; he had even given them
hopes, that the time was not far diftant, when
they might obtain what they fo earneftly defired:
In this feffion, the motion for repealing the teft March 2d and
act was prematurely brought forwards by Plum- 12th.
mer, who fupported it in a very able fpeech.
Though the minifter oppofed the motion in the
prefent inftance, he did it with fuch candour and
moderation, and, " expreffed himfelf fo cautioufly,
" with regard to the church, and fo affection-
" ately, with regard to the diffenters, that neither
" party had caufe to complain of him. The pub-
" lic has been long informed of all the argu-
" ments urged for and againft the motion, as al-
" moft every year produced fome event that re-
" vived them, therefore they are omitted here. Negatived.
" The motion was negatived by a majority of 251
" againft 123." *

Although

* Tindal, vol. 20, p. 323. Journals.

Period V.   Although the minister thus oppofed the repeal
1734 to 1737·of the teft act, he warmly patronifed and fup-
Quakers' bill. ported a bill for the relief of the Quakers, who
prefented a petition to the houfe of commons.
March 2d.   It ftated, " that notwithftanding the feveral acts
of parliament made, for the more eafy recovery of
tythes, and ecclefiaftical dues, in a fummary way,
by warrant from juftices of the peace ; yet as the
faid people confcientioufly refufed the payment,
they were not only liable to, but many of them
had undergone grievous fufferings, by profecution
in the exchequer, ecclefiaftical, and other courts,
to the imprifonment of their perfons, and the
impoverifhing and ruin of them and their families, for fuch · fmall fums as were recoverable by
thofe acts ; and therefore praying, that the houfe
would be pleafed to afford them fuch relief, as
to them fhould feem meet." *

Though the minifter and the majority of the
houfe were difpofed to favour the petition, and a
bill was framed accordingly, yet the great intereft
of the eftablifhed clergy, rendered it a matter of
much difficulty.   Counter-petitions poured in
March 26.   from all quarters, fetting forth, " That fuch a law
would be extremely prejudicial to themfelves and
brethren, excluding them from the benefit of the
laws then in being, for the recovery of tythes and
other dues, and thereby putting the clergy of the
eftablifhed church, upon a worfe foot than the
reft of his majefty's fubjects ; and praying to be
heard by counfel againft the bill." †

                                                Notwith-

* Chandler. Journals.   † Ibid.

Chapter 46.
1736.

Notwithſtanding all obſtacles, the diſpoſition of the houſe was very ſtrong in favour of the quakers. Their petition was not conſidered a party affair; and the proceedings againſt many of them, had ſuch an air of perſecution, as procured them many friends amongſt all parties. The bill underwent great alterations in the committee. The main intention of it was, to make the determination of two juſtices of the peace final, as to all payments of tythes and church dues, when the quaker, who was to pay them, did not litigate the ſame, which the juſtices were to certify under their hands and ſeals, without fee or reward. But in caſe the quaker ſhould litigate the payment, then either party, who ſhould diſſent from the adjudication of the juſtices, might have recourſe to the courts in Weſtminſter hall. The payment of all church and chapel rates, if refuſed by quakers, were, upon the complaint of the churchwardens, to be levied by diſtreſs, by order of two juſtices, upon their goods, in the ſame manner as the poor rates are levied, and no quaker was to be ſued or proſecuted for not paying any church or chapel rates, in any other manner.

Such was the main purport of this famous bill, though clogged with a great number of other clauſes; when after long debates, and ſeveral diviſions, it paſſed the houſe of commons, by a majority of 164 againſt 48. *

Paſſes the
co.nmons,
May 3d.

In the upper houſe it was ſucceſsfully oppoſed by Rejected by
the lords.

* Chandler. Journals.

the interest of the church and the law; a considerable number of courtiers were also non-contents. The two great lawyers, lord chancellor Talbot and lord Hardwicke, made a strong impression by observations on the incorrectness and imperfections of the bill, for the amendment of which, the short remainder of the session would not afford time. "The speakers on both sides displayed great abilities and temper, but when the question was put, for committing the bill, it passed in the negative; by a majority of 54 against 35." *

Dissatisfaction of the minister.

The minister was highly dissatisfied with the rejection of a bill which he was induced from various considerations to promote. He was strongly averse to all measures which bore the appearance of persecution in religious matters. His conduct was also influenced by personal considerations. A large body of quakers were established in the county of Norfolk, and particularly in the city of Norwich, who had always supported the candidates whom he favoured at the general elections, and he was anxious, from a principle of gratitude, to prove that he was not unmindful of past favours, and deserving of future assistance. These motives operated so strongly in its favour, that few circumstances ever ruffled his temper, or affected his equanimity more than the rejection of this bill. He bitterly complained of the vindictive spirit which reigned in the house of lords, and his resentment was principally excited against the bishop of London; to whom he attributed its defeat.

Resentment against bishop Gibson.

* Tindal, vol. 20, p. 315. Lords' Debates.

defeat. That prelate had prevailed on the bench of
bifhops, to give their decided oppofition to the
bill, and had exhorted the clergy, in all quarters
of the kingdom, to petition againft it, as highly
prejudicial to the interefts of the church. In
confequence of thefe exertions, the minifter, with
a fpirit of acrimony very unufual to him, withdrew
from the learned prelate the full confidence which
he had hitherto placed in him, and transferred
into other hands the conduct of ecclefiaftical affairs with which he had been chiefly entrufted.

Edmund Gibfon was born in 1669, *, and educated at the free grammar fchool at Bampton, in
Weftmoreland, the place of his nativity. At the
age of feventeen, he was admitted a fcholar of
Queen's college, Oxford, and raifed himfelf into
early notice by various publications, which proved
his claffical erudition, his accurate acquaintance
with the Northern languages, and a correct
knowledge of the Roman and Saxon antiquities,
and Britifh topography. His great talents and
extenfive learning, introduced him to the patronage of archbifhop Tenifon, who made him li-
brarian of Lambeth, and appointed him his domeftic chaplain. By the archbifhop's interest, he
became precentor and refidentiary of Chichefter,
rector of Lambeth, and archdeacon of Surry. In
1713, he gave to the public that great and laborious
work, intituled, " Codex Juris Ecclefiaftici An-
glicani, or the Statutes, Conftitutions, Canons,
Rubricks, and articles of the church of England,
metho-

* Biographia Britannica.

methodically digefted under their proper heads; with a commentary, hiftorical and juridical, and with an introductory difcourfe concerning the prefent ftate of the power, difcipline, and laws of the church of England, with an appendix of inftruments, antient and modern, in folio."

Being a great friend to· the proteftant fucceffion, he was promoted, in 1716, to the bifhopric of Lincoln, and in 1720, tranflated to the fee of London.

In this eminent ftation, he enjoyed the full confidence of the king and miniftry, and was principally confulted by lord Townfhend and Sir Robert Walpole, in all ecclefiaftical matters, particularly during the long decline of health which incapacitated archbifhop Wake for tranfacting bufinefs. He was always zealous in fupporting the eftablifhment of the church of England, and uniformly oppofed the repeal of the teft act. He declined a tranflation to Winchefter, * and looked forwards to the primacy with fuch confidence of expectation, that he was called by Whifton, heir apparent to the fee of Canterbury. Thefe wellfounded hopes were fruftrated by the indignation of Walpole for his oppofition to the quaker's bill. On the deceafe of Wake, the fee was conferred on Potter. And when, on his death, in 1747, it was offered to Gibfon, he declined it on account of his advanced age and increafing infirmities.†
He died on the 6th of February 1748.

The

* Letter from bifhop Gibfon to Sir Robert Walpole. Orford Papers.
† Letter from bifhop Gibfon to the king, communicated by the bifhop of Salifbury (Dr. Douglas.)

The inveteracy difplayed againft this eminent Chapter 46. prelate for the confcientious difcharge of his duty, 1736. reflects no credit on the memory of Sir Robert Walpole. His efteem for the bifhop of London had been fo great, that when he was reproached with giving him the authority of a pope, he re- plied, " And a very good pope he is."* Even after their difagreement, he never failed to pay an eulogium to the learning and integrity of his for- mer friend.

On the 20th of May, the king put an end to this Prorogation of parliament. late feffion of parliament, by a fpeech, in which he acquainted both houfes, " that fince the preli- minary articles had been concluded between the Emperor and his moft Chriftian majefty, a further convention, concerning the execution of them, had been made and communicated by both thofe courts, and that negociations were carrying on by the feveral powers engaged in the late war, in order to fettle the general pacification." He ex- preffed himfelf with great concern in relation to the feeds of diffenfion that had been fown amongft his people, exhorting his parliament to cultivate unanimity, and promifing impartial protection to all his fubjects. He then acquainted them, that being obliged that fummer to vifit his German do- minions, he hoped that they would make the ad- miniftration of the queen, whom he had refolved to appoint regent during his abfence, as eafy to
her,

* Etough's Minutes of Converfations with Sir Robert Walpole.

Period VI. her, as her wife conduct would render her go-
1734 to 1737. vernment agreeable to them. *

Horace Wal-
pole declines
the office of
fecretary of
ftate.

At this period, Sir Robert Walpole and his
brother gave a memorable proof of their prudence
and moderation. The king being diffatisfied with
lord Harrington, propofed to difmifs him from the
office of fecretary of ftate, and queen Caroline
offered the place to Horace Walpole; but confcious that the elevation of two brothers to the
principal pofts of government, would augment
the jealoufy and popular outcry which already
prevailed, and fearful left fo important a change
fhould increafe the divifions among the minifters,
he declined the offer. The king, however, would
not admit lord Harrington's attendance at Hanover, and though he acquiefced in the refufal of
Horace Walpole, yet he infifted on his undertaking the employment of fecretary of ftate during his refidence abroad; an order which Horace

Accompanies
the king to
Hanover.

Walpole, though he attempted to elude, could
not venture to difobey, and accordingly accompanied the king to Hanover. †

Confidential
correfpond-
ence.

As the king was extremely jealous of being governed, and yet as his ignorance of the Englifh
conftitution, and his natural attachment to German meafures, rendered it expedient that he
fhould be advifed by thofe who were refponfible
for the adminiftration of affairs, it became neceffary to convey this advice in fo delicate a manner,
that he fhould appear to guide the reins, which
                                                    were

---

* Tindal, vol. 20. p. 325. Journals. Chandler.
† Horace Walpole's Apology.

were conducted by another hand. With this view, a confidential correfpondence was carried on between the two brothers; and as the king always expected to fee any private letters which paffed between them, an arrangement was made, that oftenfible letters fhould be fent for the perufal of the king, and confidential ones to Horace Walpole alone. A part of this correfpondence is ftill preferved; thofe letters of Sir Robert Walpole which relate to foreign affairs, prove, as ufual, his extreme caution in avoiding, as much as poffible, any continental embarraffments, which were not immediately neceffary to the prefervation of external peace and internal tranquillity.

The letters on domeftic occurrences, are chiefly concerning the murder of captain Porteus; tumults in Spitalfields, on employing Irifh manufacturers, and the riots on account of the gin act. They difplay his good fenfe and prudence, in endeavouring to prevent rather than punifh difturbances, and yet indicate no deficiency of vigour, when it was requifite to act with fpirit. *

Befides the difficult tafk of fettling the difputes between the Emperor and the allies, which encountered continual obftructions from the difcordant views of the contending powers, three foreign objects of great importance principally occupied the attention of the king at Hanover, and gave fufficient employment to the fagacity of Walpole: The regulation of the fucceffion of Berg and Júliers: the project of a league with the northern powers;

* See Correfpondence.

powers; and the mediation between Ruffia and the Porte.

John William, duke of Cleves, Juliers, and Berg, dying in 1609 without iffue, his dominions were claimed by the houfes of Saxony, Brandenburgh, and palatine Newburgh. After a long conteft, the difputed fucceffion was regulated by a family compact, and divided between the great elector Frederick William, who was defcended from the eldeft fifter of John William, and Philip William, duke of Newburgh, afterwards elector palatine, who was defcended from the fecond fifter. Frederick William obtained Cleves, La Marck, and Ravenftein; Philip William, Juliers and Berg. By the family compact, it was ftipulated, that fhould the male iffue of either branch become extinct, the other fhould inherit the whole fucceffion.

As at this period Charles, fon of Philip William, having no iffue, and being advanced in years, the fucceffion of Berg and Juliers was claimed by Frederick William, king of Pruffia, grandfon of the great elector. But his claims were oppofed by Charles Frederick, prince palatine of Sultzbach, of the collateral line of the houfe of palatine Newburgh, as being lineally defcended from the third fifter of the laft duke of Cleves. He accordingly remonftrated againft the family compact; and was fupported in his pretenfions by the elector palatine, to whom he was prefumptive heir. This fucceffion had long been a favourite object of Frederick William: He was

4   prepared

prepared to affert his pretenfions with his whole
force, on the death of the elector palatine, and was
fecure of wrefting these duchies from the houfe of
Sultzbach, had not the latter been openly fupported or fecretly abetted by other powers.

It became an object of common prudence and
policy, to obviate the difficulties which were likely
to arife on the death of the elector palatine, and
to regulate, if poffible, the provifional fucceffion
to the difputed provinces, in fuch a manner as to
prevent the difturbance of the public peace. But
the difcordant views and complicated interefts of
the powers who were capable of interfering with
effect, gave little hopes of a fuccefsful and ftable
arrangement.

France had given her guaranty to the houfe of
Sultzbach, but fhe had given it at a time when
fhe was interefted to fecure the palatine family,
and as that motive no longer operated with the
fame force, it was probable that fhe would act in
conformity to the fituation of affairs at the time
of the vacancy.

The Emperor, with his ufual duplicity, had
fecretly guarantied the provifional fucceffion to
both the contefting parties; but although he had
lured Frederick William with the moft folemn
profeffions to fupport his pretenfions, yet he was
known to be fecretly inclined to favour the houfe
of Sultzbach. In all events, however, he was
unwilling to offend either Pruffia or the palatine
family, and was no lefs anxious than France to
avoid

avoid a public declaration of his future resolutions.

The Dutch, whofe territories bordered on Berg and Juliers, were more than any other power interefted to prevent difturbances on the death of the elector palatine, and extremely anxious to propofe fuch an accommodation as fhould remove the apprehenfions of a war. They therefore applied to the Emperor and France, and defired the king of England's concurrence to propofe inftant and proper meafures for obviating the troubles by an accommodation between the contending parties, and preventing all hoftile aggreffions while that accommodation was negociating.

George the Second, highly difgufted with the king of Pruffia, was averfe to fupport any meafures which might tend to his aggrandifement, and would not eafily be prevailed on to guaranty his fucceffion to Juliers and Berg, unlefs fome advantage was ftipulated for himfelf. For this reafon, the Dutch had propofed that Eaft Friefland, to which both he and the king of Pruffia had pretenfions, fhould, on the death of the reigning fovereign without iffue, revert to George the Second as elector of Hanover, the right of maintaining a garrifon in Embden being referved to the Dutch. They farther recommended, that in confidération of renouncing all claim on Eaft Friefland, fuch a portion of Juliers and Berg, as might be adjudged to the king of Pruffia, fhould be fecured under the guaranty of England.

The

The king feemed inclined to confent to thefe
ftipulations; but the minifter, ftrongly averfe to
complicated and diftant guaranties, expreffed his
objections, to all interference; declared himfelf
againft prematurely agreeing to guaranty the fucceffion of Berg and Juliers, in which they might
be left fingly with the Dutch, or making any
declaration which might difoblige either Pruffia
or the palatine family. He ftated the great inconveniencies which might arife from blending
that affair with the general tranfactions then in
agitation, when the Emperor and France had
agreed to poftpone the confideration of it, till
the chief bufinefs of the prefent negociation fhould
be concluded. His opinion prevailed, and all
thoughts of interference were relinquifhed. *

The nothern league was the object which moft
embarraffed the minifter, and reduced him to
the neceffity of oppofing the king's inclinations.
Rofencrantz, the Danifh minifter at Hanover,
with a view to benefit his own country, and Mr.
Finch, the Britifh envoy at Stockholm, from a defire of favouring the court at which he was employed,
had reprefented to the king the good policy of
forming a league between the maritime powers, and
Sweden and Denmark. The king, who underftood the interefts of Hanover better than thofe
of England, and who could not fufficiently appreciate the great commercial and naval principles by which the minifter was actuated in forming

---

* Sir Robert Walpole to Horace Walpole, June $\frac{18}{29}$, 1736. Cor-
refpondence. Thoughts on the Succeffion of Berg, Juliers, and Eaft,
Friefland, by Horace Walpole. Walpole Papers.—Hiftory of the
Succeffion to the Duchies of Juliers and Berg.

ing alliances and giving guaranties, eagerly embraced, and zealously supported the scheme; and
with a view to keep the king of Pruffia in awe,
propofed * the acceffion of Ruffia. He communicated his wifhes to the queen, and requefted
the opinion of Sir Robert Walpole in fuch a manner, as fufficiently proved to which fide he inclined. The minifter difapproved the meafure,
and confidered it not only as highly inexpedient,
but as abfolutely impracticable. He was convinced that fuch an alliance with Sweden would
offend the Czarina, unlefs fhe was invited to accede, and that her acceffion could not be obtained but by guarantying the poffeffion of Livonia
and Ingria, which would no lefs offend Sweden.
In his oftenfible letter to his brother, Walpole
frankly ftated his objections to precipitate refolutions, recommended cautious proceedings, and
particular attention not to offend the Emperor
and Ruffia, and reprobated expenfive and burthenfome guaranties.

Counteracted
by Walpole.
Auguft 15.
As the negociation became more and more complicated, and the king feemed inclined to perfevere in his opinion, Walpole prudentially infinuated, that a matter of fuch extreme delicacy and
importance, fhould be tranfacted by an official
correfpondence, rather than by private letters between the king and queen. The king having approved this propofal, Horace Walpole was ordered
to prepare the project, and received hints from
his brother in what manner it fhould be drawn.
Being

* Horace Walpole to Sir Robert Walpole, Auguft 5. Correfpondence.

Being fubmitted to the king, he highly approved
it, and was eager for the conclufion. It was then
tranfmitted to Sir Robert Walpole for the confideration of the queen and the lords juftices, and
was accompanied by a paper of private obfervations againft the treaty. The minifter found this
paper fo convincing, that although intended for
his own ufe, he communicated it to the queen.
Convinced by the foundnefs of the arguments,
fhe promifed to conceal any knowledge of this
paper from the king, and to write her fentiments
in conformity to that opinion. At the fame time,
Sir Robert Walpole wrote an oftenfible letter to
his brother, informing him that he fhould decline
laying the project before the cabinet council, left
the fudden difclofure of fo important a tranfaction, might create furprife and alarm, and propofed to delay the communication until the negociation was farther advanced, the inclination of
the norther courts founded, and the fituation of
affairs more fettled, " that we may fee" he adds
" who and who are together, before we form
new fchemes, that may clafh with we know not
whom nor how." Thefe prudent meafures were
attended with the defired effect, and the king
finally confented to abandon his favourite project *.

  This whole tranfaction reflects equal honour on
the minifter and the king: On the minifter, for
frankly delivering his fentiments, and perfevering
in them, though oppofite to thofe of his fovereign;

* Correfpondence.

reign ; on the king, for yielding to the arguments, and wifhes of his faithful counfellor. Thofe who confider the impatience of contradiction, and pertinacity of opinion, which marked the character of George the Second, will highly appreciate the merit of his fubmitting to the guidance, and conforming to the advice, which fo ftrongly contradicted his own wifhes.

War between Ruffia and the Porte.

In the midft of thefe tranfactions, hoftilities broke out between the Ruffians and Turks, which, in confequence of the alliances of France and Sweden with the Turks, and of the Emperor with Ruffia, appeared likely to excite a general war; yet, contrary to thefe expectations, this event contributed more than any other caufe to accelerate the pacification in Europe. The Emperor, divided between the fear of irritating the Czarina on one hand, and of retarding the peace on the other, and tempted with the hope of fharing the fpoils of the Turks, became lefs averfe to the aggrandifement of the houfe of Bourbon.

Walpole declines mediating.

A mediation between the contending powers had been propofed by Calkoen, the Dutch minifter at Conftantinople, and too eagerly adopted by the Englifh embaffador, Sir Everard Fawkener. Walpole was apprehenfive left the Czarina fhould conftrue a premature officioufnefs into a partiality for the Porte, and confider it as an attempt to ftop the career of that fuccefs with which her arms were crowned.

He was alarmed, left the dignity of England fhould be lowered by offering the mediation be-

fore

fore it was defired, without a certainty of its being accepted. He was convinced, that any attempt, to reconcile Ruffia and the Porte, would
be fruitlefs and ineffectual; and he obferved, in a letter to Horace Walpole, " For my
part, I think you may as well hope to break in
upon the conftancy of two lovers in the honey-
moon, as to ftop the career of two powers juft
engaged in war, in the heat of their refentment,
and before they have had time to feel, to reflect,
and grow cool." * His advice prevailed alfo in this
inftance, and the mediation was declined.

The fignature of the preliminaries between Difficulties in
France and the Emperor, did not, however, pro-reconciling the
Emperor and
duce an immediate pacification. Several months the allies.
elapfed before the kings of Sardinia and Spain
could be prevailed on to accede, and when their
concurrence was reluctantly obtained, difputes
occafionally revived between France and the Emperor, and a long feries of negociation took place
before the final ratification.

Nor are thefe delays to be attributed folely to Capricious dif.
the allies. The Emperor, though a prince of high pofition of the
Emperor.
fpirit, and by no means deficient in capacity, was
of fuch a changeful and capricious temper, and
appeared fo different at different intervals, that to
define his real character and fituation, confounded
the wifdom of the wifeft, and baffled the conjectures of the moft enlightened.

At one time he was fo exafperated with England, that he threatened to feparate himfelf from
her

* Sir Robert Walpole to Horace Walpole, Anguft ⅘, 1736. Correfpondence.

Period VI. her for ever, and was so devoted to France, as
1734 to 1737. to induce Mr. Robinson to observe, in a letter to
lord Harrington, "This court is too much in the
June 20. hands of that of Versailles, not to do every thing
that the other wills, or to do any thing that
the other wills not." At another time he courted
England with the greatest eagerness; denounced
the house of Bourbon as his irreconcileable enemy,
and offended cardinal Fleury by the most arrogant
and presumptuous demeanour. With a prince of
such a changeful temper, it was no easy task to
negociate. His ministers were no less intractable;
and Vienna exhibited a motley scene of pride,
humility, cabal, intrigue, and procrastination.

Dissatisfaction   Another great difficulty arose from Francis
of the duke of duke of Loraine, who had espoused the eldest arch-
Loraine.
duchess, Maria Theresa; and was unwilling to
renounce his family inheritance. He required,
that if Loraine was ceded to France before the
death of the grand duke of Tuscany, an adequate
compensation should be secured to him. Mr.
Robinson, in one of his dispatches, gives a pathetic and interesting account of his extreme distress and agitation on this occasion. * "In an
audience which I demanded of him, to announce
the marriage of the prince of Wales with the
princess of Saxe Gotha, he interrupted me in the
midst of his compliments, to pour out his joy at
the marriage, and his respect and veneration for
the king, which he first expressed aloud. But
left

* Mr. Robinson to lord Harrington, May 30th, 1736. Walpole
Papers.

left any of his attendants in the next room might overhear, he retreated with me to a window 'at the farther end of the apartment, and said with the greateſt emotion, " Good God, where are you, where are the maritime powers ! As for my part," he continued, " I rely upon the king " ſingly, not upon treaties, not upon formal pro- " miſes, but upon what his majeſty has told me " over and over again of his goodneſs for me by " word of mouth." If his words expreſſed the higheſt agony and diſtreſs, his geſtures and ac- tions expreſſed no leſs : " He threw himſelf, in a reclining poſture, and in an inconſolable man- ner, upon the arms and end of an adjoining ta- ble and chair." " Such alſo," adds Mr. Ro- binſon, " is the extreme agitation of his mind, that his health is affected by it ; he owns that he has no friend to look up to, and that next to God and the Emperor, all his fortune depends on the king of England."

Perhaps theſe complicated diſputes would ne- ver have been ſettled without another war, had not the pacific ſpirit of Walpole and Fleury in- terpoſed, and had not the Emperor, eager to make war againſt the Turks, with a view to in- demnify himſelf on the ſide of Boſnia, for the loſs of Naples and Sicily, found it previouſly ne- ceſſary to ſecure the peace of Italy, that he might draw his troops into Hungary.

Views and con-
duct of the
Emperor.

The French, aware of his inclination, refuſed, under various pretences, to evacuate the Mila- neſe ; the Emperor was induced to make repeated conceffions, and finally to yield the immediate poffeffion of Loraine, for the eventual fucceffion of Tufcany. He was fo eager to conclude the definitive treaty, that he paid 600,000 florins more than he had ftipulated. He gave to the king of Sardinia, eftates among the Langhes, as fiefs of the empire, which never belonged to the empire, and fuffered that monarch to mark the limits of his dominions according to his own conveniency. *

In the courfe of thefe various negotiations, Walpole had ufed every effort to conciliate difcordant parties, and to effect a general accommodation. He well knew that the great obftacles to a general peace, proceeded from the intrigues of Chauvelin, who, from the time of his appointment to the office of fecretary of ftate, and keeper of the feals, almoft invariably ufed the afcendency which he had gained over cardinal Fleury, in counteracting the defigns of England. To obtain his co-operation, Walpole directed his principal attention, and even adopted the chimerical project of bribing him to compliance. The profpect of fuccefs was principally founded on the extravagance of Chauvelin. He lived in a ftile of great profufion. He had laid out, and continued to expend large fums in beautifying his favourite villa of Gros Bois, which vied in magnificence with the royal palaces.

With whom or in what manner the fcheme originated, the papers under my infpection do

not

* Thomas Robinfon to lord Harrington, Auguft 5. Grantham

not supply specific information. Sir Robert Wal- Chapter 46.
pole was too cautious to make such attempt, had 1736.
not some favourable circumstances occurred. It
is not improbable that a hint imparted by Trevor,
and insinuated in a letter from Horace Walpole to
queen Caroline, might have suggested the first *
idea. It was an experiment which the minister
deemed it imprudent to reject, though he never entertained sanguine hopes of success. Perhaps the
first opening was afforded by Chauvelin himself,
who, to support his own declining interest, was
desirous of securing the assistance of Sir Robert
Walpole; with whom Fleury was anxious to co-
operate in establishing the peace of Europe. But
he had no sooner effected a temporary re-establish-
ment of his credit, than he discontinued this private correspondence, rejected all pecuniary grati-
fications, refused to give any farther information,
and became, as before, the inveterate enemy to
England.

The commencement, progress, and termination
of this intrigue, are detailed in the private correspondence which passed between Sir Robert
Walpole and the earl of Waldegrave, and was
communicated only to the king. In the succeed-
ing year, Chauvelin made another attempt to renew his secret offers, in such a manner as induced
the earl of Waldegrave to conclude, that he
would accept a bribe. Walpole wrote to the
English embassador, to avoid being again deceived;

---

* Horace Walpole to queen Caroline, August $\frac{1}{12}$, 1735. Correspondence.

to offer a large bribe, of not lefs than £. 5 or
10,000, and if that was not accepted, to obtain the
removal of one whom he calls our quondam friend,
but now our greateft enemy. *

Fleury pro-
pofes an alli-
ance with Eng-
land.

While this intrigue was in agitation, cardinal
Fleury, in a confidential converfation with the
earl of Waldegrave, made heavy complaints againft
the conduct of the Britifh minifters abroad, and
propofed, through the channel of Horace Walpole alone, an alliance with England, † to check
the ambitious defigns of the Emperor, and keep
in awe the reftlefs fpirit of the queen of Spain,
who had fo often convulfed Europe to aggrandife
her own family. The anfwer of Horace Walpole
began with a fpirited remonftrance againft the
weaknefs of the cardinal, in liftening to all the
idle and malicious reports of thofe who endeavoured to fow diffenfions between the two crowns;
ftated the impoffibility of acceding to the propofal
of a particular union with France in the prefent
juncture, becaufe Chauvelin would obftruct and dif-
appoint all hopes of bringing it to a fuccefsful iffue.
He concluded with reprefenting, that the king had
always had in view the prefervation of the tranquillity and equilibrium of Europe; that the numerous
treaties which France had made before the late troubles, and the complicated negotiations for the execution of the preliminaries, in which the king
had not participated, rendered it impoffible to determine

---

* Sir Robert Walpole to the earl of Waldegrave, September 26,
1726. Correfpondence.

† Horace Walpole to the earl of Waldegrave, Auguft 8. 19th,
1735. Correfpondence.

termine what meaſures or alliances would be moſt
proper for preſerving the balance of power, until
the whole plan of the league ſhould be propoſed;
that if the plan ſhould appear conformable to that
great end, the king would ſupport it by every
means in his power ; and concluded with repreſenting, that the cardinal would always find the
king diſpoſed to preſerve a good underſtanding
with France.

Foiled in this attempt, the cardinal endeavoured
to ſucceed by opening a private correſpondence
with Sir Robert Walpole, the knowledge of whoſe
pacific ſentiments, inſpired him with the confidence and hopes of impoſing upon him, and drawing him in gradually to abet the alliance with
France, and by that means to ſeparate the Emperor ſtill more from England. Two converſa-
tions which the cardinal held with the earl of
Waldegrave on this ſubject, will ſerve to ſhew the
art with which he endeavoured to amuſe the Britiſh cabinet. *

After delivering his ſentiments on the murder
of captain Porteous, and recommending lenity to
the miſled populace who were concerned in that
tranſaction, he repreſented the neceſſity of curbing the overgrown power of the Emperor ; hinted
as his opinion, to be ſolely communicated to Sir
Robert Walpole, that the beſt method of effecting that end, would be a league of the proteſtant

princes

* The earl of Waldegrave's letters to Sir Robert Walpole, October 23d, and November 21ſt, 1736. Correſpondence.

princes in Europe, to be propofed by England,
and fupported by France. In reply to thefe friendly communications, the minifter commiffioned lord
Waldegrave to exprefs great refpect for the cardinal, and an earneft defire to cultivate his friendfhip, for the mutual honour and intereft of the
two kingdoms. At this, the cardinal interrupt-
ing him, expreffed the higheft opinion of Sir
Robert Walpole's diftinguifhed abilities, and particularly expatiated on his integrity and fpirit,
characteriftics highly neceffary in the compofition
of a great minifter. He then propofed a fecret
correfpondence, through the channel of the earl
of Waldegrave, to which, in France, no one fhould
be privy but the king, and in England, only the
king and queen; trufting, on his part, that no
advantage would be taken, and no hints given of
this intercourfe.

Although Sir Robert Walpole was not ignorant,
that during thefe overtures, the cardinal had been
endeavouring to perfuade the Emperor to conclude a definitive treaty, exclufive of the maritime powers, he neither reproached him for his
infincerity, nor declined the offer of a confidential
communication. He on the contrary affected to
difbelieve, while he hinted the report, becaufe,
he faid, it contradicted the declarations fo frequently and folemnly made by the cardinal, that the
maritime powers fhould be included in all the definitive tranfactions for a treaty, as alfo, becaufe he
did not doubt his fincerity in defiring a particular
alliance with England. Uniformly attached to his

grand

grand principle of promoting peace by whomfo-
ever, or in whatever manner it was effected, he
expreffed his readinefs to concur in all meafures
which might be juft and honourable to the two
nations, and requefted him to draw up the heads
of a definitive treaty.

Although the earl of Waldegrave juftly remarked, from his knowledge of the cardinal's character, that much could not be concluded from
thefe private tranfactions, they ferved, however,
to preferve harmony, and to foften the immediate
effects of that inveterate jealoufy which had fo
long divided the two nations. The mutual in-
terchange of friendly difcuffion ftrengthened the
pacific fentiments adopted by both minifters, and
prevented the hafty renewal of offenfive meafures.
The outlines of the definitive treaty were fettled,
and the conclufion of the general pacification accelerated.

Another confiderable advantage was alfo un-
queftionably derived from this private tranfaction.
It gave to Sir Robert Walpole and the earl of
Waldegrave, opportunities of reprefenting the
malicious conduct of Chauvelin, and occafioned,
or haftened his downfal, which took place in the
commencement of the enfuing year, and to which
the reprefentations of Waldegrave greatly contributed.

Before the difmiffion of Chauvelin, an interefting correfpondence had paffed between the
two brothers and the other minifters, relating to
a curious incident that happened to the earl of

Waldegrave

Period VI. Waldegrave at Paris. Chauvelin having, among
1734 to 1737 other papers, by miftake, put into his hands. a
letter from the Pretender, the embaffador fent it
by a courier to the queen. Immediate information
was forwarded by Newcaftle to the king at
Hanover, with the remarks of Sir Robert Walpole. Several letters paffed between the minifter in
London, Horace Walpole at Hanover, and the
earl of Waldegrave at Paris, which prove the extreme uneafinefs and jealoufy excited by this
difcovery.

Jacobitifm at that time produced a tremor
through every nerve of government; and the flighteft incident which difcovered any intercourfe between the Pretender and France, occafioned the
moft ferious apprehenfions. It was no wonder,
therefore, that this event fhould fpread alarms,
which the obfervations of the two brothers were
calculated to obviate. The letters which paffed
on this occafion, are given in order of date, and
are fufficiently explicit without any farther illuf-
trations. *

Riots in Lon-
don.

During the abfence of the king at Hanover,
where he remained till the beginning of January,
the fpirit of difcontent and infurrection was bufy
at home; and various tumults took place in the
capital, and other parts of the kingdom. In the
capital, thefe difturbances were occafioned by the
weavers in Spitalfields, who took umbrage that the
Irifh were employed at an inferior rate of wages;
and by the difcontent of the populace, excited
by the execution of the gin act.

Thefe

---

* Correfpondence. Period VI. Article, the Pretender's Letter.

These alarming riots, which were notoriously
fomented by the disaffected, were scarcely suppressed, when a more atrocious outrage demanded
the attention of government.   One Wilson, a daring smuggler, was sentenced to be hanged at Edinburgh, for having robbed a collector of the revenue.   This man, having abetted the escape of
a fellow criminal, in the time of divine service,
and from the midst of his guards, the magistrates
of Edinburgh increased their usual precautions for
the execution of the sentence, by ordering the officers of the train bands and the city guard, provided with arms and ammunition, to attend for
the purpose of preventing his rescue.   The procession passed along; the sentence was performed
without the smallest appearance of riot, and the
executioner was at the top of the ladder cutting
down the body, when the magistrates retired.   At
this moment, the populace rushed forward towards the gallows, part forced their way through
the guards, with intention, as was supposed, to
carry off the body, under the hopes of recovering it.   Others threw large stones, maimed several
soldiers, and struck captain Porteous, who was so
provoked at this outrage, that he ordered the
soldiers to fire.   Five were killed, and several
wounded.   Porteous was immediately apprehended,
and tried, for having directed the soldiers to fire
without the orders of the civil magistrate, and was
condemned to death.   But so many favourable
circumstances appeared on his trial, that seven of
the fifteen jurymen acquitted him, and the verdict

dict which condemned him, acknowledged that " he and his guards were attacked and beat with " several stones of a considerable bigness, thrown " by the multitude, whereby several of the sol- " diers were bruised and wounded." * In con- sequence of this ridiculous inconsistency in the verdict, and other favourable circumstances, the queen regent sent down a respite of six weeks, for the purpose of inquiring into the circumstances of the case.

On the 3d, the reprieve was brought to Edin- burgh, and on the 4th, vague reports were cir- culated, that the populace had resolved, on the evening of the 8th, to set fire to the prison, if Porteous was not executed on that day, according to his sentence. But the magistrates, on inquiry, could not discover any foundation for the report, and no precaution was taken to remove the pri- soner into the castle. On Tuesday the 7th, about a quarter before ten at night, the magistrates had notice, that a few boys had seized the drum in the suburb of West Port, and beat it in the Grass Market within the city. About six minutes be- fore ten, they sent to call out the guard imme- diately under arms; but a few minutes before the clock struck, a mob suddenly rushed in upon, and surprised the guards, drove them from the guard room, seized all their arms, being ninety firelocks in number, besides several Lochaber axes, and almost at the same time made themselves

masters

* Trial and Sentence; Political State, 1736; and Gentleman's Magaz'?.

masters of the city gates. They then provided
themselves with shot, by breaking open the shops
where ammunition was sold, attacked the jail,
drove out the provosts and magistrates, who attempted to disperse them, and wounded several of
their attendants. They next set fire to the gate
of the prison, and rushed into the wards, forced
the turnkeys to open the doors, released all the
prisoners, seized Porteous, and dragged him to the
Grass Market, where they broke into a shop, took
out a coil of ropes, and hung him upon a dyer's
cross post, close to the common place of execution. * Lindsay, member for the city, found
means to escape from the town, and to convey
information of the tumult to general Moyle, commander of the king's troops, who were quartered
in the suburbs ; but as he was obliged to make
a large circuit, he did not reach the head quarters till near eleven. General Moyle had already
collected his own troops, and sent for those who
were quartered at Leith, but made no attempt
to force the gate of the city, which was occupied
by the armed populace. He persisted in refusing
to act against the insurgents, on the faith of Lindsay's intelligence, without an order from the civil
magistrate ; and as he deemed it impossible to obtain an order from the magistrates in the city,
he dispatched a messenger to Andrew Fletcher,
lord justice clerk of Scotland, who was at his
villa at the distance of above two miles and a half.
Fletcher being in bed, no answer was procured
until

* Narrative of the Tumult. Correspondence.

until one o'clock, and by some miftake, it was then delivered not to the general, but to Lindsay. Meanwhile the execution of Porteous had taken place, the exertions of the military were rendered unneceffary, by the difperfion of the rioters, and in the morning, Edinburgh was in a ftate of perfect tranquillity.

Lord Ilay was fent to Edinburgh, as the only perfon capable of bringing the offenders to juftice. The accounts * which he tranfmitted to Sir Robert Walpole, proved that a regular fyftematic plan had been formed with the utmoft fecrecy and order; that feveral made this infamous murder a point of confcience; and that one of the actors went to a country church, where the facrament was given to a large number of people in the church-yard, and boafted of the fhare which he had taken in the tranfaction. He obferved, that perfons who affected fanctity, fpoke of the murder as the hand of God doing juftice, and reprobated all endeavours to bring the actors to condign punifhment, as grievous perfecution. He added alfo, that although feveral perfons had been imprifoned, and large rewards offered, no difcoveries had been made of the perpetrators or inftigators of this atrocious act.

* Correfpondence.

CHAPTER THE FORTY-SEVENTH:

1737.

Meeting of Parliament.—Speech from the, Throne.—Proceedings:—On .the Bill refpecting the Tumults at Edinburgh.—On Sir John Barnard's Scheme for the Reduction of Interest.—Licentioufnefs of the Stage.—— Origin and Progrefs of the Playhoufe Bill.

THIS feffion of parliament, which opened on the 1ft of February, was as unquiet and ftormy, as the laft had been eafy and tranquil. Meeting of parliament.

The parliamentary proceedings which it is ne-ceffary to notice, are the debates refpecting the tumults in Edinburgh; Sir John Barnard's pro-pofal for the reduction of interest; the playhoufe bill; and the motion for an addrefs to the king, to fettle £.100,000 per annum on the prince of Wales. Parliamentary proceedings.

The fpeech from the throne noticed the late difturbances, but without any fpecific mention of the tumult at Edinburgh. It was anfwered by loyal addreffes from both houfes, expreffing their abhorrence of fuch outrages, and their refolu-tion to fupport the royal authority in fuppref-fing all riotous and feditious attempts, which threatened the very being of the conftitution. The minifter, however, feems to have been embarraffed in what manner to introduce the inquiry. For-tunately, lord Carteret relieved him from this di-lemma. Although he was in violent oppofition to the meafures of adminiftration, yet he juftly thought On the murder of Porteous. In the houfe of lords.

thought that the indignity committed againſt the
eſtabliſhed government, ſhould not remain un-
puniſhed. He accordingly referred to that part
of the ſpeech which alluded to the tumults in various parts of the kingdom. After arguing that
theſe riots did not proceed from diſaffection to
government, and complaining, that notwithſtanding the power with which the civil magiſtrate
was armed, the military force had been employed
in ſuppreſſing them; he adverted to the murder
of captain Porteous, which he particularly ſtigma-
tiſed as a moſt atrocious deed; obſerving that the
conſpiracy which had effected it was the more
dreadful, becauſe it was concerted and executed
with great deliberation and method, and was attended with no other diſorder. He was of opinion,
that ſome citizens of Edinburgh had been concerned in the murder; that the magiſtrates had
encouraged the riot, and that the city had for-
feited its charter; he concluded with expreſſing
hopes that an inquiry would be made into the
particulars and circumſtances of the caſe.

The duke of Newcaſtle and the lord chancellor,
after contending for the neceſſity of employing
the military force in ſuppreſſing riots and putting
the laws in execution, and juſtifying the reprieve
of captain Porteous, did not reſiſt or promote the
inveſtigation propoſed by lord Carteret; they only
argued for a general inquiry into the cauſes and
circumſtances of the riot, and not for a ſpecific
inquiry into the diſturbances. Carteret, in reply,
maintained the neceſſity of a particular inquiry,
and

and of confining it to the tumult at Edinburgh.
The earl of Ilay, after oppoſing the forfeiture of
the charter, and obſerving that the outrages had
originated from diſaffection to government, declared himſelf in favour of a particular inquiry,
and expreſſed his readineſs to join in any propoſition for that purpoſe. A motion was accordingly
made by Carteret, for the attendance of the magiſtrates, and other perſons who could give the
neceſſary information, and for an addreſs to the
king, that copies of the trial of captain Porteous,
and the account of the murder, ſhould be laid
before the houſe.

In conſequence of this motion, which paſſed
without oppoſition, the reſpective documents
were produced. In examining the proceedings of
the trial, it plainly appeared that Porteous was
fully juſtified, from the principles of ſelf-defence,
in firing upon the mob, and that the reprieve
granted by the queen was founded on law and
juſtice; and as the conſtitution of the criminal
law in Scotland was different from that in England,
it appeared incomprehenſible to moſt of the peers,
that a perſon could be condemned to death, upon
a verdict ſo inconſiſtent with common juſtice.
Accordingly, it was ſuggeſted by Carteret, to declare the verdict erroneous; this propoſal was oppoſed by the earl of Ilay and the lord chancellor,
and no motion was made. *

Having thus juſtified the proceedings of government, the next object was to diſcover thoſe
who

* Lords' Debate.

who were concerned in the murder, and to punish all who either concerted or connived at it. The magiftrates of Edinburgh, the commander in chief of the forces, Lindfay, member for the city, as well as the Scots judges, were feverally and feparately examined at the bar. Their allegations, however, were confufed and unfatisfactory; but proofs appeared that the magiftrates had not been fufficiently active in preventing the rifing of the mob, or in fuppreffing it when excited. Yet no legal evidence was obtained to convict them, nor did it appear that any of the citizens had been acceffary to the murder, and not a fingle perfon was difcovered who had been concerned in it. Notwithftanding this deficiency, the majority of the peers thought it neceffary to bring in a bill of pains and penalties againft the provoft and city, for conniving at, or not preventing the perpetration of fo atrocious a deed.

The bill was oppofed in a very animated fpeech by the duke of Argyle, who contended that it was an ex poft facto law, punifhing a whole community for crimes within the reach of the inferior courts of juftice. It was neverthelefs carried by a

May 11.
majority of 54 againft 22, and fent down to the commons, under the title of " An Act to difable Alexander Wilfon, efquire, from taking, holding, or enjoying, any office or place of magiftracy, in the city of Edinburgh, or elfewhere, in Great Britain, for imprifoning the faid Alexander Wilfon, and for abolifhing the guard kept up in the faid city, commonly called the town guard; and

M

for

for taking away the gates of the Nether Bow Port
of the faid city, and keeping open the fame.''

Such was the title, and fuch were the penalties
of this famous bill, as it was fent to the commons. It is certain, the minifterial party in the
houfe of peers, had not thoroughly confidered the
nature of the Scottifh conftitution, as left by the
act of union; nor was the evidence fufficient for
juftifying the feverities contained in the bill. Wilfon, the lord provoft, was a weak well-meaning
man, and had acted to the beft of his courage
and capacity; and the greateft imputation fixed
on him by evidence, was his not having been active in arming the citizens the day before the riot
had happened, when only vague rumours were
whifpered. With refpect to the penalties inflicted upon the city of Edinburgh, doubts were
raifed whether they could regularly be impofed,
even by a Britifh parliament, confiftently with
the articles of union. *

Accordingly, the oppofition was violent and
ftrenuous; moft of the perfons who had appeared
at the houfe of lords, were again examined before
the commons; petitions were received, and counfel heard againft the bill. The Scottifh members
who were affected by the ftigma to be affixed on
their capital, and looked upon the queftion as a
national concern, uniformly oppofed, and many
of them, particularly Duncan Forbes, the lord
advocate of Scotland, difplayed great abilities.

On

* Tindal.

On every reading it produced frefh debates, and in one inftance, was carried only by the cafting voice of colonel Bladen, the chairman of the com-mittee.

Walpole fpoke only on the firft reading, and then he faid but a few words in reply to thofe who object-ed to the bill, becaufe it originated in the houfe of lords. He obferved, that he was as jealous of their right as any other gentleman could be, but thought too fcrupulous a jealoufy at this time might be attended with the worft confequences. In reply to an obfervation of Duncan Forbes, that tendernefs ought to be fhewn to the corporations and boroughs which the commons reprefented, efpecially thofe of Scotland, he urged that the commitment of the bill was the greateft mark of tendernefs which could be fhewn. It was to punifh, in an exemplary manner, a practice that had been too much encouraged ; a practice, which if not fuppreffed, muft deftroy the right of all corporations, and perhaps abolifh the privileges of the houfe, and the very form of the conftitution. He concluded, by faying, that gentlemen would not oppofe the bill without better reafons than any that had yet appeared. He did not enter into the merits, or difcufs the proofs of the objections urged by the Scottifh lawyers, but left thofe points to be argued by the attorney and folicitor general. He by no means made it a minifterial queftion. In the houfe of lords, fome of his friends had promoted and others refifted it, and on one queftion, the duke of Newcaftle and lord

chancellor

chancellor Hardwicke had voted on different fides. The fame circumftance occurred in the houfe of commons. Some of the moft violent oppofers of government befriended the bill, and others ab-fented themfelves while it was depending. He was moft anxious that the queen fhould be jufti-fied for granting the reprieve, and that fome punifhment fhould be inflicted on the magiftrates, as an example to deter others, and to render the civil power refponfible for outrages committed in their jurifdiction : a falutary and effential act of policy.

When thefe points were gained, he was not in-clined to enforce the penalties. He fuffered there-fore the bill to be modified and mitigated. That part which ordered the abolition of the city guard, and the demolition of the gates, was omitted, and in the whole was reduced to an act "for difabling Alexander Wilfon, the provoft, from taking, hold-ing, or enjoying, any office, or place of magiftracy, in the city of Edinburgh, or elfewhere, in Great, Britain, and for impofing a fine upon the faid cor-poration, of £. 2,000, for the benefit of the widow of Porteous." *   The bill, however, thus miti-gated and rendered " ftinglefs †," met with un-ceafing oppofition, and after having narrowly efcaped being thrown out, was fent back to the, lords, who agreed to the amendments, and it finally received the royal affent.

While this act was in agitation, another paffed the

* Tindal.   † Ibid.

the lords, and was fent down to the commons, " For the more effectual bringing to juſtice, any perfons concerned in the barbarous murder of captain John Porteous, and puniſhing ſuch as ſhall knowingly conceal any of the ſaid offenders." This bill was of a ſevere nature, and was directed to be read, for a ſtated time, by the eſtabliſhed clergy of Scotland, in their pulpits, every Sunday. Amongſt other clauſes, it contained an indemnity to any perfon who was concerned in the murder, provided he difcovered and convicted an accomplice, before the firſt of February. This clauſe was added to the bill by the commons, as was alfo another, promiſing " a reward of £.200 to any one who ſhould difcover, and convict, by their evidence, any perfon concerned in the murder." Thefe proviſions were by many thought too fevere, and cenfured as giving too great encouragement to informers. The Scots, when the act was read to them, treated it with the utmoſt contempt ; and though many thouſands were publicly concerned in the murder, and fome of them tried, yet none were legally convicted. *

These proceedings augmented the unpopularity of the miniſter, by inflaming the refentment of Scotland, and facilitated the efforts of the duke of Argyle, to return, at the next elections, a majority of the Scots members in favour of oppoſition.

Sir Robert Walpole incurred great cenfure by
the

* Tindal, vol. 20. p. 344.—The reader is referred for the above particulars, to the Correfpondence—Lords' Debates—Chandler— Journals—Tindal—Political State of Great Britain.

the alienation of the finking fund; and has been
expofed to no lefs obloquy, for his oppofition to
Sir John Barnard's fcheme, for reducing the intereft of the national debt. He has been accufed
by party, prejudice, or mifapprehenfion, of the
meaneft motives for adopting this line of conduct : motives fo contradictory, that they refute
each other. By fome,* he was fufpected of having clandeftinely promoted the introduction of
the bill. It was infinuated that, at firft, he intended it fhould pafs; and that he only deferred
the meafure until the queen, who was fuppofed
to have a million in the funds, could fell out to
advantage. Others,† on the contrary, afcribe
his oppofition to the mean fpirit of jealoufy, and
reproach the minifter with having exerted the
whole power of government, that he might deprive Sir John Barnard of his due applaufe.

In the committee of fupply the minifter moved
a refolution, that a fum of one million fhould
be taken from the finking fund, and applied to
redeem a million of old South Sea annuities. The
motion was oppofed by feveral members, principally of the minority, who argued for the expediency of appropriating that fum to the difcharge
of the debt due to the bank, becaufe the intereft
paid to the bank was fix per cent. whereas that
on the other parts of the public debt did not exceed four. They accordingly propofed the amendment; but the original motion was carried without a divifion.

On

* Opinions of the Duchefs of Marlborough, p. 45.
† Sinclair on the Revenue, chap. 5.

D D 3

On the 14th of March the resolution was reported and agreed to. * On this occasion, Sir
John Barnard proposed, that the house should
resolve itself into a committee, to take into consideration the national debt, and to receive any
proposal which might be made to reduce the interest to three per cent. The minister, after a
few observations on the danger of meddling with
public credit, or taking any step which' might be
likely to affect it, without the most mature reflection, declared that he had no objection to a
committee; because time would be allowed for
deliberation; and concluded, that if any reasonable scheme for reducing the interest should be
then proposed, he should readily agree to it.

On the 18th, the account of the national debt,
which amounted to £.47,866,596; was produced.
On the 21ft, the house resolved into a committee
of supply, and Sir John Barnard brought forward
his scheme. With a view to popularity; it was
called, a proposal towards lowering the interest of
all the redeemable debts to three per cent. and
thereby to enable the parliament *to give immediate
eafe to his majesty's subjects*, by taking off some of
the taxes which are most burthensome to the poor,
and especially to the manufacturers, as likewise *to*
give ease to the people, by lessening the annual taxes
for the current service of the year. †

Though

* Journals.
† The proposal was as follows:
" That an offer be made to the proprietors of the South Sea Annuities, as well old as new, at such times as the respective transfer
books shall be shut, in the following manner; viz. That all persons
be

Though the principle of the meafure was fuch
as to intitle its founder to expect much popularity,
yet as the interefts and prejudices of many perfons
were to be combated, great oppofition was excited,

be at liberty to make their option for the whole, or any part of their
capital of one or more of the particulars undermentioned, for which
books be laid open at the South Sea houfe, for fo long time as fhall be
thought proper; viz. All who defire to be paid their money, to enter
their names and fums in one book. Thofe who fhall chufe to have
annuities for certain terms of years, and the capital to be annihilated,
may fubfcribe in particular books for that purpofe, at the following
rates:

" For 47 Years at 4 per Cent. per Ann.
  31 Years at 5 - - -
  23½ Years at 6 - - -
  19 Years at 7 - - -
  16 Years at 8 - - -
  13¾ Years at 9 - - -
  12 Years at 10 - - -

" That the proprietors of fo much of the capital, as fhall not be
claimed in money, nor fubfcribed into fome of the annuities for terms
of years, fhall, for the future, be intitled to an annuity of 3 per cent.
per annum only. And for the encouragement of the annuitants to
accept of 3 per cent. per annum, it is propofed, that they be not fubject
to redemption or diminution of their annuities for the term of 14
years. And that all the annuities for terms of years be transferable
at the South Sea houfe, without any charge; as well as the annuities
which fhall be continued at 3 per cent. per annum. And that all the
annuities for terms of years, commence from the determination of the
annuities of 4 per cent. without any lofs of time. It is apprehended,
that this offer will be more beneficial to the proprietors than the remaining in their prefent fituation, and receiving a million at a time, to be
divided alternately between the old and the new annuitants, which muft
affect them in a very high manner, as it tends greatly to reduce their
capital, by continual laying out the money paid off in new annuities
at advanced prices.

" If the parliament fhould be willing to indulge any perfons, not
being foreigners, who may be advanced in years, with annuities for
term of life; the following rates are fubmitted to the confideration of
gentlemen who have turned their thoughts to this fubject; viz.

To perfons 44 Years old, or upwards, 7 per Cent. for Life.
  53 - - - - 8
  59 - - - - 9
  63 - - - - 10

" If thefe rates for lives, or any other rates, fhould be thought
convenient to be offered; it is then propofed, that the old and new
annuitants

cited, and the stores of argument and calculation exhausted in defending the plan.

March 21. Sir John Barnard moved, in a committee of supply, " that his majesty be enabled to raise money, either by sale of annuities for years or lives, at such rates as should be prescribed, or by borrowing at an interest not exceeding three per cent. to be applied towards redeeming old and new South Sea annuities, and that such of the annuitants as should be inclined to subscribe their respective annuities, should be preferred to all others."

This motion occasioned long debates. It was principally defended by the landed, and resisted by the monied interest, and the minister's friends were divided. The house did not appear inclined to adopt any specific determination ; some of those who were averse to the measure, declared themselves incapable of giving their opinion, without due reflection and more information. They moved, therefore, that the farther consideration should be deferred till that day se'nnight, which was agreed to without opposition. This point being carried, the adversaries of the bill made another effort, which was attended with success. It had been urged as an objection, that a considerable part of the South Sea annuities belonged to widows

<hr>

annuitants be permitted to subscribe any part of their capital, they being within the limitation of years above expressed ; and that none of the proposals foregoing be made for ready money ; because it is reasonable that the present creditors should have the preference in any advantageous offer made by the parliament, as this is apprehended to be, since money may be raised at 3 per cent. per annum, with a liberty of redeeming the same at pleasure."

widows and orphans, and to perfons who were proprietors of fmall fums: this fuggeftion had a great effect upon the houfe. Willing therefore to take advantage of this impreffion, they moved on the following day, that an account fhould be laid before the houfe, of the quantity of old and new South Sea annuity ftock, holden by any executors, adminiftrators, or truftees; which accounts were prefented on the enfuing Friday.

Hitherto the minifter took no public part, either for or againft the fcheme; although he was generally fuppofed * to be inclined in its favour. But from this period he was determined to oppofe it, though he thought it prudent to act with circumfpection, as many members, who were perfonally attached to him, favoured the meafure. In this fituation the minifter had watched the progrefs of public opinion, and found it decidedly adverfe to the propofal, which excited the moft violent clamours among the proprietors of the funds.

During the adjournment of the bufinefs, the minifterial papers were filled with objections to the meafure, and a perfpicuous ftatement †, expofing

---

* Robert Trevor to Horace Walpole, April 19, 1737. Correfpondence. Opinions of the duchefs of Marlborough.

† " As I can by no means approve of the fcheme, publifhed in your paper of Saturday laft, for reducing the intereft of the national debt to 3 per cent. I fhall, for the fake of thofe who are not acquainted with calculations of this kind, make a few obfervations on the propofed method of reduction, that fuch proprietors of the public funds may fee how far their interefts are like to be affected by it. And, in the firft place, I obferve, that the annuities propofed for certain terms of years are calculated at compound intereft, allowing the annuitants 3 per cent. for their money, and the furplus of the annuity is to reimburfe them their purchafe money at the fame rate of intereft.

" To

poſing its inexpediency, appeared in the Whitehall Evening Poſt, which was either drawn up by the miniſter himſelf, or approved by him. In the ſame paper, of the 26th, an appeal was made to the feelings and paſſions of the public, in which the

" To explain this, I ſhall fix upon the firſt annuity propoſed, which is 4 per cent. for 47 years, at the end of which the capital is to be annihilated. By this proposal, the purchaſer is to receive 3 per cent. intereſt, and the remaining 1 per cent. is to reimburſe the purchaſe money in the term propoſed at compound intereſt; but I cannot think this a fair method of computation in the preſent caſe; for, although it be true, that £.1 per annum will, in 47 years, amount to £.100 at compound intereſt; yet it is highly improbable, if not impoſſible, that intereſt upon intereſt, or, indeed any intereſt at all, ſhould be made of ſuch ſmall ſums for 47 years running, as muſt be done, to raiſe the ſum advanced; and therefore ſuch a method of calculation muſt be fallacious, and nothing but the ſurplus of the annuity can be ſafely relied on for reimburſement of the purchaſe money; and then it will be evident to the meaneſt capacity, that if the annuitants are allowed 3 per cent. for their purchaſe money, they will, at the end of 47 years, have received no more than 47 per cent. of their principal; and in all the other caſes the purchaſers of the propoſed annuities will be conſiderable loſers; only it is to be obſerved, that the ſhorter the term is, the leſs the loſs will be: for if the annuity be 7 per cent. for 19 years, the purchaſers will receive back 76 per cent. and if 10 per cent. be allowed for 12 years, they will receive back 84 per cent. of their principal money: the reaſon of which is very obvious to thoſe who know, that compound intereſt is a ſeries of geometrick progreſſion.

" Secondly, I obſerve, that if, out of any of the propoſed annuities, there is annually reſerved a ſum ſufficient to reimburſe the purchaſe money, the annuitants will not receive an intereſt of 2 per cent. upon their principal. And for the proof of this, I ſhall only take notice of the two extremes and middle term in the annuities propoſed; by which it will appear, that if £.2 out of £.4 be reſerved for 47 years, it will raiſe no more than £.94, and if £.5 out of £.7 be reſerved for 19 years, it will amount to no more than £.95, and £.8 out of £.10 for 12 years, will give only £.95.

" Thirdly, It is to be obſerved, that the method propoſed will not enable the parliament to give immediate eaſe to his majeſty's ſubjects, by taking off ſome of the taxes which are moſt burthenſome to the poor, and eſpecially to the manufacturers; for, by the firſt propoſal, the ſame annual intereſt which is now paid, viz. 4 per cent. is to be continued for 47 years; and conſequently the taxes by which that intereſt is raiſed muſt be continued for that term, which will give but ſmall relief to the preſent generation. And in all the other caſes, the annual intereſt muſt be augmented, inſtead of being reduced: for if the proprietors of £.20,000,000 of the public debts could be ſuppoſed to accept any of theſe annuities upon the terms propoſed, the annual

the bill was defcribed, as tending to ruin trade, to
depopulate the capital, to impoverifh widows and
orphans, to reduce the farmers to day labourers,
and the fons of noblemen and gentlemen to
farmers,

.. Thefe exaggerated declamations made a deep
impreffion on the public mind. When the houfe,
met on the 28th to refume the confideration of
the bill, Sir John Barnard entered into a full explanation

annual intereft muft then be increafed in the following manner;
viz.   £.
For 31 Years	- - 200,000 per Ann.
23½ Years	- - 400,000
19 Years	- - 600,000
16 Years	- - 800,000.
13¼ Years	- - 1,000,000
12 Years	- - 1,200,000

" Fourthly, I obferve, That the other part of the fcheme, which relates to annuities upon lives, is liable to the fame objection : for if the
propofed annuities are taken at a medium of 8½ per cent. and the lives
are fuppofed at a medium to continue 18 years. (which very nearly
coincides with the rules laid down for finding the number of years
due to any given life) then it will be evident that a further intereft
of 4½ per cent. muft be raifed to pay fuch annuities, which will more
than double the prefent annual intereft.

" Fifthly, It is to be obferved, that this fcheme is not calculated
for the good of the whole, but, according to the old proverb, to rob
Peter to pay Paul, or, to remove the burthen from one part of the
community, and lay it upon another, and upon that part too which
hath already contributed no lefs than fix fhillings and eight-pence in
the pound towards leffening the public debts. I am unwilling to
charge the author with an intention to opprefs the proprietors of the
public funds, though his fcheme manifeftly tends to it : but why does
his tendernefs lie all on one fide ? Is there no part of it due to thofe
widows and orphans, who have no other way of fubfiftence, but the
income of fmall fortunes in government fecurities ? For my part, I
cannot perceive the honefty or policy of eafing one part of the community, by diftreffing another ; neither can I apprehend any wifdom or
juftice in making invidious diftinctions between the landed and monied
intereft, fince it is in a great meafure owing to thofe, who ventured
their fortunes in the public funds, that the Proteftant part of this nation have any lands or liberties left. I do therefore hope that their prefent intereft will not be leffened; but if nothing elfe will ferve, I am
perfuaded I can propofe a way of doing it that will be the leaft injurious
to them of any that can be thought of, which, if called upon, I am
ready to publifh."

planation of his fcheme, and laboured with great
addrefs and ability to obviate thefe popular objections.   He went over all the grounds of political expediency, and in the courfe of a very long
and ingenious explanation, urged, that in every
view of the fubject, relating to the extenfion of
commerce, both domeftic and foreign, to the encouragement of induftry, the increafe of population, the augmentation of the manufactures, and
the improvement of agriculture, this plan would
be attended with the moft extenfive and beneficial confequences.   He faid, that even thofe public fecurities which bore an intereft of three per
cent. only, were fold at a premium in Change
Alley: he was, therefore, perfuaded, that all
thofe who were willing to give a premium for a
three per cent. fecurity, would gladly lend their
money to government for the fame intereft, fhould
books of fubfcription be opened for that purpofe,
with an affurance, that no part of the principal
fhould be paid off for fourteen years.   He expatiated on the national advantages that would ac-
crue from a reduction of intereft.   From a long
feries of calculations, he inferred, that in a very
little time the intereft upon all the South Sea
annuities would be reduced from four to three
per cent. without any danger to public credit, or
breach of public faith ; that then the produce of
the finking fund would amount to fourteen hundred
thoufand pounds per annum, to be applied only
towards redeeming the capital of the feveral trading companies : he proved that this meafure would
bring

bring every one of them fo much within the power of parliament, that they would be glad to accept of three per cent. intereft on any reafonable terms; in which cafe the finking fund would rife to one million fix hundred thoufand pounds per annum. Then the parliament might venture to annihilate one half of it, by freeing the people from the taxes upon coals, candles, foap, leather, and other fuch impofitions as lay heavy upon the poor labourers and manufacturers: the remaining part of the finking fund might be applied towards the difcharge of thofe annuities and public debts, which bore an intereft of three per cent. only, and afterwards, towards diminifhing the capitals of the feveral trading companies, till the term of fourteen years fhould be expired; then the finking fund would again amount to above a million yearly, which would be fufficient for paying them off, and freeing the nation entirely from all its incumbrances *.

Walpole, among others, replied to this ftatement, but his arguments were confined to fhew that the time was improper for the reduction of intereft †. He was fully convinced that the propofal, in the fhape it was offered by Sir John Barnard, was neither expedient or practicable. It became neceffary therefore either to amend or throw it out. To throw it out by direct oppofition, was not in his power, as notwithftanding its increafing unpopularity without doors, it ftill feemed

Indirectly oppofed by Walpole.

---

* Chandler. Smollett's Hiftory of England, vol. 2, p. 521.
† Chandler.

seemed agreeable to the general sense of the house, and was warmly supported by many of the members who were personally attached to him. His confidential friend, Mr. Howe, afterwards. Lord Chedworth, had proposed the scheme in the highest terms of approbation. He said that the country gentlemen would be benefited by the reduction; that the landed interest required, and were intitled to relief, that the land had hitherto been loaded with all the burthens, while the funds had borne none; and that their necessities had arisen from the abundance of the stocks *. Under these circumstances, Walpole, apprehensive that it would be carried with all its imperfections, adopted indirect

Proposal extended.
means of throwing it out. At the close of the debate, his friend Winnington proposed to extend the reduction to all the redeemable debts. He observed, that he would not enter into the question, whether a reduction of interest would tend to the advantage of the nation, or whether the natural interest of money lent on public security was below three per cent. But should both be resolved in the affirmative, according to the principles of the bill, he must condemn the injustice and partiality of confining the reduction to the South Sea annuities. He was of opinion, that it ought to be extended in its operation to all the public creditors. These, he concluded, were his sentiments, and if they were approved by the house, he should move for resolutions to redeem

all

* Heads of Mr. Howe's Speech; Parliamentary Memorandums, Orford Papers.

all public debts that were redeemable by law, and
to enable the king to borrow money at three per
cent. for that purpose.

These observations seemed to meet the general
sentiments of the house, and Sir John Barnard
could not venture to oppose them. He observed,
however, that the proposal was intended to frus-
trate his scheme, by introducing such amendments as must render it abortive, according to
the old proverb, " Grasp at all, and lose all." He
added, that although government could borrow
money at three per cent. sufficient to pay off so
many proprietors of the South Sea annuities as
were willing to accept that interest, because their
united stock did not exceed twenty-four millions
yet it would be extremely difficult to obtain such
a loan as would discharge the whole of the redeemable fund, which amounted to forty-four
millions. But as the scheme, even thus amended,
might be productive of signal advantage to the
nation, he should not oppose it, and he hoped
the honourable gentleman would move for such a
resolution as he had just intimated. Two resolutions were accordingly moved for by Winnington.
They contained in substance, " That all the public funds, redeemable by law, which carry an interest of four per cent. per annum, be redeemed
according to the respective provisos or clauses of
redemption contained in the acts of parliament
for that purpose, or (with consent of the proprietors) be converted into an interest or annuity, not
exceeding three per cent. per annum, not redeemable.

able till after fourteen years. That his majefty be enabled to borrow from any perfon or perfons, bodies politic or corporate, any fum or fums of money, at an intereft not exceeding three per cent. to be applied towards redeeming the national debt." *

March 30. ‧ Thefe refolutions being reported, and carried by a majority of 220 to 157, in which divifion Walpole appeared in the minority, Sir John Barnard, Wortley Montague, and the mafter of the rolls, were ordered to prepare a bill accordingly. †

Motion for abolition of taxes. ‧ ‧ Sir John Barnard, however, had not fufficient difcretion to be fatisfied with this partial victory; inftead of weakening the refiftance to his favourite fcheme, by making it as much as poffible a great national object, he on the contrary united a numerous body of adverfaries, loft the vantage ground on which he before ftood, and reduced it to a mere party queftion. He followed up the report by moving, " that the houfe would, as foon as the intereft of all the national redeemable debt fhould be reduced to £.3 per cent. per annum, take off fome of the heavy taxes which oppreffed the poor, and the manufacturer." ‡

His view in making this unprecedented motion, was to attach popularity to his bill; but it had a contrary effect, for it was proved to be fallacious, illufory, and irregular. It was fallacious, becaufe it affumed as facts, ftatements that were

not

---

* Chandler, vol. 9. p. 452.   † Tindal. Chandler. Journals.
‡ Journals.

hot true ; that the public imposts fell more heavily upon the poor in England, than in other countries, and implied, that the reduction of the interest from four to three per cent. would compensate for the loss of the revenue, if those taxes were abolished. It was illusory, because it held out a prospect of taking off the taxes several years before the reduction could be effected ; and it was irregular, because it bound future parliaments to the adoption of a measure which might not at a future time be feasible. It was ably and unanswerably argued by the minister, and those who opposed it, that to agree to the resolution, would be exposing the public to unavoidable disappointment, " that it would be time enough to come to a resolution to abolish some taxes, when the scheme had taken effect, for if such a previous resolution should be adopted, and the scheme should afterwards prove altogether abortive, the whole world would laugh at their precipitancy."

In the speech which Sir John Barnard made in defence of this motion, he betrayed such a confusion of projects, and indistinctness of ideas, assumed so many principles which were untrue, and so violently transgressed the bounds of parliamentary engagement, that the motion was negatived, by 200 against 142, and the public clamour very much heightened.

Under these unfavourable circumstances, the bill, prepared on the basis of Winnington's resolutions, was presented to the house by Sir John Barnard, and it was read the first time. On the

Rejected.

Bill introduced.

April 22.

29th, the bill was read a fecond time, and a motion being made for recommitting it, it was no
lefs refolutely fupported than vigoroufly attacked.
Several fpeakers on both fides had been heard before Walpole delivered his fentiments.

He began by denying the truth of an affertion,
which had been affiduoufly diffeminated, that Sir
John Barnard had held private conferences with
him, and fettled the fcheme then in agitation.
He proceeded to review his own conduct during
its progrefs; acknowledged that he had acquiefced
in the committee, but that on the firft reading,
feeling fome doubts on the propriety of the meafure, he had defired time to weigh maturely its
beneficial againft its evil confequences. " But
whatever doubts," he continued, " I might then
entertain, deliberate reflection has removed them,
and convinced me of its inefficiency.

" The meafure is founded on plaufible affump-
tions, that it is better to pay three than four per
cent. and that it is defirable to difcharge the debt
of the nation. Thefe pofitions are undoubtedly
true, but the queftion is, whether the method
propofed to effect them is juft and adequate?
We muft take care not to confound public neceffity with public utility. Public utility differs
effentially from profit or benefit gained to the
public; for when profit accrues to the public, at
the expence of many individuals, it lofes all claim
to confideration under the title of public utility.
This houfe, in carefully attending to their duty
as guardians of the national purfe, muft not for-
                                                        get

get that they are truftees for the creditors. We muft not affume a right to prejudice the public creditors, or to convert the right of redemption which we poffefs, into a right of reduction, to which we have no claim. Debts not originally fubject to reduction, are, in that refpect, in the fituation of irredeemables, and the faith of parliament is equally pledged, to prevent any reduction without the confent of the proprietors. If we advert to the time and manner in which thefe debts were created, every argument againft the reduction of intereft, acquires a great additional force. At that difaftrous period, the creditors of the South Sea and Eaft India companies had a power to demand the whole amount of their bonds. Their forbearance was effentially neceffary to the defence and well-being of the community; for, had they perfifted in claiming their principal, the whole muft have fallen on the landed intereft, or the refult muft have been fuch as I dare not mention, or hardly think of. And is the fervice then rendered to the country, to be now repaid by a compulfory reduction of their dividends? I call it compulfory, for any reduction by terror, can only be defcribed by that name. If they are to be fo reduced, the pretence is, that it will eafe the current fervice, or take off taxes; but that would be only to take the taxes off others, to be impofed on them, in the moft cruel and infupportable manner. It would be equally juft to take away one fourth from the income of every individual, or to deprive him of one fourth of his

E E 2   lands

lands or ftock in trade; or rather the injuftice would be lefs in fuch cafe, becaufe the national creditor is, by exprefs contract, exempt from all public taxes and impofitions.

" Nor is it true that the intereft propofed is equivalent to the value of money; for though money cannot be invefted in the funds without an advance above three per cent. at par, yet all loans on real fecurities, on eftates, or on perfonal fecurities, bear a much higher intereft. The preference given to the funds, arifes from various caufes; from the facility of receiving intereft, cheapnefs of transfer; and from none more than the faith placed in the national honour, which is bound to fuffer no lofs to fall on the public creditor. Stock, while the credit remains untarnifhed, is but another name for ready money bearing intereft, a property which in no other cafe can attach to ready money; and if the confidence now placed in the guardians of the public honour is diminifhed, even that advantage will not in future tempt individuals to truft their money out of their own cuftody. No diminution of taxes, or other contingent advantage, can compenfate for fuch a privation; nor is it to be compared to a repayment of the principal at any time, however inconvenient, for it is not to be fuppofed that any one would prefer a fudden and abfolute privation of one fourth of his whole income, to the cafual and diftant refumption of 10 or 15 per cent. on his capital, not to be effected without

an

an equivalent payment, which may be delayed by
accident, or fruſtrated by neceſſity.

" The injuſtice of the preſent plan appears in
this, that it is calculated to mark out all the
great companies, and to benefit the borrowers at
the expence of the lenders. But this is not the
whole extent of the evil. A double duty is incumbent on the legiſlature; to uſe their utmoſt
exertions towards paying the national debt, and
to avoid creating diſtreſſes and diſcontent. Now
the whole number of perſons intereſted in the ſtock
to be affected by the propoſed meaſure, is about
23,000, of theſe, upwards of 6,000 are intereſted
as executors, adminiſtrators, and truſtees, and
upwards of 17,000 are poſſeſſed only of ſums not
exceeding £. 1,000. The executors and truſtees
muſt be greatly embarraſſed, eſpecially if the ſums
committed to them are ſmall, in perfecting the
purpoſes for which they are confided; and thoſe
who poſſeſs ſuch ſmall ſums as do not amount to
£. 1,000 muſt be much diſtreſſed by ſo unexpected
and wanton a reduction of their income."

The miniſter, in the courſe of theſe obſervations, took an ample review of the bill, which he
ſhewed to be unequal to the ends it was deſigned
to anſwer. He proved that the alternatives of
the propoſition, produced repugnant and diſcordant effects; and that the plan was deſtructive of
the purpoſes, and inadequate in benefit to the
ſinking fund.

On this head, he ſhould beg leave to take notice of a circumſtance that perſonally alluded to
him. Gentlemen had diſcuſſed, in the courſe of

the

the debate, *the advantages which had been derived from the* plan of reducing the national debt from six to five per cent. which he had the honour of proposing to the house. They had conceived it impoſſible for him to reſiſt a ſimilar reduction from four to three per cent. without the groſſeſt inconſiſtency. But he was free to declare, that he could oppoſe the preſent ſchéme without ſubjecting himſelf to that imputation. It became his duty, on the authority of the former ſcheme, to give his negative to this, becauſe no two ſchemes ever differed more widely in their intention, effect, and conſequences.

He then ſtated the difference between the preſent ſcheme, and that which he had propoſed. "This ſcheme," he obſerved, "is compulſory, mine was optional. On the former occaſion, money was prepared; on this, it was yet to be raiſed. My ſcheme laid the foundation; this reverſes the whole ſyſtem of the ſinking fund. Mine was founded upon converting numbers of years at higher rates, into perpetuities at lower rates. This plan eſtabliſhes terms of years at higher rates, in lieu of perpetuities at lower rates, after an expiration of twenty years of the former terms. This was intended to lock up the ſinking fund for ſeveral years; of which the ſhorteſt term was not leſs than twelve, and the longeſt forty-ſeven. During this time, all reduction of intereſt would be prevented, all abolition of taxes rendered impracticable, and a neceſſity impoſed of laying freſh burthens in caſe of emergency. Whereas mine had a contrary tendency; a million of the debt

I   might

might be annually difcharged, or fome of the exifting taxes might be abolifhed, or the impofition
of frefh taxes prevented, by applying the furpluffes of the finking fund to the current furvice.

" The declared intention of the bill is, to give
eafe to the fubject; and the title fpecifies *immediate* eafe. But its tendency is calculated to vio-
late this very principle, and to falfify the title, for
no eafe can be given, until the reduction has taken
place, and that event is diftant, uncertain, and
precarious. In fact, the prefent difadvantages of
the fcheme propofed by the honourable gentlemen, evidently appear from the affectation with
which he expatiated on *his love to pofterity*. For
certain it is, that his fcheme cannot benefit the
prefent generation, but its falutary effects will
principally be confined to thofe who are yet un-
born."*

Sir John Barnard faid in reply, " I am very
much obliged to the honourable gentleman, Sir,
and therefore, I thank him for vindicating me from
the imputation of having had any private converfation with him, or of having ever had any concert with him, and if he is afraid left people
fhould fufpect his having had a hand in the
fcheme I propofed to you, I fhall be equally juft
to him, by declaring, I never had any private
converfation with him about it, nor did I fo much
as afk his approbation or confent to what I was
to

---

* The fubftance of this fpeech is taken from parliamentary minutes in the hand-writing of Sir Robert Walpole.' Walpole Papers.

Period VI.
1734 to 1737.

to offer; but as to the fcheme as it now ftands, every gentleman that hears me, knows it is very different from what I offered; and every one like-wife knows, that the new model, which is the model we have now before us, if it was not of-fered by the honourable gentleman himfelf, it was at leaft offered by fome of his friends; and what they propofed was agreed to by other gen-tlemen, in order that we might have their affift-ance in carrying it through. Therefore the fcheme now before you, cannot properly be called mine; and it is very remarkable, that all objections made to the bill, are only to thofe articles and claufes of it, which relate to the improvements and ad-ditions made to my fcheme, by the honourable

Bill rejected.

gentleman's friends." * The houfe divided, and the queftion of committing the bill was negatived, by 249 againft 134. †

Walpole's mo-tives.

It is difficult, without farther documents on this fubject than I poffefs, to afcertain all the motives

* Chandler, vol. 9. p. 479.

† I have dwelt thus particularly on the confideration of Sir John Barnard's fcheme, becaufe the accounts given by moft writers, who have fallen under my obfervation, are fuperficial and inaccurate, Even Tindal is unufually fhort and barren of information. Tindal, vol. 20. p. 348.

Smollett, excepting a good abftract of Sir John Barnard's fpeech, which I have adopted in the text, is extremely deficient. He fays it produced other debates, and was at laft *poftponed* by dint of minifterial influence. The falfity of this account is evident. Smollett, vol. 2. p. 627.

Belfham obferves, " A bill was, however, ordered upon the bafis of Winnington's propofition, which being in the fequel warmly at-tacked, and *faintly defended*, was *finally poftponed to a diftant day, by a motion of the minifter.*" In this fhort account there are three errors. It was warmly attacked, but by no means *faintly defended.* It was not *finally poftponed to a diftant day*, but the fecond reading was only put off for feven days; and it was then *negatived*, but *not on the motion of the minifter.* Belfham, vol. 1. p. 389.

motives which induced the minifter to refift the
reduction. It may be fufficient, perhaps, to at-
tribute it to a full conviction, that the meafure
was highly and generally unpopular. He had relinquifhed his favourite excife fcheme, notwithftanding the certainty of its beneficial tendency,
folely on that account. It was not to be fuppofed that he would promote this fcheme, of the
good tendency of which he was not affured, and
which in many refpects was partial and unjuft.

But in addition to this motive, I can fuggeft
two others, which influenced his diffent. Firft, he
forefaw, from the difputes with Spain, which then
began to rife, that the nation might be involved
in a war, and that government could borrow with
greater facility at four per cent. than at three.
He was ftill more fwayed by another motive,
which he could not venture to difclofe. He had
already appropriated part of the furplus of the
finking fund to the current fervice of the year,
and as the meafure was extremely popular, he
had refolved, in cafe of emergency, to alienate
the whole. But his defign would have been fruftrated by this bill, which would have locked up
the greateft part of the finking fund for feveral
years, and have rendered it neceffary to impofe
new taxes for the purpofe of fupplying the inci-
dental expences. *

An

* A reduction of intereft took place in 1749, upon a plan, which
has been defcribed as fimilar, though it is effentially different from the
original fcheme propofed by Sir John Barnard. It was finally carried,
though not without great oppofition, by the united influence of the
minifter (Pelham) and Sir John Barnard.

An act of this feffion, which is commonly de-nominated the playhoufe bill, has expofed the minifter to no lefs obloquy, from fubfequent writers, than his oppofition to the reduction of intereft.

Thofe who thus load him with indifcriminate cenfure, and impute this act folely to his *defpotic influence*, have not paid due attention to the hiftory of the English ftage, to the power of the lord chamberlain over the players and theatrical reprefentations, and to the opinion of the moft moderate and beft informed magiftrates at the period of paffing this act, which has been fo much calumniated, and fo little underftood.

It is needlefs to difcufs the queftion concerning the neceffity of fixing fome bounds to the licentioufnefs of the ftage. The neceffity muft be allowed, except by thofe who think it fitting to fubject to public mockery, law, government, and religion, and to expofe magiftrates, judges, and kings, to the perfonalities of fatire, buffoonery, and low mimicry. In all well regulated governments, the fact has been univerfally admitted, and wherever it has not been adopted, the moft fatal confequences have followed. Even the freeft democracy which perhaps ever exifted, that of Athens, after having experienced the effects of unreftrained licentioufnefs in their theatrical performances, found it neceffary to remedy the evil, and to limit the ftage within the boundaries of common decency and juftice.

It appears from the hiftory of the English ftage, that no period ever exifted when it was not fub-

ject

jeft to fuperintendence,. when players were not
licenced, and when plays were. not reviewed and
amended, allowed, or. rejected. · Before the reign
of Henry the Eighth, the power of fuperintend-
ing the king's hunting parties, the direction of
the comedians, muficians, and other royal fervants, appointed either for ufe or recreation, was
exclufively.vefted in the lord chamberlain.

Under him, and fubject to his controul, was
an inferior officer, who exerted himfelf on particular occafions for the purpofe; of regulating pa-
geants, public feftivals;: and mafquerades. This
man was. called :by, the fanciful names of the
Abbot of Mifrule, or *Lord of Paftimes*. But in the
reign of Henry the Eighth, this temporary office
was rendered regular and permanent by letters
patent, and. called the office of *Mafter of the
Revels.* *

. Under Elizabeth, fome wife regulations, with
the advice of Walfingham, and co-opération of
Burleigh, were made for allowing the ufe, but
correcting the abufe of the ftage; particularly,
when the earl of Leicefter. obtained the firft general licence for his theatrical fervants. to act ftage
plays.in any part of England, a provifo was added
in the patent, enjoining that *all comedies, .trage-
dies, interludes, and ftage plays, fhould be examined
and allowed by the mafter of the revels.* Thus.that
authority which was before confined to the paftimes of the court, was now extended to the
theatrical exhibitions of the whole kingdom.

During

---

* Officium magiftri jocorum, *revelorum* et mafcorum.

During her reign· alfo,· the privy council exercifed an authority, legiflative and executive,
over the ·dramatic world. They opened and fhut
playhoufes ; gave and recalled licences ; appointed
the proper feafons when plays ought to be prefented or ·with-held ; and regulated the conduct
of the lord mayor of London, and the vice-chan-
cellors of Oxford and Cambridge,· with regard to
plays and players. The privy council gave Til-
ney, ¯the mafter of the revels in 1589,·two co-adjutors, a ftatefman and a divine, to affift ·him in
reforming comedies and tragedies.

. .Thefe prudent regulations, and the wifdom with
which they were exercifed,· were attended with
the moft beneficial effects. The· mafter of the
revels, by regulating the ftage, ¯ and ·reftraining
the number of ·theatres, .gave·greater refpectabi-
lity to the profeffion of a player, and the genius
of the drama ·expanded ·and. foared to a greater
height, although its ·limits were. contracted and
its flight circumfcribed.

Had not thefe wife regulations taken place,
Shakefpeare might have confined to burlefque
·farces, and low buffoonery, thofe vaft powers of
invention and defcription which his own language
can alone adequately. delineate. ·

" The poet's eye in a fine frenzy rolling,
Glances from heav'n to earth, from earth to heav'n,
And as imagination bodies forth
The forms of things unknown, the poet's pen
Turns them to fhape, and gives to airy nothing
A local habitation and a name." *

By

* Midfummer Night's Dream.

By the wife and temperate ufe which the mafter of the revels made of his power, his weight
and influence increafed, and he gradually appropriated to himfelf the greater part of that antho-
rity, which had belonged to the lord chamberlain. During the latter part of the reign of James
the Firft and Charles the Firft, it was held by Sir
Henry Herbert, * nearly allied to the earl of Pembroke, lord chamberlain : under his prudent management the reputation and confequence of the
office increafed, and produced the moft falutary
effects, until his functions were wholly fufpended,
by the troubles and confufion of the civil wars,
and the fanaticifm of the republicans.

On the reftoration of Charles the Second, the
mafter of the revels endeavoured to re-affume his
former authority, but met with infuperable oppofition from the proprietors and managers of the
king's and duke's companies, one of whom had
obtained a frefh licence to act plays, the other a
renewal of a former grant. In vain the mafter of
the revels applied to the courts of juftice for redrefs ; in vain he appealed to the fovereign, or to
the lord chamberlain ; he was neither fupported
by the one, or countenanced by the other ; his
authority, though not overthrown, was confiderably fhaken, and his regulations were combated
and defpifed.

During this fufpenfion of his power, the particular

---

* Brother to the eccentric lord Herbert, of Cherbury, and of George
Herbert, rector of Bemerton, known by the name of the divine
Herbert.

Period VI, ticular differences, pretensions, or complaints, were
1734 to 1737, generally settled by the personal interference of the
king and duke, or referred to the decision of the
lord chamberlain. In consequence of this relax-
ation of authority, and the libertine character of
the court, the theatre was disgraced by the grossest
ribaldry and obscenity, and the best authors vied
who should produce the most licentious comedies. Ladies could not venture to attend a new
play without masks, then daily worn, and admitted
into the pit, the side boxes, and the gallery.

On the death of Sir Henry Herbert, the mastership of the revels was conferred on Charles Killigrew, manager of the king's company. The
union of these two functions increased the evil,
and the smallest check was not imposed on the
glaring immorality of the stage.

At the revolution, the power of the lord chamberlain over the theatre was revived without restric-
tion. He opened and shut playhouses, imprisoned
and licensed players, corrected and rejected plays.
Under him the master of the revels seems to have
recovered some part of his former power, and to
have had his share in the revolutions of the
theatre. He revised and sanctioned plays, and his
aid greatly contributed to the celebrated conquest
which Jeremy Collier, by the publication of his
short view of the stage, obtained over the immorality of the drama. In this publication, the most
profane and obscene passages in several modern
plays, which had been written by Dryden, Van-
brugh,

brugh, Wycherley, Congreve, and the most admired dramatic authors, were detected, and expofed. The truth of his obfervations, which all
the wit and talents of the authors who were defervedly chaftifed could not controvert, produced
a furprifing effect; a general outcry was raifed
againft the licentioufnefs of the ftage, and king
William fent the following order to the playhoufes: " His majefty being informed, that notwithftanding an order made in June 1697, by
the earl of Sunderland, then lord chamberlain of
the king's houfhold, to prevent the profanenefs
and immorality of the ftage, feveral plays have
lately been acted, containing feveral expreffions
contrary to religion and good manners: And
whereas the mafter of the revels hath reprefented,
that, in contempt of the faid order, the actors
did neglect to leave out fuch profane and indecent
expreffions, as he had thought proper to be omitted: therefore, it is his majefty's pleafure, that
they fhall not hereafter prefume to act any thing
in any play, contrary to religion and good manners, as they fhall anfwer at their utmoft peril."
At the fame time, the mafter of the revels was
commanded not to licence any plays containing
irreligious or immoral expreffions, and to give notice to the lord chamberlain, or in his abfence to
the vice-chamberlain, if the players prefumed to
act any thing which he had ftruck out. *

But this reformation did not continue long in
its full force. As foon as the firft awe and panic
of

* Tindal, vol. 14, p. 478.

Period VI. of the actors. had subsided, the stage nearly re-
1734 to 1737. lapsed into its former immorality, all attempts to
reform it became the object of theatrical wit, and
were ridiculed in plays, prologues, and epilogues.
Although the new plays were usually more decent
and moral, yet the old plays were frequently
acted, without being freed from their exception-
able passages.

Either in consequence of these proceedings, or
of some disputes which arose between the actors
of the royal theatres, and produced the desertion
of the principal performers from Drury Lane to
the Haymarket, the nuisance of playhouses, and
the conduct of the performers, became so flagrant,
that a bill, in the twelfth year of queen Anne,
included players, who acted without a legal settlement in the places where they performed,
among vagrants, and subjected them to the same
penalties as rogues and vagabonds. But before
the beneficial effects of this act could have time
to operate, the death of the queen produced a
new revolution in the drama.

Soon after the accession of George the First, the
power of the master of the revels, which had been
considerably circumscribed, was almost annihilated;
a new patent was injudiciously granted to Sir
Richard Steel, Colley Cibber, and Booth, for acting plays without subjecting them to the licence
or revision of any officer.

In consequence of this grant, the master of the
revels was abridged of his power, and defrauded
of his dues, and his emoluments were reduced to
a small

a small salary from the exchequer, to lodgings in
Somerset Houfe, and to occafional fees.

At the death of Charles Killigrew, the office,
thus mutilated, was conferred on Charles Henry
Lee, and the decline of his power was fufficiently
fhewn by the growing licentioufnefs of the ftage,
and the numerous pieces which offended equally
againft religion, decency, and common fenfe.

Although, in all the letters patent for acting
plays fince the time of Charles the Firft, no mention was made of the lord chamberlain, yet he
was ftill confidered as poffeffing an abfolute,
though an undefinable authority over the ftage,
which he had occafionally exercifed. The performance of feveral theatrical pieces had been prevented, particularly Lucius Junius Brutus, a prologue of Dryden to the Prophetefs, Mary queen of
Scotland, and recently Polly, the fequel to the
Beggar's Opera.

But as this exercife of his power had been always attended with much unpopularity, it was
feldom exerted. Numerous theatres were erected
in different parts of the metropolis, in which the
actors performed without licence or authority.
To prevent this, feveral attempts were made to
enforce the laws then exifting. An actor, who
performed on the theatre of the Haymarket, without licence, was taken from the ftage, by the
warrant of a juftice of peace, and committed to
Bridewell, as coming under the penalty of the
vagrant act. The legality of the commitment
was difputed; a trial enfued; it was decided, that

the comedian being a houfekeeper, and having a vote for electing members of parliament, did not come within the defcription of the faid act; and he was difcharged amidft the loud acclamations of the populace. The iffue of this. trial gave full fcope to the licentioufnefs of the ftage, and took away all hopes of reftraining the number of play-houfes.

From this reprefentation of the ftate of the drama, it is evident, that fome reformation was indifpenfably neceffary. The minifter himfelf had long feen that neceffity. The obloquy which purfued him was not confined to the prefs; the ftage was made the vehicle of the moft malignant farcafms, not expreffed in the elevated tone of tragedy, or couched in fentiments and language perceptible only to men of refined underftandings; but his perfon was brought on the ftage, his actions maligned, his meafures mifreprefented and arraigned, and his conduct made the fport of the populace, in all the petulance of vulgar farce. He was unwilling, however, to make this a perfonal confideration, but rather a public and national queftion, in which the good of the law, conftitution, religion, and morality, was intimately involved, and fuch an opportunity feemed to prefent itfelf, when Sir John Barnard March 5, 1735. brought in a bill " to reftrain the number of houfes for playing of interludes, and for the better regulating of common players of interludes."

Bill for reftraining the number of playhoufes. On reprefenting the mifchiefs which theatres had done to the city of London, by corrupting

youth,

youth, encouraging vice and debauchery, and greatly prejudicing trade, the proposal was at firft received with contempt and ridicule, until it was feconded by Sandys, Pulteney, and warmly fup- ported by the minifter himfelf. It was obferved by a member, in the courfe of the debate, that there were at that time not lefs than fix theatres in London. The houfe being fully convinced of the neceffity of the bill, leave was given to bring it in without a fingle diffenting voice. It was accordingly, on the 3d of April prefented, read the firft time, and ordered to be printed; not- withftanding petitions againft it from the proprie- tor of the theatre in Goodman's Fields, and from the mafter and comptroller of the revels. It was read a fecond time on the 14th of April.

The minifter conceived this to be a favourable opportunity of checking the daring abufe of thea- trical reprefentation, which had arrived to a moft extravagant height. It was propofed to infert a claufe, to ratify and confirm, if not enlarge the power of the lord chamberlain, in licenfing plays, and at the fame time infinuated to the houfe, that unlefs this addition was made, the king would not pafs it. But Sir John Barnard ftrongly objected to this claufe. He declared that the power of the lord chamberlain was already too great, and had been often wantonly exercifed, particularly in the prohibition of Polly. He fhould therefore withdraw this bill, and wait for another opportunity of introducing it, rather than

eftablifh

eftablifh by law a power in a fingle officer fo much under the direction of the crown, a power which might be exercifed in an arbitrary manner, and confequently attended with mifchievous effects.

The attempt of Sir John Barnard having thus failed, the immorality of the drama increafed, and the moft indecent, feditious, and blafphemous pieces were performed, and reforted to with in- credible eagernefs. Among thofe who principally fupported this low ribaldry was the celebrated Henry Fielding, who, though he never fhone in the higher line of perfect comedy, wrote thefe dramatic fatires in a ftyle agreeable to the popu- lace. One of his pieces, called Pafquin, which was acted in the theatre at the Haymarket, ridi- culed, in the grofleft terms, the three profeffions of divinity, law, and phyfic, and gave general of- fence to perfons of morality. " Religion, laws, government, prieft, judges, and minifters," ob- ferves Coliey Cibber, " were laid flat at the feet of the Herculean fatirift, this Drawcanfir in wit, who fpared neither friend nor foe, who to make his poetical fame immortal, like another Erof- tratus, fet fire to his ftage, by writing up to an act of parliament to demolifh it."

This piece was peculiarly offenfive to the mi- nifter, becaufe it contained many perfonal allu- fions and invectives. But as he was not willing to employ the power of government in a mere temporary prohibition of this and other perform- ances, which would have been extremely unpo- pular,

pular, and not attended with permanent effects, he wished to avail himself of the present flagrant abuse, to prevent future reprefentations fo difgraceful and indecorous.

In the courfe of the feffion, an opportunity offered, which he did not omit to feize. Giffard, the manager of Goodman's Fields theatre, brought to him a farce, called the Golden Rump, which had been propofed for exhibition; but it is uncertain whether the intentions of the manager were to requeft his advice on this occafion, or to extort a fum of money to prevent its reprefentation.

The minifter, however, paid the profits which might have accrued from the performance, and detained the copy. He then made extracts of the moft exceptionable paffages, abounding in profanenefs, fedition, and blafphemy, and fubmitted them to feveral members of both parties, who were fhocked at the extreme licentioufnefs of the piece, and promifed their fupport to remedy the evil. With their advice, concurrence, and promife of co-operation, he read the feveral extracts to the houfe, and a general conviction prevailed, of the neceffity of putting a check to the reprefentation of fuch horrid effufions of treafon and blafphemy. He acted, however, with his ufual prudence on this occafion. He did not bring forward, as is generally fuppofed, an act for fubjecting all plays to the licence of the lord chamberlain, and reftraining the number of play-

F F 3 houfes,

houfes, but contrived to introduce it by amend-
ing the vagrant act.

The bill was called, " A bill to explain and
amend fo much of an act, made in the twelfth,
year of the reign of queen Anne, intituled, an
act for reducing the laws relating to rogues, vagabonds, fturdy beggars, and vagrants, and fending
them whither they ought to be fent, as relates
to the common players of interludes." * Leave
was accordingly given to bring it in, and Pelham,
Dodington, Howe, the mafter of the rolls, the attorney and folicitor general, were ordered to prepare it. During its rapid progrefs through the
houfe, certain amendments were made, and two
claufes were added. The firft, which occafioned
fo much obloquy, empowered the lord chamberlain to prohibit the reprefentation of any theatrical performances, and compelled all perfons to
fend copies of any new plays, parts added to old
plays, prologues and epilogues, fourteen days before they were acted, and not to perform them,
under forfeiture of £.50, and of the licence of the
houfe. The fecond, which is faid to have been
added at the inftigation of Sir John Barnard, operated in reftraining the number of playhoufes, by
enjoining, that no perfon fhould be authorifed to
act except within the liberties of the city of
Weftminfter, and where the king fhould refide. †

The

---

* Journals.

† 1. Every perfon who fhall for hire, gain, or reward, act, reprefent, or perform, or caufe to be acted, reprefented, or performed,
any interlude, tragedy, comedy, opera, play, farce, or other entertainment of the ftage, or any part or parts therein, in cafe fuch perfon

The bill is generally faid to have been warmly
oppofed in bóth houfès; but it is remarkable that
no trace (excepting the fpeech of lord Chefterfield)
of this oppofition is to be found in the periodical
publications of the times, which are filled with
accounts of the other debates. It is alfo certain,
that not a fingle petition * was prefented againft
it,

fon fhall not have any legal fettlement in the place where the fame
fhall be acted, reprefented, or performed, without authority, by virtue
of letters patent from his majefty, his heirs, fucceffors, or predeceffors,
or without licence from the lord chamberlain of his majefty's houfehold for the time being, fhall be deemed a rogue and a vagabond,
within the intent and meaning of the faid recited act, and fhall be liable and fubject to all fuch penalties and punifhments, and by fuch
methods of conviction, as are inflicted on, or appointed by the faid
act for the punifhment of rogues and vagabonds who fhall be found
wandering, &c.

2. Any perfon having or not having any legal fettlement, who fhall
without fuch authority or licence, act, &c. for hire, &c. any interlude,
&c. every fuch perfon fhall, for every fuch offence, forfeit the fum of
fifty pounds, &c.

3. No perfon fhall for hire, &c. act, &c. &c. any new interlude,
&c. or any part or parts therein, or any new act, fcene, or other
part added to any old interlude, &c. or any new prologue or epilogue,
unlefs a true copy thereof be fent to the lord chamberlain of the king's
houfehold, &c. fourteen days at leaft before the acting, &c. together,
with an account of the playhoufe or other place where the fame fhall
be, &c. the time wherein the fame fhall be firft acted, &c. figned by
the mafter or manager, or one, &c. of fuch playhoufe, &c.

It fhall be lawful for the faid lord chamberlain, as often as he fhall
think fit, to prohibit the acting, &c. any interlude, &c. or any act,
&c. &c. &c. thereof, or any prologue or epilogue; and in cafe any
fuch perfons fhall for hire, &c. act any, &c. &c. before a copy
fhall be fent as aforefaid, or fhall for hire, &c. &c. contrary
to fuch prohibition, every perfon fo offending fhall, for every fuch
offence, forfeit the fum of fifty pounds, and every grant, &c. (in
cafe there be any fuch) under which the faid mafter, &c. fet up or
continued fuch playhoufe, &c. fhall ceafe.

4. That no perfon or perfons fhall be authorized by virtue of, &c.
from his majefty, &c. or the lord chamberlain, to act, &c. any interlude, &c. in any part of Great Britain, except in the city of Weftminfter, and within the liberties thereof, and in fuch places where his
majefty, &c. fhall refide, and during fuch refidence only.

* * * * * *

5. If any interlude, &c. fhall be acted, &c. in any houfe or place,
where wine or other liquors fhall be fold, the fame fhall be deemed to
be acted, &c. for gain. &c. Statutes at large, 17 G. 2. c. 28.

* Sir John Hawkins, in his Life of Johnfon, afferts, that the ma-

nager

it, and not a fingle divifion appears in the journals of either houfe. Striking proofs, if any were ftill wanting, to fhew the general opinion in favour of its neceffity,

The difpatch with which it was carried through both houfes, affords additional evidence that it fcarcely met with any refiftance. The bill was ordered to be brought in on the 20th of May, read the 24th, a fecond time on the 25th, and committed to the whole houfe; ordered to be reported, with amendments, on the 26th, reported on the 27th, all amendments but one agreed to, and the bill ordered to be engroffed; paffed on the firft of June, and Mr. Pelham ordered to carry it to the lords. It was read the firft time on the fame day, the fecond time on the 2d, after a debate, carried in the affirmative; the third time on the 6th, returned to the commons on the 8th, without any amendments, and received the royal affent on the 21ft.

It is moft probable that lord Chefterfield alone fpoke againft the bill, and that his fpeech fo defervedly admired, has been repeated by fubfequent writers who copy each other, until a violent oppofition to the meafure has been fuppofed, which never exifted,

Chefterfield did not confine his exertions to the houfe, but wrote againft the new act, in a paper called Common Senfe; his arguments have little to recommend them, at a time when the

proving

hager of Goodman's Fields prefented a petition againft it, and was heard by counfel, but this petition was prefented againft Sir John Barnard's bill in 1735.

propriety and utility of the meafure againft which
they were directed, is generally conceded. The
fatal evils which were predicted as the certain
confequences of this bill, perpetual flavery and
the introduction of abfolute authority, have not
followed; the good effects which were expected
from it, have been confirmed by never failing
experience. While it fuppreffed the licentioufnefs, it has not deftroyed the fpirit of the drama;
wit has not appeared lefs lovely and attracting, in
promoting virtue and curbing vice with decency,
than in recommending treafon and obfcenity;
nor are the fhafts of ridicule rendered ufelefs, becaufe, while they have preferved the power to do
good, they are divefted of the power to do mifchief. " The facts, which have been detailed,
evince, with fufficient conviction, that this act of
parliament merely reftored to the lord chamberlain, the ancient authority which he poffeffed before the appointment of the mafter of the revels;
armed him with legal power, in the place of cufto-
mary privilege; and enabled him to execute, by
warrantable means, the ufeful, but invidious truft,
which experience had long required, and policy
at length conferred." *

* Journals of the Lords and Commons. Chandler, for 1735,
Lords' Debates, 1737. Colley Cibber's Apology. Jeremy Collier's
View of the Immorality and Profanenefs of the Englifh Stage. Tin-
dal, vol. 20, p. 350. Oldmixon, vol. 3. p. 192. Introduction to
Biographia Dramatica. Gentleman's and London Magazine, 1737.
Maty's Life of Chefterfield. Hawkin's Life of Johnfon, p. 75;
Smollett, vol. 3. p. 525. Burn's Juftice, article Players. Chalmer's
Apology for the Believers of the Shakefpeare MSS. p. 471 to 543; to
whofe elaborate refearches on this fubject I have been principally in-
debted,

CHAPTER THE FORTY-EIGHTH:

1737.

Origin and Progress, of the Misunderstanding between the King and Prince of Wales.—Application to Parliament.—Conduct of Walpole—of Lord Chancellor Hardwicke—of Opposition.

Period VI.
1734 to 1737.

THIS year was marked by two domestic events, which proved highly prejudicial to the influence of Sir Robert Walpole, and greatly contributed to hasten the close of his administration; the public opposition of the prince of Wales, and the death of queen Caroline.

Frederick Louis, prince of Wales, was born in 1707, and continued at Hanover until he had attained the twenty-first year of his age.

Causes of the misunderstanding.

George the Second had found, from his own experience, the embarrassments to which government might be exposed from the opposition of the heir apparent, and dreaded the arrival of a son who might irritate the state of parties, and increase the ferment arising in the kingdom against the measures of the cabinet. He from time to time deferred his removal from Hanover, and did not send for him to England, until a concurrence of circumstances rendered it impolitic to permit his longer residence on the continent.

Clamours were justly raised in England, that the heir apparent had received a foreign education, and was detained abroad, as if to keep alive an attachment to Hanover, in preference to Great Britain.

Britain. The ministers at length ventured to re-
monstrate with the king on the subject, and the
privy council formally represented the propriety
of his residence in England. The king, however,
still hesitated, when an event occurred, which decided his choice, and induced him to accelerate
the prince's departure from Germany.

. A long negotiation had taken place between
the houses of Brunswick and Brandenburgh, for
a double marriage between the prince of Wales
and the princess royal of Pruffia, and the prince
royal of Pruffia and the princess Amelia. This
negotiation had commenced in the reign of George
··the First, and was eagerly promoted by his daughter Sophia Dorothy, who had espoused Frederick
William, king of Pruffia. Both parties seemed
to have desired this union with equal anxiety; but
the capricious and brutal temper of Frederick
William, and his sudden secession from the treaty
of Hanover, had so highly offended George the
First, that he ceased to favour the proposed inter-
marriages. Still farther obstacles were thrown in
their way at the accession of George the Second.
The two kings, from their early years, had formed
a violent antipathy to each other. The system of
politics adopted by England increased this misunderstanding. Frederick William had been lured
by the Emperor to join the allies of Vienna, in
opposition to those of Hanover, and his recruiting
officers frequently made illegal inrolments on the
Hanoverian territories.

In

In vain the queen of Pruffia endeavoured to reconcile her hufband and brother, and to promote the conclufion of the family union, which fhe fo earneftly defired. The antipathy of the two monarchs increafed inftead of abating; and the king of Pruffia was endeavouring to arrange another alliance for his fon and daughter, which both they and his queen highly deprecated.

During the progrefs of this affair, the prince had formed an attachment to the princefs of Pruffia, and by the fecret information of his aunt, the queen of Pruffia, was apprized that her daughter felt an equal affection for him.

The prince was now twenty-one; his paffion was inflamed by oppofition, and being filled with apprehenfions of lofing the object of his affection, he adopted an expedient which proved the ardour of his attachment. He fent La Mothe, a Hanoverian officer, to Berlin, who obtained a private audience of the queen, in which he told her that he was commanded by the prince to declare his refolution of repairing incognito to Berlin, and fecretly efpoufing her daughter, if their Pruffian majefties would fanction this ftep with their approbation. At the fame time he entreated the queen that it fhould be communicated to no one but the king. The queen received the meffage with a tranfport of joy, approved the defign, and promifed to keep the fecret inviolable. The next morning, however, fhe difclofed it to Dubourgeay, the Englifh envoy, obferving, that fhe believed

believed him to be fo much her friend as to par-
take of her fatisfaction. Dubourgeay expreffed
his concern that fo important a fecret fhould be,
confided to him, and declared it his duty to fend
immediate information to the king of England.
The queen, confcious of the error which fhe had
unwarily committed, conjured him not to betray
her confidence, but he perfifted in his refolution;
and a meffenger was immediately difpatched. *
The queen was greatly embarraffed at this unexpected incident, but trufted that the affair might
he concluded before the return of the meffenger
from England, and fo fanguine were their hopes
of fuccefs, that the king of Pruffia came from his
hunting feat to Berlin, expecting the daily arrival
of the intended bridegroom.

But while they were indulging thefe hopes, information was received that the prince had been
fent for to England. George the Second, on the
intelligence from Dubourgeay, difpatched colonel
Launay, to Hanover for that purpofe. The prince
received thefe commands with refpect, and inftantly obeyed them. At the conclufion of a ball,
he fet out from Hanover, accompanied only by
Launay and a fingle domeftic, traverfed Germany
and Holland as a private gentleman, embarked
at Helvetfluis, and arrived at St. James, where he
was coldly received by his father.

For fome time after his arrival in England, the
novelty of his fituation, his little acquaintance
with

* Polnitz, Hiftoire des quatre derniers Souverains de la Maifon
de Brandebourg Royale de Pruffe, tom. 2. p. 182-184.

with the language, his total ignorance of the conftitution and manners of the country, and the
dread which he feems to have entertained of his
father's indignation, kept him in due fubmiffion,
and prevented him from openly teftifying his diffatisfaction. But as he increafed in years, and
became confcious of his dignified ftation, the
eftrangement of his father, and the reftraint in
which he was kept, naturally difgufted a young
prince of high fpirit, and increafing popularity,
and the refentment which he had conceived againft
his parents, excited an antipathy to the minifter,
in whom they had placed implicit confidence. As
he had a tafte for the arts, and a fondnefs for literary purfuits, he fought the fociety of perfons
who were moft confpicuous for their talents and
knowledge. He was thrown into the company
of Carteret, Chefterfield, Pulteney, Cobham, and
Sir William Wyndham, who were confidered as
the leading characters for wit, talents, and ur-
banity.

His houfe became the rendezvous of young men
of the higheft expectations, Pitt, Lyttleton, and
the Grenvilles, whom he afterwards took into his
houfehold, and made his affociates. The ufual
topic of converfation in felect fociety, was abufe
of the minifter, and condemnation of his meafures, urged with all the keenefs of wit, and
powers of eloquence. The prince found the men
whofe reputation was moft eminent in literature,
particularly Swift, Pope, and Thomfon, adverfe

to

to Walpole, who was the object of their private and public satire.

But the person who principally contributed to increase his resentment against the king, and to foment his aversion to the minister, was Bolingbroke, who was characterised by the first poets of the age, as the " all accomplished St. John, the muse's friend." The prince was fascinated with his conversation and manners. His confident assertions, and popular declamations, his affected zeal to reconcile all ranks and descriptions, the energy with which he decried the baneful spirit of party, and his plausible theories of a perfect government, without influence or corruption, acting by prerogative, were calculated to dazzle and captivate a young prince of high spirit and sanguine disposition, and induce him to believe that the minister was forming a systematic plan to overthrow the constitution, and that the cause of opposition was that of honour and liberty.

So early as 1734, the misunderstanding between the father and son had increased to a very alarming degree, and the prince, encouraged by opposition, took a very injudicious step, which was calculated to provoke the king, and occasion an immediate and open rupture. He repaired to the anti-chamber, and without any previous arrangement, reqested an immediate audience. The king delayed admitting him till he had sent for Sir Robert Walpole, on whose arrival, he expressed his indignation against his son, and would have proceeded to instant extremities, had not the mi-

nister

nifter contrived to calm his refentment. ;; He ftrongly inculcated moderation, and perfuaded the king to hear with complacency, what the prince wifhed to communicate.

On being admitted, the prince made three re-quefts, in a tone and manner which indicated a fpirit of perfeverance. The firft was, to ferve a campaign on the Rhine in the Imperial army; the fecond related to the augmentation of his re-venue, at the fame time infinuating, that he was in debt; the third was, his fettlement by a fuit-able marriage. To the firft and third points, the king made no anfwer; in regard to the fecond, he fhewed an inclination to comply, if the prince would behave with due refpect to the queen.

The king had fuppreffed his anger on thefe de-mands of his fon; but his refentment broke out with redoubled violence, when rumours were cir-culated, that the prince would apply to parlia-ment for an augmentation of his revenue. The queen exerted all her efforts to foften the king's indignation, and the minifter ufed every argu-ment which policy fuggefted to incline him to moderation, and to induce him not to drive the prince wholly into the arms of oppofition. Thefe exertions had a temporary effect. * The rupture was fufpended, and the hopes of oppofition were difappointed.

Marries the princefs of Saxe Gotha.

The paffion which the prince had entertained for the princefs Frederica, being thwarted by his parents, preyed upon his mind and increafed his **difguft,**

---

* Lettre de Monf. de Lofs à Monf. de Bruhl, fans datte; de Monf. John à Mont. Von Hagen, 16 de Juillet 1734. Correfpondence.

difguft, and when the propofal of another union was
imparted to him, he remonftrated with great marks
of offended fenfibility, and expreffed his repugnance to efpoufe a princefs whom he had not feen,
inftead of one whom he had feen and approved.
When the arrangement was made for his marriage
with Augufta, princefs of Saxe Gotha, the prince
of Wales fent for baron Borck, the Pruffian minifter, and complained, with much indignation,
that the king his father compelled him to renounce all hopes of efpoufing a Pruffian princefs.
He requefted him to lay his grief before the king
his mafter, and to affure him that he was determined to have refifted all compulfion, and was
only induced to agree to the alliance with the
princefs of Saxe Gotha, on being informed by
his mother, that the king of Pruffia had refufed
to give him his daughter in marriage. He expreffed his heartfelt regret that he was not permitted to have the honour of forming an union
with a family which he loved more than his own,
and to which, from his earlieft infancy, all his
defires had been directed; he hoped, neverthelefs,
that the king would not withdraw his favour and
friendfhip. He teftified his concern, that he was
to be connected with a houfe from which he
could not expect that fupport, which he fhould
have found in the king of Pruffia, and lamented
his hard fate in being condemned to remain under the fevere controul of the queen his mother.
He concluded by obferving, that he muft fubmit
to his deftiny, that he could not fee, without

grief, the king of England difdaining the friendfhip of a great monarch, without which the ruin ·
of his houfe muft infallibly enfue. * The letter,
in which Borck gave an account of this indifcreet
conference to his mafter, fell into the hands of
the king, and greatly irritated his inflammable
temper.

. On the 27th of April 1736, the prince of Wales
efpoufed the princefs of Saxe Gotha, in whofe
beauty, accomplifhments, and virtues, he forgot
his former paffion. But the marriage did not remove the unfortunate mifunderftanding between
the father and fon, it rather had a contrary tendency. The increafed expences of the prince's
houfehold, without an adequate increafe of income, rendered his fituation ftill more irkfome.
His revenue, although enlarged from £.36,000 to
£.50,000, with the emoluments of the duchy of
Cornwall, did not amount to £.60,000, a fum the
prince and his friends deemed infufficient to fupport the dignity of his ftation. It became matter
of public animadverfion, that out, of a civil lift
of £.800,000, he received only £.50,000 a year,
although the king, when prince of Wales, received £.100,000 out of a civil lift of only
£.700,000. But while this was induftrioufly circulated, it was not confidered, that George the
Second, when prince of Wales, had a large family, and that he had feveral younger children,
for whom he was to make a provifion out of the
civil

---

* Letter from Borck to the king of Pruffia, December 23, 1735.
Orford Papers.

civil lift, which was not the cafe of George the Firft.

The marriage of the heir apparent greatly increafed his popularity. The affability of his manners, the courtefy of his deportment, were contrafted with the phlegmatic referve of George the Second. His protection of letters, his fondnefs for the polite arts, and his rifing merits, became the favourite theme of popular applaufe, and of parliamentary declamation among the members of oppofition.

It is remarkable, that the addrefs of congratulation to the king, on the nuptials of the prince of Wales with the princefs of Saxe Gotha was moved by Pulteney, and that the principal fpeakers in the prince's praife, were thofe who uniformly oppofed the meafures of government. It was on this memorable occafion, that William Pitt made his maiden fpeech, in a ftrain of declamation, which a contemporary hiftorian defcribes as not inferior to the great models of antiquity, " it being more ornamented than Demofthenes, and lefs diffufe than Cicero." * Both he and his friend Lyttleton, who alfo firft fpoke on the fame occafion, defcribed the prince as a moft dutiful fon; defcanted on his filial obedience and refpectful fubmiffion to the will of his royal parents, and expatiated, with oftentatious energy, on his generous love of liberty, and juft reverence for the Britifh conftitution. ✗ In affecting to praife the

king,

* Tindal.

G G 2

✗ Neither Pitt nor Lyttelton deserve these encomiums on this occasion they were set speeches; scarcely above mediocrity

Period VI.
1734 to 1737.

king, for having gratified the impatient wifhes of
a loyal people, they gave the prior merit to the
prince, for having requefted a marriage fo neceffary to the public good, and afcribed only a
fecondary merit to the king for granting this requeft.

The manner in which this debate * was conducted, the warm panegyric beftowed on the prince,
the cold praifes given to the king, and the acri-
monious cenfures of the minifter, gave great offence, and tended ftill farther to widen the breach.

Joins oppofi-
tion.

At length the mifunderftanding arofe to fo great
a height, that the prince threw himfelf into the
arms of oppofition. Bolingbroke, who had long
advifed the moft violent meafures, now laid down
a fyftematic plan of proceeding to be followed by
the prince, the firft ftep of which was an emanci-
pation from all dependence on the crown, by the
acquifition of a permanent allowance of £. 100,000
per annum, which the king fhould be compelled
to grant, at the remonftrance, and under the
guaranty of parliament.

Requires an
increafed al-
lowance.

From the time that this fcheme was firft fuggefted by Bolingbroke, and which had been un-
advifedly infinuated to the king, in 1734, before
it was maturely weighed, the prince feems to have
perfifted in his refolution of appealing to parliament. Soon after his marriage, he mentioned
his intention to the queen. The queen, perceiving that any advice would be ineffectual, affected
to confider it as an idle and chimerical fcheme;

fhe

* Chandler, vol. 9, p. 222.

fhe treated it as a jeft, and declared that there
was not the leaft profpect of fuccefs. But her
remonftrance had no effect. Urged on by Bolingbroke, whofe laft advice, before his retreat into
France, was to purfue unremittingly this one favourite object, the prince at length determined to
lay his cafe before parliament. He accordingly
applied to the moft refpectable members of oppofition, without any previous intimation, not with
a view of afking advice, but of demanding fupport. Pulteney, though furprifed at the unexpected requeft, declared a hearty inclination on
his own part to promote the meafure, but added,
that he muft confult his friends. Finding, however, the prince determined to perfevere, he engaged for the unanimous confent of his particular
friends, and offered to make the motion himfelf.
Sir John Barnard promifed his fupport, and Sir
William Wyndham anfwered for the Tories; obferving, that they had long defired an opportunity
of fhewing their regard and attachment to the
prince. He alfo declared, that all his party were
anxious to prove by their zeal, the falfity of the
reproaches caft againft them, that they were Jacobites, and to fhew that they were mifreprefented
under that name.

Dodington, afterwards lord Melcombe, was
the firft perfon connected with government, to
whom the prince imparted his defign, and to
him it was declared only on the 7th of February.
Dodington gave a ftrking proof of firmnefs and
integrity, by declining to fupport a fcheme preg-

nant

nant with fo many evils, and made ftrong and
fenfible remonftrances to induce the prince not to
prefs any farther a meafure which muft render all
who voted defperate either with the poffeffor of,
or fucceffor to the crown; but all his efforts were
ineffectual. *

No information was conveyed to the king, and
the minifter did not receive the leaft intimation
of the bufinefs, or even fufpect it, until the 13th
of February. He was never before engaged in
any tranfaction which gave him more concern or
greater embarraffment. He was aware that £. 50,000
a year was inadequate to the dignified ftation of
the heir apparent, and yet convined that the king,
incenfed as he was againft his fon, could not be
perfuaded to increafe that allowance. He was not
however intimidated by a dread of offending the
heir apparent, who might one day become his
mafter, and did not fhrink from his duty to his
fovereign and to his country; but refolved to fupport the king in his juft prerogative, and to oppofe a meafure which he confidered as no lefs unconftitutional than difrefpectful. He lamented,
however, that the king had imprudently delayed
to make the prince a permanent allowance of
£. 50,000 a year, in the fame manner as George
the Firft had granted his allowance when prince
of Wales, and that he had not fettled a jointure
on the princefs. Walpole was not ignorant that
the prince derived from thefe circumftances juft
caufe of complaint, and that until that was removed,

* Dodington's Diary.

moved, the oppofition would have great advantage Chapter 48.
in the argument. In confequence of ·thefe fenti- 1737.
ments, he ufed all his efforts to obtain a concef-
fion of thefe points, and finally conquered the repugnance of the king.

But the ungracious manner in which this was Proceedings in the cabinet.
offered, widened rather than repaired the breacn.
The minifter fummoned a meeting at his own Feb. 19.
houfe, at which were prefent, the dukes of Newcaftle, Grafton, and Devonfhire, the earl of Scarborough, Horace Walpole, and lord Hardwicke,
recently nominated lord chancellor, on the death
of lord Talbot. * Walpole informed them, that·
he had, though not without the greateft difficulty,
prevailed on the king to render the prince's allowance independent, and to fettle the princefs's
jointure; and that his majefty had been pleafed
to give him authority to ·announce to the houfe·
of commons, when the motion was made, his
confent to both thefe points. The chancellor ob-
jeted, that if this declaration fhould be firft made
in the houfe of commons, without properly acquainting the prince, or his treafurer, it would·
have the appearance of an intended furprife. He
added, that the friends of the royal family might
think themfelves ill ufed, if they were reduced
to fo great a difficulty as that of voting in a difpute between the king and the prince, when perhaps

---

* Lord Hardwicke has left a circumftantial narrative of this important tranfaction, from which I have felected the moft interefting
particulars. Hardwicke Papers.

haps fuch previous information as he recommended might have-prevented the motion.

To this fenfible reprefentation, the minifter, replied, that it was in vain to imagine the king could be reduced to fo low an act of fubmiffion, as to permit any private communication of this kind, after the fteps the prince had already taken. The fuggeftion, however, of the chancellor made a due impreffion, and Walpole perfuaded the king to fend a meffage to the prince, by fome of the lords of the cabinet council.

Accordingly, on the day in which lord Hardwicke received the great feal, while he was waiting in the antichamber with the dukes of Newcaftle and Argyle, the earl of Wilmington, and other lords of the council, Sir Robert Walpole came out of the king's chamber in a great hurry, holding a paper in his hand. Calling all the lords of the cabinet to the upper-end of the room, he read to them the draught of a meffage, in his own hand writing, and acquainted them, that it was the king's pleafure, it fhould be immediately carried to the prince by the lord chancellor, lord prefident, lord fteward, and lord chamberlain.

The draught was not fairly tranfcribed, and feveral of the lords complained, that the whole bufinefs was tranfacted with fuch precipitation, that fufficient leifure was not allowed to confider the terms of the meffage. The time preffed extremely, and the place was highly improper for fuch momentous confultation. For the company which affembled to attend the levee filled the room, and could

. not

not avoid hearing many of the things which paſſed
in the courſe of converſation. The chancellor,
however, ventured to object to the expreſſions,
" *the undutiful meaſures which his majeſty is informed
your royal highneſs intends to purſue;*" but it was
replied by the miniſter, that the king inſiſted on
the word *undutiful,* and that it was with great difficulty he was induced not to add ſeverer epithets.
The chancellor, however, perſiſting in his objection, the word *intends,* was changed for *hath been
adviſed to purſue.*

The chancellor took Walpole aſide, and expoſtu-
lated with him on the hardſhip of making ſuch
a diſagreeable errand the firſt act of his office.
The miniſter anſwered, that he had hinted this to
the king, *as far as he durſt venture in ſo nice a caſe,*
but the king prevented all farther diſcuſſion, by
exclaiming, *my chancellor ſhall go.*

The expoſtulations of the chancellor, however,
produced a variation in point of form; inſtead of
only four officers of the crown, the whole cabinet
council was ordered to attend with the meſſage.
It then growing late, Sir Robert Walpole acquainted them that buſineſs of conſequence was
expected in the houſe of commons, that he and
Sir Charles Wager muſt attend, and they both
went away, leaving the foul draught of the meſſage. Lord Ilay, under a pretence of attending
the houſe of lords, alſo retired.

When the ceremony of giving the great ſeal was
over, the remaining * lords of the cabinet deli-
berated

* The Lord chancellor, the earl of Wilmington, the dukes of
Dorſet and Grafton, the duke of Richmond, maſter of the horſe, the
duke

berated in the council chamber on the mode of executing their charge. The meffage was not yet copied, and a rumour was circulated, that the prince was going to the houfe of commons; the lord fteward and the lord chamberlain were deputed to inform him, that the lords of the cabinet were ordered to attend with a meffage from the king, and requefted to know where he would receive it. He anfwered, in his own apartment. As foon as the fair copy was compared with the draught, the lords went to the prince, and being fhewn into the levee room, the chancellor kiffed his hand, on being appointed to his high office, and received his congratulations. The door being then clofed, he read the meffage over audibly and diftinctly, as follows:

"His majefty has commanded us to acquaint your royal highnefs, in his name, that upon your royal highnefs's marriage, he immediately took into his royal confideration the fettling a proper jointure upon the princefs of Wales; but his fudden going abroad, and his late indifpofition fince his return, had hitherto delayed the execution of thefe his gracious intentions; from which fhort delay his majefty did not apprehend any inconveniences could arife, efpecially fince no application had, in any manner, been made to him upon this fubject by your royal highnefs: and that his majefty hath now given orders for fettling a jointure upon the princefs of Wales, as far as he is enabled by law.

duke of Argyle, commander in chief, the duke of Newcaftle, the earl of Pembroke, groom of the ftole, the earl of Scarborough, and lord Harrington.

law, fuitable to her high rank and dignity, which
he will, in proper time, lay before his parliament,
in order to be rendered certain and effectual, for
the benefit of her royal highnefs.

" The king has further commanded us to acquaint your royal highnefs, that although your
royal highnefs has not thought fit, by any application to his majefty, to defire, that your allowance of £. 50,000 per annum, which is now paid
by monthly payments, at the choice of your
royal highnefs, preferably to quarterly payments,
might, by his majefty's further grace and favour,
be rendered lefs precarious, his majefty, to prevent the bad confequences which he apprehends
may follow, from the undutiful meafures, which
his majefty is informed, your royal highnefs has
been advifed to purfue, will grant to your
royal highnefs for his majefty's life, the faid
£. 50,000 per annum, to be iffuing out of his majefty's civil lift revenues, over and above your
royal highnefs's revenues arifing from the duchy of
Cornwall, which his majefty thinks a very competent allowance, confidering his numerous iffue,
and the great expences which do, and muft neceffarily attend an honourable provifion for his
whole royal family."

The chancellor having concluded, there was a The prince's
fhort paufe, and a profound filence enfued. The answer.
prince looking about him, faid, my lords, " Am
I to return an immediate anfwer ?" to which the
chancellor replying, "if your royal highnefs pleafes,"
the

the prince then delivered a verbal meſſage to the
following import :

"He defired the lords to lay him, with all humility, at his majeſty's feet ; and to aſſure his
majeſty that he had, and ever ſhould retain, the
utmoſt duty for his royal perſon ; that he was
very thankful for any inſtance of his majeſty's
goodneſs to him, or the princeſs, and for his majeſty's gracious intention for ſettling a jointure
upon her royal highneſs ; but that, as to the meſſage, the affair was now out of his hands, and
therefore he could give no anſwer to it." After
which, he uſed many dutiful expreſſions towards
the king, and then added, *Indeed, my lords, it is in
other hands, I am ſorry for it*, or to that effect. He
concluded, with earneſtly defiring the lords to reprefent his anſwer to his majeſty in the moſt re-
ſpectful and dutiful manner." *

When this anſwer was reported to the king in
the evening, by the lords, he looked difpleaſed,
but made no reply.

Situation of the   The fituation of the miniſter was rendered more
miniſter.   embarraſſing at this particular period, from the ill
health of the king, who was at that time ſo in-
difpoſed as to give real apprehenſion, that he could
not long ſurvive. Hence Bolingbroke, in a letter †
to Sir William Wyndham, expreſſes his aſtoniſh-
ment at Walpole's imprudence, in offending the
heir apparent, who was likely to become his maſter,

---

* Chandler, vol. 9, p. 301, 303.
† Correſpondence, Feb. 3, 1738. Period VII.

ter, and the duchefs of Marlborough thought his Chapter 48.
conduct no lefs incomprehenfible.* This circumftance had given to oppofition a great acceffion of ftrength, but had no effect on the conduct of Walpole.

On the 22d Pulteney made his motion for an Motion in the houfe of com-
addrefs, requefting the king to fettle £. 100,000 mons.
a year on the prince of Wales, and the fame jointure on the princefs as the queen had when fhe
was princefs of Wales, affuring the king, that the
houfe would enable him effectually to fulfil the
fame.

The great points which Pulteney, and thofe
who fupported the motion, laboured to prove,
were, that the prince had a claim to the propofed
alowance, founded on equity and good policy,
and a legal right, founded on law and precedent,
and that the revenue of the civil lift had been
granted to George the Firft, and afterwards augmented under George the Second, on the exprefs,
or at leaft implied, condition, that, out of that
revenue, the fum of £. 100,000 fhould be referved
for the prince of Wales, as a permanent and independent eftablifhment, which the king had it
not in his power to withhold. Pulteney fupported the principles on which the motion was
founded with great ability, and with a long feries
of hiftorical references to heirs apparent and prefumptive

---

* [Feb. 6, 1736.] Heard this day, from a pretty good hand,
that his majefty has been worfe than they cared to own, but upon
remedies they applied, his fever leffened, and was better. However,
the phyficians fay, that if he does get over this illnefs, he cannot
live a twelvemonth. Opinions of the Duchefs of Marlborough, p. 36.

sumptive to the crown, who, he maintained, had received an independent and permanent allowance. He concluded by anticipating several cogent objections to the proposed address, arising from the impropriety and indecency of interposing between the king and the prince, between the father and the son, and of interfering with the prerogative of the crown.

The minister in reply, began by observing, that he never rose to speak upon any subject with a deeper concern, and a greater reluctancy, than he did on the present important affair. He expressed the concern and embarrassment under which most members of that house must lie, in giving their votes or opinion; if they declared in favour of the motion, they must seem to injure the royal father, their sovereign, or by declining the motion, seem to injure the royal son, and apparent heir to the crown. But he would declare his sentiments with freedom, because from his *personal* knowledge of the two great characters, he was satisfied that neither of them would think himself injured, because any gentleman gave his opinion or vote freely in parliament; and he was convinced that the prince of Wales had so much wisdom, and such a true sense of filial duty, that he would never consider as a favour bestowed on him, what had the least tendency towards offering an indignity to his father.

He supported the prerogative of the crown, and the right of the king to dispose of his civil revenues, without the interference of parliament, and

to

to suffer no controul in the management of his own family. In the course of his speech, he communicated the substance of the message which had been sent by the king to the prince, and declared that £.50,000 a year, exclusive of the revenues arising from the duchy of Cornwall, was a competent allowance, and as much as the king could afford out of the civil list. He expatiated on the impropriety of interposing between the father and son, deprecated the attempt to make a breach between them, entered into an historical examination of the several precedents mentioned by Pulteney, and denied that any foundation for such a parliamentary interposition could be found, except a single precedent under Henry the Sixth, whose reign was so weak, that the parliament found it necessary to assume several rights and privileges, to which they were not properly entitled. He declared, that the prince had neither a claim from equity or good policy, and still less a right, founded on law or precedent, and he mentioned that the revenues of the civil list had been granted unconditionally to the king, without the most distant allusion to a stipulation, that £.100,000 per annum should be paid to the prince of Wales.

The reasons urged by Walpole, in contradiction to those advanced by opposition, sufficiently proved, to all dispassionate persons, that the motion was not founded on law, good policy, or precedent, and were not invalidated by the reply of Pulteney, in summing up the arguments on both sides.

But

But a confident and plaufible aſſertion, advanced by a fupporter of the motion, made a deep impreſſion on the houſe, and ſeemed to vindicate the proceedings of the prince, and to arraign the conduct of the king.

" By the regulation and fettlement of the prince's houſehold, as made ſome time ſince by his majeſty himſelf, the yearly expence comes to £.63,000, without allowing one ſhilling to his royal highneſs for acts of charity and generoſity. By the meſſage now before us, it is propoſed to fettle upon him only £.50,000 a year, and yet from this fum we muſt deduct the land tax, which, at two ſhillings in the pound, amounts to £.5,000 a year, we muſt likewiſe deduct the ſixpenny duty to the civil liſt lottery, which amounts to £.1,250 a year, and we muſt alſo deduct the fees payable at the exchequer, which amount to about £.750 a year more, all theſe deductions amount to £.7,000 a year, and reduce the £.50,000, propoſed to be fettled upon him by the meſſage, to £.43,000 a year. Now as his royal highneſs has no other eſtate but the duchy of Cornwall, which cannot be reckoned, at the moſt, above £.9,000, his whole yearly revenue can amount but to £.52,000, and yet the yearly expence of his houſehold, according to his majeſty's own regulation, is to amount to £.63,000, without allowing his royal highneſs one ſhilling for the indulgence of that generous and charitable diſpoſition with which he is known to be endued in a very eminent degree. Suppoſe then we allow him but £.10,000

£. 10,000 a year for the indulgence of that lauda-
ble; difpofition, his whole yearly expence, by his
majefty's own acknowledgment, muft then amount.
to £. 73,000, and his yearly income, according to
this meffage, can amount to no more than
£. 52,000. Is this, Sir, fhewing any refpect to
his merit ? Is this providing for his generofity ?
Is it not reducing him to a real want, even with
refpect to his neceffities, and confequently, to an
unavoidable dependance, and a vile pecuniary dependance too, upon his father's minifters and fervants ? I confefs, Sir, when I firft heard this motion made, I was wavering a good deal in my opinion ; but this meffage has confirmed me : I now
fee, that without the interpofition of parliament,
his royal highnefs the prince of Wales, the heir
apparent to our crown, muft be reduced to the
greateft ftraits, the moft infufferable hardfhips." *

Full credit was, at the time, given to this ftatement, as well becaufe it was oftentatioufly difplayed by two of the prince's fervants during the
debate, as becaufe the minifter, to prevent great
heats and animofities, made no immediate anfwer,
and feveral perfons were induced by this reprefentation to vote in favour of the motion, which
was negatived by a majority of only 234, againft
204. †

This fmall majority of 30 would have been
reduced to a minority, had Sir William Wyndham been able to fulfil the promife of fupport,
which

* Chandler.   † Journals.

which he made to the prince in the name of his party. But forty-five Tories confidered the interference of parliament as hoftile to the principles of the Britifh conftitution, highly democratic, and fuch a dangerous innovation, that they quitted the houfe in a body before the divifion; an act highly honourable to thofe who refufed to facrifice their principles to their party.

In the lords. On the 23d, the fame motion was made in the houfe of peers by lord Carteret, and a fimilar debate enfued. It was negatived by a large majority of 103 againft 40, and a proteft was inferted only by fourteen peers. *

Mif-ftatement of oppofition. But although this unconftitutional propofition was thus thrown out in parliament, yet the fmallnefs of the majority in the lower houfe, proved the difficulties under which the minifter laboured. His caufe was highly unpopular. The oppofition introduced the queftion in every fhape and form which was moft likely to attract the public attention, and in the periodical papers and pamphlets, written with all the addrefs and fubtlety which the talents of the great leaders of the minority could fupply. Among other pamphlets which were circulated with zeal, and read with avidity, was one intitled, " A Letter from a Member of Parliament to his Friend in the Country, on the Motion for addreffing the King to fettle £.100,000. per Annum on his Royal Highnefs the Prince of Wales." This work was written with fuch an air of candour, and plaufibility of argument, and yet contained

* Lord's Debates.

tained fo much bitternefs and acrimony, that the minifter himfelf revifed the anfwer, which was compofed by lord Hervey, called " An Exami-nation of the Facts and Reafons contained in a Pamphlet intitled, A Letter, &c." In this work, Sir Robert Walpole made feveral infertions, which prove the importance of the letter, and which are ftill extant in his own hand-writing among the Orford Papers. He here commented with greater free-dom than he could venture to do in parliament; and anfwered the arguments in favour of the mo-tion with more fpirit than moderation, and more indignation than temper.

That part of his infertions which is moft wor-thy of notice, was the anfwer given to the ftate-ment made in the houfe, refpecting the prince's eftablifhment, faid to have been regulated by the king. From a fair inveftigation of the paper which the prince's officers had fhewn to the houfe, he demonftrated, that it was not an *eftablifhment*, but a calculation founded on the expenditure of pre-ceding years; that it was exaggerated and over-charged in almoft every branch, and that fo far from having been regulated by the king, his majefty had not even a knowledge of its exift-ence.

The indifcretion of the prince in bringing fo unconftitutional a queftion before parliament, contrary to the judgment of his real friends; the violence of his counfellors, and particularly the petulant and indecorous infinuations thrown out

H H 2 againft

Period VI.
1734 to 1737.

against the queen * in the course of the debate, highly offended the king, and rendered the breach between the father and son irreparable. Coldness, reserve, and distance increased. The prince considered himself a state prisoner in the palace of his father, pined for a release, and seized the first plausible pretence of emancipating himself from the controul of his parents.

The prince leaves Hampton Court.

July 31.

The royal family being at Hampton Court, the princess of Wales was seized with the pangs of child-birth, and the prince, without the least intimation to the king and queen, hurried her away to St. James's, where she was that night delivered of a princess, before the queen, or any of the officers of state, who were accustomed to be present, could arrive.

The prince apologized for his abrupt departure to the queen, who went the next morning to visit the princess. He observed, that the suddenness with which his wife was seized, rendered it necessary to obtain immediate assistance, and that it was thought most prudent to return to London, where good assistance was to be obtained, than wait till the physicians and midwives could arrive

at

* Walpole having in his speech maintained that the parliament had no right to interfere in the creation or maintenance of a prince of Wales, and that in the case of Richard, who on the death of his father, the Black Prince, was created prince of Wales, in consequence of an address or petition from parliament, that measure was in all probability directed by Edward the Third: In reply to this assertion, the opposition indecorously alluded to the influence of queen Caroline over the king, and her preference of the duke of Cumberland to the prince of Wales, by observing, that Edward doated in his old age, and was solely governed by Alice Pierce, and *his second son* the duke of Lancaster. *The conclusion of this note is entirely a mistake. It was mr. Pitt (first earl of Chatham) who first mentioned Alice Pierce, in a debate ten years after this period. In the life of lord Chatham, I avoided the mention*

at Hampton Court, which might be too late;
he entreated the queen to explain to the king
the motives which induced him to retire from
Hampton Court, without intimating his defign,
which the hurry of his departure had alone prevented; and he profeffed alfo his intention of
waiting on the king that morning. The queen
advifed him to delay this vifit for a few days, in
which the prince acquiefced. He repeated the
fame apology to Sir Robert Walpole and lord
Harrington, who had come by the king's command to be prefent at the birth. The king,
however, was not moved by this juftification, but
refolved to exprefs his refentment in a manner
no lefs public, than that in which he conceived
the indignity was offered. A draught of a meffage
was accordingly prepared by Sir Robert Walpole, and fubmitted by him to the confideration
of the lord chancellor, lord Wilmington, and
lord Harrington. The chancellor, with a view
to fhew great tendernefs to the fituation of the
princefs, and to gain time for conciliation, before the moft aggravating circumftances of the
rupture were rendered permanent, and incapable
of modification, by being committed to writing,
difapproved the draught, and propofed another in
more foft and gentle terms.

" The king hath commanded me to acquaint
your royal highnefs, that his majefty is moft
heartily rejoiced at the fafe delivery of the princefs, but that, on account of certain circumftances
in your royal highnefs's behaviour relating to that

* H H 3   event,

event, which have given his majesty juft offence, he thinks it not proper to fee you, with the particular reafons whereof he will caufe your royal highnefs to be acquainted in due time."

Lord Wilmington, who feldom declared himfeif explicitly on any fubject, fupported, however, with unufual warmth, the original draught ; and as lord Harrington was filent, the chancellor's alteration was rejected, and the original carried. On the 3d of Auguft, it was fent to the prince by lord Effex, the lord of the bedchamber in waiting, and contained thefe words :

" The king has commanded me to acquaint your royal highnefs, that his majefty moft heartily rejoices at the fafe delivery of the princefs, but that your carrying away her royal highnefs from Hampton Court, the then refidence of the king, the queen, and the family, under the pains, and certain indications of immediate labour, to the imminent danger and hazard both of the princefs and her child, after fufficient warnings for a week before, to have made the neceffary preparations for this happy event, without acquainting his majefty or the queen with the circumftances the princefs was in, or giving them the leaft notice of your departure, is looked upon by the king to be fuch a deliberate indignity, offered to himfeif and to the queen, that he has commanded me to acquaint your royal highnefs, that he refents it to the higheft degree."

In reply to this meffage, the prince wrote a letter, in which, after expreffing his mortification

at

at having difpleafed the king, he juftified his
conduct, repeated the fame motives as he had
ftated to the queen in perfon, and requefted permiffion to wait upon the king the next morning.
This requeft having been rejected, the prince
repeated, in another fubmiffive letter, his earneft
hopes of being reftored to favour. No anfwer
was returned to this application, but a meffage
from the king was conveyed by the earl of Dun-
more, appointing the baptifm to be performed on
the 29th, declaring, that he fhould fend the lord
chancellor to ftand god-father as his proxy, the
queen's lady of the bedchamber for the queen,
and defiring the princefs to appoint one of her
ladies of the bedchamber to reprefent the dowa-
ger duchefs of Saxe Gotha, the other god-mo-
ther.

The prince took this opportunity to reiterate,
both to the king and queen, his application for
pardon, with increafing earneftnefs and humility.
His entreaties, however, had no effect. The king
adopted the violent refolution of making a total
feparation between his family and that of the
prince, by difmiffing him from his refidence in
the palace of St. James's. In taking this refolution, he was, if not confirmed, at leaft not oppofed by the minifter.

The prudence and moderation of the chancellor
faw the danger of fuch a feparation. However
difagreeable his interpofition might be, both to
the king and Walpole, he thought, it his duty to
prevent, if poffible, fuch extremities. With this

H H 4. r view,

view, he went over to New Park, and had a long and interefting conference with Sir Robert Walpole. *

" He laid it down as a principle, that in this nice affair, two great points were always to be purfued. Firft, the real and effential intereft of the king and his family, in which the whole of the kingdom was involved; and next, the fupport of that authority and reverence, which was due to his majefty. That it was the duty of his minifters and fervants to endeavour to combine both thefe views, and in their conduct not to lofe fight of either. That he could not help thinking, that if there was a difpofition to it, a reconciliation might be effected confiftently with both; but if that fhould be found impoffible, a total feparation muft indeed be. fubmitted to. However, he begged leave to lay before him feveral confiderations, which feemed material in this great queftion, fome whereof diftinguifhed the cafe from that of the quarrel in the late reign, and made the prefent breach more formidable.

" 1. That it ought to be confidered what influence it would have on the fide of the queftion, which had been once moved in parliament, and was expected to be brought there again, viz. the prince's demand of a larger allowance, and this upon different fuppofitions. It appeared to him, that if the king fhould be finally in the right, and the prince continue, as he was certainly at firft,

---

* This conference is given verbatim, from lord Hardwicke's interefting narrative before mentioned,

firſt, on the affair of the departure, in the wrong,
it would ſtrengthen the king as to that queſtion;
for nobody could, with any ſhadow of reaſon,
maintain that the king could with decency be
addreſſed to increaſe his ſon's allowance, while he
was ſtanding out in defiance. But on the other
hand, it muſt be attended to, that this offence
was ſuch as to admit of a ſatisfaction between a
father and a ſon; and if the world ſhould think
the prince had made a proper ſubmiſſion, and yet
the king turn him out of doors, it would ſtrengthen
the prince in his demand; ſince it might then be
ſaid, that the king had cauſeleſsly obliged him to
live by himſelf, with an increaſe of family, at a
great expence. He added, that it muſt be expected that even thoſe who leaſt wiſhed a reconciliation, would adviſe him to make ſuch a ſubmiſſion, when they were ſure it could not, or
would not, be accepted.

" 2. That in the next place, the ſituation and
circumſtances of the royal family deſerved the
greateſt attention. In the late reign, the difference concerned only the king and prince; there
were no other children to be affected by it. The
moment the breath was out of the late king's
body, it was at an end as to the royal family,
though particular ſubjects might feel its effects.
That now the caſe was far different. A queen
conſort, the duke and four princeſſes, not to include the princeſs of Orange, muſt neceſſarily be,
to a degree, involved in it. If the prince ſhould
ſurvive his father, he muſt, and by the courſe of

law

law and nature, ought to reign. All thefe will be more or lefs in his power. The queen poffibly leaft of all is; but how far the honey-moon of a new reign may carry men as to her large jointure, no one can forefee. The others abfolutely. Yet thefe muft now, as they juftly deferve, live at court in the fun-fhine of the king and queen's favour, the prince being excluded. This will naturally breed an alienation of affection, great envying and much ill blood, which may break out into fatal confequences when the prince fhall find himfelf their fovereign. Add to this, that it is not probable that any fettlement will ever be obtained from the parliament to make cadets of the royal family, independant of any perfon who fhall wear the crown.

" 3. He next confidered the cafe of the prince's children. Either the king muft take the cuftody of them, or leave them with his royal highnefs, If he fhould take them, having a favourite younger fon, and feveral daughters, juftly dear to him, what jealoufies and fufpicions may not arife in cafe of accidents. Malice may even fuggeft what was once believed in France, of the late duke of Orleans. If the king fhould fuffer thefe branches of the royal family to remain with the prince, will it not greatly weaken the former, and ftrengthen the latter? And at length, they will be bred up under the fame influence which is now objected to their father.

" 4. As to the adminiftration, what an inundation of penfions did the breach in the late reign produce!

produce ! What a weight did that bring on my
lord Sunderland's miniftry ! And it fhould be
confidered whether even that miferable expedient will, be found practicable under this king.
The prefent demands of mankind will rife on one
fide in proportion as greater hopes are held out
on the other. It put lord Sunderland on ftrong
meafures to fecure himfelf, which yet he could
not carry. Witnefs the peerage bill, wherein
were feveral provifions tempting to the Whigs,
and yet they rejected it.

" 5. It will make a coalition between the
Whigs defperate and impoffible. Before this,
the Whigs in oppofition wanted a head, became
liable to the difagreeable imputation of conftantly
acting with the Jacobites; had no profpect of
ever coming into any fhare of power, but by re-
uniting with their old friends. They will now
find a head in the prince, and he, being the immediate fucceffor in the proteftant line, will be
an irrefragable anfwer to the reproach of Jacobitifm. Befides, the Whigs, as a party, will, in
good policy, not wifh fuch a coalition, unlefs it
could be accompanied with a reconciliation between the father and fon, left it fhould throw the
fucceffor wholly into the hands of the Tories, and
make their caufe defperate when he comes to
take poffeffion; whereas, by having one fet of
Whigs in the prince's favour, the party will have
a fair chance to be preferved from ruin when that
event fhall arrive.

" 6. Laftly,

" 6. Laftly, it muft not be forgot, that if the king fhould carry his refentment fo far as to remove his fon out of his palace, it will be neceffary that fome account of a tranfaction of this high nature in the royal family, fhould be given to foreign courts. This meafure was taken in the late reign. If the prince fhould at length fully fubmit himfelf to his father, and do that which the world fhall judge a complete fatisfaction for the late offence, what reafons can openly be affigned to juftify fuch a conduct ? He would nòt fay that reafons might not be fuggefted, from a feries of conduct offenfive and provoking in many other refpects; but when once thofe come to be coolly examined, he fufpected whether they would be found fuch, as it would be extremely difficult, if not impoffible, publicly to avow and explain."

" The minifter allówed all thefe to be confide-. rations of great weight, without attempting to take off their force, except as to that of the prince's children, who, he faid, were intended to be left with their parents, whilft of tender age, only for nurture. The great point on which he laid his ftrefs, was that the king had now an advantage, by the prince having put himfelf fo much in the wrong, which ought not to bé parted with. That he was apprehenfive there muft be a total breach before there could be a complete reconciliation; and to make up the particular difference about carrying away the princefs from Hampton Court, without the grand point, would not

not be fo much as fkinning over the fore, which
would infallibly break out again worfe than ever.
That it was impoffible to reconcile the whole without money, and that could not now be obtained ;
neither was it fit to advife the king to make fuch
an advance, until his fon, by proper acts of fubmiffion, and declared alteration of conduct, fhould
put himfelf in a condition to deferve it.

" As to the fubmiffion already made, he enlarged much on the offenfive behaviour to the
queen ; and in particular, objected that, although
the king in his meffage had charged the *fact to
be a high indignity to himfelf and to the queen*, the
prince had not in any of his letters afked her pardon, or fo much as made an excufe to her majefty for what he had done."

" Hereupon, the chancellor took occafion to
obferve, that this was manifeftly the game of thofe
advifers of the prince, who intended to prevent a
reconciliation ; and as this laft was their point,
they could not play their cards better. That
confequently the moft effectual method of difap-
pointing it muft be the beft play, on the other
fide : and as the queen had great talents, as well
as great power with the king, would not it become her wifdom to fupprefs the woman's refentment, and take the contrary part to that into
which thefe men wifhed to drive her ? That in
his opinion, if her majefty continued unmoved by
their ill ufage, and in fpite of all their provoca-
tions would reconcile the father and fon, fhe
would endear herfelf to the nation more than

ever,

ever, and make an abfolute conqueft of all her enemies at once."

Thefe fenfible reprefentations not only had no effect on the minifter, but even feem to have made a contrary impreffion; for he faid afterwards to fome of his friends, " The lord chancellor made me a long vifit, and talked like an angel on the fubject of the prince, yet I thought his arguments made for my conclufion rather than his," which induced the chancellor to lament the fhortnefs of human forefight, and exclaim, in the words of Virgil,

" Nefcia mens hominum fati, fortifque futuræ,
" Et fervare modum rebus fublata fecundis.
" Turno tempus erit, magno cum optaverit emptum,
" Intactum Pallanta et cum fpolia ifta diemque.
" Oderit." *

Conduct of
Walpole.

Although it cannot be denied that the conduct of the prince had given great and deferved offence to the king and queen, and that in particular his behaviour to the queen had been highly difrefpectful, yet it cannot at the fame time be fufficiently lamented, that the minifter involved in the interefts of party, the feuds of the royal family. He confidered the ftruggle as much between himfelf and oppofition, as between the king and

* " O mortals! blind in fate, who never know
" To bear high fortune, or endure the low!
" The time fhall come, when Turnus, but in vain,
" Shall wifh untouch'd the trophies of the flain,
" Shall wifh the fatal belt were far away,
" And curfe the dire remembrance of the day."
DRYDEN's VIRGIL.

and prince, and knowing the prince's averfion to
his miniftry, viewed a cordial reconciliation as
tending to his removal.

Under thefe impreffions he had drawn up, by
order of the king, the fubftance of a meffage to
be delivered to the prince, ordering him to remove from the palace of St. James; and he communicated it confidentially to the lord chancellor,
the duke of Newcaftle, and Pelham, for their
opinion, before it fhould be fubmitted to the
whole council. He produced two letters, fent by
the prince to the king and queen after the chriftening; and acquainted them, that the king was not
fatisfied with the fubmiffion made by his fon.
He added, with regard to the king himfelf, they
were mere words, and calculated to be offenfive
and provoking to the queen. None of the letters
contained any affurance of a change of conduct,
or of acting in fubordination to his father's will
for the future. The prince was entirely under the
influence and direction of perfons whom the king
had thought fit to remove from his councils and
fervice, and who were in a determined oppofition
to all his meafures; and lord Chefterfield and lord
Carteret were known to be with him in private
every day, and were called into his clofet after
the levee, as regularly as the king's minifters were
called into his. He recapitulated many particulars, to fhew that the prince had avowedly fet
himfelf at the head of a faction in oppofition to
the king, and that thefe letters were underftood
by the king to proceed from their dictates, and
intended

intended only to amufe and deceive him. That things being in this fituation, the king had re-folved not to permit his fon to refide any longer, in his palace, but to fend an order for his de-parture, with his whole family, as foon as it could be done without prejudice or inconvenience to the princefs, and had commanded him to prepare a draught of a meffage for that purpófe, which he then read.

The chancellor and his friends having exprefled their concern, and delivered their opinion, that fuch a meffage fhould be avoided if poffible, con-fiftently with the king's honour; the minifter re-plied, that fuch was the king's final refolution. It was then propofed, that a meffage fhould be fent to the prince, acquainting him with the kind of fubmiffion which was required of him, and the alterations in his conduct, which the king ex-pected as the terms of the reconciliation. But the propofal was rejected by Sir Robert Walpole, as likely to beget mutual altercations, and produce a paper war between the king and his fon, which would be attended with ftill more fatal confe-quences than taking it *fhort at firft.* *

The draught of the meffage was then taken into confideration. It was couched in very harfh and improper terms, and contained indecorous reflec-tions, inconfiftent with the dignity of the crown, and the ftation of the difputants. A paragraph towards the conclufion, exprefled a fevere re-proach on *perfons in general* reforting to the prince, who

* Lord Hardwicke's Narrative.

who did not pay their court to the king, but oppofed his measures, called them a FACTION, with
other ftrong and harfh words. To all thefe, the
chancellor objected, as a ftyle improper between
princes, and indecent from the king to his fon.
He thought, if a meffage of this nature muft go,
it fhould be ftrong, but full of decorum. Sir
Robert Walpole declared his opinion, that, as
the prince had plainly fet himfelf at the head of
the oppofition, it was right to carry the war into
the enemy's country; and as they attacked the
king through the fides of his minifters, to return
it by falling on the prince's advifers. To this the
chancellor replied, that, as to fuch advifers as
fomented this fatal divifion in the royal family,
the harfheft words which language could furnifh
were not too much; but his objection was, that,
as the draught then ftood, it comprifed more, and
might extend to all that came to the prince,
who happened to differ from the king's minifters
in parliament, and did not come to court. That
this would include fome perfons of the firft quality and eftates in the kingdom, befides great
numbers of others who were only mifguided; and
as it was probable this paper might one time or
other be laid before the parliament, it might give
rife to very difagreeable debates and queftions
there. The duke of Newcaftle and Mr. Pelham
acceded to his opinion; whereupon moft of thofe
expreffions and epithets were at length ftruck out,
and that remarkable paragraph entirely changed
and confined to the *advifers* of the prince, who

fomented

fomented the division in the royal family, and thereby
weakened the common interest of the whole.

On the 9th of September, this meſſage was
laid before the lords of the cabinet council who
were not abſent from London. *

Sir Robert Walpole acquainted them with the
ſeveral cauſes of the king's diſpleaſure againſt the
prince; he ſaid, for theſe reaſons the king was
of opinion that the families ſhould be ſeparated,
and deſired their advice on the method of doing
it; he had, by the king's order, and with his
approbation, prepared the draught of a meſſage
to the prince, which he ſhould now ſubmit to
their conſideration. He at the ſame time intimated, that the king thought the ſtyle of the draught
full gentle enough. He then read the letters which
had paſſed between the prince on one hand, and
the king and queen on the other; and directed
them to obſerve the difference between the narrative of the fact contained in the firſt letter to the
king, and the accounts which he gave to the
queen, as well as to lord Harrington and himſelf,
the morning after the labour, which laſt he read
from ſome minutes to which lord Harrington had
agreed. He obſerved, with great emphaſis, that
theſe letters were ſpecious empty words, without
any

---

* Preſent. Archbiſhop of Canterbury (Potter)—Lord chancellor
—Lord Godolphin (lord privy ſeal)—Duke of Grafton (lord chamberlain)—Duke of Richmond (maſter of the horſe)—Duke of Newcaſtle—Earl of Pembroke (groom of the ſtole)—Earl of Ilay—Lord
Harrington—Sir Robert Walpole—Sir Charles Wager.

Abſent. Lord Preſident (in Suſſex)—Earl of Scarbro' (in Yorkſhire, and not ſufficiently recovered to attend buſineſs—Duke of De-
vonſhire (in Ireland)—Duke of Dorſet (at Namur)—Duke of Argyle
(in Oxfordſhire.)

any affurances or alteration of conduct; and laid
great ftrefs on the variations between the letters
to the king, and thofe to the queen, and particularly requefted them to remark, that in the letter to the queen, the words, *your majefty*, were
never ufed, but only *madame* and *vous.* He then
read the draught of the meffage.

The lords fufficiently teftified their concern, by
their looks and expreffions. They underftood'
this to be a communication of the king's determined refolution, which was not to be changed.
They agreed that he was undoubtedly mafter in
his own family, and as he had been highly offended, he was to judge whether he would forgive or refent. They confidered that their advice
was only required as to the *method*, not the *meafure*, and therefore proceeded to take the draught
into confideration. A few exceptions were made
to the terms. Two were made by the lord chancellor, the firft to the words, *I cannot fuffer myfelf
to be impofed upon by them*, as too harfh, and not
adequate to the dignity of the perfonages concerned; he propofed to infert, *I cannot, confiftently
with my own honour and authority, fuffer them to
have any weight with me.* But this alteration was
not adopted. The fecond objection was to the
word *rendezvous*, as too low and coarfe; and as
all the lords concurred in the fame opinion, it
was omitted, and the word *refort* fuffered to ftand
alone. In the place of, *you fhall not refide in my
palace*, inferted at the propofal of the archbifhop;
lord Godolphin offered, *I think it not fit that you fhould*

refide

reside in my palace; an alteration which was approved by the chancellor, as expreffive of the king's opinion, and properly introductive of the fubfequent command to leave St. James's. This was rejected on the obfervation of Sir Robert Walpole, that thofe words could not be confidered as fufficiently ftrong.

After making a few other verbal alterations of little confequence, the meffage was agreed to, and fubmitted to the final approbation of the king. *

The manner of fending it to the prince was propofed to be by a meffage figned by the king at the top, with his name at length, and with the two firft letters at the bottom, after the form of inftructions; and that an order, figned by his majefty, fhould be delivered to the perfons who fhould be charged with carrying it, reciting the meffage in the very words, and commanding them to read it to, and leave it with his royal highnefs. It was alfo agreed, that copies of this meffage fhould be privately delivered to the feveral foreign minifters, in England, and other copies fent to the king's minifters refiding abroad, as a *fpecies facti*, or narrative of the king's reafons for this proceeding with his fon.

Other particulars were mentioned, and it feemed to be the general fenfe of the lords that they fhould be regulated in like manner as upon the *feparation* in the late reign; but it was thought proper to leave them to the perfonal direction of the

* Narrative.

the king himſelf, without offering any particular
advice thereupon. On Saturday, September 10th,
this meſſage, ſigned as before mentioned, was ſent
to the prince by the duke of Grafton, Duke of
Richmond, and earl of Pembroke, who had a
ſigned order, as above deſcribed, for their juſtifi-
cation.

" The profeſſions you have lately made in your The prince ordered to quit
St. James's.
letters, of your particular regard to me, are ſo
contradictory to all your actions, that I cannot
ſuffer myſelf to be impoſed upon by them. You
know very well, you did not give the leaſt intimation to me, or to the queen, that the princeſs
was with child, or breeding, until within leſs than
a month of the birth of the young princeſs : you
removed the princeſs twice in the week immediately preceding the day of her delivery, from the
place of my reſidence, in expectation, as you
have voluntarily declared, of her labour; and both
times, upon your return, you induſtriouſly concealed from the knowledge of me and the queen,
every circumſtance relating to this important affair : and you at laſt, without giving any notice to
me, or to the queen, precipitately hurried the
princeſs from Hampton Court, in a condition not
to be named. After having thus, in execution
of your own determined meaſures, expoſed both
the princeſs and her child to the greateſt perils,
you now plead ſurpriſe, and tenderneſs foi the
princeſs, as the only motives that occaſioned theſe
repeated indignities offered to me, and to the
queen your mother.

I 3   " This

" This extravagant and undutiful behaviour;
in ſo eſſential a point as the birth of an heir to
my crown, is ſuch an evidence of your premedi-
tated defiance of me, and ſuch a contempt of my
authority, and of the natural right belonging to
your parents, as cannot be excuſed by the pretended
innocence of your intentions, nor palliated or diſ-
guiſed by ſpecious words only.

" But the whole tenor of your conduct, for a
conſiderable time, has been ſo entirely void of all
real duty to me, that I have long had reaſon to
be highly offended with you.

" And until you withdraw your regard and
confidence from thoſe by whoſe advice you are directed and encouraged in your unwarrantable behaviour to me and to the queen, and until you
return to your duty, you ſhall not reſide in my
palace, which I will not ſuffer to be made the re-
ſort of them, who, under the appearance of an attachment to you, foment the diviſion which you
have made in my family, and thereby weaken the
common intereſt of the whole. In this ſituation
I will receive no reply; but when your actions
manifeſt a juſt ſenſe of your duty and ſubmiſſion,
that may induce me to pardon, what at preſent I
moſt juſtly reſent.

" In the mean time, it is my pleaſure that you
leave St. James's, with all your family, when it
can be done without prejudice or inconvenience
to the princeſs. I ſhall for the preſent leave to
the princeſs the care of my grand-daughter, until

9   a proper

a proper time calls upon me to confider of her
education."

All farther application from the prince being
ineffectual, he retired from the palace, to Norfolk House, in St. James's Square, where he took
up his refidence, and his houfe became the centre,
of political oppofition.   The king accordingly
iffued an order, forbidding all perfons who paid,
their court to the prince and princefs of Wales,
from being admitted into his prefence at any of
the royal palaces.

All the correfpondence which paffed between
the king, queen, and the prince, on this unfortunate occafion, was publifhed, by authority of the
court, and diftributed to each of the foreign minifters in England, and to the Britifh embaffadors
abroad.

As the meffage delivered on the 10th of September, contained many reflections on the prince,
which no man of honour could forgive, * the
meafure tended ftill farther to irritate him, and
to fupply an excufe for his refentment to the king,
and his deteftation of the minifter, who incurred
the principal blame in this whole tranfaction, and
was accufed of fomenting the mifunderftanding,
to ferve his own finifter purpofes.   The prince
gave credit to thefe imputations.   Walpole was
held out as the man who having fo often, nay, fo
conftantly facrificed the national intereft to his
avarice, his ambition, and his fears, had now facrificed

* Opinions of the duchefs of Marlborough.

crificed to his paffions the peace of his mafter's family, and taken that opportunity to make him declare a profcription to all thofe who oppofed the minifter. *

In reviewing the conduct of Walpole in this delicate tranfaction, he cannot be wholly exempted from blame; nor is it eafy to afcertain in what degree he was culpable. He had, on former occafions, earneftly laboured to reconcile the father and fon, and had infufed into the king a fpirit of moderation and forbearance. This cafe was attended with peculiar difficulties, which can never be fully appreciated. Lord chancellor Hardwicke himfelf fays, " Sir Robert Walpole informed " me of certain paffages between the king and " himfelf, and between the queen and the prince, " of too high and fecret a nature, even to be " trufted to this narrative; but from thence, I " found great reafon to think that this unhappy " difference between the king and queen, and his " royal highnefs, turned upon fome points of a " more interefting and important nature, than " have hitherto appeared." †

It is, however, juftly remarked by the fame candid obferver, that thofe who attempted to reconcile the breach, were not liftened to on either fide. On the part of the prince, thofe who wanted to fet him at their head, againft his father's meafures, feemed to have it in view to write fuch·

* Lord Bolingbroke to Sir William Wyndham. Correfpondence.

† Lord Hardwicke's Narrative.

fuch letters to the king as might read well when
publifhed to the world, be taken for a fubmiffion,
and at the fame time effectually prevent that
from being accepted, by provoking the queen,
and thereby cut off the chance of mediation, and
fhut the only door through which any reconciliation could enter.   On the other fide, Sir Robert
Walpole feemed to think, that they had now an
advantage over the prince which ought not to be
parted with, and that it would be better for the adminiftration to have a total and declared feparation, than that things fhould remain in the precarious ftate in which they then ftood. *

In the courfe of this unfortunate tranfaction, Lord Hardwicke's inter-
view with the
prince.
the prince gave figns of high fpirit and extreme
fenfibility; a ftriking inftance of which is recorded
by lord chancellor Harkwicke, which I fhall relate
in his own words. ✝ " On the fourth of Auguft,
the day of proroguing the parliament, I went to
St. James's in my way to Weftminfter, in order
to enquire after the health of the princefs of
Wales, and the new-born princefs.   After I had
performed that ceremony, I went away, and was
overtaken at the further end of Pall-mall, by one
of the prince's footmen, with a meffage that his
royal highnefs defired to fpeak with me.

" Being returned, I was carried into the nur-
fery, whither the prince came immediately out of
the princefs's bedchamber, and turned all the
women out of the room.   Having faid many civil things, and made me fit down, he fhewed me

* Lord Hardwicke's Narrative.   ✝ Ibid.

a meffage

a meffage which he had received the day before from the king, which he faid, he prefumed I, being one of the cabinet, muft have feen before. Without ftaying for an anfwer, he made a long apology for his conduct, much to the effect of his firft letter to the king, with this addition, that if the king, who was apt fometimes to be pretty quick, fhould have objected to her going to London, and an altercation fhould have arifen, what a condition would the poor princefs have been in ? He then faid, he would read me two letters he had written, the one to the king, and the other to the queen; whereupon I afked him whether they had been fent, for if they had not, I was determined in my own mind not to have feen or heard them read. He anfwered, they were fent the day before by my lord Jerfey, and then read them. He afked me what I thought of them ? at which I bowed, and faid nothing. He went on, that upon thofe letters the king fent word he would not fee him; but he did not think fit to let it reft there on his part, and had fent another letter by lord Carnarvon that morning, which he read, and afked me, if it was not very refpectful; to this I anfwered, *very refpectful*; and indeed, it was a much more proper letter than the former.

" I then proceeded to tell his royal highnefs, that I had heard nothing of this unhappy affair, till my going to Hampton Court on the Tuefday before, to congratulate the king and queen on the birth of their grand-daughter. That I then found

found their majefties highly offended with what
had paffed, and I fhould be unjuft to his royal
highnefs, if I concealed from him, that, from the
circumftances preceding and accompanying the
carrying away the princefs, they underftood it to
proceed from a deliberate intention to take that
part without their privity. I added, that incidents of this nature gave the deepeft concern and
affliction to every one who wifhed well to the
whole royal family, and to none more than myfelf. That every occafion of that kind ought to
be removed; for that *union* in the royal family
was moft effential to the true intereft and prefervation of it. That the contrary gave the moft
formidable advantages to their enemies; whereas
nothing could hurt any branch of it when united.
That I hoped his royal highnefs would fhow fuch
a fubmiffion and dutiful behaviour to the king
his father in the prefent juncture, as would tend
to bring about this union, and that I was fure it
would be the zealous endeavour of the king's fervants, and in particular of myfelf, to do every
thing that might facilitate it.

" He anfwered, my lord, *I don't doubt you in
the leaft, for I believe you to be a very honeft man;*
and as I was rifing up, embraced me, offering to
kifs me: I inftantly kneeled down, and kiffed his
hand, whereupon he raifed me up and kiffed my
cheek. The fcene had fomething in it moving;
and my heart was full of the melancholy profpect
that I thought lay before me, which made me almoft burft into tears. The prince obferved this,
and

and appeared moved himself, and said, *let us fit down, my lord, a little, and recollect ourselves, that we may not go out thus.* Soon after which, I took my leave, and went directly to the house of lords."

CHAPTER THE FORTY-NINTH:

1737.

Illness—Fortitude—and Death of Queen Caroline.—Virtues.—Grief of the King.—Affliction of Sir Robert Walpole.

Illness of the queen.

I SHALL close the transactions of the year 1737, with the illness and death of queen Caroline, an event highly disastrous to the country, to the king, and to Sir Robert Walpole. This illustrious and amiable woman, had been for some time in a declining state of health. The disorder under which she had laboured, and which occasioned her death, was a rupture, which, from motives of delicacy, she had communicated only to the mistress of the robes, her favourite lady Sundon: she was even so imprudent as to conceal the cause of her illness from the medical men who were called in to her relief. This false delicacy, which was incompatible with her usual magnanimity, was the cause of her death. For the medicines which were administered, and the methods taken, were diametrically opposite to those which would have been adopted, had her disorder been known. Judging from the symptoms, and from her own declarations, the physicians treated it as the gout

in

in her ftomach, and adminiftered ftrong cordials, which aggravated the malady. When the danger became fo imminent as to render the concealment impoffible, it was too late. She fubmitted in vain to the moft painful operations, and the furgeon who performed them declared, that if he had been acquainted with her real fituation two days fooner, her fpeedy recovery would have been the confequence. *

Although racked with extreme agony, almoft without intermiffion, during twelve days and nights, fhe bore her fufferings not only with patience and refignation, but almoft without a groan, maintaining, to the moment of her diffolution, ferenity, temper, dignity, greatnefs of foul, and an unaffected fubmiffion to the ways of Providence. In all this melancholy fcene, fhe behaved with fuch invariable courtefy to every one about her, that one of the phyficians obferved, he had never met with a fimilar inftance in the whole courfe of his practice. She repeatedly expreffed to her attendants, her grateful fenfe of their laborious watchings, and diftinguifhed each of them with appropriate marks of regard.

She recommended her fervants, in the moft affecting and folemn manner, to the king's favour and protection; extended her concern to the loweft of them, and was equally warm in her folicitude for their welfare; recounting to him the faithfulnefs of their refpective fervices.

This

* Letter from Charles Ford to Swift, November 22, 1737. Swift's Works.

This firmnefs and refignation were not the effect of infenfibility or ftoical indifference, but
derived from the ftrongeft exertions of reafon and
religion. On the fecond day of her illnéfs, fhe
was obferved to fhed fome tears, occafioned either
by the lownefs of her fpirits, the anguifh of her
fufferings, or by tendernefs for the defpair of her
family; fhe foon, however, recovered from this
debility, and refumed her accuftomed fortitude.
Apprehenfive that during a painful operation, fhe
had fo far forgotten herfelf as to ufe peevifh expreffions, fhe reproached herfelf with having fhewn
an unbecoming impatience.

She frequently declared that fhe had made it
the bufinefs of her life to difcharge her religious
and focial duties; fhe hoped God would pardon
her infirmities, and accept the fincerity of her endeavours, which were always intended to promote
the king's honour, and the profperity of the nation. She declared that fhe was a hearty well-
wifher to the liberties of the people; and that if
fhe had erred in any part of her public conduct,
it arofe from want of judgment, not from intention.

Death.   A little before fhe died, fhe faid to the phyfi-
cian, "How long can this laft?" and on his anfwering, "Your majefty will foon be eafed of your
pains;" fhe replied, "The fooner the better."
She then repeated a prayer of her own compofing,
in which there was fuch a flow of natural eloquence, as demonftrated the vigour of a great
and good mind. When her fpeech began to
faulter,

faulter, and she seemed expiring, she desired to
be raised up in her bed, and fearing that nature
would not hold out long enough without artifi-
cial supports, she called to have water sprinkled
on her, and a little after desired it might be repeated. She then, with the greatest compofure
and prefence of mind, requefted her weeping re-
lations to " kneel down and pray for her." Whilst
they were reading fome prayers, she exclaimed,
" pray aloud, that I may hear;" and after the
Lord's prayer was concluded, in which she joined
as well as she could, she said, " So," and waving
her hand, lay down and expired. *

Having already difcuffed the character of the
queen, I shall only add a few traits to the pre-
ceding sketch. † She was bleffed with a natural
ferenity and calmnefs of mind, and often expreffed her thankfulnefs to God, that he had
given her a temper which was not eafily ruffled,
and which enabled her to fupport every difficulty.
It was truly faid of her, that the fame foftnefs of
behaviour and command of herfelf, that appeared
in the drawing room, went along with her into
her private apartments, gladdened every body that
was about her perfon, accompanied her as well
in the gay and cheerful feafons of life, as under
the moft trying circumftances, and did not fail
her even in the hour of death itfelf.

One part of her conduct, which reflects the
highest

---

* The principal circumftances of her death, are extracted from Dr.
Alured Clark's Effay towards the Character of Queen Caroline.
† Chapter 31.

Period VI.
1734 to 1737. higheft honour on her memory, was her maternal attention to her children, and particularly to her daughters. She fuperintended their education, directed their behaviour, formed their manners, and tempered her reproofs with a mixture of proper feverity and kindnefs, which rendered her equally beloved and refpected.

Afperfions examined.

The enemies of queen Caroline, have reprefented her as being of an unforgiving temper, and even reproached her with a want of maternal affection. It was malicioufly fuggefted, that fhe fomented the mifunderftanding between the king and the prince of Wales; but on the contrary, fhe exerted her utmoft influence to abate the petulance of the fon, and the irritability of the father. Once in particular, when an action of the prince had been reprefented to the king with malicious aggravation, the queen defended her fon, and good naturedly obferved, " Ce n'eft qu' une indifcretion de page :" 'Tis nothing but a youthful frolic. * The tongue of flander has even reproached her with maintaining her implacability to the hour of death, and refufing her pardon to the prince, who had humbly requefted to receive her blefling. To this imputation, Chefterfield alludes in a copy of verfes, circulated at the time :

" And unforgiving, unforgiven dies."

Pope alfo has configned to pofterity this afperfion, in terms of malignant irony :

" Or

* From lord Orford.

    "_Or teach the melancholy mufe to mourn,
    Hang the fad verfe on CAROLINA's urn,
    And hail her paffage to the realms of reft,
    All parts perform'd, and ALL _her children bleft_. *

I am happy to have it in my power to remove this ftigma from the memory of this great prin-cefs. She fent her bleffing and a meffage of for-givenefs to her fon, and told Sir Robert Walpole, that fhe would have feen him with pleafure, but prudence forbad the interview, as it might em-barrafs and irritate the king. †

" Her charities were limited only by her re-venue; though fhe avoided all appearance of of-tentation fo much, that many perfons who fub-fifted by her bounty, were wholly ignorant of their benefactrefs; and fhe was fo liberal that her public and private lifts, with the occafional fums expended on the fame account, amounted to near a _fifth_ part of her whole income." ‡

                          Her

Liberality.

---

* See Epilogue to the Satires, Dialogue 1, l. 79. The fatirift, with a duplicity not unufual to him, has affected in a note to repair the infult offered to her memory, by obferving, that her laft moments manifefted the utmoft courage and refolution. It is, however, juftly obferved by Dr. Warton, on this paffage, that, " no fubtle com-mentary can torture thefe words to mean any thing but the moft poig-nant farcafm on the behaviour of this great perfonage to her fon on her death-bed :" and adds, that " about the fame time, Pope wrote a couplet on the fame fubject :"

    " Here lies, wrapt up in forty thoufand towels,
    The only proof that Caroline had bowels."

The evidence that Pope was the author of this infamous quibble, which is generally attributed to Chefterfield, is not given by Dr. Warton. Lord Mansfield had it from Pope himfelf, told it to lord Orford, from whom I received it, with a variation of " feven-and-twenty," inftead of " forty thoufand towels."

† From lord Orford.

‡ Character of Queen Caroline, p. 12.

498

Her difpofition was fo humane and benevolent, that the unfortunate in all fituations and religions were fecure of her protection. She paid a particular attention to thofe Roman Catholics, whofe zeal in favour of the Pretender had expofed them to the rigour of the laws. Several Popifh and Jacobite ladies, and particularly the duchefs of Norfolk, were admitted to private conferences Their reprefentations procured liberal fupplies of money to many of the moft indigent. In fome inftances, fhe even carried her protection to an impolitic extreme, and in a manner which diftreffed Sir Robert Walpole. Archibald earl of Ilay, who principally managed the affairs of Scotland, having been reproached for permitting fo large a number of Jacobite meeting-houfes in Edinburgh, and in other parts of the kingdom, in open defiance of the laws; acknowledged the fact, and exculpated himfelf, by declaring that he had laid a fcheme for fuppreffing them before the minifter, who difcouraged his attempt, by obferving, their friends had a ready accefs to the queen by the back ftairs, and all his efforts would be defeated. *

Patronage of learning.

A confpicuous part in the character of queen Caroline, was her great patronage of learned men. The protection fhe afforded to the firft luminaries of the church has been flightly mentioned. She diftinguifhed Clarke, Hoadly, Butler, Sherlock, Secker, and Pearce, with peculiar marks of regard.

* Etough, imparted by Archibald duke of Argyle.

gard. The gracious manner in which fhe liftened to recommendations of literary eminence, is well difplayed in an anecdote relating to the celebrated author of " The Analogy between Natural and Revealed Religion." Secker *, while he was king's chaplain, mentioned, in converfation with the queen, Butler, who was then rector of Stanhope. The queen faid, fhe thought he was dead, and making enquiries of archbifhop Blackburne, if he was not dead, his anfwer was, " no madam, but he is buried." Soon afterwards, without folicitation, fhe appointed him clerk of her clofet, and he ufed to attend her every day, from feven to nine, in the afternoon. She alfo caufed his name to be inferted on the lift for a vacant bifhopric.

Obfcurity, difgrace, and banifhment, were no obftacles to her bounty and protection. She conferred benefactions on Stephen Duck, who from a common labourer, had raifed himfelf into notice as a poet. She obtained the pardon of Savage, who was condemned to death for having committed a murder in a drunken fray, in fpite of the oppofition of his unnatural mother, and fupported him with an annual penfion. † She fhewed

her

* Life of Secker.

† " When Savage was difappointed in his application for the place of poet laureat, which was given to Colley Cibber, he applied, in the bitternefs of diftrefs, boldly to the queen, that having once given him life, fhe would enable him to fupport it; and therefore publifhed a fhort poem on her birth-day, to which he annexed the odd title of volunteer-laureat. Not having a friend at court who would get him introduced, or prefent him, he publifhed the poem, which was not ill calculated to ftrike the queen. The queen fent for the verfes, and in a few days after the publication, Savage received a bank bill of fifty

pounds,

500

Period VI.
1734 to 1737.

her efteem for the memory of Milton, by confer-ring a prefent on his grand-daughter. She ob-tained the recal of lord Lanfdowne, and of Carte, the nonjuring hiftorian, who had both been obliged to abfcond for fufpected principles. *

Grief of the king.

Words cannot fufficiently exprefs the fenfibility

and

pounds, and a gracious meffage by lord Noith and Grey: That her majefty was highly pleafed with the verfes; that fhe took particularly kind his lines relating to the king; that he had permiffion to write annually on the fame fubject; and that he fhould yearly receive the like prefent, till fomething better (which was her majefty's intention) could be done for him. After this, he was permitted to prefent one of his annual poems to the queen, had the honour of kiffing her hand, and met with the moft gracious reception." Johnfon's Life of Savage.

From thefe now-forgotten poems, may I be permitted to quote one paffage which alludes to the beneficial confequences of the pacific fyf-tem, planned by Sir Robert Walpole, and fupported by queen Ca-roline.

" Here ceafe my plaint—See yon enlivening fcenes!
Child of the fpring! Behold the beft of queens!
Softnefs and beauty rofe this heavenly morn,
Dawn'd wifdom, and benevolence was born.
Joy o'er a people, in her influence rofe;
Like that which fpring o'er rural nature throws.
War to the peaceful pipe refigns his roar,
And breaks his billows on fome diftant fhore.
Domeftic difcord finks beneath her fmile,
And arts, and trade, and plenty glad the ifle,
Lo! Induftry furveys, with feafted eyes,
His due reward, a plenteous harveft rife!
Nor (taught by Commerce) joys in that alone,
But fees the harveft of a world his own.
Hence thy juft praife, thou mild, majeftic Thames!
Rich river, richer than Pactolus' ftreams!
Than thofe renown'd of yore, by poets roll'd
O'er intermingled pearls, and fands of gold.
How glorious thou, when from old Ocean's urn,
Loaded with India's wealth, thy waves return!
Alive thy banks! along each bordering line,
High cultur'd blooms, inviting villas fhine:
And while around ten thoufand beauties glow,
Thefe ftill o'er thofe redoubling luftre throw."

* Biographia Britannica.

and affection of George the Second during her illnefs, and his regret for her lofs. He watched by her bed-fide with unabated attention, and could fcarcely be prevailed on to take any reft, till fhe expired.

As foon as the firft emotions of grief had fub-fided, he loved to talk of his departed queen, re-counted her virtues, and confidered how fhe would have acted on occafions of difficulty. He continued the falaries of all the officers and no-minal fervants who were not taken into his own houfehold, and commanded a lift of her nume-rous benefactions to be laid before him; faying it was his intention, that nobody fhould be a fufferer befides himfelf. *

On her death bed, the queen teftified her ap- The queen probation of Sir Robert Walpole's meafures, and recommends the high opinion fhe entertained of his capacity Walpole. and rectitude. Turning to the minifter, who with the king was ftanding by her bed-fide, fhe faid to him, " I hope you will never defert the king, but continue to ferve him with your ufual fidelity;" and pointing to the king, fhe added, " I recommend his majefty to you." The king faid nothing, and the minifter was alarmed, left this mode of making him of more confequence than the king, might awaken jealoufy, and be the caufe of his difgrace. † But thefe apprehen-fions were unfounded.

The king was fo affected with the queen's
death,

* Character of Queen Caroline, p. 41. † From lord Orford.

Period VI.
1734 to 1737.

death, that for a long time after that melancholy event, he could not fee Sir Robert Walpole without burfting into tears. About a fortnight afterwards, the king fhewed him an intercepted letter, in which it was obferved, that as the queen was dead, the minifter would lofe his fole protector. " It is falfe," faid he, good naturedly, " you remember that on her death-bed the queen recommended *me* to you."

Affecting
anecdote.

Horace Walpole has recorded a ftriking inftance of the king's violent grief for the death of his queen, and affection to her memory, which I will relate in his own words. " Mr. Walpole can never be able to forget a melancholy epoch, when, about ten days after his arrival from Holland, upon the queen's death, his majefty found him with the princeffes, in their apartment, and their royal highneffes immediately retiring, the king, with a flood of tears gufhing from his eyes, which drew an equal torrent from thofe of his faithful fubject then prefent, with agonies and fobs, gave a confidential detail to Mr. Walpole, of the inimitable virtues of his royal confort, that was now no more, and particularly with refpect to the great relief and affiftance which he found in her noble and calm difpofition and fentiments, in governing fuch an humourfome and inconftant people ; that her prefence of mind often fupported him in trying times, and the fweetnefs of her temper and prudence would moderate and affuage his own vivacity and refentment ; that incidents of ftate of a rough, difficult, and difagreeable

greeable nature, would by her previous conferences and concert with that able minifter, Sir
Robert Walpole, be made fmooth, eafy, and pal-
atable to him, but that he muft now lead a help-
lefs, difconfolate, and uncomfortable life, during the
remainder of a troublefome reign, that he did not
know what to do, nor which way to turn himfelf.
But then recovering himfelf a little, he faid, " as
fhe never forgot her love and concern for me to
the laft moment of her days, fhe earneftly recommended it to me on her death-bed (and his majefty emphatically added, that it was a juft and
wife recommendation) to follow the advice of Sir
Robert Walpole, and never to part with fo faithful and able a minifter; this (faid the king) is
now my only refource, upon this I muft entirely
depend." *

Some time after the queen's death, before his
hour of rifing, George faid to baron Brinkman,
one of his German attendants, " I hear you
have a picture of my wife, which fhe gave you,
and which is a better likenefs than any in my
poffeffion; bring it to me." When it was brought,
the king feemed greatly affected, and after a fhort
paufe, he faid, " It is very like, put it upon the
chair at the foot of my bed, and leave it till I ring
the bell." At the end of two hours he rang the bell,
and when the baron entered, the king faid, " Take
this picture away, I never yet faw the woman
worthy to buckle her fhoe." †

Walpole

* Horace Walpole's Apology.　Walpole Papers.

† Communicated by Theodore Henry Broadhead, efquire, grandfon of Baron Brinkman, who poffeffes the portrait alluded to in the
text.

Walpole was no lefs affected than the king. He deeply felt the fevere lofs of his patronefs in the clofet; he appreciated the difficulty of guiding the king, when the interpofition of his patronefs was no more, and anticipated the embarraffments he was about to encounter from the jealoufies of a difcordant cabinet. Impreffed with thefe fentiments, he clofed a letter to Horace Walpole, in which he fpeaks of the queen's death, " I muft have done, our grief and diftraction wants no relation, I am oppreffed with forrow and dread." *

Sir Robert always entertained a high refpect for the memory of his royal patronefs queen Caroline; and it was principally through a deference to her recommendation, that fome time after her death he obtained the deanery of Winchefter for Dr. Pearce, and placed Butler upon the bench of bifhops.

I fhall clofe this chapter with an elegy on the death of queen Caroline, compofed by Dodington. †

When Heav'n's decrees a prince's fate ordain;
A kneeling people fupplicate in vain.
Too well our tears this mournful truth exprefs,
And in a queen's a parent's lofs confefs.
A lofs the general grief can beft rehearfe,
A theme fuperior to the pow'r of verfe;
Though juft our grief, be ev'ry murmur ftill,
Nor dare pronounce his difpenfations ill;
In whofe wife counfels and difpofing hand,
The fates of monarchies and monarchs ftand.

Whe

---

* Correfpondence.   † Melcombe Papers.

Who only knows the ftate of either fit,
And bids the erring fenfe of man fubmit.
　　Ye grateful Britons, to her memory juft,
With pious tears imbalm her facred duft ;
Confefs her grac'd with all that's good and great,
A public bleffing to a favour'd ftate.
Patron of freedom, and her country's laws,
Sure friend to virtue's and religion's caufe;
Religion's caufe, whofe charms fuperior fhone
To ev'ry gay temptation of a crown.
Whofe awful dictates all her foul poffefs'd,
Her one great aim to make a people bleft.
　　Ye drooping mufes mourn her hafty doom,
And fpread your deathlefs honours round her tomb,
Her name to long fucceeding ages raife,
Who both infpir'd and patroniz'd your lays.
Each gen'rous art fit penfive o'er her urn,
And ev'ry grace and ev'ry virtue mourn.
　　Attending angels bear your facred prize,
Amidft the radiant glories of the fkies :
Where godlike princes, who below purfu'd,
That nobleft end of rule the public good,
Now fit fecure, their gen'rous labour paft,
With all the juft rewards of virtue grac'd :
In that bright train diftinguifh'd let her move,
Who built her empire on a people's love.

END OF THE SECOND VOLUME.

ERRATA, Vol. II.

Page 14. l. 25. *for* Bellendon, *read* Bellenden.
36. l. 7. *for* inviolable, *read* inviolate.
67. l. 4. *after* Spain, *insert* a colon :
69. l. 24. *for* art, *read* act.
128. l. 5. *for* confiderable, *read* confiderably.
150. l. 24. *for* Cerberes, *read* Cerberus.
160. l. 5. *read* entered into.
173. l. 3. *for* to minister, *read* the minister.
192. l. 22. *after* excife, *insert* on.
225. l. 25. *for* or, *read* of.
319. l. 27. *after* Emperor, *instead* of a comma, a colon.
339. l. the last, *for* ruptures, *redd* rupture.
340. l. 8. *after* the, *insert* propriety of.
355. l. 12. *after* Tufcany, *add* on.
375. l. the last, *after* Juliers, a comma instead of a colon.
401. l. 25. *for* at the houfe of lords, *read* at the bar of the houfe of lords.

Printed by Luke Hanfard, Great Turnftile, Lincoln's-Inn Fields.

History of Shipp[...] ch. sec 35
Page 44 &c

Page 252 childr Sypralth and Phillip
Page 171 Walfield splended Hype
first delineation of Botany [...]
in the last Anto Ministry
page 93 Account of the [...]
[...] Murder of Capt Porterie

CPSIA information can be obtained
at www.ICGtesting.com
Printed in the USA
BVHW04*1421310818
526160BV00008B/47/P

THE REPUBLIC OF
TEXAS
2022

THE REPUBLIC OF

TEXAS 2022

TEXAS' LAST STAND FOR FAITH AND FREEDOM

GARY BRAY

TATE PUBLISHING
AND ENTERPRISES, LLC

Published by Tate Publishing & Enterprises, LLC
127 E. Trade Center Terrace | Mustang, Oklahoma 73064 USA
1.888.361.9473 | www.tatepublishing.com

Tate Publishing is committed to excellence in the publishing industry. The company reflects the philosophy established by the founders, based on Psalm 68:11,
"The Lord gave the word and great was the company of those who published it."

Published in the United States of America

ISBN: 978-1-63122-122-4
1. Fiction / General
2. Fiction / Political
14.03.14

DEDICATION

This book is dedicated to Marilyn and Brandon as well as all my Free Republic friends. It is also dedicated to all of those and especially those Texans and Oregonians who would like to live in a society that is based on free market economics and ideals. This fantasy allows them to take a vacation into their mind to see what such a society would look like, how it would be constructed and how it would perform. Hope they enjoy the roller coaster ride and understand how to live by faith and learn to turn your life over to God.

CONTENTS

INTRODUCTION

Steven Moses stepped out of his Black Stallion hover jet dressed in his dress khaki slacks and cowboy boots as the hot Texas wind whipped him across the face. That South wind brings not only a sweltering marine humidity but a heat that cooks you to the core. Steven was a tall man with muscular, chiseled looks you get from years of hard work in the oil fields. He grew up as a rigger where he was well known for working hard and playing harder in his early years. His well-trimmed beard looked as good on his wildcatter rigs as it did in the boardroom in his wrangler suit and boots.

Women noticed him immediately with his thick, blondish brown hair and the way he filled out his shirts with his barrel chest and wide shoulders from years of wrestling pipe in the Texas oil patch. Most were drawn to him being the most powerful man in Texas, making him the richest man in the world. Steven has been married to his job ever since his wife Sandy succumbed to cancer seven years ago. He still wore his wedding ring to remind himself of their years and a way to deal with the pain he still felt in his chest.

The turn of the century seems like an eternity ago, he thought. We had the rise of the markets, the attack on the towers and the recession, followed by the 2016 Depression, which led to Texas seceding from the Union and declaring its sovereignty. Texas in six short years has grown into the most powerful country on the planet, as Moses Oil and its conglomerates proudly stood as the largest company in Texas. Sandy would never believe what had happened.

He grew up in the oil patch as a third generation wildcatter. His dad and grandfather never made much money, but they did what they loved: gambling on oil wells. Sandy Sanderson was his high school first love, and they married after he graduated from Texas Tech with honors in engineering. They were married for eight years before she found the lump in her breast, which was malignant, and it slowly tore her away from him. He never loved anybody else and simply married his work and research, which is why he kept wearing his wedding ring.

His research had led him to a patent on a chemical compound that thins oil ten thousand feet underground, allowing companies like his to reclaim old dry wells. Oil wells previous to Moses additives were only able to profitably pump half of what was in the reservoir. They were then abandoned as they began to drill another reservoir and then another. After he invented the Moses additive, it was like pumping free oil buying these abandoned wells for pennies on the dollar as oil once again became plentiful and easy to produce without having to drill, making him and everyone around him very wealthy.

When the great collapse happened, it bankrupted almost every state in the old United States and especially those with spending out of control like New York, Maryland, and California, making hard times for their citizens and businesses. America was so desperate financially when Texas voted and offered to buy their way out of the union the rest of the states jumped at the chance. The Texas Succession Bill passed the US Congress in a couple of months and was signed by the president to form the Republic of Texas. A country built on cheap energy, and the free and unfettered energy markets was a chance Texans were willing to take.

Flying in from platform four fifty two was pretty uneventful; however, entering the Houston airways was always a touchy adventure. He thought it seemed like everybody in Texas owned a hover jet, and they were always coming or going from Houston even at this hour in the morning, which kept you on your stick. The Moses Tower stood out like a Lone Star sentinel in this energy capital as it was the tallest skyscraper in America standing as a monument to energy and free markets. It was shaped like the biggest oil rig in the world. The crosswinds and downdrafts were tricky at twenty-three hundred and fifty feet where his landing platform was located as he approached from the south and squared her up, crabbing in to a perfect three-point touchdown.

Flying was his favorite hobby when he wasn't working as it allowed him a chance to clear his mind from the stress of being the leader of this conglomerate. Danny the air porter gave him a friendly good morning and "God bless you, Steven" as he rolled the new beauty to the executive hanger. As he walked into the 230th floor of Moses Oil Corporation, the express elevator whisked him to his top floor suite, and he was met by his personal secretary, Debra Jenkins.

"Good morning, Steven. President Stewart has been calling you all morning to find out about our negotiations with China and how much oil do you think we can send them. Why haven't you been answering your earplug?"

"Easy, Debra, I was taking the new hover jet for a spin over the gulf and really didn't want to take my mind off my enjoyment. If you weren't married or I wasn't single, I would swear you were my wife with your constant need to know where and what I am doing."

"You will never let a girl get close enough to have a chance!" She giggled at their favorite joke. Debra was the type of girl who was just as pretty in a tailored suit and makeup as she did in blue jeans and no makeup in a very country, feminine way. She could have been a Cowboys cheerleader with her attractive farm-girl face and wavy, shoulder-length copper red hair. She was wearing a flowery green dress suit, which hugged her curves modestly but smartly.

She grew up in Longview, Texas, on a wheat farm and was the top of her high school class then graduated A&M with honors in business management. All the boys wanted to take her out but she had a sweet spot for awkward geeky guys, and when she met Dan Jenkins at a college church retreat, she melted. He was from Houston, and while they were playing volleyball, it was obvious he wasn't very athletic. When Dan got tangled in the net and fell in a heap, she giggled, turning him five shades of red, which she found so cute, opening the door to her heart.

Dan was studying chemistry and engineering at A&M and when he graduated summa cum laude, they married and now, seven years and three babies later, were still crazy in love. Dan worked as a head engineer at Texas Air Company, producing long-range high-speed courier drones. They were living a dream life with Debra's parents staying with them in their retirement and helping watching little Davey, Bobby, and Sandra. Debra would love to be a full-time mom, but the money at Moses Oil was great and hours flexible so she stayed in one of the best jobs in the world.

"Call it my female need to know everything. I'll get President Stewart on the line for you if you're ready. Oh, and don't forget, you have a lecture this afternoon at University of Texas up in Austin."

"Don't remind me, you know how I hate giving these boring lectures to a bunch of uninterested students on how I made lemons into lemonade. Not to mention their being journalism students and will be grilling me about everything except how this works. Give me five minutes to get the files we will need and then put him in the virtual imaging chair and send Drake in."

"Did I hear my name?" Jeff Drake walked in, who was the CFO of Moses Oil. "What does that new bird do, around six-fifty? Seven hundred? I've never seen a six seater that looks so much like a Corvette. Bet it turns on a dime and can't wait until we go checking out some platforms. I saw you coming in on the roof and knew you wanted to go over the Chinese proposal while you talked with President Stewart. Listen, these Chinese, as always, are trying to drive a tight bargain into the future and demanding we supply them before the Koreans or Australians. We have to find a way to keep everybody happy while not stretching ourselves too thin on contracts. You know they would be more than happy to continue to dominate the Asian energy markets as well as put a headlock on Taiwan. Then of course, there is the triangle of them selling their bonds to us while lending to the US, which is a bit touchy financially."

President Stewart's image appeared on the virtual chair with a big hello. "Help me out, Steve, tell me you can keep everybody satisfied and my neck out of the noose. Seems that becoming the world's leading producers of NatGas and refined oil products is making us very popular. although it is starting to put us in a vice."

"Sorry, Mr. President, but we are just getting Refinery Seventeen on line in a couple months and are buying raw crude from wherever we can get it. Our problem is with prices going up as strong as they are. We aren't able to hit the targets necessary to fill their orders at a profit. Of course we are buying futures contracts to hedge against higher priced tankers we are buying on the cash markets. In addition we expect to receive more oil from our own production as it is developed. The moderate prices in the shale production from the western United States help, but we could use a hundred tankers rather than the seventy-five available on the spot markets. The good news is once these tankers are processed, we should be able to bring on some more of our production as our new gulf deep wells start producing."

"Are you still getting grief from DC wanting us to loan them more money?"

"Of course," President Stewart mocked. "I told them as long as they continue as a socialist country and spend money without any fiscal considerations, they can buy our energy and fuels but don't expect us to finance their spending programs."

Jeff answered, "This is going to be a balancing act with these countries as they continue to go down their spiraling financial disaster. Until they bring real fiscal responsibility to the table, they are going to continue to live hand to mouth. For the time being, we will play at these levels, but in the future, we will need to rein them in a bit. Thanks for your time, David. Drake and I have a meeting down in Austin, and I have a speech to some students at the university to give. We will be seeing you later today."

The corporate shuttle to Austin was uneventful although the checkerboard of Texas farmlands and ranches never gets boring. He and Drake met the professor, June Darling, at her office as they were introduced by Dean Horford of the journalism school with a refreshing cup of coffee. June Darling was an attractive woman who was friendly in a scattered sort of way. She had deep green eyes, which looked like round emeralds the way the sunlight reflected off them. Her strawberry blond hair had a lazy curl which was pulled into a ponytail that cascaded just past her thin shoulders. She was wearing a pink flowered sundress, which showed off her feminine shape but was very conservative in a girlish style. She was transminding into her goggle screen deep in thought as she was still intuitive writing when they walked in.

"Professor Darling, this is Steven Moses. Mr. Moses, this is June Darling," Dean Horford stated.

"Oh, excuse me, I was just trying to get this article finished before I introduced you to the students. Mr. Moses, I am so honored to meet you, and the kids are thrilled you would take the time to come to talk to them."

"My pleasure, I hope they are not going to be too tough on me." He thought she was more excited than he expected on a campus, but then, these schools aren't like the ones in other countries. Her office was neat and clean with screens lining the top of her walls, allowing her to monitor events as they happened around the world.

"Well, we shall see," she teased, leading him to the large auditorium.

They walked through a side door as she went to the front of the auditorium to the main lectern. Her small frame was dwarfed by the size of the room with over a thousand students filling every chair while the back was three deep of students lining the walls. There was a full bank of remote cameras feeding home universities and web-motes for thousands streaming in around the country.

"Hello everybody, we are so glad to have you here and honored to have one of the true pioneers of industry from our Lone Star Republic. As you know, Mr. Steven Moses is here as our special guest, and we would ask that you would allow him to give an opening statement and then we will begin a question and answer session for the next ninety minutes. As you all know, he is the CEO of Moses Enterprises and its conglomerates, an innovator and pioneer who has had incredible success in the energy sector. So without any further ado, it is my great pleasure to introduce to the University of Texas Journalism School, Mr. Steven Moses!"

As he walked into the middle of the floor, a thunderous applause came up from the crowd as they stood up in unison to give him a standing ovation. He looked around the auditorium at the young faces all smiling and nodding with a few approving shouts as they continued their applause.

He finally signaled them down and thanked them for their warm welcome.

Steve didn't expect such a rock star welcome as he humbly asked them to sit down to start.

"First of all, I would like to thank God who has been with me and my family to help me through both the tough times and the good. Some may look at me in envy but being successful in many ways is tougher than being broke since so many more people depend on you. I have thousands of people working for me, so if I fail, thousands of people's lives are turned upside down just like me when I was running my own small company nobody knew or cared how I did. As most of you know, when United States collapsed, Texas was the only state left solvent financially, so we didn't want to become bankrupt like the rest of the union, which is why we filed for secession and purchased our way into sovereignty and freedom.

"We then instituted the identical constitution as the United States that ensured this would become a capitalist country based on free trade and individual rights both economically and individually. These laws value small government and lower taxes, which led to one of the greatest economic miracles in the history of the world. Texas has become the number one economy built on energy, which was a natural fit with our reconstituted wells along with the development of the hybrid turbo natural gas engine. This developed the Texas Ford NatGas auto industry, and the rest is history. Texas is not only the energy capital of the world but exports more cars and flying vehicles than any other country.

"Energy is not only the lifeblood of our country. It is the building block for our economy as it provides a cost-effective, solid foundation on which we built every other industry. An abundant low-cost energy resource gives us a price-competitive edge in the worldwide marketplace since in reality energy costs are the building blocks of everything you make or use. Energy costs are the main expense of every product, which are reflected in transportation and manufacturing. If you can control and lower your energy costs, you will lower your production cost for everything else, which is what has made us the free market economic power we have become.

"As we developed one market such as our NatGas vehicles, it naturally led us into the hover jet industry and all the engineering and aerospace transportation avenues, which naturally developed. That is the beauty of the capitalistic free market system we have here in Texas. Our industries have no government interference or needless restrictions allowing people to research and develop the products the marketplace demand which allows you to always be on the cutting edge of product evolution. Those are the basics of how the Texas miracle happened, and now I will answer your questions."

Professor Darling asked the first question, "Mr. Moses, what is it that makes Texas and the free market such a powerful economic engine so that it dwarfs other economies like the US, Europe, and China?"

He thought her hair looked really stunning pulled back in that ponytail but would look better down around her feminine shoulders and wearing cowboy boots although those sandals looked really good on her with the red toenails…what?

"Well, our economy…and please call me Steve, Professor Darling. Mr. Moses sounds too Biblical." He enjoyed how his flirtatious tone turned her a nice crimson rouge in front of her students.

He let the laughter die down to answer the question, "Seriously, capitalism is the natural basis of man which allows him to reach his full capacity. Capitalism maximizes the individual freedom and flexibility so men can test and expand the limits of their abilities. It is the only economic system ever invented which rewards a person exactly what they are worth. It is by far the most efficient transfer of goods and services ever devised by mankind."

He continued, "Capitalism allows the free flow of ideas to maximize the limits of our possibilities. Rather than having governments make every decision and determine what is good and bad, it allows the free market to decide the value in real time from one market to another. Capitalism is the ultimate open market just like you see in the old movies where people haggle over every purchase, but it moves that open market worldwide and in every transaction twenty-four seven, three sixty five. For example, a year ago, due to our abundance of natural gas as a byproduct of our production of oil products, we had a cheap source of energy to produce electricity with our NatGas electrical plants.

"An aluminum company called me from China and asked what kind of program we could put together from our electrical generation. He told me where I had to price this energy to make him come to Houston and not only did I meet that target but beat it by ten percent by transferring some of our excess production to the building of another NatGas plant, which we were planning on building a bit later anyway. So now they are making more money and keeping it while hiring another five hundred workers from the Houston area. It's a natural symbiotic relationship as it is meant to work without government interference.

When you take the government and regulators out of the equation, it makes the negotiations more efficient. We were able to put this transaction together in a matter of days rather than months or years it takes a government having decisions going up and down the chain of authority."

"Thank you, Mr....er...Steven," blushed Professor Darling. "We are now going to our question and answer session now. Justice?" she said, pointing to the black student in the front of the line of questioners.

"Mr. Moses, sir, my name is Justice Thompson. I grew up in the District of Columbia and would just like to thank you for all you have done for young men like me. I immigrated to Texas three years ago and just got out of the work and reeducation program six months ago and thank God every day I am here. I was raised in a family who loved the American system with all the free programs, but I grew up reading about capitalism and free markets, so when Texas seceded, I knew I wanted to come here and experience what true freedom would be like. I am so honored to meet you face-to-face since you represent everything right in the world. God bless you.

"You helped sponsor me through the First Baptist Church of Houston where I stayed and worked for the Texas Ford engineering department learning about the free market and everything you said is right. I am now working nights and going to school during the days to be a journalist and write the truth about how great this country is. I am starved, and I know millions of young people like me are, too, so I want to be able to explain the free market to them. So thank you, and my question is, why don't other countries follow our church welfare program and could you explain it to the students here that may not know what it is or how it works?"

"Well, you're welcome, Justice, and you are the reason we have those programs. We have a very tight immigration system since we are surrounded by states full of people who would love to come here with our two percent unemployment rate as well as high wages and low taxes, meaning more take home pay or more freedom. We allow over a million per year to immigrate, but with the understanding they want to become capitalists in every sense of the word, believe in freedom *of* religion not freedom *from* religion and are willing to dedicate three to five years of their lives to become Texas citizens.

"Most come with nothing but the clothes on their backs, so we plug them into one of the numerous churches we have in the state immediately. We found the churches work better than the government to provide food and shelter with all of their free volunteers. We call it one-stop welfare where they are not only fed physically but mentally and spiritually. Meanwhile, they go to the training schools to help them begin to reeducate themselves with economic and social classes about free markets and why they work. You would be amazed how many do not know the slightest thing about the benefits of living in a free-market economy. All they know are the risks of failure rather than any opportunities of success. Outsiders call it brainwashing, but we call it reversing their previous brainwashing and the people like Justice Thompson are free to leave if they want, but most find it to be the best thing they have ever done. Am I right, Justice?"

"Amen, Mr. Moses, it has been the best education of my life since I was starved to hear the truth about capitalism. It freed my mind to think, and I am excited to get my degree and become a self-published journalist. Maybe I'll write your story, do you need a biographer??" The entire auditorium rang out with laughter.

The next student in line was a young woman whose name was Michelle Davis. "Mr. Moses, how do you make sure that business and government are not filled with corruption like we see in other countries like the United States?"

"That is a great question, Ms. Davis, and goes to the heart of why capitalism works. First, you have to have honest people with integrity making the decisions since there are so many opportunities for corruption. You have to trust everyone involved. It comes down to the old saying that you need to work with people who will do the right thing when no one is watching. If you are not, you will have to always be watching everyone all the time which costs money.

"It helps that we are a Christian nation in that people know the difference between right and wrong or telling the truth and lying. It is no coincidence we are the most Christian nation in the world with eighty percent going to and being involved with Christian-based churches in Texas. It is also no coincidence we have the lowest crime rate in the world as well as divorce and drug addiction rates. We value God, the family, and private property so people value other people's possessions and freedom.

"The second part about government corruption is how you and our computerized system come in. We have nearly complete transparency to all of our industries. If you are doing the right thing, you have nothing to hide. Of course some of it is sensitive and can't be shared, but we want everything and everyone to share their knowledge with the public. This is where you budding journalists fit in and we want you to report the story both good and bad. Write your critical articles, but have the same vigor and passion on reporting what is going right since nearly all the businesses are honest although you never hear about them."

The next question was from a boy who looked like he was a football player. He was tall and wide with not an ounce of fat on him, and his cowboy hat only made him look like a horse on two legs. "Mr. Moses, my name is Tom Johnson. I was recruited out of Chicago to play defensive line for the Longhorns and am trying to immigrate if you can get me some help? My question is, being from Chicago, how did you keep the unions out and messing everything up, and why does nobody want an hourly wage?"

"Well, son, I don't have that kind of clout to get your citizenship but you may want to talk to Coach Brown Jr. Most think he has more clout than President Stewart in Texas. That is a good question, Tom. The short answer is, nobody wants the unions. The long answer is, every time they come down here, they find out they cannot match piecework. Once we computerized our wages, we had real-time wage negotiations and could work out a salary as the worker improved his value to the company. This evolved into piecework, and the value inputs were invented and matrices formed to pay someone for every job he did whether it was turning screws or keying in contracts, it all came down to activities the computer could track and value by the second, which is far more than the hourly could pay. The employee became his own business by being the controller of his paycheck.

"The advantage is, it encourages the workers to work harder, smarter, and more efficiently, making the companies more productive. This is how we are bringing business from China and other low-wage countries since our workers are motivated and passionate about their work and their companies. They essentially share in the success of the company by making the company more successful. We have a saying at Moses Oil, 'You are the key and we are your doorway.' It means we all work together to unlock success. That is how the free market works."

"Hello, Mr. Moses, I too am proud to have you here. You are a hero in my family. My name is Miguel Martinez, and my family has lived in Texas for five generations. I was fourteen when the Texas secession happened. Could you explain how and why it did."

Steven was moved by the statement and caught himself thinking about those events. "Miguel, it was a long process moving away from the United States. As you may know, we were a very patriotic state and loved the American ideal, but the federal government became so overbearing and regulatory that it was destroying our economy and state. When America became so overextended financially and collapsed, there was so much pain and suffering especially in the major cities. They wanted to take more taxes from us since we were still producing oil for the rest of America and the world. We were one of the only states still producing a positive budget due to being fiscally conservative and our church partnerships.

"We tried to fight it in Congress, but they wouldn't listen. As a matter of fact, since we were so outnumbered and outvoted, they doubled the taxes they were taking from us since we were an oil-producing state. The final straw was passing new regulations which were going to shut down our oil industries so we really had no choices. We drew up our own Declaration of Independence and submitted it to the president of the United States. That's when the Congress declared war on Texas and ordered all of our offices seized by the National Guard.

"When the Texas Minutemen gathered, myself and a few other prominent businessmen combined our resources together and offered the US fifty trillion dollars for our independence. American President Sanchez thought we were crazy, but when he saw the names on the declaration and which companies were leveraging their finances, he realized we could actually pay the bill. He then took it to Congress.

"Congress had me speak as the leader of the coalition, and I explained to them that not only could we pay the money, but would guarantee them energy for the following decade at a reduced rate so long as they would not take military actions against us. We enjoyed a lot of help from our senators and congressmen who guided our declaration through Congress. At that point, there was really nothing they could say or do since they knew there would be an ugly war between the states, and we had all the guns and troops we needed. So, they debated a couple of months and gave us our sovereignty with a few caveats and now here we are.

"Not only did we pay them off ahead of the scheduled payments, we have grown so fast we have expanded ten times what we would have growing as a state. This has been an amazing adventure both as a country and as an industry. We are proving to the world what can happen if a country and the free market work together rather than as antagonists. Thanks be to God for all of these events and bringing such a fine team together. I firmly believe this was an act of the Holy Spirit to free Texas and its people from the oppression we see in the US today."

Professor Darling stood and walked forward, addressing the crowd, "That is all the time we have. Ah, Steven, and we would certainly like to—"

One of the boys in the back yelled, "Don't mess with Texas!" And the entire audience stood in applause and cheering like they had just beaten the Aggies. The chant went on for over five minutes while both he and Professor Darling tried to settle them down.

Steven Moses regained himself and finished by saying, "Thank you so much for your attendance, your patriotism, and enthusiasm, which only encourages me that we have another generation of

Texans who will build on what we have started. Make sure to study hard, work hard, and pray hard for tomorrow will be here before you know it. Everybody now, may God bless Texas!"

As they walked back to her office, they enjoyed the warm sun highlighting the beauty of the campus with all the deep green grass and multiple varieties of trees and flowers. He could hear a turtledove cooing in a dogwood tree across the campus. He could smell a slight hint of honeysuckle wafting through the air, adding sweetness to the warm, humid gulf breeze.

"Thank you so much for coming and speaking to our school, Mr. Moses. It was such an interesting speech. The students enjoyed your talk, which was so inspirational for them to hear. You are so generous with your time, and we appreciate how valuable yours is."

Such an intriguing woman, Steven thought, *very pretty yet in a bit of a plain sort of way.* She carries an air of being hurt by a man at some point, and if he guessed, it would be in the past year or so, which is why she seemed so distant.

"How long have you been teaching at Texas?" He quizzed as they arrived at her small office in the Hart building.

"I have been a professor here for two years and have been a virtual author for the *Austin Gazette* online for much of that time. Before then, I was studying to earn my doctorate while I wrote for both the *New York Times* and the *Washington Post* as a syndicated writer."

"Should I consider you the enemy, Professor Darling?"

"Oh, hardly, I was the lone free marketer in those papers and was considered a persona non-grata, but they couldn't find anyone else to write for them. As a matter of fact, I covered much of the secession and Declaration of Independence. I actually interviewed you via e-mail as a graduate student."

"Well, anytime you want to interview me again it would be my pleasure. Would you like to go get some coffee? Is there a good spot around here, Professor Darling?"

"Oh, ah, well, Mr. Moses, I really can't. I mean, I am not really ready to begin any relationship or anything, besides I am kind of seeing someone and—"

"Look, I ain't asking you to marry me or anything. I just thought you might want to talk over a cup of coffee. Why is it every pretty woman immediately thinks if you want to talk, you want to get married? And my name is Steven, can I call you June?"

June began fidgeting with her ponytail. "Well, no, I mean yes…ah, no, I didn't think you were asking to marry me. What? Yes, June is fine, and there is a nice little cafe across the commons for coffee." Where did that come from, you're sounding like a babbling fool, she thought.

They both laughed at the moment as she grabbed her purse and jacket. "I would be interested in interviewing you sometime when you had an hour for a project I am working on."

"Well, sure, that would be fine, although you may find my life is far more boring than you think."

"How can your life be boring as one of the richest most powerful men in the world? You probably have beautiful women throwing themselves at you."

They walked into a crowded little cafe called the Longhorn Bistro and Brew. It was crowded with students who were enjoying good food and coffee as well as the older students having the cold beer and burger combination. Country Western music was playing in the background, making for a real Texas flavor.

"Why should you worry if women throw themselves at me?"

"Oh, ah…I don't. I was just stating the obvious." She knew she said something she shouldn't have, but he is really handsome, she thought. Stop thinking that she was still getting over Tom who was the dream of her life until he ran off with one of his students. Men are such creeps.

"What is obvious?" He was teasing her now.

"What? Oh, well you know you are rich and powerful. You have to be a very good catch for most women. Oh, brother, how do I get out of this, and is there a way out?" They both laughed at her three shades of red.

"So, June, not to change the subject, but did you grow up here, and where is your family?"

"I grew up in Tyler, Texas, where my dad is a pastor at a small church. Trinity Baptist, he was the pastor, and my mom played the piano and sang. Trinity, around a hundred and fifty members and was a real small community. I had two bothers and a sister who are very close. I love Texas and the university. Everybody knows your story. Are you also close with your parents?"

"Yes, my dad, Daniel, who has always been my hero and mentor showed me how to live my life. My mom, Helena, is the best mother a kid could want, who really kept the family together while my dad was out drilling in the gulf or in some Texas jackrabbit gulch. She just loved all of us and made a perfect home. When Dad came home, it was like Christmas since he was gone weeks at a time and sometimes months out of the country. He would always come home with a bag of candy to make it festive. He worked hard and kept us safe and secure."

"Did you miss him while he was gone?"

"Of course, he missed lots of baseball and basketball games. All the other kids' dads were the same and worked in the gulf, so we all got used to it. It was just part of growing up, but when I got old enough to work in the fields, he was my best friend and mentor, showing me the ropes. He became the best dad a guy could ever hope for to learn the important parts of life."

"Why haven't you remarried or have a wife and family?"

He laughed off the pain that question always brought in his chest. "Is that a proposal?"

"Stop it, I'm not that kind of girl," she said laughing. She sensed the hurt he still felt from his wife's death. "Did your parents take you to church, and are you religious?"

"Yes, I accepted Christ as a young boy at church camp. We went to Calvary Four Square growing up, but I strayed for a while, you know sowing my oats. When Sandy died, I became angry at God for what he did to me and punishing her with such a horrible death. I thought God was a cold and punishing God, and he liked bringing innocent people like Sandy such pain. In the end, it made me stronger and realize I could love someone with all my heart and soul even though losing her hurt, we still are together which is why I am still single. Fortunately, I had a friend on an oil rig who was a Christian, and we talked, and I regave my heart to Jesus. I don't know what I would do without him. He is my entire life now."

She looked at his wedding ring he still wore. "Is that why you still wear your wedding ring because of the pain?"

"Oh, that, yes. I have never been hurt like that in my life when I lost Sandy. For the first year, it felt like my heart was pulled out of my chest and stomped on. She saved me from a life of drinking and fighting and turned it around. She was the perfect woman for me, and I don't think there can be anyone to fill that scar in my chest. It also lets women know I am off limits since I am really married to my career and company anyway. Pretty much a stop sign on my hand. Kind of sad, huh?"

"No, not at all. She was a lucky woman to have a man so dedicated to her to still consider himself married after her death. It's charming."

"As for the 'no wife and family,' all I can say is, I am a workaholic, and I wouldn't want to raise my kids the way I was raised. If I were to have a family, I would have to give up most of my work, and I really enjoy my work. What about you? Do you love your job?"

"Oh, absolutely, this is the best career in the world. There are very few places you can help to teach kids how to not only report the news but explain how it affects their lives. Very few people really understood it when we first left the States, so it was our job to teach our journalists how economies work and retrain them to write about the wonders of capitalism and freedom. That is our job and my calling. We are pioneers in a field that was designed to take businesses down and promote an agenda. We are the new reporters who are fighting the war of words to lift up free markets and how they empower the individual spirit thorough entrepreneurship and creativity. Most do not understand a business is really an individual. It is simply an individual entity representing a group of people with a common goal speaking as one voice."

"Now I am in love." Steven teased as June playfully slapped his hand when his phone rang. "Yes, hello, Drake? How was President Stewart? Yeah, it is getting pretty hectic. We are at the Longhorn Bristo and Brew, why don't you come over?"

"What?"

"Now?"

"I can't…really?"

"Okay, I'll be there in a few minutes."

He hung up and looked at June, rolling his eyes. "Now you know why I never remarried. Apparently, I am needed at President Stewart's office to work something out. I am not sure what it is, but it sounds like something to do with the new proposals by the United Nations. Can I walk you back to your office before I head over there?"

"No, that's not necessary. I have to stop by the library first and then a couple other things I have to do. It was a pleasure, and thank you so much for talking to my students. They enjoyed it so much."

"Can I see you again, and perhaps you can have that real interview."

"Perhaps an interview, but the time just isn't right for either of us," she said, wondering if she was passing up something she had been waiting for or more trouble than she needed right now. She didn't want to get hurt again, and besides her new boyfriend David was hinting at getting married. Oh, why now?

Steven looked into her eyes and said, "Like my dad always told me, 'Never wait for the next cab when the one you may need is parked right in front of you.' I will let you know when we can do the interview." Steven looked into those sparkling green eyes, feeling them tug him in as his mind swam around in their reflective deep green pools of life. "I better get going, and it was very nice meeting you, Professor Darling." He shook her hand and turned to go heading for his shuttle over to the capital.

A STORM IS BREWING

United Nations Secretary General Salinas Margarita Polentas looked out her office down at New York City. She could remember when she first arrived at the UN as an assistant for the Venezuela ambassador. In those days before the US collapse, you could walk around the city without having to worry about your safety, which she took full advantage of and searched every corner of New York. Sure, there were places in the city you would not to be out after dark but not like now.

The rampant gangs and mafia have turned the UN blocks into an armed compound you never leave except by air, and even then, you may get shot at by a laser or missile. You wouldn't want to end up like the bloody bodies she saw this morning hanging from a lamppost with the banker sign attached to his chest. On the next post was a woman with stockbroker attached to hers. Then of course there were the human crosses. It was too gruesome to think what a horrible death they must have faced until hanging became a welcome escape.

The city has turned into complete anarchy by gangs who had taken over complete sections of the city; it was every man for himself. For a woman like herself to be out after dark was a chilling thought. The only areas that were reasonably safe were the walled sections of the Upper East Side, some of the villages, and East Long Island, which had become armed compounds with everyone working from home and not letting anybody in their cities who doesn't have proper ID. Those inner cities without natural defenses had fallen into complete chaos.

There were no cars in the city as nobody could afford gas even if they have the proper rationing chips. The streets were basically empty since everyone took the subway as it has not only become the transportation hub, the tunnels were also the black market centers of the cities. Everything from fuel to people were traded down there out of the way of the police and authorities who could never patrol the labyrinth of tunnels.

Looking out over the dead city, you could see the skyscrapers with missing windows. The electricity only worked periodically since coal had been outlawed, and nuclear powered plants shuttered while renewable sources were unreliable even when they were maintained. The rails and subways only worked on occasion, not that anybody would want to go down there to be robbed or raped during blackouts. When trains shut down, the people on board were free game by the gangs.

There is only one answer to this problem Secretary Polentas thought and that was to have Texas provide America with cheaper electricity and begin paying taxes like every other country in the world. It was not fair that they should have all their excessive wealth when so many people were suffering from hunger and poverty around the world. There was just so much good she and the UN could do; if the Texans would just pay their fair share they could solve those problems. It was not right that a country should be so wealthy and not help the world pull itself out of this worldwide depression.

The citizens were becoming ungovernable ever since the collapse. Sure they were paying seventy-five percent taxes, which was hard, but the UN and America needed more revenue to provide the services the people required. *Why didn't they understand the simple fact we were doing what we could to keep the people from starving on the four corners of the world?* She thought about the seemingly never-ending sirens and lights keeping her up during the night. Sure she was safe in the UN condos inside the complex, but it would be great to get a decent night's sleep without the yelling, the screams, and the sirens; guess that is the price of living in the Big Apple. If something did not change soon, this city could destroy itself, by mass riots like it had never seen before.

Her Chief of staff entered her office, snapping her out of her thoughts. "Secretary General, the United States president is here and the security council has been assembled and waiting for you in the boardroom."

She took the short walk to the elevators and down to the inner boardroom where the ten economic leaders were waiting. The UN ambassadors of the United States and the president, the ambassadors to China, Russia, Japan, Chile, Saudi Arabia, Iraq, Germany, and Britain.

She opened the meeting, "Thank you, ladies and gentlemen, for coming and especially President Chambers. You all know why we are here. We have written and are going to propose to the General Assembly UN measure 2022-311, which will require any country that wants to import or export to a UN member country will have to be a full-paying member of the UN. This of course will require all of our countries to have equal footing with other countries and will come under the UN Charter for fair and equitable trading practices. This will generate more business for every country and stop any one country from exploiting other less advanced countries through inequitable trade practices. Questions? President Chambers, you have a question?"

President Chambers was the newly elected president from Boston and came out of its Socialist Party machine. He was an ardent fighter for the nationalized health care and social programs then was a supporter to maintain the programs the United States had developed over the past century. He came from a hardworking family whose father owned a small grocery store in north Boston. The family knew everybody, and his father was well connected in the Democrat Party until it morphed into the Socialist Party as the Republican Party simply imploded into the Constitutional Party. His rise in party politics was dramatic as he went from state representative to governor and midway through his governorship ran for president and won. He had no idea how difficult this would be as the chronic unemployment would not stop increasing and currently was at twenty-nine percent.

"Madame Secretary and distinguished ambassadors, you know this resolution puts us in a difficult position with the Republic of Texas. We have been allies since their secession and have stood in the way of three other of these resolutions. There are numerous issues with this proposal that will affect us in many ways. The least of which is they are our largest trading partner as we import sixty-five percent of our oil and power from them. We will need assurances from the council that we will have our energy needs covered by your member countries.

"Our other issue is their maintaining our debt by purchasing our bonds. When they originally split from America, we agreed on a price of 50 trillion dollars over ten years, which we believed would help us with our services and infrastructure, but they paid it off in two years and we have been struggling ever since. If they were to call in our debt or not purchase our bonds, we very likely go into default on our payments to foreign countries, triggering another worldwide financial collapse.

"Our citizens have suffered under this worldwide recession, and they are not able to pay any more taxes. The rate they are paying now is seventy percent, and we have the wealthy paying in excess of ninety-five percent so where can we increase our revenue? The worst part is we are losing our most skilled people and profitable businesses to Texas. They are able to pay the highest wages with the best benefits of anywhere in the world, let alone the Americas, so they are taking the cream of the cream for their own empire. They have all the best engineers and most skilled technical workers, so the rest of the world no longer can compete. With their corporate and personal tax structures, there is no way we can keep our best people staying. The only ones who are staying are the ones who are not able to immigrate due to their stringent immigration laws.

"We still have 50 percent of our most successful business leaders who have not left but many of those have applied. As you know, they will not let anybody through their borders unless they are the top of their industry and/or have a patent they can use to expand their economy like Texas Ford. Then they have a four-year education program, which educates immigrants on their economic and government structure. After five years, you become a citizen with the right to vote and to run for offices. If they continue to take the best people and businesses in our country and the world, how are we able to compete? We need some guarantees of revenue from the UN dues and fees. We need Texas energy to survive.

"There is no way we can enter a military battle with Texas since our history as well as citizens would have a problem fighting against a former state as well as our secession agreement allows us reduced prices on all of our energy purchases. If they were to cut us off from our energy supplies, we would have some severe shortages and outages that could cripple our economy even further. We may be able to enter into a limited conflict with them, but we would need plausible deniability to free us from any connection to this action either militarily or politically.

"You should also be advised, Madame Secretary, that we have some information from inside Texas that they have some very sophisticated weapons. As you know, they are one of the major suppliers of laser and digital weaponry. They are very technologically advanced, so we are not sure how advanced they are, but our military people believe they may have some weapons being researched, which could be very effective against most attacks. They have taken the best scientists in the world for the past eight years so it is anybody's guess what they have developed or have on the drawing board.

"In addition, we all know they have the fastest aircraft in the world. Lone Star Air has dominated the transworld market with their aircraft ever since they unveiled these commuter ramjet space shuttles. While most of our aircraft still take eighteen hours to get to Asia, they are making the flight in a little over two. We have heard rumors their next generation is even faster and could operate subatmospheric and who knows what types of fighter weaponry they can put on those types of platforms? Ladies and gentlemen, let me say as a former countryman of Texas, be very diligent in your entering any type of shooting war with these people. We will support you in your discussions and negotiations with them as well as provide as much intelligence as we can, but you have to understand we are not in a position to enter into a battle that will force them to isolate us from their energy supplies."

"Thank you, President Chambers," snapped Secretary General Polentas. "We understand the difficult position you are in and have no intentions of putting you at risk of Texas cutting off your energy supplies. We thank you for your information, and our intelligence has verified everything you has told us and more. They are not only the most powerful country in the world economically but have dominated the technological and military development, which is why we would never want to get into a shooting war with them.

"The UN military generals have looked at the difficulties of breaching their multiple walls and defensive weapons, deciding it would be nearly impossible. They have been advancing their wall security to keep Americans out so they have perfected their laser tazer to the point of making it nearly impossible to get past their laser robots. They have determined they could simply upgrade those robots by installing more powerful lasers to stop nearly anything on the land or air. Texas has become a force to be reckoned with, but we think we have a way to bring them to the table, which is why we brought you here."

———⌒∿∿⌒———

Terry Thomas was flying his hover jet along the northern wall looking out into Oklahoma red countryside, making sure he stayed just inside the Texas border. It was bad enough he had to make sure nobody was able to breach the walls or fly into their airspace, but his night optics were acting fidgety tonight. His mind was filled with so many checklists to make sure the robots were functioning, as well as the Okies weren't compromising their sensors spread across the farmlands disappearing across the horizon. At night, the laser display a visual display rivaling any light show.

He knew every one of those people walking aimlessly would give their left arm to be doing what he was doing. He was in his third year of immigration, and four years ago, he was one of those in the hobo camps who just happened to graduate number three from Annapolis and became one of the best fighter jocks in the US Navy, allowing him to immigrate with a skill. The F-22s he flew were a bit more responsive than this hover jet, but he felt he was every bit as needed, and these hovers were fun to fly with all the avionics built into the joystick.

He thought back to the first year and the changes he was being taught to eliminate the communal thinking and beliefs he brought with him. He laughed at the thoughts of how he used to believe completely in the social safety net when here in Texas: they not only don't have one but have no need for it. When you have ninety-eight percent employment, there is no need for wasteful social programs. For those who are infirmed or handicapped, they would be cared for through the churches who are far more efficient than an uncaring bureaucracy. The Texas Christ Churches were able to feed the soul as well as the stomach to really fix what was hurting. As they call it, the one-stop feeding, which fed the body and soul to truly heal the person.

He looked across at the scattered hobo campfires and wondered what they would look like if they were run by the church rather than the government. Churches were far more effective than governments since they had huge numbers of volunteers, making the donated dollars stretch further. They had been throughout history the primary welfare and poverty providers, and those people would not only be fed but brought back into society and productivity. If those states weren't taxing their citizens out of their homes and jobs, there would be plenty of money to tithe the churches to feed the poor. Even though he was making a lower wage than he made as a captain in the Navy, when you factored in a fifteen percent tax rate, he could not only tithe but give to other charities like the Veterans Hospital Fund. Overtaxing and underuse of churches and faith made all of those people's lives more desperately hopeless.

He thought about his second year when he began to learn about free market economics while doing his volunteer work at his church at their food bank. After the first two years for Border Security Inc., he could not only clean his hover from the windshield to the tail fin into a mirror finish but could tear every one of these aircraft down and rebuild it blindfolded. Those were tough years as he had a full day's work followed by six hours of economics, history, government, constitution law, and energy conservation and development. It was fourteen hours of the most intensive instruction and physically demanding job he had done in his life, but it gave him a sense of pride he never enjoyed before. Now he was a mere twenty-six months from becoming a full voting citizen for the Republic of Texas. Who knows, now perhaps he could start looking for a wife?

Suddenly, something caught his eye in the brush as he was flying by, so he pulled into a silent hover. Looking closer, he magnified and saw what he thought it was: a nice jackrabbit. He dove in as two of them ran into the open. They were darting back and forth between the heavy brush and trees, avoiding hawks and coyotes, but he anticipated a small opening they had to cross and squeezed the lasers, killing both instantly. The boys back at the base are going to be enjoying some rabbit stew for lunch or maybe dinner tonight.

He did a couple of outside loops with one of his patented curly cues to celebrate and saw dozens more dashing across the ground as he set his craft down to do the dirty work of cleaning and skinning these two delicious fat beauties. Even though it was just before sunrise, it was still pretty warm and humid in the panhandle. It wasn't as humid as down by Houston, but it still stays warm and muggy in the early summer even before dawn. He made short work of the cleaning and was putting them in the cooling unit when he saw something fast coming out of the corner of his eye. A military jet screamed across the grasslands, nearly passing right over the top of him doing around twelve hundred knots coming straight out of Oklahoma about thirty feet off the tree tops with no markings or lights.

Terry jumped into his craft, fired it up, and shot straight up into the air; but there was no sign of the one that just went over the top. He flashed on his laser ops, and they picked up nothing, dead air. It couldn't be more than eighty miles by now and should be lighting his windshield like old Times Square, but nothing. He called in to border command and reported what he saw and asked if they had just scoped an aircraft from Oklahoma, nothing. He knew what he just saw and heard, but how could anybody have that good a signal diverter to counter his ops? They scrambled ten more hovers, but nobody picked up or saw anything. He thought he better get back to the base to report this and then start fixing some delicious fresh rabbit stew.

—◦◦◦—

A STORM IS BREWING

What a great day with the afternoon sun shining bright and bringing a happiness to the capital even in these tense times. He could not get June Darling off his mind with her reddish blond hair and green eyes that drew him in like a moth to a midnight lightbulb on a hot summer night. He felt a bit of aching he had not felt since Sandy was with him. Austin was a beautiful city with its artsy culture mixed with a major campus as well as the Texas capital. The gulf winds were coming out of the equator and knocking their shuttle a bit as well as fairly dense traffic at all elevations during the short hop. They landed on the top deck of the capital and walked into the president's wing and was ushered directly into President's Stewart's office, which was filled with Drake and the finance cabinet and secretaries

His office was on the top floor of the newly built Texas White House. It resembled the Washington White House from the outside except it was over twice as large and far more opulent and of course newly built with the country, which had all the latest technological advantages. His office was expansive with an adjacent board room for cabinet meetings, which had walls of monitors covering the entire world to talk to different leaders. He had a row of virtual chairs that the head of the Senate and House were sitting from their offices. His office was comfortable with couches in a semicircle facing the presidential desk. The walls were covered in deep cherry paneling with gun memorabilia displayed . His pride and joy was the Sam Houston long rifle, that was museum quality for its place in Texan history which had passed through his family.

"Steve, thanks for coming, you know everybody, Vice President Chapman and my cabinet members. The reason we wanted you to join us is you know we have been getting rumblings from the United Nations that they were in negotiations to change our tax and import export agreements. We are not sure where this is going, but they have invited us to come to New York City next month to speak to the UN Counsel and explain our positions in regards with our production and distribution of energy. The US ambassador is hearing they may be making a move to not only increase the world tax but take a more active role in negotiating and writing contracts to control production and distribution. He thinks they want to make us a full member with all the taxes and regulations which go with it.

"They are going to attempt to make us pay a tax and some are indicating it may be in the thiry-five percent range. As you all know, we have refused to pay any taxes and the United States has vetoed all of the bills they have introduced to single us out. We are the wealthiest country in the world, controlling sixty percent of the energy markets worldwide, so they want to take from us to give to their socialist economics in the guise of feeding the poor. The problem we may have is the US is falling into such desperate straits they may need to take our taxes too, leaving us alone without an ally on the security council to veto their proposal."

Steven responded, "The reason we are the economic power in the world is that we don't have one of those Marxist disasters and have succeeded on the ingenuity of the average person who wants to maximize his talents and abilities. We are proof that if you have a small government who gets out of the way of free enterprise, the sky is truly your limit. Now they want to impose their will on us—no way! We have to fight this with every ally we have just like we did last year and the year before."

Vice President Chapman interjected, "You all know me and my ancestors have lived in Texas since before the Alamo and love this land with my entire heart. I will proudly die in Texas and if need be for my great country. What we have seen since we seceded has been perhaps the greatest success story in the history of mankind with our freeing of the human spirit as well as our outward worship of the Lord. Steven, we are meeting with the Texas governors and Congress next week and would like you to speak to them about how to fight the UN and of course give them a background on the international energy sector you know so well. We know this is short notice, but the president and I think you are the best person to address this issue, you know all the various countries around the world and leaders who are pushing this tax and seizure. We are meeting next Tuesday morning here in the chambers, would you be able to be there?"

"Of course I will, Miguel, whatever you need of me I will be happy to speak to the governors and fill them in on who these leaders are and what they are trying to do. Obviously since the county governors are the local service providers they should understand how this would affect them and why we will need their support if we are going to challenge this resolution. They have benefited both by our success in building and modernizing our infrastructure as well as receiving low-cost energy and superior road building products. If we have to start sending taxes to the UN, it will force us to lower our provisions here, which could cut into our infrastructure, which will increase costs on every one of our products."

President Stewart spoke up, ""We have a uniquely close relationship with our industries as we understand they need flexibility and an understanding we are allies and not their rulers. This has been one of the main advantages we have and is our hands-off approach, which has not only allowed them to expand but they have expanded in a responsible manner. All of our inspections as well as their paperwork have shown they in nearly all cases have not only met our requirements, but always exceed all but the most absurd requirements designed to curtail production. This has made us by far the least polluting as well as the most efficient energy producers on the planet. All of this gets to the point that we have very little real power here in the capital and will be pushing our limits just to challenge this resolution, and we have no power if they decide to push the issues.

"So fellow Texans, I don't think any of us have come this far to have some two bit bunch of socialist dictators take away everything we have built. The last thing anybody in this room wants is to go back to what we left, and if you are like me, I will die holding onto my ancestors' freedom. What they really want to take away from us is our freedom and then enslave us into their World government, which they claim will end poverty. As we all know, they will only make it worse as they try to take the money from us to give to corrupt dictators they have propped up around the world. So this is the first step onto a journey we have no idea how long or far it will go. So thank you for coming and…don't mess with Texas!"

"Don't mess with Texas!" they all echoed in unison.

MOSES OIL

Steven arrived in the office later than the usual 7:00 am, knowing it was going to be a long day filled with strategy meetings. He scheduled a board meeting to fill them in on the events that he was told about in Austin and world events that were happening on a minute-by-minute basis. The heads of Moses subsidiaries were spread around the table with their assistants behind them on their two-way computer goggles, communicating updated information to be relayed as needs arose. They could all tell by the somberness of Steven this was going to be a long and intense meeting.

"Board members, I am glad you could all make it and hope you are all prepared. We have perhaps the greatest threat to our companies as well as this country we have had since our independence. I know most of you have heard through the grapevine news and rumors we are about to have a massive cost and regulatory stranglehold put on us from the United Nations. You know my thoughts on their alliance of Marxist dictators, but it does not matter they have the entire world at their disposal to pressure us, which is why we are having this emergency meeting.

"Dave, what have you heard from our customers and suppliers of oil and gas?"

David Scott was a third generation oilman whose blood was sweet Texas crude. He had either traded or owned oil commodity companies his last twenty years making fortunes in their distribution. He became a billionaire in the shutdown of the Alaskan pipeline when he controlled most of their outside production as oil increased ten times its value in six months until the government was forced to reopen it. After the Texas secession, he let Moses Oil acquire his company and made him the head of oil and gas.

"Thanks, Steven, it's everything you say and worse. My sources are saying they are being pressured by the UN and their governments to stop buying and selling with Texas until we begin paying the world taxes we have refused since our founding. They are saying it was fine when we first became a republic since we had no extra income and were strapped to pay back America, but now we are the leading energy producing country in the world and they say we should be paying our fair share.

"Our largest crude suppliers in the Middle East are torn since they have as little use for the UN as we do, but they cannot afford to look like they are siding with us. We may be able to convince some of the smaller producers like Nigeria and Israel to continue to sell to us, but even they are getting pressure from other member countries. We are pretty sure we can continue to buy from the Dakotas and Alaska, but if President Chambers and the Congress steps in, it is anybody's guess.

"Sales are going to be another story. It sounds like they are going to form a coalition against us and stop buying Texas products on the open market. They have all but stopped buying our futures contracts even though, as you all know, we have been forced to discount to the limit and still no buyers in the last week. We are shipping the existing contracts but China, Japan, and Europe have all made it clear they are going to wait until the general assembly decides what they're going to do before they step back into the market.

"America has to buy their gasoline from us as well as refined fuels, but we have heard from inside sources Chambers has agreed to go along with the UN and is willing to cut himself off to force us to comply. This could become the old Mexican standoff if they go along since it will hurt them as much as it will hurt us, then it becomes a matter of who can hold out the longest financially. That is all we know right now, Steven, we will keep you all up to speed as events develop."

"Thanks, Dave, as you can see, this may become a very large problem for our company as we have no idea how far they are willing to push this or how long. Sam, can you give us the report on our power generation?"

Sam Satterwhite has been with Moses Power for ten years when they purchased Texas General Power and Light, which he was the CEO. He had moved up through the ranks of Texas General as an innovator in the electrical power generation industry. His ability to position his companies in the most efficient and cost effective mode of electrical generation had made him legendary in the industry although a bit of a pariah among the governments who wanted to use power as a tool against their people he stayed with the most dependable. He shunned all the fad electrical plans like solar and wind in their early stages, preferring to stay with coal and gas. When gas was being found and developed in expanding quantities he was building NatGas electrical plants next to the refineries using their byproduct as his primary fuel. This has made Moses Power and himself legendary in the power generation industry.

"Thanks, Steven, we don't look quite as bleak as the oil side, although I am not going to fool you into believing we won't be affected if there is a Texas boycott. We will have plenty of NatGas from our own domestic supplies and may even see prices lower if our competitors are not purchasing from us. As far as sales go, we will be able to sell to our own markets to maintain our own plants and industries, which may or may not be cut off depending on which companies. Y'all know nobody is going to stop Texans from turning on their air-conditioners in the hot summer sun!

"The big issue is we sell nearly fifty percent of our power to the United States. We feed the grid from California to New York, and if they stop buying, we will really feel the loss. The bigger question is, if we were to cut off their power, they have no way to replace it from their lack of building power plants over the last forty years in the numbers they need. Lack of production and their antiquated grid network loses power as it escapes from their lines they have a critical shortage. If they had updated to coaxial or laser like we have, they would be fifty percent more efficient than they are now.

They have regular brownouts and rolling blackouts to keep from permanent blackouts, and if we pulled the switch, they could have a major blackout, shutting down the entire nation. So one of the issues we will need to decide is if they were to act with the UN, do we act first, or wait? Our estimates are that they would have a difficult time keeping the power on if we cut their power. Then if we do, how much misery would we cause? We are doing the analysis and will report on that later, but the initial models show massive disruptions of supplies like food, power, and necessities."

"Thanks, Sam, I think everybody here hopes we never have to make that decision, Tom, what are you seeing with the steel and aluminum companies?"

Tom Summers was one of the newcomers who moved out of the Rust Belt after the secession. He was the CEO for Alcoa and walked away when he saw the writing on the wall for his industry. America was destroying its own energy production, which was going to drive energy costs above the industry's ability to pay. There was no way in the middle of a recession to pass those costs onto his customers, so bankruptcy was the his most likely scenario. He too was a living legend in the aluminum and hybrid industries, making the production more efficient and the development of stronger lighter products, which had revolutionized the aircraft, rocket, and hovercraft industries.

"Steven and gentlemen, we obviously have two issues just like the rest of you, except we have a very competitive market to sell into. If we lose our foreign markets in airline sales as well as hover jets, we could be forced to cut back on productions. Right now, we have a market that is purchasing nearly everything we can produce, thanks to our quality and superior technology. The Asian producers have forced the markets down due to lower labor and raw material costs and have flooded the markets to some extent. The US producers have fallen so far behind in technology, thanks to the union takeover as well, as their energy disadvantage they are basically an industrial mess. The European producers have had so many shutdowns and missed deadlines the major airlines are afraid to purchase their products for fear of never receiving shipment. That said, the UN could force them to boycott us, and they would have to buy elsewhere.

"Our other problem will be having availability of rare minerals from around the world. As you all know, we have an advantage of abundant and cost-effective energy, but we have to import most of our minerals, which produce our alloys. We may be able to import many of them from Mexico and the Dakotas, but if we are cut off from them, it is going to put us in a real pinch to produce the metal and composite products we have been supplying to our vital industries.

"We have been building a surplus over the last two years to take advantage of the prices, but even at that, we only have a six-month supply. We could increase our purchasing while we wait to find out if the UN is going to take action and what they may do. Overall, I believe we will be able to supply steel and basic metals to the auto industry, but for the aircraft industry, we have very limited resources of the trace minerals we need."

Steven looked grimly over to Jake Dustin for an overview. "Well, Jake, do you want to finish up this little shindig?"

Jake has been with Steve since they were both young wildcatters and considered themselves brothers. He has been through thick and thin in the oil business, but he always had a knack of finding the wells that hit. Even though he had a gambling streak in the business, he was the one who kept the numbers in line and was the level headed one. When Steve would propose, the biggest risk they had ever undertaken to see if his theory of draining the reserve would work, Jake always provided the logistics and costs associated with such a giant undertaking as well as the potential gain. He was able to show the potential trillions they could make if they could purchase all the dry wells and turn them into gushers. After they found Steven's idea worked, it was how they could quietly purchase those wells without being discovered, which is what Jake mastered in.

"Steven, we have been looking into this for a few years since they have threatened us before. The issue we have now is we may not have the United States allying with us to stop the UN. They have gotten themselves in such horrible shape financially, they likely need the tax revenues we could provide worse than the UN. President Stewart is going to speak in front of the general assembly and has asked Steven to also speak there and give our case to why we cannot afford and refuse to pay their excessive taxes, which could be from fifteen to fifty percent, depending how they want to classify us.

"We really won't have any idea what they will be doing until they have their assembly, but if it is anything like they did to China and Iraq, we are likely going to see the upper end as well as severe regulatory laws. They may reduce our production and development and who knows what else they are capable of. This is going to be a tough fight, but one thing about Texans, we know how to fight."

"Thanks, Drake, and yes, we will fight this to our last breath. You all know how I feel about the UN and whether or not they will have our best interests at heart. They see what we have accomplished and believe they had a hand in it, so they feel they should be paid for their worldwide services. If that worked, how come there are more poor countries now then when they started? If they really wanted to stop poverty, they would copy our model, but they don't want to or are afraid to take their hands off the wheel and let their citizens make their own decisions. This is why we have been successful since we allow individuals to succeed or fail on their own merit and start over until they do succeed without government interference.

"So, gentlemen, we need to prepare for the worst and purchase as much raw material inventory as we can to prepare for this war. We do not know if it will be a political, economic, or a shooting war, but we need to prepare ourselves for a long siege to hold out as long as we can. We are the foundation of the Texas economy, so we need to make sure that foundation is as strong as we can make it. You all need to fill your warehouses and get on your knees every day because very soon we may be back in the Alamo. Dismissed."

As they were logging off their headsets, John looked over at Dave Scott. "Dave, you want to get a bite with Drake and me before we head down to Houston for the flight to Beijing?"

"Sure, Steve, give me a couple minutes to make a couple calls from my office. I don't usually like to eat anything before liftoff, and there is a great restaurant at the sky port in Beijing so I may have a quick snack."

"All right, how about we meet at my hanger in forty-five minutes, and we will take the corporate hover limo down to Houston Space and give us a few minutes to prepare for the Chinese delegation. They may be a key to this entire problem, and if we can get their support, it could be to our advantage. The Chinese coalition has some strong allies in the United Nations."

⚘

June Darling could not get Steven Moses off her mind. Was he really flirting with her and what could he possibly see in her that he doesn't see in the models and starlets she sees him around on the news programs from morning to night? He was easily the most eligible bachelor in Texas who is not only perhaps the richest man in the world but was a really handsome guy. His long legs and wide shoulders made him the kind of real man every woman would want. His handsome rugged features from working on the rigs gives him a confidence in himself that very few men have anymore. Course those deep gray green eyes and thick blondish hair doesn't hurt…what is she thinking? Why would he be interested in a journalism professor in Austin? *Get a hold of yourself, June Darling.*

He did ask her out or at least made it obvious he wanted to see her again to do the interview. Perhaps she would do the interview just to see if she was imagining things or…

She was interrupted by a knock on her door. "June, are you in?"

"Yes, come in, Sally."

It was Dean Sally Sherwood, the dean of the journalism school and her closest friend.

"Hi, June, I have a favor to ask you that means a lot to the university and our journalism school."

"What is it, and why are you asking me?"

"Well, you have obviously been following the United Nations attempted the takeover of Texas, and we have been contacted by a large donor who wants us to cover it and document it for historical purposes. Since you wrote your thesis on Steven Moses during the secession, the board has decided you would be the best person to document this and make a historical record about this event. We don't know what and where it is going, but we believe it may be one of the biggest historical events in Texas's short history and perhaps the United Nation's. Our donor wants to make sure that our side of the issue is discussed and reported, and we think you are the perfect person to handle this research.

We will be giving you a sabbatical from your teaching, and any expenses you will have will be paid by the university. I don't think I have to tell you June this is a once-in-a-lifetime opportunity for a journalist. It could lead to a book and who knows what else."

"Well, thank you, Sally. I don't know what to say. You have caught me off guard, and yes, it is very interesting for me to record the historical details of these events as they happen, but I am in the middle of the semester and my students need me."

"June, we have contacted Professor Albertson to take your place, and your students will understand. They're journalists and know the magnitude of this opportunity as well as the historical significance. This is freedom and open markets against tyranny and socialism fighting for the final death of capitalism worldwide. We need you to record this fight. Can we count on you, June?"

"I don't know, this is all so sudden, and I don't know if I can do this. It would take so much time, and I would obviously have to go to New York to report it, I don't know… Yes, I do, someone once told me, 'Never wait for the next taxi when the one you need to take is parked right in front of you.' This may the biggest mistake of my life or the taxi I need, so yes, yes, I will take your proposal…er…offer."

"Here's hoping this isn't the only proposal you get."

"Sally, Stop!" June shrieked as she turned a bright shade of red.

"Well, there are all sorts of rumors floating around about his visit during his speech. You never know, and he is available, rich, and handsome other than that not much of a catch. Some girls have all the luck!"

"Stop it, he was just being nice. I'm sure he is that way with everybody, and that is not why I am doing this. He is handsome, though."

"From what I heard, he was being way more than just nice, it sounded like he was pretty interested in our little professor."

"Quit! Where did you hear that?"

"A little birdie told me, I have my sources. You know how universities are, telegraph, telephone, or tell a professor?"

"Yes, I will cover this story, but there is no way he is interested in me."

"Something tells me you are interested in him? June Moses has a nice ring to it, don't you think?"

"With friends like you, who needs enemies? Let's go have some coffee." She giggled as they walked out her door.

Terry Thomas focused his investigation on the area of the last sighting of the intruder. There was no signal found on any of the sensors or radar. No one could understand how any farmers or even the better military craft could deflect all of the technology they had on the border. It must have been a military aircraft with advanced software, which meant it had to be a US craft invading Texas, meaning an act of war if caught. Why would America take a risk like that just to look at some jackrabbits and take a look around North Texas? If they try it again, he will be ready and will get a shot off.

He practiced his evasive maneuvers even with the limitations of this hover jet, he was able to push its capabilities. The new weapons were more responsive and had a nice feel with the visual responders and the intuitive spotters.

The techs back at the base upgraded his detection software and gave him a bit more distance and power on his weaponized lasers if he ever had a chance to take a shot. It felt like his mech techs had tweaked his engines, and handling a bit as his hover jet felt like it had more power and speed than it had before. Pretty standard when an event like the possible intruder happens. There were reasons to believe someone may be testing the response and detection technology.

He also could see the techs have been working on the wall and border zones, checking the detection lasers as well as making sure everything was working as it should. He slowed as he approached the area to see if he noticed anything out of the ordinary to explain how they could get through the illuminated wall of detection. He wasn't interested in the jackrabbits scurrying across the field, trying to avoid becoming dinner for the local predators. He was more interested in the winged predators who were hunting for another type of dinner.

He pulled on the throttle so he was hovering at a hundred feet and looked north toward the direction he thought the intruder came from. Where up there could they possibly be coming from, there were no bases for a couple hundred miles, and breaking Texan airspace just doesn't seem worth the risk of being shot down. All of a sudden, his alarms lit his windshield while pushing his craft into evasive maneuvers. "Laser lock, laser lock take evasive action. Enemy aircraft targeting."

He automatically pushed toward the deck to get as low as he could while scanning the horizon with his lasers, finding nothing. He hid behind a tree, although if somebody shot, he would have likely have bit it when suddenly a shock wave hit him. Something just roared past him, doing at least Mach 3, heading north again before he could get his targeting software aimed. He fired one distant shot in the general spread the direction he thought it may be heading.

"Hit, hit, hit." He got a hit around 150 miles out, and suddenly his Lasdar lit up with an aircraft heading northwest at Mach 3.5 as it left his range at three hundred miles. What was it and where was it going were the first questions but what was an aircraft doing here in Texas that would take a chance like that and not be detected. How has it been able to get into the country without us seeing it? He better get back to the base and see if there was any information on his computer to help identify the bogey.

He took one last look around and banked back to the base as his windshield lit up again.

"Laser lock, laser lock, laser hit." As his cockpit erupted in flames, it crashed into the brush before he had a chance to pull the ejector.

A second jet blasted invisibly past as he faded into darkness. He laid in the wreckage and thought at least he died a free man doing what he loved as everything faded to black.

Arriving at Beijing was always a shock on the body no matter how many times Steven had done it. Walking into that shuttle with the other twenty people getting ready to get strapped into a hundred-ton ramjet and shuttle glider is a nerve-wracking experience. Even though everything was perfectly safe to know that you are attached to a something that travels thirteen thousand miles per hour gets your heart racing. When you hear the countdown start and the engines begin to rumble, suddenly you are being smashed into your seat by three Gs turning you into a human pizza. Once the conventional rockets stop and the ramjet booster ignites, you either black out or nearly do for the five-minute burn. Your breathing gets forced, and you have to rely on your G suit and ventilator mask to keep the circulation into your brain. The exhilaration of accelerating to those speeds however is pure adrenaline.

In a matter of minutes from liftoff, you turn weightless as you leave the earth's atmosphere where you are surrounded by pure darkness yet the brightest sun you will ever see. In space is where you can really accelerate up to max speed before you begin reentry, and the shuttle turns into a ball of fire, dropping out of the sky until you begin lining up for the landing onto Beijing National. If you enjoy adrenaline the way Steven did, there was no more thrilling ride available, and thanks to their secretly refined propellants and ramjet technology, Lone Star Air was the only provider to have a service to those whose time was measured by millions of dollars per hour.

Sure it was only a two-hour flight, but blasting off and reentry were always tough on the body. Taking those kinds of Gs, even if it was a public craft, took a lot out of you and especially since they would be pulling the same Gs on the way back in another twelve hours. They all knew they needed to get Premier Zuan on their side or they were going to have a hard time with the assembly.

They were escorted into the main boardroom where Premier Zuan was seated with his Vice Premier Chua and the Minister of Energy Baoto as well as the oil, coal, and gas secretaries. The hall was completely covered in rich dark mahogany with pictures of their accomplishments as an economic superpower. The Workers Party posters had long been torn down and replaced with pictures of skyscrapers and giant dams and factories. The Mao jackets had been replaced with some of the finest silk suits designed by the best tailors in the world. The fit and hand tailoring were benefits from having nearly free skilled labor. Premier Zuan came around from the table to greet his guests as their hospitality was still an important part of their business culture.

"Welcome, Mr. Moses, Mr. Drake, and Mr. Scott, thank you for coming, we are honored. I hope your flight went well. Sometime, you will have to let me fly in your shuttle, such a great advancement since it takes us twelve hours to fly to Texas, and that is with a tailwind. Please have a seat. Can we get you something to eat? You must be hungry, and we cooked a special meal for our friends. We had our chefs make some lobsters and Chinese dishes you should enjoy."

Steven smiled and responded, "Thank you so much, Premier Zuan. We are honored to be here, and we have become good friends over the few years we have known you and your cabinet. We value our relationship and are determined to continue to have you as one of our largest consumers of our petroleum products. We understand your dependence on us and our dependence on you as a supplier of commercial products to Texas.

"As you are aware, the United Nations are continuing talks to begin forcing us to pay to their world fund as well as become regulated by their energy commissions. If this were to happen, we would see our production costs go up dramatically as well as being regulated into not being able to produce our resources as efficiently as we can today. This would possibly curtail our production and not allow us to be as reliable as we are now. These and other issues are our concerns for our business relationship and are hoping you will help stop this from happening with your veto vote on the security council.

"As you know, cost effective and reliable energy is a primary need for the world economies. If they were to force us to raise prices or curtail production, it would not only hurt us but you and every other world customer. Your country and people have benefited as much as any on a reliable supply of relatively low-priced oil products. We are hoping you will help us put pressure on the United Nations not to impose these restrictions on Texas and our production."

Premier Zuan looked at Steven and smiled. "Mr. Moses, Mr. Drake, and gentlemen, as you know, we have been very satisfied with our relationship. We provide the world with our goods, and to produce those items, we not only need a cost-effective labor charge but unlimited and low-priced dependable energy. We have lots of electrical energy with our coal plants, which are very powerful and clean and have many available mines in our country, but we do not have oil and gas in the amounts we need and those you supply. We are pleased with our services from Moses Oil as you have been able to produce below the rest of the world producers. This has been a good relationship between our two countries.

"Unfortunately, we are strong members in the United Nations and agree with most of what they are doing for the world. We have seen too much starving and poverty around the world, which leads to riots and wars. There is much work that could be done if we were all pulling the cart together rather than separately to pull those poor countries out of their misery and help them to become more self-sufficient. If the Republic of Texas were to help pull this cart, there is no limits to the potential the world would have.

"My economic minister has also informed me that another one of our aluminum companies is relocating to the Republic of Texas and was one of our stronger companies employing over a thousand workers. We have some very powerful coal plants that have a very low cost to produce electricity, but they cannot compete with your NatGas plants since you basically get it for free as a byproduct of producing oil and your abundant fracked gas resources. This is very concerning to us that you can take our businesses from us simply because you produce gas cheaper than we can produce coal.

"At this point, we cannot sign a long-term agreement for our oil needs into the future. We will honor our agreements for the remainder of this quarter but will wait for the decision of the United Nations on how we want to do business into the future. We are receiving offers from other oil producers and will be comparing with them what they will be available to provide from their schedules and pricing. We are not saying we will not be using your energy in the future, but we would highly advise you to cancel your contract with the aluminum company as well as becoming a member of the UN. Until both of those issues are resolved, we really have nothing to discuss."

Steven waited to let the words sink in before he spoke, "Premier Zuan, I certainly understand your concerns about the competition we are to you and the rest of the world. I also understand your loyalty to the United Nations as you have been a member since its formation. What I do not understand is why you would expect us to damage our own country and markets to satisfy some world government, which, as you know, is filled with corruption and back-scratching deals. We have been against their overreach since we declared our independence, and we see nothing that has changed or altered our opinion.

"Premier Zuan and ministers, we believe every country and industry needs to be able to compete on an equal field where the best and most efficient producers will win the day. We believe the only way you can do that is through the free market and an openly capitalistic form of government. In that environment, the human spirit is able to grow and develop to innovate and create in a healthy competition to produce the best product possible. As these products and people's ideas compete against each other, the technology and products get better and better forcing products to reach their full potential in both quality and cost.

"Premier, you need to grant your people and designers the freedom to grow their capabilities for their betterment. Your people have been enslaved to a top-down mentality rather than a bottom-up creativity. You need to show the courage to allow your people the freedom to become more entrepreneurial rather than being nothing more than living breathing machines. I know that may be an exaggeration, but you get the point of what I am saying. Why don't you take your first space shuttle ride with us tonight? There are a couple extra seats and you can visit Texas and see how freedom and a truly free market works and how it could work in your country."

"You don't understand our country or our people, Mr Moses. We were centuries old when you were just settling Texas, and our people are a proud and determined culture. We need a strong government structure to bring the different cultures together. We have been a one-party government for nearly a century, which has cleaned our country of the corruption and has helped make us more efficient than we were even five years ago."

"With all due respect, Premier Zuan, you still have so much top-down interference that your industries have a hard time competing in the free market unless you force your workers to produce below their worth. For instance, you were talking about your coal energy plants producing the lowest-cost energy of any industrial country, but you mark up the cost to your industries a thousand percent to bring revenue into your government. If you were staying competitive to the market, you would mark it up no more than double or triple and still generate good revenues allowing your industries to become profitable.

"Rather than stifling your businesses and people to generate revenues for Beijing, allow them to grow and expand the economy for everybody, including the government that is what takes courage. Why don't you clear your schedule and come see capitalism and the free market at work and take your first trip outside the atmosphere to personally experience the very best way to travel ever developed?"

"That is a very tempting offer, Mr Moses, and I see how you became the man you are. Okay, I will take my first ride in your space shuttle. Let me make the arrangements and call my wife. I will meet you at Lone Star Air in two hours."

"Thank you, Premier Zuan, we will have you back here tomorrow evening, and you will have the ride of your life even if it is for only a couple hours. If Mrs. Zuan would like to come, bring her along, and we will show her some Texas hospitality. Has she had real Texas barbecue?"

THE STORM BUILDS

Secretary General Polentas never liked waiting for anybody even when it was for a United States president. The flight down from New York was uneventful for her and her counsel other than the usual disturbances you see once you hover outside of the compound. She could see the gangs rampaging the neighborhoods and violence of the people who could not afford to move away. It did seem there were more people hanging from the lampposts than normal. They had their usual handmade execution signs attached to them; there were two bankers, a stockbroker, an oil trader, and a pastor with what looked like his family all hanging like human crosses. They were all guilty of various crimes against their community. The odd thing she had never seen was three were hanged on one lamppost, and they all had "Gangster" attached to their chests and NYTR under the word. Was there some sort of battle starting between the rival gangs?

Flying into Washington, DC, was more of the same, only the police had it pushed out a bit farther than New York had. When will these Americans ever understand that we all need to work together to make this work for everyone?

President Chambers's secretary Ann Fletcher entered the room. She was an attractive middle-aged woman with brownish-blond, shoulder-length hair woven into a tight French weave. She looked like she might be of Irish descent, obviously well put together with her tan business suit and knee-length skirt, highlighting her attractive figure. "President Chambers and the congressional leaders are ready to see you. Is there anything you would like, Secretary General Polentas?"

"No, thank you, Ms. Fletcher, please just show me the way."

Secretary Fletcher led her and to a West Wing conference room with a long table, which had the president at the head and his cabinet and congressional leaders on the right side of the table. The atmosphere was tense as everybody knew the secretary general was there to make sure there was cooperation with their upcoming talks on the Texas resolution.

President Chambers rose and came around the table to greet her. "Hello, Secretary General, welcome to the White House. I hope you didn't a long wait as we were having some extensive discussions and hope you will understand. Have a seat at the head of the table and let's get right to business."

"Thank you, President Chambers, Vice President, cabinet members, and congressional leaders. We are so glad to be here at this time. Washington, DC, is so beautiful this time of year. I truly understand why you are so proud of your historic city. I used to visit this city when I was a child with my father when he was an ambassador and just loved all the monuments and parks that make this city so special.

"As you all know, we are working on a resolution ensuring the Republic of Texas will become a full member of the United Nations. There is no reason for them to continue to use and exploit all of the infrastructure and protection the United Nations provide and not have to share in the payment of those benefits. They have the free and safe passage of their products to and from ports of origin to their port facilities and pay no duties or fees for those services. They trade on our markets and use our banking arrangements as well as all of our international armies and currencies and pay nothing to our United Nations funds. We have allowed it, since for a certain time from their secession, we agreed with you that they needed time to establish their industries, but now they are the most prosperous nation in the world and in large part, thanks to our infrastructure, we have provided for their marketplace.

"Everybody knows they have contributed nothing to the International Military Fund or contributed troops for our peacekeeping missions around the world, giving them the stability to conduct their business. This gives them a distinct advantage in their markets by not having to pay the investments the rest of the world is paying to keep up the infrastructure, aid programs, and peacekeeping forces, which is unfair to the world. If we and you have to purchase their products, then they should contribute to the world we have made for them to operate which is why UN Resolution 2022-311 has been proposed."

President Chambers adjusted his seat forward and interrupted, "Madame Secretary, everyone here is in agreement with everything you have said and support the concepts you are proposing. Texas has enjoyed a free ride on the backs of the rest of the world with their unregulated exploitation of the earth and all of its precious minerals and energy products. We, too, believe it is time for Texas to contribute their fair share to maintain all of the world government infrastructure and security they use to produce and promote their economy. We think there are going to be some issues they may resist since they are so stuck in their ways of free enterprise and capitalism without government intrusion. Do you plan to enforce the UN World Environmental Agency regulations on them, and will you have UN officials there to verify that enforcement?"

"Well, of course, President Chambers, the World Environmental Agency is all that is protecting our air and water to make sure it is healthy to drink and clean air to breath. The agency has evidence they have been using unapproved technology for their industries and are polluting well beyond the levels we have mandated as safe. So of course, we would to need to monitor their emissions like every other UN member to maintain and validate those emissions. It is simply to not only protect the earth's air and water but to level the playing field for the other nations. We are proud to say last year was the most pollution-free per capita throughout the world, thanks in large part to the World Environmental Agency and their enforcement agencies."

Vice President Victoria Price spoke up, "Madame Secretary, we certainly understand the need for the WEA and the wonderful accomplishments they have made around the world to help save our precious environment. You also have to understand the precarious position we are in being a former country with them as well as our necessity to use and maintain their power generation. Energy Secretary Phillips has made a detailed study over the past year and has found we are purchasing forty-five percent of our energy from Texas, and if they were to cut us off, we would have an immediate power blackout as our power substations would fall like dominoes across the country. We have an antiquated transmission system that loses over ten percent of what we produce or buy in the transmission of our energy through the grid. Obviously, New York would also be affected, so do you have any suggestions how we can replace their production?"

"I understand your concerns, Vice President Price, and we have some of the same concerns having our headquarters in New York, so we have made some concessions into the agreement. We have contracted both Canada and Mexico to use them as alternative providers. They have agreed to call for emergency rationing of their countries to supply you an additional ten percent each. We can also pass an emergency war waver to lift the mothballed coal-fired plants on a temporary basis until the potential crisis is over. This should give you enough energy to maintain your own emergency rationing to maintain the grid to keep the basic services and governments as well as the strategic industries for at least six months. We do have some concerns about more unrest as there would be more shortages, but the added revenues would bring more prosperity to the world."

"Excuse me, Secretary Polentas," Vice President Price responded. "It will take months to acquire the necessary coal and recommission one of those aging plants. We closed those coal mines years ago, and bringing it from the Chinese miners in the West would cost too much. We need a more immediate solution, or we could have massive blackouts."

President Chambers replied, "We have our concerns about the security and peace of our country. As you know, we already are having security and gang problems inside our cities with multiple lynchings and violence and really don't know how much more chaos we can withstand. Six months is a long period of time for us to watch this continue to collapse before we can expect any recovery. We would obviously not have to go through this and would like you to convince Texas to agree without any military action. If you take military action, we would want it to be a very short event to begin to recover. Have you addressed the economic and labor issues they would need to address to become a member of the UN?"

"We will have to address their lack of labor representation in their workforce. They will have to have to accept fair and equal labor laws as well as maintaining a department of labor fairness to make sure they have a fair and equitable living wage and all the living benefits that go along with those laws. They also will have to report to the UN economic fairness panel to share their technologies as well as equalize their contracts with our member countries. By our estimation, they are completely out of balance with the UN economic rules and regulations."

Senate Leader Dalton Young spoke up, "As you know, Madame President, they are also out of compliance with the UN hate speech resolutions by maintaining numerous churches, which discriminate against homosexuality and women's rights as well as other intolerant dialog and would like to know how you would address those issues?"

"Of course, Senator Dalton, and congratulations on your daughter's election. We would have to have them agree that their church leaders take a more tolerant stance to their extremist rhetoric like they do in the US and other countries. Unfortunately, some of those pastors have had to be jailed or relieved of their duties for their insistence to defy our resolutions. We have made some progress since the Bible ban and may have to institute that, of course, to maintain the peace. They will find in short order these adjustments will make for a more civil and respectful dialog both inside and outside their churches. We still have some resistance, but for the most part, the churches have learned to moderate their messages to become more tolerant of other people's freedom of lifestyle.

"We would like to invite President Chambers to speak in front of the UN General Assembly in preparation for the writing and issuance of the Texas Acceptance Resolution 2022-311 two weeks from this Friday and have invited President Stewart and his delegation to also speak before the assembly. Nobody is going to say we didn't give them every opportunity to make their case."

June Darling opened her e-mail to chat with her father when she saw a high-priority mark. It read: June Bug I received this e-mail from someone I don't know and thought you may be interested in seeing it:

Pastor Darling, I call myself the Texas Ranger, and I need some help advancing the name of Jesus. I have scrambled my destination so you can't get in touch with me and more important, neither can the United Nations. I belong to a group called the Texas Christ Church of New York, and we are taking back our church and America. We sell Bibles on the black market and need more than we have available. We are importing them and have a very large and growing network of Christians wanting their Bibles back, and we are able to smuggle them to the closed churches.

We have also formed a peacekeeping group that is taking back New York City one neighborhood at a time. We have caught, tried, and convicted a number of gangsters who have been punished accordingly. We need somebody to help us acquire Bibles, but just as important, we need someone to get our message out to America and the world without risking their own lives. We know your daughter is a very-well respected journalist in Texas and would like to have her publish our story and let people know we are out here. Can you help us? I will call tomorrow night at eight your time if you can help me please answer so we can talk.

June returns:

> Daddy, please have him contact me, it may add to my new research project.
>
> Love, June Bug

The flight back was uneventful for Steven, but Premier Zuan had the ride of his life. He was sweating like a convicted man walking to the gallows on takeoff, but when he went weightless, he began playing like a five-year-old boy. He wanted to know everything there was about the flight and how fast they were crossing time zones around the world. He had everybody spin him and floated from one end of the shuttle and back. He had them spin him in somersaults till he got a bit dizzy before the descent started. He even got strapped in with the pilots on the landing while seeming to have a smile chiseled into his face. He apologized that his wife Laoa wouldn't come since she said she was too afraid to ride the shuttle and tried to talk him out of it, but nobody could do that.

On landing, he came over to Steven and shook his hand while bowing. "Thank you, Mr. Moses, that was a thrill of a lifetime. It was everything you said it was and more—what a flight! I felt like I weighed a ton on the liftoff, and the speed the shuttle could travel was so surprising, and then within minutes, you are weightless. To see the world from space and looking out into space with all the stars and moon was something I will never forget. Then to finish it off, you reenter in a ball of fire as you fall like a rock from over a hundred miles up, leaving your stomach in space was terrifying yet exhilarating. I almost vomited on the way down, but the thrill was more than I ever imagined. What a ride, Mr. Moses, you have an unbelievable aircraft!"

"Call me, Steve, Premier," he said as he handed him an "18,000 MPH Club" shirt. "Yes, it is quite a bit of technology, but it serves a very valuable purpose as a time saver for us. We needed to be able to travel back and forth to your capital on a regular basis, which would normally take three days minimum and a recovery time of another two days. That is a full week for people who are making multibillion-dollar transactions day in and day out.

We realized a long time ago we could not afford taking those people out of circulation for those lengths of time so one of the first things we did when we became a country was to develop faster and faster methods of flight until we were able to travel anywhere in the world in three hours. Once we were able to combine the technology advancements with fuel development, we had a commercial rocket shuttle that was ready for public use. This made business sense as well as a flight like no other. That is what capitalism and ingenuity does for the economy and society. Let's take the corporate hover limo, and I will give you the tour of our company and south Texas."

They took the short walk over to the Moses hangars where the eight-man limousine and pilot were waiting to take them on the tour of Moses Industries. It was a sleek craft, which was simply a luxury limousine built to fly at over three hundred knots from site to site while talking with your guests. It had good speed and power yet was quiet as an empty church inside. The pilot loaded the premier's luggage into the trunk and gave him the copilot seat, which had the best view of the ground while speaking to him on the headphones. Once the passengers were on board, he started the hover jets, lifting them to height before the turbo thrusters fired and headed them toward the port facilities.

Steven looked out as the south Houston coast came into view and the oil port covered the horizon. "Premier, this is our main port where we receive the inbound oil tankers as well as your outbound gas and oil mixtures that come from and go to every country in the world. These tankers will go through our expanded Panama Canal, which we have widened and expanded into two-way traffic for more efficiency. There are normally around a hundred tankers coming or leaving this area at any given time with no accidents over the past twenty years. Tankers are able to arrive and load or unload at one of these in port or offshore terminals in less than three hours.

"As we travel inland, you can see our refineries, which are the largest and most efficient anywhere in the world. Our oil cracking separators are producing at rates double the world average, each one cracking a tankers worth of oil every fifty minutes. This process produces enormous volumes of natural gas, enough to supply the world's needs every day, which we have converted into the electrical generation you were asking me about in our meeting. Yes, we have very low costs for our electricity as a byproduct of our oil production.

"As you look down, you will see over five hundred NatGas electrical generation plants. We not only produce enough electricity for all of Texas but sell our excess to the United States and is a large part of why we paid back our loan before it was done. We are continually investing in more plants and grid infrastructure to give us the lowest cost energy of any country around the world. We are very close to having the ability to send electricity across the ocean floor through high density submariner cables that could reach Europe with very little bleed loss. We know you have the second lowest cost, but as we talked in your meeting with your corruption and province costs, those low prices for coal power are lost . Imagine if you were able to expand your low-cost energy and send it to Japan, Korea, and the Middle East?

"Now, down below us is our high-energy usage manufacturers such as aluminum, steel, aircraft, computer, and strategic metals production. These companies are not a part of Moses Industries but are located here due to the low cost and short transmission of our power plants. They receive discounted energy rates during the off-peak hours or seasons helping both their production costs and the energy companies using the surplus energy. These companies have found not only a low cost of energy but our low tax rates gives them a cost advantage very few countries can offer. They have fled from the high-tax countries like the United States or the European Union to set up shop here just as they do in China."

"I understand completely, Steve Moses, you are taking many of our companies who are able to lower costs the same way they have come to our country in the past. This, of course, is of concern to us since you have an advantage of not having to pay the United Nations funds that the rest of us pay."

"Premier, I understand your concerns. However, we would work much better as partners rather than competitors on these issues. We can help you build your economy in a more free market framework rather than the communist model you are following now. This will make you more competitive as you learn efficiencies in your industries. You know as well as I do that you are not getting what you are paying for with the United Nation taxes. We can help you take advantage of the natural technological advancements the free and unfettered ingenuity that comes from the entrepreneurial spirit.

Once you take the controls off the human spirit, they are free to try new ideas and let the power of trial and error to develop new and advanced technologies that can compete in the marketplace. As you can see across the Texas horizon, there is business after business, all producing goods and services for both the local economy and the world's. Every one of these started as somebody's idea or dream and is his way of reaching his dream without interference of an overregulating and frankly corrupt government. You will not see this anywhere else in the world, and just look how well it is working with your own eyes."

They flew over hundreds of miles of businesses, watching trucks running every direction as evidence of commerce being transacted by the invisible dance of capitalism. This dance has been going on for centuries; however, now it was playing to its own music and the results spoke for themselves. The only thing that appeared constant was the activity and the growing miles of businesses on the edges of the horizon. The pilot banked the limo jet to the east as they headed to the Moses Tower where some Texas-sized brisket and baby back ribs were being prepared for their most honored guest.

Steven welcomed Premier General Zuan with a few words of tribute to the Chinese leader and finished with, "Premier Zuan, we hope you will become our partner in the new world we are building with our free market model. It has brought prosperity to more countries and people than any other economic system. Tonight, though we hope to show you how Texas is truly famous for two things, oil and barbecue, and as chef Holt says, his baby backs will make you want to slap your grandma they're so good! Welcome to Moses Tower and enjoy your stay."

Premier Zuan looked confused by the translation but saw the crowd laughing; he joined along as he was handed a black cowboy hat and alligator boots with the state of Texas engraved on them to try on. After he was dressed up for real Texas barbecue, he was grinning from ear to ear.

"Hello, is this professor Darling?"

"Yes, who is this?"

"Hi, Professor Darling, I call myself the New York Texas Ranger and your father, Pastor Darling, gave me your headset number. He said you would be expecting my call and gave your permission to talk to me and hear our story."

"Yes, I did, but why all the secrecy and why is your number scrambled, showing a Brazilian identifier?"

"You don't understand, Professor, we are some of the most wanted people in the United States and especially in New York. We are considered enemies of America and the UN police for smuggling Bibles into the United States. We can be jailed for ten years for spreading hate. We are one of the fastest-growing underground organizations with some of the most talented people in New York, so we can communicate very well to the outside by scrambling our locations. We are a closed group and are continually on the move, so it is very hard for the government police to find or capture us. This is also a safety measure for you as my voice is altered as is the background noise to throw off the authorities who will be able to locate this in less than four minutes."

"Sounds very James Bond, but I suppose I understand since you are technically breaking the law by smuggling Bibles and running an underground church. Why did you choose me to tell your story?"

"One of the main reasons is, you are from Texas where you still have freedom of the press. If I were to tell my story to a journalist here, they would be required to report us to the police if they weren't already working for the government to help find churches. We have read your stories, and we see you give free market economics and businesses a fair voice, so we wanted to give you our story and thought you would report it accurately.

"We have been a movement for nearly three years and are the largest organized church in New York. We are selling over two million Bibles a year on the black market as well as all types of outlawed or restricted items. This has given us a strong monetary position that has helped us in our latest movement while fighting the gangs and sweeping the streets of these murderers. We have set up a neighborhood police force which is taking back the streets one block at a time.

"You have to understand what it is like to live in New York nowadays. The city has become a human jungle where survival is New Yorkers' single thought from minute to minute. The gangs control the neighborhoods, and they are always fighting over territory and control of the black markets.

"Anybody who can't afford to get out of the city or is not a member of a gang is going to be a victim of the gangs to be robbed, raped, or killed. They have targeted capitalists such as bankers or stock brokers as criminals who they lynch as a warning to others. They consider making money a crime against the community. There are no safe places left in New York anymore, and especially at night, it becomes a survival zone.

"There are a number of gangs, and the police are all owned by them, so they have free reign to terrorize the people. They control the streets through violence and intimidation as well as taking protection money from all the businesses that are paid to the unions. The strongest gang is the Dockworkers who control all the gangs through a complex network. We aren't exactly sure where they get their funding and weapons, but they seem to have a connection with the government. We're trying to figure out their connections, although we suspect they are directly or indirectly controlled by the UN.

"They use their intimidation tactics to threaten and kill anybody who stands in their way or attempts to stand up to them. They are also in control of the banking and finance, and if anyone crosses them, they will soon end up on hanged from a lamppost, and then one of the gangs' people will be taking over their position, which keeps them in a constant state of terror willing to do whatever the gangs demand.

"Many of the rebel gangs are simply anarchists who will go in and murder families for whatever reason they consider a hanging offense. The bankers and finance people as well as Christians have been so vilified they are often killed for little or no apparent reason. The gangs consider all types of violence an open season on anybody who crosses them, and the common citizens are simply available for their convenience to rob, beat, or rape for whatever reason they deem an offense.

"If a girl is raped on the street and reports a protected gang to the police, her family will be lynched within days. You don't cross the gangs and especially the Dockworkers. This is who we have been targeting for our own retribution. We have our own courts with witnesses and a defense but if we capture them it is for a reason.

"We have started a Christian group called the Texas Christ Church, which is beginning to fight the gangs and bring justice to the neighborhoods. We are growing quickly as the victims are looking for safety in numbers as well as a small revival moving across the city from people looking for something to hold onto in Jesus Christ. Our members are all wanted criminals by the gangs since we have fought them in numerous neighborhoods and have tried and punished many in their own manner.

"We have been smuggling Bibles into the city, which has the police and authorities trying to stop it and put us in jail. Those of us who have been jailed are usually turned over to the gangs and hanged with the others being shipped to prison camps around the country. It is a dangerous job and larger than we can succeed in doing, but we believe we are making a difference, and we have some Texas Church neighborhoods where the gangs have been thrown out and have agreed to leave them be, so there are some victories we are seeing block by block.

"We are hoping you will tell our story and let the world know what is going on in New York. We don't know everything but are finding out more and more every day as our movement grows.

We have our suspicions of what the structure of these gangs are, but nothing is confirmed. We are hoping you will report it as we find things out and will be our voice to the outside world."

"Thanks, Ranger, I would be happy to send your story to syndication. Your timing is amazing since I have just accepted a project that will mirror with your story from another angle to expose what is happening in New York. There are winds blowing that are going to affect both New York and Texas, and I want to report the entire story including yours. I look forward to talking to you in the future. Good-bye."

"Good-bye, Professor Darling."

TEXAS RESPONDS

Terry was leading a group of four hover jets along the border, looking for any signs of crossings by the aircraft that shot him down. He was laid up in the hospital for four weeks recovering from his injuries. Fortunately, the crash beacon went off, and thanks to the quick action of the medic craft, he was able to get to the emergency room in time to save his life. Texas has the best hospitals and doctors on the planet, and his recovery from his injuries were simply more evidence to him. They wanted to keep him longer, but they didn't have strong enough rope to keep him tied down. He wanted to find out who or what was crossing this border.

Texas not only has the best medical system in the world but has some of the most creative medical insurance money can buy. Most Texans have policies like Terry, which is employer-assisted pay plans with higher deductibles and a cafeteria-style benefit program. You can have as many benefits covered or as few, but all of them take care of major medical for catastrophic events. His deductible is partially paid by his employer, and the remainder is paid in a twelve-month payroll deduction plan. This makes sure the doctors and hospitals are paid as well as making it affordable for the patient. After twelve months, everybody is paid, allowing protection for the providers of the health care industry. Doctors enjoy the highest level of medicine through competition and innovation exploring new and intensive specialization. They are able to go wherever their knowledge and training takes them assuring they and their patients are the decision makers of the treatment required. This allows the doctors to explore the frontiers of medical treatments.

In America, if he survived he would have been in a hospital ward for months; however, with the technology and techniques these hospitals have, he was out in only weeks. They wanted him to go a week or two longer, but he was going to get out as soon as he could and wasn't going to let some overprotective quack tell him no.

He really didn't remember much about the crash other than he was flying in the same area as he was before and suddenly was hit by a rogue aircraft that had entered Texan airspace. Why would they be invading Texas? What were they up to, and who was it?

"Rattler to wing, be prepared for a slow hover as we are approaching where I was hit and crashed."

"Roger that, flight leader. Bronco here, do you want us to fly a perimeter as protection or stay close?"

"Roger that, Bronco, scatter and fly a ten-mile perimeter, and Chance will stay on my wing. You both know there have been a few other sightings here so stay on your toes and monitor a hundred miles out."

Terry fluttered to a stationary hover to take a good close look at what remained of his craft. The company had taken most of his hover jet back to the shop for forensics, but it was clear where he had crashed by the blackened brush and ground. He tried to look in the direction he felt he had been fired from and where the invader had come and fled. Nothing was coming to his mind as he cruised over to the north wall to see exactly where the sensors would have been located, trying to find how they were defeated.

Even the latest stealth technology shouldn't have allowed jets to cross undetected, but they did.

Suddenly, his display lit up from an aircraft coming over Mach 2 from the north at three hundred miles and closing. As he tried to focus on a visual, it suddenly dropped off the screen and disappeared. Scanning the horizon, he saw nothing, although there was a contrail being formed by what must have been the jet when it suddenly turned vertical and twisted back north. He strained to see the shape and any markings, but even with his face mask magnification, there was no way to make out exactly what type it was, perhaps a Mirage 2020, but it was impossible to tell. At least he did get an initial track before it disappeared, and perhaps the techs can get an engine match off it, although the chances of that were between slim and none.

—◦◊◦—

The Republic of Texas assembly was loud and filled with congressmen and senators from around the country. Each county had one senator and a congressman for each hundred thousand citizens, and the country was set up exactly like the founders of the United States with their three branches of government. This allowed for balance between the urban and rural areas of Texas giving the republic equal representation. This assembly was the largest event since the secession as the president was going to discuss the upcoming fight against the United Nations resolution 2022-311 and what it would mean to Texans. It was not only being broadcast across Texas but around the world. Even though the president was not a powerful office, he still was the figurehead of the Republic of Texas and would be the person who informed as well as represented the country in nationwide events. In this instance, because this resolution would have such powerful economic ramifications, he asked Steven to speak to the economics of the issue.

The vice president walked in with Steven who sat at the side with Drake and the presidential cabinet. Vice President Chavez approached the lectern. "Ladies and gentlemen, fellow Texans and people watching from around the world, this is not a time we have asked for and would prefer to not have an assembly like this. It is my great honor to introduce President Stewart of the Republic of Texas."

President Stewart entered from the side door in a tailored charcoal suit with black cowboy boots. He looked determined and stoic with his jaw set as he stood behind the podium looking over the crowd as he began, "My fellow Texans, you have worked so hard to bring us to the point we are. This has been the greatest experiment the world has ever seen, going from an energy-producing state in America to forming our own country and, within eight short years, rising to one of the most powerful economies in the world.

"As you know, the United Nations is in the process of writing a resolution that will handicap, if not destroy, this great economic engine, which literally powers the world. We have built this engine through the unleashed power of free market capitalism and freeing the human spirit to turn Texans' dreams into a reality. They have accomplished this since Texas believes it is better to have a healthy environment to grow their businesses than for the government to stand in their way with high taxes and stifling regulations. We believe in sensible taxes to encourage businesses to invest in people and regulations that strike a balance between protection and production. We believe businesses are respected citizens of Texas first and corporations second so they maintain a healthy work environment as well as a healthy business environment. We trust these businesses to watch out for their people and have shown the transparency to look out for their neighbors and neighborhoods.

"We trust in businesses to be honorable managers of their resources and environment, which has provided us with the cleanest most efficient industries on earth. Our businesses are the safest anywhere as their records will attest, which is one of the reasons we have the lowest regulatory costs and government interference, working efficiently for all those involved. This has added to our efficiency, allowing these industries to have the highest compensation of anywhere in the world without the conflict and cost of unions. These and numerous other free market forces lower costs allowing Texas to have some of the most cost effective energy and manufacturing pricing of any producer in the world."

As Steven looked around the assembly, his eyes spotted someone in the balcony toward the back who he had not seen in quite a while. He noticed the wavy strawberry blond hair immediately and could make out she was wearing a white suit and a yellow ribbon in her hair. He suddenly imagined the sweet lilac smell of her perfume she was wearing when he saw her at the university.

"We have been warned we will be expected to pay the standard thirty to 35 percent tax the rest of the new UN members pay. They say it is unfair for us to use the oceans and byways without having to pay for the protection they provide in the commerce lanes. We don't believe we should have to pay those fees and are willing to provide our own protection for those shipping lanes. We believe the shipping lane protection is only a small amount of the funds the UN takes in.

"Too much of their money is used to pay off corrupt governments and wasted for their own unethical activities, which have been documented numerous times. We do not believe in their Marxist ideals of income distribution from the wealthier countries to the poorer. It's simply more of the same socialism we left when we separated from the United States. This is another government redistribution program that takes from the producers and gives to the nonproducing countries. We understand the only reason these poorer countries are struggling is due to corrupt communist governments stealing from their people. This is where they want to send our tax revenues and where we would rather see these governments' corruption cleaned up.

"I could go on about this, but Steven Moses has prepared a report of what this potentially means to the Texan economy and our oil industry. So to speak on the economic factors this would have on our republic, I would like to introduce Steven Moses."

A polite ovation spread across the chamber as Steven walked to the podium with his eyes and jaw set as he looked around the room.

"Ladies and gentlemen of Texas, you know who I am and the industries I represent. We are about to be asked to give up not only a large percentage of our income here in Texas but an equally large amount of our sovereignty. We have built the strongest economy in the world through hard work and innovative development and technology. Our entire economy and country is built on the free flow of oil and our ability to produce it as cost effectively as possible. These taxes will be adding as much as 35 percent to our costs, making our product less competitive to our businesses and industries. This not only punishes Texas but will punish our customers around the world, including the United States, Japan, and China.

"Some will say this is only fair since the rest of the world must pay taxes to the United Nations. The rest of the nations chose to join the UN, and we have chosen not to join and now are being forced to without our free will. We believe all countries should be free to join unions or not join such unions and is a God-given right to individuals, countries, and industries. We see this UN Resolution is restrictive to our freedom and will hamper our sovereignty in numerous ways both economically and socially.

"We have chosen to not have workers unions for the same reason. We believe it stifles a person's ambition and creativity, so we allow workers to vote if they want unions. Repeatedly our workers have freely voted against unions, and the unions no longer try since they know our workers understand the shortcomings of forming unions and accepting mediocrity and watered-down achievement as well as income potential. This is one reason we have the highest productivity and wages of any country in the world.

"Just as on a small level, such as unions you have the same affect with a worldwide union, which stifles a country's ability to compete and achieve under the guise of fairness. Economically, it will affect the oil industry in both the cost and further development of our vital resources. In addition to adding the direct costs of taxes, we will also be subject to strict United Nations regulations over our industries, which will hamper our production and development.

"We have identified over ten thousand regulations that will interfere with the production and refining of oil and gas that will cause production to fall and costs to rise. These costs have projected to increase costs anywhere from eighty to over a 100 percent of current expense. In addition, these regulations will interrupt much of our production and refinement, decreasing our output from 20 to 35 percent, depending on how the laws are interpreted.

"These costs will be passed on to our other industries, which depend on low-priced energy, causing their costs to increase, making their products less competitive on the world market. Many will be forced to move to countries that have lower expenses in other areas to compensate, such as labor or living expenses. This will be a major disruption to our industries and will drive up the costs worldwide for energy and production. The increased prices of oil and gas will affect both costs and supplies on an already stretched commodity, which can potentially drive up demand and prices exponentially to the end users. This is going to be a burden to the entire world and affect the poor nations the worst. The poorer nations are exactly the ones who cannot afford these higher costs on their people, making them even more desperate.

These costs will affect the very people who cannot afford them the worst.

"In Texas, we believe in the freedom of the individual to pursue his dreams and desires without government interference. Whether that means raising a crop of wheat, drilling a well in hopes of hitting it rich, or casting a lure on a lake in hopes of catching a bass, we believe the individual has the right to decide what is best for him. We also believe the ultimate individual is the corporation, which is a collection of individuals pursuing their dreams and desires as an individual entity. The corporation should be free to chase their dreams without the interference of the government but should be allowed to decide what is best for it just as the individual fishing for bass on the lake. Only they know what their own plans and dreams are in their own individual case.

"Finally, we are a Christian society that not only believes in God and Jesus Christ but that our churches have an absolute right to their freedom of worship. We cannot abide to the UN charter, which closes down any church that preaches anything the UN finds offensive or hate speech. We will not allow our pastors and priests to be censored for what they believe no matter how many people may deem their beliefs offensive. Jesus said that the world would find his words offensive and that the world would hate his words. Jesus said to love the sinner but hate the sin while the world wants these churches to tolerate sin and in many instances to celebrate the sin. This goes completely contrary to Jesus' teaching, against our Constitution and denies Texas its religious sovereignty. For these reasons and many more, we recommend this body and Texans to continue to stand against the membership into the United Nations. Thank you, and may God bless Texas."

As Steven turned to sit back down, someone yelled, "Don't mess with Texas!"

A thunderous applause rolled across the chamber as every seat was emptied into a loud standing ovation and a chant of "Don't mess with Texas!" Every corner of the building was standing and chanting as the defiance was made clear, not only in the building but the message was also being sent across Texas and around the world that there was a unity for freedom and sovereignty by the entire country. By this display, the vote was now a mere formality.

Steven looked across the assembly; his eyes went up into the balcony where he could see just the slightest hint of strawberry blondish hair where he knew Professor Darling was standing. It appeared that from what he could see she too was standing and applauding, and for whatever reason that was all that mattered to him at the moment. He knew because of her applause he had said what needed to be said.

He exited the stage before the politicians began the formal debate and votes for the passage of the Texan resolution to reject membership to the United Nations. It was more a formality as congressmen got air time and let their constituents know they were standing up for them. He shook a few hands as he made his way to the door where he met Drake, asking him for a few minutes to go run a quick errand. Walking up the stairs to the balcony, he found the one person he was looking for as she sat transponding notes of the governors' debate.

He tapped her on the shoulder and watched her turn around in surprise and delight. He motioned her into the hallway where they could talk and reacquaint.

"I really liked your speech. It was brief and to the point, but you really spoke for all of us Texans. You not only covered the economics of the issue but the religious aspects of the takeover, which are just as important to our freedom."

"Thank you, June, but that isn't why I came up here?"

"Oh, really, why did you?"

"Well, if you remember, you…ah…owe me a chance to take you to dinner, and I owe you an interview."

He enjoyed the way she turned into her pinkish shade of red as he stumbled on his words. "You mean now, you remembered our last conversation when I couldn't go? I have to cover this event. I mean I am working on this project and—"

"You know as well as I that this is only a formality before they vote unanimously for the resolution, and besides it is going to be recorded for later. You promised me the last time I could take you to dinner, and I have a very special restaurant I think you will like if you enjoy seafood."

"Where, what, I have to go see Senator…oh, wait, what the heck, I do love seafood. When do you get a chance to have dinner with the wealthiest man in the world? Am I being too obvious?"

"No, not at all, grab your things, and I will take you downstairs where I can rearrange my schedule with Drake to take the rest of the afternoon off."

"How did you know I was here? I didn't tell anybody I was coming. I just got my press pass and slipped up here in the balcony so I could record the event. Who told you I was here?"

"You were the only person I saw in the audience. Didn't you notice me staring at you?"

"No, I thought you were just looking at the audience. Let me grab my purse and things then we can go."

She didn't know what to think about this: Steven Moses was treating her more than the mousy professor she was? Why wasn't he going after all those models or high society women who were always around him on TV? Why did she have to wear this old suit she wore a hundred times and her makeup was a mess in this humidity, let alone her hair? Why was her hands shaking? Maybe a quick trip to the ladies' room? Was she asleep or was this real? She pinched her forearm while she gathered her things just to make sure. They took the elevator down to the dignitaries' lounge where David Drake was waiting. He seemed thrilled to see her and was happy to take them back to the office where his private hover jet was waiting.

They changed hover jets, putting her things in the hatch while she got into his new Black Stallion. It was deep black with silver trim while having the streamlined shape of a sports hover that was built primarily for speed and looked like a flying Corvette. It was frightening yet thrilling all at the same time as she settled into the deep seat as the body bars lowered locking her comfortably into place.

"Get ready for takeoff. This one has more speed than most and will be a little bouncy as we accelerate. I want to take you to one of my favorite spots in the gulf."

"Are you sure you know how to fly thi—"

The Black Stallion blasted off by two powerful jets with a stabilizer fan to allow for the hover while the two jets rotated horizontally giving its thrust and power. She felt herself pushed straight back in the seat and could no longer feel the body bars on her chest from the force of the acceleration. She felt a sense of terror and thrill all at the same time as she hoped he was able to fly this as well as he seemed.

Once they reached cruising speed and altitude, she was treated to one of the most spectacular views of the gulf she had ever seen. They were flying straight south over the water, and she could see the sun lowering toward the water reflecting to the east, casting the skies into a blue-pink warmth, lighting the horizon into a pinkish-blue rainbow. They were flying at dizzying speeds as Steven quickly proved he was an accomplished pilot, pointing out the different landmarks and oil derricks spread across the gulf. He would drop down every once in a while to point out a certain landmark as he gave her a tour of his workplace as they talked about the day's events.

After an hour, they turned east, and she could see islands and derricks as well as ships coming and going as they screamed across the gulf at speeds she had no idea existed in hover jets even though this one made almost no noise while he played some very nice gospel jazz on the sound system while she tried to take it all in.

"How fast are we going?"

"We are just a little over the sound barrier about 760 miles per hour."

"Can you tell me where we are going yet?"

"It's a nice little restaurant in the Keys that has some of the best seafood in the gulf."

"Oh my, a restaurant in the Florida Keys. I guess it was worth the wait since I only took you to the Longhorn Bristo, and you are taking me to the Keys! Do they allow peanut shells on the floor like the Longhorn? You are sure not very good at making trades."

He looked at her with a wink and laughed. "Oh, I don't know about that, seems a fair trade from my eyes," making her smile and blush.

She responded, "You really like embarrassing me, don't you?" making them both laugh.

She sat back and enjoyed the beautiful view of the gulf as he flew in a meandering flight, pointing out more sights and islands as the sun sank lower into the west. Then he said, "Here we are, the world-famous Platform 276!"

He brought the hover jet over the platform of an abandoned oil derrick 150 miles southwest of the Keys. It was rebuilt into a nautical-theme covered with Greek statues between jumping dolphins. There were around thirty hover jets parked on the deck and at least that many boats tied up to the docks around the base of the derrick. She noticed a chartered fishing service on the far end of the derrick that looked like it had a half a dozen boats. There was a huge sailfish over the entryway of the elevator. He escorted her to the entrance, which was a glass elevator taking them straight down into the sea where there was a glass-enclosed restaurant on the floor of the gulf, which was the shape of a sunken submarine.

The windows were over foot thick but were crystal clear, and you could see fish swimming in every direction around a nautical scene that resembled the Greek Acropolis. The ocean was lit up with a backdrop of a wall of bubbles while there were schools of every type of multicolored fish swimming around from groupers, tuna, to schools of shrimp, creating a colorful kaleidoscope of sea life, making a ever moving seascape. The floor was covered with lobsters, crabs, and clams sitting on coral outcroppings. The fish were being fed by multiple divers in different colored neon suits with trained dolphins swimming through the scene herding the different schools of fish through a series of tunnels and arches. It was as if they were at the bottom of a giant aquarium. This had to be the most charming and beautiful place she had ever been.

"How did you find out about this place?"

He just laughed and said, "You forget, I've lived my entire life on the gulf oil rigs, and I sold this one to the owner. Here he is now. Terrance Jasmine, you have any fresh fish? I want to introduce you to my lovely friend, June Darling."

Terrance Jasmine was a large black man who had a wide girth and an even wider smile with a shaved head with two laughing brown eyes. He was a Creole from New Orleans who grew up in the Cajun restaurants and learned to cook and brought his family recipes to their customers who became followers of his uniquely spicy seafood, chowder, and gumbo. By the time he was thirty, he had his own restaurant, and within three years, he had one of the busiest places in the French Quarter. That is when he had the idea for the Platform restaurant on the bottom of the gulf.

"Welcome to the Submariner Restaurant, Ms. Darling, you are aptly named, how did you end up with this long tall drink of water? A beautiful lady like you can do a lot better than him!" His laugh filled the room.

"I saw your speech tonight, Moses, and what an inspiration. You gave those UN dictators a piece of your mind and told them who and what Texas is about. Makes me wish I built this off Texas with the rest of you freedom lovers, but unfortunately, I have too much invested here, and you can't just move an oil derrick. Tonight, my brother with another color, whatever you want is on me!"

"Thank you so much, my dear friend, but I insist on paying. Anybody who can cook swordfish like you deserves to be rewarded for it, besides who is going to pay the divers? They all look a bit skinny!"

Terrance's face lit up and he laughed. "Well, even God knows you can afford it, my friend. Come sit down and let me make you the best meal you two have ever tasted. Now, Ms. Darling, tonight the diet is off, I am going to fix you some food that when you taste it you will wish you were fat like me. My momma was the best cook in N'Orleans, and she taught me everything she knew. Welcome!"

June enjoyed the fun teasing and responded, "You don't have to worry about me. My daddy is a preacher, and he told me two things: you don't order fish in Omaha or order steak in New Orleans. I think I will have the swordfish and gumbo."

"Ah, Cheri can eat and laugh! I like her already. You better grab this one, Mr. Moses, before she spits the hook. She is what we say in the Keys, a woman with a spirit that ignites your soul."

Now Steven became a bit tongue-tied. "There you go, my friend, that is what I have kept telling her, but she just won't hear of it. She seems to think we have to get to know each other or something? I just think she's waiting for something better to come by."

June just sat down and smiled contently.

"I'm sorry if we embarrassed you."

"Not at all, taking me here is amazing. Terrance really is a sweetheart, and he has a really special restaurant. How often can you say you have eaten seafood with the fishes on the bottom of the ocean?"

"Not very often, this is one of the best-kept secrets in the gulf and one of the hardest restaurants to get to. We are a 150 miles southwest of the Keys, and the only way to get here is by air or boat, and it is always filled. People who have found out about Platform 276 come back as often as they can. Not only is it a unique dining experience seventy feet underwater, but Terrance is one of the best chefs anywhere. What more could you ask for?"

Their waitress arrived at their table with the first course of seaweed wrapped shrimp and scallops, spicy calamari, crayfish tails along with some Creole bread, and a cup of jambalaya with garlic croutons. She spoke in a thick Jamaican accent, "Hello, my name be Charlene, your waitress for the evening. Mr. Terrance says to enjoy our specialty for an appetizer, which is our submariner seafood starter. He says to enjoy the chowder and your fresh swordfish will be swimming by shortly."

June laughed as she left and looked at Steven in a serious manner. "Steven, I have to tell you something. I recently received a grant at the university to write a paper about this battle between Texas and the UN, and I wanted you to know about it."

"Really? That is amazing and, what perfect timing. Texas needs someone to explain our side of the story and we understand the New York and world media will only tell the UN side and make us out to be the villains. We need someone to professionally document these historic events. Maybe you can turn it into a book? How did you get this opportunity, and should I be careful what I say around you from now on?"

She laughed at that. "No, of course not. This is going to be an academic record of our history and documenting the events as they occur. The university approached me to do this since a company donated enough to cover my sabbatical and expenses. That is the reason I was at the speech today and had no idea you would see me from the stage, let alone come up and find me. Did your company give the grant to the university?"

"I have no idea. If you are asking if I paid it, the answer is no, but I have no idea if Moses Industries or one of the affiliates did since that is not part of my responsibilities or knowledge. Although I do enjoy the idea of having you writing this paper and having you around, it certainly brightens up the room."

"Haha! Aren't you clever, Steven Moses? How serious do you think the UN is about forcing you to join the Union?"

"I have no idea, but you know they are going to push it as far as they can to get the tax dollars. They are having serious financial and worldwide control problems due to the ongoing recession, so they are going to attempt to get us to join. Whether they are willing to use military options to make that happen is anyone's guess, I pray they don't. What do you think?"

"Me? Why does it matter what I think, I have nothing to do with this."

"Apparently you do, and who could possibly know more about the subject than you right now? I want to know what you think will happen."

"Well, if you need to know. I think they will push it to the military solution and make Texas submit to their authority. They have too much to lose if you were to successfully stand up to them. What would stop other countries from breaking away from their control and taxing authority if you defied them and succeeded? I think this is a very dangerous situation and is one of the main reasons I want to write about it. This may be the final battle between capitalism and communism, and we have no idea how it will turn out. This is the ultimate dream for a journalist to record a great battle between two economic theories. Who could ask for more?"

"That is the main reason you want to write about this? I feel slighted. Now look at us here, we are at one of the most romantic restaurants in the world, and all we do is talk about the potential end of the world. Don't you like the surroundings or the company? Did anybody tell you your eyes sparkle like green pearls underwater?"

Her face lit up, and the twinkle in her eyes brightened in their intensity. He had not felt like this since Sandy and he were dating in college. Why does she remind him so much of Sandy, and how is he falling so fast and so hard?

"I bet you use that line on all the girls you bring here," she said teasingly.

"Nope, the only other girl I brought here is my executive secretary, and it was with the entire board of directors, so I never got a chance to use it. Not to mention her husband would likely made hamburger of me if I did. I really am glad you came here, and I really enjoy when we have time together. And yes, I know we barely know each other, but it just seems like we have known each other longer than we have."

June smiled a very warm smile as her eyes reignited and simply said, "Yes, I know, I feel the same way."

Charlene returned with Terrance and their dinners of swordfish stuffed with rock crab served on rice pilaf and garnished with lemon, mango, and parsley served on a banana leaf. It smelled and looked absolutely mouth-watering. Terrance walked over and said, "I hope this dish proves to you, Cheri, you're not eating fish in Omaha."

"Terrance, Jasmine, this doesn't look anything like Omaha, and you proved that my daddy was wise beyond his years."

Terrance laughed and clapped his hands as the lights inside dimmed to candlelight as multicolored bubbles began falling from the ceiling and the stage lights on the Greek stage brightened. The divers began line dancing to the "Yellow Rose of Texas" while the dolphins with saddles on them were doing an intricate choreography swimming in and out of the columns as stage was immersed with the multicolored schools of fish. As the song ended, the divers all lined up with neon sign boards reading, "Don't mess with Texas!

Terrance just laughed and loudly said, "Ladies and gentlemen, I would like you all to welcome my good friend and Texan, Steven Moses and his lovely guest, Professor June Darling." The restaurant erupted as the diners stood in unison to give them an ovation.

June leaned over to Steven and whispered, "Is it always this friendly down here?"

RESOLUTION 2022-311

Secretary General Polentas sat at the head of the conference table with her cabinet as they prepared for the Texas Conference coming the following week. She was wearing a cream-colored business suit with a large eagle broach on the left side of her chest. Her cabinet consisted of the ambassadors to Nigeria and Iran, as well as Great Britain, the United States, Canada, Germany, Russia, Japan, and China. There were another fifteen countries sitting in virtual seats who could not attend.

She opened the meeting, "United Nations ambassadors, thank you for your time. I am so glad to have you attend this very important meeting. As you know, we are trying to negotiate a treaty with the Republic of Texas, and so far, they have resisted all of our offers. I hope you know the importance of their participation with our Union of Nations.

"It is critical that they no longer exploit the world's resources and assets without having to contribute anything back to those of us who maintain these assets and protect their profits. This is a great financial burden for the UN, and as everyone here knows, we can no longer afford to pay for their use of our infrastructure uncompensated.

"We also insist they become a better world neighbor and stop exploiting the air and water resources we have tried so hard to maintain. They have not allowed a world monitoring of their pollution levels or water standards, and this potentially affects all of us and especially their neighbors in Mexico and the United States. We demand they begin allowing our inspectors to verify the implementation and verification of their industrial production.

"Our final requirement is that they also verify the fair wage resolution we have instituted in 2019 to protect the workers from exploitation. We have had reports of Texas companies not complying, and we do not find it equitable to the rest of the world neighborhood as well as the questionable exploitation of workers. We need to know they are paying a fair living wage and that those who are working have a wage, which allows them dignity and value in their neighborhoods We believe a good working environment is a worker's right and not a benefit. These issues, we are afraid, are human rights violations and demand they comply immediately.

"We believe these are fair requests for a country using our world banking and transportation facilities as well as becoming a responsible world neighbor. This will make the United Nations a more effective manager of the world economies helping all our countries become stronger together. We can obviously assist some of the more needy countries to help keep the peace in those regions. We need to be unified in these requests so they know they are isolated in the world community."

The first to respond was the German ambassador: "Madame Secretary General, we are in complete agreement. We are very good business partners with the Republic of Texas since we export car and truck engines to them, and they export shiploads of refined oil products to us. As valuable a trading partner as they are, we understand and support the position of the United Nations. If we don't work as a unified world, then many nations will suffer while others like Texas will have unfair advantages.

We need to level the resources and eliminate the advantages for all nations."

Next was the Congo ambassador: "Since we found our oil reserves five years ago, which are estimated to be one of the top five finds in the world, we have been one of the top suppliers of the Texas refineries. They have always treated us fairly and are a good trading partner. We have been able to feed our people, but there is much work to be done in our region. There is only so much we can do, and many countries can use additional United Nations help. For this reason, we will support the UN resolution 2022-311 to bring Texas into the world community."

Finally, the ambassador to China spoke: "Madame Secretary, we support your resolution with some reservations. We are Texas's largest customer for petroleum products, and our economy demands a consistent supply of these products. We have a very complicated relationship with them as they are both a supplier and a customer as well as a competitor for many of our businesses to relocate to. They have many advantages over our country of which their lack of a world business tax is a very attractive benefit. We would be very well pleased to have them begin to have a tax similar to ours and the rest of the world's. The concern we have is if this was to become a protracted negotiation or action. We cannot afford to have our gas and oil supply cut off for an extended period of time. Has the Madame Secretary or her military advisers discussed this possibility and how to move things along in a timely manner?"

"Ambassador Wong, yes, we have discussed this as this has been a common concern for many of our member countries including the US. We plan on putting a naval and air blockade in place to stop all shipping and transportation, which we believe will have an immediate impact to the Texas economy. We believe this will end either immediately or certainly in a matter of weeks. We have estimated they will be feeling this disruption immediately and will bring them to the negotiating table very quickly. In the event we need more aggressive measures, we will look at those on a case by case basis."

"Madame Secretary, if this lasts longer than a couple of months, many of the less-developed countries could start running out of fuel and food which could bring critical hardships to their people. Many of our member countries can barely keep their industries producing now, so what would happen if they run out of petroleum products due to this disruption? They could have a hard time feeding their people. This action could lead to mass starvation. We need assurances that this will not be a long and protracted war. Texas is a very powerful country that can sustain itself for a long time. Much longer than our countries especially with the economic disruption this war could inflict on the entire world. They are the suppliers of our basic energy needs, and this could harm us in ways we are not foreseeing. I simply hope Madame Secretary has thought through all of the different scenarios. Thank you for your time, Madame Secretary, and my fellow ambassadors."

Secretary Polentas finished, "We have discussed all of your concerns, which is also our concerns, and we believe we have the basis of a plan that would be a very short action to bring this to a positive resolution. We thank you for all of your time, and we welcome all of your suggestions."

❦❦❦

"Rattler to air command, we are in hot pursuit of a bogey pilot who has crossed the Texas border and is now returning north to the border in Mach 4.8. We will be crossing the Oklahoma border in two minutes and request your approval to stay on our target outside Texas airspace."

"That's a negative, Rattler, we do not want to commit an international incident, which could be considered an act of war. We can't afford to be pulled into this type of action, which could have unintended casualties. Break off of your pursuit and that is an order!"

"Roger that. What is going on through this corridor? Did you get any computer or engine signatures from our sensors?"

"Negative, Rattler, whatever they are using is able to diverge our sensors with no trace. Our tech guys have no idea what they are using or how they are doing it. You can bet they will figure it out, it will just take some time." Terry Thomas knew he had to get back to headquarters and check his data.

He understood the cat-and-mouse game of testing their defenses, but to actually cross the border is a highly risky tactic if they were to get caught. They had to be doing more than that, but what could it possibly be? Were they planting sensors of their own or photographing areas they couldn't get from satellite? It just didn't make sense. All he knew is he would like to give that guy another shot and even things up.

"Hello, Professor Darling, this is the Texas Ranger, do you have a minute?"

"Yes, hello? Why do you sound upset?"

"The authorities have declared martial law for the upcoming UN summit. They are cracking down on all of the freedom groups and especially ours. The city has become a fortified prison camp, and they are declaring curfew at sundown and rounding up everyone they can. They have built an electronic web that can detect anything or anyone moving for over a square mile around the building. Anybody caught moving around is immediately being jailed, and if they belong to the Texas Christ Church they are being sent upstate. Are you coming to the summit? I would like to meet with you if possible."

"Yes, I am coming with the Moses group and the Texas delegation since I am recording this event as a journalist. How can we meet?"

"Don't worry, my people can make it happen. Are you going to be staying in the same hotel as the Moses group?"

"I don't think they will be spending the night. They are taking the Texas air shuttle and flying around Florida, which only takes thirty minutes. I am a bit anxious flying on that rocket, it sounds terrifying."

"Sounds like an amazing ride. I will have my people contact you inside the UN to pass on what is actually happening in the city. It's too dangerous to transmit you these files electronically, but we will find a way to get you the videos and pictures we have explaining the conditions here and what we have found out about the gangs. There are some direct links we need to show you. You will find much of what we are finding very interesting. I have to go before they trace where I am. We will reach you when you arrive. God bless you, and don't Mess with Texas."

"God bless you, Ranger, and God bless Texas!"

Steven met his team at Moses Tower before sunrise to get prepared for their day at the UN General Assembly. They would meet President Stewart and his team at Texas Space as well as June for the flight to New York. His prep team had been working all night, analyzing what they believed would be the proposals the assembly would have for Texas. They expected the worst since the worldwide recession had brought the tax revenues down every year for the last five years. His secretary Debra Jenkins brought in Drake and June Darling as well as the catering staff with a breakfast buffet for the staff and his team.

Debra asked, "Well, Steven, is this the young lady everybody has been talking about? It is so glad to meet you, Professor Darling. I hope you have a great flight to New York. That big bird is only terrifying for the first twenty minutes, and then it is like falling out of the sky in a brick. Other than that, there is nothing to worry about."

June laughed nervously and looked over at Steven who locked his gaze on her as he said, "I hope your flight down here was good. It isn't as bad as she says and you may just enjoy it if you like that kind of thing. We have a big day so get something to eat and we will be on our way. Have you been to New York lately?"

"Not lately, I worked for the *New York Times* before they went bankrupt and have not been there for five years. After they reorganized, I went on my own and earned my doctorate at Columbia like every other journalism professor. I knew the city pretty well. It's changed since I was there and not for the better. I've never flown anywhere near those speeds before so I don't know if I can eat, I'm pretty nervous."

"Oh, don't be, it's like flying any other plane it just takes off a lot faster, and we won't be going out of the atmosphere on this flight. Normally, we wouldn't use it for a short hop like this, but we really don't have anywhere safe to spend the night in New York so we may as well fly in and out. We aren't exactly going to have the welcome mat put out for us. It's a half-hour flight, and we will be over the ocean the entire time to avoid sound corridors and keeping with US sovereignty laws. You should get a bite as this is going to be a really long day and you will be needing to keep your strength."

They flew down to Houston Space with Drake and Dave Scott who would focus on the oil issues they would be discussing. After they met with President Stewart, Vice President Chapman, and Senate Leader Gerald Crockett, they boarded the ramjet shuttle and prepared for their flight. June settled in next to Steve and held his hand as the booster rockets fired and blasted them into the sky. Once they were ten miles up the booster's shut down and then they could feel the power of the ramjet taking it to the speeds she had read about as she was pushed into her seat making her stomach a bit queasy.

She squeezed Steven's hand for all she was worth as terror rushed through her veins, and then it became exciting beyond description. They were gaining speed and altitude as she watched the earth turn from a flat horizon into a round globe, and then the engines just stopped, and they silently glided back to earth. She had never imagined what the earth would look like at these heights, and as soon as she was amazed by the power and speed, they were preparing to land in New York. It was a breathtaking flight even though it felt like going to Dallas it was so short.

They landed at La Guardia, and now it was perfectly named since it was an armed camp. The entire airport was walled with guard towers every hundred yards armed with laser tasers to keep the gangs out. They could hear the gun battles being fought across the river and smoke rising from a few buildings in downtown Manhattan. They flew separate hover jets for security with all the gangs waiting for their arrival and were inside the UN in another thirty minutes being escorted to a conference room next to the assembly. Everybody opened their files in preparation for their presentation.

President Stewart began the meeting. "I don't think I have to tell you this room is not secure, so we need to keep our conversations very generic and let's not disclose too much. We all know what we are going to be saying, but we need to be prepared with our speeches. We are going to be basically following the same format as our speeches in the Texas assembly but will have to focus on informing the people who will be watching around the world. They have given me a half hour to speak, and Steve will have fifteen minutes. Then the secretary general will give a speech, followed by President Chambers. We will then have a chance for rebuttal and the entire chamber will begin the debate with our team answering their questions. We need to pray for guidance and strength before we go into this chamber. Any questions?"

Steven spoke first, "Yes, David, this is going to be a very high stakes battle between Texas and the United Nations. You know they are looking at more taxes than any other country. How hard do we want to hit them in this address?"

"Well, Steve, like we have said in our past meetings, they need to know that we are not ready to back down, so why shouldn't we tell them just that. There is really no point in pulling punches since at this point, it is likely their minds are already made up. We can hopefully reach one or two countries who can stop this with a veto, or we will simply have to go to the next step, whatever that could be. Is everybody ready? Let's say a prayer, will you lead us, Steven?"

Terry Thomas was meeting with the technology geeks to find out how these bogeys were still crossing the borders undetected. These laser detectors had some of the most advanced technology Texas Instruments in partnership with the most advanced engineering companies could develop, which should not be able to compromise their laser detection grid yet did.

Bill Branson was an immigrant from Florida who had graduated the top of his class at MIT and became a head engineer for a defense contractor in Miami. After immigrating to Texas four years ago, he installed and updated the laser detection pods as well as the transmission system to the central computers. He and his team of technicians have developed the most sophisticated system in the world, yet somebody has invented a stealth system to counter his units.

"Terry, we have been going over the data, and not only is there no record of the intruder, there is a blank spot of twenty seconds on the devices. We can't tell if there is an override on the device or if it is in the transmission back to headquarters. This means one of two things, either they have a counter measure on their aircraft, which can shut our detection devices down, or we have somebody compromising our system. Either way, it is serious, but the second is obviously more concerning, since it would mean somebody in our tech program is compromising our security for some reason."

"Is there any way to determine which it is?

"Not really at this time. We are analyzing the units to see if they had shut down and so far we see no evidence of that, but we aren't sure they actually shut down or were compromised by a stealth jamming system. We have another problem that is more serious though. As we began checking these detection units and the other units around the country we began finding the same thing on others. It appears there are a number of corridors that have been compromised and we have been invaded by these aircraft for around the last twelve months numerous times without detection."

"Where are they coming in and where are they going?"

"They are coming in from two areas in the north, one on the east, and one on the west. We figure they are not coming across the south due to all the traffic that could detect them or perhaps see them. They are coming through the least populated areas so they won't be heard or seen, which are also the most difficult to spread our laser detection pods tightly enough so it is easier for them to compromise."

"We need to step up our patrols in those areas and upgrade our weapons to hopefully get a shot at one of these bogeys. We also need to find out if we are being compromised by our own people so we need to compartmentalize all of our systems so no one can know the entire system or compromise it. Other than myself and my immediate staff, nobody will understand how and what the different pieces are to our defensive system or how they fit together."

"I agree, we will only report to each other and those in our departments who need to set up the counter measures. If there is a mole, we can't let him know we are looking. He is obviously good enough to be able to compromise the system without detection, so if we let too many people know about these jets, he may disappear and would not find who he is working for and why. There is also a real possibility there is no mole and they have found how to electronically manipulate our defenses or are infiltrating our border and manually compromising them. The odds of either of those are slim with our countermeasures but any counter measure can be compromised by someone so anything is possible."

Terry asked, "Do you think there is a possibility they were coming here and dropping surveillance electronics inside our country. Is it possible they could have been on some type of spy mission inside our borders rather than simply testing our defenses?"

"That is exactly the same thing I have been thinking, Terry. Nothing else makes sense, but we have no idea what they were doing. Needless to say, we are looking for electronic spying devices, although if they are preparing for war, they may not get activated until later when they need them. Either way, it is the old needle in a haystack to find them even when they are running, let alone if they are sitting dormant."

The United Nations chamber was filled beyond capacity with ambassadors and dignitaries from around the world. This was the largest assembly since the decertification of Israel as a nation vote two years ago. Bringing the newly formed Texas into the United Nations was as critical an endeavor as any in its history. The Texas delegation was seated at the front on the left in a dignitary box while the UN leaders were seated in the front, facing the assembly. A silence came over the crowd as Secretary General Polentas strode up to the lectern.

"My fellow ambassadors, senators, Texas delegation, and citizens of the world, thank you for coming to this historic world assembly. Since their secession and formation as a nation, we believe we have given the Republic of Texas ample time to become economically viable before they were offered membership to this world union. We are here today to debate and vote on United

Nations resolution 2022-311, which is the Republic of Texas membership ratification. They have been a valuable member of the economic world, and now it is time for them to become as valuable as a member of our world organization. We look forward to welcoming them as full United Nations members. With that designation, they will receive all of the benefits that go with that membership such as protection and settlement of disputes throughout the world in the world court.

"As a nonmember of the UN, they have been able to make use of our military security and commerce infrastructure without having to contribute to the expenses of those services. They have been allowed to ship their products around the world using many of our port facilities without having to pay the costs of keeping those port and shipping lanes open. This was understandable as they were a new nation and not yet economically stable. However, now they are not only viable but have become one of the leading financial forces in the world and need to begin sharing the expenses.

"In addition, we as citizens of the world need to be environmentally aware of the natural resources such as clean air and water. This has become a burden to their neighboring countries who have been breathing their pollution and drinking their polluted water both on the surface and throughout the various aquifers. We will help you to attain and maintain our standards to help you stay within the UN agreed drinking water standards to protect the earth from excessive pollutants and contaminants.

"It is our duty as citizens of the world to protect our children and grandchildren from dirty air and water, so we need to install and maintain the UN environmental team to help make sure their industries are not polluting the worldwide air and water inventories. We will need to monitor and maintain their ocean platforms and production facilities to make sure the quality of the seawater is maintained to worldwide United Nations standards.

Our ocean life demands a quality of water be maintained to the strictest measurements as it is throughout the member nations. We don't have to remind anybody of the great 2018 Brazilian spill and the hundreds of square miles of destruction it caused to both fish and wildlife. If that were to occur in the gulf, there would be millions of people affected and a biological disaster of epic proportions.

"Texas will have an equal voice in all of these issues from the moment they became a member of this body. They will be allowed on the UN Security Council which would give them a veto vote on any military actions we were undertaking as well as many UN resolutions. They would be allowed an exemption seat on any committee they are nominated or elected onto. This would allow them a voice on the energy committee or a commerce committee to give them a real influence in the UN government.

"Texas will have full voting privileges immediately which would make them a powerful voice in the world. Their citizens would be immediately covered under the UN health care program as well as the fair workers' living wage assistance treaty and our World Social Security retirement program. We have had the most successful health care program in the history of the world as we are covering seven billion people with quality health care with little or no costs to the patient. They would have the option of using ours or their programs depending on their preference.

"We are offering Texas an interim membership we offer to our new members. It will initially be 15 percent of gross profits from your industries for the first year and increasing over five years to our full membership of 35 percent. This will allow them time to adjust their industrial and governmental responsibilities while they transition into a full membership. The obvious advantages are the military and social protections as well as the added benefit of having most of their governmental duties being handled by our UN continental offices. We are looking forward to a long and prosperous partnership. Let me speak for everybody in this family of Nations, we would be honored to add the Republic of Texas as one of our new members. Thank you."

As the secretary general sat down, the president of the general assembly, Uganda Ambassador Mohamed Achmed Julestuli stood and walked to the podium.

"It is my honor to open this session to discussion and the first person on the forum to speak is the president of the Republic of Texas, President David Stewart."

President Stewart made his way from the tables on the floor up the steps to the podium and began to address the over two thousand dignitaries assembled in the large hall.

"Secretary General Salinas Margarita Polentas, President Juletuli, assembled ambassadors, dignitaries, worldwide viewers and fellow Texans. I come here in both humility and honor that this body would consider us for this invitation. We as Texans are honored and proud you would offer us for this position in as short a time as we have been a country. We have discussed this offer at length, and I am here to say we have to respectfully decline your generous offer. We as Texans need to keep our sovereignty and economic freedom from outside intervention that would have to be mandated through the United Nations Charter. No country has been forced to accept membership of the UN before, and we do not believe this is the time or situation that requires this precedence."

"We as a country would be willing to provide for our own protection of our shipping lanes and port facilities with our own ships and weapons to protect us from sea-going pirates and other dangers. We would even be willing to pay the UN a fee for that protection on the open seas from rogue countries attempting to hijack ships like we have been victims of in the recent past. We would even be willing to work out an agreeable fee for those costs of sea transportation for our goods to cross those sea lanes so we would be willing to drop the maritime protections and costs.

"The people of the Republic of Texas have met and voted on this measure in its Congress and find it both restrictive and excessive, which compromises our sovereignty as a country. We are a deeply independent country which is a major reason why we seceded from the United States. We feel the entrance into the UN would hinder our independence as well as our ability to maintain our economic freedom, creativity, and viability.

"Our senate met and discussed this resolution at length and has unanimously voted to reject it at this time and to keep our republic an independent country. We are very satisfied with our system of government, which values small, localized governments rather than a massively large centralized government, which is why our federal government is purposely weakened compared to our local county officials.

"We have organized our country so the local municipalities make decisions on where to spend their resources and how to tax and spend them rather than from a central capital like Austin. We feel the local officials have a better idea of how to use their funds on local items which is in their jurisdiction and expertise rather than someone a few hundred miles away. To turn our control over to a worldwide government in New York City goes against our basic form of governance and why we seceded in the first place.

"The final issue is your elimination of the Christian Church's right to freedom of speech and religion. Over eighty percent of Texans are God-fearing Christians, and the churches are a primary partner of our welfare system. Texans in general not only worship in the church but the church is a place where people come to be fed both physically and spiritually. Many of our food and poverty programs are directly attached to the churches in Texas which we consider a one-stop shop for the soul.

"Our churches not only feed the stomach, but they heal the heart through the salvation of Jesus Christ while offering counseling as well as every type of health care assistance. The church offers job search and family guidance to completely heal the person in need and get him back on his feet. Your incitement speech regulations would put our pastors' jobs at risk with their Biblical beliefs and destroy our social safety net to be replaced with the UN government programs, which turn people into wards of the state. We believe our churches are far more effective and have the results to prove it.

"For these reasons, our congress voted to respectfully reject United Nations Resolution 2022-311. My friend and CEO of Moses Enterprises, Steven Moses, would like to address the economic issues in regards to our decision. Thank you for your time."

There was a polite yet sparse applause, which spread across the assembly in response to his remarks. As Steve rose to address the general assembly, he looked up in the balcony where he saw June applauding his upcoming remarks.

He glanced over the United Nations General Assembly and thought how a kid could go from working on an oil rig spitting chaw to this moment. He knew God had guided his path as well as his father and mother's encouragement who taught him to do everything the right and honest way. Now he was about to give a speech to the entire world about one of the most important issues in an attempt to avoid a world war between Marxism and free market capitalism.

"Madame Secretary General Polentas, General Assembly President Julestuli, United Nations ambassadors, distinguished guests, and people of the world, it is in humility we come to you tonight. We have become a powerful nation in a very short period of time, and it is our hopes and prayers every country in this assembly could become economically everything and more than we are. We have accomplished this by using our resources, hard work, and ingenuity to become one of the most powerful countries in the world.

"I am the son of a wildcatter and through long hours and an innovative patent allowed my company to recover oil, which had not been recoverable. This innovation allowed me and my team to build one of the largest oil companies in the world. We believe in giving our customers the best value for their money, and Texas has followed that same path. We are now the largest energy producer in the world, not only in petroleum products but also in electrical generation as we produce a large percentage of the electrical energy for the United States, Mexico, and most of South America. We have developed underwater trunk lines and are now powering Hawaii and in the future Japan and parts of Africa.

"We look at the world market as one worldwide open air market. Just like in ancient days with the open public market or in underdeveloped countries where people put out their wares on a blanket or table and haggle over the prices, so too does our marketplace. We have millions of people making millions of transactions every minute of the day, negotiating the value of a product or service and what that product is worth. Each person makes those decisions without the help or interference of a government entity which makes those transactions easier and more efficient, but by what those people decide the good is worth to them.

"By shrinking the size and power of the government, we increase the power and creativity of the individual. This is the basis and how the free market economy works by making the individual free to invent, develop, and market his products then let the market decide what is good or bad as well as what is a fair price. He will have to go against someone trying to get the same order, so he will have to keep his prices in line or find ways to make his pricing more competitive. We have used this basic concept to become the world leader in energy products as well as many related industries.

"The key requirement to this form of economics is honor, trust, and integrity. Unless you can trust the person you are dealing with to provide or pay for what he says he will do, you cannot have a free market. A free market requires you to trust the person you are dealing with or it all falls apart. Without trust, you have to bring in lawyers or more levels of government to make sure everyone will perform to the levels they claim they will. In our case if we agree to provide a million barrels of oil by a certain date, we are required to deliver it by that date, at the agreed on price and the customer is required to pay for it in full.

"Another large part of Texas's success is the low levels of taxation and regulation required from our government. We work together as a partnership since we believe in Texas that the government which works best is one that works least to give the freedom to use their own independence and ingenuity to become the best they can be. This makes for a fertile environment for business to grow and expand into the economic success Texas has become. This is a unique relationship which is more fertile for a healthier economy and stronger government as the revenues go to the local municipalities where funds are distributed much more efficiently directly to the people.

"Our businesses would have a difficult time surviving let alone thriving if we were to have the UN tax of thirty-five percent on top of our present tax structure. We would also lose our ability to work efficiently with the regulations you have on our class of industries. We already have some of the cleanest plants in the world, but your regulations are unclear and excessive in our view and would adversely restrict our ability to develop and produce our products. This would not only an be added burden on us but an added hidden cost for all the countries that import our products due to higher costs being added to our pricing. This would adversely affect every country in the world and especially the weaker countries as our energy price increases would hurt them the most.

"We have the most innovative and generous wages and benefits of any country in the world. We allow our workers and management to become the best they can possibly be on an individual basis. Our two-year waiting list for immigration is testament to these wage structures. The World Union would destroy our ability to maintain our pay and benefit programs as well as divide workers from management. This relationship is one of the main factors making us the most productive and competitive work force anywhere. We cannot allow the World Union to destroy what we have built between worker and management over these years.

"Our economic advancements and business models have allowed us the lowest unemployment rates of any nation as well as the highest levels of income. This has allowed us to become the most generous county in the world as we have come to the aid of all natural and man-made disasters for any country and provide nearly as much assistance as the United Nations by ourselves. I only point this out to bring us to our worship of God as we are a Christian nation. We are deeply religious and believe in helping our brothers no matter who or where they are. Over 80 percent of Texans are regular attendees who consider themselves conservative spirit-filled Christians.

Steven looked around to see how his speech was being received and searched up into the balcony to try to spot June only to see an empty seat. He expected she was coming down to join them or stepped out for a minute, as he continued. "We believe all nations and people are born free and independent as sovereign countries. We have provided not only some of the strongest economic industries, but they are also good stewards of their resources. We have exceeded all of our targets in clean air and water to provide a clean and healthy environment for our citizens. All of our industrial discharges are monitored and open for review on the company websites twenty-four hours a day for anyone's inspection. Texans are excellent managers of our resources and are conservationists for both the water and air quality. We are not polluting the air in any measurable amounts that would ever reach across our borders to the US or Mexico.

"Finally, as to the protection provided by the UN for our shipping lanes. We as a business community would be willing to either provide our own protection or assist the UN in their protection with our assets as we develop them. Our preference would be to purchase the protection from the countries we do business with on a country by country basis but would be open to purchasing that protection from the United Nations as a separate revenue for the UN. We believe this is something that can be worked out while we are allowed stay independent of the UN and keep our sovereignty which we value more than life itself. I thank you for your time and ask that you consider our arguments thoughtfully. , God bless you, and God bless Texas."

THE GREAT DEBATE

June Darling had received a call from the Texas Ranger to meet a girl in the entrance bathroom on the first floor of the UN. She had no idea how the girl would be able to get inside the compound and didn't ask.

As she entered the bathroom, she was met by a young woman named Susan Bennett who took her to the handicapped stall. Once inside the stall, she opened a hidden door that went into the catacombs of the UN building and eventually into the network of tunnels below the building. Once they were down in the habitat tunnels, she was met by a group of men who escorted them outside the compound and up to a street where a waiting convoy of around ten vehicles picked them up. She didn't know if they were armed but assumed that they were. Tessie warned her that even with these men escorting her, they couldn't protect her from the larger more organized gangs or the police who were looking for the Texas Christ Church.

The first thing she noticed when they left was the sound of gunshots all around the car and the acrid smell of smoke and rotting flesh. She had no idea where they were coming from or what they were shooting at but she could tell they were both close and in the distance in every direction. It sounded like a jungle war zone. She also saw the bodies hanging from the lamp posts throughout the city. They were all ages and sexes as you could see entire families hanging with their signs attached to their chests and some were hanged with stretched out arms. "Why are all these people being hanged? Is this the retribution gangs that are lynching people because they are bank executives or business owners? This is the most horrific scenes I have ever seen as she recorded the video on her handheld computer."

"A man in the front seat turned around in a black ski mask and said, "Yes Professor Darling, they are still purging all the capitalists from the economy. These gangs are both organized groups or mercenaries who we believe have coordination from certain groups we are attempting to identify and expose. We think this is the systematic elimination of anybody who is a leader in the business world. We are fighting these gangs using their own tactics and have eliminated a number of them and their leaders. We are in a fight for our city and we want it back."

She recognized the voice, "Are you the New York Texas Ranger?"

"Yes, pleased to finally meet you Professor Darling. Excuse the mask but it is for your and my safety. If either of us are captured you will have nothing of value to give them and will get you out of the situation faster. Believe me, your life is in extreme danger being with us and the danger factor doubles with me. I am the number one prize for the gangs and the UN. Thank you for coming and having the courage to cover this and tell our story."

He gave her some computer pods he said contained all the information she needed to cover the story he had and wanted to take her on an inside tour of New York. She was amazed how old and destroyed the buildings of New York were compared to how she remembered them. Windows were broken out and doors were laying on the ground with people wandering in and out without the least regard for their maintenance. There were entire walls of skyscrapers which were missing and debris laying in shambles. She saw rats scampering everywhere as the garbage was piled up over two stories in every ally and side street in giant mounds. The smell was sickening from the putrid oily fragrance of rotting garbage floating in the air.

The convoy rambled down through downtown Manhattan in a tight formation. They obviously knew what they were doing as the lead cars would continually peel off to stop traffic on side streets in case of ambushes. They left the island and headed north toward the Bronx. The intensity of Manhattan lessened and the gunshots were less frequent and there were no bodies hanging from any lamp posts except for the occasional gang member who was clearly marked with a cardboard sign attached with a bayonet formed into a cross in his chest.

June looked at Texas Ranger and asked, "Did you kill those men?"

Texas Ranger looked at June and said, "I can't say who killed them. All I can say is they likely had a better trial than the people they killed. You don't want to know who or why they were killed except we are in a war, and if anybody is caught in our group, they will likely be hanging from a street light within an hour, and that includes you, Professor Darling. When you are in the middle of a war, there will always be the casualties of war.

"I don't know who that gangster is or what he did, but I do know his type. My father was a hardworking stockbroker down on Wall Street working for Goldman Sachs. He raised us right and never cheated a person in his life. He rose through the ranks specializing in pensions and retirements, helping a lot of people during the collapse to save what they had. You know how he was repaid? He was followed home one day eighteen months ago. They broke into his home then beat my mom and sister in front of him then took them out in the street and hanged my mom and sister the way they hang Christians. Before they hang them they stretch a two by four behind their neck and over their shoulders and then nail their hands to the ends of the board to form a cross. After they made my father watch them get tortured and hanged they beat him and hanged him. He was guilty of being a greedy corporate banker. So no, I don't know or care what this guy was caught doing, but you can know he deserved what he received."

June looked him in the eye. "I don't know who you are and that is a horrible story, but two wrongs do not make a right. No matter how many you kill to get vengeance, it will never bring your family back or make the hurt go away."

"You are right, Professor Darling, but that guy hanging from the lamp back there won't be attacking the next family he decides is guilty of crimes against the community."

They pulled into a deserted warehouse that said Tramboli's Clothing Warehouse on the side. The lead cars doubled back and blocked the gates and stayed outside while they went into the warehouse. When they got inside, they found a refurbished building that was turned into an auditorium with a cross at the front and a large sign saying Texas Christ's Church of New York. Texas Ranger motioned for June up onto the stage as the crowd stood and applauded his arrival.

Walking to the podium, he spoke with a booming voice as there was no speaker system for fear of the authorities monitoring their services. "Brothers and sisters in Christ, we have just come from the United Nations Building where you all are aware of the debate to force Texas into the United Nations. We have brought a special guest with us from Texas who is going to tell our story to the outside world. Let me introduce Professor June Darling who is from the University of Texas, 'Hook 'em Horns.' She is here to report our story."

The entire auditorium gave her a standing ovation as she walked forward and waved.

"Professor Darling, would you mind saying a few words?"

"Why thank you, I really was not expecting to say anything. I guess I would like to say how honored I am to be around people who are willing to take a stand while being persecuted and killed for your faith. In Texas, we have no idea what it would be like to be hunted all the time for being a Christian and that is what we fear would happen if we were to accept the membership into the United Nations. It is known for its persecution of any religion that strays from their official acceptable language.

"I hope I am able to tell your story to the world and give the respect each one of your lives deserve. This is a story that needs to be told, and God willing, I will have the skill to provide this vision to the world. Thank you all."

Steve was starting to become concerned about where June could be. It was not like her to just disappear, and this was not the place to do that without telling him or anyone else. His security people told him the last time they saw her she was talking to someone near the exits at the food courts, and when they looked again, they had disappeared during a rush of people between sessions. They have searched the buildings, and she wasn't answering her phone. The next speaker was the ambassador of Iraq and was approaching the dais.

"Madame Secretary General Polentas, General Assembly President Julestuli, United Nations ambassadors, distinguished guests, and citizens of the world. I come to you in humility as a member of this most great assembly of countries. We have a very difficult decision to make today as we have heard some strong arguments from both Texas and the United Nations. What the people of Iraq understand is the United Nations has been a powerful force for good in this world for nearly one hundred years, and hopefully will be here for long after we have passed this great assembly to the next generation.

"We understand the reservations of Texas to enter into the world community for all of the reasons they have stated. We believe we should give them a grace period to acclimate to their admission and have a sliding scale for their payments and adherence to our world agreements. This would allow them time for their citizens to adapt to our democracy.

"Texas is a good partner and valuable customer of ours since they purchase over sixty percent of our oil. If they could also contribute to the revitalization of their supplying countries' infrastructure, we could more efficiently produce more oil. We have millions of people who are suffering because we cannot produce enough oil to sell on the world market, so many of our people are suffering from hunger and poor roads and services. I know I not only speak for Iraq, but I have toured many of my neighboring countries, and they to are suffering from the lack of proper nutrition, education, and medical care. Why should these people suffer when there is so much wealth and luxury in countries like Texas?

"We would also like to address their concern about the control of hate speech in their churches. As many know, we have had our problems in the past over the spreading of hatred from imams inside our Islamic mosques and the violence that occurred when we accepted the hate speech charter. It has been an ongoing struggle, but after our imams accepted the cameras and monitoring regulations, our country has had a decrease in violence of nearly fifty percent over the past five years and is seeing continued improvement. This has been a large improvement for our citizens and is overwhelmingly supported by our people. I would like to reassure our friends in Texas that after your citizens have accepted the incitement restrictions, they will come to appreciate them.

"We hope our friends in Texas will reconsider their opposition to this and look forward to having them as a fellow member of this great union. We look forward to continued economic prosperity for both countries and expect Texas to be a strong addition to these United Nations. Thank you very much."

President Stewart stepped forward to have a chance to rebut the arguments that were made by the previous speakers. ""Madame Secretary General Polentas, General Assembly President Julestuli, United Nations ambassadors, distinguished guests, and citizens of the world. With all due respect to the speakers who have all spoken, we have heard you and would like an opportunity to discuss it again with our senate, although there is nothing we have heard today that we have not already considered. We believe in a free market that should be allowed to grow and provide jobs and benefits without interference of government management. This not only applies to the UN but our own government is structured in such a way as to give the individual and business as much freedom as possible to follow their own hopes and dreams. To add another level of government from the United Nations only goes against everything Texas and Texans believe in.

"We also have an overwhelming issue with the regulating of free speech and the freedom of religion. Unlike many religions around the world, with all due respect, we do not have a problem of violence from our churches or church leaders. What one man considers discussing the societal issues from the Bible, another man considers hate speech. We have read your charter, and there are some real issues from the broad interpretations that will limit our churches from preaching and teaching what they believe are the holy scriptures from God. We believe the freedom of religion is one of the most basic rights men have and to limit their worship is an infringement between worshipers and their relationship with God. How do you allow a government to interfere and in truth say it has more authority than God? Texans are not going to allow that Right to be taken away. I hope you will reconsider UN Resolution 2022-311 and table this proposal. Thank you very much."

Steven was panicking; nobody had heard from June in over four hours, and her phone was not working. The security team checked the cameras, and all they found was her going into one of the bathrooms and never coming out. They had later found her earphone in bathroom garbage can so she had no GPS locator, and it looked as if she had been kidnapped, but by whom?

Jason Tyler, head of security, was motioning Steven and President Stewart to move to the hover port on the roof. Jason Tyler was six-foot-four and built like a linebacker, although he was a running back in high school before doing two tours of duty in Afghanistan in special forces. He had lost track of how many battles and missions he had been on before he began working for international security teams. He was not all that concerned about New York City, but he knew to not take chances when flying exposed over areas that were not controlled militarily. His team was good, but you can only be so good when you know there are random hostiles out to kill you. If they were to capture the package, the results would be final and immediate, but he wasn't planning on them having that opportunity. "President Stewart, Mr. Moses, we have to get moving. I have talked to the security here, and if she turns up, they will escort her to the airport. It's beginning to get dark and that will only make things worse from a safety standpoint. We have to get moving, now!"

Texas Ranger was giving a rousing sermon, and the entire crowd was involved, which began giving testimonies of how they have been harassed and threatened by the New York gangs. They told of the most horrific murders, rapes, and beatings from survivors, families, and friends; but the one thing that kept them together was their faith in God. "Brothers and sisters, we are witnessing a monumental change in history. We are finally seeing neighborhoods fighting back against the murdering gangs and corruption that has taken over the Boroughs. We have fought back entire neighborhoods here in the Bronx, Queens, and Long Island and have secured neighborhoods in Manhattan and Newark, but we need to stay strong because they know they have to destroy us to completely own New York and the United States. We are the last surviving toehold of America and freedom outside Texas. So far, we have captured, tried, and eliminated over a hundred and fifty gang members caught lynching innocent victims.

"Professor Darling has come here in spite of the dangers and will tell our story about our group and what we stand for. She will tell our story to the world of how a few resistance fighters are willing to risk everything to keep the hope of returning freedom from this oppressive dictatorship. She has risked her safety to come here and record our stories to take them to the world . We have to get moving before their locator drones find out we are here, but let's give another hand for Professor Darling!"

A loud ovation came up as the entire crowd stood and gave another thunderous applause, overwhelming her. The crowd then began to sing "The Star Spangled Banner" in such an emotional sound from people who knew what each and every word meant to their lives. The music wafted as the tears flowed in unison. They understood what the author must have imagined and had the same dreams in their minds when they echoed, "The land of the free and the home of the brave."

Suddenly, she heard the crackle of gunfire erupting in the streets behind her, obviously coming from behind the trucks and cars that they had arrived in. The room immediately came to life as all the men pulled out hidden weapons, running to the windows. Texas Ranger was on an earphone and giving orders to the outside men and showing the ones inside which doors to exit and where to go.

"June, stay down. We are being attacked by the Union Gangs. It is a large, well-armed force and appears there are a number of splinter gangs with them. We can get you out through some escape tunnels we have, or if you can call in some help, we can get you to an area out the back that is pretty well secured for a hover jet landing. We don't have any time. Here is a secure phone you can make a call to escape. This may get pretty bloody and no telling how many they have coming. We need to get you out now. Take this phone, and Susan will take you toward the tunnels."

June was terrified; she had never been this close to gunfire, and she could see and hear the bullets hitting the walls and hear the men screaming in pain. "Let me call Steven and see what he can do." She made her way away from the fighting as the men and a few of the women went toward it with faces set against the enemy. She dialed the number.

Steven saw the strange number with no ID and answered it, only to hear June's terrified voice and what sounded like a war in the background. She was shouting to him, and he quickly understood she was in trouble.

"Jason, June is in trouble in New York and we have to go get her. Get your men and let's take my Stallion and get going. It sounds like a war. She just pinged me her GPS , and we can follow it in the Bronx, but we have to go now. I will fly the hover jet. Let's go."

Jason didn't like the idea of the person he was to protect going on a mission like what he envisioned who didn't have experience in these matters. He was going to be more trouble than help. "Mr. Moses, I can't let you go. Give me the coordinates, and my guys will go get her. We know what we are doing. This is nothing you want to get involved with."

"Jason, I am paying the bill, and I am the best hover jet pilot we have. Besides I am going with or without you, and this is too important for me to sit and wait. Either you let me go or I go by myself." He jumped into the pilot seat and fired up theStallion, checking the instruments.

Jason didn't hesitate. "Men, armor up and let's go. Check your weapons, this LZ is going to be a hornets' nest."

The three men climbed in as the Stallion lifted off and Steven headed straight for Bronx, knowing he would be the biggest prize of their lives to have him hanging from a lamp post. Jason was going to make sure they never got that reward.

The river slid behind them as they cruised four hundred feet off the ground flying into the Bronx. They saw the smoke and explosions rising ahead of them and knew this must be what she was talking about. Taking a wide arc, they could see what looked like hundreds of people firing small arms at each other with bodies lying everywhere. Jason had seen skirmishes like this around the world as one warlord fought another. He never expected to see it in a Borough of New York City, yet here it was. Coming around the back, they pinpointed the beacon and could see people crouched down in a small alcove between some buildings protected by cars and rubble.

The fighters who were attacking the warehouse saw the hover jet and began firing at it, knowing it was in the wrong place at the wrong time. Steven pushed the throttle and pointed the nose straight for the pavement. The gun and laser fire became intense as he headed for the deck like a rock thrown from the sky. Fifty feet from impact, he pulled on the stick and leveled it out, hitting the hover break for all he was worth and hit the ground with a huge bounce and then settled down.

The security team raced to the corners of the hidden alcove and began laying down cover fire on all the surrounding buildings. There seemed to be a hundred men in the windows and roofs of the surrounding buildings and the hover landing attracted all of their attention knowing there had to be a valuable target they were rescuing.

Steven looked across the alcove and saw June coming his way with a couple of strangers. He jumped out of the hover and ran over to her, hugged her, and swept her up in his arms, protecting her with his body while running back to the Black Stallion. He shoved her into the back covey while jumping over into the pilot seat, revving the jets while motioning for Jason's team to get back in.

Jason and his team straddled their seats and the outside jump steps continuing to fire at every target they saw hitting one after another.

Jason shouted over the confusion, "Go, go, go!"

Steven hit the throttle on both the jump jet and the forward thrust to get as much speed as the hover could possibly produce. It was a trick he learned on some small derrick platforms when he had to fly in bad weather. "Hold on!"

He banked and corkscrewed straight up in a zigzag, making it impossible to be a clear target as every warning light in the cockpit went off at the same time while the men were holding on for all they were worth until he leveled off at a thousand feet, speeding off back to La Guardia taking less than a minute.

Jason looked over at Steven while securing his rifle. "Any time you need a job as a special ops jock, give me a call. That was some pretty fancy flying for a civilian. I don't think I have ever seen a landing or takeoff like that before in one of these. You are a pretty good stick and glad you were there, but don't ever try that again."

Steven smiled and answered, "I had this one juiced up a bit to get a bit more performance out of it for when I'm out on the gulf. I never really thought it would come in handy when I was being shot at. Guess that Kevlar plating can take a hit or two."

He looked over at June and asked, "What in the world were you doing in the middle of a war and why did you leave the UN meeting?"

June still looked like she was in shock and quietly answered, "I can't tell you now, we will talk later."

Ninety minutes later, they were lining up on the Houston Space runway as the shuttle made its final approach from its glide path. June was obviously more relaxed as she returned to Texas after her experience, and Steven was still mystified what she was doing in the Bronx in the middle of a gunfight.

He grabbed her hand as they landed, and she looked over and smiled while a small tear leaked down her nose, which made his heart skip a beat. "Look, I don't know what you were doing, and it really isn't important. The important thing is you're safe, and we are together. If you don't want to tell me, that is fine since I trust you knew what you were doing. You are in no condition to drive, so let me fly you home, and I will have someone drive your car to your place in the morning."

She smiled and said, "That would be fine. This has been a really exhausting day."

After they landed and got into the hover limo, they dropped June and Steve at Moses Towers where they got into a company hover jet and flew to Austin while she enjoyed the lights below. "You know this is the most beautiful country on earth and so peaceful. I couldn't talk when we were with the security guards since I was there to cover a story.

June explained to Steven how and why she was in the Bronx while they left Houston.

He reached over and grabbed her hand again, and she squeezed it as she leaned over and rested her head on his shoulder. He could hear her breath soften as she gently fell asleep from exhaustion while he flew the rest of the way into Austin, taking a long circle as he enjoyed the feeling of her head on his shoulder while her hair cascaded down his chest. Finally, he found her house and parked on her driveway as she was awaken by the landing.

"Are we here? Did I fall asleep? I'm so sorry I must have dozed off, I am sorry."

He smiled down at her and said, "Don't worry. I kinda enjoyed the feeling of you sleeping on my shoulder. I could get used to that after a while. Let me walk you to your door. We don't want anyone attacking you again."

She let out a small laugh. "Thank you for everything. This was a day I will never forget, and I am so sorry to drag you into that situation. I had no idea it was going to be that dangerous. Those Christians needed, me and they are some of the bravest people in America. You saved my life, and I really don't know what to say. That was really brave and heroic. I was stunned."

"Now why would you be stunned? I would prefer shining white knight but hero will work." The moon shimmered off her hair, blinding his eyes with a rainbow-colored sheen while they talked about the day. He looked into her two deep pools of emerald green that swallowed him up like a flower swallowing a bee. Reaching around her small waist, he pulled her to him as she looked up into his eyes as their lips met. It was everything he knew it would be as he found who completed him again. This was more than a kiss but a possession of two people by the other as they bonded into a ring forming between them. Both of their lives up to that point was past, and this kiss pointed them to the future, which was their new horizon. Then as quickly as it began, the kiss was over, completing the moment.

"Well, good night, June. I will call you in the morning."

"Ah yeah, call me. Good night, Steven," she said as she fumbled at the code pad dazed, wobbled, and in shock, knowing this was more than a good night kiss.

Steve hopped back into the hover jet, gave it everything it had, and corkscrewed it into the sky, repeating the maneuver in New York as she smiled and slumped against the door. "What have I gotten myself into?" She reached over to her left forearm and pinched herself twice.

Midnight was a tough hour for any pilot, and Terry Thomas was no different. He was pretty tired but with all that was happening in New York, he felt something may be happening tonight to test the sensors. Finding the beam diverters next to the pods was a great discovery by the tech crew, so now, those bogeys may find it a bit tougher to get through undetected, but they have found out by now and have found a way to counter act it.

He and his wingman Snakebite were issued the new craft with the mini-ramjet engines connected to the hover technology, which allowed him to hover as well as travel at Mach 5. In addition, they juiced up the weapons to maximum stun so whatever they hit would be disabled and have to land immediately if they were within thirty miles. He was hoping he would get a chance to use them when suddenly one of the ground monitors lit his screen with an alert and coordinate of a bogey traveling at Mach 4 crossing the border. He saw it as he locked and was counter locked at the same time. Kicking in the ramjet while firing in unison, he saw the laser attaching to his craft but the deflectors diverted the beam as he headed for the sky while his beam had a hit on the target. He saw it fall out of the sky, tumbling across a cornfield as the pilot ejected and his powerchute motored lazily back across the border.

The adrenaline rush he felt from knocking down his first intruder as a Texan pilot was exhilarating. He had to keep his head in case some of his buddies came in to either attack him or destroy the downed craft. He and Snakebite set up a perimeter and circled until backup arrived to begin recovery and identification of the intruder's craft. As they watched, a charge went off in the wreckage, exploding it in a hundred yard circle of debris.

June woke up early, got ready to go into work, fixed herself some coffee, and had a grapefruit half with an English muffin for breakfast while she prepared for her day. She had so much to read and analyze with all the data she picked up from Ranger's people it will take weeks she thought. She began searching the news sites to see what she could find out about the attack on the church when the doorbell rang. Looking at the door monitor, she could see it was Steven? What was he doing here, and she was looking a mess just out of the shower with wet hair and no makeup.

She spoke into the monitor, "What are you doing here? I wasn't expecting you this morning. Give me a few minutes." She quickly blew her hair and made herself up as best she could without making him wait too long on the porch. She put on a pair of sweats, drug a brush through her hair, while putting on some lipstick and a bit of eyeliner then met him at the door.

"Good morning, Steven, did you forget something last night?"

"Yes, I did, I forgot you, I am not letting you out of my sight from now on, and I came here to pick you up before we attended the States' council meeting."

"What are you talking about? I can go down there myself in a couple hours and get some work done here and run some errands. I don't have time to go to the council meeting. I haven't had a chance to get ready!"

"Look, June. You want to document this event, and so do I. How close a look inside can you get than being with me, and I will get you into all of the important meetings you want to be in on. Besides, you are one of the most knowledgeable people on the United Nations so you can be a valuable asset for these discussions."

"So you just want me for my brains, I should be offended?" she teased.

"Well, your brains are a good start. I think I proved that to you last night, or have you forgotten already? Now, get ready and let's go. We are meeting President Stewart and the security council in ninety minutes. Have you had breakfast yet?"

"That's okay, I already ate. I have some things I need to take care of on the hover computer while you change and we will take off as soon as you are ready to go."

Steve gave her a quick kiss and a hug as he headed out the door, leaving her head spinning while she stumbled to the bathroom to make that small miracle she had to make happen in fifteen minutes. She just wished she would have taken the time to buy that black pencil skirt she saw last week in Austin.

—◦◦◦—

Terry Thomas and Snakebite had been circling over the crash site all night waiting for the crash forensic crew to arrive. They would be able to get some identification off the craft and find out who these invaders were and hopefully get into their data and find out why they were coming in. All they needed were some small pieces to find out who was sending these intruders.

He saw the convoy rolling across the horizon off in the distance. They would be here in about thirty minutes and then they could begin putting this jigsaw aircraft back together again. Hopefully the computer memory survived the mandatory crash destruction. All these guys needed were a few molecules, and they would be sucking data off the virtual pieces. Still, any government worth their salt knows to turn all their data into dust once the crash was occurring, which was likely the case with this crash. A spy plane will be especially hard to get a signature, but if anybody can, it's the guys approaching from the south.

A woman's voice broke the still Texan morning dew, "Hello, Captain Thomas, this is Major Morgan. We are about thirty minutes out. Are you the pilot who called in the intruder's crash?"

"Yes, Major, I am the pilot who was attacked and counterattacked, hitting the aircraft and downing it. The pilot was able to escape back across the border with a power-chute, but we have this craft spread across this cornfield underneath me. Do you want me to land and wait for you now?"

"Negative Captain, please keep the area secure. We don't want you to contaminate or compromise any of the evidence, we will be there in a few minutes. By the way, nice shooting, Captain!"

"Thank you, Major Morgan."

Steven and June walked into the capital from the VIP hangers directly into the presidential wing. There seemed to be more security around the capital and in the chambers than you would normally notice. They were escorted by two Texan National Guard hovers from ten miles out all the way to the capital building.

President Stewart's personal secretary Sarah Masters met them as they walked in. "Hello, Mr. Moses, excellent speech yesterday. I heard you had some interesting times after the meeting too. Glad you are all safe and sounds like it got pretty frightening for a while. Is this Professor Darling? We heard you had a pretty scary situation in New York."

June smiled and responded, "Scary really doesn't cover it, terrifying was more like it. If it wasn't for Steven and the bodyguards, I don't know if I would have made it out of there. Thanks for asking."

"Let me show you the way to the president's office, do either of you need anything? Coffee and juice is in the office, and we have a breakfast prepared if you would like?"

Steven responded as they walked to into the president's office, "I would love some sausage and eggs with some hash browns and toast if you don't mind. Can she get anything for you June?"

"No, thank you, I just ate but I would really like some orange juice and coffee? I will set up over here and begin recording the meetings if that's all right with you and President Stewart?"

"Did I hear my name?" President Stewart said, smiling as he walked over to greet them. "Certainly, Professor Darling, if you want to record our meetings it is fine. We just ask that you withhold anything sensitive on security matters and ask you to not divulge them until later. We have nothing to hide in here, but much of it will be sensitive and want this recorded for future generations, God willing."

"Please call me June, and yes, I appreciate that and will not reveal anything sensitive until after all of this is over. I am more interested in the actual history of this event than the details of the security issues."

"Thank you, June. Steven, I know it was a short night last night, but we have a full day today. After we grab a bite here, we are going to meet with our security people, it sounds like they have something that occurred last night. They apparently shot down an aircraft invading our airspace so they want to brief us on that and then discuss all the possibilities they believe could happen with this embargo. After that, we meet with the Congress.

We have to discuss all the options they are going to be expected to deal with in relation to the social and economic realities of a severe economic downturn. So enjoy your breakfast, you're going to earn this meal."

The security council consisted of Major General Sutton, Border General Landrus, and Technology General Martinez. Major General Sutton was a native Texan who grew up in the army and was rose quickly through the ranks from his exploits in Iraq and Afghanistan as a multidimensional battlefield expert. He was one of the originators of the combat coordination through AWACS and fast attack tank warfare as well as warthog and helicopter support for the ground troops and their armored support. His strategies were copied throughout the Pentagon. He was then moved into the inner corridors of the Pentagon helping develop strategies and tactics used around the world.

The clouds were dark and thick over New York City as Secretary General Polentas sat in her office. Sitting across from her was her NY City mercenary squad leaders headed up by Stazi Ramone and Shelton Liston. These two controlled the mobs of New York and handled all the insurrections. She looked at them through narrowed eyes. "How can the Texas Christians still be causing us problems? You said you would have them taken care of months ago, and not only are they not taken care of, they are growing stronger and fighting in broad daylight. They are lynching your people and the locals are sympathizing with them. I want them stopped, and I want them stopped now!"

Stazi was a thick Italian American who grew up on the streets promoting his Sicilian roots. He dreamed of becoming a big mafia boss but took a detour into the Union mob. He became a strong arm guy, losing count of the number of broken arms and promises to his family he had made in his lifetime. He always could break a knee or issue a contract on a troublemaking leader to settle the dissension, but these Texas Christians and their leader, the Texas Ranger, were different. Nothing scared them or intimidated them as they were Christians and had a belief that couldn't be silenced by threats or intimidation.

He looked at Secretary General Polentas and said, "Secretary General, you don't understand. We have armies of unions and gangs who have been fighting them when we can find them, but they are like fighting smoke. You can't corner them and when you do they fight like they have ten times their troops. We had them cornered two weeks ago in the warehouse district and had them beaten and then the wind and rain came in and they just escaped like ghosts. We killed a dozen of them, but there are thousands now and we are having a hard time finding them."

She looked at them both and raged, "You listen and you listen good, I want them dead. Do you hear me? I am putting a bounty on each and every one of them of one hundred thousand dollars and ten times that for their leader the Texas Ranger. We are about to go to war with Texas, and the last thing we need to worry about is the security of New York so if you two can't do this then I will find people who can, do you understand?"

Shelton Liston was quietly listening and felt the anger begin to well up in his belly. He was a large black man who grew up in the drug gangs in Harlem. He came from a single mother family and grew up on the streets in the gangs who were his real family. He quickly became one of the leaders and was especially bright in the drug trades unifying the gangs into one mega-gang that controlled the entire city.

When his organization joined with the unions, they became one of the strongest forces in the city virtually controlling the streets. Then came this Texas Ranger group who began fighting his gang and taking over entire neighborhoods using residents as snitches who pointed out and coordinated the attacks knocking his shooting galleries out of the blocks and shutting down entire neighborhoods.

"Listen, Secretary General Polentas, nobody wants these Christians out of the city more than we do. They are interfering with our entire operations. We will take you up on your bounties and we will double the bounty on their leader. Just give us a little more time, we are getting closer and closer, but Stazi is right. These guys are hard to corner and fight like nothing we have seen before. They are well organized and understand how to fight and find weaknesses as well as knowing the tunnels and passages of New York. Just give us a bit more time."

She looked at the two and wondered how she ever found two so incompetent leaders and answered, "That is just the problem. We don't have more time. I am going to meet with the security council later today and propose they give me the power to declare war on Texas. They will give me that power and then our entire focus is going to be to destroy and level their country and get it over quickly. The last thing I need is a street battle going on here while we are running people in and out of this city. I will patch you into our security people who are connected with the police and intelligence communities to find out who this guy is and his organization. We need to kill them and we need to start yesterday. If we don't we have a chance of having the sympathizers beginning to join them and then our problems will multiply overnight. Our people will get in touch with you this afternoon and help you find these pests and put and end to them. Do you understand me? I want them dead, and especially this Texas Ranger!"

They looked at her and answered, "Yes, we understand, and we will have his head on a platter within twenty-four hours. We have to go and meet our troops. We won't disappoint you this time. We will find this instigator, and when we do, he will be dead. Thank you for your time."

She could hear the continual gunfire throughout the city. It had a sort of dark rhythm like a Caribbean drum beat that made your heart pound from the passion and violence coming off in the distance. The street battles were getting more and more pronounced as the gang wars became a way of life in the city. She did not have time to be concerned with the problems in the city when she had a renegade country causing her potential problems within her own coalition. Many of her political enemies were sympathetic with Texas and wanted her to take a softer tone then she was willing to. She didn't want to begin a war with Texas but to hold the world together she knew she had to enforce the resolution to the full extent of her power and make sure it is over quickly. When this was done, the world will know there is truly one government, and she will be the one leader of this government.

Her personal assistant knocked on her door and brought in President Chambers and UN military general and ambassador of Brazil. Ambassador Herrmoza who was a large chocolate-skinned man with a distinguished face and a well-trimmed black beard. His beard matched his dark eyes, which were narrow and cold from his wars against the drug cartels in the late teens. He was known as a great tactician and completely ruthless in his abilities to find a weakness in an enemy and then scorch the earth behind them. His treachery was only matched by his corruption as he was known to take bribes and drugs for the cartels' protection.

Secretary General Polentas rose and welcomed the two men. "Gentlemen, you know the reason I called you here. We have passed the resolution, and now we need to explain to them what it means to them and the world. We need for them to acquiesce to our demands and become a full member of the UN. If they refuse, we need to force them to do this immediately, which means we have to throw the full force of the world government behind our enforcement. I want this to be short and dramatic so no other nation will dare to show such resistance as we have seen from Texas. We are going to offer them a forty-five-day period to accept our demands, and if they don't, we have to be prepared to use anything at our disposal both economic and militarily."

President Chambers spoke up, "Madame Secretary, I want this as much as you do, but don't you think we should fight this war diplomatically and strategically with sanctions like we spoke of before rather than militarily? And if I am hearing you, it sounds as if you are not ruling out nuclear weapons. We can't—"

"President Chambers, you are in no position to say what we can or can't do. You and your people are only able to survive, thanks to the generosity of the UN and our ability to provide you assistance. You know what would happen to your country and your presidency if we were to cut off your power or funding to run all of your utilities and industries. We have enough countries like yours that use the world's resources to provide for your ungrateful citizens like the ones fighting in the street, we need more countries that understand the power and might of this world government. Now, Ambassador Herrmoza, what have you got for me?"

Ambassador Herrmoza placed a minicomputer on her desk, which put a visual on the wall opposite them with a map of Texas and the surrounding area. "Madame Secretary, we have been working on this problem for over a year and have come up with a plan we believe will bring them to acceptance if and when we decide to go forward.

"We have been testing their defenses and we believe we have found a number of weaknesses, which we can exploit to gain access to their infrastructure. You will notice they have a series of oil wells throughout the gulf, which are largely undefended. We can begin by knocking them out and then move in and destroy their refining capabilities here on the coast. We can have them completely unable to produce oil or export though their ports by sinking tankers and container ships, making them unable to import or export bringing them to the negotiating table. We predict this will get their attention that we mean business and will be ready to accept our demands as well as making a statement to any other countries who would be a world renegade."

Secretary Polentas responded, "You don't understand the Texans. If this plan would work and you would be able to close down their ports and refining, what would stop them from fighting back and rebuilding their facilities? These Texans have backbones and I doubt a few destroyed refineries and oil wells are going to make them quit. What would stop them from digging in and wanting to fight harder, I want them to understand we are not going to stop at destroying a few oil terminals. These Texans and the world have to know and fear us. What else do you have?"

"I am glad you asked, Madame Secretary, since we agree with you, and this is simply the first phase. If and when they turn down our offers for peace, we will have already defeated their defenses and completely rule the air and space over their country, which means we will have access to their infrastructure and buildings throughout their industrial centers here around Houston, Dallas, and their capital here in Austin. Our first target will both be strategic and symbolic, which will be the Moses building and the surrounding buildings destroying their financial and energy centers. At the same time we will be leveling the Houston area as well as the Dallas metro complex and eliminate Austin so there will be no communication or coordination throughout the country.

"Once we have neutralized the country we will send in our troops from Oklahoma, New Mexico, and from the gulf. We expect the fighting will last no more than thirty days due to the lack of communication and the knowledge that their most important landmarks and communications have been destroyed making a chaotic militia which will quickly be dispatched and neutralized making them and their people demanding a peace treaty."

President Chambers stood up protesting, "This is insane, Madame Secretary! You are talking about killing perhaps hundreds of thousands if not millions of people and causing untold destruction that will take decades to replace. There are better ways to do this without all this death and destruction. You can't be serious about doing this. I refuse to be a part of this!"

"You have no choice, President Chambers. Without our help, you will be in a deeper recession without power or fuel within forty-five days. What do you think will happen to your political career once that is done?"

"I don't care about my career you can't making threats or wholesale killing entire countries to make some sort of sick example so you can become the ruler of the world. My career isn't worth my soul, and I won't go along with this. I am going to the security council to have this stopped."

Ambassador Herrmoza touched him on the back with a baton and hit a button, sending President Chambers heart into a severe arrhythmia, forcing him to slump to the carpet as he stared in disbelief at the secretary general. She simply stared at him without blinking as he slipped into his black envelope of emptiness.

"I told you he wouldn't go along with this, but there is no way we could allow him to talk. Call the authorities and let them know this is an emergency, but there will be no way for them to trace this, it is impossible to tell it from a heart attack. Call his Secret Service team."

"Before I do that, what is your plan if this doesn't force them to acceptance of the resolution?"

"Like you said, Madame Secretary, we are willing to use all options both conventional and nuclear."

"That's what I thought now get that thing out of here while I call his secret service."

"I will give you two minutes before I call them in."

Ambassador Herrmoza walked out the door and into the foyer past the secret service on his way to the elevators. As he entered the elevator, he slid the thin baton between the door and the wall and could hear it start to fall the seventy-five floors where it shattered into a thousand pieces.

TEXAS DECIDES

Steven Moses, President Stewart, June, and the rest of the room stared in disbelief at the monitor as they had over the last twenty-four hours while the United States Supreme Court Justice swore in Vice President Victoria Price as president. The entire world stood in absolute shock that President Chambers would die of a sudden heart attack in the UN. The timing and location seemed too convenient to be a heart attack, and the Grassy Knoll crowd had already begun posting conspiracies. Everything was moving so fast it was hard for them to keep up and then the UN votes to enforce their sanctions with military force put them in a direct line toward World War with the United Nations.

"Well, there you have it, she's president," remarked President Stewart, breaking the silence. "I felt I could deal with Chambers, but I have no relationship at all with Price. I know she had a pretty famous father who was a senator for years, but I have really never met her. My guess is she will rubber stamp everything coming out of the UN, which doesn't help us at all."

Steven looked over at him and around the room. "Do you really think he died naturally in Secretary Polentas's office?"

"We will never know, since whatever happened will be covered up by the authorities and their friends in the media. I wouldn't

137

put anything past them, but I have no proof, so it really doesn't matter. Unless they have some evidence this could just be another conspiracy rumor. Our problem is, do we go to war with them, or don't we. If we decide to go to war, we will be in for the biggest nightmare of our lives, and we have to consider the millions of Texans who will be hurt or killed."

Vice President Chavez spoke up, "Either way, it is going to be our biggest nightmare. If we agree to their resolution, we will lose our economic future through having to give away so much of our revenues to the UN, and if we fight, we will lose untold lives and massive economic destruction to our industries. We have never set ourselves up to be a military power, so we have very little to fight them with. If they did kill President Chambers, we know what kind of person we are dealing with. That said, whatever you decide, I and the Texas people are behind you."

Steven spoke up, "What if we try to buy some time to develop some weapons? We have a number of them on the drawing boards, and we have the platforms for weaponizing our aircraft as well as some of our armored vehicles, but we need some time to begin production. What if we agreed to their terms on a trial basis for six months?"

President Stewart responded, "Can we manage for six months in their control, and would the Congress agree? We would have to surrender to their terms without them finding out what we are doing. In the meantime, we would have to negotiate with them while we were developing our weapon programs before they discovered since we know at some point they will find out what we are doing. I would guess we could get somewhere between two days to four months before we would be found out, and then war would be declared. How long would it take before you could be producing weapons if we were to agree to their terms?"

"Well, Stew, we have been actually working on weapons for years and have a number of mock-ups of pretty conventional stuff like energized lasers and missiles, but we have some ideas in the pipeline that we must have to fight such overwhelming forces. We will be outnumbered and outgunned by a hundred to one as well as all the advantages they have in satellite cover and having us surrounded. Even if we get the time and can work out some of the bugs in these new technologies it will take a miracle to keep them from our complete annihilation, and that is if they do not use nuclear weapons which we have never developed.

"We need to take this to our Congress in a closed session to hammer out these choices, but if it comes down to my decision, it will be to keep the embers of freedom burning. This is bigger than a few million Texans, this is about keeping the hope of man being able to choose his life as well as his government, which has only occurred a few times in history. Texas is the last stand of freedom just like our forefathers at the Alamo. Remember them?"

As they walked into the hall, June's phone rang from a scrambled number. Answering it, she heard the familiar voice of the Texas Ranger. "Hey, Professor, that was a pretty close call we had when you came to visit. I've been holed up and on the run, but it looks like we finally shook them, although they seem to becoming more aggressively hunting us. There are all sorts of rumors floating around about President Chambers's death and if it was an assassination. Most think they had some sort of undetectable drug to stop the heart. Nobody is sure how they did it, but he died in Polentas's office, which is just too convenient. What are you hearing?"

"Nobody here has any idea of what happened other than what is being reported. It sounds suspicious that he would have a heart attack in the UN secretary general's office at this time. Either he was under unbelievable stress or someone had a hand in it. We will never know. It is so good to hear your voice, how did you get out of there?"

"It was pretty lucky, but we have a lot of ex-military, and they always have contingency plans, and this was one of those. Let's just say we were able to give more than we took and left them in pretty bad shape. That brought out their big guns and pretty much our church and a few other meeting houses, and it has become open season on Christians. That's okay, the church always grew the fastest during the harshest persecution. I just wanted to let you know we are good, and we have some big things coming up, our numbers are growing and we are really making headway against their forces. Take care, and I will be in touch."

"Hey, I wanted to tell you what I found in your data?"

"Not right now, I will call you next week when you have a chance to talk. See ya, I have to go!"

Rev. Ranger closed his phone just as his detection sensors started beeping. He had now been triangulated again, and the hovers were closing in. The bullets and lasers began lighting up the area as a large force of union gangs and UN support started firing from airborne platforms. His men began firing back, and the perimeter forces began taking on the hovers. The new anti-air handhelds were a godsend as they began dropping a couple and holding off the ones closing in. He heard the ground vehicle sirens coming in, which were likely the police coming to quash his fellow rebels.

His men and he began to counterattack to allow the bulk of his forces to escape into the maze of buildings, tunnels, and sewers that made up Brooklyn. That is when he saw the largest hover he had ever seen come out of nowhere. It was the deepest black he had ever seen as it came banking out of the south river and circled their positions firing from every angle. It was a full city block large and had at least fifty lasers shooting in all directions using computer identification and targeting. In addition to the firepower, it had some type of digital panels that stopped the airborne platform's lasers and redirected them back at the platforms, blowing them to pieces. He watched as his men and weapons fell ten stories to their deaths. His heart fell the ten stories with them as he knew his strategy was going to make over fifty families fatherless.

Although the size and mass of this machine was immense, it had speed and agility to move faster than any hover he had seen while having the ability to maneuver between buildings to get near street level. It was targeting all of his men in perimeter and their anti-air weapons had no effect on this craft as it killed them in microseconds. This is when he gave the order to disengage and fall back to a safer location. He watched as his men were slaughtered or captured while he and his main group were able to hide under the overpasses and maze of tunnels to escape this latest weapon of destruction.

His men returned to their most secure hideout below Queens and assessed the damages. His officers reported to him that they had lost seventy-eight killed and dozens wounded and captured, although he would not be able to assess until they had a chance to regroup. They all knew the captured would be given a quick trial and either hanged or shipped to the work camps in upstate or Montana and the Dakotas. As they talked and he reassessed their situation, he knew the tide had turned and his groups' days were numbered.

He spoke to the hundreds assembled, "Ladies and gentleman, you all know what the situation is: we are all outlaws in our own city. We have become outlaws by defending our city from the gangs and unions who are supported by the One World Government of the UN. We have been fighting for our freedom and only by the grace of God have we survived this long. We lost some good men today who have fought with us side by side. We lost Peter Summers and Josh Carpenter who have been fighting with us since this movement began. We lost many friends who are with Jesus tonight, and we are all hurting for them, but they are in glory.

"I am releasing everybody here from their pledges to fight this battle against these impossible odds. You need to go now and raise your families and live long, happy lives rather than get killed fighting against something we can't overcome. We have made a statement and they are only after me, so it is time for me to do the right thing and turn myself in before we are all wiped out. So I am disbanding our army so you can all be safe again."

David Thomas, a twenty-two year old ex-punk rocker, walked forward and spoke loudly, "Who are you to tell us when and where we can lay down our lives for freedom? What good is living a long and happy life if you live that life under the fear of a government that can take your life from you whenever they want? If they have you, it won't stop them from doing what they did tonight, they will only hunt us down harder. I, for one, will fight with you or someone else who will take your place to the death with me and my wife. I would rather die fighting to breathe the cool breath of freedom than die of old age breathing the stench and acrid smell of oppressive government slavery. Just like Patrick Henry said in our revolution hundreds of years ago, 'I regret that I have but one life to give for my country. Give me liberty or give me death.'

"I remember when I was a young boy and we had a free country but we gave it away. We let the government grow and intrude in our lives more and more, thanks to apathy and selfishness. We have perhaps one chance to get that country back and only by the mercy of Jesus Christ our Lord and savior will we be able to do that. As for me, my wife, and my family, we will give our dying breaths to return that liberty to this once great country; America. Who is with me?"

In the back to the room someone started singing, then the entire room began to sing that chorus, " Ohhhhh, say can you see, by the dawns early light…"

Steve, June, and President Stewart entered the senate chambers, which was completely filled to standing room only. President Stewart went straight to the podium. "Thank you everybody for coming. You know the gravity of this meeting and need to remind you this is the highest security for everything that is going to be discussed today. Only the highest security clearances are to be attending today and anybody without those security clearances must leave now."

A number of aides and assistants shuffled out of the auditorium, leaving only senators, congressmen, and military who needed to be part of the decision making process.

"Ladies and gentlemen, we have one of the most difficult decisions we have ever had to make. I don't believe I have to remind you, you cannot speak of anything we are going to be discussing today. You should consider as of this minute we are in a state of war, and anything you say outside of the proper channels could not only compromise our plans but cost thousands of lives.

"You are all aware that we have been given an ultimatum to sign Resolution 2022-311 or face the consequences of force, which would certainly mean a sea blockade and very likely military action. We should expect the worst since we all know they need to make an example of any independent country that is willing to stand against the United Nations and its governing authority. They will show what can happen to countries no matter how big, and they have warned us there would be mass casualties and destruction with no mercy being shown.

"We all remember the brutal atrocities that were shown by the UN forces in the uprisings in India, Brazil, and Spain. You can imagine what they are capable of with a Country like Texas which they need to be made an example of what can happen if you cross the UN Security Council? This may or may not include nuclear weapons if they see the need.

"The worst part is we have not completed our weapon-making capabilities, so we are essentially defenseless minus a few hovercraft and jets with light laser capabilities. We have some old missiles from when we were a state that were left to us, but without any stealth technologies or reflective digital, they would be lucky to make it out of their silos. We do have a number of advanced weapons in the design and testing stages, but they will need time to be turned into usable weapons so we need time to develop them.

"Everybody understands the UN and the world have all of the wartime weapons they are using and developing constantly in their peacekeeping activities. This means they have and know how to effectively use their military, which would likely overwhelm us before we can get our weapons developed or deployed. So what we need to do is one of two things, either we comply with their resolution or we appear to comply while we are buying time. Every one of you has to understand what this means if we are exposed, and they decide to punish us for it. We are looking at a real possibility of being completely leveled if we go to war or economically destroyed if we agree. If we buy some time and fail to do it, we will likely be at war within twenty-four hours, and you all understand what that would mean. Does anybody have any questions?"

Major General Thompson asked, "I am in complete agreement that we need to buy time if at all possible, but does everyone here believe these congressmen or Texans are going to accept giving up their freedom and sovereignty to as untrustworthy an institution as the UN. They are all ready to fight as you see every night on the net streams, how do you think they will react if we accept the proposals and have to keep the actual reasons secret? The Texas National Guard are not going to want to begin fighting Texans when they are ready to fight the Blue Helmets."

"That is a good point, General Thompson, and right now, we are not sure how we are going to present this to the Texas people," President Stewart responded. "Our initial thought is that we should promote the idea we are attempting to protect them from death and destruction a war would wreak. We have to explain we would lose most of our manufacturing facilities including the oil terminals and refineries as well as the auto and surrounding industries in the first two weeks as they are completely defenseless. There would be mass casualties inside those facilities and surrounding communities through the fires and destruction as well as collateral damage and casualties. We would have to make that clear to our fellow Texans yet not give any indication we are developing our fighting capabilities behind the scenes."

Senator Stanson from Houston spoke up, "Well, I for one do not like this program for one second, but if what General Thompson confirms what President Stewart has to say, then my county will go along with the program as long as we have an understanding there will be payback in short order. Now a couple of things I would like to suggest as I was thinking and this discussion was going on. First, we can still buy some time before the UN regulators come in to shut down all of our so-called polluting industries in Houston and elsewhere. What if we were to offer to buy our sovereignty for a sum similar to what we paid the United States?

"Perhaps at the drop-dead date, we could offer a buyout to get us a few months' time before they come in and not only hurt our manufacturing but will be looking over our scientists shoulders as they continue to develop these programs. This would not only buy us some time with the UN but would give us time with our citizens who are ready to start World War III.

"Let's also not forget the United States needs our petroleum products as well as electrical generation that if we shut down they will be crippled worse than we will. There are a few levers that we can pull to make them think twice about attacking us and destroying our energy production. They would be cutting off their nose to spite their face.

"They need to understand that if they were to drop a nuclear weapon, they would suffer as much as us from the destruction of our energy generation. They could only survive a few months without our power plants, and although we would suffer the deaths immediately, they would suffer as many or more deaths from the lack of power and from the mass anarchy that would come from our destruction."

Rattler was flying the converted F-22 over the gulf taking it through its paces enjoying the feel of an aircraft with such precision and power. He had flown US Air Force fighters, which were supposed to be identical but these had far more updated technology and power than anything he had ever flown before. The weaponry was far advanced of anything in the arsenals of any of the air forces around the world since Texas Instruments supplied most of the world's military. He was happy to move back to fighters from the hover jets he had been flying. The power and maneuverability of the fighter gave him a feeling of power he had not felt in many years. These fighters had far more acceleration and maneuverability than anything he had ever flown plus the computer assisted flying reacted as fast as you could touch the joystick.

"Rattler, give the ramjet a try, you need to get used to the speed of this aircraft. Hit the ramjet booster, and you will accelerate to Mach 7 for ten minutes. This will allow you to escape any aircraft or attack an enemy before he has any chance to detect you on laser."

"Roger that, Commander Jackson, scanning the horizons and satellites, horizons scanned, I will be going ramjet in five, four, three, two, one, fire." He hit the ramjet trigger and heard the air intakes surge in power as the aircraft began to shudder and was immediately thrown into the back of his seat as his helmet molded into his headrest. He could feel the G suit inflate while he pushed hard on his abdomen, feeling the blood begin to leave his head and his eyeballs sink into their sockets. His jet immediately shot up to ninety thousand feet and was flying at nearly four thousand miles per hour in ninety seconds, yet he kept complete control of his aircraft.

The feeling was more exhilarating than he had ever experienced, knowing there was nothing that could come close to staying with him other than the shuttle and rockets yet very few air to air or surface to air could begin to catch him if they could were to detect his signature. The aircraft diversion software protection would deflect any laser weaponry and have him out of range in seconds. After the ten-minute burn, the ramjet stopped and he switched back to jet power doing a few loops, rolls, and spins to let off the excitement while testing the maneuverability of aircraft. *This will be a formidable weapon in the war against the UN*, he thought.

Senator Stansen spoke up, "I don't know why we are dancing around when we know this is going to be a war sooner or later and most likely sooner. I say we need to tell them to take their resolution and stuff it where the sun don't shine. Sure they are going to blockade us and most likely attack us, but, if we can hold them off for two months and starve the world of refined petroleum and power, they will be begging for the UN to settle this. We all know this is going to end at the same place, so why not just get it over and be done with it? I can tell you, my constituents in Houston are ready and willing to fight and then deal with the consequences. We have had enough of the UN bullying us and every other country around like they own us."

A loud cheer swept across the chambers as the mood in the hall began to turn.

Senator Davis followed up, "I agree with Senator Stansen. We may not be ready and perhaps we will be in better shape in a couple of months, but why should we cower to their demands. Did our forefathers negotiate with Santa Ana at the Alamo? No, they fought like Texans and died with their boots on. I say we push as hard as we can to get our weapons up and turn off the power to the US to let them know what they can expect and let them know we are not going to bow down to their demands. I want them to know there are still Texans who are willing to die with their boots to take that final breath of freedom. They need to know that nobody messes with Texas and that goes double for the United Nations! Remember the Alamo Texans!"

Another loud cheer arose with shouts of "Remember the Alamo" as the members of the chamber began to become excited.

President Stewart looked over at Steve and asked him to the podium. "My fellow Texans, you all know Steven Moses, and we can see that many of you are serious about going to war, let him speak to you about the ability to cut the power off of the United States and what that would potentially mean."

Steven walked forward. "Well, as you all know, this has never been attempted, let alone accomplished, but we have been studying it and sending test models through the grid over the last six months. What we have found is there are a number of weak points in the grid in both the midwest outside Chicago and Columbus as well as Philadelphia, Newark, DC, and New York, which we call junction breakers that could likely cripple the entire network.

"What our engineers have found is that if we were to trigger these weakened transmitters and cause them to fail, they would not know we had turned off the power and they would be blacked out for anywhere from twenty-four to seventy-two hours and perhaps up to a week in certain areas. It would look exactly like a grid malfunction that just tripped substations like dominoes. When they did get back on line, they would find we were not generating, but it would look like we had a back surge knocking out our transmission lines and stations. Now they may eventually figure it out, but it would get us a couple weeks while the United States was completely dark in many of the populated areas. Any questions?"

Senator Stansen stood up. "Mr. Moses, does this have a chance of permanently destroying their electrical grid, or would it simply be temporary and could you aim this at certain cities like New York and Washington, DC?"

"No, it wouldn't physically damage anything other than a few transfer stations, which would be repaired, and no, we cannot aim it. Once you trip the switch, it will simply spread across the trunk lines and transformers like a spiderweb blacking out state by state with no real way of stopping it. Once the web starts building, there is no way of knowing how or where it would go or what cities would be blacked out.

"Now, understand this is all theory since we haven't actually done it on a massive scale like this, but you will remember the brownouts these cities had two months ago from failing substations? We are pretty confident we can make this happen. They will then route power down from Canada and up from Mexico, which will be on limited power for the duration, blacking out cities they decide can be blacked out to save energy."

The debates went on well into the night, offering resolution after resolution until the final ballots were cast and President Stewart stepped to the podium. "Ladies and gentlemen, the resolution is passed, and we have decided to reject United Nations Resolution 2022-311 and are now considered in a state of world war. God help us all and may God watch over Texas."

After the vote, June and Steven took off in the Black Stallion and flew south into the gulf. He suggested they fly out one last time since the gulf will probably be a no-fly zone as soon as the UN finds out that the resolution agreement was voted down, and they would soon be making military blockades. June enjoyed the watching sun melt into the blue and violet curved horizon fading behind them. It did not feel like they were at war although she could feel a knot in her stomach saying otherwise. This was an emotional day sitting as a witness to one of the most historic events in Texas history. She was mind scribing on her computer as she watched all of the shipping, hover traffic, and fishing boats working their nets for one of the last times in who knows how long.

She marveled at all of the seemingly chaotic movement, yet it was the dance of commerce as everybody pursued their own dreams, which only they knew where they lay or where they were going. She looked over at Steve and wondered what he was thinking as he carried so much of the world on his shoulders and had to know he could lose everything in a matter of days.

She put down her mind scriber and asked, "Are you afraid of this war?"

He looked over at her and simply smiled, "No, what can they take from me? I have everything I want now, I have my faith, my health and family, and I have found you. I have been blessed more than any man deserves. If it goes away, I have lived a life I only dreamed of as a child. As long as you will never leave my side, I have all I want."

She just smiled as a tear moistened her cheek and laid her head on his shoulder the remainder of the flight, knowing she too had everything she ever wanted; soon she saw the flight beacon of Platform 167 appear on the horizon. She could see the platform covered with hover jets and boats tied up to the docks all around the platform. He fluttered to a hover and settled down landing in the middle of the last parking space on the deck. They got out smelling the sweet salty breeze of the Florida Keys blowing across their faces as they walked to the entrance.

They took the elevator down into the sea, and as they entered the Submariner restaurant, they were met by Terrance Jasmine with his wide smile and wider blue tuxedo as the entry was filled with his laugh. "My favorite customers delighting me with your company again. What brings Steve and June Darling to my ocean floor paradise? I couldn't be happier to have such a lovely couple dining with me tonight."

"We just wanted to get down here one more time before who knows what happens. Things just seem to be spinning out of control up on top, and we wanted to get away from it all for an evening together and escape into the sea."

"Well, that sounds ominous, but you are in my place and there is seventy-five feet of sea, barracudas, and sharks between you and the real world. Come, you can have our best table we have, and we will get you started with some drinks, appetizers, and entertainment."

Terrance led them to the center table by the windows as they sat and had some pineapple drinks served in a coconut shell. He started the music, which began the water show. The dolphins swam across the stage and did their choreography swimming in and out of the Acropolis columns and statues, followed by schools of multicolored fish being herded by another set of dolphins. The divers swam through their dance routines moving with the music that flooded the room and finally two divers swam from opposite sides of the stage one man in a tuxedo diving suit and the girl wearing a bride's veil, unrolling a sign that said "Will you marry me, June Darling?"

June looked over at Steven who was on his knees, holding a small black box and the largest diamond ring she had ever seen. Under the diamond was a triangular-shaped ruby set in a white gold setting.

"The diamond represents the sunlight you are in my life, and the ruby is the scar in my heart from Sandy's death. One represents my broken past and the other our bright future together."

Her eyes filled with tears as she covered her face. He looked up into her eyes and said, "June, you know I love you, and I know you love me. I want to spend the rest of my life with you however long that will be. Will you please be my wife?"

June was in shock as the tears began to flow out of her eyes while she reached out to hug and kiss him while she sobbed. "Yes." He slipped the ring on her finger, which was lit by a spotlight somewhere in the ceiling. The setting had two tiny golden dolphins swimming around the ring with a large derrick-shaped diamond in the middle, sitting above the triangular ruby.

Just then, the lights lowered and multicolored bubbles began falling from the ceiling with a multicolored laser display lighting the underwater columns and divers as the restaurant applauded while Terrance came walking out grinning from ear to ear with both of their parents. "He got you, Cherie! Congratulations, to you both, although I don't know what you see in this man. You could have done a lot better, Cherie!"

June looked weakly as her tears flowed freely. "Mom? Daddy?

"June Bug, we are so happy for you. He called us last week and asked for your hand in marriage, and I said only if I am able to marry you two . Your mother and I had a pretty good idea you would say yes, so we agreed to come out here. What a place! I ain't crazy about being on the bottom of the ocean in a glass bubble, but this is beyond beautiful."

Her mother was dressed in pink chiffon that made her look like an underwater fairy with the light glittering off of the sparkles. Her eyes were filled with tears as she came over to hug her daughter. "This is so beautiful, and you make such a handsome couple. I know you will both be happy. Welcome to the family, Steven we have been waiting for you." That made them all laugh.

Daniel and Helena Moses stepped forward and congratulated Steven and June and hugged them all.

Daniel Moses looked at June. "We couldn't be happier for you to be his wife. You have no idea how hurt he was when he lost Sandy. It was as if he had his arm cut off and we watched as he retreated into his work and ignored his personal life. You have changed all of that, and we could not be prouder of him or happier for you two."

Tears rolled down her cheeks as she hugged both of them.

"I am stunned, Jasmine. How did you two pull this off?"

"Cherie, he called last week, and we put it all together for him. For you, we provide anything, now be prepared for the best crab stuffed mahi-mahi you have ever tasted. I hope you brought your appetite, Cherie, you are going to need it!"

"Of course I did. Today was the longest day of my life and now it is the happiest, but yes, I am starved. Thank you, Steven, I love you so much it hurts! Can we get married right away? I don't believe this is happening."

The restaurant began applauding and wishing them a happy future together as the party was just beginning.

NEW YORK
CHRISTIAN CHURCH

The New York Texas Ranger rose to give his speech in a deserted school auditorium in front of over two thousand cheering fans and parishioners. "As you all have heard, last week Texas rejected UN resolution 2022-311, and now the they are deciding what actions they are going to take. You all need to pray for our brothers and sisters in Texas for their protection and safety as the winds of World War III is surely about to reign down on them. I also shouldn't have to tell you, we are all in even more danger than we have ever been before.

"We have no way of knowing what this means for us in New York City, but we should be prepared for martial law as well as tightened security throughout the city if that's possible. We are all going to have to take some extra precautions so we are not seen or captured in the city sweeps coming our way. We will not be having any more of these large rallies as we need to have our assemblies on the secure net and use all of your masking software to confuse the spyware and spiders. From this point on, we all need to be considered even higher priority targets than we have been in the past.

"Folks, how did we get here? For all of you Americans and New Yorkers who grew up here, you have to ask yourselves, how did this tyranny ever come to be? How in America does a group that simply wants to enjoy freedom become public enemy number one of the United States let alone the world? And how does one of our fellow states that seceded become the enemy of the entire world simply for wanting to hold onto its sovereignty? It is simple how this happened, good people stopped paying attention and caring about their country, and their country vanished. It has now been taken over by the very people who we considered our enemies ten years ago. Little by little, they took more and more until we became their subjects.

"Brothers and sisters, you have to remember who you are. You are proud God-fearing Americans who do not need the government to make your every decision and provide your every need. You are the people who conquered the oceans, crossed the prairies, and those western mountains in wagons. You are the people who fought off the most powerful tyrannies around the world numerous times and now we need to be those people once more. They are here in New York and throughout the country, Americans who are all starving for the truth and looking for leadership. We need to reach out to those people and recruit them into our ranks. We need to cause the tyrants as much problem as we can while their focus is on defeating Texas. We need to distract their focus so the Texans can have a chance of winning.

"Even though there will be a crackdown on our movements, it is doubtful they will be able to fight the war and have enough men to find us with our underground routes. We still can use our subway avoidance methods of overcoming their detection monitors. The past five years have taught us ways to get in and out of places nobody in the city even has a clue on where these tunnels go or our hidden entries.

"We owe it to our Texan brothers and sisters to make things as difficult for the United Nations to fight this war. You all know that if you're caught you are likely going to be sentenced to imprisonment or hanging . We need to have their heart and courage to maintain a war in the belly of the beast. Many of you will not make it out of this war, but you will have given everything you have to the cause of freedom. The advantage we have is we know these people better than they know themselves. This is the last stand for freedom or we will all die trying."

A chant started across the crowd: "Freedom, freedom, freedom or death! Freedom, freedom, freedom or death! …

"Yes, my brothers and sisters, this is our fight for freedom. We have been oppressed and taken advantage of for far too long. We can go back to the times where they had fair and free elections when people's votes were counted. We can go back to self rule and bring our republic back to be represented by the people and where the people rule."

Just then, the entire outside of the building lit up like a movie set as they could hear shooting begin on the roof. Spotlights were shining from police hovers as well as the street spots being directed from the tops of the skyscrapers lighting the entire area like it was the middle of day.

"Battle stations everybody! Women and children hit the escape routes and get moving. We will give you a twenty-minute head start and be right behind to meet at the designated meeting locations for your teams. Prayer warrior teams, say some prayers for our victory!"

The gun battle was in full combat as Ranger moved outside. They were surrounded by UN police and gangs as well as some of the special union forces. The air was covered with hovers darting in and out of the New York canyons. An anti-air laser opened fire on one coming at them as you could see the digital deflection shield was lit up like a fireworks display when all of a sudden, it lit up deep red and exploded into a giant ball of flames crashing into a warehouse. They knew they were outnumbered and outgunned as they fought with a ferocious tenacity to give the women time to escape down through the maze of tunnels. The prayer warriors continued praying for a miracle to allow their escape and to allow a victory.

Then they heard the now familiar screech coming from up the East River that froze the spine of every man on the ground. A Hover Fortress came roaring over the battle field, firing lasers in every direction, killing men by the dozens. The battle turned to chaos as they retreated back toward the school side entrance, which was cut off by the block-sized killing machine. It was impossible for them to cross as the entire parking lot was lit by spotlights being shown from the tops of tall buildings on either side. The loud speakers were demanding their surrender and to put down their weapons or face certain death. His entire force was pinned down behind abandoned cars and trucks and hid under the school walkways as the police and gangs were fighting their way toward them it was only a matter of time before they were captured or killed.

Susan Bennett was leading the women and children through the tunnels as quickly as she could. The leaders had night vision headlamps, and she knew these underground mazes as well as anybody in New York. She grew up with her brothers playing and transporting Bibles through this network, which allowed her travel below ground faster than most New Yorkers could above. Just as they turned the corner that linked into the subway rendezvous, the entire tunnel lit up from rows of overhead lights as they looked and saw around fifty police officers waiting for them in an ambush. They looked behind, and there was another group of gang members blocking their exit behind them, carrying portable spotlights turning the dark into the brightest day with nowhere to hide.

One of the policemen spoke through a megaphone and said, "Ladies, don't move or try to escape. We won't hurt you, but you must surrender and come out of those tunnels. Now come over here nice and slow! If you have weapons, drop them and surrender peacefully, you owe it to your children, we won't harm them or you if you cooperate."

The Ranger huddled together with his captains and discussed whether to surrender or fight it out and try to break through, when something caught his eye across the river and started seeing white explosions and buildings going black. It quickly moved their direction as they heard what sounded like shotguns going off and large flashes followed by darkened blocks when suddenly a flash lit up the transformer across the street in a spark cascading explosion as all the lights around them went dark, including the spotlights covering their escape. There appeared to be mass confusion as this happened and could hear the police yelling for instructions as their radios and computers went dark. That's when he yelled to make a break to the school building, and they ran for all they were worth getting inside the school and down through the tunnels and into the blackened city.

Susan Bennett was praying as the police portable spotlights went black, giving her a chance to take the side tunnel leading to their designated rendezvous. She heard the confusion of the police behind her as they replaced the false brick covering of their escape tunnel and headed to the emergency meeting site while praying for the men's safety. She had no idea why the lights went out, but it was a miraculous answer to her prayers.

President Stewart, Steven, June, Vice President Sanchez, and Sam Satterwhite Texas, Secretary of Energy, watched the giant wall monitor of the US grid as the rolling blackout moved across the country until the entire screen was dark. After it finished like an intricate rolling domino fall, they looked at each other knowing that this was going to cause untold pain and suffering in their old country. They all knew this had to be done to buy some time before the military attacks began. If they waited, the attacks would likely be coming in the morning, and who knows they may come anyway, although it was very likely they shut down the United Nation's communication for the short term. They would have very little time to organize an attack on Texas while trying to figure out how to stop the people from rioting from no electricity.

Sam looked at the screen in amazement and then turned to the group. "Well, it looks like the surge torpedo worked. We had our questions as to whether this would cause isolated blackouts with some brownouts rather than a rolling blackout. There is no way for them to trace it since when they isolate it they will find a substation outside Cleveland is what tripped this event. A blown transformer will be found to be the culprit. You may have your usual suspicions, but after they run their tests and models, it will always point to Cleveland rather than Texas. That is some amazing technology that could send a surge torpedo through the power lines and begin tripping breakers all along the lines. The final piece of this technology is it destroyed our power bridges across the border, so it will take weeks to repair them on our side to potentially bring us back on line. We can delay repairs up to eight weeks due to our lack of adaptability to United States technology before they know we are dragging our feet, but they will be expecting that.

"Right now, any building that has emergency power or diesel backup is trying to get on line and restore as much power as they can. The governments including the UN and US are trying to reroute to Canada and Mexico although some of those may have been damaged in the blackout. This is going to take three to five days and perhaps a few more before they are back to functioning on a limited basis. Once they begin to recover, they will have to decide how to ration the power, which means they are going to have to decide which are the most vital cities and which are not. The rest of the cities will be dark and will have critical food and fuel problems complicating their recovery. Right now the UN is functioning at around ten to 20 percent and have nobody to communicate to or have any idea of what is left with power. The next forty-eight to seventy-two hours they will be assessing the damage as will we."

Steven walked to the front of the room, "Folks, we have just caused our old friends to become basically a third-world country in a matter of minutes. They may as well be in the middle of Brazil as far as they have no power, water, or transportation. The difference is, even though they have had hard times over the last few years, they have never experienced life with limited electrical power, and we must return it as soon as we can. We now are the most powerful and advanced country on earth since we have unlimited power and only a week or two before this war will begin in earnest. This also will give them an idea of what to expect if they are to destroy our generating capacity, they will suffer along with us.

"We have a short window of opportunity to prepare for battle. With the rejection of our stalling tactics from the Texas Congress, we have to make every minute count and begin to set up defenses and design weapons. Everything has to be put on a rush schedule and become usable yesterday. This is our chance to produce as much advanced weaponry as we can and my companies will work around the clock to make sure this happens."

President Stewart looked around the room. "This was a truly amazing event. How your engineers made this happen is beyond me and a miracle it actually took out the entire US. I understand your feelings for them, Steven, but they declared war on us, not the other way around, and they deserve whatever punishment they receive. They won't be worrying about Texas when they and the United Nations begin destroying our industries and cities or wiping out oil platforms. Texans will potentially be dying and that is what I care about, not whether a city is lit up or a gas station is working, they should have considered that possibility when they allowed the UN to use them. We now have an upper hand for a couple weeks and it is time for our people to make the most of it."

———⟨◦⁄◦⁄◦⟩———

Ranger and his forty best fighters had been driving all night to get to the Rome NY Reeducation camp that held twenty-five thousand political prisoners. With the power out and the mass confusion in the streets, they believed this would be the ideal time to help some of their friends and allies escape and swell his ranks. They pulled up on the south side of the camp with the lake on the opposite side. They could see that it was still lit up under emergency power and could hear the generator rumbling, but there were large areas were darkened without good lighting, which was where they were heading.

The only good part of being on the run is they always had fuel in storage depots or used the underground network to provide enough for missions like this. Most city dwellers had given up on owning cars due to the lack of gas, but his network was filled with underground survivalists who had stockpiles of staples like fuel. They parked the cars five hundred yards from camp while Ranger addressed the group, "Men, you all know this is going to be a high-risk mission. You may be killed or captured, and then you will be spending ten years inside this prison. You also know this is our opportunity to grow our army with thousands of our experienced Christian warriors back from the camp. These men and women were some of our best trained fighters and technicians, and we have a real chance to get them back, so here is how we are going to get inside.

"I want the technicians and scouts to take out the auxiliary generator in the middle of the compound, which should be guarded. I need you to knock it out and make the prison yard dark. Tommy, you know how to get your guys over the fences without being detected, you are the key to this. Once you black out the grounds we will cut through the fences while you are getting into the cell blocks and opening the doors. We will be thirty seconds behind you once the lights go out, and you take care of the tower guards. When the prisoners begin filling the camp, the guards should give up and worry more about getting home rather than being killed by their prisoners. We will definitely have the advantage of surprise as there is no way anybody is expecting this. Let's say a prayer and get going. You guys ready?"

Tommy Davis led a group of five men to the darkest section of fence and took off his backpack. As a one-time jewel thief who had broken into the tightest museums in the world, this was child's play. Inside the pack was a digitally synchronizing ladder and paralyzing Kevlar razor wire cover. It was in a spring loaded catapult which shot it over the razor wire and digitally censored the fence detection and electrification. Once his ladder contacted the sensors, it eliminated their signal and allowed the men to climb up and over the fence. Once they got inside, they made it to the generator shack where they shot the men with laser stun guns while their engineers shut down and disabled the generator, making the prison completely dark while opening the magnetic door locks to the cell blocks as a safety feature. They headed for the prisoner barracks as they could see the rest of the teams coming through the fence, which is when the shooting started from the guard towers.

Ranger's men systematically returned fire and had the upper hand of not only having the advantage of surprise, but they all had night lenses while the guards were searching for theirs, making them easy targets. The rest of the guards had no night lenses and began surrendering immediately once they realized the attackers could see while they were blind men. The barracks began emptying as the remaining guards started running toward the lake and into the surrounding woods. His men fired a few shots in their direction, but they knew they wouldn't be back as they entered the prison to free the prisoners.

When they turned a corner, they saw they were in what looked like an infirmary except all the people on the beds were dead.

Both men and women were on gurneys with tubes coming out of their arms, but there was no movement and as they checked them they found them warm with no pulse. Just then, prisoners came around the corner, and they stopped to look at the room full of dead bodies as the horror hit their faces.

They all walked through the room to the double doors out the back, which led to a large morgue and crematorium oven that had multiple doors to dispose of the bodies. It looked as if they could burn hundreds of bodies at any given time.

One of the prisoners spoke up, "Hi, my name is Tom Shelton. This is the Adirondack death camp. There are fewer than a thousand of us left. We make furniture as long as we can provide free labor, but once we are unable to provide that, thanks to the starvation rations, we join these people and become ashes for the corn fields. They dispose of over five thousand of us per month, mostly political prisoners."

Ranger just shook his head. "My name is Ranger, and I am their number one political dissident. There are supposed to be more than twenty-five thousand prisoners here, how long have you been here, and how long has this been going on?"

"I have been here almost a year, which is longer than most last, especially during the winter when they turn the heat off in the barracks. This has been going on longer than I've been here. We have heard rumors there are around twenty or thirty of these camps spread across America."

"Is this everybody, and are there a women's barracks?"

"No, there is only one women's cell block. They are brought here immediately since they are considered expendable unless they are attractive to temporarily become the guards' mistresses or they are exceptional accountants or another needed skill. Of course they don't want much of this reported so those positions are pretty scarce. I believe there may be five or ten left on the north end of the camp. Do you want me to show you where it is?"

"Sure, take some of my men and bring them out we will be leaving in ten minutes. Take plenty of video of this infirmary, boys. We need this news to get out to the United States and the world."

The horror of this camp reminded Ranger of the death camps in Germany and Russia, but he never imagined he would ever see one in America. He had a rage that went to his core, knowing his brothers and sisters were being murdered by the tens of thousands for the crime of being Christians and fighting for freedom. This was a crime against humanity, yet there was nobody to enforce it. A feeling of helplessness began at the base of his spine, making him dizzy until the rage stepped back in.

They could see the lights of the bus convoy coming in the distance as they pointed the prisoners where the hole in the fence was and to head over to the now lighted trucks they had just arrived in. Ranger's men guarded the escape to make sure no guards decided to be heroes and begin shooting at his new recruits although after seeing what he just saw he wasn't sure if he would start shooting first.

Madame Secretary Polentas addressed the assembled security council, "Ladies and gentlemen, thank you for making the effort of coming to this security meeting to address this issue of Texas's rejection of UN security resolution 2022-311. Even though we are experiencing extreme power blackouts in many regions of the United States, we have been assured by the United States government that they will have a majority of New York City back to full power within forty-eight to seventy-two hours. We have enough diesel fuel to provide emergency power, until then. The local citizens continue to conform to emergency protocols and the UN compound will soon be back on public power.

"As for the matter at hand, we must decide what options we have to convince Texas they need to join the world community.

Until we have our power back on line, we recommend we simply declare and enforce a sea and land embargo of all goods going in and out of Texas. This is manageable and would allow us to negotiate with Texas to provide them an opportunity to return to the negotiating table and accept UN 2022-311. A blockade would show we are doing everything we can to negotiate while projecting strength under these circumstances. The world needs to understand Texas is being unreasonable while we are reaching out to avoid military action. The floor is now open for discussion. Mr. Shabaz of Swaziland is recognized."

"Madame Secretary, how do we know this power outage was not caused by the Texans, and if it was, it would be an act of war that would allow us to respond in kind. We have a major country out of power as well as a rebuff from Texas. If they can rebuff the United Nations, then what power do we have? Speaking for myself and a number of my colleagues, we recommend a retaliatory attack and destroy their oil storage facilities as punishment for their attack on the energy infrastructure of the US."

"Mr. Shabaz, the United States and our people are investigating this outage, and although it is very early in the investigation, the analysis is pointing toward a mishap having to do with the age of the grid. I do, however, agree we have to be careful with the appearance of weakness in this situation and need to be strong and forceful in our response. That is why we believe a full blockade on all Texan ports of commerce is the proper step while we assess and help repair the power infrastructure. If we had not had these blackouts, we would have full access to our spy and satellite network as well as more efficient communication to coordinate an attack along their Gulf coast. Much of our military structure and communication is down, so we need to restore those assets before we can be at full capabilities. Does that answer your question, Ambassador Shabaz?"

"Yes, Madame Secretary, I yield my time to Ambassador Herrmoza from Brazil."

Ambassador Herrmoza was a decorated general of Brazil and became the vice president of Brazil before being appointed to the UN post. "Madame Secretary, as you know, there is a growing sympathy for the Texan movement in South America, and I would just warn you and this chamber of the dangers a long negotiating period could have in our hemisphere. A number of our countries down there are oil-producing suppliers who have long-term economic relationships with Texas, and they are not firmly behind with this action. Can you guarantee this will be short and decisive action that will not drag on, because the public sympathy will not stay on our side for very long?"

"Ambassador Herrmoza, and to all the ambassadors of South America, we have been in communication for a long time with your continent and are very aware of the economic realities of your region. Your people have to understand they and their countries have been exploited by the Texan oil industry for decades. When they come into the world community, they will have to share their wealth and make those contracts for your oil more fairly written for your underprivileged countries. Your people have to know one of the reasons we are taking this action is for them and their futures. They deserve to share in the wealth of Texas rather than being exploited by them. When Texas does sign this resolution, and yes, there will be a very short action, we will have the world finally working in unison to solve our shared problems of poverty, starvation, and inequality.

"Yes, Ambassador Wong of China."

"Madame Secretary, we too have been close trading partners with Texas and have built strong alliances both economic and technologically. We admire much of what they have accomplished although they are very tough competitors. China agrees with you that we need to make them agree to the resolution and stop the exploitation of small undeveloped countries around the world and especially in the Asian continent. That said, we also do not want to destroy their ability to provide and produce many of the products they provide efficiently and on time for us and the world. We and many countries rely on their production as you can see from the blackout. We would prefer this can be negotiated to a satisfactory outcome, but if we do need to use some sort of force, let it be short and swift with as little collateral damage as possible. You need to understand we are walking a dangerous tightrope with the economy of the world. The last thing we need is to fall into another massive Depression like 2016.

"Ambassador Wong, you have my word that is exactly what our generals are planning to do. We will only use whatever amount of force is necessary to accomplish the task. We expect this will be a very short surgical action causing as little damage and casualties as necessary. You must also understand if we allow Texas to stare us down, then which country will be next and who after that until we have no member countries in the United Nations. We need to stand together and make this happen so the Texans will comply quickly rather than trying to wait us out."

—⟨⟩⟨⟩⟨⟩—

Steven Moses looked around the board room, which had a magnificent view of the Texas horizon stretching across the Lone Star landscape of over a hundred miles from the top of Moses Tower. "Ladies and gentlemen, you all know why I called this meeting and the critical nature of it. You have been briefed, and I expect you can tell us what you have found from your departments. As you know, this is a meeting between our energy, technology, and weapons development groups in hopes of designing a system to protect our energy facilities.

"We need to install some more advanced defensive and offensive systems that will protect our facilities from the attacks, which will be coming in the next days and weeks. Ideally we will be able to protect our refining and shipping ports as well as the production wells off the coast. Those well caps, of course, are mostly below water and with automatic shutoff valves controlled from here the damages would be minimal and easily repaired after this is over. We also expect very little attack on our electrical power generation since these will be powering America when we are able to get back on line. Their main targets will likely be the oil refining and storage facilities. Am I correct, Major General Summers?"

"Yes, that is our assessment. We expect they will attack those oil storage and production facilities first to knock out our primary products and cause the most damage possible in a high-priority target. Our most vulnerable refineries are offshore refineries one, two, and three. Being built five miles out on twenty-acre platforms makes them inviting targets for their ships and planes. This is a two-edged sword in that it is a rather small area with a maximum amount of damage per attack, but it is also very defensible in a narrow kill corridor if we can develop and deploy some weapons to defend them.

"The good news is, unless they do something completely out of character militarily, we know exactly where they are coming, so we can use our target as bait for their weapons. I warn everybody, though, there is an old saying that all of the best laid plans go out the window after the first shot is fired."

"Thank you, General, and that is sound advice. We are working on those weapons, which is why we invited Bill Branson our Tech Leader and what his teams have been working on, Bill."

"Thank you, Steven, hopefully we will give the general some mousetraps for his giant piece of cheese. As most of you know, we have been supplying most of the weaponry around the world, which were applied to many of the weapons platforms we produced. Our engineers have been working double shifts since we got drift of our acquisition by the UN and have made some significant developments with our weapons systems.

"A couple of the defensive advances we have developed are advanced digitally protective skins for our fighters and hover jets. Think of them as skins that are computer screens which projects the background on that screen. Also, they will deflect any lasers hitting them as well as detection wavelengths. They have multiple advantages since they are a perfect camouflage blending into whatever background they are against. They simply put the background on the skin and become invisible to the eye as well as electronic detection.

"We are developing the ability to make a surface digitally protected with a series of lasers to jam any laser weapon on the planet for short periods of time. Our problem is we can only cover limited areas for limited periods of time since this technology uses vast amounts of memory to jam such large numbers of codes enemy laser weapons' possess. We are trying to miniaturize as much as we can, and it will also stealth any guidance systems for conventional bombs with laser targeting. As of now, we have no capability to defend since we haven't deployed any of these weapons we are completely defenseless to an attack.

"As most of you know, we have retrofitted our F-22s with a ramjet booster to make them a crossover between a jet and a rocket, giving us the fastest aircraft in the world. We are training our pilots and working out the issues with making them maneuverable at these supersonic speeds. We are also working out the details of how do our weapons systems work at those speeds. We have made great strides in developing intuitive mind-control targeting, thanks to our gaming industries. We definitely have the best fighter on the planet. It's just that we only have around a hundred of them compared to over twenty thousand UN aircraft. I guess you can say we have them right where we want them."

The room chuckled in appreciation.

"Along those same lines, we have been developing some multi-Mach drones that have been showing great promise. Again, we have not deployed any of these weapon systems or aircraft. We will begin these systems as soon as we finish testing them. Any questions?"

President Stevens spoke first. "I appreciate all you are doing and how hard your men are working, but do we really have time to completely test these weapons since we may be attacked any day now? This rolling blackout will only last a few days, and perhaps a week, and then they will have the ability to attack us."

"I agree, President Stevens. However, we would be putting people at risk if these are not tested, and we don't have enough man hours to make things happen any faster. We should have these systems ready to go in two or three weeks and then begin deploying."

Steven rose to speak. "Bill, this is our number one priority. Whatever you have to do and whatever it costs, these weapons have to be deployed. I want them completed and deployed in three weeks from today, even if you have to use every person at Texas Technologies to get that done. Can we count on you?"

"Yes, sir, I have no idea how, but we will get it done."

June's earpiece rang, and the midair halo display said it was unknown, which meant she knew who it was. "Hello?"

"Professor Darling, Ranger here. I have something you need to know. We made a raid on a prison camp during the electrical blackout, and we found something absolutely unfathomable. There was a camp up in the Adirondacks set up to hold political prisoners, which we raided to help some of our prisoners escape and were expecting to release around twenty thousand or more to help us with our battles in New York. When we broke in we found a death camp."

"What do you mean by a death camp?"

"Just what you think, it was designed to kill political prisoners. We found less than a thousand people still there and found they were killing over five thousand per month and that there are camps like this scattered around the country. I have a file we have made with video and interviews we need you to share with your people and the rest of the world. I am sending that to you when I hang up and hope you pass it to your news distributors to let the world know."

"Ranger, are you telling me there are concentration camps like in Nazi Germany and Mao's China killing people simply because they are politically disagreeing with the government? Are you sure these weren't actually criminals who were guilty of capital crimes or that the political prisoners were not being transferred somewhere else?"

"No, we found people in the infirmary with IVs of cyanide in their arms who were dead and rows of corpses being prepared for cremation. It was a death factory, and we have the video and interviews to prove it. We…what the—" Just then the connection went dead.

"Hello, Ranger? Hello?" June frantically tried to reconnect, but the connection could not find the source.

She tried all of her redials and reconnects and searches for a connection and nothing, causing her to fear the worst. All she could do was wait and hope that his download was sent and could reach her memory base. Were they actually killing their enemies in New York, can that be true, and if it was, she needed proof to let the rest of the world know. She would wait through the night, but if there were no files in the morning, she knew she would have to go find Ranger. She had a sense he was in real danger, and nobody knew it but her so she had to help.

The next morning, she checked her memory banks at home and the office, and there was nothing with no messages on her phone, which meant he was either captured or deep underground. Either way, she knew she had to go find those files to confirm what he had told her. She rode the shuttle down to the Moses tower and met Steve for an early breakfast.

He lit up when he saw her, giving her a kiss and a hug as he offered her to sit at the executive cafeteria. She ordered an Alaskan crab omelet with a cup of tea while she looked out over the horizon, staring far beyond it.

Steve noticed he distance and quiet mood. "What is it, June? Is something wrong? You seem to be worried about something, second thoughts about getting married?"

She laughed and shook her head as a tear rolled down her cheek. "I think they have captured Ranger, if they have it is his death sentence!" She explained the phone call and everything he had told her about the concentration camps. She told how she waited and worked all night to get his connection back to get the files and find out if he was safe. Steven was in shock as he listened.

"Steven, I have to go to New York and find him and bring back him and his files to get this story out. I contacted the girl who escorted us out of the subways, and she said they are looking for him too and have some tips where he might be. I have to do this to get the truth out. With this upcoming war, there is no way we can allow this story to be buried, the world needs to find know what they are doing and who is doing it."

"Then I am going with you, I'm not taking a chance of losing you again up there. The last time you went on your own was too close, and I don't know what I would do to lose someone else I love. Besides we are a team, and I can fly you to places you can't go without me."

"You can't go, they know who you are, and they would be watching your every move and you have too much to do here. I can go as a journalist who is covering this story and will have a certain amount of anonymity. You would draw attention to me and that is the last thing Ranger needs right now. There are still domestic flights to New York, and even though they may watch me, I will not be that valuable a target as a professor and a member of the press. And yes, I know, I will be careful, but this story is too big and can destroy their entire smokescreen as a guardian of the oppressed. I have to go and find Ranger and those videos."

"Look, June, everything you say is true, but I need to come with you. I will go as an official ambassador to continue some last-minute negotiations with the UN. This will keep the focus on me and can allow you to be in the meetings as an official reporter, and we can look for Ranger together. Besides, you are recording this for history, and whether we like it or not, I am a big part of this story. I am not going to let you up there again without any help or protection. If there is still a chance to stop this, war we need to take it. If there are death camps being run by their government, it needs to be exposed so the world will know about their existence." He was used to the times when his fame was a hindrance, and this was one of them except this time he could be a divergence. She could be found by Ranger's group, and she was the only one they trusted, so she was the only one who could possibly pull this off.

He looked over at her. "We can only go for a week. If we can't find him or the camp in that amount of time, then you are not going to be able to and things will be getting too dangerous as the war will be imminent. I hate going there in the first place, but we have to do this, and they won't be suspecting us, although they will be trying to follow us, so I will be using the stealth upgraded Stallion and keep them off our tracks. I have had it retrofitted with some upgrades and will be very helpful in this situation."

June relented. "I love you for helping, and I really don't know why you put up with me. We have to do this, and bringing anyone else will only endanger them, and we won't be able to get around as easily. I need to be there as a reporter who is just trying to get the story at the UN and not draw too much suspicion while you are negotiating. They will be suspicious of us as Texans, but I don't want to be looking like we are there for something else. I know this is dangerous, but we don't have any choices if these camps are real. I don't know why you put up with me, must be love."

"Must be," as they both laughed.

———◦◦◦———

Captain Thomas was getting the feel of his new jet and was now able to target, maneuver, and fire while entering and leaving ramjet speed. He had learned to bank and change directions faster than any of the other pilots in the training group. It was as if he had always flown this jet and was becoming a part of it as his senses began to adapt to the speed and technology of the fighter. The new advanced lasers were far more powerful than anything he had ever seen and had kill power out to fifty miles. This should give him an advantage of nearly twenty miles over anything the UN had in their arsenal and, with the advanced targeting electronics, will be far more advanced of what they will be seeing. In today's battles, there is a saying, "Microseconds make the difference between flying, spying, and dying."

They practiced their mock dogfights over the gulf, knowing in a few days they would be in real air battles protecting Texas and these oil facilities, which they all knew would be the primary targets. They practiced their attacks from over a hundred thousand feet to make full use of their ramjet boosters. This was a riskier attack mode since pulling out going over four thousand miles per hour was difficult, but from a strategic standpoint with their stealth technology they would be appearing from space and should be looking at a shooting gallery. The plane shook and groaned every time it bottomed the trough from the heavy G forces, but the more times he practiced, the better he got until the plane actually floated through the bottom. This may be how they could overcome the huge advantage the United Nations Air Force had in numbers of aircraft.

He saw the attackers on his down screen attacking out of the south and nosed down hitting the afterburners shooting past Mach 4. He was slammed back in his seat as the 3D screen filled his windshield while he squeezed the targeting computer as he looked at the various targets. The visual targeting tagged all the aircraft as they lit one after another with hit and kill lights, making their way across the horizon just as he pulled back feeling those heavy Gs forcing him deep into his seat as the ramjet fired, turning his aircraft into a blur across the gulf climbing back to subspace just as the booster cut out well out of the fray. He felt himself going back to conventional as he banked back from off the Jamaican beaches then coasted back to Bush Air Force Base north of Houston.

After he landed, he was called into Commander Jackson's office for his debriefing. As he walked in, he noticed another half a dozen generals who all turned as he entered the room. He knew he was either in big trouble or something good to have all those full birds in one place.

"Captain Thomas, enter. I hope you know everyone here but let's just say we are all very impressed with your flying ability and how you have quickly adapted to our ramjet booster technology. For most of our pilots, it is a bit overwhelming to fly at those speeds with as much information and speed coming at you, but you seem to thrive on it. What's your secret?"

"I'm not sure, Commander, I think I just have flying in my blood and want to do my part to help Texas. It just seems, sir, that when I hit those burners and ramjet, all of a sudden, not only does the plane begin accelerating but so does my body and mind. It is as if I become a part of their speed and the entire world slows down to normal even though I know we are rocketing through the Machs. It is then when everything becomes clear and the targets look like they are all moving in slow motion compared to my speed and they become sitting ducks on a pond.

"Sir, I am not trying to be cocky, but when I am up there, it is not like I am flying at all, but every single muscle and nerve is a part of the control panel and taking the plane places it never has gone. I have complete confidence in her, and I know it is the best fighter ever developed. I also know these jets are very likely all that is standing between winning and losing this war and our freedom. These few planes may be the only thing standing between thousands or even millions of Texans living or dying. It may be like Winston Churchill said in the Battle of Britain, 'Never has so many owed so much to so few,' and I am one of the few. Does that answer your question, sir?"

"Yes, it does, Captain Thomas, and we have been going over your results along with the other pilots who are also impressed with your abilities, some who have been flying for years as fighter pilots, but you have exceeded all of their results. We have decided to promote you to wing commander and begin sharing your skills with the other pilots. Frankly, Captain, you are the best pilot we have seen go through here and are the best pilot we have on the ramjet F-22. So, Captain Thomas, come here and let me pin on your squadron commander wings. Along with this comes your Texas citizenship, so congratulations, Texan Air Force Wing Commander Thomas."

Terry Thomas was stunned. Not only was he promoted to being the squad leader, but he now had his dream come true of being a Texas citizen in only two years. He was gob-smacked as he looked up at Commander Davidson saluting him, and he quickly snapped a salute back and shook all of their hands. He knew now was not the time to tear up although he had never been so moved in his life. He walked out of the room thinking he was already flying higher and faster than any jet he flew. He thought to himself as he walked across the tarmac, Captain Terry Thomas "Texan," and his eyes began to swell up as he thought how proud his parents would be. That would all have to wait as he headed for postflight drills and breaking down the latest video.

Steven stepped into the Stallion and checked over all the gages while June looked across the river. He lifted off from La Guardia heading toward the United Nations Compound. A few minutes later, he and June sat in Secretary General Polentas' waiting room looking out over the East River wondering if Ranger was dead or alive. She had to keep that out of her mind as she was about to have the interview of a lifetime between her and the most powerful woman in the world and the man holding the fate of nations in his hands. Does she know about the concentration camps or is someone on a mission of their own? She wondered if she could get a clue during this interview. The secretary motioned to her and Steve. "Madame Secretary General will see you now."

Steven's hair on his neck stood on end as his senses moved to a heightened state. He was fully aware that the president of the United States had died in this office under very suspicious circumstances so he had to be aware of his and June's safety at all times. He entered the office and no matter what you thought of the United Nations or New York City the view of Manhattan from these heights was inspiring. You couldn't see as far as you could from the Moses Tower, but you could see skyscrapers and cityscapes spread across the horizon and stretching out to the Atlantic Ocean.

He looked at the diminutive UN Secretary General Salinas Margarita Polentas standing and coming around her desk to shake his hand. He noticed standing next to her was Ambassador General Herrmoza of Brazil who also shook hands and greeted them through cold squinted eyes—eyes you knew you could never turn your back on.

"Hello, Madame Secretary and Ambassador Herrmoza, you know Professor Darling who is a journalism professor for the University of Texas and documenting all of our negotiations for historical record if you do not mind. We wish we were meeting on more friendly terms and are hoping we can ease some of those tension we are all feeling right now."

"We share your hopes, Mr. Moses," she replied. "Things seem to have spun out of control, and we are hoping that in our meetings cooler heads can prevail and we can come to an amiable agreement. What exactly brings you here, Mr. Moses?"

"Well, Madame Secretary, the president of Texas has sent me, and we are hoping we can find a way to avert a military solution and be able to maintain our sovereignty which we have worked so hard for generations to acquire."

"What do you propose, Mr. Moses? You have already turned down our final offer for peace and will not join the United Nations as a fully partnered nation, so there doesn't really seem to be another solution unless you have something we have not yet discussed. Do you have something new?"

"Well, yes, Madame Secretary, we are proposing something that we believe can be beneficial to both parties and allow us to begin to work with the UN. What we want to offer is, we will pay half of the United Nations dues you are asking and would renegotiate that in twelve to twenty-four months so we can begin to adapt to some of your regulations and procedures, which would be mutually negotiated. We also believe you can save much of your expenses if we would suspend your regulations and regulators from actually having to physically come to Texas and maintain our practices. We will send you audited results from our companies on a hourly basis to verify our compliance with your pollution standards.

"As you know, we fall well below the World Pollution Commission mandates for our own emission controls and there is really no need for you to send all those people to monitor something that is already being taken care of. We have all of our industry emission monitoring on the Internet for anyone to look up day or night in real time. We would also expect to pay our full expenses on the UN protection of our trade routes we use for international commerce. We are hoping these compromises would be satisfactory to avert any military actions which may be considered by this body."

"Mr. Moses, you cannot be serious. Why would we ever agree to not only Texas not become a full member, but you would most likely never become one? This proposal is not acceptable and if this is all you have then you are wasting yours and my time. Certainly you did not come all the way from Texas to offer this, did you?"

"Please, Secretary Polentas, of course, we didn't fly up here to waste your time. Just tell me what we can do to an equitable compromise and make this agreement work. You have to understand our countrymen are very proud people that value their freedom and liberty. What is it we can offer to potentially give both of us what we want?"

"Well, Mr. Moses, pride is the type of thing that can start wars. Time for compromise is over. The minimum we will accept from you is the complete acceptance as a full member of the United Nations. We have already discussed this in the past, and you should understand this completely. Unless you accept our resolution, we will be putting a full sea and air blockade on your country in one week. I will be announcing this in the morning, now do you have a more appealing offer?"

"Not at this time, Madame Secretary. Let me talk to President Stewart and see what else I can offer you in the morning. Before you make this announcement, I would like one more opportunity to discuss another proposal with you. Can we meet first thing in the morning?"

"Unless you are willing to agree to our resolution, I see no point in carrying these discussions any further."

"With all due respect, Madame Secretary Polentas, we are potentially talking about starting a world war. Surely you would want to exhaust all opportunities to avoid that. I guarantee you, Texas does not want to go to war if we can avoid it. You and I know we have very limited resources to fight such a war and do not want to face the possibility of having our fellow Texans killed. We see this resolution as a complete surrender of our sovereignty to the UN and a giving up of our country's independence. This is not acceptable for Texas. You don't seem to understand, we have been a proud hardworking people for over two hundred years, and after we won our secession from the United States, a long-held dream had come true. We were once again a fully sovereign republic.

"We then worked hard to pay off our debt, and through resource development and free market capitalism, we were able to not only survive but flourish. This has led to the highest standard of living in the world as well as the lowest poverty and best education of any country anywhere. We have used competition to expand our lead in all areas and you want us and are actually forcing us through military force to give up our freedom and turn it over to the United Nations. Well, we Texans are not going to give up our freedom willingly and would like to be able to negotiate an arrangement that will allow us to keep what we have built as a country and pay you a reduced tax for greatly reduced monitoring and UN services. Surely you can understand our side of the issue and will give us an opportunity to offer another proposal before you declare an act of war such as a blockade."

"Mr. Moses, we are not the freedom-stealing monsters you portray us. We are simply trying to help as many of the poor and hungry around the world as possible by leveling the playing field. Many of those countries don't have access to the resources and facilities a wealthy country like Texas has. We are simply trying to give more help for the poorer countries and trying to make things more fair and equal for everyone."

" What would be fair and equitable is to let the free market determine who succeeds and who fails, that is what is truly fair. You would have, within a generation, a worldwide economic recovery that would truly begin to eliminate hunger and poverty. If you would give us an opportunity, we could teach these countries how to make that happen and begin to see real progress in all of those poverty-plagued areas that have been hurting around the world.

It isn't their resources or will to work or an unfair advantage, it is repressive governments that take the resources and waste them for their own enrichment through political corruption"

"Not every person or country had a father who passes oil wells and refineries down to their children like you have, Mr. Moses. You may believe the capitalist system is fair when it is anything but fair. Those who have, get rich or stay rich while those who do not, don't."

Steven was obviously getting angry as he raised his voice, "As you know, Madame Secretary, I made my success from developing a way to extract oil from dry wells, which not only helped me but helped people all around the world with lower oil and energy prices. My invention not only made thousands of people wealthy beyond their dreams but alleviated the pain of the poor around the world to have affordable energy helping them to avoid more pain and suffering. This argument doesn't really accomplish much, and I would ask you to indulge me tomorrow to see if we can make some progress before you begin to use military force."

"Very well, we will meet tomorrow morning at 9:00 am to see if we can avoid an armed confrontation. Ambassador Herrmoza, can you escort them to the hover port?"

Ambassador Herrmoza escorted them to their hover jet and returned to Secretary Polentas's office and saw the look of anger in her eyes. "They are gone, what do you think about tomorrow morning? Are you going to hold off on your announcement for the blockade?"

"No, I doubt he is going to offer anything of value. He's simply trying to stall and has something else up his sleeve. He is a danger to us. He won't negotiate or budge off his position. He is more troublesome than President Chambers and needs to have an accident, just like the president."

"I understand, Madame Secretary, that would truly be a shame. New York City is a dangerous place."

THE STORM HITS

Steven and June were walking around the inside of the pockmarked warehouse where he rescued her from the attack. They could see bloodstains on the outside as it was obvious there was a fierce battle rather than the usual gang fights you would expect in the surrounding neighborhoods. The area had become bleaker than it was when they saw it the first time since the union gangs were completely in control of the city. There were the now numerous bodies hanging from lampposts on every corner, giving the city the putrid stench of rotting flesh.

June looked over at Steven. "She said she would meet me here, I hope nothing happened to her?"

"I don't know, but let's see if we can find any clues of who these people were and how the women were able to get down into the subways. That may lead us somewhere? You said they took you through a passageway to get you to the alcove I found you, do you remember where that was?"

"We all went to the back of the building over here behind some storage bins. It seemed like they were well hidden, but the worshipers knew exactly where they were and where they went. It seems like they were back here in this corner behind these barrels."

June searched in the back of the warehouse in a cluttered area that likely wasn't straightened up since the attack and everything was turned upside down. She found a small door hidden behind some large refrigerator sized boxes and clutter.

"Steven, come here and help me lift some of this stuff. I think this is where they took me out."

"Here, let me move some of that stuff, and we can get down to that doorway. It looks like the handle is either broken or not working on purpose. Is there anything that we can use to force this door open? Hold on a second, I think I have seen one of these latches before on a rig in Mexico, let me try this. It seems to be jammed."

The handle suddenly began to turn counterclockwise by itself and the doorway slowly began to open. A blond-haired women peered around the corner and asked, "June, is that you?"

"Yes, are you Susan?"

She nodded.

"Steven, this is Susan Bennett, and she is the one who helped us out of the warehouse and through the tunnels to the rescue area you found me."

Susan handed them each a pair of night vision goggles and motioned, "Follow me, and I will take you to the safe house where we have the files and some help. It isn't far."

They bent down as they entered the small entryway, which was about waist high. He reached back for June's hand as he crouched in the dark and moved forward, following Susan. They were inching down a pathway inside a false wall coming down to the end of the warehouse and a dead end.

She then led them down into a stairwell. At the bottom of the stairs was a hatch on the brick floor which was locked and crossed with white caste iron handle that was partially exposed.

Steven turned the handle and pulled it up, exposing another set of stairs heading into the darkness. They quickly walked down the steps that led to the New York sewer system. The sewage smell and humidity hit their nostrils like a day old skunk kill on a hot Texas highway. When they reached the bottom of the stairs, the tunnels went four separate directions with worn trails in the raised brick shoulders.

"Follow me and stay close behind, this is very treacherous walking," she said, pointing to a darkened tunnel heading east toward the river.

They walked cautiously along the brick walkways near walls while the water and sewage flowed inches from their feet heading toward the treatment facilities. The smell and darkness was like an invisible umbrella engulfing them in an eerie cloud. The goggles barely lit up fifty feet, but it was pure smelly darkness after that. You could almost see the smell rising off the acrid water. As they rounded a corner, they could hear some men off in the distance echoing through the tunnels. They couldn't tell which tunnel it was coming from, but it sounded like a pretty large group of men.

Susan and Steven crouched lower and moved quietly toward the voices. June held on to the back of Steven's shirt trying not to breath as she tried to feel the bricks along the wall and under her feet and not making noise or falling into the water flowing beside them. There was no way to tell if they were friend or foe, but there was only one way to find out. They moved closer and closer, trying to make out what they were saying. As they inched nearer, the words became clear.

"The boss said we need to clean up these neighborhoods before they can declare martial law. There is no way we can continue to fight the resistance while we are trying to maintain the order in the city. If we could finally get the Christians under control, we would finally have New York working properly. We have them pushed out of Brooklyn, but they are still well established in Queens. At least we got that pesky Ranger, we won't be having any trouble from him again." They all laughed and nodded at that comment.

June and Steven looked at each other. He whispered, "Maybe they will give us a clue of where he is or if he is still alive? Let's move a bit closer."

As they peered around the corner, they could make out a large group of men lit in the dingy dark tunnel that widened out and lit by some work lights for the subway. Some were smoking and others had their union jackets and hats on with a large Italian man who was obviously the leader doing most of the talking.

"We have been given some special orders to rid them of some other pests. As you know, that oil baron puke from Texas has been a thorn in our side and we need to take him to the same place upstate we took the New York Texas Ranger to get on ice. Jeff, I want you and your boys to make this guy disappear just like you did our other problem. The bounty on him is double what you received for the Texas Ranger."

Jeff whistled and said, "Tell your friends we appreciate their generosity and soon they will be sharing the same cell."

"Tommy, you keep rounding up the Christians, they've been hitting our supplies pretty hard, and you need to stop them. Like we always say, the only good Christian is a hanging cross, and we need more good Christians!" That brought another round of laughter and clinking of beers.

Susan, Steven, and June began backing away from the group. June was shaking from head to toe but needed to get out of there before they were seen. As they were backing up, two rats came scurrying out of one of a hole and startled them, causing June to make a muffled scream.

The group stopped talking and looked their way. "Who is that?" Tommy yelled.

They started running back up the tunnel, and the group of men started after them. Steven was pulling on June's hand, trying to keep her running in the right direction while his light barely made out the small ledge they were running on. Just as they were rounding the last corner to reach the stairs back up to the warehouse, someone came flying out of the darkness and caught Steven square in the ribs, driving him into the water. More men came in behind and held him underwater, trying to drown him. June and Susan began screaming as they let him up and began punching him the face and stomach until he slumped back into the water.

They all began walking them back to the meeting. As they came into the light, the leader had a look of surprise and said, "Well, well, look what we got here. We didn't even have to go find him he came right to us like a mouse to cheese in a trap. Jeff, you and your boys just got yourselves another big bonus. This is the richest man in the world, Mr. Steven Moses. All the money in the world ain't going to help you now Mr. Big Oil money!"

Jeff walked up and gave Steven a look of disgust and punched him in the stomach once more, bending him over as he tried to catch his breath through blood covered lips. He grabbed Steve by the head, holding it while he kneed him in the face sending him sprawling on the ground while his nose and mouth exploded with blood. "You rich guys ain't so tough when your bodyguards aren't around, are you?"

Stazi Ramone barked, "Stop that, we have to have the goods in decent shape if we want to get our reward. If anybody else touches them, you are answering to me! So clean him up and make sure he doesn't have any weapons and let's take him over to the boss at the UN. They will have a nice surprise for him. Make sure you have him and the girl secure while you clean them up. Hold this other one here and try her then hang her for trying to help these spies. We don't want anybody to notice when we take these two upstairs. So, Jeff, you going to take your wife on a cruise with all this reward money?"

They dragged him between two men with June following in the grasp of another through the tunnels until they reached a subway station and walked him up the stairs. When they made it up to the street, they had a man on each side and two in front and back but they didn't want to look like they were kidnapping him so they held him loosely while June was being escorted behind them. They just looked like a couple of homeless people covered in filth.

He could see the van they were heading with the Dockworkers emblem on it when he slowly slid his hand on top of his belt buckle and pushed the button on his hidden remote hover key. This activated the emergency GPS retriever on the Black Stallion, making it take off and come flying over the top of the building directly to the right of them and barreling across the street straight for them in silent mode.

Steven saw it coming directly at them as he slowly lowered himself into a crouch like he was beginning to pass out, while it bowled over the two lead bodyguards he threw his shoulder into the one on his right and punched Jeff on his left with a shot he hasn't thrown since his days at the Wildcatter Brew and Pub, dropping him like the last cowboy he caught insulting Sandy when they were dating. He dropped him like a sack of potatoes opening a lane of escape.

This shocked the group for a moment as he grabbed June and threw her into the Black Stallion with himself right behind and hit the throttle as the doors closed shut. Within twenty seconds, they were out of sight and flying over the Atlantic, leaving his captors in the jet wash. Stazi's men picked themselves up and asked each other what had just happened while they tried to wake their boss from his knockout punch.

Steven looked over at June, catching his breath, and declared, "How do you like our date in New York City so far? We better find somewhere upstate where we should be safe and pick up some new clothes."

"What about Susan?"

"There is nothing we can do. We have no idea where they have taken her and can only pray she gets away."

June looked out over the ocean at the melting darkness. There was a silent calming beauty of the boats bouncing toward their home ports while the lights of the boats started to flicker in the dusk. She could see most of the seaboard from their height stretching from the boardwalk of Atlantic City all the way up to Providence.

Even though she knew she was now a hunted person, she felt a comfort knowing she was with Steven who she saw in another light after their escape. He wasn't the calm and reserved business negotiator she had come to know but he had a rugged side that was protective and manly. The first escape was not a fluke, this is who he is. She leaned over and laid her head on his shoulder and let the warmth of the night drift her eyelids closed as her dreams spread peacefully across her eyelids.

Captain Thomas and his wingman Firefly were flying reconnaissance over the gulf. He was monitoring the military ships moving into the Texas shipping lanes. He had been watching thirty-four combat ships fanning out across the gulf, which he was taking computer readings on their size, speed, and weapons. Most were cruiser class from all nations around the world although the largest group were US ships, which included a carrier group with some of their latest aircraft. He had no idea if his jamming and stealth technology of his F-22 would be able to counter their detection although he had a hunch he would be finding out soon.

He continued on his mission getting computer signatures of the Carrier UNN Kofi Annan making sure he stayed out of its fifty-mile shoot-down zone. His stealth-tronics said the carrier's counter laser was attempting a contact although they were not able to get a lock on him. He knew their techs were likely going crazy as they could tell someone was sweeping their ship from somewhere and were likely doing everything they could to trace it back to the source. Just then, his alarms went off and maximum stealth systems switched on as his warning showed aircraft closing on him from his nine o'clock. His radio broke silence with Firefly screaming, "Let's get out of here, Rattler, they found us so let's hit the deck and get back home."

"Roger that!" He pushed full throttle, kicking in the afterburners, hitting the deck below the sensors and banked back north toward home, knowing this would give the carrier a brief signature, but he was found anyway from aircraft. The bogeys followed him sweeping him the entire ten minutes while he was able to sweep their systems, both knowing if this were a shooting match one or both would be spinning into the gulf. This should be some great signature data for his boys back in the Spooks Cave even if he was a bit peeved they were found. He knew there had to be a hole in the laser masking if they were able to spot him before he could spot them, which better be corrected. The good news is they didn't let them find out about his ramjet, which he knew he would reveal to them at the proper time. The only thing he was focused on now was skimming the waves and getting back to Bush Field safely without revealing his entire stealth system.

⟁⟁⟁

Steven and June found a little bed and breakfast called the White Pine Inn in the Adirondacks they looked up on the net, which guaranteed no Internet or phone services since he thought would have the best chance of not being recognized and reported. It was a cute little log lodge design with four bedrooms overlooking a small pond. It had individual cabins scattered across the grounds. He rented two cabins on the lake near the lodge since they didn't seem to have many renters. Although he never slept, he stayed up and used the Black Stallion GPS satellite service to identify three locations south of Syracuse that were potential prisons, which could be holding Ranger. June, on the other hand, looked absolutely stunning to him as she walked into the lodge. She obviously had a good night sleep and had a cheery good morning with a peck on his cheek.

"Good morning, hero! How did you sleep? I slept like a princess up in this crystal mountain air."

"Good morning, sweetheart. Hero? I don't know about that, but thanks anyway. I couldn't sleep, so I stayed up and did some satellite searching and found a few locations, which may be the prison Ranger told you about."

"I thought we came here because you can't get any service up here?"

"Anytime I am within five hundred yards of the Black Stallion, I have communication anywhere in the world. So I used my time last night to take a look at these sites and gave a call back to Texas to tell them what was happening and got some updates for my software. We can fly over the top of the potential spots this morning and get some close-up video and see what we can find. After all, we are not going to be going to be having breakfast at the UN this morning so we may as well use our time wisely. Now what are you hungry for?"

Stazi Ramone was not thrilled about the meeting with the ambassador and looked around the opulent office nervously. He was a large thick Italian who had worked his way up through the union leadership and was now the head of the Dockworkers for all the New York ports. He was not looking forward to explaining how his men let the most wanted man in the world slip through their fingers. Shelton didn't look much better as they sat in the secretary general's waiting room.

"The secretary general will see you now, gentlemen. Follow me." She led them back to the impressive office overlooking the East River and filled with a dozen men and Ambassador Herrmosa, Secretary General Polentas, as well as a number of assorted ambassadors and military officers.

Ambassador Herrmosa addressed them, "Gentlemen, you have put us in a very difficult position since you now have exposed our connection with your unions to Mr. Moses. We were expecting to have one of two things happening this morning. Either he was going to be caught and simply disappear or he would be here this morning to negotiate the treaty and avoid the sea blockade of Texas. Now we have neither option available, and he has disappeared and we have not picked up any detection of his hover jet. How did you idiots manage to let him escape?"

"We thought we had him and were taking him to the van to bring him here, but he had some sort of autopilot attack software on his hover jet, which knocked down a couple of our men, and in the confusion, he was able to get in and escape. I have never seen an aircraft actually knock somebody off their feet and then set itself to make an escape. Who would have thought that could happen? We were caught completely off guard."

Secretary General Polentas walked from around her desk. "Who would have thought of that? You are bringing in the richest man in the world and you are not expecting the unexpected? You men have no idea how difficult a position you have put me in. This has forced my hand, which means we are going to have to begin to enforce the blockade today. Major General Mohamed Almach, can your technicians find a single hover jet here in New York City, that is, if he is even in the area now?"

Major General stood up. "Madame Secretary, we had been tracking it from the time it arrived in La Guardia to the UN yesterday and out to Brooklyn; however, when it made the maneuver during their escape, it engaged some sort of stealth with a laser detection scrambling technology we have never seen. When we hit it with our lasers and radar, it shows over fifty aircraft in locations spread over a hundred miles and traveling in a hundred different directions. The targets moved around our screens randomly and would simply drop off until they all disappeared and had no idea which one was him. So he could be anywhere from Boston to Philadelphia from what we were tracking. Our teams were using everything we have to find it from satellites to lasers and we simply cannot find it."

Captain Thomas was flying at ninety thousand feet with two squadrons of ten fighters working as two wings spread over fifty miles. He could see the contrails of the commercial aircraft below him as well as the wakes of the numerous ships moving every direction. At this height, you could still make out the tiny triangles of the ships spread across the gulf. He could see on his heads up laser some of those small triangles were the two carrier groups working the gulf practicing war games preparing for the upcoming war.

He looked over at his two squadron captains and spoke into his mask, "Okay, Firefly and Sagebrush, let's take a run at those two flattops on our screens but make sure not to be too threatening. Follow me, boys, and try to stay in a tight formation."

Steven and June were searching the forests of northern New York and soon discovered finding a settlement or prison in the mountains was like trying to find a flea on a black dog. They flew over the first two suspected locations on the computer, the first was shuttered tight and turned out to be an abandoned work camp while the second was a closed-down hardwood mill. They flew across the hills, looking at the thousands of lakes and forested areas getting readings of small groups of people but nothing sizable. With one small hover jet, it was a monumental task knowing he would have to be on top of the prison to actually find it, and he had one potential site left. They looked across the mountains, wondering if people out here knew what was going on in the city or were they completely tuned out from the world.

Just then, the heat sensors flashed, revealing a large population under them even though there was nothing on the maps or satellite imagery. June and Steve looked at each other in surprise and she asked, "What do you think that is? It isn't a town or a city can we go down and take a closer look? Maybe it is the prison?"

He nodded and circled back over the area to get a closer look. He turned the Stallion on silent mode and put the stealth on maximum deflection then closed in close to treetop level and see what they could find. From a satellite, there would be no detection as the upper skin was a computer screen that would show a video of the ground and trees beneath and the sky when looking from below the hover.

It didn't appear to be a prison although there were lots of tents and temporary structures so it could be a work camp of some sort. He used the high-zoom cameras to see what he could make out, but there didn't seem to be any real structures or modern technology you would expect from a work camp or prison.

The censors said there appeared to be over two thousand people living in these temporary structures and tents. They came around to the south and rose up over from behind the largest hill to get a better look at the main building; the people seemed to be congregated in and aimed their camera on the largest building in the center of the clearing, and as the camera focused on it, they looked at each other at what they saw. It was a large log structure that appeared to be over a hundred feet long and eighty feet wide. The roof was covered with Mylar, making it invisible to overhead cameras and satellites. Gunshots sounded behind them and bullets began zipping past them and a couple bouncing off the Kevlar skin, telling him he had been detected and determined a threat. Let's hope they don't have anything with some punch.

He quickly dropped down in an evasive maneuver, building more speed from his jets to slingshot the Stallion up and out of the fire zone. They quickly climbed to fifteen thousand feet and out of the range of anything they may have. He replayed the video and as clear as could be you could see the cross on the log structure. He looked over at June who was staring at the video in amazement.

She looked up and said, "There are Christians down there. We haven't seen a cross since we left Texas, so we have to go back and find out who they are and if they can help. They may be part of Ranger's church and help us find him."

"I know, honey, but we have to check out the last location, which is about a half hour away. We can come back and hopefully not get shot. We will have a better chance of getting in at dark than now. I think we have to figure out how to get in without getting shot. That said, I really think we may have found a good lead on where Ranger is. I have it marked, and we will scout it when we get back."

Secretary General Polentas entered the grand chamber to a standing ovation. The chamber was filled to overflowing with every ambassador attending this historic event. The back wall was filled with cameras as the news feeds from every country was represented. You could see the network anchors up in their boxes introducing the secretary general to their audiences.

She stepped to the podium with the two small microphones extending out toward her mouth as she began her speech. "Ambassadors, delegates, leaders, dignitaries, and we especially reach out to the people of Texas to whom I would like to say, we have arrived at a time the United Nations did not want to reach. We believed we could find an agreement with the Texan president and senate, but they have rejected our multiple offers and there is nothing more we can do to bring them to the negotiating table. They have abandoned the Texan people and are pushing us toward military action. We even tried to avoid this action with a last-minute meeting with industrialist Steven Moses yesterday, but have not heard from him today even though we had a deadline for this morning. From his absence, we have been forced to move forward with an action we have tried to avoid.

"Starting tonight at midnight, Greenwich Mean Time, we will begin a full naval and air blockade of the Texan sea and airports. We will not be allowing any military and commerce ships or aircraft in or out of Texas in an effort to bring them back to the negotiating table. We will also be closing all rail lines except for humanitarian supplies. We in no way plan on harming the Texan people from receiving necessary food and water but will stop any shipments that contain commercial goods or weapons. All ships attempting to leave or enter Texan ports will allow a full inspection by United Nation ships, and any resistance will be considered an act of provocation and will be responded to accordingly. Any flights outside the Texas borders will be considered an act of aggression and an international act of war.

"This action has been approved unanimously by the security council as well as the full assembly and hopefully we will have a short duration and we can move forward with the incorporation of Texas into the world Family of Nations. We welcome any discussions that will lead to the immediate agreement of Texas joining this world community. I know I speak for the entire Union of Nations when I say we hope this action will end quickly and peacefully as my phone will always be open. Thank you very much and continued peace around the world."

The room was solemn in its silence as the ambassadors quietly sat in their seats, wondering what the next move would be. The secretary general and her entourage filed out in a somber procession as they walked to the security council chambers.

Captain Thomas was cruising at fifty thousand feet across the gulf with his two four-plane squadrons when a voice came over the headset, "All aircraft and shipping in the Gulf of Mexico, now hear this. This is the UNN Carrier Kofi Annan, and we are declaring an international blockade of all shipping and flights both military and domestic beginning tonight at twenty-four hundred Greenwich Mean Time. We are ordering all ships and aircrafts to return to their ports and bases to avoid any conflict. We are taking this action according to international laws within the United Nations Charter. We recommend any military aircraft to leave the area and stay grounded immediately. Thank you for your full cooperation."

Captain Thomas called the airbase for confirmation although they had been expecting this announcement for weeks. "Hello, headquarters, this is Rattler. Do you copy?"

"Yes, Rattler, we copy."

"Is the announcement of the air and naval blockade legitimate?"

"Yes, it is, and you are ordered to land immediately. We do not want to start an international incident."

"Yes, sir, and we will be heading in as soon as we can get turned around. We are pinched between these two carrier groups and will need to keep a wide birth while we maneuver back to the base without being detected."

"That's an affirmative, Rattler, make it back to base as soon as you can possibly return safely and keep your eyes and ears peeled. Make sure to follow all the protocols you have been trained to follow, we are no longer in peacetime."

"Copy that, over and out."

Captain Thomas and his squadron continued flying south between the two carrier groups planning to roll west and come back around along the Panama coast. As they were making their turn, their passive displays lit up showing they had been detected by the ships and fighters coming from the east and closing.

"Squadrons, climb out of here and let's get up above them and move away." Just as they began climbing, their alarms went off, indicating lasers were being lit and hitting the sides of their planes but foiled by their deflection technology.

"Change your deflection frequencies and go to multiplier mode. Hit the ramjets!"

Rattler hit his ramjet booster to gain altitude and get up to Mach 7 as he rolled over and dove through the displayed laser mazes. As he dove, he could tell there was no focus by the navel weaponry as they were shooting randomly. He dove for the carriers and began lighting up fighters as he dove down, knowing he could see them but they were blind to him. His speed was above anything he had ever attempted as the deck was screaming at him.

The carriers and support ships were firing their lasers as well as Sidewinders and Phalanx guns using shoot and hope mode. He looked down through the fountain of lights and fire as he went in for the big prizes. He flew by visual intuition, letting the plane become a part of his mind for his final maneuver, which wanted to pull the plane and him apart.

He was diving at Mach 8 when he began to pull up and releasing his array of lock and leave ordinances while the plane structure was vibrating and groaning from the stress of the maneuver. As he skimmed the waves and slingshot back into the clouds, he saw the reflection of the explosions hitting their targets. His squadron came in behind him, finishing the support ships and the few aircraft left in the sky. The air and water was empty of military ships and planes.

As they turned back to home, they were able to see the results of their fifteen seconds of aggression. Every ship was sinking and only perhaps sixty minutes separated these giant ships from their watery grave. He never in his wildest imaginations believe these planes had the power they had when they passed the speed of the defensive algorithms of these warships. These speeds made missiles obsolete and lasers had no affect on his deflection skins. The only possible weapon was a bullet that was lucky enough to hit the plane at those speeds would tear it apart, which was avoidable with the flight assist computers.

He called the Texas Coast Guard to send rescue ships, but although he was surprised at the power of his fighters, he was very keen of the fact he was now at war with the world and they would be looking for retribution. He could also see the desperation below him as thousands of men and women were heading to the same watery tomb as their crippled ships.

—◦/◦◦—

Steven set his Black Stallion down a quarter mile to the south of the camp where they saw the people they believed were Christians. He scanned the ground for human activity as the sensors showed them still in the camp and scattered around but nothing in this quadrant, which was hidden by some dense forest. He landed in silent mode, making sure to get in and see exactly what this camp was about. He and June exited the Black Stallion and quietly made their way toward the compound.

When they closed within a dozen yards of the first building, they crouched behind it and looked around at the grounds. It was fairly well lit with scattered overhead lights and the trails were all marked with solar ground lights. They could see families walking together, and most everyone was headed for the main building with the bronze cross on top.

He suddenly had an idea and grabbed June's hand and pulled her around the waist and began walking toward the building with the rest of the families while looking at the ground. She caught on and simply began some idle chitchat with her hand on his shoulder as they walked together toward the main building and up the stairs then into the back of the building and off to a side hallway out of the main traffic while nodding to the people as they found a darkened spare room they could hide in without being detected.

June whispered to Steven, "That was a gutsy move, hiding in the middle of a crowd. Now what?"

"We need to find out if this is the Ranger's church or a branch of the church and we should be able to hear everything that is going on in there."

He was right as the music started and they began singing "Amazing Grace" followed by a number of old gospel hymns they both grew up with. After a brief set of announcements, the pastor came to the main stage and gave a powerful message on individual freedom and responsibility given only through Jesus Christ and the Holy Spirit. Finally he mentioned the Texas Christian Fellowship as he finished his sermon. At that point, Steven grabbed her hand again and said, "This is enough for me these people are our friends, let's go meet them."

"Okay, if you think it is safe?"

She was frightened but had faith God had delivered them to this church. They walked together though the back of the auditorium, which was very large with cathedral ceilings and stained glass windows sparkling from the setting sun while they walked up the aisle. The pastor looked down at them and then recognized Steven and his eyes went wide and bewildered at the same time. He was just under six feet tall with light brown hair and a demeanor which was cheerful yet serious. He tried to say something and could barely get the words out, "Are you Steven Moses, and what are you doing here in our church?"

"Yes, I am, and this is my fiancée, June Darling. We came up here to try to find the Texas Ranger, but we were captured last night by a union gang. We were able to escape and have been searching for the prison they may be keeping him in when we found your compound. We found our way inside, and after we heard how spirit-filled this church was, we decided to come out and meet you."

"Yes, we are part of the Texas Christ Church of New York, and I am Pastor Davis. We have been searching for Ranger too. We believe we have found him in a prison about a hundred miles from hear on the Canadian border. We hope he is still alive, and we are planning a rescue attempt in two days. We can give you details later, but we would be honored if you had a few words to say."

Steven walked up on stage and looked over the crowd of desperate faces. "Brothers and Sisters in Christ, I have to praise God we found you, and I am honored to be with so many Christians standing up in the face of persecution. How many of you were in the warehouse June was in when you were attacked?"

A number of hands went up.

"I want to thank you for protecting her, and we are glad you were able to escape that battle. We are on the brink of war. We heard this morning that the UN was placing a blockade on Texas and I can guarantee you the Texan people are not going to tolerate this type of outward force. Just like everyone in this church, we are not the type of people who are going to roll over and go along with the shutting down of our livelihoods."

"We came up here to try to accomplish two things. One was to find Ranger since he was supposed to send some files to June when his phone suddenly went dead. We were afraid he was captured and came up here to find out. The second reason was to attempt to work out a negotiation with the UN, which would avoid this war from starting. We met with Secretary General Polentas yesterday and made no progress and were supposed to meet with her this morning, but we were captured last night while we were searching for you. We managed to escape while they were taking us to the UN for who knows what and began looking up here for a prison or work camp holding Ranger. Sadly one of your members, Susan Bennett, was captured with us and they took her to possibly hang her.

"Folks, we are the very last vestiges of freedom. If we are defeated, then freedom is defeated, and it will be decades if not centuries before it returns. You have lived under a totalitarian government for almost a decade now, and if they force Texas under their control, then all hope for liberty is completely lost. This is what we are fighting for here, and when we go back to Texas at the end of the week, it is what we will working toward there.

"America changed when there were more people who wanted to be ruled than those who wanted to be free men. Once those who wanted to be ruled outnumbered those who wanted individual freedom, the entire country had no choice except to be ruled. As the government got larger and more powerful, it restricted more and more freedoms to where you are now living under a totalitarian world government.

"The countries like America are no longer sovereign but continue to be subjects to this corrupt world dictatorship. You are no more than slaves to the UN and must submit yourselves to its authority with little or no debate while they make all the decisions and mandate regulations. In the end, there is only one way to begin the first steps of freedom and that is separation and independence from the UN "We are with you, and I am sure I speak for all Texans when I say your courage and strength makes us proud to stand with you in this fight for freedom around the world. Let me just say, don't mess with Texas and God bless America!"

In the back of the church, a group began singing the "Star Spangled Banner" and began ringing throughout the building as they sang all four verses louder and prouder than the previous bringing goose bumps and tears to the entire room.

As they were beginning to leave, a deacon came to the microphone and excitedly made an announcement. "There has been an attack in the Gulf of Mexico. It just came across the net and the details are still sketchy, but it appears a number of United Nations ships including two aircraft carriers were sunk by the Texas Air Force. The war has begun!"

Captain Thomas sat in an after action room filled with generals and colonels waiting to hear what he and his fellow pilots had to say. The news of this victory spread around the world and certainly through the Texas military moments after the attack was a success. The offensive and defensive systems worked well beyond their wildest expectations. The technological superiority was dramatic and the brass wanted to find out how.

Commander Jackson began the questioning, "Captain Thomas, what exactly started the attack?"

"Commander Jackson, it all happened so quickly we did not have any time to think but looking over the recordings we have reconstructed the attack. When the blockade was announced, my squadron was running maneuvers identifying aircraft as we were flying between the two carrier groups the UNN Kofi Annan and the UNN Fidel Castro so we continued in an attempt to get south to some open water. Myself and Captain Jameson on my wing both were painted by both the Carrier Annan and an unidentified enemy aircraft. We were then hit with some lasers, which is when I ordered to switch over to the multiplier stealth and to counterattack. We had no idea if they were going to knock us out of the air or how well our technology would work. Once we switched over and hit the ramjets, we had around fifteen seconds when everything happened before it was over. Once we gained altitude to escape the bogeys, we simply turned over and attacked at a sixty-five degree angle and could see with our laser illumination they were not aiming at us but using a random scatter, hoping to detect or hit anything. You could easily make out the path to take, and it was simply a matter of the computers dodging the tracers for the track in then releasing the lock and leave ordinances."

Air Force General Brighton asked, "Captain Thomas, you said you were identified and hit by lasers. We have verified that by the marks on your aircraft as well as the data collection. Have you or your techs found out how they were able to defeat our basic stealth software or diffusers?"

"Yes, General, the techs are telling me from their initial findings the enemy had randomly found a hole in our disrupter software. While we have been upgrading for the possibility of war, there is a lot of basic systems upgrading, which has not been completed, and this software was part of it. Once we clicked over to the newer upgrade, we were able to hide ourselves again and you could see that they went completely blind to where we were."

Commander Jackson responded, "Captain Thomas, once again, I have to commend you on your resourcefulness in the counterattack. We have never used the ramjet before, how do you feel it responded?"

"Commander, I know it is very early in this war and the use of our ramjet F-22 fighter, but I don't believe there is an aircraft that can stand up to this fighter. The proof is on the bottom of the gulf and we could have caused more damage if we didn't call the attack off almost immediately after our first run. Between the different stealth and weapons technology plus the speed and agility of this aircraft we may have air superiority which puts you at a distinct advantage in this war. They now have two real choices, to send untold numbers of aircraft and ships at us or use ballistic missiles. We need to be prepared for both since we are completely outnumbered, and they will eventually destroy enough of our weapons to organize an attack on the country. We need to keep bringing ramjet fighters on line and boost our anti-missile capabilities, begging your pardon, sir."

"No, Captain, don't bother. This is an open discussion and you are making very important points. We do have to prepare for war and be prepared for any contingency. Our large victory changes the dynamics of this war in both the timing and execution. They and we have just realized how large a technological distance we have between each other."

Secretary General Polentas met with her military cabinet to receive a briefing of the attack and loss of the aircraft carriers Kofi Annan and the Fidel Castro. Her top generals were at the table including Naval Admiral Romelov of Russia, Air Force General Davis from the United States, and Ambassador Herrmosa.

The secretary general brought the committee to order and asked, "How did this happen? We had every ship with the highest technology tracking these planes and they were able to destroy our entire Atlantic Carrier Fleet?"

Admiral Romelov responded, "This was the largest attack on the UN Navy in the history of our government. The speed and strength of the attack was beyond anything we had seen or heard Texas had in their arsenal. We are trying to recreate the attacks on the recovered data, but it appears they may have found a way to put a ramjet engine on their fighters and they were able to hit those kinds of speeds. There was no way for our defense matrices to adjust to the attack that was over in less than thirty seconds. The survivors said they identified a hostile jet and locked and had direct laser hits on it and then it changed its stealth frequency and simply disappeared. They described the stealth as suddenly there were hundreds of targets on their screens going all directions. Then out of nowhere, they were being attacked by invisible aircraft that began hitting their ships with laser-guided smart bombs, which were devastating at the speeds they were traveling. They went to the bottom of the ships where they detonated vaporizing the bottoms of our hulls."

Air Force General Davis added, "Our technicians have been pouring over the data, and it is disturbing. We too had a brief signature on these aircraft when they both accelerated beyond anything we are capable of and simply disappeared off our screens like they said multiplying into hundreds of craft. Unless we can solve this advantage, we are sending our assets to a certain death. You cannot see them visually due to their masking stealth technology, you can't pick them up on laser, and if you do get a hit, they simply change to their multiplying program and you cannot guess where they may be. Other than the fact we have them outnumbered by over a thousand to one, we are at a disadvantage by a large distance. We may have to rely on our cruise missile assets to get through their defenses.

"Their final advantage is their speed. We have the tracking on the ones which actually attacked us which showed them reaching Mach 7.5 on their attack runs. We know they have been perfecting their ramjet engines and have likely incorporated it into their fighter jet arsenal, but our engineers cannot understand how they are doing this. They do not understand how they can carry and deploy weapons at those speeds or how the craft holds together at the bottom of the run? By their calculations, it is physically impossible to do what they did, but they did it. We really don't have a counter to these jets since at those speeds and stealth, we are attempting to shoot down ghosts. We are working on how to break through their stealth, but it is very advanced."

Ambassador Herrmosa finished up, "Secretary General, this is a critical time in this action. We are not even a day into it, and we are seeing we have no advantage against these Texans in conventional weapons. We can bring more planes and ships into the area, but they will be at risk of being destroyed, and frankly we cannot afford to lose any more carriers since the cost and time to construct is more than we can afford. I would suggest we park our ships out of their range and use our cruise missiles to counterattack their port and airports to ground their military and commerce.

"We should start with the oil production and refining capabilities. We can easily reach them from anywhere in the United States or our missile bases in Cuba, and we can use bomber deployed cruise missles. They can launch from a thousand miles out and hit their targets. The Texans may be able to shoot down some, but they will never get all of them and we can pinpoint target their production targets. We need to make a statement after such a devastating attack.

"We need these Texans to pay for what they did. Until we do, the world will be waiting and questioning our authority and strength. We need to develop technology to defeat these fighters so we can knock them out of the sky.

"While we are working on defeating their technology, we can overwhelm them with our sheer numbers. We outnumber their fighters by the thousands, and we can take them down by wearing them down one by one. If they are using ramjet technology, it will only work for a few minutes at a time and then will fall back to conventional. This is when we attack and take them out one by one. We will lose lots of our fighters, but it will be worth it to take out these weapons. As long as they are flying, they have a distinct military advantage.

"We also need to send a message immediately that we are serious and will not take these attacks—that we will look at other options we may bring to bear. I want you men to get together and come up with a comprehensive plan to win this war and I want that plan in the morning. I want these Texans to pay for this."

THE WIND'S RAGE

Steven and David Goldstein were flying in his Black Stallion over the suspected prison holding Ranger. He had it in silent mode with the full stealth invisibility, which made it very unlikely they would detect him. Just to be safe, he was hovering over a thousand feet up and was scanning the grounds with the thermal sensors. They noticed the guard towers were only half filled, and it seemed there were not very many guards or prisoners in the prison compound if it was indeed what they were looking at. If Ranger was taken here, it was unlikely he was down there, which made Steven think the worst possibility. He circled back to where the assault team was preparing to attack just east of the compound. He quickly landed and moved over where the assault team had gathered.

David jumped up on a raised beam and addressed his men, "We just scouted this facility and have some mapping laid out to help you enter where we have found some weaknesses. These two towers here on the northeast side of the compound are not manned, and you should be able to gain entrance through this fence. We have trained you on how to get through this fence, and once in, you need to go straight for the prison barracks on the south edge and the two next to it, which is where we detected people who we expect are the prisoners. We need to be ready for anything since these guards are war ready and will be shooting to kill. I will be flying with Steven, and we will give you real-time information of what is going on in the towers on two way and what the guards are doing on the ground. Let's say a prayer and start the attack on our signal."

Steven and David climbed into the hover and took off again over the prison. He lowered it down next to the guard towers silently and brought the Stallion within five feet of the east tower where two guards were looking out over the darkness with a complete lack of interest. The early morning had them off their peak performance even if they could see them. Steven set the hover laser on stun and fired at both guards simultaneously, knocking them both to the floor.

David called to the assault team, "Begin the attack. It is all clear on the east tower. The entire east wall is unguarded, and we will give support suppression fire for your assault."

The men cut through the wire fence using metal cutting lasers making holes big enough for two or three to go through at the same time. This set off the security alarms, but the towers were now empty as all of the guards were all either stunned or dead. The ones coming out of the main control center were being cut down by both the Stallion or the first wave of attackers coming through the wire laying down suppression fire. The battle on the grounds only lasted a few minutes before it went inside the complex for a short time where the leaders called out the all clear.

Steven turned off the stealth deception software as he landed and headed inside to help find Ranger.

General Davis was addressing Secretary General Polentas on the conclusions they had come to after working all night on the solutions. "Madame Secretary, we have some difficult decisions to make as we have some very complicated issues with the attack by the Texas Air Force. They have some very advanced technology, and as we detailed with you yesterday, much of it is more advanced than our weapons. Our biggest concern is their fighter jets and their ability to control the air.

"We were surprised by their speed and stealth abilities, and we believe we were caught off guard by these aircraft, and we will not have the same disadvantage in our next attack. We should have known they would have brought their ramjet technology to their fighters, but we did not think they had the time to make that happen. Our spy flights over their research complex or satellites never picked this up. We also should have known they would have the best technology since they have been supplying these advancements to countries including the UN for a couple years through Texas Instruments. They have apparently developed the next generation of stealth-cloaking skins, which are undetectable to our systems, many of which they developed or were in development. The good news is we were able to see them at the beginning of the confrontation, and when they went into ramjet mode due to the heat generated on the skins were detected but our algorithms were confused by the speeds.

"We do believe we can fight them with some of our most advanced fighters, and we have a couple of other strategies to beat them. Their ramjets only can fire for one to two minutes so we believe we can attack them after they return to conventional power. If that is the case, we need to spread our fighters at the ends of their runs and between their targets as they return to Texas. Our engineers believe we can get a targeting signature off the planes during their acceleration and then determine where they should end up after they run out of burn. Even though we know we will take a number of casualties as they are in the attack, we believe we can beat them with our overwhelming number of conventional fighters. If we can take out these aircraft one by one until they are gone, we will then take control of the skies, which will be the end of their protection overhead. After that, it will be simply a few attacks on their infrastructure before they realize surrender will be their only option."

Admiral Romelov spoke up next, "Madame Secretary, we have looked at all the data we were able to retrieve from the attack, and we have some encouraging news from the air battle. When we initially detected the enemy aircraft, we were able to document some engine signatures as well as defeat some of their stealth technologies. Our technicians are working on their coding and believe we can solve their advantage in a week or less. We believe we can overwhelm them with our pure numbers of ships and aircraft to begin to eliminate their air force.

"We also think we should use our advantage in cruise missiles as well as range to take out some of their strategic targets. We can position our ships a thousand miles off their coast and launch a barrage of missiles that can fly through their laser defenses. Many will be destroyed, but enough will get through using different codes to get to their targets. We need to focus on Bush Air Force Base and destroy it to eliminate their ability to get their jets in the air. If we have a coordinated attack with thousands of missiles, enough of them will get to their destinations to send a message. This will not only cripple them and their efforts to fight us but will buy us some time to defeat their technological advantages. We will overwhelm them with our sheer numbers."

Secretary Polentas replied, "I am not sure you men understand the seriousness of this attack. We do need to have a decisive and immediate counterattack to maintain our strength to the rest of the world. Right now, our member nations are discouraged and not sure if we can defeat Texas. We have to make a statement, which means these attacks must be successful and decisive. If not, then you will need to use a more aggressive solution to cause the maximum amount of damage to force them to rethink this war."

Major Thomas was leading his squadron, checking the waterfront facilities of the gulf. They were on maximum alert while every precaution was being taken. They knew they were now targets and staying well within the Texas international waters even though Texas claimed half of the gulf. Their primary mission was locating and detecting enemy aircraft coming from South American or the Mexican bases. Nothing had been detected, although that did not mean nothing was there if the UN had more advanced stealth technology as they have found out weeks ago.

Their secondary mission was testing their ground based anti-aircraft batteries. They crisscrossed the batteries at different altitudes, stealth codes and speeds to try to defeat their ability to track as they prepared for the potential attacks. This was exhausting and monotonous, but they knew they had been compromised in the past and it only takes one to get through and thousands could be killed. The drills went on for hours and hours as their bodies began to mold into their seats like a catchers mitt in late innings when the radio broke, "Rattler, we have an unidentified aircraft nine hundred miles south of Houston we have detected and need you to get a better reading. It is on a north-northeast track and need you to see if you can ID it."

"Roger that, send me your coordinates, frequencies, and programming codes to locate."

"Firefly, this is Rattler. We have a hostile due east of us detected nine hundred miles south southeast we need to ID. Take your squadron to the east of his position, and we will fly to the west to try to get a reading and triangle. Be careful, this could be a trap and let us know if you get any reading on him. You will be getting coordinates and codes momentarily."

"Roger that."

Thomas and his squadron rolled east with their cloaking on max spectrum while they scanned the horizon, looking for any breaks in the bogie's stealth software. They traveled halfway when his displays started showing blinks across their screens. It looked like there was some type of software malfunction with dots blinking on and off across the heads up monitor as well as the three dimension positioning display with dots looking like the stars of the entire solar system.

He spoke to his right wing, "Coyote, I am having software problems with my Laze-lume display. There seems to be a lack of stability and getting random reflections covering my screen. What are you seeing?"

"That is an affirmative, Rattler, my screen is acting up and looks like a nightsky blinking off and on. Either my software is off and needs a reset or—"

Just as he said that, there were laser detections from every direction. The 3D illuminator looked like water fountains as streams of red were coming from every direction and raining down on his squadron like an inverted fire hose. He watched as three of his squad jets exploded while he screamed into his helmet, "It's an ambush! All fighters hit your Ram with maximum deflections and go to up to a hundred thousand—*now!*"

Thomas hit the ramjet shooting him to Mach 9 as he began taking out bandits ten at a time. His counter was over a hundred shot down as he saw an explosion next to him, knowing it was one of his squadron having a midair unable to fly through the gantlet of enemy fighters. Once he got up to the ceiling and out of their range, he had the advantage; he called into his mike, "Firefly, are you still there?"

"Roger that, Rattler, we took some hits and lost two and one limping back. What are your orders?"

"Move your squad east, and we will veer yours for a pincer attack and then refire your Rams and fight our way back to the base. There has to be over a thousand aircraft up here. Let's do this!"

"Careful, boys, by our ground estimates, there are over five thousand fighters up there and are coming out of your south like a dark cloud of locust. You need to get up above them and work your way back to base. Try to stay above them if you can. We are scrambling everything we have and you should have help in a few minutes. Godspeed!"

He slammed back in his seat once more as he and his intuitive fire computers were hitting enemy after enemy while they weaved above the swarms of jets back to the Texas coast. He had never seen this many fighters in one place even when he was doing international maneuvers with the US Air Force. Once he leveled off at fifty thousand, he hit the ramjet one more time as he saw a flash of another one of his aircraft exploding. He was hit repeatedly but never with enough energy to destroy his deflectors. Lasers were hitting his deflection skin from every direction constantly, and it was doing exactly what it was made to do. He could see the mass of fighters following him like a speeding cloud of death toward the Houston refineries, which could only mean one thing.

"Base, this is Rattler, you need to scramble all your jets and have a refuel team ready for me as I need to do a rolling refuel. You need a crash team for some damaged aircraft you have coming in with me. We have over a thousand aircraft heading toward the south coast area, and we need to get as many aircraft up as fast as we can."

"Listen, squadron, any planes with major damage, land first but get to the fire rescue zones as fast as possible since any planes that can fly need to get back up here with more fuel. Keep the tankers on the ground since they would be target practice up here. Anyone with nonthreatening damage needing repairs stay up until we can get the rotation done and back up. Okay, those needing to get down, land now."

Rattler and Firefly's squadrons made the turnaround in ten minutes with fresh fuel and recharging the deflectors. They were up with every fighter Texas had, which was currently around three hundred. They headed straight south to join the dogfights going over Houston refineries. They could see the smoke coming from the fires, which covered dozens of square miles.

Thomas's monitors were lit up from horizon to horizon with targets. He had streaked back up to a hundred thousand to begin his attack dive through the hundreds of fighters on his screen. Hitting the ramjet, he targeted for his computers to hit targets dozens at a time with the counter over three hundred kills. There seemed like there was no end to the number of dots just like there was no end to the lasers hitting his plane. As he negotiated between the explosions, he heard distress calls from his fighters as their planes were getting knocked down one after another.

His warning light on his deflectors lit up, which told him they were just about to fail forcing him back to the base. He had already logged over a three hundred and fifty kills and hit the ramjet one last time to get out of the fray. As he turned, he noticed the remaining bandits were turning to the south and heading back. He wasn't sure if they were out of fuel or aircraft, but in his mind, he didn't care. He was just hoping the fight was over as he was bone tired and needed some rest.

Just as he thought it was rolling back to the barn, he noticed a spark on his left flap. In a flash, his panel went black and a laser ripped across his wing, cutting it from the fuselage. The plane immediately went into a twelve hundred mile per hour death spin, hurtling toward the gulf. The centrifugal force had his hands pinned to the sides of the plane without enough strength to reach down for the ejector lever as the ocean surface came racing at his face.

"Eject, eject, eject, 452, eject!"

The church hall was filled with men and women full of anticipation as the chatter grew louder among their families. The church had been transformed into a dining hall so tables could be spread around for the potluck and celebration. The families were dressed in their Sunday best, although living in the woods for six months or a year did not exactly make for the finery of a New Year's ball in the city. That did not put a damper on the festivities as the band played, and a choir sang some of the old time gospels raising spirits of the entire compound.

Pastor Davis, Steven, and June walked in from the side of the stage, pushing the Texas Ranger in a wheelchair. He looked gaunt and weak as he had obviously been beaten severely including a cast on his left leg and his fingers were wrapped where his fingernails were torn out. His face was swollen and bruised as he had a black eye and numerous cuts on the side of his face and arms. The crowd erupted as he looked out over them and slowly lifted his hand to wave and give the thumbs-up sign. He smiled at them through broken and missing teeth as the entire hall began signing "Amazing Grace." As the song went higher, the tears flowed faster as it continued to grow louder and louder and the hall rang with power and hope. When it ended, the silence was deafening as they stood in silence anticipating the Texas Ranger's words.

Steven rolled him forward then handed Ranger the microphone; the ovation grew and grew as the members responded with the love they were feeling for his return. "Thank you so much, brothers and sisters! God is so good, and he has been giving me my strength back every day since the rescue. It was miracle you found me and even more that you were able to get into that prison and break me out. Your timing was amazing.

"After they caught us in the ambush down in the city, they took me to the UN compound and beat me for hours to get the names and addresses of our members. They kept me there for two days and beat me every six hours for two hours until the moved me up to the prison. I was supposed to be killed immediately, but they thought they could get the names and locations out of me since we were a pretty big thorn in their side. They would beat me one day, let me heal a bit the next, and then beat me the next the entire time I was there. They offered me all sorts of enticements and temptations if I would just give them a few names or locations of our safe houses, but God gave me the strength to endure it one more day. I just tried to remember what my savior went through for me and the beatings did not compare.

"I was driving them crazy since I never broke and was always in a joyous mood, singing and praising God throughout the ordeal. They could not understand why I wasn't bitter, angry, or complaining but continued to give God the glory, recite scripture, and sing gospels. I was able to share the gospel with two of my guards, and they eventually came to Christ, which filled my heart with even more joy beyond their comprehension. They never could understand why I wasn't angry and bitter, but singing and praising God.

"The warden realized I was not going to break or give them any names or information, so I was scheduled to go to the death chamber the next day before God rescued me. Thousands of men went to that death ward and none of them ever returned, so I was sure they were going to kill me. I was ready as I knew the Lord Jesus Christ had given me a life I could only dream of and was ready and praying for his will to be done. I was praying daily this movement would continue to sustain and grow stronger. I prayed for all of your health and protection and you rescued me, praise God."

A huge roar went up as the people jumped to their feet praising God for his safety.

"When I saw Steven's hover jet lights landing and heard the gunfire, I knew God was saving me from my death and then when I saw Steven, I knew God was truly in control. He is in control of this entire war, and he has told me to take our battle back to New York and go to the center of this battle. We are to attack and take out the United Nations compound. While they are focused on Texas and their defeat of them, they will not be looking for an attack on the compound, which is exactly why we need to go there.

"You must know, on paper, this looks like a suicide mission, but as we say, 'One man with God is an unbeatable army.' We must have faith in him, and we will have the advantages of surprise as well as knowing the area better than our enemies do. We have built a network through the subways, which will allow us back into the city without detection. We know the gaps in the security and can get a strong force into the compound area and can develop a plan to accomplish our mission of taking down the Secretariat Tower.

"With that, I want to thank you for all of your prayers, which helped sustain me through some pretty dark times, and it is now time to celebrate. Those dark times however were the times I felt closest to God and have had a purging affect on me. One of the beatings I remember feeling I was going to die and the Holy Spirit spoke to me to keep hanging on and stay strong since God had a plan for me. He told me to dig in and give more of my life to him and then the pain simply disappeared, and it's as if I was no longer in my body and the torture never was effective. It was like a cleansing fire bringing me to a higher level of faith. So, brothers and sisters, let's celebrate God's mercy on all of us and begin to take our faith to the next level and truly live our lives by faith."

As the band stuck up, they could hear a low rumble building in the distance. It was the sound everyone in the hall knew and feared. Outside they could hear the anti-aircraft batteries going off on the surrounding hills and those batteries taking incoming laser and missile fire. The hall lights began flashing, letting everyone know they were under attack as the women and children headed for the basement the men grabbed their Kevlar deflector gear and weapons and headed for their battle stations outside.

When they ran from the building, their worst fears were realized. A giant Hover Fortress was over the middle of the compound with UN stormtroopers repelling down ropes to the ground in full battle gear. Loudspeakers were blaring for the people to surrender as they were surrounded and overpowered. The men were firing from their fortified positions, but the troopers were wearing deflection Kevlar, making their weapons less than effective. They were able to make some concentration hits, knocking a couple of troopers to the ground but with the Hover Fortress over their heads kept them pinned down with no way of escape.

The Fortress was firing from position to position taking out the defenders without any real affect from the anti-aircraft batteries. Either they were already taken out, or the fighters were not wanting to be detected until they had an open missile strike, which would mean certain death in return. The compound looked like a raging forest fire rather than the peaceful compound it had been a few minutes earlier.

Steven looked over at Ranger and said, "I'm taking up the Black Stallion to fight that thing. It is the only chance we have."

Ranger looked at him. "Do you really think you can stop that Fortress?"

"I don't know how I can, but like you said, 'One man with God is an unbeatable army.' I have to try."

June looked at him and added, "You can do this, honey. They are depending on you. We will be praying for you and God will help you find a way." She knew there was a good chance he would not be coming back, but he was their only chance of stopping the Hover Fortress.

As Steven sprinted towards the nearest building to hide behind with laser blasts hitting all around him, Pastor Davis and June began to take Ranger downstairs when he objected, "I am not going to hide down in the basement. take me to the second level balcony so I can watch the battle. Let's go!"

They pushed him up to the balcony where he could see the lasers and missiles flying in every direction, lighting the evening in a crisscrossing maze of lasers. It was a spectacular light show and deadly at the same time.

Outside, there was mass confusion as the troopers were working their way toward the main hall. Steven dashed around one of the cabins and looked across the meadow where the Stallion was hidden. He pushed his emergency remote, and the Stallion fired up and shot across the meadow where he could jump in the cockpit. He shot straight up and banking around he could not believe the massiveness of this Fortress. It had to be more than a full city block across and had no visible weakness. His only thought was to somehow hit the intakes if it were possible.

He dove straight down behind it, hoping he could remain invisible for a few seconds which he apparently was unless it was setting him up for a trap. His screen was showing search detectors hitting his skins but nothing was marking him. He crept up over the top and looked down at the massive blades spinning below the huge air intakes. He could feel the swirling tornado of wind buffeting the Stallion as he attempted to get close enough for a shot when a downdraft pulled the Stallion into the intake blades. This was worse than landing on a derrick in a raging hurricane on the gulf. Hitting his full reverse power, he attempted to pull away from the instant death staring at him in the enormous whirling blades.

He was two feet from the intake with the Black Stallion fighting with everything it had to stay out of the thundering egg beaters. The powerful winds were rocking and shaking the craft in a violent fight for survival as he fought the controls with every fiber of his being. He felt this instant was his only brief chance before becoming sliced into a million pieces and pulled the trigger. The laser cut the blades with a surprising ease as the as the titanium shrapnel went screaming through the massive hulk tearing electronics and aircraft as the metal parts flying at ten thousand RPM did their mortal damage to the giant beast. One superheated shard shot through the fuel tanks, starting an initial explosion, illuminating the entire compound, igniting secondary and tertiary explosions. These explosions sent fireballs into the sky, throwing the Black Stallion back over a hundred and fifty yards while Steven fought the controls while his Black Stallion cartwheeled through the air out of control and eventually landing in the top of an ancient oak tree.

The massive hull of the hover rocked right and then left before it suddenly fell out of the sky and into the ground, causing a final immense fireball as the storm troopers looked on in stunned disbelief. A cheer went up from the compound defenders as they made a final charge at the enemy troopers who were dropping their weapons and raised their hands in shocked surrender.

Steven shook his head, trying to get his bearings and figure out where he was. Once he did and chuckled how he ended up in the tree. After he caught his breath, he restarted the Stallion and limped it back to the church while the entire compound erupted in cheers, pulling him out of the cockpit.

June met him with tears streaming down her cheeks. "I knew you could do it. I knew God would protect you, and I love you so much. God is so good!"

THE EYE OF THE STORM

The Texas Security Counsel met three floors under the capital building in a reinforced bunker, which was built shortly after Texas declared its sovereignty from the United Sates against the likely chance of war. The commanders of all the armed forces were in the room with President Stewart, Vice President Chapman, Senator Jackson, and Jeff Drake representing Moses Enterprises along with leaders of the other strategic industries.

President Stewart spoke first, "Ladies and gentlemen, we are at a critical stage as we are in a difficult situation with our fighter aircraft. We are down to eighty-five combat-ready fighters, and if we have another attack like we had today, we will be defenseless to their attacks by noon tomorrow. This would make our skies empty of our fighters so they could attack our industries unopposed. Barring a miracle, we must seriously consider our options including our surrender."

Senator Jackson burst out, "There is no surrender in Texas! Our history began at the Alamo against impossible odds where we fought to the last man. Texans will fight to their last heartbeat, and I swear I will fight until my last breath on this earth as a free Texan!"

A cheer rose and echoed off the mahogany paneled walls of the bunker.

"That was all I wanted to hear and exactly the way I hoped you would react. I don't know how we can fight this war against these overwhelming odds of the pure might and numbers with the world against us. We need a miracle to save us and our great country from its demise. General Thomas, can you update us on our situation in both aircraft and land based laser systems."

"Thank you, Mr. President, as you stated earlier, we are down to eighty-five fully operational aircraft with another five to ten, which can be repaired by morning. Every able-bodied mechanic and pilot has volunteered to help, and they are working as hard as they can around the clock. We cannot survive another attack like today, but we can hopefully withstand another two days if all goes well.

"Our land-based lasers are in good shape, and we should be able to stop any low-flying stealth missile attacks as well as conventional warheads however subspace and space based missiles are generally in a directed free fall and will hit close to whatever they are programmed to hit. In addition, high-altitude bombers are outside of the effective range of our lasers and would likely avoid a downing hit, especially with their newly advanced deflectors. Our fighters that can get in at close range are the only effective weapon against a fully stealth armored aircraft."

"General Martinez, can you give us an update on any technology and weapons development which may not be aware of?"

"Well, President Stewart, I wish I had something in hand, but we are advancing on improving the distance of our lasers as well as improving our stealth technology. Our techs have been working overtime for the past three months and is why we are able to have the successes we saw today. Our main issue is the time and expense of producing more fighters. We do not have the capabilities or resources of the entire world combined.

"Tomorrow we are going to launch our newest weapon into the war which is a ramjet drone fighter. As everyone knows, we have been flying messenger drones around the world at supersonic speeds, although they have been limited by power and payload but can stay in the air as long as they have fuel. To have the weaponry generation, we have to have to generate the lasers and cloaking we have had to miniaturize power generators beyond technologies we have used in the past. We have incorporated a ramjet booster into the propulsion system, although unstable there is nothing that can match the speed although their maneuverability is the question. Our engineers have been coordinating from every industry to make these aircraft weapon systems work. We have had some breakthroughs in the past two weeks and have been testing our initial prototypes, which we will take into combat tomorrow. We are going to test fly twenty-five, but if they work, we can bring on over two hundred per day which can buy us some more time.

"We do not know how effective they will be as they have only been tested in our labs and test flights to recreate dogfights in West Texas, but to put them in actual combat situations is anybody's guess. We do believe we have some pretty good remote pilots who have been flying these for years, however, how are they going to react and avoid detection in combat is the question. They have never shot at live aircraft in combat situations. If they are marginally effective, we can buy some time and defend against these overwhelming odds. If not, we will have to improve their designs and weapons until we can have a working drone fighter."

Jeff Drake spoke up, "If these drones work, we will provide any funding and engineers you may need to produce five hundred per day. I have spoken with Steven Moses, and he has assured us to put his company's entire resources at the disposal of the war effort. If there is anything you need, simply say the word and we will try to provide it."

All of the industry leaders confirmed their support with the effort.

President Stewart responded, "I expect these drones will do the job very well as they have been the best craft in the world, so it really comes down to the weapons systems, which it appears you have perfected or are close to perfection so we will see tomorrow. In any event we have no real options so we would like to set a goal of producing five hundred per day. Is that possible? If we can it would offset their advantages in a few days and would overwhelm them in weeks."

General Martinez answered, "I suppose we can attempt to make that happen, but we really don't have the space or facilities to manufacture at that level. We would need some help from other industries. Perhaps Texas Aircraft could help us if we sent them the schematics and programs to manufacture these drones and weapons. Is that possible?"

Drake answered, "I will talk with Davis Thompson, their CEO, tonight. We will make this happen, and it is possible that Texas hovercraft may take some of the manufacturing to help produce these drones. It would take some modification and engine design work, but they should be able to produce them too. We will get our engineers over there working tonight to make this happen."

President Stewart finished the meeting, "Gentlemen, this may be the weapon we have been needing to even things up against their overwhelming numbers. Nobody is sleeping tonight and perhaps tomorrow, but let's give this push everything we have, our people are counting on us."

The pilots' meeting had been going on an hour when Terry Thomas walked in shocking everyone. He was hobbling and favoring his right leg with his arm in a sling and looked like he had been in a fight with a mountain lion, but his smile was still there as was the familiar sparkle in his eyes. The room erupted in cheers as he waved and walked to the front and looked out over the pilots.

His squad wingman Firefly looked shocked. "How in the world did you survive that hit? I saw you get blasted by at least twenty lasers taking your wing off and then death spin into the ocean at over twelve hundred knots and no chute?"

"You're right, it was a miracle since I was hit by a multifocused shot, which sheared off my wing. I was in a spin that plastered me into my seat completely immobile with the centrifugal force holding me fast and thought I was a goner. If not for the audio backup ejection pod, there would have been no way to survive. I barely got out the fourth eject vocal command before I passed out, and the plane splashed then exploded. Even though I must have ejected, I hit the water so hard it felt like a parking lot as the retro rockets barely had time to fire let alone make for any controlled landing. The plane must have been at just the right angle for me to not be pancaked.

"I was knocked out cold by the impact, and thankfully the rescue crews were on scene in short order to save me from the pod capsizing and drowning. The long and short of it, I used another of my nine lives in that crash, I should be dead right now, but thank God, I am still alive and ready to fight more than ever. Just a little bruised and stiff all over. Hopefully we have a replacement fighter for me to get back up tomorrow and get me some more UN bogeys. I look much worse than I feel. The good news is, I am meeting a lot of nurses with these trips to the hospital. Who knows one more crash and I may be married?" The room broke up in laughter.

Commander Jackson responded to his request, "Squad Leader Thomas, make sure to get yourself checked out. Some of the soft tissue damage won't show up until tomorrow morning, but if everything checks out, I am sure we can find an extra aircraft for you to go up and shoot down more bad guys. Thank you for the job you have been doing, Thomas, you are leading the air force in confirmed kills at 1487 with today's total alone at 339. Congratulations."

The room erupted in applause as his fellow pilots gave him a standing ovation while chanting, "Thomas."

"Gentlemen, let's get back to the business at hand. We expect another massive attack in the morning as the UN has to believe we are pretty much out of fighters, which we are. We are down to eighty-five functional aircraft This means we will have only half the fighters we have pilots to fly. Which brings me to the second part of this meeting.

"We have a new weapon being rolled out in the morning, which is a fighter drone with ramjet boosters. They are an upgrade of the shuttle drones we have been using for high-speed courier deliveries around the world. These drones were pretty fast and nimble to begin with, but they have completely reworked them to turn them into potentially an equalizer since they can produce these drones in the hundreds rather than the dozens they make fighters now.

"That said, we need to have the pilots who do not have a fighter and can fly some of these aircraft while training the techs who are test flying them now. It will be similar to being in a simulator without all of the hydraulic movement. The visuals will be shone inside three-hundred-and-sixty-degree visual goggles for your intuitive targeting and defense systems. You will have the same electronics and displays you have in your fighter and all of the weapons systems will feel the same. I really think these drones can become the difference makers in the war. That said, who will volunteer to fly those drones rather than your fighters?"

Terry Thomas slowly got up out of his seat. "I will volunteer to fly a drone, Commander. I may be a bit stiff in the morning, and this sounds like a new challenge and where I can be the most effective."

"Thanks, Thomas, how about you be the wing commander down at Johnson Space where they will be controlling these new drones. Who else would like to volunteer?"

Pilots stood up around the room as they lined up to do their part and stay in the fight.

—◦◦◦—

The main clearing of the compound was covered by the wreckage of the Hover Fortress. They had recovered twenty-nine bodies from the airship and found three still alive who were in the infirmary recovering. The massive size of the craft was incredible even after the explosions and fires had consumed much of the fuselage it still covered two football fields. The fact it landed in the middle of the clearing away from the compound log buildings was the most stunning miracle of all.

It was ten thirty in the morning, so the men stopped the weapons salvage and clearing of the wreckage and began walking over to the main chapel where the strategy meeting was being called for the next four hours before they began packing and leaving. There had been a large increase in the number of people inside the compound over the past couple days as word of their victory had spread among the church groups.

Ranger was wheeled up to the podium and began speaking to the overflow crowd. "It is time to take the fight directly to the United Nations compound. God is with us and showing his glory and will now finish revealing his power. Over the last year, my leaders and myself have been designing ways to defeat many of their defenses and now we have faith in the plan that we believe will work.

"We all know they are being distracted by the war effort, and there is no way they are expecting an attack on New York. One of the benefits of being hunted by them for all of these years is we know how to get in out of the city without being detected. We know all of their defenses detection locations and techniques as well as how to defeat them. We are going to need to get over a thousand men into their compound area to fully engage their security forces. While they are engaged with you we will be bringing in the real strike with Steven Moses's hover jet.

"These men with the aid of some of our armored trucks are going to mount an attack from the south to draw all the fire from the compound in their direction as well as their troops and hovers to defeat this attack which should leave the northern sector of the compound open for the real attack.

"Steve, are you ready for one more mission with the Black Stallion?"

Steven looked up and replied, "Of course I am ready if it will help end to this war, but I don't think the hover can go since it was pretty damaged in the attack. It is not very stable and the crash knocked out my stealth computers. We can attempt a remote download for upgraded software to see if that will help, but any way you slice it, getting close enough to the UN building for a kill shot is suicide. I just do not know how I can get in past all of the security."

"Leave that to us, Steven, there is more than one way to skin a cat, and in this case, we will get you in. I will be flying shotgun and can show you the way in without their seeing you. We will have to fit the Stallion with stronger lasers and install some launchers we have, which can deliver enough payload to level the building."

Steven replied, "You mean you want me to destroy the entire building and everyone in it? I don't know if that is the right way to fight."

"Steven, I understand what you are saying, but you kill a snake by cutting its head off and the United Nations building is their head. They declared war on Texas, and you know they were trying to take us out with the attack two days ago. We are going to do to them what they tried to do to us and God willing will put an end to the UN and this war!"

The building erupted in cheers.

"Okay, let's divide into our groups and go over the details. After the meeting with your leaders, we will be loading the men who are going to be on the ground so do your packing and be ready to leave at twenty-thirty hours tonight. We have to do this right since we only will have one opportunity to surprise them."

—◊◊◊—

The city was quiet and Secretary General Polentas could see for miles across the light-speckled horizon. There were more and more swaths of black but there was still beauty in the night as she could see for nearly sixty miles of the Atlantic shoreline from her office. She thought of how the people in all of those houses were sleeping peacefully while she and her team were spending most of the night preparing their war designs.

It was nearing midnight, and she was a bit annoyed but curious why Ambassador Herrmoza had called an emergency meeting with just her. She had an idea why but decided to let him explain what he was there for.

"Madame Secretary, thank you for your time. I have been speaking with our air force generals and we have a very troubling development beginning to materialize. Our pilots are refusing to go up and attack the Texan ramjets. They are afraid of the numbers that are being shot down and even though they know they are close to finishing the job of defeating Texas from the air, they don't like their odds of who will be coming back.

"Unless we defeat them decisively tomorrow, we may not have many pilots willing to attack the next day. We need to do something powerful and dramatic to force them to the negotiating table for surrender and that is a nuclear attack on Dallas."

" I gave my word to the generals, we would wait until tomorrow to decide on whether we would use nuclear weapons or not?"

"I understand, but things have changed and I have spoken to Admiral Romelov and Air Force General Davis, General Davis disagrees with a nuclear attack, but we really don't have time to wait if we cannot defeat them tomorrow. We have to use everything at our disposal and do it while we have a window of opportunity for victory. You have the authority to call an attack during a time of war and deploy any weapons you deem necessary."

"Thank you, Ambassador Herrmoza, the wholesale killing of upward of two million people or more is not something I can decide like this in the middle of the night. I will call an emergency meeting in the morning, and we can discuss and decide this at that time."

THE FINAL FURY

The sun was just rising over East Texas as the flight crews readied the flight lines for battle. The pilots fired their jets as they pointed their birds into the golden rising sun. They headed south over the deep blue gulf, expecting an attack from all directions; however, it was surprisingly quiet this morning. It was as if they were flying routine patrol before the war began except they all knew the war was here. The only noticeable difference was the lack of shipping and the smoke billowing from the refineries surrounding Houston.

Firefly looked over at his wingman. "Titan, be on your toes. This feels like the calm before the storm and we have a class-five hurricane coming straight at us. We are severely outnumbered and outgunned, which means we have them right where God wants them. They want today to be the final battle of the war, and we have to make sure that doesn't happen. Say your prayers and be ready to fight like you're at the Alamo and this is Texas' last stand."

As soon as he finished the statement, his display Christmas treed like it had never lit up before. Next, the air ignited with laser tracers bouncing from every direction as the Texans fired their ramjets and climbed to a hundred thousand, escaping the red glowing spiderwebs of death. While they climbed and watched the earth fade below as they cut the gulf into sectors while they accounted for the hundreds of aircraft they were about to attack.

As Firefly pointed his squadron down into his quadrant of bogeys, he screamed into his mask, "Y'all don't mess with Texas, ya hear?"

Firefly felt a edgy calm come over himself as he suddenly become a part of the jet like much as a wing or a rudder understanding how the plane reacted before he touched the stick. He was hitting everything he saw while looking at his 3D interior display light up with mini-explosions sparkling in every direction, giving the cockpit a celestial look. His kill counter seemed to be rolling like a slot machine quickly passing a hundred, and he had only been up for twenty minutes while he looked to go for more fuel and a recharge. When he rolled back toward Bush Air Force Base field, he was hit by a multiple burst, making a surge in his defensive software, causing it to fail, momentarily exposing his aircraft to all of the enemy fire. In a split second, it was enveloped by lasers from every direction as his jet exploded instantaneously.

Terry Thomas had been familiarizing himself with the controls of the drones for the last four hours. It seemed to have many of the same motions; however, they seemed to be more responsive with a much tighter turning response on the trainers. They seemed to dart like jackrabbits rather than bank and climb like a jet. This was something new, something he only dreamed his planes could do without the mass and controlled velocity. He now sat in the actual control seat and slid on the flight goggles as he gave the drone flaps and engine a once-over before he taxied onto the runway. He had never been this nervous since his first training flight in the air force, feeling an anxious anticipation in his gut.

"Squadron, prepare for takeoff. Okay, hit the burners and let's go into the Texas blue yonder."

The actual feel of the plane was nonexistent, which meant he had to adjust to not flying by feel, but on the other side, he could dart without any concern for G-force or the muscle fatigue that goes with it. His goggles lit up with targets as he entered the kill zone and ordered into his microphone, "Hit the Rams and let's get above this battle. Techs, could you lay out some quadrants for us when we get up to a hundred thousand?"

When they were up to altitude, he gave the order, "Okay, boys, point them at the water and let's go see what these birds can do."

He made his maiden dive while hitting targets with his intuitive targeting. It had the same power in weapons if not a bit stronger, and the banking ability was very surprising at the speeds his plane was flying. The flight computers kept the plane stable even when he tended to overcorrect as he tried to match what he was seeing with his lack of feel. The size of his plane made it even harder for bad guys to detect as the power and quickness made for a deadly combination. He made numerous runs on his targets, making the kill counter spin like an old-fashioned gas pump. Thinking of which, his fuel tanks showed they better get back on the ground as he called out, "Let's get our drones back on the deck and refuel. I don't know about the rest of you, but this fighter is as good as any craft I have flown."

The battle that day was as fierce as any they had ever experienced, as the sun was setting, they had only lost thirty fighters and two drones. The losses for the United Nations was well over eleven hundred fighters. As Terry turned his drone back to base for the last time, he took one more ramjet booster up to a hundred thousand when his monitor showed a giant flash from the north. He could see the flash coming his direction and then hit his drone, knocking it backward as a monstrous electrical pulse hit his electronics.

Once he began to regain control of his craft, he rolled in the direction he saw the flash, and within minutes, he saw the massive mushroom clouds rising above Dallas.

⟞◉⟋◉⟍◉⟝

Ranger burst into the prayer room where Steven and June were in prayer, "They destroyed Dallas with a nuclear attack last night! The news is reporting there is nothing living for a fifty-mile radius. There has to be millions of dead and who knows how many injured. This is the worst attack in history, and we have no idea how many more nuclear warheads they have aimed at Texas. We need success in our attack today."

June was stunned as they lifted their heads and began to take the ring off her finger. "Steven, this is an impossible mission, but you have to try it to end this war, and I am so afraid you may not be coming back. I want you to wear my ring as a memory of both Sandy and I, to help carry you back to us. I love you more than I have ever loved anyone and want to marry you and give you a house full of screaming children, but this is bigger than any of that. Take my ring as a symbol of both of our hearts while the world seems like it is falling apart we will be kneeling on your heart in prayer. Perhaps our ring will heal the wound aching in your chest from her death. So I will be praying that Sandy is still be looking down from the hands of Jesus to watch over you. All the women will be here praying a hedge of protection over both of you."

Steven was touched, "I do not deserve either of you women, let alone both. This ring is the greatest gift anyone has ever given me. I can't guarantee the pain of Sandy's death will ever go away, but I am so blessed to have a woman who understands my wound. I can never thank God enough for bringing you into my life. You know I will be coming back to hold you to that promise of a house full of kids."

June blushed through cheeks covered with tears as she gave him a wet kiss good-bye and hugged Ranger. "I have never been so proud of anyone in my life, you two are the bravest men I know."

Walking into the shed, Steven nodded to the mechanic as he looked up from his diagnostics readying the Black Stallion. "Brady, have you been able to download the repairs from Texas for my stealth software?"

"Yeah, we were able to repair most of it, as well as a new upgrade they just developed; however there are a couple of bugs and viruses you picked up in the crash that I was not really able to fix and completely load. Your hardware took a pretty big hit when you crashed into the tree. You will be visible to certain frequencies, and there will be flashes of the software just stopping for a reboot so be on your toes they may have some looks at you when it has software conflicts. This will be especially dangerous when you get in range of the compound as they have the most sophisticated detection outside of Texas. You may be invisible or visible, I just can't tell what will happen. It simply has some code in it which was corrupted into something I and the guys in Texas have never seen before so it is anybody's guess how it will respond under attack. There is a good chance this mission just became even more risky."

"Thanks, Brady, I know you did everything you could and say a prayer for the Black Stallion."

"I will and Godspeed."

———

Secretary Polentas sat in the war room on the twenty-fourth floor of the Secretariat Tower with her top military generals who were directing the war. It was a crystal-clear morning although there was a feeling of defeat in the room as they were not able to eliminate the last of the fighters the day before.

Secretary Polentas opened, "I understand the consequences of yesterday's defeat, but what I want to know is what we can do in the future to turn this war around to our advantage. We may have to change our strategy if we are going to defeat the Texans.

General Davis, can you and Admiral Romelov give us a rundown on where we are from the air force's perspective."

"Yes, Madame Secretary, we have analyzed our losses overnight, and it does not look good. We lost over twelve hundred jet fighters and brought down only twelve Texan jets as well as only two of their new fighter drones. We are completely outgunned when it comes to a technological standpoint. We are not able to defeat their software or break through it unless they have a software glitch which reveals themselves to our LASAR detection.

"The other side of the coin is they have broken our codes and our stealth software is ineffective against them, and they are able to target our aircraft in multiple targeting sequences making our fighters easy pickings. Now we have to battle their new ramjet drones, which are even harder to find and faster as well as more maneuverable than their fighters. By all measures, they have air superiority over Texas and the gulf."

Admiral Romelov added, "Madame Secretary, I have to agree with everything General Davis just reported, and it has caused a serious demoralizing affect on our pilots. They know the odds are stacked against them and have no trust in their aircraft when they go up. Add to the fact we have lost most of our best fighter pilots, and we are in a situation we have the least experienced pilots flying older and less advanced aircraft going against the most advanced aircraft in the world, and is getting worse by the day. We cannot simply overwhelm them with our numbers since we cannot pierce their defensive weaponry."

"Ambassador Herrmosa, do you have anything to add?"

"Yes, Madame Secretary, we are in a difficult position, although not as impossible as the generals are making it out to be. We really have two choices, since we do not have air superiority we have no way of destroying enough of their aircraft to accept the resolution, then we either negotiate a surrender agreement or send a message that wars have consequences. We only have one advantage they do not have which is our nuclear arsenal."

General Davis spoke up, "There is no way we can make this a nuclear war. It was bad enough you two decided to launch an attack on Dallas against my demands, but I am not going to agree to a nuclear war on Texas. They were part of the United States, and my country will not tolerate your destroying one of our fellow states. There is still a kinship between us and Texas, and the attack has Americans in shock."

Secretary General Polentas broke in, "Gentlemen, we are not going to decide this right now whether we are going to escalate this into a nuclear war. It is true we have two choices, either negotiate a surrender or use the nuclear option. We will meet at noon and discuss our options back here."

Instantly the alarms in the building began howling, and the generals' phones started ringing when General Sanchez came barging in the room with a look of concern, "Secretary General, there is an attack on the compound coming up First Avenue from the south. It looks like a well-organized militia with over a thousand men."

Steven and Ranger had been hugging the earth under the power lines to avoid detection over the past two hours. The electron leakage of the antiquated power lines made a perfect electron field to avoid satellite detection. There were no people around as these lines took the roughest mountain paths and had been off limits for the past five years from wheeled traffic, making them a perfect route to be unseen from the normal traffic allowing them to save computer power. They slowed to a hover as they approached New York City at Woodlawn station on the Green Line waiting for the nine fifteen to pull out as they watched from a thousand feet away.

"Now you are going to have to get right in behind the train as it enters the subway. There is an invisible envelope that extends ten feet behind the train that is a dead spot in their detection system. The electric motors cause too much static electricity for the sensors to see through. They never expected people to be there, so they never picked up on the gap in their system, which is how we have smuggled people, guns, and Bibles into the Burroughs."

The train rolled out toward Manhattan as it entered the subway tunnel while Steve brought the Stallion inches from the back window just above the taillight. The drafts behind the train swirled violently as the downdrafts came off the top of the train pushing his hovercraft into the tracks while the side drafts made a whirlpool of turbulence. If the Stallion were to touch the middle rail, they would both be electrocuted and then hit by the next train.

He could almost reach out and touch the window as he was within two feet of the people standing inside the car. He must have been invisible, but he had no idea what would happen if his cloaking were to stop from the bugs in his software, but he had no time to dwell on the possibilities. All he knew is he had to get through this maze and put an end to this war. He would get a short break to relax at each station as the train took on more passengers filling to capacity. He now had over fifty people within fifteen of him without them having any clue of he was outside the window staring right at them.

He sat there hovering behind the train waiting for it to move. When it finally pulled out of the station, he kept the Stallion within inches of the window even though the wind continued to buffet and rock him as he stayed in the backwash of the train as it gathered speed. He continued this flying attached to the window while people looked straight at them thinking they were seeing the tunnel behind him on his Mylar cover. They continued this game of cat and mouse until they pulled into Grand Central Station where Ranger showed him a secret series of tunnels taking them up to Forty Seventh Street exit flying out an abandoned service tunnel and straight up toward the East River and the United Nations Tower Plaza.

Ranger looked over at him. "Turn off your software and let them see you!"

"What? Are you crazy? It is all we have to survive."

"Have faith and turn it off and let them see us! Let God take control of this."

"Okay, here goes."

As they openly banked into the skyscraper, the lasers began hitting the Stallion. It wasn't designed for this much energy even though most of the firepower was still being directed at the street attack. He did just as Ranger had told him and began circling the tower, letting the lasers hit his hover at will and returned fire on the tower's firing positions. He waited for it to explode as the temperatures were shooting past critical stages. Circle after circle, the direct fire intensity increased and increased as they waited for the inevitable failure of his titanium.

Tommie Davis had his men ready inside the Queens midtown tunnel. They were part of ten teams of two hundred and fifty each. They had to work their way into position before the morning shift change. After ten years of being chased and hunted, these men knew how to creep into positions and blend into their surroundings unseen. This exercise was different than most as the guards were on full war alert.

All the men had heard about the nuclear attack on Dallas and were ready to exact their payback or die trying. At nine o'clock, the attack began as two fully armored panel trucks came speeding up First Avenue, firing lasers and rockets into the compound and hitting the Secretariat Tower causing minor explosions throughout the compound. The men cried out, "Don't mess with Texas" as they came out of their hidden positions and attacked the compound in full view.

The UN troops began the counterattack as well from the wall and roof-mounted lasers, keeping Ranger's troops pinned down. Ranger's forces were firing from all angles on the South sector of the compound behind their armored trucks. They were combining their laser intensity on the laser mounts on the tower walls forcing the operators and spotters to keep their heads down. That is when they heard the sound they all feared most coming up the East River. Appearing from behind the tower was another Hover Fortress with the loud whining of its powerful turbines and multiple power lasers lighting a maze of misery on the troops. It looked like a thousand-legged spider being held up by thin lights spinning a web of death.

The black Hover Fortress blocked out the sky with its immense circumference. It immediately began firing in a hundred different directions, hitting men or destroying their covered positions. It immediately took out the first armored truck while the second one was firing at the hovering monster in a futile attempt to engage it with little if any affect. It was putting up an impressive fight, although they knew what the ultimate outcome was going to bring about their deaths. The ground troops could all see the Black Stallion flying up the street with no camouflage and bank around the back of the tower which reignited the spirits and caused the helpless truck to drive full speed right at the hovering Fortress.

From the north, over a thousand men swarmed down First Avenue with ten more armored trucks firing on the building and surrounding troops. They began hitting the building taking out troops stationed around the building as the battle immediately was now on three sides of the compound.

Ranger yelled to Steven, "When you finish the seventh trip, you have to go inverted and give this battle to God."

"What are you talking about? That would be instant suicide. I have almost no deflection on the bottom of my hover."

"Steven, you have to trust God completely and go inverted."

"Here goes!"

On the seventh trip around the tower, the army below blew all of their air horns they brought as a call out to the Lord and then it happened. Every one of the UN lasers from all sides as well as the

Hover Fort hit the inverted Stallion at the same time, knocking the Stallion downward as a surge shorted the computers turning the mylar into a blinding silver mirror reflecting the energy back into the side of the tower while the lasers intertwined, forming a nova laser, cutting the building in half. The steel girders were severed and immediately collapsed from the weight above them, beginning the pancake collapse. Everyone watched as the entire building began to tip and slowly collapsed upon itself into a giant cloud of dust engulfing half of the compound. Within minutes the entire tower was nothing more than smoldering mountain of rubble turning into a raging pyre of paper, plastic, and wood furniture with the screams of people dying inside.

The Black Stallion spun out of control from the hit and spun into the middle of the river bouncing numerous times before settling upright. The armored truck exploded in a giant fireball just as the tower began to collapse. The Hover Fortress pilot never saw the collapse as it was directly behind the tail structure when a huge chunk of tower structure came crashing through the center of the massive black beast. This destroyed the entire engine compartment and fuel tanks causing it to lose control as it came apart with an orange ball of fire and sending the death machine spinning out into its own watery grave.

A huge cheer came up from the troops as they began surging toward the compound and firing on anything that was moving inside the smoldering pile of debris. Within minutes, the compound guards were raising their hands to get away from the intense heat of the burning building. They could hear screams and cries coming from inside the twisted remains as the heat and flame reached into the depths of deepest caverns and bunkers beneath the footprint where the tower just stood.

The Ranger's ground troops continued down the street toward Central Park, taking out the gangs and union troops who were running aimlessly while the Ranger's numbers swelled as they conquered block after block. The gangs lost their courage when they saw the collapse and either surrendered or ran from the vigilantes as they saw the upcoming retribution from the Christians.

Steven unbuckled his chest harness as the Black Stallion began to sink into the frigid water. The river was pouring into the gashes and damage covering the right side of the craft. He looked over at Ranger, who was unconscious and began to shake him. "Ranger, wake up, we have to get out of here."

He began to stir and looked over at Steven and then began to comprehend the situation, looking down at his lifeless legs. "I can't get out of my harness, and my legs are trapped against the crushed metal of the hover. Can you reach over and open my harness bars?"

"Here, let me reach in there. It seems to be jammed, but I think if I pull this emergency release, the harness bars come off. Okay, there we go. Grab my hand and let me help you out."

"Steven, my legs are crushed into the wreckage. The console is completely smashed against my legs, and I think they may be broken. Unless you have a blowtorch or a Jaws of Life, I don't think I am getting out, and this water is pouring in pretty fast."

"We can get you out of here. Let me over there and see if I can free your legs."

Steven looked down Ranger's legs and could see the metal had crashed down on his thighs, and his feet were completely hidden under the crumpled metal. He tried pulling him out by lifting his shoulders and soon found it impossible to move him.

"Steven, this is the end, when your faith is really tested. I learned in prison they can take everything from you, including your dignity, but they cannot take away your faith in God. So I may not survive this, but my faith is stronger now than it has ever been in my life. I am ready to see my family again for eternity. This will be my final baptism, and in a few moments, I will be meeting my Savior. Steven, do not ever feel sorrow for me or have sadness since I will be waiting for your arrival in glory.

"Look over there at that pile of rubble, which used to be the UN. Our faith did that. Years from now when our story is told, they will know we put our faith in God and turned off the deflectors, flew inverted to change the world. Save yourself, brother and we will see each other again soon."

The Black Stallion filled completely with water and sank straight to the bottom, taking the Texas Ranger into the dark depths of the icy blackness as Steven slowly swam back to the bank. He pulled himself up on the gravel as he began sobbing while he looked over at the empty flowing river.

The wedding was being held at Ground Zero in Dallas. The reclamation crews had been working twenty-four hours a day, six days a week for the last six months to haul the radioactive material out of the blast zone and haul in ten feet of landfill making the ground they were on completely safe. They had accomplished the impossible with help from around the world. They moved over a million lead lined truckloads of blast material and dirt out of the Dallas blast zone and were replacing it with new fill dirt twenty feet deep.

The open air ceremony was on a stage on a newly planted grass field with new landscaping, which would become a ground zero park commemorating the over two million deaths from the nuclear attack on Dallas. The beginning of the park was starting to reveal itself and was absolutely breathtaking with the rolling hills and large reflecting pools, lakes with newly planted trees from around the world. There were already streets being laid out surrounding the park area and foundations being dug for the rebuilding of Dallas city center. The largest building would be the new Moses Tower II, which was being designed to be an exact copy of the Houston tower. While the Houston tower was considered the energy capital of the world, the Dallas tower was being built to become one of the world's financial capitols.

The ceremony was located on a large rolling hill overlooking the park's Ranger Memorial Lake in Dallas Memorial park a perfect sunny afternoon with a crowd as far as the eye could see. A VIP section including President Stewart, US President Victoria Price, Chinese Premier Zuan, along with every major leader in the world was set on a podium to the right of the stage. The Texas delegation included all the senators and congressmen was to the left. Also attending was the newly admitted sister state representatives of Oklahoma, Louisiana, Arkansas, New Mexico, and Mississippi. It looked as if the entire Texas Christ Church of New York had traveled to be there in celebration. Pastor Darling was officiating the wedding while Jeff Drake was Steven's best man. Steven was dressed in a black tuxedo and tails with a white bow tie. Jeff was dressed in a matching tuxedo with the exception of a bolo tie and a gold nugget slide as they made a striking image waiting for the ceremony to begin.

The entire crowd was wearing their cowboy best. The men were in cowboy boots and hats while the women were wearing the biggest dresses they could find with their Easter bonnets. Moses Industries provided a fully stocked costume pavilion for anyone who did not have their own boots and hats which had been fully stocked. Even Premier Zuan was wearing his hat and boots with a cowboy-tailored suit while his wife was wearing a silk flowing dress and ornate hat, which looked right out of a Western saloon.

The wedding started with the slow entrance down the boulevard of a single completely refurbished 1890s stage coach being pulled by six matching white stallions. The stagecoach was decorated by bouquets of flowers and multicolored mylar strips woven in the wheels. When it arrived, a half a dozen cowboys helped June Darling out of the coach as Dean Sherwood, her maid of honor, helped her with her wedding gown and train. As the wedding march began, the entire crowd turned to look at the bride. She was blazingly radiant as she looked like a princess with her long, flowing gown trailing ten feet behind her and her wind-blown veil billowing down her front. She slowly made her way to the lectern where she could see her father waiting with moistened eyes.

"Ladies and gentlemen, I have the rare opportunity to do what every father dreams of one day doing, which is marrying his own daughter to the man she loves with all her heart. Steven Moses, I have always loved my June Bug from the moment she was born and always will. I am proud to give her over to you since I know you will guard her heart, her spirit and her mind like I have for the rest of your life."

"I promise I will, sir."

"June, it's about time!" he said, making her and the crowd laugh.

"It is about time. It is about you June Darling promising to give the rest of your time with Steven, and Steven Moses promising to give his name and the rest of his time with you for all eternity. So you are making this promise in front of your family, your friends and God to spend the rest of your time devoted to each other."

"Steven, do you have the ring?"

"Yes, I do, Pastor."

"Call me dad." The crowd laughed again.

Steven reached over to Jeff who handed him the ring. The ruby was gone and only the large diamond was left in a silver and gold setting. June's eyes teared as she understood its meaning while looking into Steve's eyes as he nodded yes.

"Steven Moses, this ring represents the endlessness of time which thanks to Jesus' promise is how long your love will last with June. Steve, do you promise to love and lead June through good times and bad, through sickness and in health, for better or for worse, forsaking all others through all the days of your life, till death do you part?"

"I do, and I will."

"June, do you promise to love and respect Steve through good times and bad, through sickness and in health, for better or for worse, forsaking all others through all the days of your life, until death do you part?"

She choked out the words as the tears flowed freely down her cheeks. "I do, and I will."

"You may kiss my daughter, your bride."

He lifted up the veil to see an angelic face filled with tears of joy as he leaned her back for a wet and lingering wildcatter kiss. Not any kiss but the kiss he had missed for years. This kiss not only made his heart stop but cleansed his entire body of the tightness, which suddenly disappeared as June completed him again. He could finally catch his breath for the first time in nearly a decade. This was a kiss to make a man look forward to the rest of his life with his woman.

June nearly fainted from the emotion she felt with his kiss. His passion and depth tore through her heart like an arrow through a hay bale. She understood the healing he felt from this moment as the past pain was washed away and their new life began as her husband was now completed as was she.

"With the power given to me by the Republic of Texas, I now pronounce you man and wife. May I introduce you for the first time Mr. and Mrs. Steven Moses."

The "Yellow Rose of Texas" began playing amid an emotional applause as they walked out arm in arm to the sweet smells of mesquite and hickory smoke wafting in the wind. The line dancing went on throughout the day and even Premier Zuan and his wife were kicking up some dust in their boots and hats whooping it up.

As the day wore on and the festivities were waning, Jeff Drake stood up and made an announcement. "Steve, we couldn't think of what to get a guy who has everything and there was only one thing you loved nearly as much as June, and I don't mean a new oil gusher. He reached in his pocket and clicked a button. In the distance, you could see a speck growing and coming right at them and fluttering to a stop next to Steven and June. It was the Black

Stallion painted with "Just Married" on the sides being flown by General Thomas. On the driver's door was painted two Hover Fortresses and the United Nations building.

General Thomas explained the details of the craft, "We had it rebuilt from the ground up and added a bit more power for you. If you look underneath you will see we added a ramjet booster to it in case you want to get up to Mach six or seven. Go easy on it at first, so you learn the power and feel at those speeds. We just want to make sure you are not shooting down anymore Fortresses or anything. Congratulations Steven and June."

Steven was caught off guard and found himself a bit choked up. "I just don't know what to say, Jeff. Last I saw the Stallion, it was sinking into the depths of the river with the Texas Ranger. How did you find it? How did you…? Oh well, you got me the perfect gift for a perfect day. I think this is a good time for its shakedown ride since we are taking our honeymoon down in the Caribbean there is a special restaurant I want to stop at with June."

"Let me help you into your carriage, my lady."

"Who said chivalry was dead?"

Steven helped June into the Black Stallion and jumped into the pilot's seat while firing it up.

Jeff yelled, "Hit the horn!" When he hit it, it blared, "Don't mess with Texas!"

They both laughed and waved to the crowd while the applause and cheers rang out as he blasted off at full throttle and corkscrewed into the sky then banked it toward the southeast, where they saw the ramjet fire streaking it across the dimming sky like a shooting star shooting across the purple Texan skies as they disappeared into the Texan blue yonder.

The End

After the collapse of the United States in 2016, Texas petitions and purchases its sovereignty to become a free republic. As an independent country, Texas is able to become a purely free market economy without the restrictions and roadblocks of government. Texas soon becomes the most powerful country in the world and draws the interest from the United Nations to become a tax paying member country.

This story is a look at a world as it could be if the producers were not only trusted but encouraged, and the welfare state was to be replaced by a more self-reliant society. This is the age old battle between government control and free market forces.

"I just finished your book, and was very impressed by your ability, imagination, and style. Of course, the storyline kept my attention since I'm as Texan as anybody could be. I can honestly say that, even though my family is somewhat newcomers. I'm only third generation Native Texan because my Great Grandfather came to Texas as a small boy in 1856. Gary, I don't read novels, mostly histories and biographies, but I could hardly put down *The Republic of Texas*."

—Uncle Sam

Gary Bray is a native Oregonian, who has been lumber wholesaler for the past twenty-five years where he learned how the free market works. He has been writing political satire for twenty years and this is his only novel he has ever written.

TATE PUBLISHING
AND ENTERPRISES, LLC